'SCUSE ME WHILE I KISS THE SKY

JIMI HENDRIX: VOODOO CHILD

'SCUSE ME WHILE I KISS THE SKY

JIMI HENDRIX: VOODOO CHILD

DAVID HENDERSON

ATRIA PAPERBACK

A Division of Simon & Schuster, Inc..
1230 Avenue of the Americas
New York, NY 10020

First Atria Paperback edition July 2009

ATRIA PAPERBACK and colophon are trademarks of
Simon & Schuster, Inc.

For information about special discounts for bulk purchases,
please contact Simon & Schuster Special Sales at 1-866-506-1949 or
business@simonandschuster.com.

The Simon & Schuster Speakers Bureau can bring authors to your
live event. For more information or to book an event, contact the
Simon & Schuster Speakers Bureau at 1-866-248-3049 or visit our
website at www.simonspeakers.com.

Manufactured in the United States of America

10   9   8   7   6   5   4   3   2   1

Library of Congress Cataloging-in-Publication Data
Henderson, David
'Scuse me while I kiss the sky : Jimi Hendrix, voodoo child / David
  Henderson.
viii, 449 p. : ill. ; 25 cm.
Discography (p. 426–433) and index.
Hendrix, Jimi. 2. Rock musicians—United States—Biography.
ML410.H476 H46   2008
787.87/166092 B 22   2006042974

ISBN 978-0-7432-7400-5
ISBN 978-0-7432-7401-2 (pbk)
ISBN 978-1-4165-3434-1 (eBook)

Dedicated to the memory of
Walter "Porky" Ellison of Throgs Neck

ACKNOWLEDGMENTS

Grateful acknowledgment is given to those who have given the benefit of their direct contact with Jimi Hendrix, in the form of an interview and/or conversation:

Jimi Hendrix, Al Brown, Betty Davis, Willie Chambers, Joe Chambers, George Chambers, and Julius Chambers (of the Chambers Brothers), Claire, Stella Douglas, Alvenia Bridges, Dave Holland, Albert King, Len Chandler, Ed Kramer, Ronnie Drayton, Myrna Friedman, Jim Brodey, Derek Taylor, Ray Cepeda, Quincy Jones, Alexis Korner, Devon Wilson, Buddy Miles, Chuck Wein, Denny Green, Ray Warner, James "Vishwamitra" Scott, Richie Havens, Ram John Holder, Ellis Haizlip, Rahman Ali and Miles Davis, Clara Schuff, Hugh Masekela, Noel Redding, Herbie Worthington, Kenny Rankin, Ed Sanders, Phillip Wilson, "Bobo" Shaw, Peter Orlovsky, Arthur Lee, Blanche Sands, JoAnne and Mark, Alan Price, Curtis Jones, Les Perrin, Juma Sultan, Howard Scott, Finney, Yvonne Rankin, Dan Cassidy, Patricia Jiminez, Ronnie Spector, "H," Fayne Pridgeon, Monika Dannemann, Dennis Armstead, Sue Cassidy Clark, Timothy Leary, Sam Silver, James Williams, Fred Rollins, Diana Rollins, Joe Boyd, Colette Mimram, Alan Douglas, Don Moye, Avotcja, Nora Hendrix, Cosmo Deaguero, Bill Graham, Marcia Herskovitz, Carl Lee Jr., Sharon Lawrence, Jim Robertson, Rudy Costa, John Mayall, Chrissie Charles, Bobby Taylor, Rahsaan Roland Kirk, Albert Goldman, Media Brown and Diama, Floyd Sneak, "Snip" Milton, Willie Dixon, Buddy Guy, "Rocki," and Taj Mahal. Don Foster and Caesar Glebbeek of the Jimi Hendrix Information Centre in Amsterdam, Holland, Jess Hansen of the Jimi Hendrix Archives in Seattle, Washington, and Don Menn of *Guitar Player* magazine in Saratoga, California, made very important files, documents, and tape recordings available. Through Don Menn of *Guitar Player* magazine unedited, tape-recorded interviews with Eric Barrett, Chuck Rainey, Cornell Dupree, John Hammond Jr., and Gerry Stickells were made available to me. Cecil Brown gave me sections from his interviews with Truman Capote that referred to Jimi Hendrix.

I also extend my thanks to those who helped me in various tangible and intangible ways:

Derek Taylor, George Melly, Ed Knowles, Mike Reynolds, Randa Nova, Craig Street, Michael Gray, Joyce Cole, Peter Bradley, Pat Dennison, Lezley Saar, Arne

Passeman, Bari Scott, Rex Griffin, Mary Frank, Gail, Calvin C. Hernton, Teri Turner, Nancy Chandler, Ornette Coleman, Cyn. Zarco, Touraine, Marie D. Brown, Yvette Guerrero, Cordell Reagan, Teddy Stewart, Paul Williams, Leo Branton, David Hammons, Garry George, Karen Kennerly, Zaid Darweesh, Butch Morris, Ray Holbert, Olly Wilson, Mike Ashburne, Lyle Hill, Angela Davis, Bruce Talamon, Mr. H. V. Cox, Eliot Mazur, Pat McCurdy, Bruce Langhorne, *Rolling Stone,* Lewis McAdams, John Rockwell, Cecil Hollingsworth, Barbara Harris, Michael Gray, Daphne Muse, Tommy Mims, Bob Merlis, Ellen Sanders, Jerome Rimson, Calvin Keyes, Loren Means, Vernon Gibbs, *Circus, Fusion,* KPFA-FM in Berkeley, California, KSAN-FM in San Francisco, California, and all the beautiful people of the Alternative Chorus-Songwriter's Showcase, Hollywood, California.

Special thanks to typists Grace Rutledge, Eleanor Arge, Damali Cruz, Mary Golden, and J. C. Reilly.

Special thanks to Dr. Barbara T. Christian and Ishmael Reed.

And most special gratitude to my family, Barbara, Najuma, Malik, Myrtle, Henry, Ray, and Juanita, and my friends who have stood by me throughout.

And to Lawrence Jordan, my original editor, with abiding respect and gratitude. My additional thanks to Alan Rinzler of Bantam Books; Denise Shannon of the Georges Borchardt Literary Agency; Barry Gruber, Charles Blass, Ho Jung Audenaerde, Caitlin Cahill, and Deirdre Scott; for conversations with Juma Sultan, Steve Roby and Juma Santos; and especially Michael Fairchild for his important chronological notes on *Jimi Hendrix: Voodoo Child* . . . and also for his new information regarding Hendrix's death.

And thanks for essential assistance in this new, revised edition to: Juma Sultan, Juma Santos, David Kramer, Taharqa Aleem, Tunde-Ra Aleem, Tajaddin Aleem, Chris Charlesworth, Ram John Holder, Kathy Etchingham, Lonnie Jordan of War, and special thanks to Dr. Christine Meilicke, Ammiel Alcalay, Maxine Bartow, Anne Seidlitz, Gabrielle David, and DeAnna Heindel of the Georges Borchardt Agency. And, as Langston used to write, "especially to" Malaika Adero, my editor, and her assistant, Krishan Trotman, of Atria Books.

. . . the story
of life is quicker
than the wink of an eye

the story of love
is hello and good-bye
until we meet again.

—JIMI HENDRIX
SEPTEMBER 17, 1970

PROLOGUE

At 12:45 P.M. on Friday, September 18, 1970, Jimi Hendrix was pronounced dead at St. Mary's Abbot Hospital in the Kensington/Chelsea section of London. Immediately the London offices of the major wire services reported that Hendrix had died of a drug overdose.

Monika Dannemann, the woman in whose hotel suite he was found, spoke to reporters, associates, and friends about Hendrix's whereabouts and states of mind that Thursday night and Friday morning.

Eric Burdon, lead singer of War (and formerly of the defunct group the Animals), had discovered a poem she said Hendrix had written shortly before his death. It was in Dannemann's sketchbook. "The Story of Jesus," titled after its first line, is also known as "The Story of Life," a title Dannemann may have chosen. It was a poem conceived as a possible song lyric.

The poem could be interpreted as the last words of a man about to die. But suicide was unlikely for a wealthy man who was in the prime of life and held in open adoration by so many. Those knowing Jimi's writing were familiar with his constant referral to hearing his train coming, or in other words, having or expecting to have some premonition about his death. Perhaps it was a farewell message written under duress. Comparisons of samples of his handwriting reveal a haste not often found in his even most casual notes or song lyrics, or even in simple messages to friends or employees. The poem begins with Jesus and ends with Jimi in the first person: "The story of Jesus / so easy to explain / after they crucified him / a woman, she claimed his name."

The message is rather amazing, especially as a last word. Jesus's life story is dominated by his crucifixion, even though he is considered by many to be the savior of humanity. The last line in the first stanza refers to a mysterious woman who "claimed" his name. Jimi then goes to a Jesus roaming the desert where he found a rose. Then in the next stanza he refers to a popular premise where Jesus was "married ever / happily after / for all the Tears we cry."

Then Jimi explains that there is "no use in arguing"; there are moans "when each man falls in Battle, His / soul it has to roam."

Jimi revisits the themes recurrent in his notebooks of angels and flying saucers, but then concludes a stanza referring to Easter Sunday, the resurrection, as "the name of the rising sun."

Here Jimi brings himself directly into this story: "We will gild the light / this time with a woman / in our arms." Instead of death being symbolized by the cross, the mysterious woman prevails: "the woman's always mentioned / at the moment that we die." As he ends the poem Jimi writes that Jesus's story "is the story of you and me." He makes it clear he is referring to himself. He cautions not to feel lonely, "I am you searching to be free." Life can end "quicker than the wink of an eye." But love is the real story, in greeting or farewell, "until we meet again."

Dannemann and Burdon agreed to keep the poem from public knowledge. They felt that it might indicate a "suicidal" state. She said that she had called her brother in Germany and indicated that Hendrix had been exhausted and wanted to sleep for several days; and that was why, apparently, he took so many sleeping pills.

Several other versions of Hendrix's death were to quickly surface, some preposterous, some perhaps not. One account has Hendrix being the victim of a contract on his life, where the regular delivery of an array of drugs was sabotaged and the regular deliveryman substituted. Whether this "delivery" also included the strong-armed drowning of the subject could not be established as being a part of that version. One had to do with COINTELPRO, the counterintelligence program of the Federal Bureau of Investigation, which sought to neutralize, by any means necessary, an array of black leaders and potential black leaders who were considered to be potential messiahs. Agents were to act to discredit groups and individuals within the responsible Negro community, and the Negro radicals and also the white liberals who have sympathy for militant black nationalists. It has been said that the FBI sought to encourage Martin Luther King Jr. to commit suicide up until his untimely and mysterious assassination.

Hendrix had publicly acknowledged support for the Black Panthers in high profile concerts and in national magazines. He had agreed to play a benefit for the Panthers at the Oakland Coliseum. He had been the biggest name in popular music to play an anti–Vietnam War benefit concert.

There are FBI documents that verify the agency's activity around Hendrix and his participation in benefits for white and black radical leftist causes. A clipping from an underground press paper that announced Hendrix playing in support of the infamous Chicago Seven (disrupters of the Democratic National Convention in Chicago in 1968) was annotated by the Bureau. These seven defendants included representatives of an array of radical organizations: Black Panther Bobby Seale, Yippie Jerry Rubin, and Students for a Democratic Society's

Tom Hayden, among others. There is a striking juxtaposition between the date of that annotation and Hendrix's suspicious bust at the border in Toronto, Canada, a few days later. Another FBI-annotated clipping announced Hendrix's appearance for the antiwar Vietnam Moratorium Committee at Madison Square Garden at the beginning of 1970. His strange, suspicious poisoning at that event prevented him from performing and had many observers suspecting sabotage. A special feature of COINTELPRO was often called "dirty tricks," but serious prison sentences, blackmail, and death have been associated with these government-sanctioned "black-bag" activities.

Author Alex Constantine links the FBI, the CIA, and other intelligence agencies. ". . . As regards the presumed paucity of FBI files on Hendrix. Students in Santa Barbara [University of California] sued and laid hands on some of them. The FBI held most back. . . . There is a common misperception concerning COINTELPRO. It was a PART of Operation CHAOS, an immense interagency attempt to counter the anti-war movement. CHAOS was international, so it was THIS operation that interfered with the Panther concert. The FBI and police hit squads killed 28 Black Panthers." Constantine considers Tupac Shakur as the twenty-ninth. Several significant members of Tupac's extended family were Black Panthers. His first recorded song was entitled "Panther Power." Hendrix had donated money to the unfairly imprisoned New York City Panther 21, which included Tupac Shakur's mother, Afeni.

Other accounts of Hendrix's mysterious death had him overdosing on superpowerful heroin at a friend's house on the outskirts of London and then taken to Monika Dannemann's place. Yet another account had him flown to Hollywood in a private jet, where he was murdered, and then flown back to London. Another account had him dying at a well-known rock star's apartment with Devon Wilson by his side.

Yet another account had Hendrix mistakenly receiving a lethal dose of heroin that had been given to Alan Douglas by Michael Jeffery in order to eliminate his successor as manager.

The following are Monika Dannemann's responses at the inquest on September 28, 1970, with commentary in brackets.

I am an artist and I live at the Garden Flat, 22 Lansdowne Crescent, London, W11. I have known Jimi Hendrix for about two years; we met in Germany. I had been in touch with him by telephone and letter while he was in the States. I met him when he came to this country in August. I have not known him to consult a doctor while in this country. I would say that all the time I knew him he was exhausted. As far as I know he always fulfilled his engagements. He took sleeping tablets from his doctor because he was nervous, but they were not that strong. I have not known him to take hard drugs, he tried them out just for experience. I do not know whether he took amphetamines. I have not known him to have a vomiting attack.

He had been staying with me since Tuesday, 15th September. Nobody else was staying at the flat. He slept well on the Tuesday and Wednesday night. [It is well documented that Hendrix spent Wednesday night at Danny Secunda's home in Knightsbridge.] *I do not know about Thursday night. We did not spend a tiring day on Thursday and arrived home about 8:30 P.M.* [That time is disputed by several persons.]

I cooked a meal and had a bottle of white wine about 11:00 P.M. He drank more of the bottle than I did. He had nothing to drink other than the wine. I had a bath and washed my hair and then we talked. At this time there was no arguments or stress, it was a happy atmosphere.

When we came back [from picking him up from Peter Cameron's party] *we were talking. I took a sleeping tablet at about 7:00 A.M.* [One researcher opines that a whole tablet would put someone of her size out for many more hours than the two or three she had testified to sleeping.] *I made him two fish sandwiches.* [Terry Slater was certain there was no food in the house when he arrived that fateful morning to help "clean up."] *We were in bed talking.* [He was taken to the hospital fully clothed, rather "flamboyantly" at that, according to one doctor. Hardly pajamas, or sleepwear of any kind.] *I woke around 10:20 A.M. He was sleeping normally.* [According to the ambulance attendants, "He was covered in wine and vomit." There was "tons" of it all over the bed and the pillows.] *I went around the corner to get cigarettes, when I came back he had been sick, he was breathing and his pulse was normal* [the ambulance attendants say he was dead when they arrived], *but I could not wake him. I saw that he had taken sleeping tablets, there were nine of mine missing. I phoned for an ambulance and he was taken to hospital, where he lived for a short time.* [Doctors at the hospital that day said Hendrix was dead on arrival. And that he had been dead for a long time.]

I had forty Vesperax sleeping pills at the flat. There were nine missing, I think he knew exactly what he could take in the way of sleeping tablets. When I last saw him before he went to sleep he was quite happy. [Since she says she fell asleep while Hendrix was still awake she would not know if he slept at all.] *The tablets were in a cupboard, he would have to get out of bed to get the tablets.*

He said he had had cannabis. There was no question of exhaustion on this particular evening. He was not a man to have moods. He was not tensed up. I have never heard him say he wished he were dead or that life was not worth living. He had business stresses but this did not worry him.

Later, the inquest returned an "open verdict," as it was called.

The death certificate listed as cause of death:

Inhalation of vomit.

Barbiturate intoxication (quinalbarbitone).

Insufficient evidence of circumstances.

Open verdict.

The "open verdict" was greatly dependent on the testimony of Monika Dannemann and Hendrix's road manager, Gerry Stickells.

The "open verdict," according to *The New York Times*, "meant that the court was unable to decide the exact reason for Mr. Hendrix's death . . ."

The admitting doctor at St. Mary's Abbot Hospital stated on the record that Jimi Hendrix's death was by drowning.

Although Gavin L. B. Thurston, coroner for Inner West London, is listed as informant, he did not sign the death certificate. A time of death was never officially determined.

Later, to the press and to friends, Dannemann was to reveal more about the evening. After the inquest and the "open verdict," Dannemann publicly revealed the untitled "The Story of Jesus" poem.

Further analysis of the pathology report indicated that Hendrix had a very low level of alcohol in his blood, much lower than the amount of wine that had been suffusing his organs and coming out of his nose and mouth when he arrived at the hospital. It would seem, according to the state of his body, that he had had an impossible amount of red wine after the party at Peter Cameron's and early the morning of September 18, yet the alcohol level in his blood remained unusually low. Hendrix did not drink like that, in crazy, sloppy overindulgence that would produce wine all over his clothing and even cake in his hair.

The cursory nature of the original inquest was a clear message to the youth culture and the black consciousness movement that the British authorities would not do what was needed to rule out any crimes that may have been done to Jimi Hendrix's person. There would be no investigation.

Those who followed the death and the aftermath noticed many inconsistencies in the official inquest. It was an open-and-shut affair that managed to hide its racist intent behind the public perceptual hoax of Hendrix as a substance abuser.

The initial reports in London newspapers, radio, and television misstated the facts of his death in accordance with the misinformation that was afloat. These reports took wing, and the initial contentions of death by drug overdose would seldom be altered by subsequent news media. The fabled British press would do no investigative stories.

As a result, millions of people all over the world thought that Hendrix had died the typical rock star death: drug overdose amid fame, blondes, opulence, sex. Decadence is usually associated with drug deaths. But it seems that Hendrix could very well have been the victim of foul play, foul play with extreme prejudice.

Jimi Hendrix did not die of a drug overdose.

As the immediacy of Hendrix's death faded, Monika Dannemann and Eric Burdon began to alter and expand their stories and reveal more of their involvement with and around Hendrix's last hours alive. At the same time, other stories began to surface. What may have seemed like a cut-and-dried accidental death began to acquire serious complications.

On September 21, very soon after Hendrix's death, Eric Burdon went on the BBC-TV program *24 Hours,* hosted by Kenneth Alsop, and declared that he believed, from the Hendrix poem that was discovered after his death, that he had committed suicide. Burdon may have been believed had he not been so obviously stoned while making those assertions.

Warner Bros. is said to have collected one million dollars from a Lloyd's of London insurance policy as a result of Hendrix's death.

A fluke interview that Dannemann was said to have given to the German-language *Enquirer*-like magazine *Bild* the day after Hendrix's death seemed to be quite revealing. One can imagine, after reading her broken English accounts of what happened, that she must have been more at ease speaking to a fellow German in her own language. Upon checking out of the hotel she had retreated to after Hendrix's death, with Eric Burdon and others, she had had a dispute over the bill and then had trouble finding a taxi. Egan F. Freheit, the reporter from *Bild,* helped her out, rode in the taxi he had procured for her, and got an exclusive interview.

The article, considered a scoop, ran under the headline "I Gave Jimi the Tablets" (*Bild,* September 24, 1970). Dannemann is quoted as having said, " 'We looked forward to getting married. We already thought about how everything should be. I would then have designed the sleeves for his records.' The blonde girl talks about the evening when Jimi Hendrix died. 'The intrigues of the people who he worked with finished him off. He could not sleep so I gave him the tablets. . . . He died from that. No drugs were involved.' And about the many girls who he was supposed to have had? Monika: 'All a lie. I was the only one with whom he was together until the end, the whole time before the end of his life and that for every minute.' "

Monika would later deny giving the interview in any formal way, but she admitted riding with and talking to the reporter. The accompanying photo of her and Jimi in 1969 could have, at that time, only been obtained from her, according to author and researcher Tony Brown.

Later, Dannemann made a slight change in her story. Where she once said that she saw he was sick and called the ambulance, she began saying that she had called others before she called the ambulance, that she had not acted alone, as her initial statement in circulation indicated. Her time of awakening also changed. She told a police officer named Shaw on September 18 that she woke at 11:00 A.M. But at the inquest the time changed to 10:20 A.M. Later, the time would be 9:00 A.M. To Officer Shaw she did not mention going out for cigarettes, as she did later. Nor to any of the authorities did she mention her interactions with Eric Burdon, Alvenia Bridges, Judy Wong, and Terry Slater.

Years later, in 1986, Burdon published his memoir, *I Used to Be an Animal but I'm All Right Now,* and made some pretty serious admissions. He stated that he had answered Monika's telephone call as "the first light of dawn was coming through the window." He called her back to make sure she had called the ambulance. "She said, 'I can't have people around here now, there's all kinds of stuff [drugs] in the house.'" He states that he caught a minicab to the hotel shortly afterward. This is an admission that he had met Dannemann at the Samarkand rather than at the hospital. Dannemann maintained that Burdon's recollection was unreliable because he was still under the influence of drugs. But from his account and other interviews with him, this event sobered him up and woke him up completely. He quickly became aware of how bad it could be.

Dannemann's story is dependent on a time line that does not implicate her in Hendrix's death (she had been accused of waiting too long to call the ambulance). Burdon's statement that the time was at "first light," or around dawn, 7:00 A.M., when he first talked to Dannemann about Jimi's being in danger, makes the time consistent with the doctor's statement that Jimi had been dead for hours by the time he arrived at the hospital just before 11:30 A.M.

Five years later, in 1991, in a conversation with Kathy Etchingham, he seemed to have thrown all previous caution to the wind. Burdon stated, "It was early morning when I got the call, in fact, I thought it was earlier than early morning. I thought it was like in the early hours." He reiterated that he yelled and screamed for Dannemann to get an ambulance and those screams happened "on more than one occasion." He thought she was stalling because of being frozen with fear of being implicated and even prosecuted for drugs (the police report noted how "smartly clean" the premises were). Burdon, thinking that she would not call for help until the place was clean, went over there to take care of that business. "When I arrived there [at the Samarkand], I remember quite clearly the door being open, and I think maybe I got there and he was there and I didn't want to, you know, look at it, you know, I didn't want to look at the mess. We had to be there before. We got the guitars out, we got the drugs out of the place . . . she [Dannemann] didn't leave in the ambulance, she was with me."

Terry Slater, a former Animal employee, was also there. He told *Earth* magazine in December of 1970, "I had been at the flat [the Samarkand Hotel suite] on Thursday night, and although he [Jimi] wasn't happy, it was impossible to envisage what was going to happen." He would make a statement to Scotland Yard in 1992 to the effect that he had been at the Samarkand that morning and had helped clean up "the mess." For some reason he stated that "there was no food whatsoever in the flat and no evidence any had been cooked." But Slater may have solved the mystery of a call Jimi made that morning in which he said, "I need help bad, man." Slater: "When he called Eric that morning he called a friend, not his manager or any of his hangers-on—he went straight to a friend."

Slater was the one who had phoned Gerry Stickells between 8:00 A.M. and 9:00 A.M. in the first place to tell him there was a problem with Jimi at the hotel. Stickells had been delayed because he went at first to the Cumberland Hotel suite where Jimi was registered.

Eric Burdon went to the Samarkand Hotel and helped Monika clean up before the ambulance was called. They would clean the place of drugs and paraphernalia. Other sources said that some stuff was buried in the garden. Keith Altham, the journalist, has mentioned in a documentary that "Eric Burdon supposedly hoovered the place and got rid of drugs and things, in which case the ambulance was delayed before it got there."

Author Tony Brown adds to Burdon's and Slater's statements. In one of the many interviews he conducted with Monika Dannemann, before and after Etchingham's conversation with Eric Burdon, she mentioned that Gerry Stickells and Eric Barrett—both road managers of Hendrix in Jeffery's employ—were also in the flat that morning, possibly before the ambulance was called. "Gerry Stickells and Eric Barrett, they took some of Jimi's stuff. Mainly, like messages, that kind of stuff. That was funny, that was so strange. They were only interested in all messages Jimi had received. Clotheswise they didn't bother at all. And the guitar, that was one of the things they wanted to take. I explained to them that in 1969 Jimi said to me, if ever he would not come back I could have his guitar. And I told them this, and Gerry Stickells still wanted to take it away from me, and I was completely in tears, naturally, not because of the guitar but because of the whole, you know, what happened. And it was Eric Barrett who sort of said to Gerry Stickells, let her have it."

It's possible they knew he was dead before the ambulance was called. If he was still alive they would have understood that their delay could have been a factor in his death. The doctors in the hospital emergency room (who ought to know) noted that Jimi Hendrix had been dead a long time. Although no one claimed to have checked Hendrix's life signs before the ambulance arrived, there is an implication that he was dead. That means that Dannemann, Slater, Bridges, Burdon, and possibly others may have had some idea of how Hendrix died, or at least more than is commonly known.

Another source said that the investigation carried on during the attempt to reopen the inquest discovered that the ambulance had been called from the public telephone within eyeshot of the Samarkand Hotel, suggesting that those who were there had left, called the ambulance, watched as the ambulance came, and then followed it to the hospital.

And what does the huge amount of red wine have to do with anything?

Vesperax is unusually strong; one pill is a barbiturate equivalent of 200 milligrams—with 150 milligrams of quinalbarbitone, a quick inducer of sleep, and 50 milligrams of brallobarbitone, which as an intermediate induces a longer sleep. It also contains an antihistamine of 39 milligrams of hydroxyethyl hydroxyzine dimaleate.

Author Tony Brown points out, "The normal recommended dose of half a tablet of Vesperax would induce an eight-hour sleep for a normal man weighing one hundred sixty pounds. If Monika had taken one of these sleeping tablets, as she had stated—which would be twice the stated dose—on top of drinking so much red wine earlier in the evening, it would be nigh on impossible for her to wake up early and refreshed after only having three hours of sleep."

Does the content of Jimi's blood as determined from the autopsy indicate his having taken nine pills? And does the alcohol content of his liver and urine indicate the vast amounts of wine exuding from his orifices? His blood "Ethanol was at not more than 5 mgs percent. Extractions revealed a mixture of barbiturates consistent with those from Vesperax. The amount calculated as quinalbarbitone is 0.7 mgs percent." There was also 1.3 mg 100 ml of Seconal in his blood and 3.9 mg 100 ml of Seconal in his liver. His liver extractions also revealed properties consistent with those of brallobarbitone. Quinalbarbitone in the blood was at 3.9 mgs percent. The search for toxic drugs failed to reveal any hydroxyethyl hydroxyzine dimaleate. A mysterious compound was isolated, which they said "might be a metabolite," and was found not only in the liver but in the urine as well, where there was a 46 mgs level of alcohol. It was thought "the blood-alcohol level was probably at 100 mgs at the time when he took the Vesperax." There was also brallobarbitone and amphetamine "easily detectable" in the urine.

In 1975, on the fifth anniversary of Hendrix's death, Dannemann told Caesar Glebbeek, a Dutch collector and Hendrix biographer, that she had awakened that fateful morning at 9:00 A.M. She said Hendrix was still asleep, but she just couldn't sleep anymore. Then she realized he had been sick. She tried to wake him but couldn't. He wouldn't wake up. So she called the ambulance, which came after ten minutes, and the ambulance attendants assured her, "He'll be okay again." She then repeated her oft-repeated theory: "While we were driving in the ambulance, they seated Jimi on a chair but with his head backwards, which I found out later was the worst position they could have put him in, because through this he couldn't breathe proper, because he has been sick." One can see the problems with her syntax. Her lack of fluency could give rise to all sorts of interpretations, but her concluding remarks are unequivocal: "I do believe that he got poisoned, that he actually got murdered. Well, there are some proof, but, well, you can't go to the police with it. There is something really behind the whole thing, and there's quite a powerful group behind all that. I think it is the Mafia."

The two ambulance drivers who on September 18, 1970, responded to the distress call from 22 Lansdowne Crescent and took Jimi Hendrix to St. Mary's Abbot Hospital were allowed by their employer, the London Ambulance Service, some years later to override their contractual restrictions and give interviews regarding that particular situation involving a celebrity.

The following is a statement issued on London Ambulance Service stationery and signed by David Smith, the press and public affairs manager:

TO WHOM IT MAY CONCERN: 3.1.92/ J Hendrix, deceased (18th September 1970)/ In the light of our extensive enquiries it is apparent that the ambulancemen acted in a proper and professional manner./ There was no one else, except the deceased, at the flat (22 Lansdowne Crescent, LONDON W11) when they arrived; nor did anyone else accompany them in the ambulance to St. Mary Abbot Hospital./ I hope this clarifies the situation.

Reg Jones was the senior man of the two ambulance drivers. "I knew he was dead as soon as I walked in the room. You get a feel for it. I can't explain, but you do and I knew he was dead. . . . It was horrific . . . the door was flung wide open. . . . The room at first was dark . . . we had to pull the curtains. He was covered in vomit. There was tons of it all over the pillow. Black and brown it was. We felt for any pulse between his shoulders, pinched his earlobes and nose, showed a light in his eyes, but there was no response at all. . . . We had to get the police. We only had an empty flat. . . . I didn't know who he was. Jimi Hendrix? A bit out of my age group. When we got him to the hospital, full lights and sirens, we had to clean the ambulance out, it was really a mess, his bowels and bladder, all that goes when you're dead. That flat must have needed a good clean, too. . . . Sit him up! No, you don't sit people up when they've choked. Them steps up the flat was steep, and you had a natural incline on the way up, but no, he wasn't sat up."

The other ambulance attendant, John Saua, said, "We got down to the flat, and there was nobody but the body on the bed . . . he was on top of the bed, dressed, but I didn't recognize him. . . . We knew it was hopeless. There was no pulse, no respiration. He was flat on his back when we got there. . . . When we moved him the gases were gurgling. You get that when someone has died, it wasn't too pleasant. The vomit was all the way down . . . we had a hell of a time trying to suck him out; I mean, the vomit was dry and there was a hell of a lot of it. The aspirators in those days were all right . . . [but] they couldn't shift that lot. . . . I don't know if anybody would've recognized him. His own mother wouldn't have recognized him."

Ian Smith, one of the two police officers called to the scene, recalls that if anyone else had "been in the flat, they [the ambulance attendants] would have never called us to come in . . . he [Jimi Hendrix] would have been identified. . . . They could have just taken him off, but in the circumstances, you know—just the body, well, they radioed their control to get us in . . . nobody knew who he was . . ."

Dr. Seifert was one of the casualty doctors who received Jimi Hendrix's body at St. Mary's Abbot Hospital. Seifert was also the medical registrar. "Jimi was rushed into the resus[citation] room. He was put on a monitor, but it was flat. I pounded his heart a couple of times, but there was no point in doing anything else as he was dead. . . . I never spoke to or saw anyone about Jimi—no woman in admissions. . . . No one would have been allowed to look at him or stand over him. That would never have been done. I would have done anything to save him, but it was too late, he was dead. . . . No nurse went out to say we'd revived him, because we didn't—that just never happened. We didn't work on him anything like an hour, just a few minutes—he was dead."

Dr. Bannister was the surgical registrar at St. Mary's Abbot Hospital. He told the *London Times,* "He didn't have any pulse. The inside of his mouth and mucous membranes were black because he had been dead for some time. He had no circulation through his tissues at any time immediately prior to coming to the hospital. . . . Masses" of red wine were "coming out of his nose and out of his mouth. It was horrific. The whole scene is very vivid because you don't often see people who have drowned in their own red wine. He had something around him—whether it was a towel or a jumper [sweater]—around his neck that was saturated with red wine. His hair was matted. He was completely cold. I personally think he probably died a long time before. He was cold and he was blue. He had all the parameters of someone who had been dead for some time. We worked on him for about half an hour without any response at all. There was a medical registrar, myself, nursing staff, and I think one other doctor. . . . The medical staff used an eighteen-inch sucker to try to clear Hendrix's airway but it would just fill up with red wine from his stomach. A heart monitor did not register. Hendrix had been dead for hours rather than minutes when he was admitted to the hospital."

The testimony of the ambulance drivers and the examining doctors directly contradicted Monika Dannemann's statements that she was with Hendrix the entire early morning of his death, that she could account for all but a few minutes of his last hours alive, and that they retired to bed and rested peacefully for several hours. (We assume he did not bed down with his clothes on.) According to her testimony, when she called the ambulance, Hendrix was still alive, and within the hour he was at the hospital. Yet the ambulance attendant said he was dead when they arrived, that he had no pulse. And both doctors say he had been dead a long time. A long time is much more than an hour.

Jimi was at the center of a number of dilemmas at the time of his death, and most of those dilemmas were chronic situations that had been going on consistently for a good while in his life as a star.

One of the most serious of his dilemmas had to do with women, and that may have proved fatal one way or the other. Hendrix often brought out the best and the worst in women, depending on what degree of moral analysis they brought to the picture or what level of Jimi's rock star libidinal behavior an individual thought justifiable. However it was cut, Jimi had a woman problem. Women lined up at his door or knocked at his door at all hours of the night and early morning. The Plaster Casters and others raved about his superior physical endowment. His erotic stage act made grown women scream like teenage girls (long before male strippers came on the scene). Jimi's act was notorious, although it seemed that he had toned it down at the beginning of the 1970s, perhaps more sensitive to the enormous effect he had on people.

This woman problem also extended, logically, to his friends, acquaintances, fellow musicians, performers, and business associates: employees and partners. Although not as obviously enchanted as the screaming fans, many of the wives, girlfriends, secretaries, and personal assistants of his associates were known to pounce when the time and proximity were right. Jimi, a king of Flower Power and the resultant sexual freedom, operated consistently as an uncommitted, sexually open individual. But many of his male associates were threatened by the possibility that their significant others would be drawn to Jimi.

One of the massive complicating factors was that Jimi Hendrix generated so much money that most of the people around him made their living directly or indirectly from him.

It was in the realm of marriage that Hendrix faced his greatest danger. Although musicians and performers were not known for successful marriages,

Jimi's business associates often prided themselves on their normal, traditional lives and committed personal relationships.

Hendrix's sexual conquests were so vast that they often ceased to have any real significance for him. Many women around him acted as if they, too, were sexually liberated, open in their sexual relationships, but few really were.

Hendrix's involvement with Angie Burdon, estranged wife of Eric Burdon, was a very public affair. In at least two incidents they got into actual physical violence. The first was witnessed by the roadie "H" (Howard Parker), a local music-scene insider in whose London flat they had fought. The second time was in the Londonderry Hotel on Jimi's return to London for what would turn out to be his last tour. The aftermath of the violence of that early morning in his hotel suite—where he, Angie, and another woman had spent the night in bed together—was witnessed by his former girlfriend, Kathy Etchingham. Angie had summoned her to the hotel so she would intervene and allow the girls to retrieve their clothes, which were inside the bedroom with an angry Hendrix. Angie and Eric Burdon shared (separately) a good portion of Jimi's final moments on earth.

Jimi's return to London as a headliner at the Isle of Wight festival had a big effect on the small, tight London scene. He had had a big impact in the recent past and his presence in town was keenly felt. Alfreda Benge—the girlfriend and later, wife, of Robert Wyatt (Soft Machine)—was candid about her attraction to Hendrix's flamboyant sexuality. Benge told Charles Shaar Murray, "For my generation of white females, he was the first person who transcended the sexual barrier between black and white. . . . It had never occurred to me to fancy someone black. He was a big breakthrough for antiracism. From then on, black people became fanciable."

Pete Townshend of the Who had found Hendrix's early London performances very sexual, not in an "appealing way," but rather, more "threatening." When he asked his girlfriend Karen Astley (who he married in 1968) if she thought Hendrix's act was sexual, and she replied, "Are you fucking kidding?," Townshend had been unaware of how "aroused" his girlfriend had become seeing those shows.

Eric Clapton could have been speaking for many men on the set when he revealed a frustration with Hendrix's sex appeal in remarks made to *Rolling Stone* in 1968: "You know, English people have a very big thing towards a spade. They really love that magic thing. They all fall for that kind of thing. Everybody and his brother in England still sort of think that spades have big dicks. And Jimi came over and exploited that to the limit . . . and everybody fell for it." Robert Wyatt doubted Clapton would have said such things to Hendrix's face.

Just over two weeks after Hendrix's return to London and the night before his death, Daniel Secunda, who was hosting Alan and Stella Douglas in his London flat, took his guests, Jimi, and Devon to dinner at a Moroccan Restaurant on Fulham Road. It was clear to Secunda that Alan Douglas was "hustling to take over as Jimi's manager." Michael Jeffery, who was thought to have solid under-world and intelligence-agency connections, had Jimi "by now, very worried." It was a strange night. "Jimi and the girls were so smacked out that, through the meal, they barely ate anything or even said a word. When we got back to my place," Secunda said, "Jimi went off to bed with Stella and Devon. He loved a ménage à trois."

Alan Douglas, who is described by Sharon Lawrence as a "white man who affected the look of a black man, complete with Afro hairstyle, goatee and, often, deep tan," had many times been in contention with Hendrix's manager, Michael Jeffery, for influence and a working relationship with Jimi. He had a meeting with Jeffery just after Hendrix's death. Said Douglas, "When I arrived he was bent over, in misery from a recent back injury. We started talking and he let it all hang out. It was like a confession. The one thing he said that I'll never forget was, 'Every time I had a woman I cared for, at some point I would realize that she was with me only to get to him.'" Douglas added, "In my opinion Jeffery hated Hendrix because Jimi had slept with Lynne Bailey [Jeffery's girlfriend]. Being so open, Hendrix couldn't have understood why Jeffery might be upset."

But Hendrix's potential conflicts were not limited to jealous husbands, wives, girlfriends, and boyfriends. He was also having a serious conflict with drug smugglers who were pressuring him to allow them to use his tour appara-tus to make it possible for them to smuggle large amounts of cocaine and other substances. Some, who had made him frequent gifts of coke, hash, marijuana, methamphetamines, LSD, poppers, and other substances, felt he owed them a favor. Others had used their entree, through gifts, to increasingly pressure him to comply.

Throughout his life as a star, Hendrix had frequently been dosed with drugs by fans and friends who meant well. But since the beginning of 1970, he had to deal with some of the most severe dosing he had ever encountered.

Jimi could handle most substances. Though often challenged, he could usu-ally get through a set. But during his last European tour his behavior had been seriously affected on several occasions, and he had been unable to play.

Jimi would not be as totally disoriented as Billy Cox had become, yet they were affected in similar ways by dosing. Jimi could still function impaired, could keep on moving and eventually rebound, but Billy Cox was another story. Once Billy returned to the States, Jimi was relieved of having to care for him, but he lost connections with that survival energy. And, as it appears, Jimi was still susceptible to being dosed.

·   ·   ·

Dannemann published a book in 1995, *The Inner World of Jimi Hendrix,* in which she describes fantastic plans she and Hendrix had allegedly made to marry, to have a child, to live in Europe. He encouraged her painting, he telephoned her mother, he was concerned about her father, who she maintained had recently had a heart attack. She understood that they could not officially announce their wedding yet, since the press would surely challenge her father's recovery. On the cover and title page of her book she prefaced her name as author with: "by his fiancée."

Most of Hendrix's close friends doubted that he would even consider marriage to Dannemann. Jimi proposed marriage on many a one-night stand, but it was understood to be essentially an amusing extension of/variation on a pickup line.

Dannemann's variances in her stories of Jimi's last days are now legend, and many of them have been completely discounted. Her statements at the inquest perhaps began these fictions. Researchers have pretty well established that Hendrix was not living with her at the Samarkand Hotel. He had no clothes there other than a headband, but his most important possession was there: his Fender Stratocaster. It has been established that he was changing clothes and taking meals at the Cumberland Hotel. He didn't often sleep there, but neither did he often stay at Monika's.

Another little-known piece of the puzzle that took years to surface concerned three people who encountered Jimi and Dannemann as they drove in traffic on the afternoon of September 17, hours before Hendrix would die under extremely mysterious circumstances.

Phillip Harvey was tooling along in his 1968 Mustang with two young and attractive teenagers in the front seat with him. The girls saw Jimi and waved, and Jimi waved back. They came up next to each other and got to chatting. Harvey invited Jimi to his home for a drink, and Jimi accepted, but first they followed him to the Cumberland Hotel, where Jimi got his messages, and then Jimi, with Monika driving, followed Harvey to his nearby home.

Monika parked her sports car in front of Harvey's fashionable town home. It was clear he was a wealthy young man of status. One of the young women was Anne Day, a redheaded Canadian folksinger of nineteen who was staying there with Phillip; the other one was Penny Ravenhill, who was sixteen. They were, according to Harvey, "very attractive in a natural kind of way, they were both wearing tight blue jeans without any makeup or adornment at all." Harvey contrasted their appearance by commenting that Dannemann appeared to be about thirty years of age, "an overly made-up lady with dyed blonde hair."

Harvey waited for more than twenty years before coming forward to recount Hendrix and Dannemann's visit to his home. The good scene turned ugly at the end with Monika becoming violently angry with Hendrix when he retired to a small room with one of the girls. Dannemann stormed out of the house, shouting loudly on the respectable street that Hendrix was a "fucking pig." Embarrassed, Jimi followed her out. She refused to return and Jimi came back inside to apologize profusely. He left and Harvey watched them drive off noting that the time of their departure was about 10:30 P.M.

Phillip Harvey, the son of the prominent politician Lord Harvey of Prestbury, a Conservative member of parliament, is nowadays known as the Honorable Phillip Harvey. He had remained silent about the encounter because of his family's prominence in public service. But after his father's death, in 1994, he felt it was all right to reveal this significant prelude to Hendrix's death.

Dannemann maintained at the inquest and in statements to the public and to writers and others that after the encounter with Harvey, Anne, and Penny, she and Hendrix went to her hotel suite at the Samarkand. But others maintain that he went on to a party at the home of Peter Cameron very soon after the visit to Harvey's. He did not take Monika in with him. Devon was there; Stella and Alan Douglas; his old nemesis, Angie Burdon; and several others. Dannemann maintains that Jimi asked her to pick him up after a short time, but those at the party indicate that Jimi came, ate Chinese food, hung out, and was cool until sometime later when Dannemann began ringing him on the intercom. He put her off but she persisted by coming back in half an hour. This became a heated thing. Stella got on the intercom and was extremely rude to Monika. This did not put her off. Pretty soon, Angie recalled, guests were hanging out the window yelling at Monika. They cried, "Fuck off" and "Leave him alone," yet Dannemann persisted. Then finally he went to the intercom, mumbled something, and then without saying anything, just got into the elevator and split. "That was around three in the morning by then," according to Angie Burdon. This may have angered Dannemann all the more since Jimi had stayed so long at a party where she was not welcome, and in fact had been ridiculed, insulted, and cursed.

Monika Dannemann turns out to be quite the mystery woman. There is little if any biographical information on her in England, the United States, or in Germany. She may or may not have been who she said she was. Suppressed information that has come to the fore provides a surprising turnaround from Dannemann's long-disputed versions of her story of Hendrix's last days. Also to consider are the various monumental motivations of the characters interacting with Hendrix during his last days.

Monika Dannemann is at the top of that monumental motivation list. Although maniacally opposed to any notion that she may have indeed been just another "groupie," Dannemann's suppressions tended to reinforce that notion of her own groupiedom. Other black musicians, such as Ram John Holder, Al

Anderson (lead guitarist with Bob Marley and the Wailers), and Jerome Rimson (the itinerant African-American bass player), all spoke of a close relationship with her before Hendrix came along. Her unrealistic fantasies of married life with Hendrix, and her great anger with him and the girls they encountered with Phillip Harvey, reveal an irrational, volatile, dangerous side to her carefully constructed image. Her struggle to express herself creatively and be validated seems to lie behind many of her public statements and actions. In fact, no one ever heard of her until Hendrix died in her bed.

According to several of his close friends, Devon Wilson was the closest Hendrix had been to having a real girlfriend. They had an open relationship that was unorthodox in many other ways as well. She lived with him at 59 West Twelfth Street in New York City, an apartment she had found for him to rent. Hendrix had made it clear that he did not want her in England during what turned out to be his last tour. The fact that she showed up in London did not please him. He told Judy Wong that he and Monika would marry, he knew that Wong (who was married to a member of the rock group Jethro Tull) would tell Devon. The object of this obvious intrigue was to needle Devon. She responded, threatening Monika physically. Hendrix had to know that would be her reaction. He purposefully pissed her off. They had a history of doing this kind of stuff to each other and then making up. Hendrix, a participant in innumerable one-night stands, was known to often play newlywed or at least fiancé with many he bedded. He had long played with the sanctity of marriage: lately it had been a preoccupation. He had expressed a desire to marry angelic model/actress Kristen Nefer, whom he had recently met and who had been his companion from just before the Isle of Wight gig at the end of August 1970 until his leaving for the Isle of Fehmarn, Germany, about ten days later. Nefer might have continued touring with him, but she was filming a movie. She had managed to accompany him on his Scandinavian gigs, and he had stayed with her and her family in Denmark. Somehow the local papers had reported they were to marry.

There was no doubt that at the time of his death Devon was provoked and angry with him, as, strangely enough, it appears Dannemann was also. And so were others close to him. Alan Douglas, Michael Jeffery, Eric Burdon could have been angry—although they could have never expressed anything that would alienate themselves from Hendrix, the king of the music scene, and necessary to their success in the music business.

Michael Jeffery had several things going with Hendrix. On one hand Jeffery had made Jimi's dream, Electric Lady Studios, a reality, even though Jimi provided most of the funds. Jimi had become a very wealthy man, but mainly from his live performances. He had cash. But a lot of that cash had been lost, and other funds had been documented as missing. Jeffery was not above impacting Jimi's creativity. He was against Jimi playing with black musicians. Taharqa and

Tunde-Ra Aleem (the Ghetto Fighters, aka "The Twins," Jimi's personal backup singers) laughed at how Jeffery and the all-white office staff would always refer to them—Billy Cox, Buddy Miles, even Jimi—as "the boys," totally unaware of the insult.

It seemed like Jeffery was not only against Jimi getting involved with black musicians, black politics, or radical organizations, like the Black Panthers or the anti–Vietnam war movement, but he also kept mainstream politics away from his star, which Jimi learned after the fact. In 1968 Robert Kennedy tried to reach Jimi after the Martin Luther King Jr. assassination to help offset unrest that summer. Jimi was being recognized as a person of power who could help influence the course of the nation. But Kennedy himself was assassinated that summer, never having heard from Hendrix because Jeffery refused to deliver the message to Jimi. The same happened the following year when Richard Nixon sought to include Hendrix in a countercultural conference the White House was sponsoring for its own edification. Again, Jeffery failed to deliver the message. And Jeffery's employees would publicly insist that Hendrix was color blind, unaware of race.

Hendrix had made it public on several occasions that he was dissatisfied with Jeffery's management and wanted a change. Alan Douglas seemed anointed by Hendrix to succeed Jeffery. In September of 1970, Douglas, a noted producer, was doing well with his Last Poets album, which was in the *Billboard* Top 30 best-selling LP list. Jeffery knew that if his management deal with Hendrix ended in December 1970, less than three months away, was not extended, everything about that management history and his other partnerships with Hendrix would be up for review—and there was a lot of money missing and a lot of other inconsistencies that have been revealed in the subsequent years.

Alan Douglas was the point man, trying to help Hendrix with the transition. But it was, kind of, all in the family. His wife, Stella, was very close to Hendrix. This situation was a factor in Hendrix's trust of Douglas. Stefan Bright, Douglas's recording engineer and employee, believed Stella, Devon, and Colette, Stella's design partner, were "very intriguing women. Especially Stella and Colette, who were so sensual. The attraction was mutual. They were both beautiful but at the same time very sad people. Their relationship with Hendrix was intimate; it wasn't just, 'Let's go down to the Scene and listen to Jimi,' it went way beyond the club scene. Stella and Colette were more emotionally stable than Devon, who was in and out with Jimi so many times it was unbelievable, but in the end he always came back to the three girls."

Strangely enough, Alan Douglas would come to control Hendrix's music after his death and—with Stefan Bright as recording engineer—would make numerous serious creative decisions about Jimi's music.

Eric Burdon was strangely connected to Hendrix throughout his London days and especially in the hours leading up to the early morning of the day he died. Hendrix had sat in with his group War at Ronnie Scott's jazz club the night before in what would be his last performance. Burdon admitted (some twenty years later) that he had gone to the hotel suite where Hendrix lay dead or dying and helped "clean" the place. Burdon had been very close to Michael Jeffery, manager of the Animals, the group Burdon had been lead singer of. They were in court due to money missing from the Animals' bank account in the Bahamas, which Jeffery oversaw. Hendrix's funds had also been deposited there and then "lost." In the early morning of September 18, Hendrix had just left the party at Peter Cameron's house where Angie Burdon was with Stella and Devon. Eric and Angie had married while Hendrix was emergent in England in 1966–1967 and Hendrix may have been a factor in their eventual divorce.

Just about everyone who was with Hendrix during his last hours either worked for or was in some way financially connected to Michael Jeffery, or was part of the extended family of Alan Douglas.

Eric Burdon: "The business killed him and I just can't put it any better."

Jimi Hendrix did not die of a drug overdose. He was drowned.

Devon Wilson died a mysterious death at the Chelsea Hotel in New York City early in 1971. Some say she leaped or was pushed from a hotel window or the roof. Others say she was found at the Chelsea badly beaten, perhaps to death, with a needle sticking from her arm.

Michael Jeffery perished when his commercial flight collided with another airplane over Majorca, Spain, in March 1973.

Angelina "Angie" Burdon eventually divorced from Eric Burdon. She moved to Australia, where she was murdered by a boyfriend in 1992.

Monika Dannemann was found dead in April of 1996 in a small seaside town in England. A hose attached to the exhaust pipe of her Mercedes and routed through a window was said to have been responsible for her death, which was officially termed a suicide.

CHAPTER 1

eptember 18, 1970, the Notting Hill Gate section of London. Samarkand
Hotel, 22 Lansdowne Crescent, garden suite. The front door is wide open.
The bedroom is dark, blacked out. A solitary figure is on the queen-
size bed.

The bed is extremely wet. Jimi is fully dressed. He is on his back spread-
eagled like Christ upon the cross. His black jacket is covered by a towel across
his shoulders, both soaking wet. Vomit and red wine cover him and are all over
the bed. The stench is strong, dominated by the smell of the cheap wine. The
stain that suffuses his clothing and the bedding is red, from the red wine, something Jimi Hendrix seldom drank.

Lately it has been no secret that he has big enemies. His loving friends are
around him always, yet as spaced out as they usually are, what could they do if
he was seriously threatened?

He is alone in the room.

A body, so still against the thin gray mute of London dawn. A room deep
somewhere. Misty in soundless sleep. A gray aura murmurs from the long thin
body upon the blanket and coverlet. Gas heat whispers underground where the
earth rumbles with the sound of machine against concrete. Rising against the
pale blue India-print curtains, tiny slits of dawn filter through the top rows of
the gauzelike venetian blinds. The potted tree in the tiny sunken courtyard
stands against a wide barred window next to the white front door with a gold
engraving of a young Buddha. The white door faces a spiraling staircase with a
wrought-iron gate at the top. Two lions sit before each of the three gray-white
town houses that form the Samarkand Residential Hotel.

On the long residential street of Lansdowne Crescent, the Samarkand is opposite a block-long private park, fenced and locked. The key belongs only to the
residents of the crescent. Down the well-kept street, solid brick gray-white
town houses sweep in a curve past the Pakistan Embassy residence, twisting on
through the groves of high trees that surround the fine homes of upper Notting
Hill Gate. At the top of the hill are lines of shops and stores along Latimer Road,
where during the dawn hours strange-shaped vans and trucks of English manufacture energetically deliver their wares. The weekend is just about here. The

early morning will throb with the energy of people expecting their pay and a holiday.

Past Lansdowne Crescent, the hill begins a steep descent into the flatlands of Notting Hill Gate where the West Indians, East Indians, mulattoes, hippies, and poor whites live. There, the view from below Lansdowne Crescent shows trees so prolific they become a solid mass of green rising like a natural mountain.

At dawn, solitary figures appear at various points along Talbot Road, where the buses and the Underground station converge. Posters and leaflets line the boarded-up storefronts, wooden fences and posts announcing the latest West Indian dances and house parties. The great flea market of Portobello Road will be held tomorrow. Throngs of bargain-seekers and fun-lovers will come from all over London to rub shoulders and mingle in the ghetto at a safe time. Crews of locals will be lined up at points along the mile-long route, drinking beer spontaneously in outdoor pubs. Street musicians, solo and ensemble, will play before clusters of casual spectators. Bargains ranging from good antiques to various concoctions of West Indian and East Indian foods will be sold.

Back up on the crescent his body is still. Opposed to the grind of the daily workers' toil and time, his body often sleeps through their day to see some of them in his day, which is night.

Above London, moving across the world, a massive storm of fantastic colors sweeps voluminous currents and waves across hundreds of miles of landmasses and water at an incredibly fast pace. Sunrise over the Pacific Rim. Seattle. The sun is bright over the city on the hill. Fall, Indian summer; in the quick tinges of wind that hit with swift force, the harbinger of winter nights and the waters of the storms.

Time moving so fast, backward and forward, people and places move into scenes and then out again so quickly as if in the blink of an eye, they shift from one sphere of vision to another.

Seattle 1912. He sees sticking outward from a pinnacle, a hill, the high granite arm of a statue of an Indian man, tall and stately, pointing out over the buildings of downtown Seattle, out toward the lakes that lie before the Pacific Ocean.

People are crowded from the edge of the knoll to the top of the hill where, before the statue, a rotund man in a black frock addresses them with a megaphone from a reviewing stand. He is dwarfed by the statue he points to. He gestures broadly, shouting something about Indians. Then he rapidly reads a quote from the dedication: "When the last redman shall have perished and the memory of my tribe shall have become a myth among the white men, these shores will swarm with the invisible dead of my tribe . . . when your children's children think themselves alone in the field, the store, upon the highway, or in the silence of the pathless woods, they will not be alone. . . . At night when the streets of your villages are silent and you think them deserted, they will throng with the returning hosts that once filled them and still love this beautiful land. The white man will never be alone. Let him be just and deal kindly with my people, for the dead are not forever lost. Dead, did I say? There is no death, only a change of worlds."

The statue is of Chief Seattle, the Indian chief the city was named after. He is wrapped in a granite robe that appears strangely tattered. His left foot forward, his right arm raised toward the bays, he looks like he might either be beckoning or waving good-bye.

The tiny officious figure orating is the new reform mayor of Seattle, George Cotterill. He takes the occasion to reaffirm his liberal nature and to belittle the former administration, noting that its former chief of police was at this moment serving time in the penitentiary at Walla Walla.

The crowd roars with approval. On the outskirts of the crowd stands a group of blacks. They laugh, throwing up their hands; the two women are dressed in very fashionable clothes from the East; the three men wear tailored dark suits, their hats tilted and broken in Chicago style.

Nora, the youngest, laughs with the rest but she knows they really have little to be happy about. Black vaudevillians stranded in Seattle, they were wearing their stage clothes and wondering about their survival. Nora, whose full name was Zenora Rose Moore, twenty-nine going on thirty, was flirting with being an old maid, as the other showgirls would tease. Ross Hendrix was seventeen years older and had been married before. But she loved him, and their years on the road had strengthened an already natural bond.

A Model T Ford moves along the Pacific Northwest shelf, heading for Canada. The Pacific Ocean coming in and out of view on the left, faded white streamers trail and break off the speeding black car in the dust and wind. JUST MARRIED has been scrawled in white along the rear of the auto.

Nora and Ross Hendrix are the newlyweds. They have decided to live in Canada and quit the show-business life. Their colleagues accompany them for the ride. They all sing the big song from the hit black play *Darktown Follies*:

First you put your two knees close up tight
Then you sway 'em to the left, then you sway 'em to the right
Step around the floor kind of nice and light
Then you twist around and twist around with all your might
Stretch your lovin' arms straight out in space
Then you do the Eagle Rock with style and grace
Swing your foot way 'round then bring it back
Now that's what I call "Ballin' the Jack."

It was a great song that swept the nation and was adopted by the "colored" jazz musicians of New Orleans, who were doing a new thing that they called "jazz."

Ross desired to escape Jim Crow, a discriminative segregation against blacks in America, but he had to acknowledge that the black showtunes, dances, and plays were changing the nation, at least as far as entertainment and recreation went.

The rickety black Ford sped for Victoria Station and the ferry that would take them across the waters to another country.

Al Hendrix, Jimi's father, may have sounded a bit comical in his sincerity, yet he held you spellbound as he spoke, in his offhand way, about the early years of his life. It was not often Al Hendrix spoke this way. It had to be a long quiet Sunday afternoon with perhaps a few beers and a couple of shots of hard stuff. He would look off straight ahead and his eyes, which were usually sheltered by his dark creviced brow and high, close cheekbones, would shine with a liquidy light through the mahogany brown.

Al Hendrix: "My mother was born in Georgia [November 19, 1883] and raised in Tennessee. My mother and dad got stranded here in a show tour. That was before the First World War. And he wanted to go to Canada, so they went up to Canada to live. They took out papers and became Canadian citizens. My mother was a dancer. She was a chorus girl. A chorus girl back in those days used to wear tights and all such as that. My dad didn't do any entertaining, he was a stagehand.

"My father had a long name: Bertran Philander Ross Hendrix. He was born April 11, 1866, in a small town in Urbana, Ohio.

"I met a fellow in the army who had been through there. We had a hard time finding it on the map. My daddy had been married before. I don't know if they were separated, divorced, or what. I remember him telling me one time that he had been a special policeman in Chicago.

"My mother's sister was in the entertainment business, too. Her name was Belle Lamarr. That was her stage name. They always used some fantastic kind of name."

Belle and Zenora's mother, Al's grandmother, Fanny, was a full-blooded Native American of the Cherokee Nation. She had married a half Native American and half Irishman named Robert Moore in Tennessee in 1881.

Zenora Moore and Bertran Hendrix's marriage produced four offspring: Leon Marshall in 1913, Patricia in 1914, Frank in 1918, and James Allen Hendrix in 1919, the baby of the family. Bertran and Zenora became Canadian citizens in 1922. James Allen was called "Allie" by his mother and became simply

"Al" from then on. He worshiped his older brother Leon Marshall, who played both the violin and piano by the time Al became aware of music. Leon was long and lean with long tapering fingers on his large hands. He read and wrote music so well Bertran and Nora hired a piano teacher to help him advance. During the last part of the twenties Leon played the new jazz music so well that he had a discernible style of his own. He also was an excellent dancer who was very popular with the women. He had a regular dancing partner and they were often called upon to perform at public events, where they would do the generally popular waltz, tango, and even the Apache dance. But Leon shone when they got to the popular black dances: tap, the Charleston, the Lindy Hop. Leon often looked after Al and, at his youngest brother's insistence, taught him those dances he had mastered. Al never forgot those lessons, those steps. When Leon died suddenly of a ruptured appendix in 1932, Al, only thirteen, was devastated. His father died two years later. The family was plunged into insecurity and poverty, but they held on. It was the height of the Depression and Al began to hustle for every cent he could earn. The family soon adjusted to their losses. Al took up boxing and went out and got a job waiting tables at Jean Fuller's Cafe, an afterhours chicken place where his mother also worked on the weekends, supplementing the money she made doing laundry. Between orders Al would do some of the dancing he had cultivated and often received tips. The jitterbug craze grew and he and his sister Pat grew closer since he was the natural selection to escort her to dances, something Leon would have done. Frank was a wallflower, not very social. Pat and Al were photographed dancing to a Duke Ellington Orchestra appearance and it was printed on the front page of the *Vancouver Sun*. After that Al had local fame as a dancer.

Al Hendrix: "Duke Ellington came to Vancouver in 1936. That was the first time a big band came to Vancouver in years. Jitterbugging was in then. We used to have jitterbug contests. But they used to separate the whites from the blacks for the contests, because the whites thought they wouldn't have a chance against the blacks. Once four of us entered the contest: Buster Keeling, Alma, myself, and Dorothy King. We were the couples in the black group. They had a hundred dollars for the prize. They brought a jitterbug group from L.A. and they danced on the stage to show the folks what the jitterbug was all about. That's when jitterbugging first became a craze. Man, I picked it up real quick. I mean, shoot, I had all the timing, because I used to do a lot of tap dancing. We went down and put in an application for the contest. That night there were only two black couples in the thing. I thought we had it made. So I said, 'Well heck, we'll split the purse whoever wins and that'll be twenty-five dollars apiece.' But the girls went and chickened out and that made us so mad. They didn't want to go on. That just about killed me. I was so disgusted.

Twenty-five dollars back in those days was equivalent to about a hundred nowadays. I wasn't working or nothing.

"I used to go out and dance with a group, with a white band. But they couldn't play my type of music. They didn't have the rhythm. They'd flow the music along. I would try to tell the pianist to play stop-time music. So you'd get that *do do doot doot . . . duu duu.* I mean all the breaks in between the music. But man, he'd flow it all together. So I used to go out with them and dance, but I wouldn't dance to their music. I would be humming to myself in my mind when I danced. I would go along with it. But I had to steel myself. Still, I enjoyed it. I mean, I always thought I would be scared in front of a crowd. But shoot, the bigger the crowd, the better I felt. I would be enjoying myself, and entertaining myself, too. I used to dance in between breaks at intermission. This group would go around to different dances, and they'd call me and I'd go along. I wasn't able to make a living at it. I had other jobs. But I was able to make more in one night dancing than I could in a whole week of hauling wood.

"When Canada declared war against Germany, I knew it would only be a matter of time before the United States got into it. I knew the Canadian Army would come for me, because my brother served in the Canadian Army. I got my hat and headed for Victoria. I told Ma, 'Well, I'm on my way.' I tried to get a job on the railroad. But the old guy would never hire me. He'd tell me I was too daggum short. I wasn't too daggum short, he just wanted to fool with me. I was around twenty, but I was about at my full growth then. This was during the Depression and I decided to go on for myself. I told my mother I ain't coming back this way. I'm gonna go out and make something. So that's what I did. When I left I went over to Victoria and worked there for about two weeks, made myself a little capital shining shoes, and then came to Seattle. I had always planned on going to New York or Chicago, the big places. I'm glad I didn't go to those places. They were wild, cold-blooded. So I wound up here."

Al Hendrix liked the unconscious part of jazz dancing the best. It was like a dream, all the people watching while he lost himself in the dance, and he would perform by sheer improvisation, reacting spontaneously to the music.

Al's mother, Nora Hendrix, would laugh at his excitement over the new dance craze. Years ago, she used to tell Al that before he was born there was a dance introduced in the Negro musical *Darktown Follies* called the Texas Tommy that was the same as the jitterbug. This was in 1912 and 1913, when Nora and her husband were still very much in show business.

While others called the jitterbug the Lindy Hop, it made no difference to Al. He would add many steps of his own, steps he had seen done in movies by Bill "Bojangles" Robinson, or Fred Astaire, or Buck 'n' Bubbles. Preferring to dance alone, Al would start off in the basic jitterbug steps: two box steps with the accent off the beat, a kick and three hops on each foot, then the breakaway, and he was off on his own, flowing toward the space in his mind where he lost conscious awareness of his own dancing, the crowd, and the music. The music seeping into him as he moved in a semitrance, performing feats he could hardly remember when they were described to him afterward.

Al had benefited from his mother and brother's dancing ability. Nora had showed him some of his very best steps: how to "fall off the log" or do the Lazy Walk. The times had demanded they pursue non-show-business jobs, yet they never skipped an opportunity to work out the way they used to. As a child, Al had often seen his mother and aunt Belle perform the acrobatic dance steps so favored in vaudeville—African crossover dances such as Ballin' the Jack, the Texas Tommy, the Ring Shout, Cakewalk, Charleston, and other dances of the minstrel, vaudeville, and ragtime eras.

Al had a formidable array of dance steps to add to the largely improvised jitterbug. His steps seemed new to the youngsters who crowded around to watch him perform, first at high school dances and then at dance halls and ballrooms. Just over five feet tall, Al dressed in the style of the times, a zoot suit: a long jacket and ballooned pants that bellowed out at the thighs and knees, tapering to narrow cuffs. The suit was perfect for the acrobatic steps due to its outsize proportions. On the dance floor Al's size was no problem. Jazz dancing often featured extreme sizes, either very fat, very tall, very slim, or very short. His size did make dance partners a problem, however. Usually Al danced alone. When he could find a partner who could keep up with him, she was usually too big for him to do the acrobatic air steps, such as the Hip to Hip, Side Flip, and Over the Back.

Al could do more floor steps than anyone in Vancouver. Many touring vaudeville troupes would pick up local black youngsters who were very talented dancers and insert a gang of them in their show as an act. Some "picks," as they were called, went on to be big stars, while many, hired only for the town they lived in, were left to descend back into obscurity.

As a solitary "pick," Al would come to the center floor of the dance hall. Space would be cleared for him and a spotlight trained on him. The band would play one of their hottest numbers and Al would go into his thing. A top jazz dancer was certain to turn on the orchestra and the dance patrons, propelling the vibrations to a fever pitch. With dance halls competing for the crowds, an act like Al's was essential. Even though he danced alone, Al could turn the people on.

Benny Goodman had become nationally famous as the King of Swing through his coast-to-coast radio broadcasts. "Swing" had caught on as the name of the new dance fad, and became almost solely identified with Benny Goodman's orchestra.

Fletcher Henderson had actually solved the problems of large orchestras playing hot jazz. But Goodman received much of the credit. Unlike the confusion apparent in Dixieland, when several saxophones, trumpets, and other horns tried to mix in the cacophony, Henderson had arranged many of his songs along the call-and-response patterns of African music. The horns alternated riffs and also played the melody as an ensemble. When Henderson sold his arrangements to Goodman, the precision of Goodman's style, coupled with the marketing expertise of the eastern recording companies, made Goodman indeed the King of Swing. Fletcher Henderson and many other black orchestras had been playing these arrangements for almost ten years in Harlem, but few people outside of New York City had ever heard them play.

Al Hendrix first came in contact with swing through the radio broadcasts from New York, but he had already intuitively recognized in Louis Armstrong the roots of jazz.

One night in Seattle he danced with Armstrong and outdid every solo he had ever done. From the basic lindy steps, he had gone into Ballin' the Jack, swaying his knees together left and right, doing a beautiful time step as if he were stepping on feathers, then, stretching his arms out in space, he did the Eagle Rock. Arms high over his head, he swayed his entire body from head to toe, going into the Georgia Grind, rotating his pelvis in a circle to the beat of the music, then coming out into a Charleston for a moment. He parlayed the kicks into air steps, took a solo flight, landed in a split, and rose without the aid of his hands and arms into the jitterbug right on time with the music.

Eventually Al found a dancing partner who was just the right size. Lucille Jeter was shorter than he, tiny, yet very shapely, with very light brown skin and a smile of great promise. She was actually strikingly beautiful, but still too young to realize it. Her delicate features contrasted with the amount of energy she generated on the dance floor. She danced as if dance was life in essence.

Al had met Lucille at the home where he lived with friends from Canada, Donald Green and his sister Christina. Lucille was a schoolmate of the landlady's oldest daughter, Berthelle, and she had just happened by when Al and his roommates were heading out to a dance. Fats Waller was headlining with a local orchestra and it was quite exciting, as with anyone famous in the East who would make it to the out-of-the-way Pacific Northwest.

Berthelle brought Lucille directly to Al and introduced them, and then boldly suggested Al take Lucille along to the dance. She looked kind of young. Berthelle said she was nearly seventeen. Lucille was definitely quite attractive, and just the right size for the diminutive Al.

They went to the dance that night. No one except Al would dance with her because she looked so young. Al discovered she was only fifteen, and would be sixteen next month, October 12, 1941. But they had a good time, and danced well together. After a couple more dates they began to smooch and then began going steady, so to speak. It got to the point where Al met her parents.

Lucille, the youngest of eight children (two deceased and two given up for adoption) was born October 12, 1925, two months premature, to Clarice Lawson Jeter, thirty-one years old, and Preston M. Jeter, who was nearing fifty. During her early childhood Lucille was often without the care of her mother, who suffered from physical and mental ailments, and her father was also not well. It would be ten years after her birth that her family would be able to get back together. From birth she had only known insecurity in her family life. While her mother, Clarice, recovered from her illnesses, Preston's health problems began to merge with old age. Although still in high school Lucille was well aware of the burden she was on her parents.

They had no strong objections to their daughter's relationship. Preston Jeter's facial expressions and mannerisms reminded Al of the blustery white actor Wallace Beery. He seemed to be a stern and unyielding man, but Al's sincerity grew on him. Lucille's parents may have been relieved that Lucille was with someone older (six years), who was a serious workingman. Lucille could have been considered somewhat fast for her age. She had already established herself as a local jitterbug champ. Her little frame could really go. She reveled in the nightlife of jazz and had great enthusiasm. She had a great sense of humor and loved to laugh. Al and his family knew all the blacks in Vancouver, B.C., as there were so few, and he knew through experience there was no woman there for him. But here in Seattle he had found love.

Although the war in Europe had been staring everyone in the world in the face for several years, the United States' entry into the war came as a shock to the citizens of Seattle.

Seattle shared the Pacific Ocean with Asia, so things were especially weird there. Almost overnight Seattle became a closed town. The city had been making civil-defense preparations for some time, and when the U.S. entry into the war was announced, a secret command took over the city.

Some places not far from the center of town became off limits overnight. Curfews sprung up. Blackouts and bomb drills became an immediate way of life. The air of hysteria channeled into passionate patriotism; everyone was threatened. Paranoia became intense. Japanese Americans were quickly interred in detention centers out in the countryside of Washington State and in other locations on the West Coast. The storm of war settled over Seattle. Anxiety about life and death became a strong element in everyone's mind. The cruelties of existence under strife were taken for granted.

Lucille Jeter had just turned sixteen years old when war was declared. The war hit her hard, as it did all of Seattle, especially those just attaining adulthood. They had to make heavy decisions fast, decisions that could span their lifetimes.

Lucille and Al had just discovered that she was pregnant and he had received his draft orders.

They married just before he left to join the army. That was not so unusual. The couples they had gotten to know, most of them regulars at the jitterbug dances, swing clubs, and ballrooms, were faced with similar situations. Every week the ballrooms had more and more couples dancing their farewell dances, very often with the male already in military uniform. It seemed as if the entire swing world had joined the military overnight.

The music became a focus for unity, especially among the youth of America. The ones who had loved to dance now had to fight a war. The big swing band became a symbol of the unity of purpose of America. Glenn Miller and Benny Goodman conducted in uniform. The big bands were going overseas to entertain the boys on the front lines.

Jazz had a fantastic impact on the war. Hot jazz, or American swing, became an immediate rage in England and Europe. It was like the bugle call of the cavalry. Jazz became synonymous with the swinging American youth, the jitterbugs and cultural epicureans, who had adopted the music of black Americans. Europe in her history had felt the distant strains of Moorish martial music before. The dark Arabs and North Africans had ruled much of Europe for several hundred years, and the fighting ability of the Moors was well remembered in European history. The black Americans were jitterbugs, the white Americans swinging Lindy Hoppers. Jazz brought a great morale lift to the European fighting forces. Jazz was relatively new music to the Europeans. Although the cultural elite had always expressed an interest in it, World War II exposed the masses of Europeans to jazz. They flipped. Jazz was a balm that at the same time lifted their spirits. It gave them the intense joyous detachment of the Harlem hipster. Listening to jazz was like meditation, yet it did not cut you off from the world. In fact, jazz made you want to dance, to act, to express. Jazz became the dominant cultural symbol of the triumph of the Allied forces in the war.

Al and Lucille soon began to hear a new and exciting musician on the national coast-to-coast broadcasts of the Benny Goodman band. Featured with the band was a name new to the devotees of swing, Charlie Christian. Never before had a new and unknown person had such an impact on the music within such a short time. The reason was the amplified guitar Christian played. Christian could play rhythm with the best, chomping along and adding some nice tone colorings, as well. But Christian could also play intricate melodies with his electrified guitar. The sound was thrilling and immediate; it opened up new realms of meaning for the dancing swingers and the followers of the music itself.

Few "colored" musicians had ever had the exposure of Christian. It had been rough going for the white bandleader to even include a black player during those Jim Crow times. Benny Goodman had used Teddy Wilson in New York, but had to go through a lot of changes to do it in 1936. In 1941 things had changed in the States. War seemed imminent. The Jim Crow laws in the South and the racism in the North began to quickly recede as national unity became the only posture reasonable in the face of Hitler, who, by the way, thought jazz one of the strongest elements threatening the destruction of the pure white Aryan race.

Charlie Christian's electric guitar sent the banjo back to folk music. Electrically amplified, the guitar was able to top the rhythm with beautiful and strong sound, and then to step out of the background and deliver solos that gave definite blue tonality to the blues-inspired jazz, with slurs and fading vibratos and long sustained lines that were perfect for dance and for listening.

At the same time, uptown in Harlem, Christian was also contributing heavily to a new and secret music based on black rhythms, blue tonalities, and shouts with the likes of "Dizzy" Gillespie, Thelonius Monk, and Kenny Clarke. This music, "bebop," would, in a few years, change the face of jazz irrevocably.

The sweet swing music of Goodman tremendously limited the genius of Charlie Christian. He gave more of his tradition than he received in inspiration. Many nights he would go uptown to Harlem after his gig with Goodman to sit in with some young and crazy black musicians who had all of Harlem in an uproar over the new music they played. Minton's, located in the Hotel Cecil on West 118th Street, was the room for the new music. Goodman's rhythm section usually played straight 4/4 rhythms with the drummer hardly ever varying from the straight jazz march beat. Uptown in Harlem, Kenny Clarke had pioneered a drumming style that had expanded the drum polyrhythmically. Kenny Clarke's drums would talk to the soloists, exploding bombs according to the peaks of intensity of the music, rather than by arrangement. Keeping time with his right hand rather than his right foot, Kenny Clarke also expanded the use of the ride cymbal and high-hat, thus giving wide rhythmic material for the soloists to feed off.

Charlie Christian became an underground hero to the jazz aficionados who flocked to Minton's from all over the tristate area to hear the new thing in jazz. At the same time he was a mainstay of the Goodman band downtown. While other guitarists such as Lonnie Johnston with Louis Armstrong and Floyd Smith with the Andy Kirk band had been important in the evolving of the guitar as a solo instrument, it was Charlie Christian who took it all the way in.

For the bop musicians, old standards such as "I Got Rhythm," "Stardust," and others became vehicles for solos, their melodies inferred, just as the blues tonalities in jazz had been inferred for so long. The wild and emotional soloing at Minton's would become the dominant jazz style after the war. In 1941 it had every jazzman looking over his shoulder for the wave that would be sure to engulf him. Even Louis Armstrong was rumored to have put down bebop as something resembling Chinese music. But the war would defer the coming of bebop for some years, strengthening its base in black Harlem while the nation and the Allies swung to the Benny Goodman and Glenn Miller bands.

Charlie Christian never lived to see either the full birth or bloom of bebop— or the U.S. entry into the Second World War. He died of tuberculosis in late 1941.

The newlyweds were only able to live together a few days before Al left for the war.

Al worried about leaving his young wife pregnant and without financial support. She was only sixteen and the baby sister of seven siblings in a family that had trouble keeping it all together. She was young, afraid, and no stranger to separation and abandonment. And in 1942 the war was especially tough.

When Al and Lucille's son was born, at 10:15 A.M., November 27, 1942, she had just turned seventeen. Without Al to consult she named the baby Johnny Allen Hendrix and received a birth certificate from the city of Seattle with that name on it.

Al and Lucille had been apart for eight months—all of her pregnancy. Lucille had wanted to join Al in Alabama, where he was stationed for a while, but he was afraid of the prevalence of Jim Crow, which was rife throughout the South and in the armed forces, as well. Al would not let her come and had been sure he would be able to return home for at least the birth. But the abruptness of the Japanese attack on Pearl Harbor and President Roosevelt's immediate declaration of war meant that wartime administration was a mess and still getting itself together a year later.

Al, Lucille, and their newborn got a raw deal, but the same was true for many others. And on top of Al's absence it took months and months for Lucille to begin receiving the monthly government allotment checks. Al sent all he could. But the pressures of separation, the anxieties of war, and the extreme youth of Lucille combined to alienate them. Their estrangement was not unlike the falling out of adolescents. After all, Lucille was only seventeen and still a high school girl and Al was in his very first serious relationship.

Apparently, after she gave birth Lucille stopped writing him regularly, and he noticed the few letters and postcards he did receive were all from different addresses. The photos of the baby and of her with the baby were all sent by others with secondhand greetings from Lucille.

Lucille was living with a friend of her family, Dorothy Harding, when she went into labor. After she gave birth, mother and child returned to Dorothy Harding's home. But a newborn baby is difficult to put up with for the parents, much less a family friend. Lucille then moved to her parents' home a few days later. The Jeters lived in a converted garage (those in the neighborhood called it a "little shack") and the heat was not sufficient. Her father was not well. Her mother was working as a housekeeper for folks who were close enough to be considered friends of the family, the Gautiers. A newborn in a freezing house with a man who was ill was a bad combination. When Lucille stayed away for a couple of days, her mother, Clarice, had to take the baby to work in a severe snowstorm and he had gotten very cold and wet. Freddie Mae Gautier and her mother, Minnie, demanded the baby stay there until the storm ended. When it became clear that all involved, including Lucille, thought it best the baby stay there for an extended time it was set up that way for a while.

Al received a formal photo taken in a professional studio of wife and son seated in a chair. His baby boy appearing healthy and Lucille looking quite beautiful just about broke Al's heart.

Then Lucille was hospitalized in June of 1943 with a circulatory illness that resulted from the concentration of blood in certain parts and organs of her body: hypostasis. Her father, Preston Jeter, died at home later that month on June 25. Lucille took a job as a waitress since she still had not received any allotment (family support) money from the government. On July 4 her baby was admitted to King's County Hospital with pneumonia. Grieving the loss of her father, Lucille entered into the first stages of becoming an alcoholic.

It is July 4, 1943. Johnny Allen Hendrix, eight months old, is held to the window of King's County Hospital by a white-smocked nurse. The display of fireworks is particularly impressive this war year.

Johnny Allen had awakened to the great flashes of lights in the sky. The nurse had found him there awake, calmly surveying the rush of brilliant lights against the darkening sky. As she changed his diaper in the dim light of the infant-care ward, the nurse wondered what the fate of this little boy would really be. His mother was not all right.

Lucille had been consumptive from birth. The weakness of her constitution and the excitement of the war years was a bad combination, especially for a lonely, very young woman. Taking care of a child required a lot of strength on a steady basis. It would mean an end to the frolic of music and dance. She had gotten back out into the world too soon. Her baby's delivery had been difficult. She had been advised to rest for a year, but as soon as she had felt strong enough she had gotten back out on the dance floor and tested her small strength to the fullest. As for little Johnny Allen, he would have to be elsewhere; he certainly couldn't stay in the infant-care ward for the months necessary for Lucille's recovery.

Al Hendrix: "They never gave me a furlough when he was being born. They told me when I went into the service that during emergencies, sickness, birth, or anything like that, you could get a *furlough*. But I was down in Alabama and all they allowed was a fourteen-day furlough. As slow as transportation was at that time, it would have taken me about fourteen days to *get home*. So I tried to get a longer furlough. I talked to the battalion commander and he told me, 'Hendrix, by the time you get home you'd have to be turning around to come back.' I was *mad*. He could see it. When I walked out he said, 'Hendrix, don't think about going over the hill.' I turned around and said, 'Yes, sir,' and I threw him a salute. Daggummit. Not a week from that day we were all getting ready to go to mess, and on the late bulletin they had the names of the guys going into the stockade. There were three of us who went to the stockade on that day. I was one of them. I asked my top kick, I said, 'What the hell am I being put in the stockade for?' He told me, 'General principles, general principles . . .' I say, 'Well, daggummit, usually a person has to be convicted of something.' I said, 'Well, I ain't did nothing.' Man, I just went to chow and come back. Sure enough the next day they took the three of us to the stockade. I said, 'Well, ain't this cold.' I was in the stockade two months, but I didn't lose any pay. I guess they were afraid I would go AWOL. That's why I was railroaded. The day before our outfit was to leave, the MPs brought me back to the barracks. We were going to embark on the train. I got my gear together, and I went back and spent the night in the stockade. They brought me back to the barracks the next morning, and I got my gear together and we got on the train. And went out there to the California coast to go overseas."

From California the troop ship stopped at New Caledonia and New Hebrides, but they did not disembark until they hit the Fiji Islands. There Al was stationed, providing security for the airbase. Al then was sent to Guadalcanal, where he saw Japanese POWs. He ended his service guarding airstrips in New Guinea.

During Al's absence Lucille's struggle with alcohol often got the better of her as she, unable to live with her parents, began a semi-itinerant existence. She always checked to see that her child was being taken care of, better than she thought she could do herself, and then went off again. She, like many others, dealt with the severe uncertainties of the war in her own way. Lucille created a parallel universe, of sorts, within the bars and clubs and many parties. She was not yet eighteen years old.

Lucille became involved with a strange, violent man named Joe Page. It is unclear whether she was being controlled by loneliness or fear of violence, but he took her to several locations in and out of Washington State before arriving in Vancouver, Oregon, where he beat her badly enough for her to be hospitalized. He was arrested for violation of the Mann Act (taking Lucille over state lines when she was still a minor) and imprisoned.

In the meantime friends and relatives had retrieved the baby, who began to live in and out of essentially foster-home situations, except it was between relatives, friends, and church members—the black community of Seattle took care of Al and Lucille's baby. They were not the only family having extreme difficulties during wartime.

Al Hendrix came back from the war in November of 1945. He was twenty-seven years old. In Seattle, departing from the troop ship, he was just another soldier returned from the war, disoriented, unemployed, looking for the loved ones he had left behind. He had been gone three years, seven months.

He had heard that Lucille had been sick. He had heard that the boy she had borne him was staying with relatives. He had not heard much more that made sense. Months of looking out into the darkness of war, the only reply a shot, an explosion, a crawling or running soldier: a sad resignation lined his face that day. He was used to uncertainty by now; the war had given him a cynicism usually reserved for a much older man. The war had bred a fatalistic calm into him.

He managed to get to his sister's all right, heavy duffel bag and all. She gave him the cries and hugs and tears, but he wanted to know about his boy. She seemed to be saving that for later, trying to act in accordance with the concept of a soldier hero returning home. But he was not a hero and there was no homecoming. He had been a simple soldier and now he was a young man trying to pick up the pieces of a life he had had to leave nearly four years ago.

Al Hendrix: "My wife and I had been separated when I came home from the service in 1945. During the time I was in the service, she had left him with this person and with that person and one thing and another. The people always kept in contact with me, the different ones that had him. I would send her an allotment home. The government had a deal for sending allotments home, and besides I was trying to send extra money home. But after she and I separated I wouldn't send nothing to her. Of course she got the government allotment. She was entitled to that. Jimmy was down in Berkeley, California. He was staying here with a woman in Seattle, I forget her name, but she died and then her sisters came from Texas and took him down to Berkeley. She lived in Berkeley. And when I came out of the service—I had kept in contact with this woman, and she had told me about her sister dying—I went down to Berkeley when our ship came in. I had come from the South Pacific. We were supposed to come in on Navy Day and I figured I would be discharged in Frisco. But on Navy Day the harbor was full of ships, and they weren't able to discharge us there. So I got discharged up here in Seattle. I immediately went down to Berkeley and got Jimmy. He was three years old. He had never seen me before. The people there had a picture of me in uniform, but it was a strange thing. I missed all his baby days and that's what I always wanted to see."

Before the war, Al Hendrix had never travelled any farther than the distance between Vancouver and Seattle. Now he undertook the third-longest journey of his life. He rode the Southern Pacific out of Washington State, through Oregon, and finally into California. Al disembarked at the Oakland depot on Sixteenth Street near the bay. A cab took him over the train tracks and headed down the East Bay streets into Berkeley.

Al was impressed by the view. The bay waters leading straight across to San Francisco, a silver-blue glistening city softly covered by a billowing fog. Veering from the approach to the Bay Bridge, the cab began driving toward the hills; the incline soon brought the bay back into sight through the receding stucco and brown-shingled homes. Al had the cabdriver slow down as he checked the numbers. They cruised along Grove Street until they came to a two-block-square low-rent housing development.

Savo Island Village was relatively new at that time and did not differ that much from the surrounding homes. Al was impressed. Berkeley seemed an affluent town. The Village looked peaceful and dignified—a nice place for his child, thank goodness.

Al Hendrix: "Those people didn't want to give him up. But she told me in a letter, 'I know you've been thinking about your son all the time you been in the service, and I'm not gonna hold him.' He knew them, he only knew me by a picture. They'd ask him who was Daddy, and he'd point to the picture and say, 'That's Daddy.' So when I got there that was a strange feeling. To see your own kid, and he's talking and walking around, and doesn't know you.

"I always wanted to be around my first child and raise him and just do things with him. When I got down there I stayed with them for about a week. I used to send the woman money all the time. They were very nice people. I often wonder where they are now. I don't remember the woman's name, but her daughter's name was Celestine. They were Texans. Everybody was taller than me. I said, 'You Texans sure do grow tall.' They were a nice family. Celestine, she was around my age, and she was way up there. They figured that I should leave Jimmy with them because he knew them. I said, 'Yeah, but this is my son, he's the only thing I thought about all the time I was in the service. Shoot, I want the boy,' I said, 'this is *mine.*' She told me in her letters, 'I know we are more accustomed to him than you are and it's gonna hurt us when you come down here to get him.' She didn't even go down to the train when we left. Nobody went down to the train. I felt bad about it, but I told them this is part of me, and I'm gonna take care of my kid.

"Of course, Jimmy was only three years old, he didn't know what was happening. All he knew was that he was going on a train ride. I had to give him his first whipping that night, though. He wanted to run up and down the aisles, and I said, 'Well, father and son got to get to know each other.' And he just kept running. Of course, he didn't pay attention to me, he didn't know me from Joe Blow. So I had to whip him. He said, 'I'm gonna tell Celestine.' I said, 'Well you tell her. She would agree with me.'"

The first thing Al Hendrix did once he had gotten them settled in Seattle, at 124 Tenth Avenue, Room 580, was to change Johnny Allen's name to James Marshall Hendrix. It became official on September 11, 1946. James Marshall, after his own first name and that of his brother, who had died in 1932—James Marshall Hendrix: a name with dignity and authority.

Al Hendrix: "When I brought him back to Seattle, we stayed with my sister-in-law. She had three girls and with Jimmy we did all right. I was getting my rocking-chair money from the government, twenty dollars a week. I was looking around for some work but there wasn't much going on. But Jimmy was with me from then on."

Jimmy became known as Buster, perhaps after the Buster Brown character associated with a boys' shoe manufacturer very popular in the fifties. Buster Brown was a happy-go-lucky blond-haired boy dressed up in a brown suit who wore shiny brown shoes and lived in a big brown shoe with his brown pet dog.

Al and Lucille's separation did not lead to divorce; they reconciled. They had never lived together yet. As man and wife reuniting just about four years after the first days of their marriage, having undergone the worst of war and now the uncertain peace, they gave it a go. But Al saw very clearly that Lucille had changed. She was naturally more worldly than the sixteen-year-old high school girl he had left pregnant, yet she was just now coming up on twenty-one.

But theirs was a poverty-stricken existence. They had moved in with her sister Dolores, leaving the room Al had rented upon his return with Jimmy. When Lucille got word that he was back she simply showed up one day. After being reassured that Al bore no grudge that would harm her physically, she suggested they give it a try and he agreed. Jimmy gave her a cold shoulder similar to the one he had given Al, seeing him for the first time in his life when he was three years old. For Jimmy those months apart from his mother probably felt just as long as those years apart from his father. Jimmy was learning emotional distancing at an early age.

The family was not able to stay with Lucille's sister very long. They were three and they needed a place of their own. Soon they rented a room in the cheap transient Golden Hotel. They all slept in the same bed; there was no refrigerator and only a hot plate for cooking. The bathroom was in the hallway, shared by several people. It was very rough, very depressing. Prostitutes worked the streets around the hotel. It was the worst of neighborhoods.

Al worked two jobs to help make ends meet. The small weekly sum he received from the government ceased.

Al, after several attempts, got a job aboard a merchant ship going to Japan. Again he had to leave Lucille and Jimmy in difficult circumstances. In Yokohama he was able to clearly see the devastation defeat had wrought physically and practically to the spirit of the Japanese and the infrastructure of the society. But the people he saw had survived and so had he. However, when he returned after two weeks to Seattle, the hotel room was locked up. Lucille and Jimmy were nowhere to be found.

He soon discovered that Lucille, after she had let her mother take Jimmy on a trip to the Midwest, had gotten put out of the room. The way Al heard it, "Lucille and this guy were caught up there in the room together and all that old stuff. So the landlady put her out." Compounding the problem was that all his clothes and Jimmy's clothes were missing, and would never be recovered, including his army uniform, his most valued possession. All he had were the clothes he had shipped out with.

Al reunited with Jimmy and they went to stay with Dolores Jeter. Soon Al and Lucille were back together again. They all knew, including little Jimmy, that their future as a family would not be easy.

Al and Lucille got housing in the Rainier Vista housing projects in 1947. Things looked up. It was a nice place in a pleasant environment with lawns and trees. They had a one-bedroom apartment and began to buy furniture. Al and Lucille were actually setting up housekeeping for the first time in their marriage.

They had their differences but they also had sweet, affectionate times together. They noticed that when they fought Jimmy would retire to the large closet in the bedroom and patiently sit it out. He was not yet five.

Determined to improve himself, Al utilized the G.I. Bill to go to school to study electronics. He went to school until 3:00 P.M., stopped at home for a little while, and then went to work at the Pike Place Market to clean up after the farmers and tourists, not returning until around midnight. Very often he would not be able to spend time with Lucille or his son.

Sometimes Jimmy would be there alone when Al returned, the lights still on, afraid to go to sleep.

Al began to notice that whenever there was drink in the house when he left, it would be gone when he returned. Lucille, it was established, loved to party.

With a drink or two in her she would welcome others to drink with her. A party would often ensue.

Jimmy became very shy. Al noticed it, but having missed his formative years could not definitely attribute the shyness to their present conditions.

Lucille's mother, Clarice, was often around. She was crazy about her only grandchild. But Al noticed that when her mother was around for two or three days Lucille would often take off, confident that Jimmy would be looked after during Al's long hours away. She began to stay away overnight, then a day, two days. Then she began spending a lot of time elsewhere.

Al maintains that Lucille had an affair with a Filipino man that resulted in a pregnancy and the birth of Leon Morris Hendrix on January 13, 1948. But Al always affirmed paternity in various official declarations. Al and Lucille stayed together and Leon was raised as theirs. Al also has written that Lucille gave birth to another child, Joey Allen, from another affair the following year of 1949. They got a larger two-bedroom apartment and Al attempted to raise the boys.

They struggled to hang on.

Leon had an early recollection of Lucille not coming home and Al gathering Jimmy and himself up and packing them in the backseat of his car and searching for and finding her. She had been with another man but came back with them. An argument ensued in the car and she almost caused an accident by pressing on the gas and the brake simultaneously. Both Leon and Jimmy were propelled forward into the front seat. As Leon reported, she hugged and kissed them, dismayed that her actions almost harmed her boys, further noting that that was the most affection he and Jimmy had received from her in quite a while, perhaps in all of his memory.

Al, having no skills and having spent his formative years in the military, had a tough time finding a steady job. Without a job, Al had to make the tough decision to send his children away to his sister. That summer of 1949, Jimmy and Leon stayed with Aunt Patricia, in Vancouver, British Columbia. The summer visit extended into the fall and Jimmy was enrolled in the Dawson Street Annex Elementary School at the age of six. The school was close to their home in the West End area of Vancouver, near English Bay. Leon was still a toddler and envied his big brother going off to school every day. His grandmother Nora made him special Indian-style clothing and treated him as a special individual. He really appreciated that. But although he was in the first grade he nevertheless had attendance problems. Al would come up Saturdays and once gave Jimmy a spanking for "lollygagging" and "dragging his butt" on the way to school.

Jimmy became even more introverted. Aunt Patricia used to laugh at puzzled visitors who wondered about his silence, and told them that he never had much to say, even to her. Tragedy struck when Aunt Patricia's husband, Joe

Lashley, died suddenly. She brought the kids back to Seattle and stayed with them. Al and Lucille were living in a small room. Economically things were looking up: he had just landed a good job at the Boeing Aircraft plant.

Jimmy and Leon returned in November. There was a birthday party for Jimmy and they celebrated Christmas with a decorated tree and presents. There was some joy and laughter but there were also fights and drinking.

Al and Lucille separated, Lucille left the house, Al assumed custody, and soon they were divorced in December of 1951.

Leon recalled that after that there were no more Christmases nor birthdays with presents. Al, he maintained, said they were just "another day," but Leon believes Al did not have the money. Leon may have also been implying that Al may have lost the will to earn enough to rise above the extreme poverty they found themselves in.

While divorced Al and Lucille still saw each other, often staying together for lengths of time.

Joseph Allen Hendrix had been born less than a year after Leon, in November 1949. Severely handicapped with a club foot, cleft palate, and one leg shorter than the other, among other things, he required extensive medical intervention. The expenses of the therapy, specialized and personal care, and medications Joseph required were judged by Al to be impossible for the impoverished family to bear, even though the state would have picked up most of the costs of surgery. Although Al would dispute paternity he never challenged it in the various family court hearings. Joseph was the baby of the family only for a year until the birth of Kathy Ira, born four months premature, weighing just over a pound and a half, and, as it would soon be discovered, blind. Just before the birth of yet another child, Pamela Hendrix, in October of 1951, Kathy Ira was declared in family court to be a ward of the state and was fostered out. Pamela also had health challenges, though not as bad as her sister's. She was fostered out, as well. And then that next summer of 1952, Joe, who had lived with his family all of his two years and eight months, was made a ward of the state by Al and Lucille, ostensibly in order for him to get the developmental care he needed. Joseph remembers waving good-bye to Leon and Jimmy and then, in his mother's arms, being driven by Al to a location where, as he put it, he was left on someone's doorstep. Actually Lucille put him in the arms of a waiting nurse, but this all took place out of doors. Joseph waved good-bye to his mother for the last time from the curb where the nurse and he sat as the car pulled away.

Jimmy, nine, and Leon, four, were deeply impacted by Joseph's removal from the household, especially since it was preceded by the disappearance of two other children born to their mother—all in the short time of less than three years. They surely must have felt their own tenure with Al and Lucille to be threatened. And since their parents were officially divorced there was only Al, who had received legal custody, to take care of them. While it was obvious both of their parents were challenged by alcohol, it was clear it was Al as caretaker or nothing.

Leon became Jimmy's responsibility those days and although Jimmy was much too young, he did his duty. Jimmy and Leon would still secretly go and see their mother, who lived in the neighborhood. She was kind and affectionate to them when she saw them, but she was not home for long stretches of time. Drinking, which before had been more of a sporadic thing with her, had now become a habit.

Demoralized, it became even more difficult for Al to make ends meet. Some thought that his drinking and gambling further depleted the family's funds. Whenever things got really bad Al would send Leon to a foster home, and then it would be just him and Jimmy. And Jimmy, a big boy mature beyond his years, could pretty much shift for himself. Neighbors would intervene with meals and temporary care, and the welfare department kept an eye on the Hendrix family situation. When Al had the funds he would hire a housekeeper.

But as Aunt Pearl Hendrix maintained, Jimmy would often be dressed virtually in rags. She would buy him new clothes, including underwear. Because of his poor clothing Jimmy had an early remembrance of being driven out of church, which he often attended alone. He did not share many detailed memories of his childhood but he never got over the outrage he felt about that incident.

Summers were the best time for the brothers. The warm weather and the lack of the strictures of school gave them a lot of freedom. They could earn some money by picking butter beans with Jimmy's new friends from Leschi Elementary School, James Williams and Terry Johnson. They would leave before sunup and return at sundown. All the long day belonged to them. Al knew Jimmy was responsible with Leon so that was not a problem. James Williams's and Terry Johnson's people would feed the boys, as would others. They were like vagabonds, Leon felt, but that enabled them to venture off, from sneaking on freight trains to going swimming to simply wandering about, taking things as they came.

In school Jimmy showed talent for art, drawing landscapes, scenes of Old Mexico, and science-fiction themes. But Jimmy's poverty was a fact established to the point that Terry Johnson would give him some of his clothing to wear. Some folks thought Jimmy had trouble with his feet because he would often walk funny, but those who were close to him knew his shoes often had gaping holes in the soles, and/or extremely rundown heels.

Terry and his family would often host Jimmy when he could not get into his own house. That was usually when Leon was fostered out.

Jimmy and James and Terry liked to refer to each other as the Three Musketeers—all for one and one for all.

James Williams and Jimmy Hendrix's friendship was solidified by a teacher who looked down on black people, Jimmy and James became inseparable. They both had paper routes right next to each other, and every morning they would meet before and after their deliveries.

James. James Williams. Slight James. Big cheeks. Like the cheeks of a squirrel filled with nuts. Incredible big cheeks and a soft voice. Slightly self-doubting, but always his friend. James had a serious face that always held a touch of humor, a glimmer, a smile. Big white teeth, not bucked but coming out at you. He would have to grow into those big teeth. Even in James's big smile there was a sadness, a forlorn air that made the bigger Jimmy want to look after him. James's sadness made Jimmy forget his own troubles. And James was a true companion. With you to the end. That is, when he wasn't sick. Often harassed by his older sisters, his mother, or seemingly by life itself, he would seem to take refuge in sickness. Jimmy would make him laugh. Cheer him up. Think up things for them to do.

They were both very poor at the point in their adolescence when they began to be attracted to the girls of their neighborhood. But their clothes betrayed them; they looked like little hobos.

Jimmy would think of James as his brother; they were able to do things together. James was the smaller and more sickly of the two. Jimmy, tall and gangly, with amazingly outsized arms and hands, would look out for James. Jimmy had two fights with bullies who had come down on James. He won them both, no one suspecting that behind this gangling, painfully thin exterior existed a fierce and determined boy who had great love for James.

Leon, his little brother, was so much younger, so unknowing of what was happening. Yet Jimmy hardly knew himself what was happening, what had happened, or what would happen in the future. He couldn't tell Leon anything, and even if he could, Leon was too young to understand. James, on the other hand, was like him in many ways. Even if they were each confused about their life and ultimate fate, they at least had their bond. They had their insecurities to measure themselves against and could mitigate the effects by sharing their emotions.

They played together on the Fighting Irish football team (composed of only black and Japanese boys), Jimmy with his long arms and speed and big hands playing end. James, because of his eloquence and low-key air, became the captain and Jimmy the co-captain. They joined the Boy Scouts. When it came time for their trip into the wilds, they wound up in Leschi Park and became the laughingstock of all the troops.

One summer day after they had picked butter beans in the fields outside of Seattle while hitchhiking back to town, Jimmy began to talk about his mother. He had had disturbing dreams and was afraid she would die. She drank an awful lot, and she was sick a lot, and very depressed.

Then when he was just on the verge of his manhood, Jimmy's mother died. This hurt him deeply, yet he never said much about it.

Lucille had married again, but in 1958 her health had turned worse.

Al refused to take Jimmy to see her, but did permit Aunt Patricia to take him. Until she came back from Canada with the two children, Aunt Patricia had never met Lucille Jeter. She was afraid for Jimmy that his mother would look wasted and deathly in the hospital bed, but to her surprise, Lucille looked very good in the face, very pretty, with a shoulder-length pageboy hairdo. As usual, Jimmy did not have much to say. He mainly stared at his mother.

Lucille passed away shortly after their visit. She had been released from the hospital in pretty good shape, and cautioned to take it easy. But she did not follow the doctor's advice. She died of a ruptured spleen.

Al was greatly saddened, his face assuming deep lines of grief. The boys had never spent much time with their mother and now they would never have the chance.

Aunt Patricia attended the funeral expecting to see Al and the boys there. But the boys never came. Al would not let them go. For the most part Al mourned Lucille privately, preferring not to mix with her family and her second husband's people. Aunt Patricia would have taken Jimmy with her, but she did not know that Al was not bringing them until it was too late.

Al had the boys take a shot of whiskey with him as a way of mourning.

Soon afterward, Leon was fostered out, though not far from where they lived. Jimmy was still able to spend time with him.

Jimmy and his father became like two roomers, two old men who moved often from place to place, always at the mercy of one authority or the other: a new landlord, the unemployment officer, the schoolteacher, the welfare office, the foster home, and now that Jimmy was a teenager, the police. He was left back and had to repeat ninth grade.

Al, tiny and squint-eyed, was a strict authority figure because of his small five-foot-two frame, and also because of his belief that life had given him a bad deal. He seemed powerless against the forces that shaped his and his son's existence. But while it was obvious that they were almost totally at the mercy of forces beyond their control, he maintained a stern silence about all that had affected them. He was the adult, the one responsible for handling things, but sometimes they seemed to be handled so poorly, and Jimmy was very aware of everything.

• • •

His father's candor came not in the words he spoke, but in the spontaneous tears that often came after drinks. Jimmy learned to sense emotion rather than fact, and then it was not too hard to deduce that their plight was just about hopeless.

His father was not one for words anyway. An eighth-grade education had left him self-conscious about his verbal skills. Even when he tried to say something, somehow the words did not come. All of the deeper meanings of what affected their lives seemed to be tied up in big words that lawyers, doctors, teachers, and priests knew. Jimmy learned not to be impatient. He studied patience as the discipline that eventually would lead him and his father to a better life. He knew that his father would not tell him the truth about his mother, his brother, his birth, and his early upbringing. It couldn't be all that sad; but the depths of emotion that the subjects wrought in his father made Jimmy afraid to ask, especially about his mother. She achieved mythic proportions, monstrous in intensity, a woman so powerful even in death that she deeply altered the lives of a man and two boys.

His father nursed a hurt that showed on his face much worse than the teenage pimples Jimmy had. A hurt that gnarled lines around his eyes and mouth, lines that grew longer and deeper every day, spreading to the cheeks and the forehead, deep-setting the eyes even more. And he seemed to descend deeper into a sadness that washed into turbulent waves, never to come out clear with the reasons, the truth of the matter. Coming back even stronger day after day.

Whenever his father seemed on the verge of telling the story, when they were close and intimate and it became obvious that the natural direction would be to mention his mother, his father would either become tearful and go outside, or become very authoritarian. He would snap shut the train of thought and bark an order. Clean up your room, sweep the floor, wash the dishes. Then he would usually go on about his life in the service, or more to the point, the obligation to duty. When the top kick said to do something you did it, or you got your head blown off; and that's the way it is here: when I say do something, I want it done or else heads will roll.

Seeing through it, Jimmy thought it funny that his father would equate the military, with its thousands of men and huge bureaucracy, property, and funds, to a boy and his father alone in a room, in the world. But Jimmy would do what was said dutifully. All he could do was obey his dad. It made his father happy in a way. There was not that much to ask of each other, so many things being out of the question, so he did whatever his father asked, with as much love and effort as he could. It broke his heart, because what he was doing was something anyone could do, and while sweeping the floor or emptying the garbage he vowed to himself that someday he would do something that few people could do, something that no one else in the world could do, something great for his father.

Al Hendrix: "The way I felt about tap dancing is the way Jimmy felt about guitar playing. I mean, it was in him to do it. He felt it. It was no job, he enjoyed it. He just picked it up all of a sudden. He had no formal lessons. He used to practice a lot. I'd come home from work and he'd be there, *plunk, plunk, plunk.* If I disturbed him or something, he'd go on in the bedroom, and he'd be in there *plunk, plunk, plunk*ing. And I'd say, 'Jimmy, sweep the floor,' or something, and he'd say, 'Okay, Dad,' and he'd do that. And after he finished doing that he'd go back to *plunk, plunk, plunk*ing. I used to hear it constantly.

"He'd be plunking away, and I could almost see his vision of himself playing for a band. I mean, that's finally what he was doing, too. While he played around the house he was visualizing himself doing that.

"He got good on that acoustic guitar. He only paid five dollars for it from this guy. He asked me about it and I gave him the money to get it. And after that I went and got him this electric guitar. But before that he used to be plunking away on this old ukulele. I found it doing some of my gardening work. These people wanted me to clean out this basement, and I found it there and got strings for it. He used to plunk away on it before he got a guitar. He used to pick up a lot of pointers from different people. So many people tell me now, 'Oh yeah, my son taught your boy how to play.' I don't think anyone *taught* him how to play. I mean *any* artist, guitar players or singers, learn so much from *other* people. They just don't go straight up from themselves. Unless they get themselves a regular musical teacher and learn straight all the way. But Jimmy just wasn't in that kind of boat. We didn't have that kind of money. So he just taught himself. He just picked it up. It was just in him, and the guitar became another part of his anatomy."

So while he waited for adulthood, he talked to his guitar. Like a new person in the household his guitar became alive. It made a world of sound. It held all the songs, all the melodies, and secrets of the universe. Though there were agonies, broken sound soon became melody, string after string the laws revealed themselves to him. It was painfully slow, yet he liked the time-eternal agony of making that guitar talk. After all, he had all the time in the world, all the ageless silence of his room late at night or any time of the day. When he got with his guitar all time ceased. He was transported to other worlds and suddenly realized that what he heard in the guitar, what it coaxed him to bring out, was something totally between them, a relationship he had nowhere else. Just the simplest song melody carried his mind deeper into the potentialities of the instrument, the medium between him and the mysteries of the universe. He began to get a sense of what he could do and how long it would take to reach the sounds in his mind. Melodies he had never heard before came to him on rainy and windy nights and days, startling in their insistence.

He had not had many lessons. He liked the ease and the agony of the long-term agreement between him and his instrument, not taking for granted and shortcutting what they had together. After every trial and error, and every head-hurting drill he had to impose upon himself to master a line or passage, the final sound became his own. New precisely at that time, coming out of nowhere, created by that moment, elongated by trial and error to triumph and release. And his guitar began to respect him and he began to love it like no other love he had known. And then the guitar began to talk. It began to talk back to him. It began to chuckle at his mistakes and lead him to new truths at the same time. It began to murmur the sound he had heard in his mind for so long. It understood the frustrations of his situation. It could re-create every moment and then show him the proper relationship and release. The release was within him all the time. The guitar revealed its secrets and filled the void of lonely silence.

Now his father would find him at his guitar. And, as if he had found him communing with a priest, he would often soften his movements in respect. The quiet was pierced only by vibrating contralto sounds. The better he became with the sounds, the more his father respected his space and solitude. Al began to treat him better. His son now had a world of his own, a world he knew, a world he could understand. Jimmy had his own concern now, and when Al would interrupt him to sweep the floor or empty the garbage or clean up a bit, it was no longer a peremptory command out of the blue. Now Al would pop over and do a little song-and-dance vaudeville routine, or jitterbug to Jimmy's playing for a moment, and then he would say, "Sweep the floor a little bit, son," or "Wash the dishes" or "Empty the garbage." But it was a love command.

One of the first tunes Jimmy played on his acoustic guitar was "Peter Gunn," the theme song from a popular network TV detective show that aired weekly, and "Tall Cool One" by the Fabulous Wailers, a popular local band who frequented the classiest music venue in the Pacific Northwest: Spanish Castle, in nearby Kent, Washington.

Once he got an electric guitar he immediately learned the changes to the exciting hit "La Bamba" by Ritchie Valens. But his most appreciated achievement was learning to play "Bad, Bad Whiskey," Amos Milburn's great blues rocker, for James Williams's mother.

Jimmy also noticed that a girl he liked, Carmen Goudy, liked the fact that he was into the guitar. She encouraged his progress. Betty Jean Morgan was Jimmy's first real girlfriend. Recently from the South, she was unpretentious, sensitive to his moods, and supportive of his musical ambitions. She would often bring her little brother over when she visited Jimmy's home. When they were in Jimmy's room they always left the door open. Al was straightforward in his warnings to Jimmy: "You've got to watch yourself. I hope you don't go around getting any girl pregnant when you can't even take care of yourself."

Jimmy's first band was a group called the Velvetones. One of his best friends, Parnell Alexander, who also played guitar, was in the group. It would have been great if James Williams, who sang, and Terry Johnson, who was learning the keyboards, could also be in the group, too, but that was not possible. The Velvetones were not that good but they did manage to get a weekly stint at Birdland, the most notable of the local clubs in Seattle's black district. Their version of "Honky Tonk," originally done by Bill Doggett, had sealed that recurring gig. "Honky Tonk" was an instrumental that one could listen to all night. It was a laid-back yet funky blues rocker that had an intriguing, relaxing quality. The fact that his band played at Birdland gave him the traditional musician's free admission to the club, where he was able to compare notes with other guitarists, as well as hear a lot of live music for the first time.

Jimmy discovered that the vibrations of music can truly bring people together. He discovered through his closer relationship with his father that music is indeed magic. Music can heal wounds and offer other worlds. The guitar brought them closer together, and it made his father proud of him. His son was investigating a mystery he himself had always been close to yet had never mastered, though he had always wanted to. A man, a father worrying about not being able to pass along knowledge to his son, now had his prayers answered. His son was entering the secret mystical covenant. Jimmy's music filled the silence, made the walls sing, made the air smell better, and heightened their lives together. A simple man, Al Hendrix did not ask that his son be a Charlie Christian, he was just happy his boy was using his time constructively.

During Jimmy Hendrix's adolescence, rock 'n' roll became an overnight national phenomenon. American popular music finally opened up to its tribal and folk roots, and the American public voted for the new music with cash money. Jim Crow had finally begun to be legally defeated in the U.S. Supreme Court decision of 1954 striking down public school segregation. The black masses finally had a major legal sanction of racism removed from their paths. American music began to release its racism, as well, and reveled in the elemental music of the country. Rock 'n' roll swept the nation. The young people of America, the babies of the Second World War, began participating in this mass puberty rite, a wild musical initiation ceremony of incredible proportions whose momentum would transform these rites into a philosophy of life.

In 1954, black music began appearing on the national charts with increasing regularity. Up until that time white pop music dominated the national charts with only an occasional black entry. White pop music was most recently descended from the 1940s smooth big-band vocal sound, which had appealed to the youth of the wartime decade. In the early fifties this sound became the dominant taste in music.

In 1949, the biggest songs in the nation were white pop, with black music subjugated to a narrow "race" market. The top songs of 1949 were "Mule Train" by Frankie Laine, "Tennessee Waltz" by Patti Page, and "Ghost Riders in the Sky" by Vaughn Monroe. "Ghost Riders in the Sky" continued as the top song into 1950, when it was joined by Mario Lanza's semi-operatic "Be My Love." "How High the Moon" by Les Paul and Mary Ford, an advanced composition in its use of electric-guitar overdubbing, echo chambers, and follow-through mastering techniques, became a hit. The monster hit "Cry," a sad ballad by Johnnie Ray, entered the charts in October 1951 and was number one through all of 1952. Vaughn Monroe's "Old Soldiers Never Die (They Just Fade Away)," became a lament to the Korean War, which was at its height in 1952.

As early as 1947, "Old Man River" by the Ravens had made the crossover from the black radio stations to the national charts. Amos Milburn was a favorite of Al Hendrix. "Rooming House Boogie" in 1949 and "Bad, Bad Whiskey" in 1950 seemed to speak directly to the Hendrixes' experiences. Johnny Otis's band, featuring Little Esther and the Robins (who went on to become Esther Phillips and the Coasters, respectively), had a trio of blues hits in 1950: "Double-Crossin' Blues," "Deceivin' Blues," and "Mistrustin' Blues." "Louisiana Blues" and "Long-Distance Call" by Muddy Waters were hits on the black stations in 1951. In 1952, Lloyd Price's "Lawdy Miss Clawdy" was number one on the black radio stations across America.

In 1953, the Orioles, a moderately popular group among blacks since 1949, recorded "Crying in the Chapel." This song became one of the first, if not the first, rhythm and blues hits that crossed over to the national pop charts to be embraced by the entire record-buying public. The group received national publicity and the song became an instant classic.

In 1954, "Gee" by the Crows entered the national charts with resounding force, followed by the Moonglows' "Secret Love," which was "covered" by the McGuire Sisters. This started a "cover" song trend among white pop singers. They would sing the songs over, often with a new "pop" arrangement for the white mass audience. In 1954, "Shake, Rattle and Roll" by Big Joe Turner was covered by Bill Haley and the Comets. "Sh-Boom" by the Chords became a classic "cover." As the song veered from the R&B charts onto the national charts, a Canadian group named the Crewcuts covered it. It went on to become *the* monster hit of 1954, with the Chords receiving moderate airplay. "Earth Angel" by the Penguins, released in November 1954, was so R&B-imbued that it was impossible to cover. It took over the number one slot from the Moonglows' "Sincerely."

By 1955, Tin Pan Alley was in a tizzy. The musical taste of the nation was changing right before their eyes. The national charts became dominated by R&B. *Billboard* magazine, the trade organ for the music industry, began to print under its weekly listings of the top songs: "Keep Pop Alive in '55." Even an R&B version of "White Christmas" sung by the Drifters edged out all the other Christmas songs as the year changed.

In 1955, "Earth Angel" faded from number one, only to be succeeded by "Pledging My Love" by Johnny Ace, who had just killed himself while playing Russian roulette. No pop star would ever do that. Johnny Ace's story captivated the nation. R&B was not only dominating the charts, it was becoming legendary as well. "Pledging My Love" was number one for *ten weeks*. Then a flukey blues number by Little Walter called "My Babe," written by Willie Dixon, took over number one. Finally white pop regained the coveted spot with "The Ballad of Davy Crockett," the theme song of a weekly Walt Disney television series. The song was played twice a week, before and after the show, on national television. The sale of coonskin caps skyrocketed. Davy Crockett, hero of Texas, had again become a hero by saving the youth of America from the scourge of rock 'n' roll. The press, parents' groups, and many older people had labelled R&B and rock 'n' roll trashy, dirty, primitive music of the lowest order. Even the *Encyclopaedia Britannica Yearbook* said: "The rock 'n' roll school in general concentrated on a minimum of melodic line and a maximum of rhythmic noise, deliberately competing with the artistic ideals of the jungle itself."

"Unchained Melody" by both Al Hibbler and Roy Hamilton had a little of both R&B and pop. When it succeeded "Davy Crockett" on the charts, it seemed that happy days for the older generation were here again. They rejoiced when "Cherry Pink and Apple-Blossom White," an instrumental by Perez Prado's orchestra, became a substantial number one hit for several weeks. There seemed to be a weird semantic battle going on in the world of song between black R&B performers and white pop singers. "Ain't That a Shame" by Fats Domino took over again, while a slew of new black heavyweights entered the charts: Chuck Berry's "Maybelline," Bo Diddley's "Bo Diddley," the Nutmegs' "Story Untold," the Four Fellows with "Soldier Boy." But then to the chagrin of those of the older generation, who believed the music came from the jungle or hell or both, whites started singing that stuff in earnest. "Rock Around the Clock" by Bill Haley and the Comets became the national anthem of rock 'n' roll, signaling to all that many whites had joined the fray—on the other side.

Bill Haley and the Comets used to be called the Saddlemen but changed their name just as the new youth music gathered on the horizon. They had had moderate hits before. They covered Big Joe Turner's "Shake, Rattle and Roll" in 1954. Bill Haley, who was also a songwriter, penned a tune called "Rock-a Beatin' Boogie" for another group. It had a refrain that exhorted the listeners,

"Rock rock rock everybody, roll roll roll everybody." Nationally syndicated DJ Alan Freed adopted "rock 'n' roll" as the name of the new music of black *and* white youths. Rock 'n' roll, though owing a great deal to rhythm and blues, also came to incorporate white country music elements, as well.

Bill Haley and the Comets' "Rock Around the Clock" became the theme song of a new movie called *Blackboard Jungle,* which featured a juvenile gang on the rampage in a New York City public high school. This confirmed, for the older generation, rock 'n' roll's inexorable connection with youth violence, even though the song had been well on its way to becoming a hit before the movie came out.

"Rock Around the Clock" was succeeded by "Maybelline." Chuck Berry, with his charismatic way of performing, became one of the most popular early rock 'n' rollers. The pop school was given further hope when Mitch Miller's "Yellow Rose of Texas," with its white choral unison sound, topped the charts for a moment. But the impetus of the new trend was solid.

The national television show *Your Hit Parade,* the showcase for white pop music, became hard pressed to duplicate the R&B and rock 'n' roll hits. Crooners from the old school—Snooky Lanson, Russell Arms, Giselle MacKenzie, and Dorothy Collins—found that their interpretations of R&B and rock 'n' roll songs failed, often miserably.

Cover songs became an industry with the advent of Dot Records. Gale Storm, a television star of her own series *My Little Margie,* covered "I Hear You Knocking," taking away from Fats Domino's initial effort. Pat Boone, sporting a clean-cut "Joe College" image from Columbia University, covered in succession "Ain't That a Shame" (by Fats Domino), "Tutti-Frutti" (by Little Richard), and "I'll Be Home," a beautiful ballad about returning home from the Korean War, as sung by the Flamingos. By the end of 1955, Pat Boone was the king of the cover artists, his flat baritone veering further and further from R&B truth.

By the end of 1955, even Frank Sinatra was "Learning the Blues," but *Billboard's* exhortation to pop lovers seemed to make a difference in 1956. "Sixteen Tons" by Tennessee Ernie Ford was number one on January 1. "The Great Pretender" by the Platters and "Memories Are Made of This" by Dean Martin reversed the trend back to pop in the first weeks of 1956. Kay Starr's "Rock 'n' Roll Waltz" made no bones about the amalgam that Tin Pan Alley was betting heavily on.

The trend might have been totally turned back to pop in 1956 if some country boys had not shown up singing about their "Blue Suede Shoes" (Carl Perkins) and "Heartbreak Hotel" (Elvis Presley). Then came little Frankie Lymon and the Teenagers' "Why Do Fools Fall in Love?" and the Teen Queens' "Eddie My Love" to prevent a complete sweep by the pop on the charts. An army of cover singers of the pop school were keeping the new rock 'n' roll back as many former country artists took to rock 'n' roll.

Elvis Presley and the Everly Brothers would hold up the rock 'n' roll banner until 1960, when Chubby Checker and the Twist came in and swept the entire nation.

But in the mid-fifties there were black recording artists who were very happy to remain in the narrow race market. Hank Ballard and the Midnighters were doing very fine with their brand of "blue" material. No one would dare copy, cover, or even sell it over the counter. Yet his music spread by word of mouth like wildfire. Their first recording of "sexually frank" material, "Get It," was a big success in every black ghetto from coast to coast. Although it got virtually no airplay, "Get It" was followed by a string of singles that used "Annie" as a sex goddess: "Work with Me Annie," "Annie Had a Baby," "Sexy Ways," and "Annie's Aunt Fannie." Etta James fashioned a reply to Ballard and "Annie" called "(Wallflower) Roll with Me Henry," which, while released commercially, was still thought to be too risqué. After several changes the title became "Dance with Me Henry," which was promptly covered by Georgia Gibbs, becoming a big pop hit of 1955. But Hank Ballard and the Midnighters continued on with their suggestive songs, doing good business under the counter. "Annie Had a Baby" and she could not "work" anymore. The song goes on to describe that she gave all of her attention to the baby, "walking" with it rather than with the narrator. Since "Annie Had A Baby" it was "Understood":

That's what happens when the getting
Gets good, so good, so good

Hank Ballard wailed on, his high Texas tenor piercing the heavy raunch of the Midnighters. It was more a pure get-down rocker than a risqué song to Jimmy, but his ears glowed anyway because he was not supposed to have heard it.

Having babies and making love were normal in Seattle's Central District. The house rent parties that were given every weekend seemed to play "Work with Me Annie" and "Annie Had a Baby" continuously. Amos Milburn and his "Bad, Bad Whiskey" was still popular and Muddy Waters was coming on strong with "Long-Distance Blues" and "Hoochie Coochie Man." But Hank Ballard and the Midnighters, with their happy up-tempo songs about "Annie," a carefree, free-loving, unattached young woman, and her subsequent motherhood, were closer to the reality of how the blacks in the projects really felt and lived their lives. Of course, the authorities felt very differently about the joy of lovemaking among the blacks in the projects, especially since the consequences seemed to make their jobs a nightmare. But the blacks had their own feelings about it that were hidden from the authorities, to be celebrated among themselves. It excited Jimmy to know that the record was banned, was a secret, but sold very well anyway. And its popularity also gave him a new sense of the emergent underground black music. He realized that there was more happy fun where "Work with Me Annie" and "Annie Had a Baby" came from.

The first bands Jimmy consistently played with in Seattle were the Velvetones, a junior high school group, which gave way to a band formed by Fred Rollins, a high school friend, called the Rocking Kings. At first he had been terribly shy and played rather badly. But his deferential sincerity and his good ear made him a good person for the young band. He listened to every kind of musical expression and idea. When they had a gig he took what was offered with sincere appreciation, whether it was a couple of hamburgers in payment or five or ten dollars. He became one of the best young R&B and rock 'n' roll guitarists in Seattle.

The Canadian border is only sixty miles from Seattle. Vancouver, British Columbia, the largest city in western Canada, was starved for the new youth music of the States. The Rocking Kings found work there and went up to play as often as possible.

The ride to Vancouver was beautiful. The boys listened to the radio on the way up. Each had certain favorites. Jimmy's were "Sleep Walk" by Santo and Johnny, "Rocking Crickets" by the Hot Toddies, "Cathy's Clown" by the Everly Brothers, "La Bomba" by the Carlos Brothers, and "Summertime Blues" by Eddie Cochran. He received constant kidding from the fellows; his spacey ways and shy, soft mumblings were always good for an impersonation when the trip got boring. The Rocking Kings played several of the Coasters' hits, things like "Charlie Brown," "Poison Ivy," "Yakety Yak," "Searchin'," and "Along Came Jones"; all were big hits in 1958–59. "Do You Wanna Dance?" by Bobby Freeman and "At the Hop" by Danny and the Juniors were surefire songs to get a crowd moving, and "The Twist" by Hank Ballard was unbelievable. Jimmy really got off on the "Peter Gunn" theme, but like "Sleep Walk," it was hardly danceable and hardly reflected the big-beat rhythm and blues rock 'n' roll the audiences preferred. "Petite Fleur," written by jazz great Sidney Bechet for the Chris Barber jazz band, was another favorite of Jimmy's. He longed to play his guitar like a horn and saw no reason why that was not possible, but his remarks along those lines never failed to bring sarcastic reactions from his bandmates.

Although spacey and spooky, Jimmy was a hit with the girls. This never failed to irritate the members of the Rocking Kings or the regular guys at Garfield High. When it got around that Jimmy, in order to protect his hands, would not engage in fistfights he began to have more trouble.

One day after school, Jimmy refused to let a bully handle his guitar. He was chased across the football field in full view of the homeward-bound students, knocked down, and beaten, kicked, and stomped. But he never released his guitar from his protective embrace.

He stopped playing with the Rocking Kings after an intrigue with another band member's girlfriend. Jimmy did not go out of his way to attract the girl, but there was something in the way he moved and joked and jived that she found attractive. Jimmy would always go into his showtime routine onstage while he played. This would enrage all of the Rocking Kings. They thought he was making a fool of himself and them, too. Jimmy would always say he was sorry, but would do it again at the next occasion, afterward saying he was sorry again. But the girls ate it up. One night before a gig at Birdland, Jimmy was called into the men's room for a private conference with the band member whose girl dug him. Everyone in the band knew what was up but did nothing to stop it. As the two boys disappeared behind the door the band members speculated on whether Jimmy would fight back or not. When they came out a few minutes later it looked like Jimmy had not bothered to defend himself. He had a bloody nose, his hair was messed up, and he was puffy in a few other places, but he cleaned himself up and went on and did the show anyway. Soon after that incident Jimmy ceased playing with the Rocking Kings.

The Rocking Kings were breaking up anyway. Fred Rollins, the leader of the group, had been scheduled to go into the army and he left soon after the bathroom incident. The next time Jimmy saw Rollins was when he was home on furlough. Rollins was decked out in an army paratrooper's uniform with a screaming eagle emblazoned upon the lapel. Everyone was really impressed and so was Jimmy.

James Thomas, who had managed the Rocking Kings, took over the band as front man, renaming it Thomas and the Tom Cats. Jimmy rejoined.

Al Hendrix had not planned on being a gardener, but after working at Bethlehem Steel hauling red-hot steel rods that would singe the double pants he wore, sometimes burning through, Al found gardening to be a relatively placid way to earn a living.

He proved amazingly strong to those who, because of his slight height, thought him to be half a man. Al was all wringing, twisting, rippling muscles, with a boxer's light grace on his feet. His centaurlike legs made short hustling steps, and seemed to slide across the garden, as if dancing, his muscles forming without concentration.

Jimmy had the same twisting, sinewy muscles, only he was much taller than his father, although not quite six feet himself. Jimmy's arms draped down almost to his knees. Sometimes his father would stop work and come over and stand by his side comparing arm lengths in jest. Then, mock-measuring his arms, Al would shake his head as he gazed down to where Jimmy's arms ended above his knees.

Al Hendrix: "Well, Jimmy slumped in school just like I did. When I was going to school I used to tell my mother, 'Daggummit,' I say, 'I ain't learning nothing. I ain't getting no further ahead.' I dropped out from Templeton Junior High School in Vancouver. I said the best thing for me to do is to go to work. That was after my dad died, and my mother was on something similar to welfare here. Public assistance of some kind. My brother and I were both going to school, but it was costing too much for us to catch the school bus. So I used to walk home in the evening. I used to catch the bus going to school to make sure I'd get there on time, and then I walked home. I had plenty of time; I didn't have to worry about being late coming home.

"I think Jimmy stopped in his senior year. I think he only had one more year to finish. I kept getting letters from his teachers saying Jimmy wasn't doing this or that. It seemed like he just lost all interest. I used to tell him, 'Man, you better finish. Finish this year.' But he didn't. After he dropped out, I went up there one day and the teacher told me, 'Well, he's got too many strikes against him. He can't make it.' And I said, 'Okay.' So Jimmy came home with me and I said, 'You have to go out and work with me. It's all for our common survival.' He tried to get jobs in some of the supermarkets as a bag carrier. He applied at a lot of places. And I said, 'That's all right, but while we wait for that to come through, you can come and work with Dad.'

"I had another worker with me named Shorty, and we got along good. I used to drive him hard. He never asked me what I was paying him. I told him it was for the common cause of survival, to make that rent money and to have some food in our stomach. Of course, on the weekend he'd sport around and I'd give him a few dollars. I'd say, 'Well okay, I know you going out with the guys, here's five or ten dollars.' Of course, cats nowadays say, 'Ooooh man, what am I gonna do with that? Where's five dollars gonna take me?' but Jimmy would say, 'Yeah, Dad, thanks.'

"I knew Jimmy had been smoking for some time. In the apartment where we lived we had to go down the hallway to the common bathroom to take a bath or use the toilet. Jimmy would go down there and smoke. Once I was walking up Madison, going to the Honeysuckle to shoot pool, and I saw him and his buddy coming down the street. I saw him before he saw me. He was just walking down the street like Mr. Big Time. I caught up to him right in front of the Honeysuckle Poolhall. 'Hey Jimmy,' I said. He had his cigarette behind his back. 'Well, you can bring your cigarette out,' I said, 'before it burns your fingers.' And he looked at me so funny. Real sheepishly. I said, 'That's all right, man, it's okay.' I always told him, 'You be truthful to me and I'll be truthful to you.' And that's the way he was. But he was surprised that day. I guess he figured I was a kind of strange dad. Sometimes I tell him no on some things and yes on some."

James Williams and Jimmy spent New Year's Eve 1960 together. It was a bitterly cold evening and they, as usual, had nowhere to go. They sat in Jimmy's room. Jimmy always wanted to play and sing. He didn't care what kind of music it was as long as it made song and melody. James liked to sing, to croon. He could sound just like Dean Martin, so they did "Memories Are Made of This," the crooner's latest hit, which was accompanied by a stylish acoustic guitar on the 78 rpm recording.

> Take one fresh and tender kiss
> And one golden night of bliss

Jimmy played guitar and sang the accompanying chorus about how sweet the memories were, and how those memories could not be surpassed. Over and over they sang that song. James did not like those wild rhythm and blues songs, but he loved the slow sentimental ballads that his father and mother preferred.

Singing such a sentimental song evoked images of loves and lost loves. Jimmy stopped to make a phone call. It became a long and involved call and soon Jimmy beckoned James to the phone. Clamping the receiver with his palm, Jimmy told James that he was talking to Betty Jean, his one big love. Unable to take her out, he had called; she was too young to really party anyway. But she knew what to feed a man for a good night of lovemaking.

"Now what you gonna give me to eat when I come over?" Jimmy asked her again. "Go on, tell me everything." She began to recite as Jimmy excitedly let James eavesdrop. As if from memory she crooned: some eggs, soft-boiled, oysters and clams, raw on the shell, lots of butter and toast . . .

James was confused; Jimmy nearly convulsed with laughter, converting it into the good cheer he projected into the receiver. He hung up. James asked him what that was all about. "That's what a woman gives her man for his sex," Jimmy replied. "That's love food that builds up the potency."

It was late for seventeen-year-olds, nearly midnight. Jimmy, who seemed to have no rules circumscribing his movements, walked James most of the way home through the chilling night winds. There was no food in the house and Jimmy wanted to eat. The Kingfish Cafe was close to James's house, so they headed in that direction. When they arrived, Jimmy asked James for some money to get food. James, who had just gotten paid, gave Jimmy ten dollars. They said good-bye again, waving. James looked back as he walked away and saw through the steaming window Jimmy sitting gingerly, shyly at the counter. It was New Year's Day 1961. They never saw each other again.

Jimmy's relationship with Betty Jean seemed to have brought out a new defiance that surprised him and also surprised his father. Along with smoking cigarettes, for the first time he became very conscious of his clothes. He desired to change what had become his trademark look: overlarge shirts with collar always up; too short pants, retro-tapered at the ankles; unfashionable, worn shoes. He began working black shoe polish into his reddish hair to achieve a slick, black effect. Then in a desire to own better, new clothes he and an accomplice broke into a store he knew well since its owner was a client of Al's gardening business. Rank amateur thieves, once they had broken in and gotten the clothing they freaked and tried to put them back, getting caught in the process. No charges were pressed but the owner had Al and Jimmy work off the damage to the premises by doing gardening work. Angry at the extra unpaid work, Al's temper flared during a confrontation and he struck Jimmy hard in the face. This was not one of Al's signature slaps, but a punch Al, as a former amateur boxer, knew well how to give. Hurt, dismayed, and embarrassed, Jimmy ran away from home. Al heard pretty readily that Jimmy was at Pernell Alexander's. He went and got him, full of mild, almost conciliatory words about Jimmy always letting him know where he was. To cap off the usually mild Jimmy's first revolt, he was caught in stolen cars twice in the same week, and arrested, spending a few days in the lockup. While he maintained he did not know the cars were stolen, it did not matter since it quickly became clear that Jimmy would be put away unless he chose his only option—join the military, a surefire way to have the prosecutor waive a trial and certain jail time.

Al Hendrix: " 'Dad, I have been going down to the recruiting office,' Jimmy told me one day. He knew he was one-A. He knew if he volunteered he would get the category he wanted. He kept going down to see this recruiting officer, and then one day he told me, 'Dad, I'm going in.' I said, 'That's all right, that's all right. There's nothing wrong with that. Get it over with.' There were no wars going on, it was after the Korean War and before the Vietnam deal. He said he wanted to get into the Screaming Eagles, and I said, 'Oh wow! You going on further than ol' Dad did.' I remember I told him when I was in Fort Benning, Georgia, we used to watch them guys jump in their practice parachutes. Man, them paratroopers were double-timing. They weren't allowed to stand at attention or anything. Double-time every place they went on the base. And I said, 'Man.' When Jimmy told me that he wanted to be a paratrooper, I said, 'Oh no!'

" 'Son, you gonna be double-timing your whole time.' He said, 'I want to get one of them Screaming Eagles, Dad.' 'Well, that makes me feel real proud,' I said. That made me feel real proud of him. He was trying to do something.

"He went to ship out, and I went down there with him and gave him some money. A helper-out. It made me feel real good. About as good as I would have felt if my dad had seen me going into the service.

"When Jimmy went into the service he didn't take his guitar with him. He had an electric guitar, but he didn't have any amplifier or anything of that sort. I said, 'Well, I'll send it to you after your basic training. Just let me know.'"

In the opening lines of an untitled long poem written in his eighteenth year Hendrix reveals something of how he saw aspects of fashion and slang.

> *Blessings on thee little square*
> *O barefoot hag with uncombed hair*
> *with thy solid peg-legged pants*
> *and thy solid hep cat stance*

CHAPTER 2

After eight weeks of basic training at Fort Ord, California, at the beginning of August 1961, Jimmy was awarded the rank of private first class. A month later he was allowed a trip back home to Seattle. He had missed a big gig the Tom Cats had had at the beginning of August. But he was able to see Leon and Al and Betty Jean, too.

He left Fort Ord in November to travel east two thousand miles to the 101st Airborne Division, Fort Campbell, Kentucky, which was right on the cusp of the Deep South.

Jump school was on tap for this paratrooper-to-be. Before they got to actual planes they jumped from a tower that was high enough to discourage several at that initial point. Jimmy experienced being "snapped like a bullwhip" on his first jump, but he had broken the ice. The physical training, which included lots of push-ups and various forms of "harassment," was designed to reinforce the command-and-control structure at the heart of the military establishment.

Fort Campbell was the place where he first made it on his own. Early on he had sent Al a drawing he had made of the Screaming Eagle patch. He had been definitely visualizing that attainment from the start. Achieving that Screaming Eagle patch would mean that he was a full-fledged paratrooper, having succeeded in that rigorous training.

He had liked the idea, the image of jumping out of planes. He had also liked the training that went with it: the rigors, the harrassments, the fussing, the trainers fighting everything they did. They could do no right. His entire life until that point had been like a preparation. Next to the emotional turmoil he had experienced as a child, the army was a lark.

Less than a month later Jimmy was ready for the real thing, jumping from planes in flight. In a letter to his father he writes of how "outta sight" the first jump was. Many, including himself, had never been in a plane before. There was a big garbage can in the middle of the area for those who needed to throw up. He describes the roar of the plane's engine and the rivet-jumping extreme shaking of the large cabin. He thinks, "Wow, a split-second thought goes through me like, you're crazy, and all of a sudden it just disappeared. And it's almost like blank and it's almost like a crying, and you wanna laugh . . ." At the door of the plane there is a "flat rush" and suddenly "you're up like that, and then you're just ohhhhhhhh . . . falling over backwards feeling in your dreams." Then in total contrast to the previous noise, "everything is so quiet, all you can hear is the breeze, *shhhhhhs* . . . you're there all by yourself and you can talk very low, you can scream or anything." But he loved it, remembering to look up and see if the parachute had opened, and thanking the Lord that it had.

Jumping out of planes also gave him a fifty-five-dollar-a-month pay bonus. Sometimes he would even take pictures with a camera while jumping. He realized that he was not afraid. He had reveled in the sound of the big plane lumbering through the air with the intense weight of its human cargo. The sound of the door opening was even more enthralling, the rush of air into the cabin, the howling singing of the wind surging in, augmenting the sound of the engine. It had been a true marriage of machine and nature: the sound, the energy. And then falling. Falling away from that sound, farther and farther toward the earth, where he would float like an angel toward its silence and its life.

He had had his father send his guitar and had begun to experiment, with his Danelectro Silvertone with matching amp duplicating the sound of the heavens. It was like the electric guitar had an earth existence and an air existence. He saw that the feat was to be able to make the guitar fly. He began to understand wind instruments totally after that and tried to emulate not the sound so much as the meaning of the sound. Like the engines of the plane and the resistance of the air made another unique quality, another unique sound, more than the air, more than the engine, more than a wind—it made a sound that sang on its own. It often made him think that there was something being said. It was the sound of speeds and heights the human body could not attain itself. The substance of that sound and the loftiness his body occupied in relation to the earth gave him a rare experience. He wondered how it would be to venture higher. Like a human spaceship beyond the stratosphere.

He could mark his life by the tunes in his head. He was able to transfer the sounds to his guitar—his traveling companion, his life companion. Sometimes he played far outside the sounds the rhythm and blues cats played, yet totally into the weird sounds of the country blues, and the weird emotions the sounds produced in him. In Kentucky, now he was hearing the rural acoustic blues, not the stuff on the radio. No one he had heard on the radio had captured the eerie mystical potential of the blues sounds in the rough, one man playing a wooden box with cat guts strung across it. From town to town the rural bluesmen traveled, playing not the huge arenas, but deep down inland, back-home places where, for decades, these bluesmen had been *the* music. Now driven into obscurity, the solid base of the people, the solid country blues, had been forgotten by the big recording and broadcasting companies. Yet, almost like a secret tradition, it lingered carefully, tenuously, only to be revealed to the true seeker.

It had not taken him long to discover after his guitar arrived that all he really wanted to do in life was play guitar. The guitar had become his entire life. It was his sister, his woman, his muse, and his release. Most of the musicians in his unit were part-time. He would amaze them with the absorption and passion with which he played. He sensed a lot of resentment beginning to build about him after he got his own instrument. Before, he would borrow someone else's guitar, or else resort to checking out the antiquated one they had at the base. Once he had borrowed a guy's guitar and while he was playing it, the guy got agitated and asked for it back, saying he was messing it up, that he was going to break it. That was stupid. The guy had been jealous because Jimmy played it so much better than him. It didn't take long for Jimmy to realize that most of the guys were pretty childish. His isolation as a child had kept him away from being close to a large group of people as he was at Fort Campbell. As a teenager he had kept pretty much to himself, even though he played a lot of music. He restricted his relationships—apart from women—as he grew older to strictly musical ones. He was known to all the young groups in Seattle as the best guitar player of their age and experience. They dug him for his ability, yet he would always be apart from their scenes. His relationship with them had been purely musical, and often they did not understand this, expecting him to hang out and pal around. Now in the army he found most of the fellows to be pretty much on the same level. Once they had worked together or jumped together or even done KP together there would be an assumed collective bond that he did not often share. Once he had his guitar it became, for many of them, an object that symbolized his separateness. And many people sought to destroy him through his guitar. Just for the hell of it.

He started sleeping with his guitar. It was no big thing. Some of the older players who had shown him a thing or two would mention sleeping with their guitars. Then he had seen an interview with Mississippi John Hurt where he talked about waking up after having fallen asleep with his guitar on his chest. It was kind of a funny topic, because the implication there was that the guitar replaced a woman in your bed.

His fellow paratroopers began to tire of his duplications of the sounds of the heavens, heavy metal flying. They began to scorn and deride his efforts. Not only was he a constant fixture in the music room, but in the barracks he was constantly working on new sounds, even without an amp. The men in his barracks began to complain that they could not sleep at night for Jimmy's arpeggios. They took to hiding his guitar and making Jimmy get down on his knees and beg for it back. He would always say he was sorry, but that would not prevent him from doing it again. One day, several of the men jacked him up and beat him up. Jimmy protected his guitar more than himself. But unfortunately for the attackers, Jimmy's boyhood friend from Seattle was Raymond Ross, the

101st Airborne's heavyweight boxing champion. He came into Jimmy's barracks soon after the incident. "I hear y'all messing with my homeboy," he said. Ross then went down the aisle beating up everyone involved and some who were not.

Although he was not attacked physically again, they still made fun of Jimmy. To them he was weird. He slept with his guitar. He talked to his guitar. He played it all the time, relating to it more than he related to the guys. He had painted the name "Betty Jean" on his guitar and began calling it by name. The men in the barracks began to say that he was crazy.

Fort Campbell, Kentucky, might as well have been the heart of the Deep South. Jim Crow, racial segregation, was the way of life. Great swarms of blackbirds would swoop over the skies, making a fantastic appearance on the low horizon. The beauty of the land kept his mind on the rural blues players. The more he learned about the blues, the more he admired the rural blues players, the Delta sound, and the guys in Chicago who had transplanted that sound to the city. He would go to Nashville—only sixty miles away—every chance he got to hear some music or just walk around. The town reeked of music. A lot of country music abounded and a new hip sound that groups like the Mar-Keys and Booker T. & the MG's were into. Their sound was hip and contemporary, yet they had a country element that was very different from the urban rhythm and blues. It was a laid-back, easily accessible music that had beautiful turns to it that captivated you after a while. He felt a kinship with that kind of sound more than the covers of the Top 10 stuff he had been playing in Seattle. Nashville, out of the way and small like Seattle, nevertheless had a distinct musical personality. He felt Nashville would be a good transition for him on his way to New York and, more importantly, he felt that he could live and learn in Nashville without the big hassles a big city would present him with.

Fred Rollins, who had played in the Rocking Kings, had gone into the Screaming Eagles before Jimmy. Although he was on a different part of the base he kept abreast of what was happening with Jimmy. He had not known Jimmy's girlfriend in Seattle, but Jimmy gave him the impression that they were very seriously involved. He assumed that Jimmy had received a "Dear John" letter when word got back to him that Jimmy was flipping out. That was the only reason he could think of for Jimmy sleeping with his guitar, talking to it, playing it as soon as he woke up in the morning, and making such weird sounds with it. Even when Jimmy went to mess he strummed the air and made noises as if his guitar were there with him.

Billy Cox heard Hendrix playing one day and was really impressed. A serious student of European classical music as well as R&B and blues, Cox recognized, upon hearing Jimmy play, a genius that ranged between "Beethoven and John Lee Hooker." Although what Cox heard indicated that Jimmy was limited to only about five keys, "and was still getting his shit together," he also recognized that Jimmy had largely mastered and extended his sound into virtuoso statements.

Cox introduced himself, checked out a bass, and they immediately began to jam. They clicked. Later they picked up a drummer named Gary Ferguson and they had a group. They gigged for a while in the service clubs on base and in clubs in Clarksdale and other neighboring towns. They played mainly the hits of the day, like "Tossin' and Turnin'" by Bobby Lewis, "Daddy's Home" by Shep and the Limelights, "Mother-in-Law" by Ernie K. Doe, "Quarter to Three" by Gary "U.S." Bonds, and "Last Night" by the Mar-Keys. Jimmy, Billy, and Gary called themselves the Casuals.

Jimmy won a small following for himself in the small towns near Fort Campbell, especially Clarksville, across the nearby border in Tennessee, and then Nashville. They would sit through set after set just to hear him solo a few times. Like Charlie Christian, Hendrix was interested in shaping his overall approach to the electric guitar along the lines of horns. He would tell his small band of aficionados that one day he would have the sound of a trumpet with a mute on it. They loved it.

Once he had reached his goal of getting that Screaming Eagle patch, Private First Class Hendrix set his sights forward. Having his guitar helped him make up his mind.

He broke his ankle on his twenty-sixth jump, having gotten his foot caught up in the sky hook, where it had become jammed. He played it, complaining of back pains, as well. Persistence paid off. Two months later, in July 1962, he was out, receiving his honorable discharge.

Within days of his honorable discharge he and Betty Jean abandoned their plans to marry and he received her engagement ring back. Teen dreams of marriage over now, he had nothing before him but an unknowable future.

Hendrix and Cox, once discharged from the army, gigged around, sleeping and eating where and when they could until they reached Nashville. They got quarters over Joyce's House of Glamour on Jefferson Street. The Casuals became the King Kasuals.

Soon they were in competition with a group of some Nashville natives led by Johnny Snead called the Imperials. Johnny Snead had named the group after the barbershop where the members all had their hair done in elaborate marcels, gleaming waves that were highly visible under stage lights. The proprietor of the shop acted as their manager. He was the owner of the Del Morocco Club, where they gigged regularly. Jimmy met Johnny at the barbershop and once Johnny heard him play he became Jimmy's and Billy's employer, protector, and benefactor. They became fairly popular in the local clubs and even made some television appearances. They were very poor, having hardly enough money for rent and food, but they attracted a following among the people in the neighborhood.

Johnny Jones was the lead guitarist of the Imperials and was quite hot. Jimmy had his first adult musical challenge.

Some of the young girls in the neighborhood became Jimmy's unofficial fan club. They looked out for Jimmy, making sure that he did not go *too* long between meals. Sandra Mathews was the ringleader. She took to calling herself and the girls who hung around Jimmy the Buttons. They would sing the blues behind Jimmy's constant playing. All he played was the blues. They also mended his clothing; that was how they got to calling themselves the Buttons. It was a private joke between them and Jimmy. He would always be missing a button or two and even worse. Jimmy kept his stage clothes together, a dark suit with a narrow Ivy League tie and white shirt, but he cared little about how he appeared when he was not onstage.

Once Fred Rollins came into town on a pass from Fort Campbell. He knew that Jimmy and Billy were gigging regularly and went straight to the club where they played with the Imperials. They were on when he got there. Fred went straight to the bandstand and took out his sax. Pretty soon he caught their eyes and was invited up to sit in. Halfway through the number Fred realized that Jimmy and Billy had advanced far beyond him musically. It was embarrassing for everyone all around. Rollins excused himself from the bandstand and sat down.

A few days later Rollins went by Hendrix's place. Jimmy was there with his girlfriend, a small black woman. Jimmy was virtually penniless. Rollins offered to treat both Hendrix and his girlfriend to dinner. They went to a local diner where Jimmy's girlfriend began to feel ill. They ate anyway, Jimmy eating her meal, too. Rollins was appalled that he had bought Jimmy two dinners. Disgusted over what he felt was Hendrix's greed and lack of will to work for a living, Fred Rollins told Jimmy off with finality.

Jimmy made his way to the Pacific Northwest and Vancouver in late 1962 to spend Christmas with his family, especially his grandmother Nora and his aunt Pat. One night he wandered into a club he had heard about called Dante's Inferno and found an unlikely duo in Tommy Chong (who would become half of the Cheech and Chong duo) and Bobby Taylor, fronting a band. Jimmy had known the guys in the band—Floyd Snead, Wes and Tommy Chong—before, and with the addition of Bobby Taylor, the band was really outta sight. It was not unusual in the Pacific Northwest to find a Chinese guy and a brother playing in a soul band, but it was kind of weird to hear Chong sing background in a falsetto tenor that was authentic soul. The band cooked. It was not long before

Jimmy was sitting in. And it was not long before Jimmy was asked to join the band.

Tommy Chong and Bobby Taylor were partners—owners of the band as well as the club. They had a good thing going. The club was packed and swung with Canadian Twist enthusiasts every night. The band had an unusual fervor. And then at midnight, when public clubs had to close, they had another club that was private right above Dante's Inferno called the Elegant Parlor.

Bobby Taylor had recently graduated from the master's degree program in music at the University of California, Berkeley, and had come to Vancouver at the request of Tommy Chong, who had offered him an across-the-board partnership in exchange for Taylor's incredible singing voice, keyboard musicianship, and composition abilities. Bobby Taylor also knew how to run a club properly. Called Bobby Taylor and the Vancouvers, the band did arrangements of popular songs of the day that were better than the originals. They had a large and consistent following.

Jimmy would play with the Vancouvers on weekends and on weekdays at the Black and Tan Club in Seattle. He stayed with his grandmother Nora and her family. It was perfect for Jimmy. He was able to cool out, play guitar, and get his energy up. Jimmy was very laid-back and quiet. What impressed Bobby Taylor the most about Jimmy was his mental strength. Jimmy said he couldn't sing but that he loved to. He would make up songs as he played, like the calypso singers. He didn't do his with rhyme, he did his with meaning.

Jimmy left the Pacific Northwest early in 1963 and went across the country. He got to Chicago. He wanted to get back through Nashville and see some friends before he pushed on to the Big Apple, but while he was in Chicago he had to go by Chess Studios and see what was going on.

Chess Records in Chicago was the home of the recorded urban blues. He did not want to seem impressed, but milling around with him were many of the greatest names in blues: Muddy Waters, Little Milton, Bo Diddley, Willie Dixon, Little Walter, Lafayette Leek, Howard Ashby, Al Duncan, and Robert "Jr." Lockwood. And a whole bunch of dudes who just sat around looking heavy. He had asked one of the cats, who walked around the studio like he owned it, about the chances of recording with his own group. Tall and paunchy, the dude just kinda grinned at him like he was crazy. Later in the day while he was fooling around the studio between sessions he saw the same dude in the booth. Jimmy started playing some of his way-out blues, changing keys while he hammered a weird obbligato, then holding a single note while he up-tempoed on the bass strings, and then sliding back into the former key and hitting some scratch rhythm chords. He thought it was pretty good. But when he went into the booth to maybe get a reaction, they started talking about the good old days. Although they pretended to be just talking, they were commenting on his playing. He got a lecture on the blues, much to the delight of the old bluesmen. Willie Dixon, the tall paunchy guy, held forth.

Right then, Muddy Waters walked in. Jimmy could not believe it—his idol stood in the tiny room nodding to everyone, moving his large frame in slow rural grace. Jimmy did not know whether Muddy Waters knew of him or not, but Muddy's remarks seemed to be only for his ears, although you would never have known it by looking at Muddy. They all started drinking some Chivas Regal. Muddy sat up there just like one of the boys, but you could tell by a subtle respect that hung in the room that he was their leader. It was not that he demanded that they pay attention to him. If one of the other guys had an essential point to make, he would think nothing of riding over what Muddy Waters was about to say. But when Muddy got to talking about the old days there was no one who had something more important to say.

He talked about Robert Johnson. He called him Robert. Alan Lomax had been looking for the legendary Robert Johnson when he had come upon Muddy Waters on the plantation where Muddy worked. Robert was dead by that time, something he had always sung about: being killed by a woman. Only he had been killed *over* a woman by her husband. But one of the hands told Lomax about Muddy. Muddy even sang one of Robert Johnson's songs: "Kind-Hearted Woman." Muddy Waters had been the youngest fellow playing in the little group they had in Stovall, Mississippi, but he was very confident of himself, mainly because he could sing. Even then, he had a powerful voice that did not pamper the blues or whine the lyrics. He sang like a man and he had just begun picking up his sliding style. At first he had mainly blown harmonica (he called it the "French harp"), but then he bought his first guitar from a friend for $2.50 and that same night got a gig where he was paid two dollars. He knew then he had done right saving nickels and dimes to get his first manufactured guitar—a Stella. Pretty soon the man at the all-night place raised him to $2.50 a night.

Although he had been "found" by one of the most significant "talent scouts" of authentic blues, Alan Lomax, it was not overnight stardom for Muddy. But by that time he had saved up and bought a Sears, Roebuck guitar that cost eleven dollars. He found that he could make a fantastic amount of money (thirty to forty dollars) playing the streets of Clarksdale. Muddy Waters's idol had been Robert Johnson. After Johnson died, Muddy's "copy" was Son House, who lived just across from him on another plantation. He would go and hear Son House often. There were a lot of blacks in the Delta who had mastered the bottleneck style, but few had the dedication of Son House, who traveled all over the Delta playing the slide guitar. Few also had the raw determination of Muddy Waters, who, although just a youngster, was determined to be "known before the world."

Muddy Waters did not know how the slide guitar first began to be played. It looked easy. Maybe easier than picking. But in order to be a master of the slide guitar you had to know the blues deeply. You had to know the feel for duration and the way the meaning was being interpreted, for when you slide you "go down in and get some of it and get out of it." It is a subtle but powerful effect that sets songs on the edge of a particular emotion. The effect can overwhelm not only the listeners but the player, as well; he has to know when to get up off it or else he ruins the whole sensibility of the song.

Muddy had picked cotton, milked cows, all the things that a sharecropper or field hand does, but his ambition was to play slide guitar on par with the greats: Robert Johnson and Son House. He had recorded for Alan Lomax, with his little group at the Stovall plantation, but he got to Chicago on his own. He worked in a paper factory and played the house parties the workers gave on the weekends. Soon the word spread and he was hired to be in the house band of a small club called the Flame. He played as a sideman for Sunnyland Slim, Eddie Boyd, and a couple of times with Memphis Slim ("Memphis Slim was the big man, he was the big man"). Pretty soon Muddy Waters put his band together. His sound was based on the Delta sound. He found that players from Texas, Alabama, and Georgia did not fit as well with the Mississippi Delta sound as those from Mississippi or Louisiana. Muddy based his style somewhere between Robert Johnson and Son House, adding a strong vocal, whereas they had depended on their playing.

Sunnyland Slim told Leonard Chess about Muddy. The first tunes Muddy cut for an unsure Leonard Chess were "Feel Like Goin' Home," "Can't Be Satisfied," "Little Annie Mae," and "Gypsy Woman," all written by Muddy Waters.

Muddy had extended the blues by adhering to strict time, speeding it up to get a drive to it. There was a lot of competition in Chicago. In the midst of World War II, a lot of people were picking up on bebop. The big bluesmen were Tampa Red, Big Maceo, Memphis Slim, and the original Sonny Boy Williamson, who had that "particular twinkle in his voice that got to people." Blues had a lot of competition, but those who knew the blues still loved the blues.

"The big drop after the beat on the drum formed the foundation of my blues. Nothing fancy—just a straight heavy beat with it," Muddy said. He remembered Charlie Patton. "He was a real clown with the guitar. He'd pat the guitar, hit the guitar, whirl it over his head." He remembered some of the old records he heard as a kid: Blind Blake, Blind Boy Fuller, Blind Lemon Jefferson, Charlie Patton, and, of course, Robert Johnson and Son House. He seemed to have a thing about Robert Johnson. He figured Robert was the only man who could beat him sliding. Probably Son House could, too, when he was younger. But Muddy felt that it was on his shoulders to bring that low-down Mississippi Delta sound up north.

"That's what makes the blues so good. When you know your blues, if you try to put direct time like you would do in pop music, I don't think the blues will sell as good. Some of my songs just have thirteen bars. I don't even count them myself, I just feel them out. We learned the beat, learned what people was moving off of. Even if it was the blues, we still had to drive behind it.

"But you see, blues, it's tone—deep tone with a heavy beat. I kept that backbeat on the drums plus full action on the guitar and harmonica and the piano in the back, then you've got a big sound. I think the best blues singers came from the church. I even thought of being a preacher myself, the blues is close to preaching. I got all my good moaning and trembling going for me right out of church."

Jimmy sat there listening in awe. He would not get to record at Chess, but he was happy he had stopped by.

Through connections from Willie Dixon and other musicians at Chess, Jimmy was able to get a gig in Biloxi, Mississippi, a sea resort town, with one of his idols, Slim Harpo ("Scratch My Back"), who was a blues legend. He also got to play behind and tour with Tommy Tucker, whose "Hi-Heel Sneakers" was a surprisingly big hit. Tucker was curious where Jimmy got those strange and weird sounds from his guitar, but all Jimmy could say was, "I don't know, man. I don't know." The sounds he produced were so intuitive that he was not really conscious of what he did. But coming from Chicago, where legends like Willie Dixon and Muddy Waters were so conscious of their methodology, he was inspired to be more circumspect with his own creativity.

In mid-March, at the end of his tour with Tommy Tucker, he wrote a postcard to his father from Columbia, South Carolina. He returned to Nashville and took up with Florence Henderson, who was friends with his former housemate, Joyce Lucas. They, Billy Cox, and Verdell Barlow, a barmaid at the Baron Club on Jefferson Street, all hung together.

Back at the Del Morocco Jimmy rejoined the King Kasuals.

Larry Lee, a younger guitarist who was playing with Earl Gaines, who had the hit "Twenty-four Hours a Day," recognizing a superior guitarist still in reach of his own abilities, introduced himself to Jimmy at the Del Morocco. He looked up to Jimmy, placed himself under his wing, and would help out in any way he could, like running errands. Soon Jimmy had him taking his place on a slow night when Jimmy found a nice young woman to take a break with.

Jimmy was given the nickname "Marbles" because many who knew him thought he had lost those proverbial elements of sanity. He would be playing guitar on the way to the gig, during the gig, and walking home after the gig. And then he was often discovered the next morning having slept in his clothes, his guitar cradled in his arms, having fallen asleep playing. To many that meant he was crazy.

Nearly a year out of the army Jimmy's guitar playing had advanced greatly. Johnny Jones was still the celebrated guitar player on the scene and Jimmy looked up to him. Some thought it was pure idolization. Johnny Jones began to appear at the New Era, Nashville's top R&B club. Jones had arrived at important elements of his own personal style and Jimmy had witnessed an evolution from when they had first played together. Jones was still developing and Jimmy hated to miss a set of his. He would often be dashing from the Del Morocco over to the New Era. Jones's advancement inspired Jimmy to grow as a player.

Jimmy's own equipment was cheap and somewhat shabby. Not only was he ashamed of it but it held him back. The amps he owned were far below even the middle of the line. But because of that he was becoming a master of the strange and unpredictable properties of damaged and broken, malfunctioning amplifiers. Billy Cox had noticed that Jimmy was already working with feedback as an element in his own development. This pioneering discovery was probably born out of necessity.

Jimmy's first gig with a big star was backing Solomon Burke, who had had two best-selling singles that featured his big R&B crooning, wailing style. He led a tour that included the up-and-coming Otis Redding, the shouter Joe Tex, and the soulful, bluesy Sugar Pie DeSanto. To top it off the comedian Pigmeat Markham was quite hilarious with his mournful, funny faces and his bits that featured exaggerated sounds of agony often because of beatings by racist cops as the agents of oppressive racial policies.

Although very competent as a guitarist Jimmy was abruptly fired for inserting his impromptu showtime routines in the midst of other acts, unheard of for a sideman.

Jimmy joined Larry Lee in a band called Joe Fisher and the Barnevilles. They played in the smaller towns, such as Centerville, Tennessee. Fisher was well connected and they became the supporting band on tours led by the Marvelettes, Motown's first girl group, and Curtis Mayfield and the Impressions.

Mayfield's sweet, melodic guitar sound was predominant in R&B. The Marvelettes, very popular in the Eastern cities, were trying to expand from their urban base. Jimmy got a chance to play through Mayfield's equipment, probably the most advanced he had ever been able to work with. Some believed he had blown out Mayfield's amplifier by playing long, loud lines, and that is what got him fired.

Until that tour his biggest gigs with Billy Cox and the King Kasuals had been when they backed Nappy Brown and Carla Thomas, who recorded on Stax Records out of Memphis and who would eventually duo with Otis Redding on "Tramp." They had also backed School Boy and Ironing Board Sam.

While playing a gig at the Baron Club on Jefferson Street with Larry Lee, a promoter who was passing through suggested Jimmy try his luck in New York City. He was convinced Jimmy could write his own ticket. Jimmy was very receptive. The promoter set Jimmy up with a recording session in Philadelphia with Lonnie Youngblood, who played saxophone and sang lead in a very tight unit that required an inventive and energetic guitarist.

Jimmy had been primed to go to New York City since he first left Seattle. But it was winter. While somewhat mild in the South it was much colder in New York. Jimmy did not have a winter coat. Larry Lee lent him one of his. Once that obstacle was removed Jimmy wasted no time in going up to Philadelphia.

This recording session with Lonnie Youngblood became Jimmy's first long-playing record contribution and began a long association with Youngblood, who became an important and loyal friend. Of the fourteen cuts Jimmy also sang on "Wipe the Sweat, Part 3." While his voice lacked confidence it did not prevent the recording from being released almost immediately in late 1963. Jimmy made the short jump from Philadelphia to New York City in early 1964.

Checking into the Hotel Theresa, just off 125th Street and Seventh Avenue, he had success at once, winning the twenty-five-dollar first prize at the Apollo Theater's Amateur Hour Contest. He would hang out in the Palm Cafe, which was less than a block away. All of the musicians who were playing at the Apollo at the time hung out in the Palm Cafe, and there was a live broadcast of the house band over WLIB-AM every weekend. Jimmy made it known among the bartenders and regulars that he was looking for work as a lead guitarist. He would run down a list of the performers he had worked with and the tours he had been on, but no one believed him. The Palm Cafe attracted many a weirdo. It was located on the main drag of Harlem, 125th Street, off Seventh Avenue, and the constant stream of characters, combined with the natural skepticism of the average Harlemite, made it hard to believe Hendrix. He looked like he was fifteen or sixteen, at most, to the hardened veterans of Manhattan Island's black city within a city. He spoke so softly and acted so spacey that they just knew he was some kind of nut. And besides, none of the Marvelettes were there to back up his story. And what the hell was Seattle?

But one night they finally let him up on the bandstand to play with the house band. They fully expected some kind of weird shit and were not disappointed. After he got up on the bandstand and plugged in his guitar, they discovered he was left-handed yet was playing a right-handed guitar—upside down, no less! Now who ever heard of that? Then he tuned up in the weirdest way by playing a crazy run of screeching notes. The Palm Cafe house band played a sedate mode of Harlem jazz, heavy on the bottom and mellow on the top. Jimmy blasted his way through their sound right away, playing weird tonics against the key and incorporating mild feedback into his soloing. His rhythm chords were on time but sounded off to the members of the band, who were of another generation. They started messing up behind him, dragging the beat, and looking at each other in disgust, as if to say that amateur hour was at the Apollo every Wednesday night, not at the Palm Cafe. Jimmy played on determinedly, even getting into his showtime routine and flicking his tongue at the girls in the first row. He got a few titters and a little applause as he walked off. But he had touched one of the young ladies there.

Fayne Pridgeon came over to his table, where he sat with a friend from Nashville, and gave him her best foxy smile. She just wanted to let him know that she enjoyed his playing and that those jerks up on the bandstand deserved to be kicked dead in their asses, one by one. Fayne was offered a drink and sat down. Jimmy was very dejected about his performance, but Fayne urged him to cheer up. She knew the cats in the band and would make them give him another chance. She had really liked Jimmy's performance. It was unusual. And his stage routine was really something else, especially the wagging of his tongue in time to the vibrato he played with one hand while down on his knees. She dug it very much. Cheered by Fayne's boisterous enthusiasm, Jimmy told her about himself and the various bands he had played with across the country. Fayne was impressed by all the places he had been and the people he had played with. Besides, he had no reason to lie. She decided right there that he was probably some kind of genius and that she would befriend him. He was also kind of cute—he might be able to do more with that long tongue besides flutter it onstage.

Fayne made Jimmy her project. She took him by and introduced him to her best friend, June Vasquenza, a Mexican-bombshell exotic dancer with the stage name of Pantera. She did well for herself and lived in the upscale Park West Village on West Ninety-seventh Street. Pantera and Jimmy were both entertainers. Fayne thought they would hit it off, and she was right. Fayne quickly helped set it up so that Jimmy could stay with Pantera. Fayne understood his situations and always seemed to have solutions.

•   •   •

One day Ronnie Isley of the Isley Brothers was scouring New York looking for a new guitarist. They had several important gigs in Canada and Bermuda and just had to have someone on lead guitar who could really play. If they disappointed their fans outside the USA, they might not be able to get those gigs again. Ronnie went into the Palm Cafe and spotted a man named Tony Rice, who used to work with Joe Tex. He let him know right away about the problem. Tony Rice had been present when Jimmy Hendrix had sat in with the house band and had been impressed. Ronnie pressed Tony; he had to be sure this guy was really good. Ronnie ran off a list of top lead guitarists who were in the R&B bag. Tony said that this Hendrix cat was better than all of them. Convinced that he was not being put on, Ronnie went up to room 406 of the Hotel Theresa and met with Jimmy. They came back to the Palm Cafe to see if Jimmy could audition for Ronnie with the house band. Tony Rice went up to the bandstand and asked if Jimmy could sit in. They could not believe their ears—of course not. Then Ronnie Isley himself went up to ask them and the answer was still no, even to an Isley Brother. Jimmy was mortified. He knew that behind that kind of recommendation he would not get the job. But both Ronnie and Tony had spotted some heavy jealousy among the house band members. Ronnie told Jimmy not to sweat. Would Jimmy come out to their place in New Jersey that weekend? Jimmy was glad to, although he had to admit to Ronnie that he did not have enough strings on his guitar to be able to audition properly.

Jimmy met Ronnie in Englewood, where the band rented a house. The Isley Brothers stayed in Teaneck. Ronnie went out and bought Jimmy some strings. Jimmy tuned up in his weird way—*wonk, woonk, wheee*—and then went straight into "Twist and Shout," "Respectable," "Shout," and "Who's That Lady?" the Isleys' last release for United Artists. He knew their songs already. There was no doubt about it, Jimmy Hendrix had the job. Ronnie was amazed to have found someone who played so well and who knew their songs, too. Jimmy Hendrix was a godsend.

Jimmy joined the Isley Brothers on the recording session of "Testify (Parts 1 and 2)" at Atlantic Studios in Manhattan in the spring of 1964. Then he immediately got to play some gigs out of the country, in Montreal, Canada, and Bermuda. In between they played Seattle and he was able to see some of his family, albeit very briefly. Jimmy loved to travel to places he had never been before. Bermuda was fantastic. The Isley Brothers were very big in that British Commonwealth country and played to an SRO-packed baseball stadium. There were even people standing on the overlooking hills. The Isley Brothers' band backed the other groups on the bill. Jimmy Hendrix caused a sensation when he went into his showtime guitar-biting and playing on his haunches with one hand. The entire stadium was in an uproar.

The Isley Brothers got attached to Jimmy. He was so unassuming and uncomplaining. He received thirty dollars a night just like everyone else in the backup band and never carped about it. He would ask for an extra ten dollars sometimes for something he needed for the gigs, like strings or an extra touch to his stage clothes—he was really into frilly shirts and chains. The Isley Brothers took to calling him "the Creeper" because he "moved so softly."

Buddy Miles was an underage drummer playing with Wilson Pickett's band when he encountered the new guitarist the Isley Brothers had with them at the Uptown Club in Montreal. "Shout" was the Isley Brothers' big number, and when they got into it their lead guitarist, off to the side, would put on a show of his own. He did flip-flops, played the guitar behind his back, ate the strings, and did splits—all at the same time, it seemed. He had a ribbon tied to his arm and one tied to his leg, and he wore an earring in one ear and had an outrageous pompadour. He turned on the crowd and the Isley Brothers, too; he lent a show-man novelty to the group, as well as an excellent lead guitar.

Later Buddy went backstage to meet this cat. He was Jimmy Hendrix, a real strange, retiring cat. Buddy was so fascinated that he kept touching Jimmy as if to make sure he was real. He was not at all like his image onstage. Buddy, who was from Minnesota, was a newcomer to the East. Though very young, Buddy Miles's muscular girth made him appear much older. He had al-ready worked with a wide range of popular musical acts, from the legendary Ink Spots, to Brian Hyland, whose song about a tiny yellow polka-dot bikini had been a huge hit of the early sixties. But it was his association with the black girl groups such as Ruby and the Romantics ("Our Day Will Come") and the Jaynettes ("Sally Go 'Round the Roses") that gave him cachet. He began to hang out with Jimmy.

Jimmy, whose long hair was in a ponytail, was a strange bird all right. Never much for hanging out or doing the things that most of the guys in the other bands would do, Jimmy would spend hours alone in his room at the Manhattan Hotel in Times Square playing on his guitar without an amp. Usually when Buddy saw him it was when Jimmy was ready to step out. He would dress in the weirdest fashions Buddy had ever seen. Zebra sunglasses, fancy vests, and red hats. Once, Jimmy said, he had even dyed his hair orange.

Thin as a rail and seemingly never hungry, Jimmy was always bustling with energy. One day, Jimmy turned Buddy on. He called it crystals. But out of his bag he produced a baby bottle with nipple, cap, and all. Thinking the white substance inside was milk, Buddy was really taken aback when Jimmy undid the cap and poured out some of the contents: sparkling white powder. Buddy cracked up. The methedrine crystals gave a weird, high-powered high. It made you want to do nothing but play. You heard the strangest of all possible sounds—and you tried to play them. Weird, high-pitched, almost supersonic whistle peals, and teeth-grinding bass notes that lathered and rumbled at the utter bottom.

Jimmy loved the new tune Wilson Pickett was doing, "Midnight Hour." It was in many ways a musician's tune, full of wailing horns, testifying vocals, and hip guitar licks that evoked a quest through the black ghetto for love. He added that song to his personal repertoire.

Pickett had just signed with Atlantic Records. He had sung lead on "I Found a Love" when he was with the Falcons and used that song as the pinnacle of his live show.

Jimmy had been recording more and more with the Isley Brothers, as well. All of their releases in the year 1964 had him playing guitar. They were also signed to Atlantic, which released the singles "The Last Girl" (with Dionne Warwick singing harmonies), "Looking for a Love," "Wild As a Tiger," "Simon Says," "Move Over and Let Me Dance," and "Have You Ever Been Disappointed?" The Isley Brothers had started their own label in '64 called T-Neck. They released one single that year and Jimmy was on lead guitar for "Testify (Parts 1 and 2)." Their biggest hits up until that time had been "Shout" in 1959 and "Twist and Shout" in 1962. But when the Beatles did "Twist and Shout" in 1964, it became number one on the national charts. Quite naturally their original version of "Twist and Shout" revived, as well, and they toured heavily behind it. Jimmy had a lot of work. He began to see how it was at the top in the rarefied realm known as the "crossover."

In late September 1964, while on the Isley Brothers' thirty-five-day tour across the country, covering most of the large cities in the Midwest, East, and South, Jimmy wrote to his father and Leon from Columbus, Ohio—about halfway through the tour—noting that from there they would go to Florida, hitting Jacksonville, Tampa, and Miami, and then into Texas, the tour winding up in Dallas.

The Isley Brothers could not help but notice something about Hendrix they had never witnessed before. As Ernie Isley put it: "He played all the time. All the time. It wasn't like a thing you were listening to, though, it was a simple observation—like the sun is shining, Jimmy's playing his guitar. Jimmy would practice phrases over and over again, turn them inside out, break them in half, break them in quarters, play them slow, play them fast." He could even make his guitar sound as if it were saying simple phrases. They had never before seen such single-minded devotion.

Jimmy purposefully missed the tour bus at a point near Nashville and returned to what had become his second hometown. It was the end of October 1964.

He had spent the better part of the year with the top R&B group in America. He had established a beachhead in New York City. He had reached close to the top of the blues and R&B realm he had aspired to and was widely recognized as a crack rhythm guitarist who could enhance the ensemble sound with the best of them. But he did have an agenda, and at that point in time it was to live in the more relaxing environment of the South, and to get into some new music.

Back in Nashville, Jimmy tried to parlay his recent status as lead guitarist for the Isley Brothers.

Jimmy set his sights on getting a deal with Stax Records, as its headquarters were in Memphis, just about a hundred miles from Nashville. Stax was the southern Motown, rivaling them in record sales. Rather than the Detroit urban sound featuring a regional emphasis, their production philosophy was different, easygoing, reflecting a southern, almost rural sensibility. They also were structured differently. Stax encouraged everyone in their organization—from secretaries to session musicians to custodians, performers, and executives—to be involved in making hit records. Their roster of artists featured performers Jimmy had worked with or had exchanged musical ideas with: Carla Staples (a solo act and also a member of the famous Staples Singers), Albert King, and legendary groups who always featured top guitarists: the Mar-Keys, the Bar-Kays, and of course Booker T. and the MG's. Stax boasted the hottest instrumental groups who often backed their solo singers and vocal groups. Booker T. and the MG's were near living legends who had already helped make Sam and Dave and Rufus Thomas famous. Their own "Green Onions" was one of a handful of early sixties-era instrumentals to become veritable standards. Their tight, smooth ensemble playing was led by Booker T. Jones on organ and featured prominently Al Jackson on drums, Donald "Duck" Dunn on bass, and Steve Cropper, one of the most successful guitarists in the music biz, on electric guitar.

Hanging out around Stax, Hendrix encountered Cropper. Cropper was more than a guitar player. He would go on to cowrite "(Sittin' on) The Dock of the Bay" with Otis Redding and "Knock on Wood" with Eddie Floyd, and his distinctive horn arrangements would become a Stax staple, especially on "Soul Man" by Sam and Dave. Jimmy's experience spoke for itself, and after giving Cropper some tips on how to play "Mercy, Mercy," a recent Don Covay hit, the logical next step was to do it in the studio. They jammed for a spell, and then they got into "Walkin' the Dog." Jimmy would have liked to have worked it so he could make a demo of his own playing to shop around, but it was not possible.

But it was a very fruitful encounter; they had bonded more through talk than playing. Jimmy had hoped Stax would be interested. He could see he still had a way to go. He had mastered rhythm guitar, but the sounds he heard in his head were not being played by anyone else. Rather than try to follow in someone else's footsteps it was becoming clear that he would either have to do his own thing or relegate his life to accompanying others, helping others achieve their ideal sound.

Jimmy met up with George Odell, also known as Gorgeous George, who wore a number of hats on the chitlin circuit, a series of set venues across the country in various black neighborhoods and communities. Jimmy and Billy Cox had met with Odell at the Hippodrome in Nashville. Cox had not been impressed with what Odell had to offer, but Jimmy had other thoughts.

Jimmy had never really played the chitlin circuit as he would do working for Odell, who worked steadily by performing any number of functions, and this factor often meant a big deal to a chitlin circuit bottom line. He would be an act in a show, copromote it, and provide valet and roadie services, as well—all for a set price that was low enough to be attractive to the very modest chitlin circuit budget. Odell, under the stage name Gorgeous George, led a band while dressed in a blond wig and wearing wild stage clothes he made himself. He did not rehearse since he was often busy with other aspects of the show, but he had the stage presence to pull his act off. Hendrix was the kind of savvy guitarist perfect for Gorgeous George's act. Jimmy was a seasoned professional, very sensitive to the needs of live performance. If his references did not do it then all one needed to do was see him interact with other musicians to know that he understood.

The chitlin circuit played to the masses of blacks who were more often than not poor, making subsistence wages, or not working at all. Often having to sacrifice even for the low prices the venues charged, they nevertheless demanded a big show, with several acts, not unlike the older vaudeville days, certainly the chitlin circuit's predecessor. Food would always be available, and a great favorite food of the black masses for reasons cloaked in mystery (in addition to the staple collard greens, yams, macaroni and cheese, black-eyed peas, fish, and chicken) was, without a doubt, chitterlings.

Chitterlings, the intestinal entrails of the pig, reek of dung since they are the passageways to defecation in the domestic animal known to eat all and anything. During slavery days chitterlings were often the only meat impoverished, imprisoned blacks could get to eat. By careful cleaning and soaking and slow cooking, the offensive-smelling meat could be made palatable, although some of the bad odor still persisted. Chitlins, as it was called in slang, could be made, with skillful seasoning, tasty enough to become even a favored food. With the end of legal Jim Crow and the more overt forms of black oppression, chitterlings had virtually disappeared from restaurants, venues, and dinner tables in black neighborhoods and communities of respectability, but hung on with persistence in the locales considered to be less respectable.

So the chitlin circuit also became a term used symbolically to indicate the poor conditions available to great black music. British rock musicians, often blues enthusiasts, were shocked by the poverty of the lives and venues of their black American musical heroes. In the early 1960s institutional racism continued to be reflected in most aspects of African-American life.

Jimmy became Gorgeous George's guitarist, but he also worked in nonperforming capacities when Odell was simply a valet or road manager. Gorgeous George Odell always had work and was also quite influential since he often dealt with so many aspects of a tour.

Odell had been working a tour that featured Sam Cooke, Bobby Bland, and B. B. King, who talked with Jimmy. B. B. King told Jimmy, almost in passing, about entirely new approaches to the guitar, and the powerful effect the Hawaiian and country and western pedal-steel guitars had had on him. They achieved a cry that sounded human, that had emotion, that sang. B. B. wanted to sustain a note like a singer, full of subtle changes. He wanted to be able to phrase a note like a saxophone player. He pointed to his "big fat" hands and Jimmy's similar ones, and noted that by bending the note and then trilling the string (something you could only do with the breadth of size and the ability born from strength) he could make his guitar sound like a woman singer's vibrato. And he could sustain that sound with the standard potentials of the electric guitar. And "by fooling with the feedback between amplifier and instrument, I started experimenting with sounds that expressed my feelings, whether happy or sad, bouncy or bluesy." He was about singing through his guitar. That was the goal. B. B. King had put enough in Jimmy's ears to keep him occupied for months, years. Jimmy knew that his own info on playing particular hits of the day paled in comparison to B. B. King's info. But he was grateful that King had acted as if they were sharing equally.

Jimmy had been hungry to check Sam Cooke out ever since Fayne had introduced them. Sam Cooke was the hottest entity in the black music world because, like the Platters, he was immensely popular with whites as well as blacks. And his appeal seemed almost effortless, as his fluid, clear voice was full of appeal and soul yet without any clichés that would signify privately to a black audience.

Before Sam Cooke had become number one on the black-male vocalist pyramid Jackie Wilson had been on top, but Wilson maintained his intensity and his velvety aplomb. Once the champ, always the champ. But it was clear Wilson targeted black audiences and always would.

For Jimmy it did not matter what his status was, just as long as he got to be near enough to witness and learn. Playing behind Cooke and Wilson was like going to school, but what bothered Jimmy the most was that Sam Cooke generated so much excitement that he never got to finish his act. The audience always became overwhelmed before the end of his set, on their feet stomping and cheering. Jimmy wanted to see all the magic.

The tour ranged as far east as Minneapolis, Minnesota, where Hendrix got to play with the Valentinos, led by Bobby Womack. But in Kansas City, Jimmy missed the bus and was stranded. He managed to reconnect with Odell in Atlanta, but the Sam Cooke–Bobby Bland tour had ended and Odell was now working for Little Richard and the Upsetters, but this time only as a valet. Odell managed to get Jimmy a job assisting him.

Hendrix started out working for Little Richard as a lowly roadie loading and off-loading luggage and music and electronic equipment. His own luggage was a potato sack and a guitar with only five strings on it. Everyone noticed this, especially Little Richard. They all laughed.

But everything changed virtually overnight once he played with Richard's band, the Upsetters, at an afterhours club. He was quickly asked to join the aggregation as a full-time guitarist. That was in early December of 1964, right around the time Sam Cooke was killed by a hotel desk clerk in Los Angeles. Hendrix felt the loss.

They toured heavily. Little Richard had been a big star not that long ago. He still commanded big respect and top billing. From Atlanta they went to Greenville, South Carolina. In January they went through Layfayette, Louisiana, then Houston, where Jimmy got to play with Albert Collins and picked up a taste for a Collins tune Jimmy would later adapt and call "Drivin' South."

By February, Little Richard and company pulled into California for an extended stay. He had some dates up and down the coast, the Fillmore in San Francisco, Ciro's club in L.A., and would record and live in Los Angeles. Jimmy, who began calling himself Maurice James, lived at the Wilcox Hotel on Selma Avenue in Hollywood.

Jimmy encountered Rosa Lee Brooks and they worked out a song called "My Diary." Brooks brought in an up-and-coming singer and vocal arranger named Arthur Lee, who would go on to form the seminal psychedelic-era group Love. Working with members of the Major Lance band, they recorded two sides for a single 45 rpm record in the garage studio of the owner of Revis Records. "Utee," the B-side, was made up on the spot by Jimmy and Rosa and Arthur to reflect a new dance in which the partners made U and T patterns on the dance floor.

Residing in Los Angeles, the road intensity lessened, Jimmy got to know Little Richard better.

Little Richard called himself the "king of rock 'n' roll." From Macon, Georgia, Little Richard added a high-keening gospel sound to the then prevalent rockabilly and came up with the most notorious of the early rock 'n' roll hits: "Tutti-Frutti," "Long Tall Sally," "Good Golly Miss Molly," "Jenny, Jenny, Jenny," "Slippin' and Slidin'," "Ready Teddy," "Lucille," "Send Me Some Lovin'," "Keep A-Knockin'," and more.

While Pat Boone and other white singers received a great deal of the credit and the loot for their versions of Little Richard's compositions, Little Richard was confined to the same race crowd that had spawned his creativity. The same is true of Elvis Presley spinoffs from Arthur "Big Boy" Crudup, Bo Diddley, and Big Mama Thornton. "If I could only find me a white boy who can sing colored," Sam Phillips had lamented, until he found Presley. While Chuck Berry was hard to cover, his incarceration in Texas for four years during the height of the rock 'n' roll craze kept him effectively out of the picture.

When Jimmy Hendrix joined Little Richard, the rock 'n' roll craze had subsided into the post-Kennedy years, and Little Richard had returned to the withering rhythm and blues circuit of the small towns of the Deep South and the West Coast. But Richard Penniman was not one to internalize his hurts. Jimmy Hendrix received lecture after lecture on the hardships pressed upon Little Richard by a public and an industry that did not reward the originators of their joy and fortune. If Little Richard was not making money, Hendrix was making less. Traveling by bus from gig to gig, sometimes stranded in strange, out-of-the-way towns, subjected to the degradations of a hurt and complex man, Hendrix nevertheless persisted, playing that same strange amalgam of rockabilly and gospel, whose simple changes offered no challenge whatsoever to his musical ability. In fact, he and others in the band, like Black Arthur and Henry Oden, would often rebel in the midst of the insipid changes and take the music out there. This would never fail to enrage Little Richard, who considered the music little more than a background for his singing and dancing and his general display of outrageous finery. He was so uptight about someone else stealing his spotlight that he became upset if they even looked good in the clothes they wore. Once Jimmy wore a fine ruffled shirt onstage. Little Richard was irate. He called a meeting. "I am Little Richard," he screamed, "I am Little Richard, the king, the king of rock and rhythm. I am the only one allowed to be pretty! Take off those shirts. . . ."

Sometimes Richard Penniman would calm down and talk about his background. A friend of his family had killed his father, who had operated a club called the Tippin' Inn in Macon, Georgia. Little Richard was "discovered" through a demo recording he sent to an executive of Specialty Records while he was washing dishes in a Greyhound bus depot in Macon. Bumps Blackwell came there to take him to New Orleans, where they recorded several songs. They went one over the limit with a new song Richard had. It was called "Tutti-Frutti." Almost overnight Richard Penniman was thrust into stardom. It seemed as if it had been too much for him. For two years it seemed like everything he wrote was a hit. He hardly had time to catch his breath. Another artist who recorded for Specialty told Little Richard one day that the type of music he was playing was evil. That thought stayed with Richard. He never thought that the pronouncement might have been inspired by jealousy. While Little Richard was on tour in Australia in 1957, the Soviets launched Sputnik. He thought of the Tower of Babel and left show business to study for the ministry with the Seventh-Day Adventists. Instead of playing music, he would tell his audiences about his conversion to God. Only two years after his first hit he left the world of music. But songs he had had in the can kept him in hits into 1959, although the last two hit songs, "Baby Face" and "Kansas City," were written by others and were not nearly as outrageous as his own tunes had been.

Little Richard would talk about his innocence during that time. He was a naive twenty-three when "Tutti-Frutti" became a hit. The first time he was exposed to anything other than alcohol was a mind-blowing experience for him. "I screamed like Aunt Jemima with no pancakes when I first tried marijuana," he would say. He would often emphasize an incident by saying, "I screamed like a white lady." Little Richard was really into screaming. He would tell Jimmy how he taught these young white boys, who had played backup for him when he toured England in Liverpool, how to scream. They were called the Beatles. Now every time they turned on the radio they would hear the Beatles screaming like white ladies. Jimmy had a lot of sympathy for Little Richard, and a lot of respect, too. Many times it seemed like Little Richard was still a lad from Macon recovering from seeing his father killed by a friend.

Jimmy Hendrix jumped Little Richard's band in St. Louis and went to Chappie's Lounge to see and audition for Ike Turner's Blues Band, which was one of the hottest R&B bands in the South. Jimmy sat in and they made fun of him and his antics as usual, but he met up with Albert King afterward and that made the whole thing worthwhile. Jimmy knew about this left-handed blues guitarist, who roamed around Memphis, St. Louis, and Arkansas, through several recordings of his: "Blues at Sunrise," "Ooh-ee Baby," and "Traveling to California." Jimmy would not play with Ike Turner long, but he could be with a virtuoso blues guitarist who played left-handed like him and had come from the blues depths.

King, too, was amused by Jimmy, yet he was kind and talkative. He was almost old enough to be Jimmy's father. He talked about Blind Lemon Jefferson, whom he had seen play in the parks around Forest City when he was a boy. He also saw Memphis Minnie, who would sing to a player piano that had custom rolls of her tunes. King grew up and began to seek his own sound as a guitarist.

He played drums with Jimmy Reed for a spell but the guitar was his heart. He was influenced by Howlin' Wolf and Lonnie Johnson. T-Bone Walker's sound entranced and eluded him until he began bending strings to compensate for the intricate runs Walker was able to do that he was not capable of. He squeezed the strings with his massive fingers rather than in the traditional bend and got a sound that was completely his own. Jimmy learned from King how to slacken his strings so he could bend them an entire step. Combined with the whang bar of the right-handed Stratocaster located close to his playing hand, because it was restrung for a lefty, Jimmy began to explore some remarkable sounds. King played without a pick and developed a tremendously tactile touch. He showed Jimmy some fingerings, using the thumb and frettings that bent the string vertically instead of horizontally. His trademark was a sound that slurred up and then dropped down. Albert King was also fascinated with horn sounds.

Jimmy had been intrigued by some of the scenes they had encountered at some of the big shows on the package tours. The saxophone players who blew the tenor usually generated the most excitement, often inciting the largely rural crowds to a near riot, so intense was the reaction. Jimmy wondered why the guitar could not do the same thing. Playing with Little Richard the guitar was used as a rhythm instrument, yet the new Fender electrics were capable of an incredible distortion-free sound, as loud as you wanted. Sometimes Jimmy had defied Little Richard and soloed, getting down on his knees and going through his whole routine. But he would get it when it was over. And there was nothing like having Little Richard shout at you for two hours. Nothing.

Jimmy wanted to get a feeling for what was being played off the beaten track, away from the Top 40 tunes of the day, back in the woods where there were no mass inhibitions.

Jimmy was always on the alert for a hot guitarist but now he also wanted to check out these saxophone honkers up close and get that sound imbedded in his mind. Hendrix was always amazed by the power of horns. Suddenly in the midst of a hot rock 'n' roll number, during the horn chorus where they riff to one note, one horn disengages from the chorus, a tenor sax, then it begins to honk, squeal, and bleat on the beat, toward a different vector from the chorus. The tenor goes beyond the music and stops the music as he gets into the pure sound of the honking reed, the sound of the slaying of a lamb, a cow, a bull, the screaming, weird sound of sacrifice heavy in the augmented air. On the hypnotic beat, the honker is on his knees; the crowd begins a low roar from the back of the outdoor arena. In the darkness a mass frenzy builds, a chain reaction. The honker is down on his back with the saxophone held straight above him steadily bleating, staggering the beat now, splitting notes and jacking chromatics. The crowd is surging against the stage now; circling bodies begin to bob up and down as the crowd turns within itself. High-crying notes in the sky, a couple roll on the ground in a mad embrace, a bottle smashes against a bald head glistening with sweat, a fight starts, the crowd rushes forward and away at the same time, cries of joy and sorrow rise in the air, and the tenor saxophone is the only thing visible onstage. It seems to be levitating, enchanted by its own sound. Then the saxophone begins to glide along the stage, going crazy in squealing elemental abandonment. Now the crowd seems to understand; it charges the stage. The honking has tranced into manic legato tenor dorians; the saxophonist has gone beyond. The crowd is both angry and thrilled; they rock the stage, clambering aboard, hallucinating mass destruction. The tenor player barely escapes.

A typical tenor saxophone climax to an outdoor concert. Hendrix, with his fascination for horns, must have seen many such frenzied endings during his music wanderings adrift from Little Richard's band.

Jimmy Hendrix rejoined Little Richard in Atlanta, Georgia. He had become as established as any young brilliant guitarist could get in Nashville and the R&B chitlin circuit, yet it seemed as if he could move no further. Little Richard's funky comeback tour had an expectant enthusiasm to it. Little Richard was crazy, but he was also wise, although the way he expressed his wisdom was outrage at its height.

Atlanta had been the only big town on the tour. The band rode the bus while Little Richard flew. They toured a lot of the out-of-the-way places in the Southwest, as well. The big cities like Denver, San Francisco, Atlanta, L.A., and Las Vegas were often only connection points for the smaller towns they actually played. And when they went into the South, they went into the heart of the civil rights upheavals.

Little Richard seemed effeminate and sometimes he could really act weird. The comeback was difficult for a man who had been a top star. Often Little Richard went into tirades, and very often the money was short all around. Many of the band members were young musicians like Jimmy. They shared the fear of being left stranded in some little one-horse town, especially in the South. Little Richard was often petulant and unpredictable. Some members of the band felt that he did not like women. But all of them needed whatever money they were paid and were afraid to protest even when they felt they were receiving poor treatment.

Jimmy maintained himself as best he could. He loved to play. Little Richard was convinced that the rockabilly change that had propelled him to stardom in the fifties would prevail in the sixties, but the audience's musical tastes were changing.

Jimmy wore a conked hairdo that he maintained himself, often with a Sterno kit and hot comb. There was hardly enough money to have it done properly by a hairdresser, and often they were nowhere near a town big enough to have a barbershop that specialized in processed hair.

Sometimes Little Richard would make them wait around his hotel room before he paid them. He liked young boys to hang around him and sometimes would go through scenes with them in front of the band while they waited to be paid. He liked Jimmy a lot and sometimes it would seem that he was directing these antics at Jimmy.

Once, in Oakland, Little Richard held the band in his room waiting for their pay while he berated a girlfriend of one of the band members. The scene got very ugly. Somebody called the cops, and the four members of the band decided to leave. They did not know whether they would have their jobs later or not. But many, including Jimmy, felt that they had had enough.

Little Richard and company were heading to New York City. Jimmy made sure he was cool until he was returned to where he had come from only a few months ago. Little Richard was known to dwell for relatively lengthy stays in various regions, California, the South, New York, out of which he would operate for several weeks at a time. It was less tiring and a bit closer to normal life than the constant touring across long distances, gigging without constantly having to pick up and move on.

They arrived in New York City in mid-April, Jimmy taking a room at the Hotel Theresa. They immediately began playing in a package-tour gig that was in residence at the Paramount Theater in midtown Manhattan. Also in the package were King Curtis and the Kingpins (a unit that consisted of sixteen pieces), the Hollies, Shirley Ellis, the Vibrations, the Exciters, the Hullabaloos (dancers), the Detergents, Dee Dee Warwick, Sandie Shaw, Joe Stampley and the Uniques, and comedian Soupy Sales. When Jimmy returned to June Vasquenza's place at Park West Village where he had his stuff, he found that things had changed. June was now with Arthur Allen, another friend of Faynes, who had a twin in the army named Albert. But Jimmy soon discovered Fayne had more personal plans for him.

Jimmy and Fayne got back together as if he had not been gone since September of 1964—six months. No woman he had ever been with was like Fayne. She became his woman. Her loyalty was absolute. She stood up for him, protected him as only a Harlem woman could. But at the same time she was always in amusement, always halfway laughing at him. But she truly loved his strangeness, his individuality, his uniqueness, and she would let no one interfere with it. She often thought of herself as the woman *and* the man in their relationship because she was always the one to "jump up in some nigger's face" about Jimmy's ways.

Jimmy was always bugging somebody with the way he walked, his soft-spoken shyness, and especially the way he played. Fayne felt protective of him. He seemed out of place in Harlem. People would always ask him where he was from. Many had never heard of Seattle, and this increased their disbelief. Some thought he was a sissy or a faggot, but he just didn't care how people took him. He was only interested in playing. Alone he played mostly old blues to himself, but he knew all the rhythm and blues changes and just about everything else that was played over the radio.

Fayne laughed a lot. She would always laugh at Jimmy. She had never met such an oddball. And he had "big titties," too, that really cracked her up. And Jimmy would be so embarrassed that she would almost die laughing. He was always good for a rise. But it was the oddity that attracted her. Used to doing her own thing, independent and bold, she was a fine and foxy fixture on the Harlem music scene. The Apollo, the Palm Cafe, Small's Paradise, Frank's, Sugar Ray's, and the fast three-for-one bars with their flashy exteriors and plush interiors, she knew them all. As fine and loud and funny as she was, she had the run of Harlem, the black capital of the world, and was perfect for Jimmy, who would have been like a lamb going to slaughter alone in Harlem.

Fayne was always her own woman. It was understood that she was not at all possessive and would not tolerate such behavior. Enamored of R&B stars and just pretty young boys, she found that Hendrix fit her fancy in the young-boy department. It had been her romantic involvement with Sam Cooke that finally got him backstage at the Apollo to hang out with the great singer. Through Fayne, Hendrix met many New York R&B artists and through his own ability he often got gigs with them, but they were unwilling to work with his musical ideas. He was just gigging—playing the same changes that thousands of young black guitarists with conked hair could play.

Fayne and her weirdo, Jimmy, came to know all the local bands that played the Harlem weekends. Most of the clubs featured live weekend music, and Jimmy thought that it would be a different scene from touring with a big-name star who had an obligation to the audience to play their hit songs the same way they were heard over the radio. But he found the club bands just as rigid. They resented him coming up to sit in and then putting on his act. Licking the guitar, collapsing to his haunches, and playing a lot of *off-the-wall* riffs. He acted as if he were somewhere else, onstage by himself, as if he were the star, instead of just another guitar player begging to sit in. Fayne would just give them hell for freezing up on Jimmy. They often got mad at Jimmy, but Fayne was always ready to take them on.

They lived all over Harlem. At first, in 1964, they lived with a friend named Bootsie at 210 West 118th Street between St. Nicholas and Eighth avenues. They lived in room 213 of the Cecil Hotel over Minton's, the famous club where bebop was invented, where Charlie Christian had established the electric guitar as a major jazz instrument capable of solos instead of just rhythm keeping. The patrons and the personnel there would tell Jimmy and Fayne the history of the place, and Jimmy, interested in all music, would check it out. Jimmy got a chance to check out Sugar Hill when they moved up to 154th and St. Nicholas, where all the "uppity niggers" used to live years ago. There were big, palatial apartment houses, where people like renowned activist, scholar, and writer W.E.B. DuBois once lived. Some were tenement slums, others still held on to the beauty of the past.

Hendrix was amazed at Harlem. This small section of Manhattan had more blacks than all of Seattle. No white folks lived up there. It was a black city. And Fayne moved through Harlem as though she owned it.

Jimmy toured with Little Richard up and down New York State and New Jersey, too, the rest of the spring, and Little Richard played the Apollo in mid-June. After that show Jimmy chose to miss the tour bus that was heading for gigs in Washington, D.C., and going back into the South. He called Little Richard's brother and tour manager, Robert Penniman, who, since both men were in agreement, "fired" Jimmy.

In July of 1965, he rejoined the Isleys, playing with their group at Small's Paradise, also in Harlem. They apparently believed his story about missing the bus in the South the year before and not knowing where they were going and having lost his guitar and therefore not being able to rejoin them. In early August he played on their recording sessions for the singles "Move Over and Let Me Dance" and "Have You Ever Been Disappointed."

After a brief flurry of gigging and recording with the Isley Brothers they, in effect, let him go. His stories about missing buses and having his guitar stolen had begun to come back to haunt him. All of the groups he had played with had received similar treatment from Jimmy and word had begun to get around in the tight-knit black music world. In order to connect with the music and study it the way he wanted to while making the meager living necessary under those circumstances, he had to have a way to leave groups without causing animosity. Missing the bus was a well-known device, but with that strategy also grew his reputation for being unreliable.

He had burned many bridges; now he had to make it on the land he was on.

Jimmy wrote to his father about his situation and his feelings at this time. He knew of a few small recording companies and felt he could make a record with one of them. "I think I'll start working towards that line because actually when you're playing behind other people, you're still not making a big name for yourself. But I went on the road with other people to get exposure to the public and see how business is taken care of. And mainly just to see what's what, and after I put a record out, there'll be a few people who knew me already and who can help me with the sale of the record." Hendrix's plan was taking shape, crude but clear. He also spoke to an assessment of the music world in August of 1965, from the perspective of someone who had played with some of the most popular acts in black music. "Nowadays people don't want you to sing good. They want you to sing sloppy and have a good beat to your songs. That's what angle I'm going to shoot for. That's where the money is . . ." Here Hendrix was making room for his own vocalizing. He did not consider himself a good singer at all. But it probably began to dawn on him that he would have to do some vocalizing in order to make it as a solo act or leader of a group. As distasteful to him as it might have been, his own singing was not ruled out. He ends the letter confiding to his father about his living conditions: "I just want to let you know I'm still here, trying to make it. Although I don't eat every day, everything's going all right for me. It could be worse than this, but I'm going to keep hustling and scuffling until I get things . . . happening like they're supposed to for me." It is obvious Jimmy was in an emotionally difficult state. "Tell everyone I said hello. Leon, Grandma, Ben, Ernie, Frank, Mary, Barbara and so forth. Please write soon. It's pretty lonely out here by myself. Best luck and happiness in the future. Love, your son Jimmy."

When Jimmy met Curtis Knight in October 1965, Jimmy had just ended a liaison with Diana Carpenter, a light-skinned black prostitute, who was a teen runaway from the Midwest. They had lived together off and on all over Times Square until she was arrested and sent back home as a juvenile offender. He moved back to the low-down Hotel America and was between guitars, having had to pawn the one he had in order to eat. He met Knight in the hotel lobby where there was a small recording studio. Knight and Jimmy got to talking. Knight, leader of his own group, could not help but be impressed by Jimmy's casual reiteration of the people he had played with. They went to Jimmy's room where Knight met Fayne, who was sitting on the bed, just about the only furniture in the room. Wanting to hear him play but discovering Jimmy had no guitar, Knight went somewhere in the neighborhood, and soon came back and presented Hendrix with his own right-handed sunburst Fender Duo-Sonic. Once he heard Jimmy play it was settled. Knight and his group had themselves a guitarist of the highest caliber. And Jimmy had work, and a guitar, even if only a loaner.

After an introduction by Knight to small label record producer Ed Chalpin, Hendrix signed a contract that would haunt him for the rest of his life.

The small sums he received for recording for Chalpin at Dimensional Studios, combined with Curtis Knight and the Squires' fairly steady gigs, helped to keep him in his cheap hotel and eating. One such session had him backing the movie actress Jayne Mansfield, who had enormous breasts and contrived Marilyn Monroe vocal and body-language mannerisms. Jimmy played on a song called "Suey." The production would become the B-side of "As Clouds Drift By," a single that would be released by London Records the following year.

Jimmy's presence helped Curtis Knight and the Squires increase their popularity at the local dance clubs, many of which were not yet over the Twist dance craze. Coming from the Isley Brothers, Hendrix was a more than welcome addition to the group.

While it had been difficult to become known while playing with the Isley Brothers, with Curtis Knight and the Squires it was much simpler. They played the local clubs of New York City and New Jersey, and as an emergent band they gave him the attention he craved and felt he deserved.

Their repertory included Top 40 R&B, some originals, and some up-tempo songs for extended boogie. They performed two of these—"Driving South" and "Killing Floor"—often. Because they played primarily discos and small dance halls, they had to maintain extended danceable numbers. While Hendrix had more chances to solo, his main job was to augment the rhythm section and melody lines in unusual ways for the dancers.

Hendrix appeared with the Squires at the post-Christmas show at George's Club 20 in Hackensack, New Jersey. The relief of finally being past Christmas was evident. The crowd was lively and plenty drunk. Curtis Knight was delighted to have such a top-notch guitarist in his group. " . . . I'd like to let everyone know that you're being recorded. This is being recorded live here at the fabulous George's Club 20 in Hackensack, New Jersey. . . . What are you going to do for the people, Jimmy, on Christmas plus one?" Hendrix slurs in a Louis Armstrong grate, "Drivin' South." Curtis Knight picks up: "A little thing called 'Drivin' South'—in D. If you ain't never been there you gonna take a trip with us now, baby. If you ain't got no car, put on some skates." The Squires hit some butt-bumping rhythm and are gone. "Drivin' South" was a one-chord back-beating tune with plenty of room on the top for continuous soloing by Hendrix, as Knight named cities and states, going deeper and deeper into the Southland. "Eat it! Eat it!" Curtis Knight shouts to Hendrix, as Jimmy displays his novelty attraction, playing the guitar with his teeth.

Hendrix's attack is sharp and piercing on treble reach. His soloing is bluesy, with long loping lines that ride over several beats of the up-tempo song. As the towns get deeper and deeper into the South, Hendrix's guitar gets bluesier and bluesier, getting down into the deeper registers of the Delta sound, where the guitar plays bass notes as well as lead figures. Hendrix climbs out of the Delta with a long upward-sliding wail that skirts the psychedelic. Toward the end, Jimmy joins the rhythm by noodling bass figures against the beat. Then Knight shouts, "Eat it! Eat it!" again, and Jimmy goes back into a riffing guitar frenzy for a while, then back to noodling with the rhythm as "Drivin' South" goes out.

Howlin' Wolf's "Killing Floor" starts out in a light whimsical rhythm with a high-ranged bass line pizzicato *Batman*-like theme, nearly happy-go-lucky. Then Curtis Knight's rhythm guitar speaks out, right on the beat, with a rhythm guitar electric *chik, chik-chik, chik, chik-chik* and then starts scratching like a twitching electrical charge inside a tube, piercing the rhythm with syncopated washboard-like percussion swinging in on the four, advancing the rhythm subliminally. And then Jimmy comes in on his Fender Duo-Sonic, playing a longer rhythm figure in harmony with the rhythm guitar. Then he joins the percussive scratching, his guitar sounding like a rattlesnake, harmonizing metamusically, creating an echo subtone scratching against the backbone in buck dance rhythm licks. Hendrix applies a slow arc of contrasting harmonies against Knight's steady rhythm; they swing in a modal arc as Hendrix explores the sound. He does not dominate the rhythm guitar; rather, he lays back in that Charlie Christian space, unobtrusive in an echo vector dewailing on the other side of the sound. Jimmy arcs the harmony completely perpendicular, his Fender Duo-Sonic creating a flashing light-ninglike stroke of complete fusion before returning to the melody stroke. Jimmy starts his solo in a low-register geechie stutter, then goes on in a legato statement that is blues, poetic and beautiful. He ranges into his personal style at the top toward another place in the melody, and then quickly returns to an earthy declamatory style full of the articulations of the blues, and comes down to hit the head of the lyric right on.

> *Lord knows I should've been gone*

Because now he's crying on the "Killing Floor" Jimmy goes crazy as they take it out in staccato rhythm. He climbs the wall with the whimsical yet sinister melody and joins the rhythm, as well, with heavy contrasting comments on the bottom. His wails scale against the ceiling, the nonchalance of the melody turning into a flash of manic murder intensity at the peak. They descend, and the song ends to a cacophony of applause, shouts, cusses, and banging glasses.

Some of the other clubs Hendrix played with Curtis Knight and the Squires were the Purple Onion, a Greenwich Village discotheque; the Queen's Inn; the Cheetah in Times Square; and Ondine's on the chic Upper East Side.

At the Cheetah they became known to a larger circle of people, some of them well known in the music business. Knight had band uniforms made out of the same cheetah-skin pattern that decorated the club's interior. It looked like the Squires were coming out of the walls. Murray the K on his AM radio show pushed the Cheetah heavily, with ads and personal testimony. Jimmy also stayed at the Cheetah to play with Carl Holmes and the Commandos. Ondine's was the cream of discotheques. The beautiful people went there. Jimmy met

Ronnie Spector, the leader of the Ronettes and the wife of legendary producer Phil Spector. She told him in a beautiful, laughing, offhand way that he was gonna make it, that he would someday be a star. He loved her for that.

Jimmy Hendrix toured for two months with Joey Dee and the Starlighters near the end of 1965, a gig each day with only two days off. He wrote to his father from Boston on November 24.

Dear Dad,
We're in Boston, Mass. We'll be here for about 10 days. We're actually playing in Beveve. Tell Ernie I'm in her home state. I hope everything is all right. We're right next to the ocean. Right across the street.

—Jimmy

When he arrived back in New York City after the tour, he was set up in a nice place when Fayne saw him again. The money didn't last long but the impression remained. This was the first time he had toured with a predominantly white band. He had played with a few white bands in Seattle, but with Joey Dee he got to savor the Twist craze right up close. The hysteria that the augmented rockabilly beat drove the myriad crowds to was amazing. It was like Joey Dee was a high priest, a messenger bringing a sacred message to all. Right there he witnessed the power of words and music, especially as promoted by big-town machinery, but more so, as ordained by the people's need for release. The Twist included all ages and all kinds of people, and it was not necessarily youth-oriented. The Beatles in 1965 were still the kings of the English sound, but they were essentially a listening experience, a pleasant experience compared to the uncouth Twist parties.

Doris Troy, then riding high on her monstrous hit "Just One Look," was present when Jimmy Hendrix auditioned for King Curtis's band. King Curtis had mellowed his sound to an approach to rhythm and blues that had resulted in a big national hit, "Soul Serenade," in 1964. Jimmy, inspired by King Curtis's style, sought to emulate it in his playing. He drove his Fender Telecaster to its highest limits in trying to give back the horn lines that had inspired him. Usually the people Hendrix desired most to play with did not like his strong musical presence; they wanted a backup guitarist, and Hendrix's interest in heavy metal funk ensemble playing was far ahead of its time. He had begun to get the message that he would have to start his own group if his ideas were to come to fruition. But again he was a hired hand. King Curtis's band, the Kingpins, was the heaviest of the R&B crossover bands on the set. Hendrix had achieved a spot with the ultimate band of his idiom. At that point he knew he would have to go out soon and do his own thing. After the King Curtis band, there would be no place else to go.

The King Curtis band was a heavyweight aggregation that was as close to jazz as rhythm and blues could come. "Soul Serenade" featured King Curtis's plaintive saxophone sliding into a get-down funk, wailing out. Jimmy shared the lead work with Cornell Dupree and fed King Curtis the pretty rhythm chords and fills that were so essential to the melody.

Jimmy got to be friends with Cornell Dupree, and with Chuck Rainey, who played a Fender bass. He did not often make friends, being quiet and keeping to himself a lot, but the frequency of contact with the cats in the band drew them together.

Jimmy grew on them. Nonchalant, very easy to get along with, and always happy to be at any gig, even if it was only as second guitar, Jimmy was never known to say anything negative. But it was hard to get close to him; he was almost too good to believe.

Jimmy had perfect pitch. This required a lot of tuning, but he was able to do it quickly. He often tuned differently for different numbers, and on occasion he employed an open tuning where he only needed to bar up the frets to change chords.

For King Curtis, Jimmy wished he had a new Stratocaster. He needed it for such a heavyweight group.

By January of 1966, Hendrix was playing full-time with King Curtis's group the Kingpins. King Curtis's own music was a sophisticated amalgam of jazz, R&B, and pop. His "Soul Serenade" foreshadowed Grover Washington Jr.'s groove by a couple of decades. King Curtis was a master of all the popular forms, including the best of jazz. He was the saxophonist who had played the solos on some of the Coasters' biggest number one hits. He was king of the recording session saxophonists just as his drummer, Bernard "Pretty" Purdie, was the best of the session drummers. They both knew from proven successful experience who had it and who didn't. Time was money. They had noticed how quickly Hendrix picked things up. Amazingly fast. If Jimmy didn't know the changes, all Purdie had to do was call them out once and they were responded to immediately and also locked into Jimmy's memory. King Curtis had distinguished himself with white romantic popular crooners like Andy Williams, rockabilly artists like Buddy Holly, and jazz masters like Lionel Hampton. The emergent gospel diva Aretha Franklin loved him.

In April of 1966, Hendrix recorded with King Curtis and the Kingpins. The first time bassist Chuck Rainey heard Jimmy play was when he was with Little Richard. King Curtis's All-Stars had shared the bill with them at the Paramount in New York City that April of 1965. But Rainey really heard Hendrix while they recorded and jammed. The lines Hendrix played had had Chuck Rainey going to his bass, trying them out. Just the way B. B. King noted the way guitarists exchanged information in a kind of shorthand, Rainey, as a bassist, found in Hendrix's lower registers such originality that he remembered "constantly going to my bass and trying to play lines the way I had just heard Hendrix play them. His lines were played with a lot of character—he didn't play them straight ahead and simple: he added feeling by using dynamics, finger tremolo, and of course his natural showmanship." After Hendrix joined King Curtis's Kingpins, Rainey was able to get a new quality to his own playing. "For the six months that Jimmy was in the group I gained an added feeling, which I label response."

Cornell Dupree and Jimmy, both guitarists, became very close. Dupree remembered a gig where the Kingpins, who King Curtis was trying to expand, had Billy Preston on keyboards and they played a gig opposite and backing Chuck Berry in upstate New York. Jimmy really put on his show that night behind Berry. Everyone who ever played with Hendrix, it seemed, experienced at one time or another his "show." Between playing with his teeth and those strange sounds he got out of the guitar, which he managed to include in his melodics, there were his acrobatics—splits, going down on his haunches and rising in time to a guitar dynamic—he was becoming recognized as a distinct entity among the black musicians, even though he remained essentially a sideman.

Jimmy recorded with King Curtis and the Kingpins intermittently throughout an extended spring.

Jimmy played with King Curtis at a party Atlantic Records threw for all their artists and wound up backing Percy ("When a Man Loves a Woman") Sledge and Wilson Pickett. Although it had been almost a year since Atlantic released "Midnight Hour" in America, it was still a favorite number and Jimmy's sly feedback tones were muted by the blaring horn section. He also recorded on several sessions with Curtis Knight.

Kim Shiroky, a young blonde woman who was friendly with Curtis Knight through his appearances at the Cheetah, had become Jimmy's first white girlfriend. They shared a room at the Hotel Lennox. Jimmy, who styled his long hair using curlers and Vaseline, jumped out of the bathroom one night buck naked to play along with "Wild Thing" by the Troggs, which had just been released. Kim thought that was funny. Jimmy's discovery of white rock was fascinating to witness since he had spent years developing an expertise in black music, from blues to R&B.

Kim introduced Jimmy to Trinidadian Mike Quashie, who performed a nightclub act across the street from the hotel at the African Room. Six foot two and almost three hundred pounds, Quashie was nevertheless an accomplished limbo dancer who was able to practically crawl on the floor on his back and still be able to regain a standing position without using his hands and arms. He wore costumes that featured scarves tied to his arms, waist, and knees. Kim noticed that Jimmy quickly adopted that fashion statement. Quashie, who ate fire and did other kinds of things that augured up voodoo associations, noted that when Jimmy would come in, often with two or three women in tow, the owner of the club "would freak." They thought the women with Hendrix were hookers. "At least they looked like hookers, and the owners thought Jimmy was a pimp, with his wild clothes, processed hair, and his doo-rag." They did not want that kind of association. Since Jimmy and Kim lived right across the street Mike would visit. "I teased him about his Vaselined hair. It was long but he was wearing it greased, and I'd say, 'You trying to be Nat "King" Cole?'" But Quashie was only giving Hendrix a Calypso style of ribbing and Jimmy was a good sport. "He'd come to see my show and I'd go and see him in his hotel room, usually to buy some speed. I was into speed a long time and I gave Jimmy ten, twenty dollars, lots of times." Jimmy's personal stash of methedrine was useful when there was no food to eat. It squashed hunger. It was also sometimes necessary when one had to play a gig without much, if any, sleep. But Quashie was also simply generous and would help Jimmy out with small loans. It was well known that Jimmy would not take a job outside of music. That was how serious he was. It helped to hang with those in Greenwich Village who lived in the bohemian tradition. Down there people understood that position and helped each other. Quashie, who lived in the Village, was a fellow traveler.

Mike Quashie kidded Hendrix mercilessly, calling him Jimmy Coon, or asking him what kind of nigger he was. But his sarcasm masked his concern for Jimmy, his living circumstances. When Jimmy needed a place to stay, some advice, or a few bucks, Quashie always helped him out.

Jimmy met Richie Havens at the Cheetah when Carl Holmes and the Commandos, a group he had begun to gig with regularly, were opening for him and Cat Mother. Havens and the huge basketball star Wilt Chamberlain watched him play from the bar. Havens could not figure out where Hendrix was getting all that sound from. He came up to the stage and peered under it, trying to discover something extra. They hit it off right away. Havens was a folk legend on MacDougal Street, living in the mysterious East Village. He urged Jimmy to come down to the Village as soon as possible and check it out. It was a perfect place for unconventional people. And Havens could see and hear that Jimmy was all that, and could grow in an artistic community that encouraged the individual.

When Kim Shiroky found out that the only thing keeping Hendrix unhappily tied to Curtis Knight was the fact that it was Knight's guitar Jimmy was playing, she went out and bought him a white Stratocaster. "That was the love of his life and he sat there for hours filing the frets down so the strings would fit in reverse. That was his baby. Then he left Curtis and Curtis never forgave me for that."

Jimmy made several recordings as a sideman in 1964 and 1965, but none of them were really where his head was at, though he had gained valuable experience. There was never enough time to do what he wanted to do, and when he was doing things he liked, he never had enough time to explore the studios. The recordings with Little Richard were standard studio rehashes of Richard's hits of the late fifties, with a few new numbers. But Jimmy's rhythm work was so innovative and his brief solos so fresh, it was amazing Little Richard did not expand Jimmy's contribution. He recorded with the Isley Brothers. "Wild Little Tiger" was more or less a vehicle for Jimmy's guitar. He concocted a wild screeching hook and then drove the tune with a rhythm line that reflected the up-tempo refrain. Jimmy achieved his effects by shaking the guitar and rolling the strings over one another. "Move Over and Let Me Dance" was another R&B rocking, shouting number of the Isley Brothers that featured Jimmy Hendrix. They gave him more freedom than Little Richard did, but could no more integrate his sound into Top 40 R&B than Little Richard could in his own brand of rockabilly.

The most dramatic of Jimmy's early work is an instrumental version of "House of the Rising Sun," Leadbelly's favorite, cut during an independent session. Recorded on fairly good equipment in Atlanta, it was the hit of those sessions. In it he uses a light up-tempo rhythm that contrasts with the tragic vocal tones and lyrics. It gives the feeling of transcendence.

Both Fayne and her mother regarded Jimmy as a trip. But his inoffensive and sweet disposition always won them over and kept them in his corner: he was simply not a threat to man or beast on a social level. All he wanted to do was play. He lived and breathed to play his guitar.

While Fayne was heavy into Harlem, she did not trust anything out of Harlem. Midtown, the Village, those were the "white" sections. She was ill at ease outside of Harlem and sarcastic at Jimmy's naïve curiosity. And when he brought home a weird hillbilly record by some dude named Bobby Dylan, she just *knew* Jimmy had gone completely crazy.

CHAPTER 3

Hendrix spent weeks walking the Village and East Village, from the Hudson to the East River, from Gansevoort Pier down West Eleventh to West Tenth then all the way across town to where West Tenth ran into the brown, austere Women's House of Detention, then past Eighth Street and Sixth Avenue, where all the street people hung out. The streets near the rivers were always empty, but here in the heart of Greenwich Village, the tempo began. Blacks, whites, Puerto Ricans, freaks, hippies, and desperadoes milled about, with camera-toting tourists smiling their way past the multitudes. He walked on Eighth Street until it became shaded by the eastern light, and the office buildings of Broadway and Astor Place loomed tall above the skyline. The continuous flow of traffic down the street that never stopped: Broadway. He thought of the Drifters' song about Broadway: *"How ya gonna make some time"*—when you don't even have enough money to buy food—*". . . and I won't quit till I'm a star on Broadway."* Yeah.

And then the tenements of the East Village low downtown. St. Mark's Place and Cooper Square where art students hung out—starving artists of the Lower East Side. Weird nationalities like Ukrainians, Poles, Yiddish-speaking Jews, Puerto Ricans, and on the last avenue, Avenue D, blacks. This little ghetto in downtown Manhattan was right off the East River.

Jimmy became more aware of the great underground movement in jazz the more he hung out. Charlie Parker was a legend in the Village. Although he had been dead for several years, people still talked about him as if he were still around. The Village Gate featured jazz, but usually only big names. Jimmy often heard the names of Sun Ra, John Coltrane, Eric Dolphy, Cecil Taylor, Archie Shepp, Charles Mingus, Ornette Coleman, and Albert Ayler spoken with awe and reverence. Most of them usually played in the clubs on the East Side like the Five Spot, the Jazz Gallery, and Slugs Saloon. Sometimes he saw advertisements for Sun Ra at the Charles Theater on Avenue B and in other unusual places. Sometimes Mingus played at the Village Vanguard. Jimmy was aware of them. Sometimes he would be at someone's house and hear some of their recordings. But he was having enough of a hard time with his own music to try to consciously incorporate some of the ideas he heard. Many of the oldtime "folkies" were mad at Dylan for taking up the electric guitar. Music was a controversial thing and he tried to avoid disputes. He listened when he could to the new and avant-garde jazz, but there were few guitarists playing in that vein. After Charlie Christian there was Wes Montgomery, but few jazz guitarists had become really well known. Sometimes he fantasized about playing jazz. But it was like a classical form of music. Usually jazz musicians read music. He could not read and would definitely not take the time out of his own development to learn. There seemed to be not much reason for it where he was coming from. In his heart he was closest to the old blues forms, and that was where he wanted to stay. But he also knew that some of the freak sounds he heard in his head, and tried to play through guitar, were closer to a jazz thing than what he was supposed to be playing.

Hendrix by now could play any rhythm and blues classic or current hit blindfolded. His departure from Harlem was not only an attempt to get away from having to play them at all, but also to stretch out more in the direction his imagination dictated. Not only was rhythm and blues still grounded in the same rigid chord changes and nuances born out of the blues, but also most black musicians had ignored the musical possibilities of the bastard forms of rockabilly and rock. While some young white rock 'n' rollers had managed to copy and cajole the correct changes of black music, they most often failed to present in their stage presentation "the show."

"The show" was the staple of every performance, especially on the southern tours and at places like the Apollo. "The show" was when the artists or band would do some wild, way-out stuff. "The show" was the height of the performance, and like the saxophone "honkers," this display often put both the audience and the performer in a transcendental state where improvisation came to the fore and the unexpected took everybody out. Very much akin to the building emotional patterns of black holiness churches, this crescendo, once reached, could be stretched and augmented and built upon all night if necessary. But for the true followers of black music, it was this transcendental moment everyone waited for. Most of the white musicians of rock 'n' roll, still heir to their racial memories and culture, remained almost classically distant in their approach to rock 'n' roll. Playing all the notes purely, but almost stock still, they seemed incapable of delivering or unable to deliver the physical keys to the higher spheres of the music.

When Hendrix put on a show, he blew minds and terrified the audience. He would just go out. Dipping down into simulated splits, whirling his guitar, gobbling his tongue, screaming with the pulsing Telecaster signal, he had consciously developed the ability to get down with the show and push the audience higher.

Hendrix, a restless, questing spirit, could not rest on his laurels as a top lead guitarist. Besides, while his rep allowed him a modest following of fellow musicians and friends, it allowed him no monetary rewards beyond the survival wages he earned as an independent lead guitarist for hire. He had nothing to lose.

Jimmy got a chance to lead his own band at the Cafe Wha?, a basement club on MacDougal Street right across the street from the Gaslight. MacDougal Street was Main Street in Greenwich Village for tourists and for those who wanted to hear some authentic music or poetry up close. Just below Washington Square Park, where MacDougal and West Third streets intersect, began the strip that lasted for only a block before turning left on Bleecker Street and continuing four blocks to La Guardia Place and New York University's south campus residential complex. The Wha? had the most varied bill of any club in the Village. The club opened in the early afternoon with a hootenanny favored mainly by the hookey players from various high schools. A flexible bill that rarely featured anybody, it reflected the transient audience it attracted. Very often the audience would also be the performers. The "hoot" in the afternoon was one way for a performer to eventually be placed on the bill for the evening's entertainment. The hoot cost nothing to get into, and the purchase of one item on the menu was enough to be allowed to sit in the cavelike darkness all afternoon.

On weekends the cover charge was a dollar. Tex, a barker of sorts for the Cafe Wha?, would stand at the doorway luring the tourists inside. The audience on weekdays was split between those who liked to discover good talent at a low admission price and made it a point to go several times a week, and tourists who wanted to go *somewhere* mainly to be able to say they had been someplace in "the Village," but who lacked the funds for the more expensive clubs, or lacked hip, intellectual, or arty conversation for the Figaro or Fat Black Pussycat coffeehouse scenes. The Cafe Wha? was the perfect place for Jimmy. Dark as all getout (a good place to mack), the shy could disappear either in the audience or on the stage. A very tolerant audience in the best tradition of the hoot, they would sit and struggle with the shy artist until he got himself together.

Only in the Village at the Cafe Wha? could he display his innovative approach to R&B, traditional blues, and the new rock. Only at the Cafe Wha? was he able to explore his imagination at length without interruption, while playing for the predominantly white audiences. The Cafe Wha? was like a woodshed for him where he worked out and exposed his compositions, and his being there regularly enabled more music people to come check him out.

Jimmy became a fixture at the Cafe Wha? Soon he had a large following, and his musical abilities attracted other musicians who wanted to play with him. Finally he had his own band: Jimmy James and the Blue Flames. The Blue

Flames—named after Junior Parker's old band—were musicians he had picked, including Randy California, a white blues devotee who played second guitar, often in the bottleneck style.

Over the Cafe Wha? at the Players' Theater, the Fugs, a local poets' band from the East Village, held forth every night. Tex introduced Jimmy to Ed Sanders, Kenny Pine, Tuli Kupferberg, and Ken Weaver, who made up the Fugs.

Jimmy and the Fugs naturally picked up on each other. Both were moving into new and exciting things, although now merely low men on the totem pole of the MacDougal Street hierarchy. Jimmy was shedding his R&B road-show image as fast as he could, growing his hair long. The Fugs were moving from poetry into music. Ed Sanders and Tuli Kupferberg were well-known poets who decided to get into some kind of rock 'n' roll. Ken Weaver, their buddy, was the drummer, and Kenny Pine was the guitarist. They picked up whatever musicians they could to round out their act, which at first had been very raw.

Ed Sanders, who knew how difficult it was to get a band together, sympathized with Jimmy. Ed would see him turning around onstage to direct Randy Wolfe, who played rhythm guitar behind his lead, and the rest of the ragtag Blue Flames. The Fugs, too, were slowly honing their raw melodies down to a personal style of performance, in the show-business sense. The Fugs all lived in the East Village, where it was far cheaper to live than in the West Village. They hung out with the poets and other post-beatniks of the neighborhood. They would talk about poetry, dope, antiwar politics, and fucking all in the same breath.

Once Ed Sanders went over to a loft on Hudson Street where Jimmy was staying with Buzzy Linhart, Roger McGuinn, and David Crosby, who were trying to get a group together. That was the first time Sanders had actually visited Jimmy in a place where he lived. Usually Jimmy would be staying with some lady or another from place to place.

Jimmy offstage was as crazy as they were, with his methedrine in a baby bottle and his comic book or cosmic riffs, which would delight and puzzle. But Ken Weaver and Ed Sanders would take all of it in with true poets' soul and insight. Jimmy's brand of blues was unfamiliar to them, but they were experienced enough to recognize the real thing, especially when Kenny Pine ran some things down to them about the music. Jimmy had started spending almost all of his time downtown, but every now and then he would take off for parts unknown for a gig. They didn't know that he doubled as one of the leading R&B guitarists, highly in demand.

But Jimmy felt at home in the funky Village. A lot of people in the Village were into blues. His weird ways and talk were not made fun of, nor was his highly personal way of interpreting the blues. Pulling off of the same bedrock as the older blues players, he was also able to infuse the blues with a heavy contemporary R&B feeling that brought the blues up to date. And he had a flair for the contemporary freak sound that screamed silently to be expressed throughout the narrow streets of the Village. He received consistently rising respect from the people of the Village, from the people of MacDougal Street, the people who lived and worked there who had watched Dylan go by not too long ago.

MacDougal Street and points around its center were the foci for the troubador "folk" singers of the time. Len Chandler, with Arlo Guthrie opening the show, was a constant at the Gaslight Cafe. Ram John Holder, the West Indian folksinger, Ramblin' Jack Elliott, Dave Van Ronk, Mississippi John Hurt, Brownie McGhee and Sonny Terry, Barbara Dane, and many others, including a peripheral Bob Dylan, orbited out from the Gaslight.

Richie Havens and John Hammond and Buzzy Linhart were the Cafe Au Go Go people. Peter, Paul, and Mary played the Bitter End. Gerde's Folk City was the traditional folk club. Tim Hardin, Roosevelt Sykes, and others, including Dylan, had preferred the out-of-the-way, offbeat insularity of Gerde's Folk City. Izzy Young and Marc Silber at the Fretted Instrument Shop were the connection for strings, advice, a sandwich, and some plain-out energy. Both Izzy Young and *Broadside* magazine were printing commentaries quickly and often on the emergent folk scene. Izzy Young's minusculely typed and printed pamphlets, filled with philosophy and quotes from Izzy himself, alerted the underground to the new energy on the folk scene. *Broadside* magazine printed new songs, commentaries, and an occasional letter on a more consistent monthly pace. Len Chandler wrote of his visit to Woody Guthrie on his motor scooter with little Bobby Dylan on the back holding on. But for all of the *Broadside* set, the folk music and blues were acoustical and often solitary. Brownie McGhee and Sonny Terry were correct while Muddy Waters and the Chicago gang were still oddities.

The lowest club on the totem pole was the Cafe Wha? While the Nite Owl Cafe was considered gross for its loud electric music and the drunk, raucous teenagers running in and out of it far into the night, they at least would feature the Lovin' Spoonful, the Raves, Lothar and the Hand People, and occasionally the Holy Modal Rounders. The Cafe Wha?, a misnomer, was considered too low for words. During a fill between songs for the folk crowd that liked a little low-key titter or two, a joke about the weird club down the street was always good for a laugh. The folk and blues crowd was kin to the beat-poetry followers who flocked to see Ted Joans and his crew of rentable hipsters perform at the Scene. Beholden to the word: phased-out over clear decipherable acoustic guitar runs, or words uttered from the lips of a beat poet, it was almost asking too much to ask these emerging hippies to behold a screaming electric blues guitar, no matter how tame.

Jimmy had only one pair of black pants. He washed them daily. That was his only stage apparel. Black did not show dirt or stains as readily as lighter colors. He still had problems with footwear, as he'd had throughout his childhood:

badly worn shoes that made him walk strangely. He had no safety net. Mike Quashie, or Lonnie Youngblood and his wife, or Fayne, or Kim helped him when they could. But they were far from well off. Because Jimmy would only take jobs as a musician, he often went hungry. And when he could not afford the cheap SRO hotels in Times Square, or the scarcer ones in the Village, he had to crash with someone, usually using the excuse that he had lost his key to his room.

The speed he took to forestall hunger and to help him with the energy necessary to gig devastated his complexion. Pimples formed as his body excreted the noxious chemicals of methedrine. And his emotions were also affected by this strong drug often full of impurities. Kim Shiroky recalled him once breaking down into tears when something went wrong onstage, just laying there crying. At other times breaking a string midperformance, he would stalk off the stage leaving sidemen there to fend for themselves. Speed kept one wired, nervous, and emotionally vulnerable, but it enabled one to do the job.

Jimmy met Linda Keith at the Cheetah while he played a gig with Curtis Knight and the Squires. The twenty-one-year-old English fashion model, having noticed him playing so excellently behind the not-so-hot Curtis Knight, sent word inviting him to have a drink with her and her two American friends. He accepted. "He was very naïve, very shy and nervous, and he didn't look at you when he spoke to you." They invited him back to their apartment, which they called the "red house." There they listened to a lot of Dylan and took LSD.

At the Cheetah that night, Linda Keith had felt mesmerized by his musical presence, and she was no stranger to listening to guitarists. She did not quite understand it all, but she trusted her instincts.

Linda Keith was connected with the Rolling Stones organization as the official "old lady" of Keith Richards, the lead guitarist. The Stones, while they were touring America, were more or less based in New York City. Linda Keith made her own arrangements to stay in Manhattan for the duration of the tour. Her involvement with Keith Richards "was running out"; their relationship "hanging from a thread."

It was no secret that the Rolling Stones regarded themselves as free agents with little if any loyalty to their girlfriends, old ladies, or even wives. Linda Keith had her own career and options, and was a person of refinement and taste. She was not dependent on the Stones for her status. Her voice alone bespoke authority.

Linda Keith was a little scary. She had money, connections; she reeked of class, status, and authority. And she was quite attractive, well bred, and always impeccably groomed.

She took it upon herself to bring out Hendrix's blues roots, perhaps unaware that he had spent a good portion of his life dealing with what he considered to be the roots of rock. He was discovering the music she was most familiar with. She knew Eric Clapton, Chip Taylor, who had written "Wild Thing," she knew the Beatles, the Stones—intimately. Just as all those Englishmen hungered for authentic connections to the blues, Jimmy was studying the present-day expressions of the crossroads of blues and rock.

But Jimmy was much too polite to turn her off. He listened intently to the blues records she insisted upon playing him. He loved the music so it was not a problem. There was always something new to hear, and every so often there was something he was glad to hear that he had not heard before. He was very polite and soft-spoken with Linda Keith.

She brought him to the red house, a large apartment owned by close friends, and then to a fancy Hilton Hotel suite in midtown near Rockefeller Center so they could concentrate on experiencing the blues, spending days on end in that pursuit.

Although he had broken up with Kim, they still saw each other and hung out and she still followed his music, faithfully sitting through many sets. And he also began to hang out again with Fayne Pridgeon, who he had taken to referring to as "Auntie Faye," as if she were some relation living uptown. Harlem was a natural boundary, off limits to Linda Keith. Fayne grounded him in her down-to-earth black-woman skepticism and she did not put on airs. That arrangement helped him to balance the precariousness of the uncertain scenes he maintained.

That Linda Keith was the classiest person he had ever been seen with was a unanimous decision among all who frequented the MacDougal Street/Bleecker Street clubs, coffeehouses, and restaurants where Linda and Jimmy would often be seen together. Jimmy himself, while safely in his shy, soft-spoken mode, could be said to have been kind of blown away by her attention.

There was something about Hendrix that excited Linda Keith intensely. Her reaction to Jimmy would presage an entire British music public, an entire white youth culture across Europe and the United States, and eventually the world. Just as the Beatles, the Rolling Stones, and the Animals were shocked to see the poverty their musical heroes, such as Muddy Waters and other blues artists, experienced in America, Linda Keith was very surprised that Jimmy Hendrix had not yet been discovered. She made it her business to rectify that situation.

She insisted Andrew Loog Oldham, the manager of the Rolling Stones, come and hear Jimmy play. She even "borrowed" a brand-new Stratocaster from Keith Richards for Jimmy to play. Oldham could not ignore her request, but he was secretly annoyed that she might be drawing him into some kind of intrigue. He was loyal to Keith Richards, and would do nothing to alienate him or any

Rolling Stone. That fact seemed to be of little matter to Linda Keith. Oldham felt that she was somehow blinded to protocol, but he nevertheless went and saw Hendrix play. He was not impressed, at least to the extent that he would be willing to risk all he had worked to establish to try to fit Jimmy Hendrix, an American black man, into the well-established Rolling Stones family.

On July 2, Linda Keith compelled the entire Rolling Stones group to come to Jimmy's performance with his Blue Flames at Ondine's on East Fifty-ninth Street. The Stones had attended after their show at Forest Hills Tennis Stadium in Queens, not far from Ondine's, just off the Queensboro Bridge. Early on in their musical careers, Mick Jagger and Brian Jones had first fallen under the tutelage of Alexis Korner. They had studied black music and especially the blues as if they were taking coursework at the London School of Economics. Bill Wyman and Charlie Watts were very enthusiastic about Hendrix's playing. Keith Richards and Mick Jagger were polite and affirmative, but they seemed to parallel Andrew Loog Oldham's stance. But Brian Jones was so effusively blown away that he might have dominated everyone's reaction. However, the Stones were on the road; they had time to dwell on nothing but the next date. They took off. But the word was set.

The Animals arrived in New York to start their American tour July 4. Linda Keith saw her friend, their bass player, Chas Chandler, at Ondine's and told him as she had been telling all who would listen that he must go and hear Hendrix play. Linda Keith did not have to tell Chas Chandler twice. The grapevine of the English rock world was perfect, and he had already heard some murmurs about this black guitarist.

The next day Chandler went with Linda Keith to hear Hendrix play at the Cafe Wha? Right away he knew he had found the man, his man. A large ethnic Englishman well over six feet tall, Chas was so excited he was knocking things over, spilling his drink, and digging his elbow into the fellow sitting next to him, Kenny Pine, a guitarist who played with a local band, the Ragamuffins. Not only had Jimmy's first number been a song Chas had been secretly keen on, "Hey Joe," but when Jimmy played "Like a Rolling Stone" it was like Chas was hearing that song for the first time, so tough and true Jimmy was to the meaning and emotion of Bob Dylan's instant local classic.

Linda Keith noticed everything. She was also aware that Chas had to still complete his American tour with the Animals. It would be nearly two long months before Chas could come back. That was a very long time in the music world.

Jimmy was excited. He knew the Animals' music and liked them a lot. But he knew better than to appear too enthusiastic.

But Chas Chandler was in quite another position. Having been the bass player for the Animals throughout their biggest-selling recordings—"We Gotta Get Out of This Place," "House of the Rising Sun," and "Bring It on Home to Me," eight Top 40 hit singles in less than five years—he was the first to acknowledge that he was not a serious musician and probably had no real future in performing. But he had done well with the impending dissolution of the Animals. His alliance with the manager of the Animals, Michael Jeffery, was a possible avenue for him to get into management. Chandler had little preparation for the business part of the music world beyond his having talent and his connection with Jeffery, who had done very well in the music business and looked as if he would continue to do well. The summer 1966 tour with the Animals was Chandler's last. The Animals would be no more. But he desired to continue in the business and do better than he had done as talent.

It was John Hammond Jr.'s fate to link up with "the craziest guitarist on Mac-Dougal Street." The son of the legendary producer for Columbia Records John Hammond Sr., he had come out of the same bag, the blues, that had made his father's name synonymous with Billie Holiday and her tremendous popularity, and also with Robert Johnson. John Hammond Jr. was meandering between folk and blues during the early sixties. Jimmy was to give him a heavy prophecy as to where the blues was going.

One night, John Hammond Jr. wandered down into the Cafe Wha?'s cellar. He had heard an unusual band was playing down there and that the lead guitarist, a long-haired black guy, played Hammond's and Robbie Robertson's guitar parts better than they did on his latest LP *So Many Roads*. Having the natural curiosity and outgoingness of his father, Hammond went down into the dark basement to check it out. Brought up on the blues, John Jr. realized the inventiveness of Jimmy's licks. He was not much on vocals, but bold and moving on instrumentals. He decided to return later and see if he felt the same way again. At that time, 1966, folk artists were more than adamant about not using electric instruments. But something had to be done about the Beatles. Nevertheless, using electric instruments was considered tantamount to selling out to the pop establishment. But it was the darkness before dawn.

The next time John Hammond Jr. went to see Jimmy James and the Blue Flames, Hammond was headlining across the street at the Gaslight, playing acoustic folk. Jimmy James had obviously mastered all the progressive R&B licks, had a good store of somber blues runs, and had an impish fluidity mixed with a quick, bright sound. Johnny had wanted to go heavily electric for some time. Even then he often doubled on a soft electric guitar to play several of Jimmy Reed's urban blues songs in the small folk clubs. "Bright Lights, Big City" was his favorite of Reed's tunes. He knew Jimmy James would be an excellent lead guitarist with him. Feeling freaky inside the Cafe Wha?, Hammond got to Jimmy as soon as he had finished his set. Jimmy knew John Hammond Jr. and his music from MacDougal Street. So Jimmy also got right to the point. The money he received for playing all night at the Cafe Wha? was below the starvation level (that was a policy of the club; that added to its reputation). Could Hammond get him a gig anywhere, anytime? He was dying to get out of that hole, even for a minute. He was sorry to be asking for a favor, but he was entirely too desperate to come on any other way. Johnny felt a rush of sympathy for Jimmy (besides, he had been wondering how they would sound together). He was happy to be able to invite Jimmy to play with him at the Gaslight Cafe.

Hendrix frequented the local Fretted Instrument Shop to simply enjoy some of their fine six- and twelve-string acoustic guitars. Recognizing his abilities instantaneously, owner Marc Silber, who ran the instrument shop by day and played bass at night with the Children of Paradise, after also noting that Hendrix could play in the style of John Lee Hooker and Lightnin' Hopkins without missing a beat, asked for serious advice on studying the electric blues tradition. Hendrix replied that it was "only a matter of the three kings." Thinking that it was a remark somehow connected to the Christian faith and the birth of Jesus Christ, it took Silber a good while to figure that Jimmy was talking about Albert King, Freddie King, and B. B. King. Excellent advice in a poetic economy.

John Sebastian, leader of the Lovin' Spoonful, had checked Hendrix out favorably, as had poets/peace activists/founders of the Fugs, Ed Sanders and Tuli Kupferberg, and Ken Weaver, who had built Jimmy his first sustain tone by fusing two Fuzz Tone boxes together. Moonlighting as a dance-band guitarist at various discotheques, Jimmy used fuzz and sustain tones to enhance the excitement of the bodies moving on the floor. But on MacDougal Street it was not a dance scene. People listened while seriously still, in the tradition of acoustic folk and blues performance, especially at the Gaslight.

John Hammond Jr.'s father John Hammond had been instrumental in Pete Seeger's and Dylan's successes, but there was no obligatory thing happening. John Hammond Jr. was very respected as being a serious bluesman in his own right. The fact that he thought enough of Hendrix to have him play on his gig at the Gaslight was huge. In fact, Hammond had so much respect for Jimmy's playing, for his pure, personalized, blues-inflected sound and sensibility, that he often just played the harmonica and sang, leaving his own guitar playing for another time. John Hammond Jr. knew the blues. He was quite a serious student of the blues—a scholar would be more like it—and given his father's expertise, he could even be called a second-generation blues scholar. He recognized Hendrix as being amazingly representative of the blues continuum.

Bobby Dylan dropped in to check out John Hammond Jr. and the new man on the block who he had been hearing about from different sources. So Dylan checked out a last set and thought Hendrix was simply "incredible." Later they all went next door to the local bar the Kettle of Fish. Dylan did not say much. That was his custom, but by simply hanging out with them it was obvious that he was positive about what they were doing. The best testimonial was sitting at the Kettle of Fish in full view through the wide windows that looked out on narrow MacDougal Street, getting drunk and laughing a lot. That was the highest endorsement. They all just got stoned. Dylan told the story of going to meet the legendary jazz pianist/composer/bebop pioneer Thelonius Monk at the old Five Spot club on nearby Cooper Square. When Dylan introduced himself by saying he played folk music on MacDougal Street, Monk had replied, "We all play folk music." They all had a good laugh.

Later Bob Dylan would say of Hendrix then: "I kinda had a feeling that he figured into things."

Hammond and Jimmy formed a group called the Screaming Nighthawks for a two-week late-August gig at the Cafe Au Go Go, which was the hippest club on the strip. They were the opening act for the Seventh Sons with Buzzy Linhart, a very popular local aggregation. Things were looking up for Jimmy. He kept his head in the music more than ever.

The Animals concluded their American tour with a gig in Central Park. Jimmy was aware of their arrival. He and Hammond were ending their gig at the Cafe Au Go Go when Chandler caught up with Jimmy there. His fears that Hammond Jr. would have somehow already arranged a deal with his extensive connections were allayed. John Hammond Sr. had come to see Hendrix at the urgings of his son, but had politely passed. Linda Keith was on top of everything, and right there when Chandler returned, as she had been for all of Hendrix's performances since they'd met.

The Cafe Au Go Go was the classiest club on MacDougal Street. Close to the Cafe Figaro right off MacDougal on Bleecker Street, the Cafe Au Go Go was also a basement club, but not nearly as steep as the coal-chute-angle plunge into the Cafe Wha? Circling elegantly to a long deep room with ample table and chair space, the Cafe Au Go Go had an array of lighting effects that many off-Broadway theaters could not match. Sexy, friendly waitresses and a menu of good food made you happy to be there.

The first set they played was a feeling-out session with Hammond using tunes from his *So Many Roads* blues album. Jimmy was sedately laid-back, soaking in the plushness of the place as compared to the zany Cafe Wha? Many celebrities were in attendance, including a contingent of English pop stars: the Rolling Stones and the Animals, the hottest English acts in the USA at the time.

But to Jimmy, the heaviest person there was Mike Bloomfield, who played lead guitar for Dylan on "Like a Rolling Stone." During the last set Jimmy went into his act. Suddenly during his solo number, "I'm a Man," Bo Diddley's signature blues song, he's down on his knees, flicking his tongue as his guitar obbligatos, stroking the strings with his teeth, using his ax as a battering ram into the low ceiling, while playing the most complex of blues changes, with strange guttural feedback sounds delicately balanced against peaking, dissolving riffs.

The audience was aghast at Jimmy James's wild antics. The British boys were stunned, also. They had seldom witnessed a black performer put on a "show." Although they were connoisseurs of rural and urban blues, their knowledge had been gained via mail-order records. Rare and obscure recordings of the old and new blues were their inspiration, especially Muddy Waters. But never in the flesh had they encountered a man as young as Jimmy who had so heavily pulled it all into a pure style of his own.

Like Dylan, Hendrix had totally synthesized his realm of musical experience into something revolutionary.

During that performance Jimmy had let out all the stops. Some in the audience thought that Jimmy was making Hammond Jr. look bad, taking advantage, but others closer to the situation knew that Hammond Jr. was encouraging Jimmy to do his thing in order to impress his potential benefactor.

Chas brought Michael Jeffery, manager of the Animals, by the Cafe Au Go Go the next afternoon to check Jimmy out. Jeffery would be Chandler's essential partner in his move into the business of music. Jeffery trusted Chandler's word on the musical aspects of Hendrix. But after he interacted with Jimmy he summed it up, once he and Chas were alone, in a single phrase: Jimmy "could be the black Elvis." He knew a good thing when he saw it. The three had a deal.

Jimmy had asked Chandler, on his return, when they were going to get serious. Now it was Jimmy's turn to be surprised, as Chandler had really thought things through. He would buy up all of Jimmy's existing contracts, get Jimmy a passport, and they would fly to London together and form a band, the Jimi Hendrix Experience. Jimmy was taken aback a bit. It was all happening so fast. He wondered if they could take the Blue Flames' slide guitarist, Randy California, along. But he was only fifteen and still a minor. That was out of the question. What about the equipment there? Would he be able to adapt to it? What about musicians? Would they be able to find the right ones? But when Jimmy asked Chandler if he knew Eric Clapton, and discovered that they were friends, Chandler assured Jimmy that he would be taken to meet Eric. And not only that, once Eric heard him play, "*he* would be falling over to meet Jimmy." That overrode all doubt; Jimmy was ready to go.

Chandler was taking Hendrix to England because his contacts were there, and they were considerably wide and carried all the important weight of the emergent youth culture. An important cult had developed around the blues, especially electric blues guitar. America was still like a mirage to the English groups. In 1966, few of them had settled there, as many would later do. Their contact with America was mainly a business arrangement intended to make the most amount of money in the least amount of time. In London the underground was small and very hip. They unanimously endorsed the underground American black music, but in England itself there were no black American stars. Here, in one man, Jimmy Hendrix, was all of it and more. Chandler could not wait to watch the impact Hendrix would have on his fellow countrymen.

Chandler's reason for leaving the music business as a performer had a lot to do with the very exploitative mess that quickly usurped many of the best young minds of the British music scene. Self-respect, personal pride, and hard-won intelligent sophistication made Chandler rebel against the hasty English musical establishment, especially the limits it placed upon him as an individual. Like Andrew Loog Oldham or Brian Epstein, Chandler wanted to use his mind and will to help manage the course of the great musical awakening of the young, not only in England, but in America, as well. Hendrix, it was clear to Chandler, could handle both very well. But first, England.

It was amazing that Jimmy could just up and decide to go with Chandler. Hendrix had no ties, no strings, and no luggage to speak of. He had not visited his home in Seattle in five years. To get an older, more established blues man to pull up roots and go was highly improbable; and it would still be an uphill fight to get the young to accept them, as they were much older, more set in their ways. But Hendrix, who could play blues with the best of them, was also young, appealing, and had his own concepts of music, which would continue to grow. Very shy, quiet, personable, and polite, he would not shatter the brittle British sensibility. But then Chandler found out just how much trouble a rolling stone could be. Their departure for England had to be delayed several weeks while they awaited arrival of a copy of Hendrix's birth certificate from Seattle. Jimmy had never before had use for such an official document as a birth certificate. Jimmy's carelessness with official documents had begun to plague Chandler. When that birth certificate finally arrived, they were then able to acquire the most important document of Jimmy's life: a passport.

CHAPTER 4

Chas and Jimi flew the Pan Am red-eye first class out of JFK, and arrived in London's Heathrow Airport at nine o'clock Saturday morning, September 24, 1966. Jimmy James was now Jimi Hendrix. They were accompanied off the plane by Terry McVay, an Animals roadie who carried Jimi's guitar case. Because of the strict admission restrictions, Jimi could not be said to be seeking work. After a hassle with the authorities, Jimi was only issued a seven-day non-work permit.

Chas arranged for them to stop by British R&B big band leader Zoot Money's house. It was on the way into London and was a communal residence of sorts for his family and band members, the home having been divided up into flats. Zoot Money lent Jimi a Fender Telecaster and they jammed for most of the three-hour visit.

Chas and Jimi checked into the Hyde Park Towers on Inverness Terrace in London W2. It was a popular musicians' hotel near many clubs, including the Scotch of St. James, where Chas took Jimi later that evening. Jet-lagged, with no sleep, wearing a scruffy U.S. Marine Corps jacket, his pimple-scarred face made him appear thug-tough. But those who interacted with him even in the slightest way discovered a remarkable courteousness that charmed and outdid the Brits at their own game. The club was so plush Jimi was almost ashamed to be there. He declined to sit in with the band gigging that night. Instead, he played an intermission solo showcase sitting on a stool onstage, improvising old and new blues. That was unheard of and a pure hit with the in crowd.

Kathy Etchingham was a nineteen-year-old, down-to-earth, long-red-haired, green-eyed, British version of a flower child who lived in an upstairs room at Zoot Money's house. She had been invited by his wife, Ronnie, to join them at the club and meet Jimi, who sat at a long table along with Chas, his Swedish girlfriend Lotta Lexon, and a number of others. Kathy and Jimi hit it off immediately. A little while later Linda Keith joined their party, and some say quickly began a row that resulted in her accusing Ronnie Money of interfering with her and Jimi's relationship. Plates and glasses began shattering as screams, shouts, and curses erupted. Amused but tired, Chas ushered Jimi and his new girlfriend out. Jimi made sure Kathy was with him. Between the club and their hotel, Jimi explained that Linda Keith was Keith Richards's girlfriend and that he did not want to interfere with the scene in England in any way.

Jimi invited Kathy to his room and she accepted. She noted that Hendrix's luggage consisted of a guitar in a case, a couple of satin shirts, one white, one black, a couple of pairs of pants, a jar of Noxema, a toothbrush, and some hair rollers. She helped him roll his hair up in them before they retired.

Jimi and Kathy spent the night in his room. That Sunday morning Kathy recalled, "We were woken up in the hotel by a girl who burst into the room, grabbed Jimi's guitar, and walked out. Jimi told me she was an English girl he'd been sleeping with in America called Linda Keith who had purchased the guitar for him. Later, after we were up, she came back, took off all her clothes, and climbed into the bed. She said Jimi could have his guitar back on condition that he get into bed with her."

The rumors took over from there. Some said that Hendrix refused the offer and sent her on her way, while others said that Kathy went home while Jimi and Linda sorted it out.

Jimi and Kathy, soon after that incident, became a solid couple in swinging London.

The impromptu show at the Scotch of St. James got word moving through the grapevine. Through transatlantic calls from the States and now during the first few days in London, Chandler made sure that his contacts were well informed as to who Jimi was, what they intended to do, and that they intended to succeed.

Chandler knew better than to allow Hendrix to ponder their hazardous course. Hendrix for his part was so gassed to be in England that he indulged in sightseeing as if he were a tourist. It was essential that they get the band together right away. Hendrix solved a lot of the problems of band members himself. He was able to play so much guitar that they would need only the barest number of sidemen; in fact, two: a drummer and a bass player.

Linda Keith spread the word, as well; Hendrix was a treat she deliciously anticipated impacting the British music scene.

Working papers were another problem—a big problem. They had to convince the authorities that Hendrix possessed a talent that could not be duplicated by any working or idle Englishman. The music people did not have to be convinced; the government authorities did. The best they could do was to issue another nonwork residence permit expiring on December 28, 1966.

Jimi called his father Al in Seattle collect from his hotel room with Kathy close by. She had moved in. Jimi gushed in his excitement to bring his father up to date. He was in England now, they were forming a group around him and auditioning a bass player and a drummer. The group would be called the Jimi Hendrix Experience. And that his first name was now being spelled J-I-M-I. Al replied, "Well, that's a little different." Kathy was so excited, Jimi put her on the phone to say hello. She greeted Al. "I spoke a few words and he said, 'Look, my boy's in England? You tell my boy to write me. I'm not paying for collect calls.'" Flustered, she returned the phone to Jimi. He listened as Al asked him who he had stolen the money from to get to England.

Jimi had to laugh: he recognized immediately Al's state of mind as he was transported back to the povery-laden world he had grown up in. Al was still there. Nothing had changed for him. Those sobering thoughts also spurred Jimi on.

The next day Noel Redding, a guitarist from Folkestone, outside of London, looking to audition for the New Animals, showed up at Birdland, where Chas was helping organize auditions for them and for Jimi. As the New Animals' spot had been taken, Chas asked Redding if he played bass. Noel said no, but that he would be willing to give it a go. Chas lent him his own instrument, a Gibson EB-2 semiacoustic bass guitar.

Redding was directed to sit in with Jimi, Mike O'Neill (of Nero and the Gladiators) on piano, and Aynsley Dunbar on drums. They went through "Hey Joe" a few times, as well as a standard American rocker and a similar rhythm and blues number, all with no vocals, and that was it. Jimi invited Noel to a nearby pub where they drank beer and talked about music. Jimi liked Noel's hair—a bouffant Afro style not unlike his own. When Jimi asked him about British music, Noel mentioned the Move, the Small Faces, and the Kinks. Noel was equally curious about American music. He liked Booker T. and the MG's (and wondered if Jimi had ever seen them play), Sam Cooke, and Ray Charles—and of course he liked the emergent American rock. They drank a couple of pints and got on okay. Jimi asked Noel if he would join his group and said that he would be rehearsing daily. Noel replied that if Jimi gave him the train fare he would return. The first member of the Experience was in.

Chas and Jimi had been kind of set on Aynsley Dunbar as the drummer. It had seemed set from early on. Dunbar was considered a masterful drummer and it would be kind of amazing if he would be available. In fact, he had been signed with John Mayall's blues band for only two weeks. The lack of any substantial tenure with Mayall meant that it would not be too bad if he changed his mind and played with Jimi.

Drummers were on their minds that night when Chas and Jimi went to the Brian Auger Trinity gig at Blaise's club in Kensington. Jimi sat in to good effect. This was the first top-flight band he had played with in London. It was incredibly apparent that Jimi was a consummate professional. The French pop star Johnny Hallyday just happened to be in the audience. The Brian Auger Trinity was supporting a minitour Hallyday was leading through France, culminating at the Olympia in Paris in mid-October, about three weeks away. Hallyday invited Jimi and his group along to open for all the acts on the bill.

This was great luck. But this also put added pressure on Chas and Jimi to finalize the group and rehearse for high-level exposure. This was the acid test.

Cream's gig at the Regent Polytechnic College was coveted by Chas as a perfect debut showcase for Jimi, who had yet to make a grand entrance onto the London scene. Due to the polite protocol of the small British music scene and the fact that both Jeff Beck and Peter Townshend of the Who had both acknowledged in intense private conversations that Jimi Hendrix was the real thing and they should treat him with the utmost respect, because of his obvious authenticity as not only a veteran of traditional R&B but also his grounding in the old blues and his ability to improvise not only melodically but with sound dynamics as well, Hendrix had broad entrée that overrode the fact that the other members of Cream did not like the idea of Jimi imposing on their very important gig. But Eric Clapton as guitarist and leader had to decide. Visiting him in his dressing room before the show, Hendrix groomed his hair with a pick that pulled the hair straight out from his head and casually requested that he be allowed to sit in. Although it was a done deal, it was the right thing to make a direct request to Clapton. His choice was "Killing Floor" by Howlin' Wolf. Clapton's spirit sunk. He knew the song and knew he did not have the technique to play it as it should be played. And then there was the dreadful symbolism. As he anticipated, when Hendrix announced the song, unfamiliar to Jack Bruce on bass and Ginger Baker on drums, and began to play, Clapton, who had not heard him play before but had only heard others' impressions of his playing, realized he could not contribute. Totally burned, he quickly left the stage, watching from the wings and then going back to the dressing room as the number extended into a long solo and jam. He shakily lit and smoked a cigarette. And to Chas, who had followed him, he asked why no one had told him of the tremendous extent of Hendrix's virtuosity. Chas was also impressed. It had taken only a few bars for Clapton to realize that Jimi was beyond him.

Clapton would begin to see the Jimi Hendrix Experience at every gig they had that he could make. At some point he had his hair permed into an Afro of sorts. His display of humility was replicated in various ways by the entire British music scene. But no electric guitarist would go head to head with Hendrix after Clapton's abortive attempt. The Regent Polytechnic College Cream concert with Jimi Hendrix as guest, October 1, 1966, became a mark in time.

Jimi and Chas rushed to get it together. When the same office that managed the Animals put out a call for drummers to audition, many quite naturally felt that they were auditioning for the Animals. When they saw Jimi that thought quickly disappeared.

The bass player had already been specifically chosen. Hendrix knew what he wanted, and what he wanted there was no model for. It had become apparent that playing with Hendrix was not easy. Hendrix, an excellent bass player himself, was able to tell Noel Redding exactly what to play. Noel Redding, having never played the bass before, had only to follow his lead. Chas Chandler also showed and told him more basic bass stuff, like how effective a running bass line could be against Jimi's improvised solos. He looked right, he acted right, and played what he was told. Perfect.

On the other hand, Mitch Mitchell, the drummer Jimi had ultimately chosen, was cocky, brash, and very confident of his abilities on drums, a typical drummer's attitude. He had played with the best R&B and rock bands in England and was a jazz enthusiast, as well. Unable to hide a strange contempt for Jimi, he channeled it into his playing, where he more than kept up; he challenged. He provided a driving tension that never let up—even beyond performances. Until a few days prior he had been with Georgie Fame and His Blue Flames, a highly regarded group, who had just had a number one UK record in 1965 with "Yeh Yeh."

The Jimi Hendrix Experience was born October 1, 1966. Once the group was decided upon—Jimi Hendrix, Noel Redding, and Mitch Mitchell—they all signed management and publishing contracts together.

A day after the Jimi Hendrix Experience was formed they flew to France, rehearsed, and did a minitour at several small locales, playing in support of Johnny Hallyday, often called the Elvis Presley of France. On October 17 they arrived in Paris, rehearsed, and before a sold-out house at the Olympia on October 18, played "Killing Floor," "Hey Joe," and "Wild Thing." At the end of the show Johnny Hallyday led all the supporting acts onstage for a grand finale farewell that featured go-go dancers in glossy white halter tops, miniskirts, and knee-high white boots. Later they joined him at a Paris nightclub where Hallyday demonstrated his hard-won ability to work and play a crowd. This lesson was not lost on Jimi.

On October 23, Chas took them to the De Lane Lea studio, a small facility where the Animals had done a lot of their recording. Chas knew the place well and his familiarity helped Mitch and Noel, who were new to recording. They did "Hey Joe," using just about the same arrangement Tim Rose had used on his recording. Jimi had listened to it so frequently that he nearly wore it out on the jukebox at the Cock 'n' Bull on MacDougal Street in Greenwich Village. He taught Noel the bass run that is unique to Rose's version, which Hendrix played against so effectively, from the opening figure on. Chas took some credit for having correctly anticipated it by teaching Noel the walking bass technique. A backing vocal group, the Breakaways—Gloria George, Barbara Moore, and

Margaret Stredder—provides the subtle, mysteriously mournful, female-undertone mixed-down harmonies representing the spirit of the murdered woman. The killer, Joe, defies the feminine by his revenge slaying along with his rebellion against the authorities. The Breakaways' role is much more instrumental to the success of the recording than they were given credit for. Although "Hey Joe" was not necessarily a vehicle for Hendrix's unique guitar work, it contained the essential power trio dynamic of the Experience, and was a just about perfect vehicle for Hendrix's singular husky-toned laid-back vocal style.

"Hey Joe" had been a song that Chas and Jimi had agreed upon almost by telepathy even before they had left the States for London. It expressed a simple, emotional defiance of authority through a tale of a crime of passion. "Hey Joe" also had a *feel* to it that they were both confident of. It didn't really showcase Jimi's guitar as much as they would have liked, but it was a rather safe vehicle for the London market.

> *Hey Joe, where ya going with that gun in your hand?*
> *"I'm going out to shoot my ol' lady*
> *I caught her messin' 'round with another man."*

The lines would have been impossible to sing legato, but Jimi's slurring rap placed the ballad perfectly in the minds of the listeners. Not only could they visualize the scene, but they could also relate—like Frankie and Johnny, the theme was universal.

The bridge was the hippest thing happening musically, Jimi and Noel dubbing long bass runs. Jimi's rhythm licks were subtle but effective, giving a hint of his virtuosity without taking away from the song as a whole.

Jimi's vocal uses two voices, the voice of Joe and the voice of a commentator. But the last voice in the song is Joe's as he flees south to Mexico, where "no hangman will put a noose around" his neck. Jimi gets a chance to take the song to another level, shouting and emoting as the song slowly fades.

The Jimi Hendrix Experience's first gig at the Olympia in Paris had been grander than they could ever have hoped for. It was a good sign, an august beginning. But Chas Chandler knew that it was necessary to deal with London—and that no matter how much they had going for them, it was still going to be an uphill battle. While the JHE recorded at a frantic pace, Chas was talking record deals. Chas and Jimi would frequent the hip afterhours clubs, hobnobbing and scouting. Jimi would usually be requested to sit in. In many ways, the requests were simply a part of the etiquette of polite English society. But Jimi and Chas began to take them up. Taking on a few select offers, the JHE played the exclusive Cromwellian Club and the hip Bag O' Nails Club. There was no serious money involved, only the right kind of exposure. One night, Jimi and company played the Scotch of St. James. Rod Harrod, the host, owed a great deal to Chas, who, as one of the Animals, had supported him when he left the Cromwellian because of a dispute with its owners. The Scotch of St. James was located in a yard off of St. James Court. The ground floor had a bar and a restaurant, and the basement level was a dance floor surrounded by tables. The Beatles and the Stones had their own private tables, which were roped off and slightly elevated. It was not unusual for Princess Margaret and Lord Snowdon to show up. The decor was Scottish baronial, with plenty of sporrans, swords, and antlers. There was a couch on one side of the bandstand. Harrod had gone out of his way (discreetly, of course) to make sure that as many of the right people as possible were there. The basement was crowded with patrons, mainly standing on tiptoes to see the action. Jimi, Mitch, and Noel played a superb set that featured "Hey Joe." As soon as Kit Lambert, manager of the Who, and an activist in the new pop youth culture, heard it, he knew the song would be a hit and wasted no time in letting Chas know that he wanted the JHE to be on the new label he was launching, Track Records.

Chas and Kit went upstairs to discuss it further. Lambert was so enthusiastic over the JHE that he was almost knocking over tables in his haste to sit down with Chas.

Chas was as enthusiastic about Track Records as Lambert was, but he tried to hide it. Track would not be launched until March. There was no doubt in Chas's mind that "Hey Joe" would be out before Christmas. But he told Lambert that he could promise the JHE to Track Records regardless of the deal made with another company. Chas gladly accepted Lambert's admittedly modest advance of one thousand pounds, and the promise of a thousand-pound budget for promotional films to go with the releases. He was broke. Chas had been talking to record companies about the release of the JHE's first single. They were interested in more than a single, but since Chas was producing the master himself, with no upfront money on the record companies' part, he really owed them nothing.

Soon Chas had the single properly mixed and in the can: "Hey Joe" and "Stone Free" as the B-side. He took it to Decca, one of the companies he had been talking to. The A&R man there turned it down flatly, adding that he did not think Jimi had anything special. Panicked, Chas went directly back to Lambert, who reassured him of the validity of the recording, adding, as a vote of confidence, that he would take the record around to the record shops himself if necessary—but he doubted it would be. Reassured, Chas went off to Polydor Records with confidence. He secured a one-shot pressing and distribution deal, with further talks scheduled for the future.

At the end of October, Chas put on a showcase at the Scotch of St. James, ostensibly for Dick Katz, ace booker with the Harold Davidson Agency. This would be the Jimi Hendrix Experience's first official English gig. But it was not just for potential bookers; a far more important influence was Paul McCartney, who had been anxious to come and sat at the table with Chas and Katz. The set was fantastic, even though Hendrix broke a string and played most of the performance only with five. That was not lost on Katz, a musician himself, who saw Jimi handle that adversity quite professionally. He was positive, saying that he couldn't wait to hear Hendrix play with six strings. But McCartney was much more direct. He leaned toward Chas and said that Hendrix would be a giant, and that he hoped Katz would have the good sense to sign him up.

Kathy Etchingham had by now become Jimi's first real long-term girlfriend in London. She was a fun-loving English girl with a sensuous mouth, fine figure, and red hair, which fell into her eyes and hung straight to her shoulders. She was outspoken and a "wild thing" by English standards, but to Jimi she was not much different from some of the progressive white girls of the Village scene in New York he had been close to.

Jimi had worried that it would have been a hang-up for Chas and Lotta for him to bring Kathy along when he moved into a flat with them. But they all got on well.

Jimi promptly painted his room black, put blackout curtains on the windows, and put black satin sheets on the bed. He wanted to create his own environment, not of cloudy London, but of pure space, the galaxy. His staying in bed for days at a time did not bother Chas or Lotta.

Even easygoing Kathy Etchingham was often astounded at his long bouts of bed rest. Sometimes he didn't even want to have sex. She *knew* that was strange. But she was as spirited as she was flexible. She would be down to go for a walk through Hyde Park at dawn, or to listen to the Salvation Army band on Sundays—a ritual he loved.

Another person who quickly became friends with Jimi was Brian Jones, the unofficial leader of the Rolling Stones when Jimi arrived in London that September of 1966. It was a natural that they would become friends. All Brian had had to do was hear Jimi's interpretation of Muddy Waters's "Two Trains . . ." and that was it. It had been Jones who had brought Muddy Waters to the Stones. He had been Jagger's, Richards's, and Jones's musical inspiration during their lean days in London.

Brian Jones's best friend, Tara Browne, had died in an auto accident right around the time that Jimi began appearing in the clubs of London. Lonely and also turned on by authentic black blues and R&B musicians, Jones turned a lot of his attention toward Jimi. Brian was kinglike, grand, gracious, and sensitive, as well. They would drink together, smoke dope together, and just hang out. No publicity or anything like that. Just two musicians with big ears. Brian was a big fan of Charlie Parker and Billie Holiday. It thrilled him that Jimi had lived in Manhattan, and down in the Village, where Parker and Holiday were legends. There was something about the way those two lived that fascinated Jones, especially "Yardbird" Parker. They pushed their bodies and minds to the limit through massive doses of drugs and booze. It was as if they had reached mystical heights through what some called self-abuse, yet no one doubted that their self-torture was real. There are some things you just cannot fake. In a world of greed, anti-art, and Big Brother authoritarianism, they had consciously sacrificed themselves to the music. In their wretchedness, in their *angst*, no one could possibly say that they were bullshitting. And the musical heights Charlie Parker and Billie Holiday achieved in spite of all the odds—social and self-imposed—gave one the feeling that they had triumphed on a truly spiritual plane. They had refused any middle ground.

Jimi and Brian often went to the Cool Elephant club, where they would be virtually anonymous among the older clientele. The Cool Elephant had a jazz policy and plenty of recordings from the bebop era that so many ignorantly hip young Londoners thought passé. Jones's musical quest was for the truly unique in sound. He embodied in his ideas a unity, a synthesis of blues, Eastern music, Moroccan trance music, and Druidian folk fragments of forgotten ages. Jimi was amused and turned on by Jones, whose enthusiasm was boundless. Brian Jones was a true bon vivant, reveling in joyous mind-fuzz classical decadence—at least for England. His flare for the outrageous supported Jimi during his first uncertain months when he was unsure which public image to project. Brian Jones was into saying "fuck it." He would let it all hang out and would not back down, no matter what the odds. Jimi's first gigs in London were models of sedateness. He was letting his guitar do the talking. But as the stories drifted to him of Brian Jones's reckless, seemingly insane come-ons to the crowds he played before, and the resultant riots and mass hysteria, Jimi began to feel that he, too, could let it all hang out. And that was the secret. London, so excruciatingly class conscious, would bow before the one who acted like a king, and kill the one who *tried* to act like a king. Brian was at the top, yet totter and teeter as he might, there was no disrupting his eminence. Jimi was honored to attend a Rolling Stones recording session for "Ruby Tuesday." It was really Brian Jones's session. He was master of the sound, and the various exotic instruments he played all fused into a melodic experience that expanded the parameters of the Rolling Stones' sound. "Ruby Tuesday" became number one as they hung out together. Brian was ecstatic over its success. He loved to hear it by chance, on the radio in his Rolls-Royce, in a club, or out of a solitary window they happened to pass. Brian would tell with great relish of how he and Keith Richards worked and worked on coloring, adding dramatic yet wispy touches here and there, alternating the mix between lead voice and background vocal harmonies, while interplaying exotic instruments. Sounds that were impossible to identify gave "Ruby Tuesday" an eternal air of mystery and yearning.

And Brian and Jimi would laugh uproariously about sleeping with their guitars.

With the single "Hey Joe" in the can the band still wondered whether it was the best they could do. After all, they had no recording history, or even gigging history behind them to help them judge.

One thing they were sure of was that the Marshall amplifiers were the ones for their sound. Jimi believed in the dynamics of high volume and the Marshalls handled it. There were things that could only be done in the high volumes, an area Hendrix believed was another realm of sound altogether.

They were moving faster and faster. The momentum helped Jimi to begin writing his own material. Chas had told him outright that he expected the B-side of "Hey Joe" to be something Hendrix had written. After all, not only had they signed a deal in America, with Schroeder, a well-established music publisher, before they left without Hendrix having anything written, but Jimi, Noel, and Mitch had signed publishing contracts with him and Jeffery, as well as management contracts.

Jimi did not let Chas down. His first effort, "Stone Free," was a basic vehicle with a driving rhythm and some autobiographical emotions in the place of facts. Not unlike "Johnny B. Goode," "Stone Free" was miles away in terms of virtuosity, yet it was a perfect vehicle for Hendrix solos. As the song was about movement and the drive to achieve, the music mirrored the emotions of that quest.

When he saw that his songwriting pretty much determined the amount of time they spent recording, Jimi quickly followed with "Can You See Me" and then "Love or Confusion"—all very basic songs with simplistic lyrics that didn't stray very much from their stated titles. But with the guitar compositions and solos and live improvisations the new material began to delineate a more complete and complex picture of the Jimi Hendrix Experience.

Another gig on the Continent, this time in Munich, West Germany, two shows nightly at the Big Apple for three days: November 9, 10, and 11. Jimi lost it after being pulled off the stage by aggressive, excited fans and then breaking his guitar as he tossed it back onstage before vaulting back up. Usually solid-body Fender guitars are difficult to break so easily. He couldn't believe it.

It was a stupid thing to do. Angry at himself for an unprofessional mistake, angry at himself for blowing the excitement, and mad at the useless, broken guitar, he grabbed it by the neck and slung it around the stage, whomping the amps a couple of times. And then he bashed it to smithereens on the stage floor. The sounds of the guitar playing back its own destruction fascinated him. But his fascination was quickly dispelled by the sound of the crowd—*they were going crazy*. Their roar was freaky and manic.

The faces of the few German youths he could see in the front rows stayed with him for a long time afterward. Jimi was feeling the *emotion* of the crowd. What he felt from that German crowd was something he had never felt before playing any gig as third guitar or as leader.

The audience had been shocked out of their minds by the sheer act of destruction. The instrument they had come to hear and had been hearing for the entire evening was destroyed before their very eyes. It was like a sacrifice, but more like a dadaist final act of truth. The ultimate testimony of an artist—to destroy his tools, as a final act ending the creation of that moment forever. It was also an incredible renegade act: total rejection of the mechanization of man and art—before many. The audience loved it. Not only was it honest emotion but it was better theater. None of this was lost on Chas.

From watching the professionalism of Johnny Hallyday, who handled his French audience with consummate skill, to discovering accidentally a key to an excitement that matched the power/noise ratios of his performance, Jimi, with Chas right there, decided there must be a way to incorporate this kind of thing into the show.

Chas sold five of his guitars in order to host a noontime reception for the JHE at the Bag O' Nails toward the end of November to announce the release of the JHE's first record, coming out in less than two weeks. They needed work and media action. Jimi's first real interview was done for the *Record Mirror*. It would be published the day "Hey Joe" hit the stores, December 10.

Although tickets were nominally put on sale, this was not really an event for the public. It was in the middle of a Friday. The few fans that were allowed to buy tickets and ordinary music business insiders were blown away by the parade of the top personages in the British music scene entering the Bag O' Nails: Paul McCartney, Jimmy Page, Jeff Beck, Keith Richards, Brian Jones, Mick Jagger, Donovan, John Mayall, Eric Clapton, Ringo Starr, George Harrison, Peter Townshend, John Lennon, and the electronics expert Roger Mayer, among others.

Jimi came on in his English military jacket, broke out his beat-up Stratocaster, and went into "Wild Thing" and simply tore the assembled guests apart. A fan, Charles Holley, described looking at Eric Clapton's reaction: "No one was more gobsmacked than Clapton—I was torn between watching his face and Hendrix's performance."

Terry Reid said, "There were guitar players weeping. They had to mop the floor up. He was piling it on, solo after solo. I could see everyone's fillings falling out. When he finished it was silence. Nobody knew what to do. Everybody was completely in shock."

Keith Altham was a journalist for the *New Musical Express,* a rival of *Melody Maker*—both weekly tabloids. Altham by that time had become an insider, a co-conspirator in the new music of swinging London. He immediately could tell Hendrix was a "brilliant" guitarist. His concern was whether Hendrix was indeed too brilliant. Was his music too advanced for the British scene, or any rock or popular market? Although Altham could readily perceive the rock orientation, might Hendrix be better suited to an avant-garde jazz group? But when he heard the finale, what Hendrix did with the simplistic melody of "Wild Thing," he then recognized how far-out Hendrix really was while still remaining in the idiom. Between the way the Experience looked and the dynamics of their sound, much of which was truly extraordinary, he knew they would make a big impact. He felt that Hendrix would be "a super-mega star."

No one missed the fact that Jimi left his Strat leaning against the amp feeding back as he left the stage. Charles Holley, following the music of his time, noted: "Two weeks later I saw Cream at the Marquee. Clapton had permed his hair and left his guitar feeding back, leaning against the amp, which he'd seen Hendrix do at the gig."

The JHE played in support of the New Animals at the Ricky Tick club. This group was managed by Chas Chandler and Michael Jeffery. Jimi and Mitch and Noel split twenty-five pounds.

Later that evening Jimi stopped by a Who recording session at IBC Sound Studios in London W1. Peter Townshend later said, "Jimi sort of wandered in looking peculiar, just really peculiar, and Keith Moon was in a nasty mood and said, 'Who let that savage in here?' I mean, he really did look pretty wild and very scruffy. Anyway, he walked around for a bit, and gave me a sort of lukewarm handshake, and then I never saw him again for a little while."

That next day, November 27, 1966, Jimi turned twenty-four.

December 1, 1966, Jimi signed a contract with Yameta, a British offshore company set up in a commonwealth country, the Bahamas, in 1965 by a lawyer named John Hillman, an associate of Michael Jeffery, who, it has been said, initiated the idea of having an overseas tax haven that would prevent certain earnings from being taxed in the United Kingdom.

Jimi and Kathy moved with Chas and Lotta to the former flat of Ringo Starr at 34 Montagu Square in London W1. Jimi's residence permit was extended to January 15, 1967, just over two weeks from the previous extension.

On December 10, Jimi's first press interview was published in the *Record*

Mirror as the Experience opened for John Mayall and the Bluesbreakers at the Ram Jam club in Brixton. Consistent with the devout British bluesman's set, Jimi played a couple of blues songs he seldom played in public: "Catfish Blues," which Muddy Waters had made famous, and Elmore James's "Dust My Broom"—and of course Howlin' Wolf's "Killing Floor." A spectator was amazed at Jimi puncturing the porous ceiling with the neck of his guitar and then using that fissure to create a bottleneck sound. Hendrix knew no one would appreciate those tunes more than John Mayall.

The next day Jimi and Kathy took in Little Richard's show at the Saville Theatre. Afterward they visited him at the Rembrandt Hotel. Jimi respectfully referred to him as "King" (as in the king of rock 'n' roll). Jimi talked about his record coming out in the upcoming week and said that it would be a hit. Just prior to leaving he conferred with Little Richard, asking him for fifty dollars. He felt he was owed several times that amount in unpaid wages when he left Little Richard's employment just about a year ago, but his request was denied.

As he and Kathy made their way home they were stopped by several police officers who took offense at Jimi wearing a British military jacket, saying that men fought and died in that uniform. Jimi's remarks to the effect that it was from the veterinary corp at the turn of the century failed to alter their views. They said they did not want to see him in that gear anymore and made him take it off. Jimi had to walk off coatless in the December cold. When they were out of sight he put the jacket back on.

On December 13, the JHE record "Hey Joe" was taped for the *Ready Steady Go* broadcast of December 16. Marc Bolan, the Merseybeats, the Troggs, and others, including the Breakaways, who sang background on "Hey Joe," were featured. Afterward the JHE continued into CBS Studios in W1, where they recorded "Third Stone from the Sun," "Foxy Lady," and "Red House," three newly penned Hendrix tunes.

"Hey Joe" was released December 16, 1966, just before the Christmas holidays. It got radio airplay at once, but there was really no way of telling how it would sell. The sound was strange and new, with supermusical effects hinting that something explosive would follow. Now the JHE had a product out on the market. Now was the time to begin to gig in earnest. On December 21, the JHE played Blaise's club—their lucky club. Although the Who was gigging at the Upper Cut, it was only a short distance from Blaise's, and Peter Townshend showed up. Jeff Beck was there, too, in the standing-room-only crowd.

The JHE got its first real write-up in *Melody Maker* in its "Caught in the Act" column. Chris Welch wrote of Hendrix's "great stage presence" and "exceptional guitar technique" and the fact that all of the Who, with the exception of Keith Moon, had been in the house. He noted that Jeff Beck, who had pretended to wander into the club, was astounded to hear Hendrix sing and play a totally original arrangement of Bob Dylan's "Like a Rolling Stone." *Melody Maker* forecasted him as "one of the big club names of 1967."

But Chas was edgy. It was difficult for him to enjoy the Christmas holiday. They were broke. The record was out. Now was the time to push through. He had to do something that would establish the JHE in the new year in London. Besides, they had no work lined up and there was no telling what would transpire in 1967. They were at a low ebb; they had to do something, and soon.

Chas decided to throw a party at the Bag O' Nails club in early January when the new record would be released and, hopefully, on the verge of peaking. It was a gamble. Although it would ostensibly be a celebration, it would also be a showcase for Jimi. Chas invited all the promoters and tour bookers and the "in" people among whom they would be most comfortable. It was a gamble in which there was also a touch of desperation. Chas knew that if this push did not take hold, then it would be virtually the end of the Jimi Hendrix Experience.

Hendrix's relationship with London's up-and-coming and premier guitarists had become bizarre. In black America competition between musicians, to challenge and be challenged, was accepted as part of the territory, and celebrated. But in England it appeared to be otherwise. The top guitarists were so in awe of Hendrix that several had questioned their continuing with the instrument. Brian May (the guitarist with Queen), Ron Wood, even Eric Clapton had made public statements about perhaps "packing it in"—"that the game was up for all of us." Hendrix felt himself becoming something of a problem. His relationship with Eric Clapton had become quite strained. He and Kathy visited with Clapton to make some kind of amends but the evening was very tense.

The first reviews of "Hey Joe" appeared on Christmas Eve. The *New Musical Express* was very positive, including the line: "This is a disc for the connoisseurs," which stuck in Hendrix's head. The *Record Mirror* thought that it should be a hit, citing the "marvelous blues feel" and that it was "a slow burner of immense excitement." A very nice Christmas present for Jimi.

On Christmas Day, Kathy and Jimi stayed home; everyone was away with family and everything was closed. They shared a supper of eggs and chips.

On Boxing Day, the day after Christmas, Jimi, Noel, and Mitch played to about thirty people at the Upper Cut Club. They tore it up.

The JHE performed "Hey Joe" live on TV on *Top of the Pops*. On December 31, they made their way to Noel's hometown of Folkestone for a gig at the Hillside Social Club. Later, at Noel's mother Margaret's New Year's Eve party, Jimi brought in the new year before a hearth in the English countryside.

The new year of 1967 found Hendrix in the middle of his first British winter. Compared with the fall, when he had arrived, the winter's cold had affected the scene: it was much quieter.

On January 9, "Hey Joe" came in on the English charts at number 48. Jeffery and Chandler had invested in the sales of "Hey Joe" by employing a standard but expensive strategy whereby they would have people buy up the records in the shops that contributed to the tally that comprised the best-selling recordings that were registered on the sales charts.

This effort had rendered Chas pretty broke. If Chas was broke, so was Jimi. Chas's general explanation was that airplay was nil, but the "ballrooms" were playing it, and it was starting to sell. But the expense of buying up records had taken him to the point where he and Jimi had "about thirty shillings left between us."

On the night of Chas's party, January 11, 1967, "Hey Joe" was moving up fast. Now for the first time there was the possibility of Jimi being more than a passing curiosity or an interesting freak.

Chas chose the Bag O' Nails because it was right off Carnaby Street, the most fashionable street of the emergent "Flower Power" youth. Many rock stars were in attendance, seated at long tables facing the stage. It was evident they were "following" Jimi. A better following was impossible to buy. But there were numerous other novelties this crowd had followed and then tossed aside after a while. George Melly, the respected English cultural commentator, author, and jazz singer, has said, "Like great fish the top groups glide from club to club, and those whose pleasure is to follow in their wake swim with them."

Chas was looking for work, not in-crowd adulation. Phillip Haywood, club owner and booker, came through; he invited the group to play as a support group to the New Animals at a series of out-of-London and in-London gigs for twenty-five pounds a night. Chas was relieved. They would be able to eat.

The next night the JHE played second on the bill to the New Animals at one of Haywood's clubs, the 7½. Immediately it was obvious that it was impossible to bill Jimi as a second, or support act. There was no question who the press and rock stars had returned to see. The 7½, a new club just off Piccadilly, was delighted to have in the audience Mick Jagger, Marianne Faithfull, Peter Townshend, Anita Pallenberg, Eric Clapton, Linda Keith, and Glen Campbell.

Jimi played his standard set of songs: "Hey Joe," "Stone Free," "Can You See Me," "Rock Me Baby," "Like a Rolling Stone," "Third Stone from the Sun," and "Wild Thing." At this point it was a pleasure for them to be working for steady money with a breaking act on tour. It was like a dress rehearsal for their break, and the way Chas was gambling, they would break out as stars or not at all.

Jimi played the 7½ club most of that week, with a one-day excursion to the Beachcomber Club in Nottingham on the 14th. On January 19, he played the

Speakeasy; on the 25th, the Marquee Club. Things were beginning to snowball. He was playing the top clubs as if he were already an established artist.

At the Marquee, Kit Lambert asked Chas to allow him to bill the Jimi Hendrix Experience with the Who at Brian Epstein's Saville Theatre. Chas was delighted. The Saville was tops, and so were the Who. Finally Jimi was sharing the bill with a group of his caliber. It began to get around London that there would be a battle royal of the groups on January 29, 1967.

One evening Jimi had a problem with some food that Kathy had prepared (funds were so low they had to prepare more meals at the flat). He thought she may not have washed the plates and utensils thoroughly. It became a yelling, screaming match and at some point Kathy dumped the entire dinner—plates, silverware, and all—on the floor. She eventually walked out and spent the night at her friend Angie's home (Angie would soon become Angie Burdon, the wife of Eric Burdon, who had been lead singer of the Animals). When things had cooled down and she returned to the flat they shared with Chas and Lotta, Jimi played her a lovely ballad entitled "The Wind Cries Mary." He told Kathy he had written it for her and all was forgiven and forgotten.

Jimi and Chas and the Experience were playing an out-of-the-way height-of-winter gig in some nether area of Yorkshire, the Kirklevington Country Club, which seated about four hundred locals who had never heard of Jimi Hendrix. They thought they had a ringer when he began "Wild Thing" since they were a strictly blues and soul venue, but pretty soon he won them over.

John McCoy, the owner of the club, took an interest in Jimi, surprised that when they shot the breeze he didn't have an attitude or anything. "Later on, we were sitting around in the back and we got into playing games. Jimi arm wrestled my bouncers, big strapping physical culture blokes, and he beat about six of them."

They upped the ante, playing a complicated game that involved doing push-ups with one arm while simultaneously removing one beer bottle at a time from a double row of bottles nestled against the wall, and "Jimi won that, as well." One of the bouncers may have thought his remark innocent: "So the nigger wins this one, too." But Chas Chandler didn't think so. "Without a second thought" he decked the guy, "laid him out," sending him "flying right over the banister."

Jimi was very impressed. Chas had also laid out an obstreperous drunk back in London who was trying to harass Kathy and Jimi when he had just arrived in England. But this was the second time, again without hesitation, and he could see that Chas was extremely hands-on in terms of making sure that Jimi only had to deal with playing. Chas made sure he didn't have to risk his hands in physical self-defense.

Jimi thought that was very cool. The strength required to do what he did with the guitar often surprised ordinary people. He was extremely fit, and, as Kathy knew well, feared no one.

Ram John Holder and Jimi Hendrix were bound to meet. They had both recently come to London from the Village. They were both guitarists, and they both would become involved with a Monika Dannemann.

Ram met Jimi at the Scotch of St. James. Ram had wandered in to get a drink and heard that a brother from the States was playing, and that he should check it out. Downstairs Jimi Hendrix was playing some shit that even made the band stop. The audience stood in amazement. At that moment, Ram felt he never wanted to play his guitar again. He felt like burning it.

Later, when he talked with Jimi, he found that they knew some of the same people. Ram had been the co-owner of the Cafe Rafio in the Village. A small club, the Cafe Rafio featured solo guitarists on acoustic in the folk tradition. Dave Van Ronk, Dino Valenti, Tom Paxton, and Richie Havens all had played the Cafe Rafio, as did Ram himself. Ram sang the blues with West Indian intonations that were lost in his sincerity. He loved the blues. He *loved* Hendrix. As a musician himself he recognized Hendrix's blues background and inspiration.

Ram John Holder had come to London to find himself. The son of a preacher from a tiny Caribbean country, he had been educated at all-black Lincoln University and had studied for advanced degrees at New York University. He had become involved in New Left politics as an outgrowth of the civil rights movement. An accomplished guitarist, he was also drawn to the stage as an actor. Ram had to decide in what direction to take his life.

Compared to Jimi, Ram was a scholar. Ram was well read and politically well informed on worldwide liberation struggles. Coming to London had been depressing for him at first. He hated the way in which black West Indians were treated in the United Kingdom. Ghettoized largely in grim towns outside of London, the blacks were no longer needed to work in the factories that had boomed when England was a world colonial power. In fact, the black population, as it continued to grow, was viewed with alarm by the staid English establishment.

Ram was tempted to jump into the political arena and champion the rights of blacks. He was well aware of the black spokesmen, and there were too few. The outstanding West Indian spokesmen were light-years apart. He admired C.L.R. James, the Marxist West Indian scholar who had written *The Black Jacobins,* the definitive book on the Haitian Revolution. He followed his writings carefully, but as an activist-speaker, James was too old to be really effective. In his late seventies, C.L.R. James did his best, but he was overshadowed by Michael X, who was much younger and somewhat in with the hip London underground. Although Michael X never really committed himself to any specific political group, his pronouncements in the press often linked the repression of blacks in London with the suppression of Flower Power. Fiery, sometimes crazy, and usually unpredictable, Michael X was the only young black able to move through many different echelons of London society (radical psychiatrist R. D. Laing thought he was great) and was, therefore, at least potentially important. But in many ways Michael X was not political enough to organize. He fashioned himself after Malcolm X and the Black Power movement, whereas Dr. James was a Norman Thomas–type figure, committed to leftist politics. The gulf that separated Michael X from C.L.R. James was symptomatic of the crisis of black leadership in Britain.

Ram John was sorely tempted to take the whole thing on.

But then again, looking at it head on, Ram felt in his heart that it would be a hopeless task. That is why he gave what support he could to Michael X. It was a hapless situation that could indeed drive one crazy. Ram tried to understand Michael X and read and relate to Dr. James, but the most he could do at the time was keep himself informed of the global situation.

Ram and Jimi became good friends. They would always hug when they met. There were not too many brothers on the set. Jimi found it amusing that Ram was an inveterate cricket fan and would rush off at a moment's notice to catch a match on the "telly." Jimi could have been an actor himself. He was an excellent mimic, especially of Harlem drag queens, and he told incredibly funny stories of his various tours with small-time bands in small-time places. Like two brothers on the block, they, each in their own eccentricities, brought each other qualities they missed in being away from home.

Ram had met Jimi the first month Jimi arrived. They saw each other almost every day. They both dug hanging out, but as Hendrix's thing began to come together he became more distant and more hassled. The big push was on, and it was not easy, or even particularly pretty to watch.

Around New Year's Eve of 1967, Ram caught an interview with Jimi in one of the smaller London papers. Jimi's rap was very spacey. As an educated man looking for substance, all Ram found were platitudes. When he came to the paragraphs where Jimi glossed over politics, revolution, and the plight of the man of color, he blew his top. It was like Jimi had sold out. Ram John was furious. He would have to see Jimi right away.

But Ram John could not reach Jimi and, having to leave on an extended trip, he mailed Jimi a note suggesting he call Michael X, who wanted to meet him, enclosing a phone number and a poem.

Jimi got the note and the poem entitled "One Flower" in the mail. Michael X wrote of building a community of "new people / who were once write-offs in the old world." While some just watched "the cities disintegrating / Princesses" viewed his work with approval. The sounds they made, "hammers and saws of the carpenters," were like music to them, even though bombs fell and some of them were jailed. "We went on. They could not tear down our town." In spite of the bombs, "one building stood / it shown like a light amid the ruins." Its "foundation was solid" because it was made of "the new material—IDEA."

After some back and forth Jimi was invited to visit Michael X at his flat. Jimi and Kathy went over one evening. Michael X and his rap had caused something of a sensation in Britain. He patterned his ideas on those of Malcolm X of the Nation of Islam and its founder, Elijah Muhammad. Malcolm X, the legendary African-American radical political spokesperson whose beliefs had included self-defense of violence against blacks and separation of the races, among other things, had been brutally assassinated in America less than two years prior after his breaking with the black Muslims to become a progressive leader of all races and colors. His death was still fresh in many minds. Jimi could not help but know of the power and the impact of Malcolm X since he had lived in Harlem, Malcolm X's base of operation, at the height of his power and influence. Jimi and Kathy found Michael X to be an overweight Brit from the West Indies who could not get over the fact that Jimi had brought a white woman to their meeting. He was quite rude, by British standards, but Jimi was polite and respectful as usual. They left at the earliest opportunity. Down the stairs and out into the London night they nearly died laughing. Whatever his ideas and insights were, all they had gotten was a ridiculous tirade that was about as far from the revolution as they could imagine. They could not stop laughing at the absurdity of it all. If Michael X was the feared British radical separatist revolutionary, then, from what they had seen, the establishment had nothing to fear.

Marianne Faithfull had just begun to live with Mick Jagger when Jimi Hendrix first appeared in London, but she was well aware of his arrival. Not only had Linda Keith informed her, but also there had been talk of an audition that Hendrix had done for Mick, who was establishing his own production company at the time. Although Jagger had rejected Hendrix, the London hip society of musicians was very much taken with him. Brian Jones raved about Hendrix. Some took that as a signal of the widening rift between Jones and Jagger, but there were others, like Eric Clapton and John Mayall, whose words of awe could hardly be disputed.

Marianne and Mick had attended the opening of the 7½ club, which Hendrix had played. Jagger, as "king of the scene," as John Lennon had dubbed him, had gone primarily out of a sense of duty. This was one of Marianne and Mick's first appearances in public and they had not stayed long. There was still the stigma of former girlfriend Chrissie Shrimpton's attempted suicide hanging over Jagger, and they had not wanted it to look as if they were flaunting anything. But they did want to establish their relationship in the eyes of the public and their peers.

Marianne was intrigued by what little she had heard of Jimi's playing. She had never before heard anyone play in his style, with his speed and apparent root knowledge of the blues.

A couple days later, Hendrix reappeared at the 7½ club in mid-March of '67 for a three-day gig. Marianne had been killing time while Mick was in the studio recording. She decided to go have an anonymous drink at the club. Although there were several empty tables the atmosphere was charged with excitement. She sat on the floor through the set, enthralled. She returned the next night. She felt some kind of bond between herself and Hendrix. It was something impossible to put into words. She felt drawn to him in a special way. Not particularly sexual, the attraction was more like a mutual recognition of each other's soul. That second night they were introduced. She knew it would be impossible not to be recognized and now that they were staring at each other, she affirmed their affinity.

Jimi was very polite, as usual, but he was also coming on to her. She was used to being come on to. She was attractive, famous, upper-class, and well-to-do. Sometimes men came on to her because they felt they were supposed to, as if there was some kind of propriety her beauty demanded that made it the thing to do. Jimi came on to her rather strongly. If it had not been for the affinity she felt they shared she might have been taken aback. But she took it as a recognition on his part that they had something strongly in common. She, too, wanted to affirm the feeling. She did not necessarily want to go to bed with Jimi. She had only been living with Jagger a few weeks; they were very happy and very turned on to each other. At another time in her life it might have been a beautiful thing to do, but that night it could not happen.

Instead, she asked Jimi if he might like to come to a get-together. She would invite some of her friends and they would hang out after the gig, get high, and talk. Although it was a substitution or a sublimation, it was also an affirmation. Of course he accepted the formal-sounding invite.

Brian Jones came. He was not too involved in the latest sessions the Stones were doing. They were laying tracks. He would come in later and add touches and whatnot (although it seemed as if he was being frozen into that role—further and further away from ever contributing songs to the Stones' effort). Linda Keith attended, as did Paul McCartney, Chas Chandler, and some young socialites. It was no big thing. They sat around and smoked and got acquainted. There were others there, Mitch and Noel not knowing quite how to act, and Kathy Etchingham, who appeared to be Jimi's old lady, although he seemed to have eyes only for the blonde and delicately featured Marianne. They had a nice low-key time, but Jimi had seemed somewhat disappointed, although his shyness made some of his emotions ambiguous. Marianne was firmly with Mick, there was no disputing that. But she was glad she and Jimi had had a chance to get together and chat. For Jimi it was almost like having tea, at two o'clock in the morning.

The Who vs. the Jimi Hendrix Experience concert, a tribute to Brian Epstein, was held on a Sunday, January 29, 1967, at the Saville Theatre. It was the JHE's most prestigious gig to date. In attendance were Eric Clapton, Klaus Voorman, Linda Keith, John Lennon, Spencer Davis, Jack Bruce, Paul McCartney, and Lulu. Right from the announcement everyone knew it would be a famous concert. The two most outrageous groups in London dueling in feedback frenzy, full amps billowing forth decibels through theater walls.

On February 4, "Hey Joe" came in number four on the *Melody Maker* chart. That was it; "Hey Joe" was a hit. The February 5, 1967, gig at the Flamingo Club was like the premiere of the Jimi Hendrix Experience as a star attraction.

The Flamingo Club was notorious for its lackadaisical approach to the best of British rock. A hip room, the Flamingo catered to a steady clientele of beat-niklike insiders of the London underground scene. They were all too hip to the machinations of the British recording industry and its sundry promotion men. This club was the last in a long line of hip London clubs Hendrix and company had had to conquer and it was the toughest. The crowd at the Flamingo usually refrained from applauding in anything but the most token fashion.

Jimi opens at once with a jam meandering in heavy tempo. Then signaling in the blues with a long-distance call tremolo, he takes the band into "Killing Floor." Straight-down boogie, up-tempo R&B chords—like an Apollo show-time theme truncated into an introduction to the Jimi Hendrix Experience. Then Jimi speaks from the wall of sound, "Thank you very much." The music ceases. . . . "We'd like to continue on with a little tune, a very straight, ha, ha . . . Top Forty R&B rock 'n' roll record. A little thing called 'Have Mercy,' have mercy on me . . . BABY."

Noel Redding comes out with a "Wooly Bully" bass beat, Jimi chording blues rhythm licks and filling in the lead, they come to the bridge, a blues chord-inverted theme that explains, as so often in R&B, with words and tune changes, the meaning of the plea.

"Can You See Me," Jimi's own tune, has the first really brilliant solo of the set spaced within an ample middle-bridge section that extends into the break, where an elongated twang sustains for eight beats on the up-tempo, and then the ensemble returns to the back-beating wall of sound. Finally Jimi slows the pace, strumming soft chords against a simple run that sounds like a coffeehouse folk song.

"Right now I'd like to try to do a song for you, a little thing by Bob Dylan, 'Like a Rolling Stone' . . . I want to dedicate this song to a few people in this club."

It comes out more like a ballad with the guitar the dominant sound, picking out the melody.

Jimi's arrangement of "Rock Me Baby" is far from B. B. King's blues-style version. It is definitely super-tempo rock 'n' roll all the way for the Experience.

Jimi slurs his announcement of the next number: "Thank you very much; and I'd like to try and do a little mixture of a whole lot of things in this one here . . . a little Muddy Waters version slightly." Jimi goes into the beginning of Muddy Waters's version of the traditional blues, "Two Trains Running" (which Muddy Waters called "Still a Fool"). From there he goes into a short solo circling about the few notes that comprise the introductory phrases and extending them. And then just as easily he slips back into the original raunchy chords with short stroking chops to sing a couple of verses. And then straight and straight up into a psychedelic solo full of blue tonality, yet not sounding like the blues at all. Then back to the verse, Jimi playing both the Muddy Waters lead and the Jimmie Rodgers second guitar of the original version at the same time.

> Well, now there's two trains runnin'
> And neither one's going my way

Jimi plays with a little feedback at the end and then the song climaxes into pure distortion, which ends in an abrupt halt. The crowd comes alive for the first time. They cheer! Jimi answers with his Stratocaster whoozing a "thank you."

Jimi buzzes into "Stone Free," the B-side of their record. The song builds slowly as he mumbles lyrics about being put down for his hair, for his clothes, and by his women, but he wants everyone to know—as the song builds to a screeching intensity—that he is STONE FREE. Without missing a beat the JHE segues right into their hit, "Hey Joe."

His solo is fantastic. His customized Fuzz Face full out creates endless peak distortions and sustains long lines that create their own vibrato from sheer force of volume. It is a thrilling sound that goes right through you. On the tag-out, Jimi makes his guitar say, "You better believe it, baby."

"Wild Thing" starts off with the fuzz hook that it was known for when the Troggs had it as their big hit. But Hendrix made "Wild Thing" a heavy, funky, mad metallic moan, full of the human sounds of the blues in primordial emotion. You *feel* "Wild Thing." In the middle passage, he goes into a little bit of the Beatles' "Day Tripper," contrasting the heavy sexual blues-laden drone of his "Wild Thing" with the flower-pop hit. Then he takes the song out. Rolling feedback in lava folds across an incredible terrain. Mitch Mitchell rolling, tramming, thunderous bombs against tingling cymbals that sound like a giant-ship emergency bell. Monster fucking sounds. Fire in pink noise. Thrashing in gargantuan moans, the overdriving amps blown full out, reporting the oscillating feedback. Pulling back into a stellar void, the deep tonic of the bass becomes apparent as Jimi sets his guitar back into the drone note that began the song.

The Flamingo Club house emcee picks up in the chaos: "Oh . . . let's hear it please for the Jimi Hendrix Experience. . . ." But the great howl makes his shout a tiny voice. The audience had responded, but their applause and occasional cheers are overwhelmed by the protesting sound system. "Okay, ladies and gentlemen. The three gentlemen you've seen on the stage have given you their very best. How about your very best for them? Would you gentlemen, everybody this time, put your hands together for JIMI HENDRIX JIMI HENDRIX EXPERIENCE?"

The crowd erupts again in a very nice hand, with scattered cheers. An incredible hand for the Flamingo.

The emcee continues, " . . . who were working out so *hard* that time. Thank you. I'm afraid that's all from those three gentlemen for the evening, but back on the stand later on goes the All Night Workers. Thank you very much for being so great and clapping so great for Jimi. . . . Here we go for a few sounds, this one dedicated to Jimi, 'Please Don't Go.'"

A British cover of "Baby, Please Don't Go" screeches out from the speakers. It sweeps the club, penetrating to Jimi's dressing-room door, as the dressing room becomes more and more jammed with well-wishers and celebrities. Well, that was it. The Jimi Hendrix Experience was officially open for business—all offers and comers lined up.

The English did not quite know what to make of this black phenomenon. The press began to ridicule him. Fleet Street stuck Hendrix with the label "The Wild Man of Pop." Could he withstand the viciousness of the establishment press? Could the London underground scene, which was just emerging itself, successfully champion Hendrix? Chas Chandler decided to fight fire with fire. He encouraged the establishment press to ridicule Hendrix. The more outrageous Hendrix would appear in the *Daily Mirror,* the more the public would be curious and the more the rebellious youth would side with him. The question was, when would they eventually make that catalyst work?

Chas purposefully fed them the ugliest photos of Jimi he could come up with. And once the Fleet Street papers got a good look, they made him the perfect antihero. One London paper called him a "Mau-Mau" in banner headlines, while another called him a "Wild Man from Borneo." They played to the racism the press was prone to exploit, knowing their readers would not ignore any aspect of the "race problem." Jimi Hendrix was denounced by Mrs. Mary Whitehouse, the leader of the National Viewers' and Listeners' Association. Donald Bruce wrote in *Pop Shop:* "For one thing, Jimi is scarcely likely to qualify for a best-looking-bloke competition." And in boldface type: "So why should Jimi worry if he looks like a wild-eyed revolutionary from the Caribbean and that he talks with the shuteye still in his big mouth? . . ."

The youth, the first generation stripped of England's vast colonial wealth, had to deal with the hard facts of a lower standard of living. The press made sure they knew this. The underground movement was an important vanguard, but very small in actual numbers. The major youth divisions were the mods and the rockers, a press invention based on upper-middle-class and lower-middle-class youths. The skinheads, the rowdy working-class kids, were considered out of it: they dug reggae and violence. They even took to hanging out with the West Indian rude boys in the reggae clubs.

But few English middle-class youths could escape the traditional discomfort with blacks, even Noel Redding and Mitch Mitchell.

Noel and Mitch would sometimes joke and use racial slurs when they talked. They would use "nigger" and "coon" as a good many regular Brits would do in banter, but it must have had an effect on Jimi and further increased the conflict among them.

The incongruity of these young fey Englishmen having taken up with "the Wild Man of Pop" did even more to project Hendrix's image in the United Kingdom. While this cooled out some of the hostility he might have received (the group was two-thirds homebred), it also was outrageous theater. Noel and Mitch, both sporting the early John Lennon short German cut when they started with Jimi, soon affected long and wild Afro-permed hair.

Rather staid young Englishmen, both Mitchell and Redding dug jazz and blues (as any English musician did who wanted to be heavy in the pop world), and both wanted badly to make it. Before Jimi they had never become tight with a black man, and especially never considered one their superior. Although the money increased, and all the side benefits were good, Noel and Mitch often found it difficult to ignore the fact that they were sidemen to Hendrix.

Hendrix had pressed the English music world to the wall, thus precipitating a brief debate over how they should react. While the English authorities put Hendrix through the mill, the English rock world got it together much quicker. Townshend, Beck, Page, and Clapton had conferred, as did the Stones and the Beatles—truth won out: Hendrix's music was unique and powerful, and his act was outta sight. And more importantly, Hendrix did not have a name in the States at all, aside from being known in the business as a good traditional rhythm and blues guitarist. So why not accept him? Make him their own, and lend even more power and veracity to English rock? They were right. Hendrix, as an English commodity, took over where the Beatles left off, and gave English music the strongest dose of real black music it had ever had.

Barely three months ago a rather morose Jimi was playing to empty tables at the 7½ club when Marianne Faithfull had first checked him out, and then he "ran away" rather than have to acknowledge their sexual attraction. Now he was just becoming the star many knew he would be. Onstage, he was surprised to see Marianne and Mick sitting at a table right in front of him. He recalled the nights seemingly long ago when Marianne had camped out at the 7½ for three days straight just checking him out. Marianne, in her own way, had helped Jimi. He still felt the same attraction he had felt at first for her. Perhaps it was assisted by Jagger's rejection of him when he was an unknown, but Marianne in her own right was a fabulous sight. Back then they had just gotten "Hey Joe" out, and he did not have the star following he had now, nor did he have his sexual burlesque stage act together. Now he physically reacted to his feedback moans, humping the guitar, playing it between his legs, grinding the strings against the microphone, and then banging the guitar against the amps as he whanged the tremolo bar. This night he really put on a show. He got down on his knees and screamed in ecstasy as the guitar moaned, then in fucking motions he panned the Stratocaster before the audience as if it were his cock, his mouth open, lip-synching with the high-velocity howl of thousands of souls in orgasm.

After the set he went straight to Marianne and Mick, ignoring the imploring arms of those who wished a word or a vibe. He ignored Mick as he sat between them. He positioned his chair in such a way that his back was to Mick and his body was directly in front of Marianne's. He had wanted for months to tell Marianne outright the way he felt. Later for all the propriety and fencing and feeling subtle vibrations. As the recorded music played over the sound system, drowning out all except the closest and most intimate of conversations, he told her, his face pressed nearly against hers, that he wanted to fuck her and that she should leave Mick who was a cunt and come with him, right now. She was taken with his audacity. She wondered if in spite of the din Mick could hear what was being said. Even if he couldn't she felt that he could suss it out anyway. She could do nothing but turn Jimi down completely. There was little else she could do unless she just got up and walked out of the Speakeasy with Jimi. Perhaps she was tempted. Given another time and another place—and maybe a little more subtlety—she just might have taken him up on his straightforward proposition. Jimi insisted, repeating his demands over and over. Marianne had to completely refuse. She sensed Jagger getting jealous. She also sensed that for Jimi it was a showdown. He was tired of the dallying around. And he resented Jagger not only for the audition but also for his best friend Brian Jones, whom he felt Jagger was driving out of the Rolling Stones, a group Jones had started—not Jagger. Jimi stood up abruptly, not even going through any formalities, not even attempting to smooth things over with Jagger, and split.

"Jimi was by now the toast of the town and on the verge of displacing Mick as the great sex symbol of the moment," Marianne Faithfull said later. "After the show, Jimi came over to our table and pulled up a chair and began whispering in my ear. He was saying anything he could think of to get me to go home with him. All of the things he wanted to do to me sexually. Telling me he'd written 'The Wind Cries Mary' for me. Saying, 'Come with me now, baby. Let's split. What are you doing with this jerk anyway?'

"I wanted more than anything to go with him, but I couldn't do it. Mick would never forgive me. Throughout the whole incident, Mick was a model of *sangfroid.*"

The next time Marianne and Mick saw Jimi perform, Mick flatly refused to go backstage and say hello. Marianne understood why.

While sitting around in the Upper Cut waiting to go on for a press party the club itself was throwing, an early gig that would begin at 4:00 P.M., Jimi started playing an intro to what would eventually become "Purple Haze," thinking of a dream he had had that previous night. Chas, always alert to what he was playing, quickly told him to "write the rest of that." So Jimi did. He not only completed the music but also the words: a long series of verses that fused the dream that had him walking underneath the sea, influenced by a story by the science-fiction writer Philip José Farmer about a purple death ray, "Night of Light." Jimi had first written, "Purple Haze/Jesus Saves . . . Beyond insane, Is it pleasure or is it pain—Down on the ceiling looking up at the Bed, See my body painted blue and red." Then he had begun again on another page the verses that would become his best-known song.

The days in London melted one into the other; he lost track of time. His life accelerated. He was concentrating so totally on his music that he felt as if he were playing one long gig in one long single night that could just as easily be an eternity. Living by night. Looking out of his blackout-curtained window, it always was twilight. The lights of the city of London coming up over the twilight haze. The dark gray townhouses of London town queued up, low blocks stretching forever. Medieval buses tramming through the narrow streets bringing the commoners, the workers home to their pubs, to their evening meals. But their plight was boring to him. They crammed into the pub below his window at six o'clock on the dot. His eyes would always turn to the sky, as if trying to discern some light, and the color for him that became the true color of his existence that year, 1967 in London, was that weird purple before the advent of night. That extreme side of the spectral haze—purple into the nights, the endless nights of his life.

Edwin Kramer seemed to have been waiting for Jimi.

Ed Kramer, a slight, blond-haired young engineer, had just started on his new job at Olympic Studios when in walked Jimi Hendrix—the most incredible electric guitarist in England.

Chas and Jimi were not satisfied with the "Hey Joe" recording they had made at another studio. They wanted to feature Jimi's guitar work more, but the more way-out stuff was difficult to record. At this point they knew that an amount of experimentation would have to take place in order to get the recorded sound they wanted. They had had their fill of the staid, middle-aged, proper British engineers. They liked Kramer from the beginning. He was different, young, and enthusiastic. He would be willing to put in the extra time and effort, as opposed to the company men who freaked out when it was past teatime and they were still in the studio. Besides, Kramer looked like an angel, a cherub, a cupid. His vibes were right.

It would be a job just to get what Jimi did onstage on a four-track tape in the studio. But they wanted more than that. They wanted to *extend* his sound via magnetic tape. They wanted the best recordings and then some. What Jimi was hearing would involve elaborate overdubbing and the most advanced devices to deliver both his quick picking and his distortion and feedback harmonics. But the total Experience sound needed something more, as well. The bass had to have absolute depth without distortion in the small speakers common to radio. The drums also needed a boost in order to feature their dynamic interplay with Jimi's lead. With only four-track machines to work with, Hendrix's music was a problem.

Not only did Kramer have constructive criticism, he was also dying to try some new things out. Recording with Jimi in the studio convinced him that here was a man who would revolutionize the music and the technology, as well. After their first sessions together, Kramer and Hendrix were most taken with each other. Studying the recordings in his time off and working with Hendrix daily in the studio, Kramer was convinced that there were some things they could do in the Olympic four-track studio that had never been done before. Edwin worked like an elf.

They worked night and day every day for a month putting the first album and much of a second Hendrix album together. Being in the studio for extensive amounts of time, where his sound could be immediately played back to him, made Hendrix a studio addict. Tunes he had written in the Village and performed at the Cafe Wha? now achieved fruition from their frail beginnings.

The studio opened Hendrix's head up musically more than it had ever been before. Finally there was a source, a place where it could all be put together.

Kramer became so important to Hendrix that it was strange they did not become close friends. They worked well together, were extremely polite to each other—but at the end of their working days/nights, they would each go back to their respective scenes.

Hendrix did not want to do anything that might alienate Kramer. Kramer was a man—and at that time one of the few men in England—who could optimize the sounds in Jimi's way-out head. He would take no risk with Kramer. Kramer was too important for Hendrix to dilute their intense work with play.

They worked out phase shifts, double-tracking, space sounds, wind sounds, even a more controlled feedback sound that could melt right into notes. Underwater sounds, spaceship and rocket sounds, refined white, pink, and blue noises—red noises. They did sound paintings right out of the avant-garde composers' backyard. Since they were using all kinds of sound contraptions to run Hendrix's guitar through, why leave the drums behind? The drums came right along and were as up as Jimi's multiple guitars on every attack. Kramer was able to get a phased timbre on Mitchell's drums that had the double-kit set almost tuned to the two guitars. Bright, liquid, and slapping, the drums walked right out of the recordings at you double-tracked and phase-shifted, just like the guitars. And in stereo, too. Although they did not publicize it, they began to mix everything in stereo. Redding's bass received several electronic boosts, as well. Special Fuzz Tone boxes were developed. But most importantly they were able to get the deepest bass effects possible without distorting the speakers, whereas in reggae, for instance, it would be years before the bass could be recorded at the depths where it was most effective. The genius of Ed Kramer made it possible for even the five-inch speaker of a common AM portable radio to deliver the full import of the Experience sound. And he was a wizard at lining up two, three, and even four guitar overdubs on one track of the four-track tapes. They had the fourth member of the Experience: Ed Kramer. Through this slim, elf-like blond they were finally able to extend Jimi's guitar into the outer heavens it had been aimed at in the first place.

Jimi encouraged his two sidemen to contribute to the Experience's first album. Noel wrote a pop ditty called "She's So Fine" and Jimi readily accepted it. Noel thought that it was a good thing to do from a public relations point of view. But it began to become clear that Noel's allegiance was indeed to pop, in the classic mode: popular acceptance. They recorded it in a breeze at Olympic. Jimi and

Chas could not help laughing out loud at Noel's singing. He really cracked Jimi up. His tonality veered close to what could be called the pip-squeak, but it gave the album's overabundance of intensity a much-needed break.

The Jimi Hendrix Experience began to move, began to fly. People joined up with the crew out of the night. Gerry Stickells was just hanging out and he had a truck, so he became the equipment manager. A weird electronic genius named "O," who made far-out "toys" for electric guitars, became an essential part of the JHE. "O" improved on Jimi's homemade wah-wah, which had been inspired by the Fugs. "O" also built a little machine they called the Octavia, which could change octaves at a touch. They were working on the highest keening treble range possible with an enhanced report to give the sound the same presence as a middle-range tone.

On March 16, Track Records hosted a launch party and press reception at the Speakeasy. The next day the Jimi Hendrix Experience's new single "Purple Haze" would be in all the stores in London and all the other major cities in the United Kingdom. Track would finally officially be in business with the hottest group on the set. Jimi Hendrix had inspired the idea for Track Records in the first place. They were tied to his rising star, and the fact that they were releasing his latest single was major, and that he was playing for them that night increased their brightness to incandescence.

"Hey Joe" had peaked at number four just a few weeks after its release. "Purple Haze," the seemingly long-overdue rocker featuring the freaky hot guitar work that had become the trademark of the Experience, was guaranteed to be a big record.

"Purple Haze" was becoming a great big hit. Spring was here, Flower Power was going hot and heavy in America and beginning to catch on in London. The *Daily Mirror* played up the Jimi Hendrix Experience German destruction bit to the hilt, especially since they were due to begin a big tour with the Walker Brothers, Cat Stevens, and Engelbert Humperdinck. The Fleet Street papers sought to link Flower Power with destruction and it seemed that Jimi Hendrix was the perfect symbol. The press seemed to be daring Jimi to destruct at Finsbury Park, where the tour would commence. Dick Katz and the tour press agents loved it, although they knew the arena authorities and theater owners would hate it. Hendrix's office leaked a rumor that Jimi would indeed destruct.

There was a massive turnout at Finsbury Park that March 31, 1967. It was common knowledge that the Walker Brothers, teen idols, would split up after the tour—a virtual guarantee that the young girls would be there in flocks.

Sitting in the dressing room while Jimi waited to go on, Chas Chandler and journalist Keith Altham were discussing some kind of punch to put into the act. Up until that time Jimi had been doing straight guitar playing, with the playing-with-the-teeth bit and his general showtime acrobatics the only departures from the norm. While this was cool for his musician and underground followers, Chas knew the teenybopper fans who would be on this tour would need something extra. Engelbert Humperdinck, Cat Stevens, and the Walker Brothers were all lady-killer sex symbols. Jimi would have to be superextraordinary just to keep up. Jimi had a tune called "Fire" that suggested to a symbolic young girl that she leave her mama's side and come to him so he could warm his body before her fire. Keith Altham thought that perhaps something could be done with "Fire" that would dramatize it more to the kids. It did not take much discussion for the assembled to figure out that the only way to dramatize fire was to create one. They sent Gerry Stickells out to get some lighter fluid and got ready.

The Jimi Hendrix Experience opened the show. "Purple Haze" and "Fire" were the new songs of the lot, with "Fire" the inevitable finale. It was basically a vehicle for shouted phrases of sexual innuendo that went as close to the borderline as possible. The lyrics were not muffled and laid-back, as had been his custom, but full-throated and haranguing. The music was simple up-tempo rock, built around Jimi's soloing and Mitch's circular drumming.

First the ensemble hits a simple boogie melody, then Jimi shouts the lyrics against the back-beating drums up to full volume. This is not the sweet-talking Jimi, but a man who does not care whether the woman of his desire cares for him or not. Nor is he concerned about her new boyfriend. He has only one burning goal, and that is, as he puts it, to be close to her "fire."

Mitch and Noel join him singing the refrain about standing next to her fire in unison several times, then Jimi hits the lyrics again, sternly ordering the girl to quit acting as if she were crazy. And then, as a giveaway that this song is aimed directly at live-at-home teenage girls, he mocks her insistence that her mother is not home. He tells her to avoid playing around with him or else she will get burned. His only interest is being close to the heat of her fire.

Jimi shouts that he will take over as he goes into a mad solo complete with all the stage tricks he can throw at the crowd! "Yeah, you know what I'm talking about. Yeah, get it on, baby." Jimi jacks his treble reach to its limit and sends the sound careening through the sky, pointing his Strat straight up from a deep crouch. "That's what I'm talking about."

Jimi soloed on the upbeat tag-out that stretched on until he got the lighter fluid out. He almost blew it. Jimi went down on his back to pour the lighter fluid over the guitar. Lighting the matches seemed to take forever. Finally he got a light. Rolling over and hovering over his guitar he applied the match to the lighter fluid and immediately flames leapt, twelve feet high. He rocked back on his haunches and then over on his back, clutching his hands. People on both sides of the stage went berserk. To many in the audience it seemed as if Jimi Hendrix had self-immolated, like the Buddhists were doing in the Vietnam War—burning themselves to death in public. There was awe, freaky terror, and delight in the crowd as Jimi bounded up and disappeared backstage. The ovation was shattering. They howled in shock.

Backstage the theater manager was threatening a lawsuit and demanding the guitar as evidence. He was outraged. The audience was still applauding.

The next day Jimi was front-page news. "Purple Haze" was burning down the charts.

The JHE organization had pulled out all the stops; now they started refining the technique. They could not let a chance like this go by. A twenty-five-day tour all over England before legions of teenyboppers with their solid British sex-symbol idols before them was set. They knew Jimi could not burn his guitar every night. But what he could do was a direct-action burlesque/satire of the whole "pop" sex symbol scene—and blow everybody's mind. Before, Jimi had only played around with the guitar: slinging it under his legs as he flicked his tongue. Now he developed it. Falling suddenly to his knees like James Brown during "Please, Please" and lip-synching a scream as his Stratocaster emitted an orgasmic howl, Jimi then moved the guitar across his body, standing straight up from his haunches and palming the instrument before him like a machine-gun cock emitting staccato bursts; humping his ax as it rumbled into low-pitched feedback, and then letting it all out as he fell back to his knees, and then over backward, feedback spilling white-hot noise all over him as he rolled around the stage, never missing a note, and the audience loved it. But the "headliners"—all static love ballad crooners—had to follow.

Soon the tour promoter was forced to act. There were complaints that Hendrix's sexual behavior onstage was vulgar and erotic. He publicly demanded that Hendrix clean up his act. Meanwhile, his tour quickly sold out.

Jimi began to incur the wrath of the headliners, the Walker Brothers. He was getting all the attention and publicity. When a French TV crew came to film only Hendrix, the Walker Brothers really blew their tops. There were all kinds of sabotage from theater owners, stage managers, and sound and light people, but the Experience stuck it out.

Hendrix IS Out of This World
Even his ex-Animal manager needed a split personality!

"Out of this world" is a much misapplied phrase, but when it's applied to that extraordinary guitarist Jimi Hendrix, it's appropriate. Looking as incredible as anything conceived by science-fiction writer Isaac Asimov, whose work he endlessly devours, Jimi is composing some numbers of equally unearthly inspiration.

There is one titled "Remember," about a manic-depressive, described as "raw nerves on record," another called "Teddy Bears Live For Ever," and a third concerning a visitor from another planet who decides that the human race is an unworthy animal to rule the earth and so destroys it, turning the world over to the chickens!

Hendrix is managed by Chas Chandler, the ex-Animal, who has developed a kind of split personality to cope with the new image.

One moment will find him the good-natured ex-pop star wearing his Lord Kitchener uniform with gold braid, and the next immaculately attired in black suit and tie as Mr. Chandler, businessman—complaining resignedly about having to buy a £2,000 mixing tape-machine instead of the Lincoln Continental his heart desires. Both Chas and his protégé share a newly acquired apartment off Edgware Road, where, together with newly acquired publicist Chris Williams, I found myself last Friday surveying a room dominated by a psychedelic painting (bought by Chas while under the "affluence of inkahol" in New York). It depicted a bleeding eye letting droplets fall on a naked woman.

There was a brass scuttle from which projected a number of empty wine bottles—relics of some bygone happening, a book about vampires, the inevitable blind eye of the TV set, and an award for the Animals' best group record, "House of the Rising Sun," on the mantelpiece, together with a model cannon.

The rest of the Chandler war souvenirs collection is yet to be installed, and the floor was covered with LPs and singles from Solomon Burke to the Beatles.

I was played tracks for the new LP by Jimi, and after one prolonged electrical neurosis, there was a mind-shattering instrumental from the three musicians who comprise the Experience.

As the last decibel faded into infinity, Chris produced an exercise in self-control by observing: "They play so well together, don't they?"

Hendrix, together with drummer Mitch Mitchell, who looks like a young Peter Cook, and bass player Noel Redding, are something new in musical and visual dimensions.

Jimi is a musical perfectionist who does not expect everyone to understand, and believes even those who come only to stand and gawk may eventually catch on.

On a tour which boasts contradictions in musical terms like Engelbert and Jimi, he has come to terms with himself.

"Most will come to see the Walkers," said Jimi. "Those who come to hear Engelbert sing 'Release Me' may not dig me, but that's not tragic.

"We'll play for ourselves—we've done it before, where the audience stands about with their mouths open and you wait ten minutes before they clap."

Originally "Purple Haze," his current NME chart entry, was written about a dream Jimi had that he was able to walk under the sea. Had the lyric been changed to make it more commercial? And was he satisfied as with the original version?

Fighting

"Well . . ." said Jimi, and there was a significant pause, "I'm constantly fighting with myself over this kind of thing—but I'd never release any record I didn't like.

"You've got to gentle people along for a while until they are clued in on the scene.

"I worry about my music—you worry about anything that you've built your whole life around.

"It's good to be able to cut loose occasionally—we were in Holland doing a TV show last week, and the equipment was the best ever.

"They said play as loud as you like, and we were really grooving when this little fairy comes running in and yells, 'Stop! Stop! Stop!—the ceiling in the studio below is falling down.' And it was, too—plaster and all," added Jimi with enthusiasm.

"I'm getting so worried that my hair is falling out in patches," he sighed, tugging at a tuft in a hedge of hair which looks as if it could withstand a clip from a combine harvester.

Trend Setter

Jimi has noted that since he adopted his bush-look that a number of other stars have been following suit—Gary Leeds is the latest bristling addition on the tour. "I just thought it was a groovy style," grinned Jimi. "Now everyone is running around with these damn curls. Most of 'em are perms—but there's nothing wrong with perms—I used to get my hair straightened back on the block."

There has been a hold-up in Jimi's first LP because of the switch to the Track label, and tapes have been damaged in the transferring of studios.

"We're calling it *Are You Experienced?*," affirmed Jimi. I smiled and noted.

"There's nothing wrong with that!" emphasized Jimi.

Full of new ideas, Jimi came up with another on recording techniques.

"Sometimes when I'm playing I make noises in my throat—almost subconsciously," said Jimi. "Jazz men like Erroll Garner do it a lot as they improvise. I'm going to get a little radio mike, hang it around my neck and record them—maybe I'll incorporate some throat sounds on a disc."

Beck Flip

Among Jimi's favourite singles at present is the flip side of the new Jeff Beck record, a number called "Bolero."

"Beautiful guitar," commented Jimi.

We talked of Mitch's new green suede boots—and how Mitch thinks high heels are coming back.

"Y'know what I'd really like to do in the act?" said Mitch, his eyes alight with the gleam of inspiration. "I'd like to pour paraffin all over my drums while the guy from Premier [drum manufacturer] is sitting in the audience.

"Then, at the end of the act, I'd set fire to 'em, and up they go in flames— just to see his face."

That was the night Jimi's guitar accidentally caught fire on stage, and "the fireman rushes in from the pouring rain—very strange!"

—Keith Altham
New Musical Express
1967

It concerned Hendrix to be touring before large audiences for so many dates with clean-cut headliners who had very little stage presence as compared to the Experience, whose love ballads were often sung standing stark still with their eyes closed, and whose audiences expected and were dedicated to that kind of presentation. The Experience would open for the headliners. Jimi said, "The first night of the Walker Brothers' tour was when I started to worry. I knew where it was at when it came to specialist blues scenes, but this was in front of audiences who had come to see the Walker Brothers, Engelbert Humperdinck, and Cat Stevens. All the sweet people follow us on the bill, so we have to hit them and hit them good."

The Jimi Hendrix Experience all had long, wild-looking Afros (Mitch had recently had his permed). Their loud stage clothes, which coincidentally had the same colors as the Flower Power spectrum, their loud music (they played with as many 200-watt Marshall cabinets as they could fit onstage, with all the volume levels at maximum), Jimi's dancing while playing, humping his guitar as he made it moan and flicking his tongue in sync with blues guitar vibrato, and his rolling around onstage while white and pink noise distortion and feedback reigned was further emphasized when he finally got Noel to join him. They drove the often surprised crowds wild.

It made stage life difficult for the headliners, but the audiences had great times and the performers got on quite well offstage, drinking and jamming to-gether. When Humperdinck's guitarist, Mickey Keane, suddenly left the tour,

Noel Redding was hired as his replacement, although he played offstage in the preintermission set that followed the Experience.

The starkness of the Experience's sexuality contrasted with the intense but well-controlled romantic emotions of the other acts, and could have been a big disaster, but it actually turned out to be a big breakthrough. This was the beginning of the Jimi Hendrix Experience's notoriety. The teenage girls would scream their names so loud they challenged the Experience's sound system, which itself was deafeningly loud. It got to the point that the JHE could not leave their dressing room. They had to run from the theaters into waiting cabs to escape the mad crowds of mostly girls who would descend upon them.

In Liverpool they had to run to the nearest pub. But the fans threatened to shatter the glass so they were forced out into the midst of the mob. Redding recalled, "We could only hold on to each other and run, praying for our lives. By the time we found a taxi who would take us, we had been stripped of everything loose, our pockets emptied so we couldn't even pay the cabbie. It was getting too frightening to be fun."

Redding felt that that tour was a turning point for Jimi. "It began to dawn on Jimi that he *could* be personally successful, that his dreams *could* come true, and that boosted his confidence tremendously."

When they returned to London "Purple Haze" was in the Top 10 at number three and Jimi had become the number one male sex symbol of London.

The *Sunday Mirror* dispatched a reporter to get a quote from Jimi about the accusations that he performed suggestive movements in his act. Jimi replied: "I think 'act' is maybe the wrong word. I play and move as I feel. It's no act. Perhaps it's sexy . . . but what music with a big beat isn't?"

I Was Lord Kitchener's Valet, the Carnaby Street clothier: Jimi being feted and fitted at the same time. It is important that he is there. The acceptance of the new London clothing styles by the "pop stars" was immeasurably important to the blitzkrieg Carnaby Street fashion designers who were waging war against the traditional London clothiers. Hip London. And who is more hip than the emergent Jimi Hendrix? He is from the States. He is photographed most often in the most appealing circumstances. Since Carnaby Street is also fighting the recent upsurge of hippie and Flower Power casualness, Jimi Hendrix's endorsement of eighteenth-century-style fop is very important to its survival, and, moreover, an important endorsement of "hip London" style.

The shop is in a flurry over him. Almost all other business is suspended; the entire shop seems to be participating in his fitting. He is of different proportions from the usual Londoner. Broad-shouldered, with extremely long legs and arms, narrow-waisted, with a protruding behind. Yet fit him they will, even if they have to completely resew entire garments. Hands are all over him. Sales-girls kneeling, salesgirls standing on all sides, the gay proprietor shouting to scurrying figures.

He feels like a racing car in a pit at the Indianapolis 500 being overhauled before going back into the race.

An Australian lady pop music writer very politely introduces herself. Her name is Lillian Roxon. She really digs what he is doing.

He sits, now stands, arms up, now akimbo, now at his sides, legs apart, now together, then he sits again. The fine hands of tailors nitting, picking, and mea-suring, smoothing and tugging.

He remembers when he first got to London, his Harlem rags cross-pollinating with his Village fashions. Fake satin shades of Lester's on 125th Street and Paul Sargeant's slim cuts on West Fourth Street. Stovepipe Levi's chi-nos and gaudy-buckled Flagg's half-soled shoes. He found everyone in London so impeccably fitted and pressed next to his rugged store-bought wear. Even the uniforms of the various bands he had played with seemed out of place. And his hair in ragged conk; huge pimples on his face. That was all changing quickly.

His first London stage costume had been a light blue nineteenth-century English cavalry jacket over black trousers. The best they could do at the time. But now he could really get into it, really get into a *look*. Might as well go all the way—the way of Sgt. Pepper.

The mainstay of the London hip underground was blues pundit Alexis Korner, who had discovered the Rolling Stones. Korner's blues band had formed in the late fifties and survived through the successive Dixieland jazz and folk crazes in London in the early 1960s. Alexis Korner had been the first blues band leader to hire Brian Jones and to showcase Mick Jagger. He also hired Jack Bruce and Gin-ger Baker for his band. Jones, Jagger, Clapton, John Mayall, and a few others were the young musicians in London who were really serious in their apprecia-tion and interpretation of the blues.

Korner had been annoyed when Chas Chandler began to publicly challenge Eric Clapton's "top guitarist" status. Chas told Korner that Hendrix was a cat who was going to show Clapton where it's at. Chandler persisted. Korner had hoped that Hendrix and Clapton would come together and just jam, but Chan-dler's remarks had destroyed the vibes for the happening, at least in Korner's mind. But they'd soon have a real meeting.

Chrissie Charles had been John Mayall's old lady. She was a free spirit. As a part of the blues purist circle, she involved herself in activities that promoted the new music of London as culture and sought to elevate blues and jazz and rock 'n' roll in the minds of the English people.

She met Jimi Hendrix while she was involved in putting together a TV special on the English rock scene. They really hit it off together. Even though the special fell through, they continued to see each other. Soon they had an arrangement.

Chrissie had her own flat outside of London. When Jimi wanted to escape from the hassles of his own scene he would give her a call to make sure everything was cool and then split to her place. Things never stopped happening at his own place. He took little holidays out at Chrissie's. The folks in the neighborhood did not know who he was. They went to out-of-the-way places, had picnics, took long walks, just had a good time.

Chrissie wore her soft blonde hair close-cropped. Tiny and perky, with a stunningly developed body, she possessed a winning way about her. She could be small and delicate, or energetic and motherly. Endearing as she was intelligent, she had a real sensitivity to the music Jimi played, and a sorrow for the plight of black people in America. Jimi did not like her to become intellectual, like when she tried to read or psychoanalyze him. He would always make her stop. He preferred her beautiful enthusiastic spirit.

They would always make love in the dark, on Jimi's insistence. This would always remind Chrissie of Jimi's room, with its black sheets and black walls. Jimi was extremely shy about his long arms and big hands and feet. Sometimes he took out a psychological race thing on Chrissie, a representative of the white race. But mostly he was too sweet to be true.

One night Chrissie and Jimi were having a leisurely dinner in an out-of-the-way restaurant. Jimi was being interviewed by a dude from *Beat Instrumental* magazine, but he was young and mellow and they were relaxed and easygoing about the whole thing. Suddenly Eric Clapton walked in. Chrissie beckoned him over. Eric Clapton, retiring and shy, was something of a recluse, and eccentric at that. Only admiration shone in their eyes as Chrissie savored the introductions. Jimi and Eric clasped both hands across the table. Holding each other's hands, they simply drank each other in joyously—hands in hands.

They all talked and got stoned. The man from *Beat Instrumental* was supposed to be interviewing Jimi, but they all got drunk instead. They had a good chat, which lasted into the dawn. The fellow from the magazine kept the tape rolling haphazardly throughout the evening.

JIMI: You can't take away the effect. You may not want to. I may not want to. . . . You might have to stay at a place now, you know, but you don't necessarily have to live there for the rest of your life, though. Do you expect to do this for the rest of your life in the same place? I mean, you know, the same scenery. Walking down the same street to go to the same office. Regardless if you're making a million dollars. Oh okay, I'll say a million pounds. But still this thing—catch yourself for a second—you're walking down the same street for thirty years, man, punching in the same clock. You might even be the whole president of it, you might even come in at eleven o'clock, or maybe even one o'clock in the afternoon. 'Cause you the president of this business that you made up.

VOICE 1: Well, it comes a time when you got to stop.

VOICE 2: When it comes to terms, well then, you got to stop.

JIMI: Well, definitely. Well, I haven't reached that yet, you know. I got a chance to make recordings for £500 a week. Now, who wants to spend one place going to the same studio and do this for the rest of their lives? My life doesn't go like that. If I got a gig doing £500, and I got bored, I'm gonna quit it, man, and go on to something else. But still I'd *try* to get into something, you know.

Quite naturally you have to make bread in order to live. . . . My own opinion of making bread is secondary. . . . You know, I keep saying these things over and over again. I'm just trying to clear the point that making bread is not that much to me. It's only the necessary things I need. Like, I see a pretty scarf, I might want to get. I get it. Like, I see a jacket—you know. . . . As far as going out and saving bread . . . and set-up money . . . setting up a contract and say that when I get to be sixty-five I get the residuals and have so much money coming in . . . you see—it's little things like that. . . .

I want to see the North Pole, I want to see the South Pole. I want to see this mountain so they say they have in the South Pole. I want to see Moscow, you know. I want to witness a slight bit of pain of what I hear about. Which might not even come about. Because it might be all propaganda. No, I don't want to witness it for too long as it was gonna hurt me. Physically, I want to witness. . . .

This is America—the heat you sweat and you be so wet . . . underground . . . I want to witness this for at least about a minute or two.

(laughter)

CLAPTON: . . . to witness it, man, for months and really die, you know—that's the way. I'd die a million times. You know when I was—

JIMI: (interrupting) . . . well over a million times walking through London. Or even around the capital of London, you fall in love a thousand times a day. You know, I look at the girls, you know. But. After I guess about after an hour after we get completely wound up and then you . . .

VOICE 1: (interrupting) Yeah, but you should never . . . because this is an immediate hangup. . . .

JIMI: But there's not—it's not nothing deep, it won't . . . there's no pain in falling in love for a second or even for three minutes. See it takes an average person, a girl, to walk—somebody you might really dig by sight, you know—from a department store to a restaurant and you might wait for a red light. I mean, like three times in less than three minutes . . . So there's no harm in falling in love that one second. For the rest of your life you fall in love. Dig, listen what I say now, you say, boy I want to marry her, I don't even know her number, first time I ever seen her in my whole life—I just seen her on the street. But then after, okay man, you go to the third workout, she's on your mind continuous—so beautiful. Then you're back to your only self again. So you shouldn't say you don't want to go and see my gigs 'cause it's so good to indulge the beauty of a girl you've never seen before. But it's not the last girl. You don't have to let something like that hang you up. Especially by eyesight, because that's nothing but memories.

VOICE 2: What happens when you meet them?

JIMI: Okay, if you meet them or something, that's *social*. I'm not talking about meeting them, I'm talking about *seeing* them. You see a girl in a green coat and purple suede shoes prancing on the corner—not over there [laughter]—well anyway, you know, so you fall in love right there in a *second*. I'd go down on her. I'd do *anything* . . . *But* after fifteen minutes you're down in another part of the street going toward your office that you intend in the first place and then you feel a love for this person—and that's beautiful because at least you still have your own mind. If you have any kind of imaginary mind it's saying that you belong to earth and earth only. That's all you can say. You belong to the people—the people go out to you. That's all you can say. You can't go by commercial values. And then, plus, you have to say to yourself. "Well, I really don't mind this person 'cause I might change my own self. So why change and then gonna be hurting on this, you know?" . . . When it's time for you to die you gotta do it all by yourself. Nobody's going to help you. Sweet words don't help nobody. That's nothing but just audio, you know, nothin' but ears, somethin' that you hear. So you have to do it by yourself, so quite naturally . . . You can owe yourself to somebody. You can give yourself to somebody. You can take yourself away from somebody if you want to. But in a split second—because don't forget—it's *your* life. All complete in your life. You understand? Okay, you have the privilege to get hung up over somebody. But still you yourself have the privilege to get *un*hung up over somebody. As soon as possible, if you want it to be as soon as possible. At any time, man. It's your own life. Freedom is the key word to this whole thing, and people don't understand that because their brains are too complex, they can't understand that. Imagination and creation are the key words to this whole earth. Why do you think you have a great part in your brain as to where you can be creative, as to where you can help your own? Like, why do you think that every single human being on this earth is so different than every other one—in one way or another, you know? There's a purpose behind this. It's because everybody has their own ways, they can do exactly what they want. Marriage, marriage, and other artificial forms that have been passed down generation to generation, say it's bad to make love to a girl or whore, or cross to the other side when you've been going berserk for three years . . . that is nothing but artificial rules. For instance, this is a very elementary for instance, but I say, but anybody would understand, right?

CLAPTON: What do you need for someone to love you because you've got your own bag? What do I need for someone to love me because I got all my own self to keep me going? . . . the people that don't create because you feel that you want to show them and teach them something and they destroy you because they can't understand you.

JIMI: That's right. Because if you get too hung up among them . . . because if your mind is too way out . . . but we take it we're talking about conventional people . . .

CHRISSIE: Am I here? . . .

JIMI: Don't be stupid. You are here (laughter).

(Chrissie talks over the conversation and all voices mix temporarily.)

JIMI: Anyway, that's the voice of Christine. Lovely Christine.

(Here the tape is confused—switching on and off amid banter and laughter of Jimi, Chrissie, and the others.)

JIMI: She is so groovy. Some girls can be so sweet. . . .

VOICE 2: Is that the girl who always answers the bell at your flat?

JIMI: That's Chas's girlfriend. She's very pretty. I mean pretty in the mind.

VOICE 2: She always sounds as if she's just got out of bed. Every time she answers the phone.

JIMI: Yeah, she's Swedish. She has this accent—an accent slightly . . .

VOICE 2: Yeah, I know. It didn't distract me at all.

JIMI: . . . I find out—even when I get sober I find out that I tell more of the truth on my own self when I am like this than when I'm sober. Music and life—the flow—goes together so closely, it's sort of like a parallel that is going like this [apparently illustrating the point to everybody] very roughly, but it's still such a parallel.

VOICE 2: But it fascinates me that you would get through life without even beginning to play or understand music. . . .

JIMI: But the reason is that they may not know. You see, music is a form of life itself and these people don't know. Like some people could tell you, "I don't know nothing about music." Okay, they don't know nothing about music, but still music enters their life some kind of way. In some ways they don't even know. As where they feel they're acting because of some kind of artificial means. But relaxation and music plays such an important part in their lives. They say, "Oh yeah, we remember the classics." They say it as if classics are not with us—they consider it as something else. But music is nobody's soul. Something from somebody's real heart. You know, that they could really express by notes. Right now people be expressing music by long hair, you know? Where you get a lot—like this song called "One Mile Long," for instance. There's different ways. Music is the whole life. People don't know it, but they . . . in music even if they work in a bank. Music, man, it means so many things. It doesn't mean necessarily physical notes that you hear by ear. It could be notes that you hear by feeling or thought or by imagination or even by emotions. You know, that's all there is.

VOICE 2: That's all there is. Is that all there is to you?

JIMI: Nothing but music . . . life . . . that's all.

VOICE 1: That's great.

CLAPTON: I am going to be a millionaire. I plan to buy myself huge cars. It sort of brings you down terribly. At the same time I have a kind of idea that money is kinda necessary.

JIMI: Yeah. Quite naturally it's going to be kinda necessary to do these things. But you know basic . . . money—you base money around what you want to do, right? It's a thing—not like saying, by the time I get to be forty-two and I have three and a half months for my birthday . . . by the time I get to forty-two I plan to have a million pounds in the bank. It isn't like that with me. I don't think—it might not be like that with you, you know. Instead of saying I want a million pounds like that, I say, by the time I get to forty-two no telling what happens but I hope I can still remember it: how I'm living now and what I do before and between now and forty-two, you know. It's a thing like that. Money, wow! Money is commercial. Human beings make money. I almost hate human beings as a certain thing that's making these beautiful ideas and commercial values like money, like real estate, and like this and that, this and this—the same old stuff. You see, human beings are so screwed. They are the most complicated animals on the earth and probably the ones who are ruling the earth. Excuse me for hanging on this. . . . Just in case anybody can hear the guitar in the background, that's me playing . . . starving . . . (laughing), anyway getting right back, you can let money rule, you have to rule money the way you want to use it.

VOICE 1: . . . two cats who say that their talent is making money and that's what they want to do, they want to make money.

JIMI: Yeah, okay, I'll tell you what. I want to make the money as where I can live when I get bald, you know—when all these little curls fall out and the teasing and the hair spray and what they call all those things I do with my hair—when all this shit falls out I want to get that money, get that money to hold me together to do what I want to do in *life*. Not my life toward money. Listen, knowing that you can get it on with a girl and really get it on with a girl—so much of a contrast, so different, man. Like wooing with, hee-hee, you can probably figure out . . . might be so beautiful there, you know.

CLAPTON: But what really hangs me up is—isn't the girl because, I mean, she's a great girl, she's having a good time, and as far as my concern, that's really great. What hangs me up is my attitude—I mean look at me . . . she doesn't even sort of . . . but she says hello . . . but she's got no craft. Except attention gets fantastic, life feels like an extraordinary game of cards, that strangers can be lovers but friends are hardly friends at all . . .

JIMI: (interrupting) Oh beautiful!

CLAPTON: (continuing) . . . and it's sort of strange you know, and this is sort of entirely something I can't understand. And this is what hangs me up, not knowing, not understanding, you know.

JIMI: Okay. Like this girl I know named Christine, like you know, I know this girl named Christine, and she's so beautiful, her mind is so together. But see, I don't even want to get caught up to her actually, you know. It's because of the thing that, I don't know what it is, it might be a phase in my life, it might be something else . . . it's not that I'm hoggish, but I want to have this freedom feeling regardless of what comes to me good or bad, you know. And she's very, very sweet, you know. Like we can be going together—going together is so beautiful. But dig, there are some things I couldn't understand about her, but I couldn't *explain*. Like . . . I want to be with her *all* the time, possibly. I want her and I go to the show. And different things. Just do different things. I like to take her anywhere I go like South America, Canada—regardless, America . . . wherever it is. But man, I might get stoned completely out my mind, you know [laughter]. Completely. And then also I might go in this funny other bag that she might not understand. She might understand it, but I can suss it through that she might not. And if she . . . All human beings are selfish to a certain extent . . . to be . . . you know . . . just . . . up and keep talking about being free and stuff. And she just doesn't understand this . . . it might even last for three minutes, it might last for five. . . .

(pause in conversation)

CLAPTON: . . . One day you gonna wake up . . . and it's all . . . gonna be gone. Because this was . . . the way I felt at the time, and I changed my life anyway . . . and she really couldn't understand. . . . She says, "Please darling, please say good-bye before you go."

JIMI: Aw . . . do this and do that.

CLAPTON: You wake up early, you know. . . . Yeah, people don't understand that you want to be free. And the thing is, you see, what is unfair about this is, I said it to her at the beginning and it hung her up. At the end she left me and it destroyed me. Because I had become her and she had become me . . .

JIMI: Beautiful, beautiful . . . oh God, that happens to me so much. Like, okay, first of all, when you—when you know what it really is? It's a thing like when you know you can have somebody—just being very, very frank—you can be, you can like a person, but that person, like when they're around, you say, "Aw well, I dig this girl, and all this. But dig this sitting at the bar, or dig this sitting about three feet away from the bandstand—outta sight." *But* deep down inside—this doesn't come out then—but deep down inside you can say, "Yeah, well, I'm digging this other girl, but she's digging me, too, you know. So you know, let me go on and, you know, cop this, what's sitting at the bar or three feet from the stage." And then quite naturally the bitch is gonna call me anyway, you know, so I say, "Well, you know, baby, it's a thing like so such" . . . you could really love somebody . . . but you still might mess around, you know, and you might . . .

VOICE 2: Aren't you caught, man, by the fact that you're Jimi Hendrix? You're the guy that magazines are going to talk about. And say—

JIMI: (interrupting) I don't know anything about that.

VOICE 2: (continuing) . . . but listen, man, this makes sense. Because, like, re-member this group called the Mersey Beat [sic] or something. They got com-pletely blown—the whole scene just fell apart—because one day they said, "Well, listen, man, you know, we see these chicks and we think, 'Great!'" So now it's great and tomorrow is no good. Because this is the way *everybody* feels. I mean it's just the way we all go. We like a girl one night and you don't like her the next—and the girls are the same. But suddenly these guys were caught by the fact that they were in the public eye . . . this is what frightens me . . . I don't want to be friends. . . . (tape skips suddenly)

CLAPTON: But I think she's really nice because she digs my work. . . . I had her in my flat for three hours and she didn't sort of get bugged at all. Now, the point is that suddenly you can change your chick every day, man. Because I might be a writer or a photographer and suddenly you're stuck by public image. This destroys me, you know, because I've got a chance as a . . . to become fa-mous. I don't want to become famous because then I'm caught by my public image. When I become famous—when I become famous I'm going to stop photographs—I'm going to become an unrecognizable character.

JIMI: That's right. Just like you might meet beautiful girls—just might be "Miss Right" and go off into something so completely. But you might meet a beauti-ful girl because of your name, you know. Somebody says, "Well, listen, I'm your manager, you know, I'm so-and-so, and I want you to meet this *model* who just came in from Paris. And she's beautiful. I want you to meet her." So you meet this model. And then that night you all might—you know, just being frank—you all might go to bed that night, you know. And she's *beautiful*. But there's a thing like, just like . . . being frank again—but mine might not look as . . . I mean, she might look so beautiful, more than this girl you might really dig. But still deep down inside you like this girl but still you gotta be around, you know . . . it's a thing like, oh God! . . . understand the fact that you might still love somebody deep down inside but still physically at such an elementary stage as you might "screw" somebody else, you know. But still deep down inside you have this deeper feeling for a person that you might've . . .

CLAPTON: I know I can screw anybody but it doesn't change . . . (he is interrupted by several voices, all indistinguishable)

JIMI: That's right. Aw, if girls could understand this. Listen, I'm'a tell you something, man. Girls really could understand this.

(This next remark by Clapton sparks a highly spirited conversation and the tape is riddled with indistinguishable voices and remarks.)

CLAPTON: No, it's not—it's what they say—if girls could understand it . . . if it's this, man. You are a man . . . so listen. I dig this girl. I think she's the greatest thing that ever happened to me and I'll always, you know, be awed by her . . . but I can go out and screw a thousand other girls and think, "I still dig Chrissie." But what happens when Christine gets up and screws another thousand blokes plus . . . (CHAOS!)

ALL TOGETHER: That's right! Then it gets really! Owww man!

JIMI: That's right, men are . . .

CLAPTON: They've got phrases like, "It's a man's prerogative" . . . I think men . . . the whole world makes me laugh right now . . . 'cause I mean, my concerts are . . .

(confusion settles somewhat)

CHRISSIE: Leave a seat for me. . . .

CLAPTON: Yeah, well, you know, baby, any time you want to come along and have a look, you know. Believe me, they're all there to look at. . . .

(repeated gaps in the tape during the following remarks by Jimi)

JIMI: . . . most [of] the time if it's somebody I really like I don't want to hurt them no kinda way. Regardless if you do it to a trip you know that somebody's liking you—really truly like you, you know that they still gonna be hurt regardless . . . of how . . . you know (large gap) . . . and don't take over forty—hey Christine, Christine, don't take over forty-five seconds, please huh . . . I don't want to be another beautiful gaiety image, you know, beautiful . . . I was sayin' to a fourteen-year-old do exactly what you want, regardless, because this is your own generation, man, and if you're not going to live this generation the way you want to you have no other ones to live, you know . . . (skips in tape) . . . see 'cause they just get in a commercial bag . . . they let it interfere with their own emotions . . . that's right, and you know what? I might make, I'll say in American terms, three dollars that year and I might not even spend it all. I don't think about, you know, the future because . . . money doesn't mean that much. If I was very gold-conscious—gold money . . . I make my little thirty dollars. . . .

VOICE 1: Somehow . . . (laugh)

JIMI: . . . and I make thirty dollars more and put it away in the bank. After about eighty-nine weeks I have a little nut. . . . (aside) That's the sun coming up? . . . But I don't look at that . . .

CLAPTON: I wish I could make more money . . .

JIMI: Aw, man . . .

VOICE 1: Like I borrowed . . . tonight, and I got five bob left. One round of drinks for all my friends . . .

JIMI: I wish I could go out on a gig for twenty thousand dollars a week, you know, I mean, not a week but I mean twenty thousand dollars a night. Anybody wishes for more money. But deep down inside . . . you make good money. And if you do, you know, mess around and make that much money that's because of yourself. *And* you don't have to give it away to nobody if you don't want to. See, there are so many contradictives. . . .

CLAPTON: I only need . . . I don't want to make money because—because of what I can buy for myself. I want to make money so I can buy things for everybody else.

JIMI: Right! That's how come I said do . . . (skips in tape) . . . make love to him, yeah. There you go making love to fairies with plastic names . . . I'm so happy now I kissed Eric Clapton, I kissed him. . . . (laughter) . . . I kissed the fairest soul brother of England. . . .

CLAPTON: Ha ha.

(tape skips)

JIMI: . . . and he comes back telling me things, like, saying, like . . . But *dig,* when peoples. . . . you go there and you try . . .

VOICE 2: If you don't like it, man, why should I . . . ?

JIMI: No no no, it's like this. I'll tell you the way my interpretation is, like, I ain't saying it exactly in the same words . . . but you know how I interpret it? . . . Right? So they just said, well, dig this cat, you know, he goes over there and the little teenybops with the little twinkling red skirts on, you know, and funny little hairdos they say that he's, you know, that they're playing too loud. But so what—they're not digging what he's playing loud, you know . . . but they gonna dig it, man. It's a thing like, oh God, you know . . . things that are so heavy are happening around me. . . .

VOICE 2: What you're going through now might, you know, might be perhaps you felt without knowing it, just be a phase, you know, I mean your set of values now may not exist in any way in the next two years. They might change so completely. . . .

JIMI: They changed a lot in the last two months. . . .

VOICE 2: At the same time don't you never stop and think about what's gonna happen at the time when you're forty-five?

CLAPTON: Yeah, of course not.

JIMI: . . . Someday he's gonna get hung up about it, scared that by the time he gets to be forty-five he might not have no money in the bank. . . .

(laughter, everyone talks)

CLAPTON: What it makes me think about . . . it's an incredible thing, it's a thing, it's a thing like nothing else, you know, like . . .

VOICE 2: . . . But it doesn't last. . . .

CLAPTON: No, of course not, and then when it starts lasting your values will be different, then you can work out what you're going to do then. But I mean it's a sick thing to be a young guy worrying about what you're going to be like when you're an old guy. . . .

VOICE 1: You're right. . . .

CLAPTON: Because sooner or later you're just going to say to yourself—right?— "I'm not young anymore" and you'll say that simply because you don't think that you were done when you were young. Then you're gonna set up some values . . . and you'll be an old man . . . and all you're going to do, man, is croak. . . .

VOICE 2: So Jimi, you just grow a new set of plastic wings. . . .

CLAPTON: That's what destroys me—how to put on real wings now. Because I don't like flying with plastic wings . . .

JIMI: You don't want to keep on doing this, right? But you might have to do a certain extent *until* you go out feeling. . . . Let's say, okay, you only hung up about memories, but the things you're doing now, that's the only way you can live is for now . . . like, if you feel like savin' up fifty quid . . . and you get paid seventy-five, well, you put [it] in the bank, you know. By the time you get an old man, just like you said, man, your life changes and you might get different ideas. But you start *then*, man.

CLAPTON: You're terribly worried about something you should never think about and that's growing old, what you going to do. . . .

JIMI: Money to me is like if you're lost in the woods, and you have to go use the restroom, right? There's no restroom for a hundred miles but there are leaves so what you do is just bend over and, you know, make sure you don't fall on your, you know, and then you just use the leaves. You *have* to use the leaves if you don't have no tissue or whatever it is. And that's exactly what money is for me—something I might have to use. I might spend about thirty bob—I mean forty bob, uh, thirty . . .

VOICE 1: Quid.

JIMI: Quid. Yeah, thirty quid tonight, you know, just getting stoned, just, you know . . . but it's a . . . you don't live up . . . Ohhh shhh . . . you know how it's so hard to explain, you know, man, I have no feel for money whatsoever except what things I need, things that I want. . . .

VOICE 1: Do you have any plans for the future? You're not going to go on making this bread forever. . . .

JIMI: Oh well, quite naturally . . . I'll be very surprised . . . plus I'll be happy if it lasts this winter, you know. I'll be so happy if it does . . . until this dies down, you know. And then get maybe, try my best to get real estate and maybe get a few clubs and manage a few groups that have creative ideas and minds. And not plastic wings . . . I'm gonna be such a big fat juicy bore. A big monotonous swine that they won't even be able to understand the second part. The first part is just saying the good things about marriage or maybe the usual things about marriage or maybe the usual things. And the second part of the record tells about the parts of marriage which I've seen. I just see both sides but I just really want to witness the first side. 'Cause I know . . . you know I'm not really gonna hurt anybody right at this particular state, you know, 'cause my mind is not together right now. So quite naturally it's gonna come out in record—it's gonna come out about all opinions. You're the writer, you can't write about—like if you made a record you couldn't say nothing about another person's opinions because you don't know their opinions really deep down inside—they might lie to you.

VOICE: Yeah . . .

JIMI: All I'm doing in that two minutes is saying my own exact opinions of a marriage, you know. Saying that I'm immature about—you know, something like that—not necessarily immature, maybe in their eyes.

VOICE 1: You ever write about . . . money and things like that?

JIMI: I have the same attitude. I don't like for money to tie me down no kinda way, you know. I don't like anything to tie me down. They always ask . . . you know, this is the longest I've ever lived in any one place in five or six years—in

England. For six months, you know. And they always ask, "Well, why do you like to move on a lot?" You know—'cause I don't like nothing to tie me down. I don't like to depend on anything actually. But you have to sometimes. You know this. Like I have to, you know. But still, you can't take away the fact . . .

(end of tape)

Just Wild
(Parents *and* Fans That Is)
About Jimi

You might think that Jimi Hendrix would appear menacingly swinging from tree-tops, brandishing a spear, and yelling blood-curdling cries of "Aargh!"

For Jimi, who makes Mick Jagger look as respectable as Edward Heath and as genial as David Frost, could pass for a hottentot on the rampage; looks as if his foot-long hair has been petrified by a thousand shock waves, and is given to playing the guitar with his teeth.

When the Jimi Hendrix Experience made its first appearance in Britain a few months ago, he was immediately dubbed "the Wild Man of Borneo," and the group was referred to as "an unfortunate experience."

And yet—his first record, "Hey Joe," went straight into the Top 10; his second disc, "Purple Haze," is currently number six, and this week his new disc, "The Wind Cries Mary" (Track), should provide him with two records simultaneously in the Top 10.

Moan

Later this month, the wild sounds from his first LP, *Are You Experienced?* should have parents moaning for the quieter days of the Rolling Stones.

The Jimi Hendrix Experience has, it seems, filled a very necessary gap in becoming the Group They Love to Hate.

Mums and dads started to like the top pop names, but they are almost guaranteed not to dig Mr. Hendrix.

Yet Jimi Hendrix is no snarling jungle primitive.

Though the gold-braided military jacket over the black satin shirt could be taken as incongruous, Jimi off-stage behaves with a quiet polite charm that's almost olde worlde.

He stands up when you enter a room, lights all your cigarettes, and says: "Do go on," if he thinks he might be interrupting you.

That "ugly" image, however, doesn't worry him in the slightest.

And he says: "Some of the fans think I'm cuddly, and as long as people buy my records I'll be happy."

He could be laughing all the way to the bank.

—Anne Nightingale
Sunday Mirror
May 9, 1967

Jimi went through Norway in the late spring of 1967 to check out a show entitled *Black New World,* which was touring Scandinavia at the time. Brian Epstein was the silent partner in the affair with Ellis Haizlip, a black producer from the States.

Jimi had not spent any time at all with Epstein, manager and mastermind of the Beatles phenomenon, in London and now he was able to hang out a bit. Epstein was quite different. With Ellis and the cast of Langston Hughes's *Gospel Show* and several others, they were in merry showbiz spirit and laughed and talked in a large dressing room.

Ellis told Jimi, much to Epstein's embarrassment, that Brian had always helped him with black productions in Europe, often as a silent partner, although they usually went fifty-fifty on cost. Brian was enjoying himself away from London and the crush of fame caused by his miraculous management of the Beatles. Here he was only coproducer of plays performed by black Americans. It was the theater, not rock 'n' roll. Brian Epstein had tried to act before, and he still enjoyed the long-term theater people, who probably worked just as hard as the Beatles but would probably never enjoy the great financial rewards that many rock 'n' roll stars did. Yet they had irrepressible spirit, bursting into gospel songs a cappella as they laughed and talked and drank.

One particularly friendly singer was a sister named Madeline Bell. She had a terrific voice matched by dark brown, smooth skin and very large sensuous lips. She was asking Jimi about living in London because she thought she might want to stay in Europe after the tour was over.

Brian was loose and happy in his surroundings. He seemed delighted to meet Jimi in these circumstances, relieved to be free of the straight-white-man masquerade he was forced to play in London.

The Great Britain release of the JHE's first album, *Are You Experienced?*, came in on the charts of June 3 at number five. Side one is the top-heavy side, featuring all the hitherto concealed genius of Jimi's guitar.

It opens with a tiny signal streaking across the horizon, peaking in freaky three-part treble harmony. A commanding abyss mode explodes before your eyes, billowing outward the words "Foxy Lady," Jimi's atonal chord gracing the top end of the figure. The boogie nation's pickup-song anthem; lady thrill song trilling, whispering, "foxy foxy" in a perfumed ear. Treble ecstatic. Slick mixed-down R&B rhythm scratching licks against the consciousness.

"You know—you're a cute little—heartbreaker . . ."

In the same breath he goes right on singing that he knows just by looking at her that her lovemaking will yield much sweetness. He punctuates the end of each line whispering dramatically, excitedly, *foxy, foxy.*

He becomes very direct and to the point as the ensemble action picks up from the meditative stagger into almost double-time. He wants to take her home, and there's nothing he will do that she will fear. But "You've got to mine," and he means all his, and then he has an involuntary exclamation in order to expel some of the shared excitement: Whew! . . . "Foxy la—dy."

He tells the backstory. He sees her at the club where everyone goes. She is so fine she makes him want to scream. He cannot stand it. He has to have her. Foxy lady, now!

"Here I come."

He solos. His elongated R&B rhythm licks stagger a counterbeat against the ecstatic sonic soprano trills this encounter will bring.

Jimi's sounds of love on the tag out, yeah, foxy yeah, yeee—aaahhh.

"Coming to get you."

Coming aw yeah, yeah.

The atonal chord staggering the rhythm and keeping funk in the straight jam, the peal comes twinkling into the coda, streaking off in an extended and developed report, and then back to the standard funk as the phased guitar wings across the sky. Hendrix's guitar has an amazing fluidity—an actual human sound of high spirituality, of high evolvement.

"Manic Depression"—with Jimi playing bass also—is built off of a massive bass drone, implying the accompanying note of the drone in atonal syncopated figures. He dubs with the bass especially during the emphasized breaks.

His opening vocal is straightforward and studied: Manic depression—a serious psychological state—he intones that this state is touching his soul. The focal point is his trying to get over, be a star, but he is unsure, he does not really know how to get there. This may be a plea theme, in the classic R&B tradition.

A plea, a hymn to his music, perhaps its origins in his emotional makeup, appealing to the spirits that control and favor the music that his emotions are wrapped around: his guitar, the medium. *Feelings, sweet feelings, drop from my fingers, Fenders, Fenders . . .*

Manic depression, the emotion that is a foundation of his music has captured his soul. Sweet music sometimes merges with a woman, but they come and go. The going stressing his emotions and depriving him of the love that was established —if only for a short time. But he has to keep on going, sweet music driving him toward the next encounter.

Tenor voices harmonize upward into the break where the guitar takes over, bucking, tossing, and tumbling. The drum kit churns. It does not keep linear time, but circular; it accents as if by random theory Jimi's rap.

> *I wish I could*
> *caress, caress*
> *a kiss, a kiss*

An extended jam ensues with Mitch keeping up an incredible pace with his circular drum rhythms straight out of Elvin Jones playing behind a hot Contrane. Only this is Jimi on public saxophone and he is kicking the long-playing recording parameters into the wild blue stratosphere.

Jimi dubbing octaves with the bass, that then takes off and departs even lower. Dubbing captivating figures that circle and resolve continuously. The tag is badass stop-time with Jimi's electric stallion neighing against the basso terrain.

"Third Stone from the Sun" opens with Noel's bass creating a tranquil and hypnotic two-note drone, while Mitch's drums tap along in the same moderate 4/4 time. Jimi strokes lightly on his guitar as background for a voice that drones off-speed at 16 rpms, as if from outer space. Sped up to 78 rpms the matter-of-fact, vérité voices of starship commanders encounter the third planet from the sun, earth, and decide to check it out.

The bass drops an octave creating a lovely surprise, then takes a step up to the first bridge, where the drums take over the time, giving the effect of a speeding up of tempo. Jimi plays the lead figure in fifths against the bass, giving the sound an Eastern effect. They come to a second bridge, where Mitch's drums move the pace even quicker, although the bass is still droning a variation of the same two-note figure and pace. Mitch's drums are mixed back down into the ensemble sound where Jimi is playing some pretty accompaniment that is as meditative as the bass is hypnotic. Here the sounds of the heavens opening up comes out in full force and they all are playing softly against its effect. They take a long break and the sound becomes airy, flying wind sounds against which Jimi very tastefully blends a subtle fuzz distortion within the total sound. Then he hits a warning midrange treble emergency signal that pulsates slowly. He speaks his lines against the hypnotic march.

Jimi, a brother from another planet, another universe, loves the look of this third stone from the sun. Will they allow him entry? He marvels at the lovely grasses of green that contrast so beautifully "with your majestic silken scenes." He finds the mountains equally intriguing: "May I land my kinky machine?"

The mellow bass line continues with the time as the drums dictate the pace.

Painting whoozy sound against the endless terrain, Jimi adds touches of distorting fuzz and airy treble tremolos:

Jimi hits the lead theme again, elongating the notes over several bars. Then free squawk crescendo taxiing out to space, the guitar splinters raw fire and static—an electrical monster in free rein. Then silence except for a flat fuzz signal that flows into a space-tracking sound that fades out slowly.

On "Love or Confusion" the set-up hook chord delineates the entire song. The strange harmony between the long sustained sitarlike chord and the overdriving Fuzz Face and Crybaby combination creates a tremolo that double-times against the 4/4 time, thus belonging to both the rhythm and the harmony. Jimi makes his guitar do a Sagittarian bow thrust, like the sound heard in cartoons when the Road Runner takes off. Mitch beats out a snare-in-the-round intro. In a fast 4/4 the funky hambone bass lines are joined by Jimi's skipping rhythm work. The bass evokes cavernous underground insurgency in echo. Jimi gets an exotic sitar sound on one guitar track and a harmonizing sustain tremolo on another. The major chord drone dips into a lovely minor mode as he shouts out: "Is that the stars in the sky—or is it raining far from now?"

A very interesting image variation on the theory of light sources from distant suns. And he contrasts the celestial with the love he feels for a woman.

The Fuzz Face/Crybaby combination is jacked to the upper registers where the loony distorted Crybaby peal takes over. Driving to a peak of oscillating intensity, it begins to solo as Jimi shouts, his voice integrated into the sound on an equal par with the rest of the instruments: "Is it love, baby, or is it a, just confusion? . . ." The hambone figures on the bass are counterpointed against Jimi's skipping rhythm figures. Keyed to rhythm against sound, rather than melody against note, Jimi's rap becomes even more powerful mixed down within the sound. The combination of guitars playing rhythm against the long drone chord and the loony wailing distress signal of the Fuzz Face/Crybaby are fantastic. The treble peaked overdriving tremolo is both a note of the bizarre harmony and an element of the 4/4 rhythm, vibrating from double time to quadruple time. Jimi peaks it into a rapturous solo. The clave chord kicks off the guitar battery again. Sounding like the rhythms of several African congas, the electronic metallic overdriving oscillating Stratocaster keeps the rhythm throb close to the pulsations of a red emergency light. With the effortless power and speed of a bird singing naturally, it becomes a totally new sound terrain. At the bridge the beat turns over on itself, giving a backward effect, moving into a higher key. Slicing, gargantuan fuzzy treble figure, Jimi's solo is driven by bottom fuzz overtones to even greater heights. So sharp, the solo seems to be on the sheer edge of flame. Gliss-sliding and double-picking, he ranges between harmonica effects and synthesizer sounds. After the bridge the caravan takes off again in its time-suspended journey. The oscillating overdrive report goes into white noise that holds the harmony just as well. Jimi begins to concentrate on the rhythm as the song goes into short breaks—only to speed off again. The coda is in several segments, all almost identical. Going beyond a normal 4/4 coda, it pushes forward after every break to the point where you are continuously surprised when it starts up again. It stops in full Fuzz Face chaos.

In "Are You Experienced?" Jimi goes right to the ladies, indicating that if they can understand him enough to really be with him then they will experience supernatural phenomena such as watching the rising sun "from the bottom of the sea." But then he goes back to the title, main question: "Are you experienced?" Was there a time in the past when she was experienced? Because he is, he can deal with the supernatural. He acknowledges the difficulties of accepting other realities, of leaving a familiar world, but, he reasons, that in a small-minded world there is nothing to prove to anyone.

The bell knell keeps time like a tuned cowbell clave throughout. The drums shuffle and bop, running up in full flurry and then back down again. The off-time bass line staggers a third beat. Then Jimi solos against the drums that are phased and recorded backward on tape. The drums go forward as the lyric picks up again.

He sings of distant violins and trumpets, heavenly musical instruments that call their names. He urges her to hold his hand and not be afraid; the experience he speaks of is not of drugs, but of the bounty that comes from love. "Not necessarily stoned, but beautiful."

The backward guitar phased sound is elongated, otherworldly, suspending time, treble fuzz going to the peak ping of the harmonic. The clave knell fades down, then swells up again and out.

In "Red House" he spins an old twelve-bar blues tale he wrote years ago to tell the ladies that if they don't come through he knows "their sisters will." "Red House" was also a direct feed to the blues purists (Jagger, Jones, Clapton, Page, and Mayall) who always had traditional blues pieces in their albums. In such a predictable form as the twelve-bar blues there is nothing to do but play—virtuosity is needed to bring something new to the standard.

> There's a red house over yonder
> Yeah, that's where my baby stays

"Red House" is also sensual and fiery love. Jimi is determined to enjoy the sensual life, the "birds" of London notwithstanding.

"I Don't Live Today" pans distances with machine-chugging vibratos that come back again embellished sharper. "Remember" is a ballad, and "May This

Be Love" is as close to corn as possible for Jimi. Obviously a song for teenage girls, but relaxed and pretty, it fills out the JHE's first album.

And in the last song of the album, the title song, "Are You Experienced?," Jimi intones to all in a musk-laden sensual voice, " . . . I am."

By midsummer the Beatles' *Sgt. Pepper's Lonely Hearts Club Band* and the JHE's *Are You Experienced?* were the number one and number two best-selling LPs on the English charts.

After the Walker Brothers' farewell tour, the JHE played two BBC-TV *Top of the Pops* shows before departing on a proper tour of Europe, seventeen gigs in fifteen days. Brian Epstein's company, NEMS, had become the booking agency for the JHE. He wanted them back at the Saville Theatre where they had done so well in early May. He was allowing them to rehearse there, and also taking an active role in their stage presentation.

Word about the Monterey Pop Festival was coming through the grapevine. It would be a major festival. Paul McCartney had suggested to John and Michelle Phillips, principal organizers of the festival, that they include the Jimi Hendrix Experience, who were burning up Europe. They quickly agreed.

The JHE's June 4 gig at the Saville Theatre became a sendoff of sorts for the Experience. Procol Harum, Denny Laine's Electric String Band, and the Chiffons were the opening acts. Epstein invited them to a dinner party afterward at his home.

Because they all knew Hendrix would indeed burn a guitar at the gig—it was almost a part of the act by now—the authorities had to be alerted. So a fireman, a fire blanket, and a fire extinguisher were in the wings of the stage as the sold-out crowd filed in. Hundreds were turned away. A veritable who's who of the English music scene was in the audience, from the Beatles on down.

The Experience shocked everyone by beginning their set playing "Sgt. Pepper's Lonely Hearts Club Band." Jimi growled out the lyrics as his guitar neighed the peaks in his signature treble freaks.

Later Paul McCartney greeted them backstage, truly moved by the tribute the JHE had given the Beatles.

At the afterparty, McCartney opened the door and ushered the JHE into Epstein's lavish and hip home. Everyone was there for the dinner to celebrate the Jimi Hendrix Experience.

People related differently to Jimi once his act broke big and "Hey Joe" and "Purple Haze" were on the charts. And once the JHE's LP hit the Top 10 all bets were off. All the other stars were happy to see him. Another star in the sky, he increased the magnitude, the brilliance, of the entire constellation. And he gave each and all of the English bands an authenticity just by his being on the scene and grooving with them. He was of the blues and for the blues. He was a hip stateside black man whom, all of a sudden, everybody wanted to know, to be near to, to say important things to. He was invited to the best parties. And now Brian Epstein was throwing a party for the Jimi Hendrix Experience.

It amazed him to hear Peter Townshend talk about autodestruct, pop art, and decibel levels of music, from the point of view of an avant-garde artist, just like Andy Warhol and John Cage and Ed Sanders. Townshend would say, "We concentrate on the concepts of dynamics and the use of crescendo," and then top it all off by saying, "Our music is cybernetic." Townshend would get so intense he would look cross-eyed.

Eric Clapton, Townshend's opposite, other side, and running buddy, would listen intently, uttering demure sounds of awe. After Jimi and he had jammed together Clapton had felt his own music changing: "My attitude toward music changed. He influenced me an incredible amount." Clapton would always quietly swing the conversation around to the blues, the old blues.

Jimi would tell them about playing the chitlin circuit with Little Richard and Solomon Burke, about his day in Chicago at Chess Records with Willie Dixon and Muddy Waters, and about the new younger cats under them like Little Walter, Buddy Guy, and Junior Wells. And then about some obscure bluesmen like Billy Butler and Robert Jr. Lockwood. When he spoke about Charlie Patton, Son House, Mississippi John Hurt, Robert Johnson, and Elmore James, they, especially the blues purists, knew what he was talking about. But they puzzled over the obscure guys Hendrix mentioned who did not front their own group, lead sessions, and put out albums under their own names. Billy Butler and Robert Jr. Lockwood were accompanying guitarists, Jimi would explain, of the highest development. They would add touches and colors that expanded the melody and at the same time would feed vocalists notes that excited their imaginations. But most importantly, to Jimi, they could play rhythm. The rhythm of the guitar, Jimi felt, was the key to the blues, jazz, and rock.

Clapton could never seem to understand what Hendrix was getting at when he would stress rhythm accompaniment. But the guitar had been a strict rhythm instrument until Charlie Christian and Django Reinhardt showed up on the scene in different parts of the world in the late 1930s and early 1940s. Now the guitar had evolved, becoming more and more a widely accepted solo instrument. Hendrix felt that Clapton was too intellectual about it, and forged his own early classical background on the subject by insisting the guitar was now an instrument of the virtuoso, just like in classical music. Jimi tried to get across the message that the funk, the feel, and the boogie of the blues came from a subtle rhythmic combination in which the guitar played an essential role but never got the credit, especially in live performances on the chitlin circuit, where the guitar put the electric fire crackling over the bass and drums, creating the dynamic that made folks want to dance and shout and work it all out.

Clapton and Hendrix, both rather shy, would never follow their disagreement through, but it always hung in the air when they met. But their points of view always excited others.

Mick Jagger, with his American teenager/English street urchin rap, would talk about his anticipation, before going to America for the first time, of seeing Muddy Waters and Bo Diddley and Chuck Berry, his idols, as stars in their own land. Only he found out that they were scarcely known to the American masses, who usually had first heard these blues people's music through groups like the Rolling Stones. Even the Beatles had had the same experience. It was an unspoken part of English rock and the blues pundits to give back to the international music world the forgotten blues and rock of the old black bluesmen.

Chas Chandler would talk about his meeting with John Lee Hooker in the States. In a way, Chas's mention of Hooker underscored Jimi's point that rhythm and feel were, in many ways, more important than brilliant virtuoso soloings. John Lee Hooker hardly played any guitar at all. But his raunchy rhythm licks, though they often sounded the same, made you get up off your feet and get to the feeling.

Elmore James had only about three solos that he used on all his recorded material. But the excitement he was able to generate with bottleneck licks in rhythm set up the audiences for his mind-boggling bottleneck flurries during his solos. People would start to shout, jump up and down, and even throw money at him.

As soon as Paul McCartney opened his mouth, everyone looked his way, even if he was trying to be unobtrusively one of the gang. He had only wanted to tell Jimi about this TV special they were working on. The Beatles were going to rent a bus and ride around the countryside playing some new songs and visiting places and seeing things they thought were way-out. Would Jimi be interested in being a part of it? Paul was so cute and polite, all Jimi could say was, "Sure. Yeah." They would talk more about it later.

In the reverent hush following Paul's rap, Marianne Faithfull got a chance to talk about the new film she was working on. It was not a big-time London studio job, but an avant-garde venture with Kenneth Anger, an American underground filmmaker. Anger was also an Aleister Crowley occult magic scholar who had come to London to be closer to his studies. He is the author of the notorious (by word of mouth) *Hollywood Babylon,* a stunning inside look at the film capital's biggest stars. His film was about demon possession and soul transmutation using many of the rituals culled from Crowley's occult writings.

Brian Jones came up, grinning like an imbecile, floating like a near-drunk angel and started talking about coloring with his autoharp, its obscurity affecting the listeners more by their not being able to identify its sound. The sound first hit the aural center and made the listeners curious because they could not identify the instrument. Brian was once head and master of the Stones, but now he did not seem to care. He always seemed close to trance. That's the way he played. That's the way he was in the studio.

Kit Lambert walked by, hustling always, talking to a dowager-looking man who reeked of having had money and lots of it for a long time. Lambert was saying as he walked by: "I certainly haven't heard a decent symphony or a decent new opera in the last eighteen months. . . . I think the whole impetus has passed to the younger generation and to the excitement that is generated in pop. . . ."

Jimi was always shy because of his appearance, his tremendously long arms and legs, his thinness, his angular big head—but even these aspects of his person were used in the development and enhancement of his heavy visual image. If Hendrix felt funny in the States about his appearance, London even further emphasized his outsize qualities; but in England it was a novelty. He had heard the black veteran soldiers in the army talk about the amazement of going into a European village during World War II, a village where they had never seen a black person before; now he experienced the awe of a people face-to-face with a person rare to their parts. He got out of a lot of his shyness by seeing that it could be used to his advantage—even the silly comments he would throw off would become a big thing; his mythological head raps became repeated and commented upon. Fleet Street journalists, especially the younger ones on the make who were supposed to be knowledgeable about the youth revolution in London, sought out Hendrix and vied to juxtapose his uniquely way-out appearance and comments with their prose of the "insider." While the young journalists were more often simply youth delegates from the conservative Fleet Street newspapers, a few insightful journalists like Tony Palmer, Keith Altham, and George Melly supported Hendrix's more serious artistic manifestations.

The Hendrix hairdo, frizzy and bountiful, was viewed by many cultural onlookers as one of the most truly remarkable visual revolts of London. For the British trendy public, who hardly ever outwardly acculturated another race's appearance, another culture, to have their youths sporting bouffant Afros and digging blues was a bit much.

Even the skinheads, who were considered an oddity for supporting reggae and the rock steady of the Jamaicans, did not emulate the Afro or make even a token protest against the oppressive racial policies directed by the English government against West Indians. In fact, they were at the other extreme: bald (or skinheaded), they were more a revolt against the middle-class mod and rocker movements among the youth of England's early sixties, who had, by the time Hendrix arrived, flowed into the Carnaby Street English rock-pop explosion. While the Bee Gees carried on the remnants of the image of the mod element, the Stones were to emulate more the skinhead, especially Jagger in his exaggeration of their working-class speech. Both the Stones and the Beatles offset their mod-rocker dress with lower-class accents—Cockney, Liverpudlian, East End hood. This effect was more pronounced when they first began to receive serious attention. On their way up, both of the groups manifested working-class dress forms. For the Beatles, the leather and cowboy getups were a large part of their initial acceptance outside of London, in Liverpool, and in Germany. The Stones were considered downright scruffy, rude, and contemptible. But around the time of Hendrix's appearance on the scene, both had cleaned up: the Beatles due to great wealth and worldwide diplomacy, the Stones in order to reach a larger public and share in the wealth of the greatest English export since colonialism—rock.

CHAPTER 5

"The First International Monterey Pop Festival." From the first hint of it—leaflets passed out at the first Human Be-in in San Francisco earlier that spring of 1967—it spread throughout the underground like wildfire. The Human Be-in had been a free-for-all affair; the Monterey Pop Festival would be a more organized event, honing and directing the energy. There was the feeling of powerful events under way, an entire recognition of the power of flower consciousness in the making.

Many of the underground newspapers that had sprung up across the country, like the *Oracle* in San Francisco and the Los Angeles *Free Press,* gave complete endorsement to the festival as a logical follow-up to the massive Human Be-in.

Thousands of young heads had been astounded at the Human Be-in to find thousands of others just like them. All across the country the returns came in on the Be-in. It was like a national election. It read: "We are in power, our shit is working, we can do what we want."

From the beginning, Monterey Pop had been conceived of as a nonprofit affair that would benefit local, national, and international causes through an ad hoc foundation set up for the occasion. Paul Simon, Paul McCartney, Mick Jagger, Brian Jones, Brian Wilson, Donovan, Michelle and John Phillips, Johnny Rivers, Smokey Robinson, and others served on the board of directors. To the usual music promoters who were used to shooting for great payoffs for their investors, a nonprofit festival was out of the question. It took the intervention of the underground press, which had been thoroughly investigating the entire setup from the beginning, to secure the important support of two beautiful people who had, hands down, the endorsement of the new youth community: John Phillips, of the Mamas and the Papas, the local music hero; and Lou Adler, a producer who could handle the finance and other business, and who was known to be honest and, more importantly, into the vibe of what was to be accomplished.

There were also other people working on Monterey Pop who were just as essential as the titular head and the business pro. Derek Taylor, the famous publicist who had accompanied the Beatles on their first tour of America, was chosen to handle the press. Used to the mass insanity, which often meant that a thousand and one things were not done as they should be, Taylor gave his witty intensity wholeheartedly to the event. One important result of his presence was that most of the underground press people (a new phenomenon) were given press credentials, just like the establishment press. In many cases they were treated better than the establishment press, often being allowed to bring in entire entourages. Tuned in to the meaning of the event, Derek Taylor ensured that the reportage would reflect the aim of the festival: international consciousness of the power of youth.

Taylor was an important liaison with the English musical scene. Used to dealing with all aspects of the music business, Taylor did not stand behind his title and deny himself to other tasks. He acted as go-between and follower-througher, and this brought the hippest array of new and established "head" entertainers to Monterey Pop. All of the artists donated their services to the not-for-profit venture. They only received expenses. John and Michelle Phillips, Paul Simon, Johnny Rivers, and Lou Adler each put up $10,000 for administrative costs. Their power, the power of music, was consciousness. The First International Monterey Pop Festival became the official recorded version of the Human Be-in.

Laura Nyro and the Jimi Hendrix Experience were the new acts at the festival.

Brian Jones and Nico saunter through the brilliantly placid Monterey Fairgrounds of California. Both he and Nico, dressed in flowing robes, look like medieval monk royalty. They each hold a can of Budweiser beer. A large iron cross swings from Brian's neck. They both affect a disdain born of their kindred personalities: Brian Jones in the supererect stature of a serious asthmatic, Nico in the shyness of a lonely child.

They are followed by a bevy of photographers. The photographers are followed by Peter Tork of the Monkees. He is waiting for Brian and Nico to stop so he can pose for a picture with them. The Monkees have a weekly nationally syndicated TV show situation comedy. On TV they are crazy rock 'n' roll stars, their roles based roughly on the Beatles' *A Hard Day's Night*. At the Monterey Fairgrounds they act as if the film crew there making a movie of Monterey Pop is filming one of their shows.

It is difficult for Brian and Nico to stop. Every time they even hesitate in their stroll, they are assailed by a mob, half of whom are working press people of one sort or another, the other half groupies and minor rock artists.

Brian Jones has flown to California from London for the express purpose of introducing Jimi onstage to the world. This beautiful act of recognition blew Jimi's mind. He would be eternally grateful to Brian Jones for this act of great faith. To Brian it was simply a testament of his belief. Besides, he loved the idea of having a holiday, attending a concert without the pressures of having to perform.

He was the first of the Rolling Stones to love the blues, to love the expressions of music coming from the history of black folk in America. To Brian, it was an honor to introduce Jimi.

Backstage everyone is smoking some excellent Mexican marijuana. Otis Redding is amazed. Jimi is happily stoned already.

Onstage, before a record-breaking twenty thousand people, Brian Jones, leader of the Rolling Stones, saunters through the dying smoke-bomb finale of the Who. The crowd hushes in mass awe; Brian Jones laughs, looking out at the crowd through the lights. He looks back at Jimi and smiles. There is a direct connection. Brian Jones, laid-back in his low-key kingly fashion, tells the audience that he has a special treat for them. Direct from England, appearing in the States for the first time—"The most exciting guitarist I've ever heard, Jimi Hendrix, the Jimi Hendrix Experience."

The lights come up to reveal the JHE onstage. The crowd roars happy approval. Thousands of tabs of Owsley's acid are taking off. "Killing Floor" moves out, down-home rockabilly rhythm and blues—its strange soprano licks almost contradicting the message.

Above them, the sky of California seems huge, endless, as the final hues of sundown disappear low upon the far horizon. The rolling muscles of a darkened mountain range form the backdrop for the stage, the sky a great rolling purple, with a light fog coming up over the sundown. Jimi feels as if he had dropped from the skies. From his London flat to a space of California he had never been within before. There was a primeval feel in the air, a fresh breath of the earth in its pure smell. And the smell is wild, from way back, the untamed smell of trees, ocean, earth, stream, and rock, pretty much the way it had always been.

Against a sky like this the sound seems to vibrate endlessly out into the darkness, the blackness. But it is so incredibly warm, the crowd so alive and eager. He is afraid. He has never played to a crowd of this size and intensity. And never before has he had this much before him in America. It was so fucking ironic. To have come all the way from England, to have seemingly all of America before him, all of America stretching out across the vast expanse. In the darkness of the cool California twilight, heads faintly illuminated, receding back endlessly, the subtle warmth of the earth blown by a slight breeze as if the warmth, the breeze was their breath.

He is at home, yet far away. They do not know him. He is a stranger to his own land, a stranger to his own people. "Killing Floor" is his musical cudgel. A song to play to challenge from the onset. But midway through it he begins to mellow. This is a beautiful audience. They are with him.

"Hey Joe" was a hit in London, but only a few here have heard it. He wonders if this will get them. So far they have been enthusiastic, but only at the same level as they have been for most of the high-caliber acts. The entire affair is high. The music is out of sight and the audience is generous and happy. They must be killed. Killed in the same sense that "Killing Floor" is a song rather than a death threat. He must do something to blow their minds and they're very high already. But he's building.

He's building. Rushing through "Hey Joe." Trying to slow down and give the ballad the pace it needs, but he's thinking about the finale, "Wild Thing." He does not want to let the audience go down. He tries to put some poise into "Hey Joe," but the vibes are too heavy. It's not his own song. The solo is nice but restrained, too keyed to the melody. He misses the dramatic vocal as he recites, but his dance is something else. He dances the story as he plays. He moves shimmering in the lights as he intones as if disembodied—"and I got me a gun, and I SHOT her." The dramatic bridge, the guitar pointing straight up in the air, Jimi's arm suspends in the air after the last chord chop. The solo begins by his fretting with his right hand while his left remains in the air, his head averted, his teeth gritting against the loony peal of the first note, looping and wildly oscillating against the ceiling threshold of possible sound. Then in a slight hunch he continues, his head going back at every thrust to the top notes. You hear something of where his head is at and what he can do delineated in the soulful grace notes and arpeggios before the solo bridge over the drone of the straightforward ballad. You hear his interpretation of the simple melody of the ballad as he screams out in agony against the helplessness and hopelessness, the horror of the murder, and the clashed-up love between it all. His guitar talks, it emotes. More than note-by-note melody line perfect, Jimi Hendrix's guitar tells its own story of love in quick, subtle, and versatile runs that peak in histrionic mourning pathos, etched high within the screams of passion and death.

By now Jimi is ready. He starts off "Like a Rolling Stone," playing the intro chords to "Wild Thing." This throws the audience off for a moment. As he talks, he begins to pick out the opening notes to "Like a Rolling Stone," laughing and joking. He mentions the name Bob Dylan and the crowd perks up; he's going to do one of his songs, but they can't figure out which one. His third reference to Mitch Mitchell looking like Bob Dylan's grandmother draws another laugh from the crowd. Then as Jimi slurs out the first few lines in perfect Manhattan street rap, everyone begins to recognize the song, and the vibrations of the audience begin to soar.

"Once upon a time you dressed so fine / threw the bums a dime / in your prime, didn't you? . . ." Right there in that moment Jimi saw himself as he had lived in America. Yeah, he had been the fine-dressing R&B entertainer, and then suffered what many of his friends of the time thought was a great fall. Ha out down in the Village with all those beatniks and hippies. Taking all that speed for energy and to stave off starvation. The slick veneer front of the R&B musician destroyed for him in the Village. Disdain from his friends "uptown"— "he's looking scruffy and acting crazy."

He saw himself walking MacDougal Street hearing the song, and every time always so amazed at how it hit so close to home. "Like a Rolling Stone" had seemed to come forth from every window, every bar. Once he had walked clear across the Village to the East Village, and stopped in a bar called the Annex on Tenth Street and Avenue B. Out of the sodden, snow-crusted streets, dark and severe and utterly desolate, he walked into the slit-windowed one-room Annex where a great swell of music greeted him, and the entire bar was singing along. The jukebox was turned up to full volume. The place was dark but packed, and they were all singing "Rolling Stone" jubilantly, as if it were the national anthem.

Although he had toured the Village like many outsiders he came to realize that anyone who did not *live* in the Village was a tourist.

You used to (ha, ha) laugh about
Everybody who was hanging out . . .

Dylan had told him in his early acoustic recordings more about the Village than he was able to see on casual visits. Dylan had started out playing the small clubs and coffeehouses on MacDougal Street and other rooms in the surrounding areas. Hendrix would go to the Village and play. He would go on his ass because he had no better way. He would live like the poor beatniks and hippies because he was poor too, and if not totally beat then at least somewhat beat. Although the money had been very poor, he had gotten a chance to play before receptive, sensitive audiences, who were not big in numbers but made up for it by their encouragement as he developed his own music. And besides, he had been able to connect with good people directly, with no jealous star or any other as a barrier. But he had been out there, alone, and he came to love those who selflessly helped him.

Go on now he calls you, you can't refuse
When you got nothing you got nothing to lose . . .

They had laughed at him in Harlem. Huge horse-laugh guffaws, he would crack them up, and always he would take the A train back down to the Village feeling very down. But when he got off the train at West Fourth Street, always being sure to ride in the front of the train so he would take the West Third Street exit, he immediately felt better, as if he had entered another world, escaping the vicious vibes uptown. In the Village people had their own ideas; many were

artists of one kind or another or broad-minded intellectuals, or straight-up bohemians, nonconformists. More and more he felt that these people were his
people, that his people could not so easily be determined by race as they had
been for most of his life.

> *How does it feel*
> *How does it FEEEEEL, baaaby*
> *To be on your own*
> *With no direction home (Look at you)*
> *A complete unknown*
> *Yeah! Like a rolling stone.*

He felt his New York City starving days strongly enough to put tears in his eyes,
to put that touch of emotion in his voice for the people to know that he was not
bullshitting. "Rolling Stone" is the kind of song you cannot sing unless you have
been through some shit. It was a song that only Dylan could sing—until now.

> *Nobody here taught you how to live out in the streets*
> *And now you got to get used to it . . .*

The days and the nights of not knowing where you were going to stay. Walking the streets, guitar dangling from your back, passing restaurants, watching
happy smiling people eat and drink, wondering who you could call on, wondering who your friends are, trying to dredge out of your memory a face, a
friendly face, a face you may have forgotten that hasn't forgotten you. Surely
there is someone you forgot, looking in all the faces that pass . . .

> *You said you'd never compromise*
> *With the mystery tramp, but now you got to realize . . .*
> *He's not sellin' any alibis*
> *As he stands in the vacuum of his eyes,*
> *And he says, Hey, baby,*
> *Would you like to make a deal?*

Jimi begins to laugh between phrases, a blues "ha ha," very much like Junior
Wells. Not in humor or in jest, but in its punctuation and indications, a gesture,
a grace phrase to the lyric that emphasizes the grim; something only Junior
Wells had perfected. Jimi is surprised that this laugh is coming out of him. He
begins to blow the lyrics as he sees vivid images of his destitute period in New
York City, a period that brought him to the utter bedrock of reality and showed
him humanity. In a perfect pause within the verses he tells the audience that yes,

he knows he missed some of the lyrics, but he doesn't really care, so caught up is he in the emotional import of the song—and neither does the audience.

Mitch Mitchell is drumming his ass off, each roll between phrases razor metallic sharp, the continuous tapping of the cymbal perfectly opposite his deep rolls, but in a strange way maintaining the emotional polarity between song and tragedy.

All of the assembled know in their hearts what "Rolling Stone" is talking about. Brian Jones in the wings smiling his weird, blissful smile, bobbing his long head in time, nodding yes, yes, yes.

How does it feel
How does it FEEEEEL, baaaby
To be on your own
With no direction home
A complete unknown
Like a rolling stone

The song ends with Jimi strumming and sustaining the strange chord that holds "Like a Rolling Stone" and "Wild Thing" together. That same chord that gets stranger as it sustains and begins to feed back ever so subtly, ever so ecstatic in its sinister mode.

Jimi had forgotten where he was, he had become so caught up in the song and the images it brought forth. It was like coming out of a trance to great applause and shouts. He had lost himself, as had the audience. They dug it.

"Rock Me Baby," another modern blues classic by B. B. King, done in quadruple time by the JHE, transforms Monterey Fairgrounds for a moment into the Apollo during a production number by the ace rhythm and blues group of the time. Jimi's voice dubs note for note with his guitar on the choruses.

"Can You See Me" is Jimi's own tune, a nice back-beating rocker with big round breaks that blossom and then explode back to the boogie. Jimi screaming distant against the funk, "Can you see me? Can you see me?" The audience responding, "Yeeaaahhh!"

He strokes a few chords from "The Burning of the Midnight Lamp" as he introduces "Wild Thing," his last number. He cautions the audience not to think he's losing his mind. He will play the combined British and American national anthems. "Don't get mad, don't get mad. I want everyone to join in . . . all those beautiful people out there."

The last phrase is mumbled as the feedback starts. A totally nonmusical frequency signal bellows from the amps, static builds underneath an overtone, harmonizes with the signal, and then a tweak of the tremolo bar leaps the signal several steps as a bass hum, as deep as can be, forms a bottom. The transformers begin to overdrive, gathering momentum upward. He teases the feedback, drawing it out, banging the guitar against his hip, shaking it quite rudely, producing the call of an electrical monster, bansheelike in the air, peaking against itself. Pink noise is driven to screams, as he runs his fingers up and down the frets rapidly getting effects that sound as if the electricity is talking. Minielectric explosions occur. He strokes the back of the neck, tapping and raising it to certain levels in relation to the position of the amps, manipulating the feedback. Then he quiets all sound and strums a few notes to make sure of his tuning. Then he sends a tiny signal to the feedback point, but holds it suspended in space, and then the first massive chord chop—"Wild Thing."

Noel singing along, dubbing flat on the note, Jimi sings on a slightly higher overtone. The controls are turned straight up to peak, the chord sounds every note distinctly, as if there were three or four guitars playing at once. The audience doesn't know what he is going to play and is quite amazed to hear the chords to "Wild Thing" coming out of the wild pink noises. The bass and drums join as Jimi sustains the chords. "Wild thing / You make my heart sing / you make everything grrrooooovy / WILD THING . . ." The song breaks, and then: " . . . Wild thing, I think you love me / But I want to know for sure / Come on and a'sock it to me one time / YOU MOVE ME. . . ." The monotony of the chords has a hypnotic effect; they seem to build within themselves, with each stroke becoming bigger within the darkened landscape of the fairgrounds. Jimi repeats the verse again and then begins to freak out midway into the second part, speeding the rhythm to double time and hitting licks even faster than that. He makes the bottom strings of the guitar feed back while he plays lightning-fast rhythm licks on the top strings. Banking left to ensure feedback control, falling down on his haunches, and then coming straight up, bobbing his head like a strobe, flicking his tongue in time with his loony vibrato fretting. Then they break back into the "Wild Thing" melody, and the crowd begins to lose control, roaring almost unconsciously, their sophisticated minds truly blown. Jimi signals the Experience back in from the break, the weird animal-sounding neighing of his guitar catching the audience off guard. They quiet down as he repeats the lyric, then he goes back into the free musical landscape where the bass is the only instrument droning something of the tune.

Within the free landscape Jimi plays a snatch from "Strangers in the Night." Jimi, down on his knees, lays the guitar down, quickly squirts lighter fluid over it, and lights a match to it as he bobs on his knees as if praying. The first leap of flames absolutely shatters the crowd. They go crazy as the flames engulf the guitar and it begins to give out a signal of its own in its weird demise. Jimi leaves the stage as the guitar burns, playing a weird death knell for itself as the controls are consumed in the flames. It plays on, as if magically controlled. The flames leap higher and higher, the audience is hollering, bellowing, screaming. The sound of the burning guitar stabilizes in a metallic tone, with full sustain.

Jimi falls into Brian Jones's arms in the wings, totally exhausted. The applause grows and grows. It builds higher and higher. The duration is out of proportion to any other act. It rises in crescendo, voices begin to howl.

The audience applauds and cheers for a good twenty minutes. They have to be hushed up. The Grateful Dead are on next. They're sick. The audience has been killed—*dead*.

Backstage was mobbed. Jimi floated through it. The audience still roared, it seemed as if they would never stop. The Grateful Dead hung in the wings, hesitant to go on. Brian Jones was chuckling in his wheezy asthmatic way as if it had been him out there. He was truly glad. He loved it. Everyone was crazy. Brian's ecstatic laugh feeding the chaotic insanity. Even Nico was moved. She gave Jimi a big hug and kiss. Everyone wanted to touch him, to share in the electric joy. Mike Jeffery was tripping about something. He was so excited; he was pissed off about a mike stand or something. Jimi, Noel, and Mitch just laughed at him as they accepted the congratulations. Hugh Masekela was shouting, "You killed them, YOU KILLED THEM!" Bill Graham was saying something about San Francisco. Jimi was looking for Chas, but he was nowhere to be seen in the multitudes. Jimi couldn't believe that many people could get backstage. It seemed as if the entire audience were crowding backstage. Then he realized they were the performers, the security guards, the roadies, and the concessionaires—the people who put it on were also blown away. He had done it. *He had done it.*

It seemed as if the roar of the crowd would never leave his ears. The audience had freaked out. They roared and screamed. They sounded as if they were going to tear up the peaceful fairgrounds. Hugh Masekela was still yelling, "You killed them, man, you killed them!"

Almost like a magical formula, Howlin' Wolf's "Killing Floor" had been a prophecy.

Several of the groups flew back to Los Angeles that night. For them the festival was still on, the vibes were so high. Everyone knew that they had made history. Every performance had been peak. Hugh Masekela, on the verge of his amazing number one single "Grazing in the Grass," had scored heavily with a total South African sound. Stephen Stills, as a part of Buffalo Springfield, had done an incredible version of "For What It's Worth." The Who had wailed. Otis Redding, with his soul sincerity, had suddenly and overnight opened up "the love crowd," as he called them, to an entire lore of soul music. But the undisputed hit of the show was Jimi Hendrix. Everyone was totalled by what he had done. What was so groovy about it was that it was part of a new movement. Jimi had the hippest people in American music surrounding him after one stroke.

Stephen Stills proposed that everyone come to his house and continue the good feelings. Everyone was into it and gave Stevie a resounding, "Yeah."

From Los Angeles International, Stevie Stills's beach house in Malibu was directly up the coast, only a few miles from the airport. They partied through the airport and out into cars and limos. Most managed to get there, but by the time they reached the house, the crowd had thinned.

The party at Stephen Stills's beach house became a legend. They jammed for fourteen hours straight. Those who had decided to go home and crash came back the next day to find the party still going strong.

Stevie and Jimi really hit it off together. Either they both played guitar, switching off between lead and rhythm, or one of them played bass while the other showed off his best licks. There were pure moments of bliss when the music would take over and they would go with it wherever it led. Hugh Masekela coming in on trumpet so fine, so crystal-piercing against the ocean's roar. It was like they were playing along with the ocean. The heaviest mama of all, she would go on endlessly; if there was a lull in the music the ocean would solo—playing bass in her elemental roar.

Masekela couldn't believe Hendrix. His music or his costume. Hugh Masekela escaped South Africa's totalitarian racism in the late fifties with a lot of help from black and white Americans. Hendrix's dress reminded Masekela of the African gold miners who would be allowed to go to town every six months or so and proceed to get very drunk. They would buy those black Spanish hats with gold bands around the crown. They would also go in for flowing red shirts and tight black bell-bottoms just like Jimi's stuff. Of course, Jimi had come from England, the source of most of South Africa's goods, as well.

If Hendrix got such a response through his personal insanity, Masekela could just as readily abandon hip pop for his own inspirational and ancestral music. When they jammed, Hendrix played nothing but blues. Funky old black American get-down blues. Just as Masekela could take recent hits or standards and give them the African sound, a little highlife, that swinging nightclub atmosphere, with his wild deep African voice making every word sound new, and then the soaring trumpet putting the icing on the cake, Hendrix had already demonstrated his abilities to deal with hits and standards and make them his own. "Wild Thing" and "Rock Me Baby" were completely transformed by Hendrix into *his* sound. He had mastered that, just as Masekela had. They had a lot to say to each other.

The day after Jimi Hendrix blew thousands of minds at Monterey he was famous in L.A. The kind of fame everyone in Hollywood believes in: the instantaneous smash! The overnight star! If Monterey had been out of sight, then

Hollywood was interstellar. Instead of receiving a symbolic key to the city, he received real keys to the city. Invitations came from all quarters to stay at luxurious houses either at the beach or in town, keys to cars, recording studios, and boudoirs. Jimi was the toast of the town.

Jimi went by Reprise Records, his American record company, which was owned by Frank Sinatra, an obligatory visit to touch base and say hello. Stan Cornyn shook his hand and welcomed him to L.A. Mo Ostin, the CEO, did the same, and also gave him an oral and written message from Sinatra: to call him if he ever had a problem he could not handle. The paper had a private phone number typed on it, nothing more. Reprise, a division of Warner Bros., was part of a multinational corporate music empire.

Jimi and company went on to play the Fillmore West. On the same bill with Gabor Szabo and the Jefferson Airplane, they played before the hippies of Haight-Ashbury and the psychedelic "flower people" of the San Francisco Bay area. The Airplane begged off early in the gig. As the headline act, they were in a dilemma. They could not follow Jimi and they could not play before him. They left the gig to Jimi and went home to practice—just as most of the rock musicians who had been in Jimi's wake were also doing. Bill Graham gave antique watches to each member of the JHE and an extra two grand in appreciation for their taking on the unexpected extra burden. Janis Joplin and Big Brother and the Holding Company took over for the Airplane. Jimi and Janis hit it off and hung out.

The JHE also played a free concert in the Panhandle, the part of Golden Gate Park that was a direct extension of Haight Street, the main drag of Haight-Ashbury, hippie Mecca, capital of Flower Power. The Jefferson Airplane donated the flatbed truck the JHE played from and some equipment. Spencer Dryden, Airplane's drummer, even let Mitch Mitchell use his drum kit. The Airplane really wanted as many people in the community as possible to hear the Experience.

Peter Tork, the chief Monkee and buddy of Stevie Stills, had just about demanded Jimi stay at his estate in Laurel Canyon. Jimi took him up on his kind offer when he returned to L.A. from San Francisco. He had an immediate entourage composed of rock stars, old friends, and hangers-on, for Laurel Canyon was like a musician's ghetto. Cass Elliot, Judy Collins, Joni Mitchell, David Crosby, and many others lived there. Mike Bloomfield was there, exulting in their reminiscences of the Village days, where Jimi had seemed hopelessly impoverished less than a year ago. Bloomfield was going on and on about how Jimi's playing had improved—even though he had been the most incredible guitarist Bloomfield had ever met, even back then. Buddy Miles was there. Vishwa, a young black cat with long curly black hair and a well-bred manner who sang, wrote, and meditated, was there. He had a flawless way of relating to people. He was very cool. The Chambers Brothers were around, too.

Everyone wanted to see the Jimi Hendrix Experience. KRLA, L.A.'s hip Top 40 radio station, was playing "Purple Haze" every hour on the hour. Offers were coming in by the hour. Bill Graham wanted them back at the Fillmore West in San Francisco. Dick Clark and Peter Tork wanted them to tour with the Monkees. Premier Talent wanted to book them for concerts in New York. Steve Paul wanted them to play the new Scene club in New York. TV offers abounded. Bill Cosby wanted Jimi to play on an album he was recording. Cosby had taken the melody to "Purple Haze" and written new lyrics called "Hooray for the Salvation Army Band." Jimi was glad he had a couple of managers to handle the deluge. He was content to do all the hanging out he could do. It had been almost a year since he had been back to the States, and over two years since he had been on the West Coast. The last time he had been in L.A. was in 1965 during one of Little Richard's endless road tours. Jimi had done a studio gig with a cat called Arthur Lee. He wondered where Arthur Lee was. Lee was a brilliant singer and musician, and one of the few bloods Jimi had met who had been into rock in 1965. Jimi heard that Arthur Lee had started a group called Love. Arthur Lee had been offered a spot at Monterey Pop but had declined because the artists were not paid.

Stevie Stills played Jimi a tape that he and Buddy Miles had recorded for a lark. It was good; Buddy had grown as a drummer. They were looking for Buddy Miles when they met Devon Wilson at the Whisky a Go-Go. Devon and Jimi had been introduced by Buddy Miles during an Isley Brothers and Wilson Pickett tour of New Jersey in 1965. Jimi remembered Devon vaguely. She had been fast, young, and kind of crazy. Most unlike just another runaway teenager in the Village in 1965, Devon had already lived in Las Vegas and had been a Playboy bunny. She was fine and worldly, an instant pleasure to be with. Jimi had been hanging out with the boys and was getting tired of the constant gang of people. The product of an interracial marriage, Devon was half black and half white, light-skinned, tall, vivacious, and voluptuously proportioned. She had just turned twenty-one. She lived in Laurel Canyon, too, in the mansion Rudolph Valentino had owned, with a mellow dude named Cosmo, a musician, who would understand that Jimi just wanted to cool out, relax, and be free from hassles.

Jimi excused himself from the boys and went with Devon. Right off of Sunset Boulevard they took a road that led upward on a narrow winding lane. In thirty seconds they were into hill country. She lived right at the Willow Glen

Road pass, straight up a private road to the Valentino complex. The mansion was white and remote, overlooking winding Laurel Canyon Boulevard and seemingly all of Los Angeles. Devon seemed to know exactly how to make Jimi comfortable. After introducing Jimi to Cosmo, a diminutive Italian musician who had a group called the Afro-blues Quintet (and whose mind was obviously blown away), Devon led Jimi to a quiet wing of the huge mansion where low floor pillows, incense, and music set a wonderful scene. Jimi spent all that evening, and a large part of the next day, there with Devon.

In late June at the Houston Studios in L.A., Devon and other friends were invited to the partylike sessions at which Jimi and company recorded a raunchy homage to acid, mescaline, magic mushrooms—the staples of psychedelia and Flower Power—called "The Stars That Play with Laughing Sam's Dice." The acronym produced STP-LSD, which represented two powerful consciousness-expanding substances the Experience had become very taken with. Unlike any other highs, LSD and its counterparts had a high that lasted for up to eight hours, featuring visually, aurally, and tactilely enhanced reality combined with profound feelings of well-being, gaiety, and laughter and also reflection, insight, and deep thought. The mind-expanding substances were very much unlike narcotics, alcohol, or even marijuana and hashish. Jimi, in an amusing takeoff in the persona of "Captain Trips," leads the listeners on a journey through inner space at the Houston Studios. Many of the Experience's friends were on hand for the several sessions it took to get it right. Devon Wilson, Frank Zappa, and many others participated in the hijinks and stoned choir vocals.

Jimi finally got to record for the first time with the wah-wah pedal and also put the Octavia, the octave-changing foot pedal box built by "O," to good use on the overdubs of the tune (and finally a master on the twenty-first take).

No "Lucy in the Sky with Diamonds," Jimi was heading for interstellar space through an inward galaxy. The high keening harmonic sounds at full report gave the feel of moving upward; at the upper pitches and upper registers of decibel it was possible to feel the sounds with the body and the emotions at an enhanced rate.

"The Stars That Play with Laughing Sam's Dice" was a joke. But Jimi was serious in the same way that an LSD trip is amusing but quite serious; as the powerful drug pulls one out of ordinary reality into a netherworld of perception, "STP-LSD" becomes a guided tour to the taking of psychedelics.

The song starts with basic rock 'n' roll, a few *Sgt. Pepper* licks and Mitch Mitchell's slight backbeat on tom-tom creating a simplistic milieu.

Jimi begins "The Stars That Play with Laughing Sam's Dice" as if it is just another rock 'n' roll song about having a certain peace with the world. The image of a zodiac as a gleaming glass before the eyes, perhaps like a kaleidoscope, becomes a promise that will soon occur. Jimi's peaceful intonation changes abruptly, as the ensemble engine reflects a drastic change, as the powerful psychotropic substance hits the brain, the entire nervous system. Jimi's guitar has the effect of myriad voices of the cosmos riding straight up on the wings of higher perceptions. "AaaaaaaaaaaaaaaaaaaaaaaaaaaaAAAAAAAAAAAAAAAAAA-HHHHHHHHHHHHHHH And away we gooooooo. . . ." The rock 'n' roll switches to psychedelia as the song climbs the scale over into higher keys, and the guitar blossoms to its upper limits.

The Milky Way express is loaded—ALL ABOARD

The guitar scaling and writhing at its upper limits, the tremolo bar jacking the sound to oscillating overdrive.

Jimi shouts as the spaceship reaches outer space, the electric guitar in one writhing, long riff strains against the heavy metal atmosphere, he warns the passengers not to throw any cigarette butts out the window. He rapidly repeats another exhortation about not opening a particular door. His change in tone indicates that his words were not heeded. He sighs "oh well" resignedly as he takes the song out.

Jimi takes a treble note almost to feedback and holds it there quavering, then hits a harmonic that takes the signal straight up—sustaining. Whanging furiously on the tremolo bar, Fuzz Tone turned all the way up through the Octavia, the guitar produces a loony wail, overdriving the amps as the song fades.

On July 3 and July 4 in New York City, Jimi played the struggling Scene club to the eternal gratitude of Steve Paul. On July 5, the JHE played between Len Chandler and the Young Rascals in Central Park. Chandler remembered Jimi from the MacDougal Street Village days. The crowd laughed when the JHE walked on. Soon the crowd was in shock. Hendrix made the audience feel that the subway had come aboveground with all its roaring cave echoes and howls.

Jimi knelt and played the Stratocaster like a koto, then ripped the strings with his teeth and threw the guitar back over his head into the amps.

In New York Jimi reunited with Arthur and Albert Allen, the twins, after his concert in Central Park. They went right uptown to see Fayne. Her skepticism was in fine form as she expressed doubt about the *Are You Experienced?* album cover Jimi showed her. "Why don't you believe me?" Jimi protested. Fayne replied, "You can have that stuff printed down on Broadway." Jimi was so exasperated that Fayne finally relented, "Okay, okay, I believe you." But Jimi felt she was just saying that. She had to tell him, "You come here with an empty damn record sleeve and you tell me that's your record? Yeah, sure." Jimi had to admit that he had left the recording back at the hotel.

The following night the twins joined him at the Mayfair Studios downtown where he was finishing up "The Burning of the Midnight Lamp." They decided to have a party back at Fayne's house. Jimi said he had something they had not experienced before, "some new stuff you all gonna love"—some LSD. He was anxious that they appreciate the mind-expanding properties of "acid," the sacrament of the Flower Power movement.

But Fayne found the new drug disconcerting. Albert Allen described how she "bolted out" of the apartment running up and down, yelling in the hallway that there were strange men in her house. Jimi and Albert hid in the apartment until she calmed down. Having removed his clothing as they hid, Jimi told Albert, well into the trip, that he was not naked but had become "invisible."

A communiqué from the Jimi Hendrix Experience's mobile "office" somewhere in the USA to Les Perrin, their publicist in London:

Jimi Hendrix played the Whisky a Go-Go in Los Angeles with the big rave there called Sam and Dave—he blew them off the stage. They have been offered the Avalon and Fillmore Auditorium in the future. Last night (Monday) they played the Scene Club, New York City. On the bill were the Seeds, they blew them off the stage. While they were in Los Angeles Jimi stayed in Peter Tork's, of the Monkees, home. After their appearance at the Monterey Festival they were offered, within four hours, to tour with the Monkees on their American trip. It opens at Jacksonville, Florida, on Friday [July 8] and goes on until August 20. How long did negotiations with Chas Chandler take? Half an hour. Jimi Hendrix is at LT 1-7000. While he was in Los Angeles he borrowed Peter Tork's GTO car. It pulled up at a filling station at Malibu and a car hit it, spun it three times, and Jimi Hendrix has received a bad injury to his right ankle—the one that was broken and had him invalided from the U.S. Army. Also in the car were Mike Bloomfield, of the Bloomfield Band, it was driven by Stevie Stills of the Buffalo Springfield Band, Billy Narls and also Dave Crosby of the Byrds. Jimi Hendrix's description of Peter Tork's house—"It was about a thousand rooms, a couple of baths, two balconies which overlook the world and Piccadilly Circus. There is a carport in which there is a Mercedes, a GTO, and something that looks like an old copper stove. In the house there is a stereo that makes you feel you are in a recording emporium. There is an electric piano, amplifier, and guitars all over the place—a cute lovely little yellow puppy-type dog.

The Monkees had "Pleasant Valley Sunday" in the Top 10. More teenyboppers than the Jimi Hendrix Experience had ever seen before screamed for the song everywhere they toured. At first it had seemed like a great idea to tour with the Monkees. Peter Tork's hospitality notwithstanding, the Monkees were a top pop act in the United States, second only to the Beatles in national appeal. The Monkees' TV series was seen by millions every week.

Jimi, Noel, and Mitch could see why Jeffery had been so eager to get them with the Monkees. They were big time. They reeked of high finance. They had their own plane, Monkees logo on the side, and Monkees insignia on the suits their employees wore. The DC-6 plane had a lounge in the back where the JHE and the Monkees would smoke much primo grass and hash while the press accompanying them were sequestered in the seats.

At the very first gig in Jacksonville, Florida, Jimi recognized that they were being put in the "death spot" just before the Monkees were to appear. Quite naturally the not-quite-fully-matured Monkee followers literally screamed the Experience off the stage with a demand chanted in high teen voices: "We want the Monkees!" That was a shock, a wake-up call. They all, including Chas, had felt this association was a mistake from the start. But as far as the numbers went co-manager Michael Jeffery's bottom line was in effect.

Yet it was clear that the JHE belonged to another audience. While the Monkees, by virtue of their TV exposure, appealed more to the stay-at-home teens, the JHE was more appealing to the hippies, runaways, and rebels. The seven- to fourteen-year-olds they toured before were puzzled, but they seemed to accept the heavy sexual set the JHE performed. However, their parents and the middle-of-the-road theater managers were scandalized. They felt Jimi was too erotic. It did not take long for everybody to agree that the JHE and the Monkees were better off apart. The JHE only had a limited time to follow through on their sensational impact. They had a tour already booked through Europe in September. They wanted to make the most of the "Summer of Love" in the USA, but it quickly became clear to all parties involved that the JHE billed with the Monkees was a mistake. Peter Tork, the main instigator behind the JHE's inclusion on the tour, had often felt stifled by the Monkees' clown-pop image. He was more at home with the serious music coming out of the Laurel Canyon musician-and-writer colony than the contrived, often silly tunes the Monkees were forced to perform on TV. Hendrix's leaving the tour confirmed for Tork the artistic conflict he felt with the Monkees. He let it be known that this would be his last tour and last appearance as a Monkee.

The Experience had had only a few days over the Fourth of July American national holiday to prepare for the Monkees tour. Noel may have spoken for the whole group when he said they were too tired and stoned to care about anything. Their explosion on the American scene had been fraught with anxious expectation and then the pressure of responding to and affirming a resounding acceptance. Success in California—south in Los Angeles, in the middle at Monterey, and north in San Francisco—was a great feat. How to follow through was a dilemma they had not really thought about. Comanager Michael Jeffery, who had been a distant figure to say the least, surely felt a connection with the Monkees was a masterstroke. But it was the associative contrasts and resultant public relations gimmickry involving an unknowing Daughters of the American Revolution that made the lasting impression.

Their tour with the Monkees had lasted only ten official days. After touring through the deepest South—Jacksonville and Miami, Florida; Charlotte and Greensboro, North Carolina—a three-day stint at Forest Hills Tennis Stadium in New York City was the end for the JHE. Whether Jimi could stand to play under such adverse conditions in the city he had launched from may have been the underlying spring. But while domiciled at the Waldorf-Astoria Hotel (Columbia Studios–Screen Gems was footing the entire bill), Chas met with TV dance-party host and tour promoter Dick Clark to sort it out. With the Monkees' consent they were allowed out of the agreement. But not before an acceptable cover story was invented and put forth.

Publicist Pat Costello handled the concept, thought up by Jeffery's publicist Michael Goldstein, that the Daughters of the American Revolution and outraged parents were protesting the Jimi Hendrix Experience's appearance on the Monkees tour. She wrote and had irate letters written to Forest Hills Tennis Stadium, Warner Bros., and the press. They had targeted the trade magazines and journals as the natural placement for the story. But it blew up and became a massive nationwide and international news story. They were unprepared for the amount of publicity they received.

This did throw Jimi off to some extent. While the publicity was okay, the momentum of the Experience's impact had been stilled. Expecting to be on the Monkees tour until the end of their stay in America, they now had to rebook six weeks in the middle of the summer.

There was an excruciating lull while Jeffery and Chandler worked overtime putting some meaningful gigs together. For a while it may have seemed that Jimi was right back where he had started. He played several gigs on MacDougal Street, sitting in with Johnny Hammond Jr. at the Gaslight, with Clapton joining once. And for some reason he reestablished contact with Curtis Knight. It was said that Knight, a former pimp, could talk anybody into anything. Jimi responded to a request to clean up some guitar parts he had recorded with them in the past. His interactions with Knight and Ed Chalpin at Studio 76 in Times Square would come back to haunt him.

Chas threw a party at the Cafe Au Go Go as a showcase for the Experience, who played there two additional nights toward the end of July. Chas married Lotta Lexon at the Warwick Hotel on July 22. Soon afterward they all took a much-needed break.

After ten days off, the Experience played the opening of a new club, the Salvation, on Sheridan Square, smack dab in the middle of Greenwich Village. They were in residence at the Salvation for five nights. In the middle of the run, Hendrix was served with papers from Ed Chalpin of PPX informing him that they were suing Warner Bros. over the proposed U.S. release of the LP *Are You Experienced?*, contending that Hendrix was signed to an exclusive agreement with Chalpin's group.

The papers were forwarded to the lawyers. It was clear to Jimi that he had been only a sideman, not a solo recording artist, with PPX, and was therefore unaffected.

The JHE played the Ambassador Theater in the Adams Morgan section of Washington, D.C., for five days. Jimi and Noel got into a joking thing during the refrain of "Purple Haze" where they went up to each other and sang, " 'Scuse me while I kiss this guy" as they puckered up and kissed at each other from a short distance.

They went through Ann Arbor's Fifth Dimension Club on the way back to California.

At the Hollywood Bowl on August 18, supporting Scott McKenzie ("If you're going to San Francisco / Be sure to wear some flowers in your hair") and the headlining Mamas and the Papas, the JHE was tolerated at best. Between the JHE's set and theirs the Mamas and the Papas and their manager, Lou Adler, wisely staged a classical string quartet to quiet the crowd down. The Mamas and the Papas were the living embodiment of flower power, they were the communal extended family unit. The crowd wholly identified with this vocal quartet and their vaulted harmonies. "California Dreamin'," indeed.

Noel Redding put it succinctly: "We died a death at the [Hollywood] Bowl."

Petula Clark, a popular British songstress, whose ballad "Downtown" was a huge international hit, chose that point in time to declare Jimi Hendrix, in particular, a "hoax." Her entire quote included no qualifiers or mitigating words or phrases: "Jimi Hendrix is a great big hoax. If he can get away with it then good luck to him. I saw him in Los Angeles. I think he's unexciting and he doesn't move me. The fact that he isn't a big success with the general public proves something."

Jimi answered her so respectfully and humbly that he dissipated whatever effect she may have wrought in public perception. He said something to the effect that he was glad, honored, that she had anything at all to say about him.

As the summer neared its end, the action slowed considerably as everyone got ready for Labor Day and autumn. Jimi grew moody. He did not necessarily want to return to London, although Mitch and Noel and Chas were eager to return home. But for Jimi, the USA was his home. He wanted to follow through immediately on his initial success. America *was* the big time. He wanted people to see that he was more than the *act* that had gotten him over into their consciousness, but also a musician, a writer, a composer. But there was no way out of their European tour. He began to sense interest in the JHE slackening off in the USA. Riding somewhere on the plane, he wrote a lyric about himself as a writer and composer. Forming the object of his conquest in the shape of a female, he wrote of a portrait on the wall and a forgotten earring on the floor and of himself. In one of his most poetic lyrics, Jimi feels his isolation begin to mount as his star rises.

In a recording studio, while playing around with a harpsichord, he had found a haunting, classical-like theme. He had used a Mellotron; its various loops of prerecorded tapes were able to concoct a female choir. "The Burning of the Midnight Lamp" was released in England as Jimi flew back to London. He loved that song and played the recording over and over.

The slow, balladlike song begins with Jimi being filled with the emotions— "All my loneliness I have felt today." He comments that loneliness has driven men to abandon their dreams, even, for some, their lives. His writing, his composing, is mostly a solitary act. For a person like himself who has felt so much loneliness and depression, it is a difficult sacrifice. But he is dedicated to his music, regardless of what it takes.

But I continue
to burn the midnight lamp . . . alone

The nascent Jimi Hendrix Experience, London 1966 *(Star File)*

Jimi Hendrix at home, London 1967 (*Petra Niemeier/Star File*)

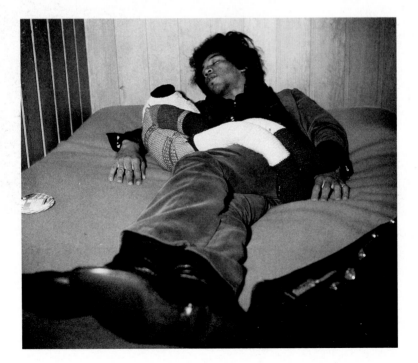

Jimi Hendrix Experience, sporting up-to-date bouffant perms—stars! London, late 1967
(*Gered Mankowitz/Star File*)

Jimi backstage (© 1968–2000 David Sygall)

Jimi, Noel, and Mitch backstage (© *David Sygall 1968*)

Jimi backstage with fans (© *David Sygall 1968*)

Jimi and Fayne backstage
(© *1968–2000 David Sygall*)

Jimi and Fayne kiss (© *1968–2000 David Sygall*)

Jimi Hendrix—Fillmore East,
East Village, New York City, May
1968 (© 1968–2000 David Sygall)

BELOW: Jimi Hendrix Experience
with light show—Fillmore East,
East Village, New York City, May
1968 (© 1968–2000 David Sygall)

Jimi and manager Michael Jeffery confer backstage (© *1968 David Sygall*)

CHAPTER 6

The JHE had no time to relax and contemplate their smash debut in the States. It seemed as if they were in England only long enough to deal with the tragic death of Brian Epstein. As they were leaving for Sweden they heard that "Burning of the Midnight Lamp" had come in at number twenty-three on the London charts.

They had been committed for some time to two small gigs in Sweden at the beginning of September. They had to be back in London for the Guitar-in Festival at the Royal Festival Hall on September 25. And there had to be an album finished by November because they were booked throughout Britain for all of November and December right up to Christmas. And then they had to return to Sweden and tour other European countries all of January 1968. In February, they were booked to lead a huge English rock tour across America.

In New York, Jimi had signed a contract with Sunn. They provided the Experience with any kind of sound equipment needed in exchange for Jimi's input on their research and development. Now the JHE had a sound system consisting of new Sunns alongside their old and battered Marshalls.

On September 3, they play a small room in conservative Gothenburg, Sweden, called Liseberg. There the audience sits completely contained, politely awaiting the start of the concert. What a contrast with Monterey and New York! Overwhelmed by their civilized demeanor, Jimi becomes even more timid and terse than usual. They are greeted by even applause with a couple of whistles and one cheer. Jimi's Stratocaster salutes the crowd with a Sagittarian bow thrust and they are off into "Sgt. Pepper's Lonely Hearts Club Band." As he sings the lyric, the beat staggers, giving the delayed effect, Jimi hitting the last figure in writhing tremolos.

The sound is splendid. Jimi gets a bell-clear summit treble, his bends balanced beautifully against the clear high tones. Now Jimi has a sound system he can work with. A Sunn cabinet with a JBL D-130 in the bottom and an L-E 100-S driver horn in the top blended with a Marshall 100-watt stack he shared with Noel's bass to seek a full-range sound at the highest power. From treble peak clusters to fuzz bottom rags, with both Crybaby and Fuzz Face pedals pressed flat to the floor, and all the knobs on Jimi's Stratocaster at ten, the system sounded good.

The guitar pipes "thank you." Jimi murmurs, "Thank you very much and now while your ears are still ringing we'll go on and do another little thing called 'I Don't Live Today,' dedicated to the American Indian."

The beat is a 2/4 tom-tom American Indian war dance with lots of accents.

Over the double-note bass drone that is almost in unison with the drums, he sounds like he is hitting two chords at once, one chord dubbing the same note he sings and the other chord a screaming soprano lament, "I don't"—Noel's voice rushing in to join Jimi's—"live today." Jimi's rap off to the side like casual remarks in passing: ". . . maybe tomorrow, uh, just can't tell you, baby—but, uh, I DON'T . . . *live today!*" Fueled by his Native American ancestry, this is Jimi's most powerful song of protest. While the words are extended lamentations, the music succeeds in delivering the message in an intense, almost crazy blues—the hardest of rock. Jimi's solo begins behind the beat in a meditative hook that moves out into long, languorous lines with vibratos at the end of phrases. The sound streaks out into a perfectly controlled synthesizer line of feedback, then quickly back to the note, only to streak out again into feedback at the very ceiling of its signal. Then a twelve-o'clock-high distort wail swoons back into the message. "I," Noel comes in as Jimi lays out, "don't," and they both sing: "live today."

The time is doubled as they take the song out in a long tag. The feedback has a beautiful feel in the upper registers. The surflike effects of the Sunn amps make the feedback sing in the upper ranges like a mezzo-soprano. The perfectly sustained tones roll out almost like liquid. Unfortunately, the lower registers of the Sunn amps do almost nothing, leaving it all on the Marshall, which is supporting all of Noel's sound, as well. The Sunn amps make a dull flat tone for Jimi's Strat at midrange and nothing below. Jimi has to content himself with the upper registers. There is not enough contrast with the lower registers for him to venture down anymore. He stays up on top of the accelerated beat and discovers a contrast between treble *wheeee* reports and sideways feedback. He rides the beat shouting, "Awww . . . there ain't no life nowhere." He shakes the Stratocaster rudely, jabbering a vibrato by force. The guitar becomes thousands of Native American souls screaming in the historic void of their violent genocidal deaths. The guitar neighs like horses shot from under Indian warriors, bows in outstretched arms blasted by Winchesters in millions of movie frames, going back in time to the original action. They churn upward, Jimi's feedback soaring above Noel's charging jag and Mitch's circular backbeat. Jimi exults in the high registers of the sound system as the rhythm section bashes to a close.

They end the set with "Wild Thing," which is beginning to sound almost traditional alongside the new material.

On the 9th the JHE discovered they had performing seals as an opening act at a fairground appearance in Kartstaab, Sweden. The seals' act did not come off well as they could not keep the balls on their noses. Jimi and Gerry Stickells had a good laugh about that.

The Diplomatic Experience Hit the Right Note with Mr. Hendrix

Britain's Ambassador to Sweden, Sir Archibald Ross, KCMG, MA, must surely now be in line for another helping of alphabet soup.

By a display of tact outstanding even for an Old Wykehamist (Motto: Manners Maketh Man) early yesterday he saved Princess Alexandra from a confrontation with the pop world's ultimate weapon.

The Jimi Hendrix Experience.

Hair

It happened as the Winchester school magazine might say, thus:

Hendrix—21-year-old guitarist-singer from Seattle, whose hair resembles a demented fright wig—returned to the Park Avenue Hotel early yesterday after a rousing reception at a concert in Gothenburg, Sweden.

With the other two members of his group, the whole known as the Jimi Hendrix Experience, he was standing in the foyer chatting.

A somewhat nervous hotel executive asked them all to move. Because, he explained anxiously, Princess Alexandra was about to pass.

The Jimi Hendrix Experience, paying guests one and all, refused.

The executive insisted.

Chords

Although they could have blasted him from Gothenburg to eternity with a few chords, the Experience refused to budge.

The executive became irate. The situation looked nasty.

Enter Sir Archibald, 65, with 31 years of dealing with difficult situations and well used to even more eccentric types than the Jimi Hendrix Experience.

He took the heat out of the situation immediately.

"He invited us to have a drink," said Hendrix yesterday, before leaving Gothenburg for London.

"He was real cool. I guess the guy at the hotel thought we were a bit scruffy and tried to tidy the place up for the Princess."

While the group members were having their drink, Princess Alexandra passed through the foyer without seeing them.

"Good old ambassador," said a spokesman for the Foreign Office when *Inside Page* informed him of this diplomatic triumph.

—The Inside Page
September 14, 1967

Jimi Hendrix showed up at the Guitar-in benefit for the British Labour Party International with a new attachment for his guitar: a vibe lever attached like a gear shift to the guitar strings, a perfected Octavia that could leap octaves at will. The crowd was wild and enthusiastic, especially compared to their ardor for the politicians who sponsored the event. As Jimi performed, a middle-aged lady stood up and walked right past him on the way out. He waved to her. "Goodbye," he said. "It's been nice having you."

Backstage Jimi posed for photos with the Liberal Party leader, Jeremy Thorpe. While Thorpe tried on Jimi's Stratocaster for size, Jimi pulled at Thorpe's short hair, intimating that he would have to go all the way out if he wanted to be a rock star. "Jimi is a very nice guy," Thorpe said to the assembled crowd. Jimi thought the whole event was very corny, but Mike Jeffery was ecstatic. There were loads of press there. They would get lots of publicity. But while the Jimi Hendrix Experience was publicizing their musical abilities, the politicians were vying for control of the British Empire, hardly an equal exchange.

Jimi's tight black bell-bottom pants, black boots, and black tuniclike cape with curly white silk brocaded flowers and birds on the back seemed to excite the press more than his words, but he gave them a few quotes anyway. "In five years I want to write some plays, some books. I want to sit on an island—my island—and listen to my beard grow. And then come back and start all over again as a bee—a king bee." Asked about what he would call the music they played, Jimi said: "It's up to you to name it. We just play it, we play what we feel." The reporters, especially one called simply "Buckley," pressed for more of a reply. After all, since Jimi's triumphant tour of the USA, he was now being recognized as an international star in London; they wanted to hear their definitions from the master now, whereas before they were content to say whatever pleased them. Jimi went on to say that their music was a blend of their individual interests: jazz on Mitch Mitchell's drums, rock on Noel Redding's bass, and blues from his playing and singing. Mitch chimed in, "There are only three of us but we need all the stage we can get, we run around a lot." "Sometimes I rub up against the amplifier," Jimi went on, "sometimes I sit on it, sometimes I jump on the guitar. I've got a gadget called the wah-wah pedal. You press it and the guitar goes *wah-wah*. Then sometimes I grind the strings up against the frets. The more it grinds, the more it whines. Sometimes I play with my teeth, you know, just for a moment. You can hardly notice it it's so fast. Or I'll be playing with my elbow for a moment so I'll just play with my elbow for a little while. I can't remember all the things I do." Jimi warmed to the subject. "Once I was playing away and there was a short circuit and the guitar went up in flames. 'What's happening here?' I said. It went over pretty well so for about three times after that I sprayed lighter fluid on it and then stamped out the burning pieces. When we played the Hollywood Bowl they were waiting for us offstage with fire extinguishers. But we didn't do it there." Jimi explained his love for low ceilings. "The Cafe Au Go Go in New York was great because the ceiling was really low and dusty. I'd stick the guitar right up into the ceiling. It was like war. You didn't even need a smoke bomb . . . it's a freaky, funky scene." Jimi yawned, "We just try not to bore ourselves. We try to enjoy ourselves and hope the audience likes it."

Mitch went on about smashing up his drum kit if he could not get the sound out of it he wanted. Noel added that they did not freak out but were "freaking in." One of the reporters suggested that the kicking and smashing were just part of the act. Jimi countered: "I get a different sound out of it if I rub against the amplifier." But he had to admit, "We have to get our amplifiers overhauled after every trip." One reporter thought that Jimi's antics were very much like the Harlem Globetrotters. Jimi had to tell them about the chitlin circuit; obviously they had no idea. "Cats used to jump on the guitar, there used to be cats playing behind their heads, or playing with their teeth or elbows. Sometimes they'd switch instruments, just for fun. We do that, too." The reporters got into Jimi's lyrics. They complained that it was often difficult to hear what Jimi was really singing. Jimi said, "We sing them that way so people have to listen again to hear what we said." Then Jimi nearly fell down laughing as the reporters, in their well-educated British accents, began to recite back to him some examples of his lyrics: "You don't care for me / I don't care about that / You have a new fool / I like it like that / I have only one burning desire / Let me stand next to your fire." That was a scream! Jimi laughed as he commented, "I don't know what it means. I just wrote it." The reporters were sure that if people really heard what he was singing, many, especially those of the older generation, would be scandalized. Buckley recited, with a little more of a Cockney twang, "Purple haze all in my brain / Lately things just don't seem the same / Acting funny but I don't know why / Excuse me while I kiss the sky."

When asked about the new attachment on his guitar, Jimi started talking about this mysterious person who was making special electronic attachments for his guitar, which enabled him to get very special sounds. The person's identity was like a high industrial secret. He was developing a high-frequency guitar that would be able to play twice as high as any models on the market, and also a light system that would be coordinated with all the instruments and amplifiers. "He's also making something he calls the 'Heavenly Sound,'" Jimi went on. "It sounds like all the heavens opening up, but don't forget about the music. We don't. All these little things happen so quick they don't really get in the way of the music. And we can't see the lights. We're constantly working, except when we sleep. Even when we go to a club, people are talking to us. This isn't as easy as it looks."

That just about wound up that session. Jimi was surprised at how seriously the London press was treating them since their return from the States. When asked for a concluding statement Jimi replied, "This is a new era in music. People are taking more time with it, taking things much more seriously."

Jimi and company are in BBC Rehearsal Studio One, supposedly rehearsing a jingle for the *Radio One* show. But he, Mitch, and Noel had long ago reached a beautiful understanding of the emotional needs of their music—to rehearse for a jingle was ludicrous. They had played for eleven months straight and were tight. They stayed in the rehearsal room to make Chas and the BBC executives happy. But rather than waste time, they jammed. Every once in a while they hit something they played in their show repertoire and would go through it for a few bars. Everything in Jimi's music fit into the constant moment of a thought, a jam, an emotion, just as physical time—past, present, future—all came from a primordial time. All of the music he had written, and would ever write, all came from this central place, heavy on blues phrasing and hip rhythm licks, with the drums driving like a jazz night train, and the oscillating deep-earth throb of the bass. They would speed up to blurs of quadruple time, and then slow down to roadhouse slow-drag intimacy, Jimi providing hair-trigger changes in direction, or key, by going off on a weird atonal figure, and then whanging back into the tonal tonic of the key, which was almost always E minor.

Chas brought a whole bunch of Motown people back to see them, including Little Stevie Wonder, and Tommy Chong, of Bobby Taylor and the Vancouvers. Bobby Taylor was not there, but Tommy said that he definitely would come by and check Jimi out.

Little Stevie stayed behind and got to hitting some licks on the drums. He played the same kind of deep metallic almost bass-tone beats that his drum mentor, Benny Benjamin, the original Motown sessions drummer, was famous for. "Can't Help Myself," "My World Is Empty Without You," "Don't Mess with Bill," and "I Heard It Through the Grapevine" were all recorded with Benjamin on drums. It seemed you did not need a bass with Benny on drums. Benny would pop the tom-toms in such a way that the sound would augment the low registers and reinforce the song microtonally.

Jimi joined in and they jammed in strict time, Stevie's clean-cut head moving sideways in time to the music, Jimi playing rhythm and lead and sometimes the bass parts, too.

Pretty soon it is time to do the jingle. The reassembled JHE goes into a heavy metal funky rag, and out of it Jimi slurs in menace:

Just turn that dial
Make the music worthwhile:

"Radio One," Jimi snarls, stole his girl but it was still his true love.

Everyone in the JHE organization was happy about the review in the prestigious *New York Times.*

A Genuine Nightmare

The Jimi Hendrix Experience is neither a pill nor a weed, but three young musicians who came over from England recently and gained some quick notoriety with a stage act that's reputedly enough to make a sailor blush. They've now got a first album out on the Reprise label called *Are You Experienced?* (6261; stereo S 6261).

The album cover reinforces the degeneracy theme, with the three sneering out from under their bouffant hairdos, looking like surrealistic hermaphrodites. It comes as a real surprise to find that the disc itself is a serious nightmare show, with genuine lust and misery; and also a highly successful blending of simple folk-blues forms with advanced electronic sound effects.

The Experience consists of Hendrix, an American Negro with a rich and primitive vocal style, and two young Englishmen. Mitch Mitchell plays the drums with a clean, almost military kind of savagery. And Noel Redding plays a bass guitar with the amplification turned up so far that it's a bit haywire most of the time—it sounds like a cello, bowed with a hacksaw and fed through a bullhorn.

There are plenty of good cuts on this disc, ranging from the straight hard rock of "Fire" to the eerie futurism of "Third Stone from the Sun." The sound is robust and hellish and tightly controlled; and Hendrix, who writes the lyrics, knows what he's writing about.

—Tom Phillips
The New York Times
Sunday, November 12, 1967

Once Jimi got famous it was like an overnight avalanche. And all of the over-the-top stuff his management did to get him known was hard to cut back from. While shooting the short film "Experience" in London, Austin John Mitchell saw Jimi's management's insistence on promoting the "Mister Black Acid, Rainbow Super Stud" persona, while Jimi was actually playful yet introspective and conscious, overall good-natured.

JIMI HENDRIX GIG LIST

October 7, 1967	Wellington Club, Dereham, Norfolk, England
October 8, 1967	Saville Theatre, London, England
October 9, 1967	L'Olympia, Paris, France
October 22, 1967	Pier Ballroom, Hastings, Sussex, England
October 28, 1967	California Ballroom, Dunstable, Bedfordshire, England
November 10, 1967	Ahoy Hal, Rotterdam, Holland
November 11, 1967	Sussex University, Brighton, Sussex, England
November 14, 1967	Royal Albert Hall, London, England
November 15, 1967	Winter Gardens, Bournemouth, Hampshire, England (two gigs)
November 17, 1967	City Hall, Sheffield, Yorkshire, England (two gigs)
November 18, 1967	The Empire, Liverpool, Lancashire, England (two gigs)
November 19, 1967	Coventry Theatre, Coventry, Warwickshire, England (two gigs)
November 22, 1967	Guildhall, Portsmouth, Hampshire, England (two gigs)
November 23, 1967	Sophia Gardens, Cardiff, Glamorgan, Wales (two gigs)
November 24, 1967	Colston Hall, Bristol, Gloucestershire, England (two gigs)
November 25, 1967	Opera House, Blackpool, Lancashire, England (two gigs)
November 26, 1967	Palace Theatre, Manchester, Lancashire, England (two gigs)
November 27, 1967	Festival of Arts, Belfast, Northern Ireland
December 1, 1967	Town Hall, Chatham, Kent, England (two gigs)
December 2, 1967	The Dome, Brighton, Sussex, England (two gigs)
December 3, 1967	Theatre Royal, Nottingham, Nottinghamshire, England (two gigs)
December 4, 1967	City Hall, Newcastle, Staffordshire, England (two gigs)
December 5, 1967	Green's Playhouse, Glasgow, Lanarkshire, Scotland (two gigs)
December 8, 1967	TV show; *Good Evening with Jonathan King*

December 22, 1967	Olympia, Christmas on Earth, London, England
January 4, 1968	Lorensberg Cirkus, Gothenburg, Sweden (two gigs)
January 5–6, 1968	Jernallen Sports Hall, Sandviken, Sweden
January 7, 1968	Falkoner Hall, Copenhagen, Denmark
January 8, 1968	Konserthus, Stockholm, Sweden (two gigs)
January 29, 1968	L'Olympia, Paris, France

Jimi took the frustrations of the hectic tour out on a Gothenburg hotel room on January 4, 1968. He had started drinking with the intention of getting drunk. Before he knew it he was a moving blackout. First he started on the glasses and lamps, smashing them to smithereens. Then the chairs began to go out of the windows. Noel Redding had the room next to him and was the first to realize what was happening. Jimi was stoned drunk and not easy to handle. He had a wild wiriness with incredibly strong arms. Gerry Stickells came in and soon he and Noel had wrestled Jimi to the floor and sat on him. The hotel authorities were outraged. This was where the royal family of Sweden stayed when they came through. Although Chas Chandler offered to make full payment for the wrecked room, the hotel authorities insisted on arresting Jimi. They could not have it be said that their hotel was an establishment that tolerated rock 'n' roll stars tearing up their premises. The police insisted on handcuffing him, arguing that he was violent. They made one concession: they allowed Jimi to wear his handcuffs in front of him instead of behind his back. Jimi was photographed for worldwide consumption being escorted from the Opelan Hotel accompanied by two policemen. He walked between them with a white mid-length fur coat thrown over his shoulders.

Jimi was released, after a mandatory night in jail. He was shocked by the confinement and very contrite when he got out the next morning. He insisted to Chas that he had remembered nothing of the incident. But to the youth of staid Sweden the incident had increased his hero stature; to them he was a true rebel. A few days later in Stockholm the Jimi Hendrix Experience was refused rooms at thirty hotels.

The movie camera slowly rode in on Jimi as he sat on a stool in the white room, made even whiter by the brilliant lighting. He wore his Sgt. Pepper red jacket and his black bolero hat and pants to match. Hunched over an instrument he never played in public—an old acoustic twelve-string—he played a soft talkinglike blues. This was a private song he had composed when he first arrived in London. A song he usually sang only to girlfriends alone in his bedroom deep into the night as they sat upon his black satin sheets:

He sings of waiting at the train station for a train that will take him from that lonely place in his being that had been with him since he was a child. People had put him through changes, even his girlfriend had put him down. He tells of his unabashed tears that are so hot that they burn his face, and that burning going way down to his heart. And amid this depression, he almost apologizes to the girlfriend as if in some way it was his fault they were apart. He will leave this town, this place of sadness and disgrace. He will become a big star and make a lot of money. This song could be a variation on "Johnny B. Goode," about a musician who will not only see his name in lights, but will achieve superstardom and wealth.

> *Gonna buy this town*
> *Put it all in my shoe*
> *Might even give a piece to you*

This is what he will do.

The twelve string rings out but Jimi's voice is sotto, intimate. The guitar hits a classic blues run in a low ramble that takes the melody all the way down in resolution.

Later, in full eccentric blues flare, the song would become "Hear My Train A-Comin' " and Jimi would add to the destiny of that lonely young man at his original train station. One of his destinies would be to go and leave this town and become a voodoo child, become a magic boy, become truly free. Magnificent blue howls fading into echo vectors, sonic fury.

The movie was called *The Experience* and would be released as a promo for the JHE's first major American tour.

During the autumn/winter itinerary Jimi also sat in on a Stevie Stills session and played lead on a song called "Good Times, Old Times." The JHE completed the *Experience* movie, appeared in writer Tony Palmer's movie *All My Lovin',* made their own "home movies" about various sex scenes with groupies, and completed work on the new album *Axis: Bold As Love,* their second album. The album would be released in the States to coincide with their giant tour starting in February 1968.

Jimi would headline a tour featuring the Soft Machine, Eric Burdon and the (New) Animals, the Alan Price Set, and Nova Express.

Just prior to his leaving London, Jimi sat in Chas's Marble Arch flat receiving visitors with Noel and Mitch. The visitors consisted of friends saying bon voyage—and, of course, the press. They took everybody as they came, smoking hashish mixed with tobacco, listening to records, and watching the laughable home movies they had made of their recent tour in England and Scandinavia.

Since his return from the States, Jimi had received more and more respect. *Are You Experienced?* had been released in the States in September and was at the top of the charts. The Jimi Hendrix Experience was booked solid in the USA from February through the summer. They were hot. In England he was a recognized force in the music business. His quotes began to be featured in the press. Young and aggressive yet cool reporters from Fleet Street tabloids and Carnaby Street glossies would carefully copy down his replies to their questions.

Jimi was rapping about some new ideas he had for stage shows. They would be playing huge halls and arenas in the States. He knew they would need a new sound system, the best that money could buy, capable of doing everything he could do in the studio. And he wanted to have speakers in the back of the halls, as well. And also lights and scenery that would create an atmosphere to suit the music. No announcing the songs at all. Tapes and films, as well. Jimi called it " . . . A complete new concept in pop—no, not even pop, I don't like that word.

"There's only so much you can do with a group—but I think that even if there were a thousand people in the group it still wouldn't be enough. Usually, of course, we don't even think that there are just three of us, and instead just think of the sound we make and try and get that sound—only more so. We have thought of augmenting with other musicians onstage, for one particular stage show we're putting together, like with maybe a string quartet—but only for one song. The group will always be us three."

Jimi laughingly said that he was planning all this mentally so that when they returned to England in the autumn of '68 they could get it together. He would be gone a long time.

Even though *Axis: Bold As Love* had just been released in London, Jimi was looking forward to the next album.

"Well, there'll be maybe two tracks from the new Bob Dylan album on it—in fact, we've done one of them, 'All Along the Watchtower,' already—just listen to this. . . . We could release it as a single tomorrow—or at least as soon as we mix it properly. But we really haven't decided yet. On the LP I'd like to do another version of 'Burning of the Midnight Lamp,' as well. I liked that song but I don't think that people really understood it. Maybe they will when we do it on the LP."

Everybody was talking about Dave Mason leaving Traffic just when the group was taking off. Dave and Jimi were friends and Jimi hoped that Dave Mason would work on his next LP. Like produce, or something like that, or just hang out and help out—whatever. "He thinks in a different way. He's got new ideas in recording techniques and a good ear for new sounds."

Jimi had just been voted Performer of the Year by both *Melody Maker* and *Disc*—the two top music papers in England. The reporters prodded him for a reaction.

"I came to England, picked out the two best musicians, the best equipment, and we started trying to create. . . . It's nice, it's really fantastically great that the kids who buy the records should realize how much we're trying to do musically. I really appreciate the compliment. But I'm still a bit worried—I think that everyone should open their minds a bit more to the fact that there are three of us in the group. It's nice to know people think about me like that but don't forget Mitch and Noel! Mitch, particularly, has so much to contribute—ideas for other instruments and things for the record. Primarily we are a group and our last LP, *Axis: Bold As Love,* was designed to show what else we do besides my guitar playing—like the words and the drumming."

Someone asked Jimi about a new release that featured him with Curtis Knight. The 45 contained "Hush Now" on the A-side, and a song called "Flashing" on the B-side.

"On one side of the disc, in 'Hush Now,' I only play the guitar. The singer's voice has been superimposed. On the other, 'Flashing,' all I do is play a couple of notes. Man, I was shocked when I heard it. I walked into a record store and saw this record of mine. When I played it I discovered that it had been recorded during a jam session I did in New York. We had only been practicing in the studio. I had no idea it was being recorded."

They asked Jimi about the meaning of some of his songs on the first LP, *Are You Experienced?,* and on the latest LP, *Axis: Bold As Love.*

" 'Little Wing' is based on a very, very simple American Indian style, you know, very simple. I got the idea, like when we was in Monterey, and I was just happening to, uh, just looking at everything around. So I figured that I'd take everything I'd seen around, and put it maybe in the form of a girl maybe, or something like that, you know, and call it 'Little Wing,' and then it will just fly away. Everybody's really flying, and [they're] really in a nice uh, mood, like the police, and everything was really, really great out there. And so I, I just took all these things and put 'em in one very, very small little matchbox, you know, into a girl, and then do it. It's very simple, but I like it, though. . . .

"*Axis: Bold As Love*? Well, like the axis of the Earth, you know. If it changes, well, it changes the whole face of the Earth, like every few thousand years, you know. It's like love in a human being if he really falls in love deep enough, it will change him, you know, it might change his whole life. So both of them can really go together. . . ."

"He's always looking for new ideas," Noel chimed in, "using either a wah-wah pedal foot-tone control, or combination of both, he extracts some very weird sounds from his guitar. And my bass, which I play at full treble, we attain a tremendous variety of effects in the recording studio and onstage. We do have one positive rule: we must have at least one new sound on each record and we must be able to produce it completely onstage."

A reporter asked about the upcoming American tour.

"They know more about us over here than over there. Now they're starting to catch on to us over there. So it's the time," Jimi cooed.

A planeload of thirty-two English rock musicians plus entourages, managers, and roadies, under the tour rubric "The British Are Coming," disembarked from their BOAC charter at Kennedy Airport and split up into limos, vans, and trucks. They had to hurry. They were expected to arrive by helicopter for a reception atop the Pan Am Building. But the helicopters, which would have taken them into the hub of midtown Manhattan, had been grounded because of poor visibility.

They arrived at the 'Copter Club of the Pan Am Building more than an hour late. The party was in full tilt. The press reporters, cameramen, photographers, promo men, groupies, stringers, hanger-outers, and hangers-on had had time to get pretty well stoned at the bar.

Jimi's was the only black face in the crowd of English accents.

He wore full finery: a black wide-brim bolero with a purple plume from which flowed his long black locks that blended into his black cape, iridescent studded black bell-bottoms, and soft-gloss boots from the Chelsea Cobbler. A totally black, caped figure from head to toe, but his cape flowed open to reveal a sky-blue silken lining, and embroidered on the back were two doves aligned vertically in upward flight. He was very soft-spoken and polite as he addressed the assembled. His reserved manner exasperated many reporters, who yelled at him to speak louder. Eric Burdon, leading the New Animals, spoke louder, as did Alan Price (an original Animal), who was leading a new group called the Alan Price Set. Also speaking were representatives of the Soft Machine and Nova Express.

Soon Jimi got off to the side and got into a good rap with Al Aronowitz, who had his *New York Post* identification pinned awkwardly to his lapel. Aronowitz was a friend of Brian Jones, and they exchanged words about how he was doing.

Jones's recent drug bust prevented him from working outside of England, and they both knew how demoralized he had become. And they felt a bond of sadness. Al Aronowitz would stab his pen at a pad every now and then but it was more like he was just going through the motions of being a columnist for the major afternoon paper in New York City, while his main interest was in simply being people with Jimi. Jimi appreciated the alliance as they both surveyed the chaotic scene going on about them. The people were going nuts in the grand tradition of the New York mass-hysteria press rout. It was definitely an event to check out and chuckle over.

A fistfight broke out across the floor just as a bearded, scholarly-looking man came up and introduced himself. He was Professor Jay Ruby, who was doing a study of various social aspects of present-day rock music. He took out his tape recorder and got right into an interview.

RUBY: What's the musical scene like in England? Is it different from here?

HENDRIX: Well, yes, it is. It's a little more together as far as the musicians are concerned. They all know each other and they get a small place and everybody congregates around London. It's not that much different really. They have their own scene and we've got our own scene over here.

RUBY: You like it better over there?

HENDRIX: As a musician, not necessarily. I like to jam a lot and they don't do that much over there. I like to play with other cats, but you just can't do that over there sometimes.

RUBY: For what you are trying to do with your music, do you feel that the trio form is best?

HENDRIX: We set out to be a trio; that's the reason we are like this. We tried the organ for about fifteen minutes and it didn't work out. It made us sound like just anybody. But it isn't ideal that it's a trio. It just happened like that.

RUBY: Are you really into the destruct thing?

HENDRIX: Not basically. There are times when we do it; but we play millions and millions of gigs, and when we do this destruction maybe three or four times, it's because we feel like it. It might have been because we had some personal problems.

RUBY: So when you do it, it's because you're mad?

HENDRIX: Yes. Maybe we might be worked up or something, you know.

RUBY: How does it feel?

HENDRIX: Oh, this is the feeling like . . . you feel very frustrated and the music gets louder and louder and you start thinking about different things, and all of a sudden, *crash, bang.* Eventually it goes up in smoke.

RUBY: Do you think about it ahead of time?

HENDRIX: No. You couldn't get that together. We did it once before and somebody said, "That's great, why don't you plan it out?" Plan what out? It just happens, that's all.

RUBY: Whom do you admire most as a guitarist? Who's doing things that you like now?

HENDRIX: Well, it's very hard to say. But as far as the blues scene goes, some of the things that Albert King and Eric Clapton do are very good. I don't have any favorites. It's very hard because there are so many different styles and it's so bad to put everybody in the same bag.

RUBY: Whom do you listen to?

HENDRIX: I like to listen to anybody as long as they don't bore me. I tend toward the blues as far as guitar players are concerned. The music itself . . . I like things from Roland Kirk and the Mothers [of Invention].

RUBY: A lot of people compare you to Clapton.

HENDRIX: That's one thing I don't like. First of all they do that, and then they say, "Okay now, blues first of all," and we just say, "We don't want to play blues all the time." We just don't feel like it all the time. We want to do other things, do nice songs or different things. But, like, the blues is what we're supposed to dig. But, you see, there are other things we can play, too. And we just don't think alike . . . sometimes the notes might sound like it, but it's a completely different scene between those notes.

MITCH: When we first started, Jimi was very much influenced by people like Dylan, and I wasn't into that scene at all. Now Jimi's gotten turned on to people like Mingus and Roland Kirk. We just learn from each other, balance each other. It's a lot better.

RUBY: And enjoy each other, right, and have the whole thing happen.

HENDRIX: Right. You should hear him really get together on drums; that's another thing that makes me mad, too. All three of us, we all have our own little scene as far as music goes. Noel likes nice gutsy rock, and he plays guitar. He's been playing bass only since he's been with us. And Mitch plays a whole lot of drums and yet people get stuck on one thing.

RUBY: Some people have difficulty making the transition from concerts to records. You have not. Do you see yourselves as primarily a live or a studio group?

HENDRIX: Either you can dig it as a record or in person. Like some want to hear one thing—when you make a record you put a certain sound in the record or a certain little freaky thing—like the sound of raindrops reversed and echoed and phased and all that. It's because you are trying to emphasize a certain point in the record. So people already have this in their minds when they go to see you, and they expect to hear that. But the main thing is the words, and they can feel the other thing and not necessarily hear it.

RUBY: The thing that turns me on to the scene today is the way everything changes so fast. For instance, what you did on your first album is different from what you did on the second.

HENDRIX: Yes, we noticed that after we listened to it. We were really deep into making our second LP.

RUBY: This is not conscious, you're not aware of the fact?

HENDRIX: No, not at all. We try to make a change. You fix your life and say, "Well, we're going to do this next time." We get ideas—groovy ideas, you know. Everything's a very natural progression. I don't know—I might not be here tomorrow, so I'm doing what I'm doing now.

RUBY: This is very different from what music has been before. No music has ever changed as fast as this has.

HENDRIX: Well, I know what you mean, like the Chuck Berry scene. I'd feel guilty if we did something like that—using the same background with every single song and only different words. That shows that you're going in the word scene. It's like anybody who's hungry—that's young and wants to get into music—anybody like that has got to go into so many different bags.

They have got so much to be influenced by, so many different things in the world.

RUBY: Is it just being young?

HENDRIX: Not necessarily, no. I mean "young" being ideas, being hungry . . . not necessarily being hungry for food.

RUBY: So maybe it's always going to change?

HENDRIX: Well, maybe. Maybe we'll settle down. There are some things . . . but some things are just too personal. They might catch up to us later. Everyone starts talking about that—they have to pick on something, and they say, "Instead of using guitar, bass, and drums, they're getting tiresome." Dig Bob Dylan. He's been in this business for ages and he's really out of sight because there's a lot of personal things. You just don't want to put a lot of junk on top of it, like violins for certain numbers, unless it calls for it.

RUBY: When you record, who does the effects?

HENDRIX: All those things are our own mind . . . all those things are coming out of us. . . . We do a lot of things. Like, on the last track of the last LP [*Axis: Bold As Love*], it's called phasing. It makes it sound like planes going through your membranes and chromosomes. A cat got that together accidentally and he turned us on to it. That's the sound we wanted, it was a special sound, and we didn't want to use tapes of airplanes, we wanted to have the music itself warped.

RUBY: When you put a song together for a recording session, what do you do? Do you play first and then put the sounds in or do you put them together at the same time?

HENDRIX: Well, it depends. Sometimes we play through Leslie speakers and then sometimes we might put it on afterward as we play. A lot of times we record the three of us as one instrument and then build around that.

RUBY: You don't do an arrangement ahead of time?

HENDRIX: Oh yes. We have ideas in our minds and then we'll add to them.

RUBY: Let's get back to the blues for a minute. How do you define it?

HENDRIX: You can have your own blues. It doesn't necessarily mean that folk blues is the only type of blues in the world. I heard some Irish folk songs that were so funky—the words were so together and the feel. That was a great scene. We do this blues one on the last track of the LP [*Axis: Bold As Love*] on the first side. It's called "If Six Were [*sic*] Nine." That's what you call a great feeling of blues. We don't even try to give it a name. Everybody has some kind of blues to offer, you know.

RUBY: What about the white/black scene? Is white blues really the blues?

HENDRIX: Well, I'll tell you. The Bloomfield band is ridiculously out of sight and you can feel what they're doing no matter what color the eyes or armpits might be. Because I can really feel it, I want it. I say, "Okay, they've got this white cat down in the Village playing harmonica, really funky." So we all go down to the Village and then, wow, he turned me on so much, I said, "Look at that." He was really deep into it and nobody could touch him there because he was in his own little scene. He was really so happy. I don't care, like I said before, it all depends on how your ears are together and how your mind is and where your ears are.

RUBY: They say that in England, it's a whole different thing. They don't make a distinction. It's sound—and it doesn't matter what color you are—you're playing. We've still got that hang-up here.

HENDRIX: It isn't really a hang-up because that's human beings—dumb-sighted anyway, you know. That's natural, just like being in a fight, nobody can go out on the street with this little boy. America's little boy. Countries to me are just like little kids, playing with different toys. But all these countries will soon grow up.

RUBY: Let's talk about jazz.

HENDRIX: Charlie Mingus and he [Noel Redding] can take care of the rest.

RUBY: How about Coltrane?

NOEL: Oh yes, he's great. There are so many cats, they've got their own little scenes. Mitch digs Elvin Jones a lot, and there's Tony Williams and the structure of Richard Davis. I like Coltrane, as well. But Kirk is nearer to what I actually like. It's very comparable to Jimi. A lot of people call Jimi a joker for using electronic effects. Well, Kirk is a joker when he plays two horns, not that I really mean that. There are only two kinds of music—good and bad—regardless of what you play or what sort of bag you might be in. We haven't even started yet. He hasn't even started yet—Roland Kirk. You can hear so much for the future. You can hear some of the things he's going into—not necessarily about notes, but you can hear the feelings. It's people like Kirk who are cutting down snobbery, because in every kind of music, even in rock 'n' roll, it exists. Where people just can't see anything outside. It's like certain jazz musicians I met in London recently who just don't want to know anything else apart from maybe Sun Ra, and it's a bad scene. If you can't sit outside your music—outside one particular scene, man, you need something done to your head.

HENDRIX: There's so much happening, especially if you have an open mind for music, because, as we all know, music is an art.

After the interview Jimi and Al talked about the barrenness of English food. Jimi said that he could really do with some soul food right now. Aronowitz said, "Let's go." They split the 'Copter Club and went down to the Village. They stopped at Seventh and Bleecker, where the Pink Tea Cup served the best soul cooking below Harlem.

Jimi talked about "the Axis" long before he formulated an album around the theme. The Axis is like the Christian cross or the voodoo peristyle—a link between the heavens and the Earth. The axis of the Earth holds everything together. If the axis of the Earth was altered, everything would be different: entirely new continents, new directions for north and south, and seas inundating shores that once lay peaceful. The axis made electricity possible, the electromagnetic energy that fed Jimi's guitar. Jimi also felt that a record spinning on a turntable was directly related to the Earth's spinning on its axis.

Manly Hall has written in *The Secret Teachings of All Ages,* "According to the mystical canon, there are always on Earth a certain number of holy men who are admitted to intimate communion with the deity. The one who occupies the highest position among his contemporaries is called the Axis *(Qutb),* or Pole, of his time . . . The *Axis* is a mysterious individual who, unknown and unsuspected, mingles with mankind and who, according to tradition, has his favorite seat on the roof of the Caaba. . . . [Caaba, kaaba: a small cubicle building in the courtyard of the Great Mosque at Mecca, containing a sacred black stone; the chief object of a Muslim pilgrimage in Mecca.]

"When an 'Axis' quits this earthly existence, he is succeeded by the 'Faithful One,' who has occupied the place at his right hand. . . . For to these holy men, who also bear the collective titles of 'Lords of Souls' and 'Directors,' is committed a spiritual supremacy over mankind far exceeding the temporal authority of earthly rulers."

Flying to London and then flying to California for Monterey, Jimi had experienced a mystical peace up above the Earth. He had understood something deep about the Earth just being above the clouds, looking down upon the land and upon the waters. As if the Earth itself was moving him to and fro, back and forth toward recognition. Making it possible for him to be able to transmit the blues on a higher level, just as Muddy Waters had done with the Mississippi Delta blues. Jimi was now extending the blues into universal dimensions, axis of the Earth, balance of the solar system. For he loved the music more than he loved himself, and for him to be able to lift it up and give it to others was the greatest gift he ever imagined receiving.

The *Axis: Bold As Love* album had just been released in America. "Bold As Love" was the title song.

The first chord Jimi strikes is the musical equivalent of anger, brusquely bringing you to attention. Then the song just as quickly mellows into the story he tells. It is a ballad with the internal rhymes and alliterations all intact, like the ancient troubadours.

He invokes a warrior standing in purple armor. His foes are jealousy and envy, as embodied by an entity of the highest rank, a queen, standing behind him. Those limiting emotion, his enemies, are also symbolized by the queen's gown green with envy and jealousy, malice, bad vibes. Jimi, in this rainbow of meaning, then summons the soothing waters:

> *Blue are the life-giving waters*
> *Taken for granted*
> *they quietly understand*

The usually happy armies of turquoise, a magical gem color for a Sagittarian, for a Native American, are ready for battle but cannot understand why there must be war. But then Jimi lets them all off the hook with his love. He says to just ask the "Axis" because they are all "Bold as Love."

He continues his tour, the colors can also enhance an understanding of the human aura as intepreted by one who sees. His red is martial, a self-assured warrior who has conquered both war and euphoria. His orange is a diminutive of red, daring yet insecure. And Jimi takes yellow, as British crooner Donovan sang in "Mellow Yellow" to say that in his case it indicates the classic definition of fear, because all the emotions he is feeling for this beautiful woman prevent him from giving his life to "a rainbow like you."

Jimi ends the song with a reiteration of the "Axis." Perhaps the love that holds the Earth on its axis—that mystical force that continues life through the will of love. *He knows everything.* Jimi's guitar croons majestic peaks as he takes this baby out.

The song modulates upward, spiraling faster and faster, until he hits its center mode. A silent missile's exhaust trailing away as it escapes into the stratosphere, the message taking the eyes aloft in yogic *trakham,* fixation on the third eye. Beyond resolution is pure emotion. The cry of the guitar solo, ranging between tears and ecstasy.

"Spanish Castle Magic," right away incredible three-guitar chorus all in unison playing, racing, challenging rhythm licks. An electric guitar choir taking you right up, creating a vortical chant. Harmonizing against electronic atonal overtones, combined with the ultrasonics of the high-volume decibel force, making another disparate, though unified, sound totally unique to the supporting bass and drum. Like supersonic locomotives flying, Jimi playing a deep dread bass figure and Mitch dubbing an octave below. Jimi signaling his trademark neigh against the beat, ending and beginning the long, looping rhythm terrain.

He pays homage to Spanish Castle, that beautiful club, the castle of his youth where he was first really heard and become known playing in a gigging band of Seattle teenagers.

Ed Kramer and Jimi laid track after track of guitar onto one track of their four-track master tape. The first guitar track is counterpoint old blues-style picking, with all of Jimi's accumulated speed. The second guitar track strums rhythm chords against the picking. The third guitar track accents single lines and takes sly mixed-down solos. Noel plays a Hagstrom eight-string bass, Jimi often in unison on a Stratocaster. It comes out like a web straining along, rapidly forming matrix after matrix. Hypnotic tones from pre-electric blues guitar revved up, creating electronic music with flat-footed blues underneath, speeding endlessly through time and space. Sound waves spiraling outward, through human heart and solar energy, challenging the cycles of heavenly lights.

Playing against the beat laid down by the bass, Jimi's guitars chatter and race against each other. The drums kick and shuffle in double time; Mitch's snare raps are precise. Jimi begins to solo. He joins the twin guitars for a moment, hitting them in the middle of their licks, creating cross-rhythms like African drum talk. The accenting lick sustains in the break. He pauses a moment, then moves off.

He makes his Stratocaster growl in the upper range, snarl and turn as if it's a savage beast he is controlling. Jimi dubs in fifths with the bass, as he loves to do. Jimi coos that "Spanish Castle Magic" is far away and it takes hours to get there "if you travel by dragonfly." And although it is definitely not in the nation of Spain the name still is "groovy," and with the right wind two magical creatures can make the trip.

The drums solo in double time, maintaining the drive. Mitch's snare make you stand at attention in the short break as Jimi shouts to his female companion to "hang on" in order to make the trip to Spanish Castle magic. They fly through the low clouds—"cotton candy and battlegrounds"—which, while visible, are all in the mind. He advises not to keep looking at negative pictures in the mind, but to "just float your little mind around." Then the song takes off; the guitar dubbing with the bass as it gets more intense and then splits off, forming a surprising fuzz wail that blends perfectly at the end of their dual figure.

> No it's not in Spain
> But all the same you know
> It has a groovy name
> And the wind's just right—HEY!

His guitar growls a sharp turn, Mitch barks the orders, snare rap on the door, and they plunge deep, Jimi churning the bass guitars into the theme plateau, away from the melody and refrain. Deep across the Spanish Sahara on horseback, bearded Moors charging for Tangier, the Straits of Gibraltar, Spain, the magic within her mantle.

"It's all in your mind!" he shouts against the wall of the music, sounding like a Pentecostal preacher as the song begins to tag out. His guitar snorts fire in staccato rays, the Fuzz Tone–splitting chords spluttering upward. On a one-chord jag the bass comes up, its three-note drone syncopating into five. Rocking out. The guitar tracks in the background move up, too, their chant creating a whirlwind. Jimi reaches the top of his summit in rooting licks. He intones that everything will be okay as they go on out, the clanging of the bell as the train leaves the station. Bells diminished, mixed-down knell. Clave.

"If Six Was Nine" had been part of a studio jam session Jimi had with Noel and Mitch. It just came out of the blue—reflecting how Jimi was feeling at that particular time. They pulled the jam out of the studio tapes and Jimi sang some words over the tracks. He had wanted to do the tracks over again, but Chas said that it was fine the way it was.

Jimi begins in a rhetorical blues mode surmising about what he would feel if the sun refused to shine. He wouldn't mind. He repeats the phrase. If the mountains collapsed into the sea, he would just let it be, it would not be about him personally. Cataclysmic events notwithstanding, Jimi had his own world that he looked through. If there were a complete reversal of phenomena, as "If Six Was Nine" again, he wouldn't mind. Even if all the hippies of flower power legend collectively cut off their hair, it wouldn't faze him. Because he has his own world to live out of, and he needn't copy anything, anyone. He is a complete individual. That is his credo. Jimi takes off on a rap about a traditional, conservatively dressed businessman pointing a "plastic finger" at him, in hopes that "my kind will drop and die." But Jimi is triumphantly defiant:

But I'm going to wave
My freak flag HIGH

He murmurs an aside that says that since his death will be his own personal demise, then he will live his life the way he wants to.

Jimi's tag is with Moroccan flutes going out in free, jazzlike peaks. Trembling in higher frequencies and challenging the heights of sound humanly heard, like the end pitch of a siren or a woman's scream in the night. Chas Chandler's "footprints" are heard on the tag-out.

"Little Wing" is so sad yet so hopeful, a ballad not of any particular category, yet blending beautifully between lyric and melody. It is a simple statement about an expression of a particular form of his personal spirit guides. An angelic being, almost always formulated in the feminine, yet it could also apply to a lover or special friend. A celestial spirit who he captures while walking through the heavens.

She has a "circus mind" that runs wild. She concentrates on unusual animals, exotic insects, fairy tales and light rays of the moon. She comes to him when he is sad, depressed, with myriad smiles and good vibes that are totally of her free nature.

> It's all right, she says, it's all right
> Take anything you want from me
> —anything . . .

Jimi had heard the entire song up on the high outreaching stage of the Monterey Fairgrounds as the throngs whooped and hollered themselves crazy. A sad bliss had come over him. He had made it. He had made it in his own land, yet in triumph there was that sad, wistful bluesy bliss. A strange country-and-western tinge comes up in the last chorus of his solo, so utterly surprising, yet hinted at in the very beginnings of the piece. This is a piece direct from his muse—*Fly on, Little Wing, fly on. . . .*

Axis entered the Top 20 on the American charts on February 24, 1968. Now Jimi had new songs to play, and new equipment for the tour, as well. They had junked the Sunn amps for the old reliable Marshalls, and had incorporated an entire array of new devices.

Jimi Hendrix's new equipment consisted of a UniVox UniVibe, a Dallas-Arbiter Fuzz Face, a Vox wah-wah pedal, a Leslie, an Octavia, and twelve stacks of Marshall amps with forty-eight beefed-up speaker cabinets. The Fuzz Tone, like a pre-amp, boosted the power tremendously and accounted for the distortion effect. He used the wah-wah pedal clear, achieving a watery effect. Parts of that effect can be attributed to the Uni-Vibe and the Leslie going at the same time, simulating rotating speakers.

Hendrix often played a right-handed Stratocaster upside down and re-strung, since he was a lefty. He could have bought a left-handed Stratocaster, but the right-handed one afforded him the speed and efficiency so crucial to the cleanliness and speed of his attack. When a right-handed person uses a standard right-handed electric guitar, the controls are on the bottom, making it necessary to cross over the instrument to work them and thus limiting speed. But with Hendrix's controls on top, actually under his playing hand, he could work the bar and all the control knobs often simultaneously, while playing and manipulating the sliding pickup switch with his palm.

On this tour Hendrix carried along what amounted to a portable recording studio, including boxes of extra Fuzz Tones, wah-wah pedals, Uni-Vibes, guitar straps, and assorted boxes of "toys," such as the Octavia, which were built especially for him. He also carried an assortment of guitars, including his old beat-up Hofner, a twelve-string Hagstrom, a Les Paul Flying V, an old Fender Tele-caster, and several brand-new Stratocasters.

The JHE *headlining,* on tour. February 5, 1968, twenty thousand attended their concert at the Arizona State University student union.

Their publicist, Les Perrin, traveling with them from London, had set up a telephone interview for Jimi with the *Sunday Mirror* back in England. The inter-view had to be done as they all prepared to leave for Anaheim, California, where they were scheduled to appear on the ninth. The call came through just in time.

February 9, Anaheim, California.

Eric Burdon and the Animals had a complete light show. During their song "San Francisco Nights," filmed scenes of San Francisco and close-up shots of Eric Burdon were projected on the screen.

The Jimi Hendrix Experience had to play harder. They had no light show to enhance their performance. They played at intensities that burned out ampli-fiers. Mitch was drumming so hard that at one point his cymbal went flying out into the audience.

On February 12, they flew into Seattle. Jimi's father, Al, his brother, Leon, and his new stepmother, Ayako, and half sister, Janie, met Jimi at the airport. The press was there to record the event. Jimi was to be honored by the city at his old high school and receive an honorary diploma. He had not seen his father or Leon for seven years. He had never before seen his stepmother or half sister. There was a reception of sorts at Al's house. Al was beaming ecstatically throughout. He had a few beers while he reminisced. With people coming in and out, he talked with awe, as if he were telling a dream.

Jimi, unnoticed, sat for a while and watched his father being interviewed by several reporters. Al was loose and loving it. Al Hendrix rapped naturally and good-naturedly, sipping from a can of beer from time to time.

Al Hendrix: "When he called me that night from London, he said, 'Dad, I could buy a home, I want to buy you a home this winter' . . . and so on and so on. We both started to cry. And I said, 'Now, lookit, Jimmy—*now don't get too ex-cited.* You take care of your scene first. You get yourself established. Ole Dad is doing okay.'

"He told me a long time ago when I was still gardening and Jimmy was gar-dening with me then. He had been playing his guitar around a few times then. And he said, 'Oh, Daddy, one of these days I'm gonna be big and famous.' And I told him, 'I hope you hurry up and do it before Dad gets too old to enjoy it.' We were just kidding and yak-yakking, and he said, 'I'm gonna make it, man.' And I said, 'Well, I believe you will.' I said, 'If you got the stamina I got, you gonna make it.' Ha ha. 'Cause I'm gonna keep on going, no matter how many obstacles are in my way. I'm gonna keep on going. I'm always gonna be plugging ahead.

"I used to tell him, when I first come to Seattle I used to sleep in boxcars and open fields, and one thing and another. Eat my meals around skid row with the bowl of beans. I said, 'I ain't no shamed. Shoot, I'm living.' I held my head higher. I said, 'I'm gonna get outta that.' And that's what I always used to preach to him: 'Always go high, get yourself higher.' You got to do it now on account of there's nothing better. 'Man,' I'd say, 'you got your sights set higher. Go higher.'

"I remember the first time I heard his record. Some of our neighbors had it in an adjoining apartment, and I knew it was Jimmy's record, even though I had never heard it before. And then they found out I was Jimmy's dad. 'Wow! Ooohh! Weeeee! Wow!' They went and give me the record. They said they'd go buy another one. '*Geee,* you really Jimi Hendrix's dad?' And I said, 'Sure.' See, I was looking for soul music, and he come out with a psychedelic job. Something new, way-out.

"They were playing the record in the apartment right next door. They had pillows all over the floor, I mean, they were way-out. I said to my wife, 'That sounds like Jimmy's record. Now, I don't know why, it's just the way that Jimmy plays his guitar, and I hadn't heard him go for a long time. But he would call from London and play us some new stuff they had just recorded.

"I watched him when he played at Birdland, the place that used to be on Madison Street here. That's where he learned a lot playing guitar. He got one stolen from him there, and I went and bought him another one. They didn't sell hard liquor at Birdland. They used to sell pop and it was more or less a place for the kids. But they used to dance to the music. And he used to be playing with a bunch of kids. I used to think to myself, 'I see Jimmy playing in a cabaret,' or something like that. I didn't know he was gonna get so international."

That night Jimi played the Seattle Center Arena. His father's face beamed up at him from the first row. Jimi put on a show. He drove the audience to a frenzy that scared the police.

Al Hendrix had remarried in 1968 to a Japanese woman, Ayako. They had a six-year-old daughter named Janie, who was very excited to be meeting her famous brother. When she saw Jimi come off the plane in 1968 she understood in her child's mind that he was a star, and therefore special, but he was also her brother and that factor became very emotional for her from that time forward.

During the concert she sat in the front row staring straight up at Jimi. He had told her how nervous he was to be playing for his family for the first time. To Janie, "It was all like a big dream; I had to keep pinching myself to make sure I was awake." It was like having a vivid, bigger-than-life dream.

Her other brother, Leon, had another perspective. He noticed that the fans who comprised much of the audience were more like businessmen, and they didn't seem to get it. There were a lot of black people, and they weren't into that kind of show, that kind of music.

Jimi was definitely challenged by the remoteness of the Pacific Northwest.

Jimi went to Garfield High School at eight o'clock the following morning. On the way, he vividly recalled his high school days. An assembly had been called for the honorary-degree ceremony and the entire student populace was there. First the principal made a speech, then Pat O'Day, of KJR, made some remarks and then called Jimi to the microphone. Jimi mumbled that he was glad to be back home. He was lost for words after that and quickly asked if there were any questions. After a long, embarrassing silence, Jimi pleaded, "There must be somebody." After another long pause a girl finally asked, "How long have you been away from Seattle?" Jimi thought for a while and then murmured, "Oh, about two thousand years." Someone called out, "Why are you wearing a hat?" Jimi laughed: "If I take off my hat my head will fall off." He stood there for a moment and then said a series of blurred words and quickly walked off the stage. The assembly was hastily dismissed. Jimi never did get his high school diploma.

On February 14, they played Regis College in Denver. There had been no time set aside for the Seattle visit. The JHE was playing eighteen gigs straight, mostly concerts on the West Coast and in Dallas. Chas Chandler and Michael Jeffery thought they would be making about $7,000 on a percentage deal—the take was $27,000. They were smashing house records.

On February 16, they played the Shrine Auditorium in L.A. Mike Bloomfield and Buddy Miles were on the bill with Electric Flag, their new group. Blue Cheer and Electric Flag had replaced Eric Burdon and the Animals and the Alan Price Set, who had continued on touring through the South. The JHE blew L.A.'s mind. Jimi wore a Spanish Gypsy tasseled vest, a paisley-nouveau silk blouse, and tight bolero trousers with flared studded bell-bottoms. They cut the amp during the "Wild Thing" finale; all at once an incredible wall of sound went silent. The crowd, caught unaware, uttered a collective surprised "Ooooooh."

On February 22, Les Perrin received a clipping of the article in the *Sunday Mirror* that had been written around the telephone interview. He took it to Jimi and they both had a laugh at the big bold headline: "WILD MAN," with an ugly distorted inset photo of Jimi in an English military uniform jacket.

Wild Man
Now He Can Laugh at Sneerers

Petula Clark called Jimi Hendrix "a great big hoax" and those American moral watchdogs, the Daughters of the [American] Revolution, branded his act obscene.

A punster added: "Man, they're right. Even his drummer uses a phallic cymbal."

Yet, on Tuesday, guitarist Jimi receives the World No. 1 Musician award from the showbiz paper *Disc*.

This is the second time in a few months he has been voted top in a British national poll. The first was a *Melody Maker* choice. Mr. Hendrix, however, will not be present to pick up his latest prize because on that same day he will be handed the keys and freedom of his hometown—Seattle, USA.

This honour from a city of over half a million citizens is no mean achievement for a man who is coloured, a pop singer, and an alleged hoaxer, and obscenity seller . . . unless he really has acquired the art of fooling all of the people all of the time.

He's the wild man of music. His hair looks as if it is standing up in fright at the sight of his face and he wears gear that makes him resemble a six-foot parakeet.

Jimi had just finished entertaining (or fooling) an audience of about 20,000 people in Phoenix, Arizona, when I phoned him.

"Man, that Seattle thing is really something," he said. "The only keys I expected to see in that town were of the jailhouse.

"Man, when I was a kid there I often nearly got caught by the cops. I was always gone on wearing hip clothes and the only way to get them was through the back window of a clothing store.

"I wonder if my old schoolteacher digs me getting the freedom of Seattle? She was a good looker, but she got me thrown out. I was talking to some chick during the lessons and this teacher got mad. I said: 'What's the matter, are you jealous?'

"That's the last time I saw her. Maybe she's a Daughter of the Revolution now."

"I Dig"

I said that Petula Clark wasn't one of the "watchdog daughters" with her "hoaxer" opinion, but was undoubtedly a prospective member of the "Hendrix Hate Society."

"Well, I figure it's nice for her to have thought enough about me to say anything," he said.

"But I dig her. I think she's great and progressive—which is more than I can say about a lot of pop stars.

"Take Presley. He's still got plenty of fans, but the only progress he's made is on his bank statement. That's not my scene. Nobody who is continually experimenting with music makes big money, but they get respect in the right quarters.

"Britain, for instance. I was completely unknown in America until the word got back that the British dug my kind of music. Now it's 'sell-out' business here."

Hendrix was, of course, a high priest of the now fading flower scene. Of it, he says:

"The flower scene was an experiment, but although it was all tied up with sensation stuff about drugs, the 'love everybody' basic idea helped one hell of a lot with the colour problem in the States.

"Coloured artists daren't go near some southern audiences in the past. But since the Flower Power craze, much of the violence has gone."

I reminded him that many Hendrix haters put his popularity down to the fact that thousands of people also go to the zoo and watch the uninhibited behaviour of monkeys. Jimi laughed. "But they don't go out and buy recordings of it, do they?"

He admitted, however, that visually, vocally, and musically his act appealed to the primitive sexual urge.

For those who aren't attuned to it, his guitar playing is an electronic nightmare, but the Beatles are only one group among a host of musicians who regard him as the pop pied piper.

When Jimi toured Stockholm, he played to capacity crowds—but thirty hotels in the city refused him a room.

In contrast, a multitude of devotees would be overjoyed to offer open house to this bizarre bundle of talent.

Provided he brought his guitar, you can include me among them.

— *Sunday Mirror*
February 11, 1968

On February 25, *The New York Times* headline called Jimi "The Black Elvis" in a laudatory review of his albums and shows.

On the same day, they appeared in Chicago, and he was waylaid by the infamous "Plaster Casters," a troupe of young groupies who made plaster casts of rock stars' genitals. In their diary of the event, they use London hip parlance.

"Plater" refers to the one who administered fellatio to Jimi's "rig," which means his penis.

> CYNTHIA: *Plater*
> DELORES: *Mold and plaster caster*
> MARGE: *Delores's assistant*

We needed a ratio of 28:28 and found this barely sufficient. He has got just about the biggest rig I've ever seen! We needed to plunge him through the entire depth of the vase. In view of all these dodgy precedents, we got a BEAUTIFUL mold. He even kept his hard for the entire minute. He got stuck, however, for about fifteen minutes (his hair did) but he was an excellent sport—didn't panic . . . he actually enjoyed it and balled the impression after it had set. In fact, I believe the reason we couldn't get his rig out was that it wouldn't GET SOFT! We rubbed a little warm water around the top of his balls and eventually it slipped out. A beautiful (to say the least) mold with part of a ball and some random embedded hairs. Dig this— the plaster cast was a flop. Delores got uptight and didn't mix enough, and then after she'd gotten it set into the mold, she got anxious to get the finished product out before it was finished, and so it all crumbled. But it was kept intact in its crumbled heap for a couple of days and it subsequently dried together and was only broken in three divisions—head, rig, and ball. A little Elmer's glue and we had our plaster cast—a little on the Venus de Milo side, but it's a real beauty.

On March 2, the JHE played Hunter College in Manhattan. Counterfeit hand-lettered tickets were sold outside the sold-out auditorium.

The next night, March 3, 1968, the JHE played to an SRO crowd at Veterans' Memorial Hall in Columbus, Ohio. In Cleveland, where the Experience was to appear on March 26, the papers reported that thousands waited in line for tickets. By March 8, a second show was sold out. The *Cleveland Plain Dealer* held a contest "to give a definition of Jimi Hendrix in fifteen words or less" for free tickets to the show.

On March 9, lawyers for Jimi Hendrix enjoined Capitol Records and PPX Productions (Ed Chalpin) in a temporary injunction to halt the distribution and sales of an album entitled *Get That Feeling*. They argued that the album cover was confusing to the public because it showed a large color photo of Jimi Hendrix and featured his name, when in fact he had been only a sideman on those sessions of Curtis Knight.

That night the JHE and the Soft Machine played the State University of New York at Stony Brook (which was often referred to as the Berkeley of the East). John Hammond Jr. opened the show. His mike did not work and he broke a guitar strap, as well. His set did not go well at all. The Soft Machine's set went on for forty minutes with a coordinated light show that burst bubbles of color that flowed as keys shifted and volumes changed. When it was the JHE's time to appear, the police and hired guards hassled the capacity crowd about smoking and standing in the aisles. They finally had to make an announcement that Jimi Hendrix would not go on unless the edicts were obeyed. The JHE blew the audience's minds even though the equipment suffered breakdowns throughout the set.

On March 15, *Life* magazine hailed Jimi Hendrix as the "Most Spectacular Electric Guitarist in the World."

On April 1, the Experience flew to Montreal, Canada, for an appearance the next night at the Paul Suave Arena. They got to see Chubby Checker at a local nightclub. They wound up hanging out in an Irish bar, drunk, singing sentimental Irish songs.

The next night the arena was so packed some thought it might have been oversold. Extra security was added. The audience was unusually hyped up. They waited until the end of the concert to rush the stage. Chaos reigned. Someone made off with Noel's microphone and stand. The audience took over the stage.

Combined with the UCLA students' storming the stage in February, this was the beginning of a stateside Jimi Hendrix Experience mania that had begun, on a much smaller scale, in England just about a year ago to date, when the Experience were on the Walker Brothers' farewell tour with Engelbert Humperdinck and Cat Stevens. There it was mostly teenage girls, here it was twenty-somethings and thirtysomethings of both sexes.

The JHE flew to Virginia Beach for an April 4 gig at the Civic Dome. Enjoying a drink at a nearby bar were Jimi, Noel, Mitch, Robert Wyatt (Soft Machine's drummer), Mark Boyle (the lighting designer of Sense Laboratory, the tour's light show) and his wife, Joan. Mark Boyle noted that they were sitting around quietly when "suddenly there were these men crowded around the bar who began to shout and laugh. And they started opening bottles of wine and drinking to the health of someone's assassin. And the waitress told us that it had just come over the radio that Martin Luther King had been shot. My Glasgow instinct was to grab a bottle and attack and I looked around at the others and saw Jimi staring away into space. I matured twenty years in two minutes and we got up and left the bar in silence. We flew back to New York immediately."

That day, through the night, and through the next day and night there was rioting all over the U.S. by black citizens, most often against largely white police and National Guardsmen, in massive shows of protest.

Newark, New Jersey, just the year before had suffered one of the worst race rebellions in American history. The JHE had a concert scheduled for Friday, April 5, 1968, in Newark at Symphony Hall. Newark, a predominantly black city, was under siege. The Experience and the supporting acts for the show all milled about the lobby of the Warwick Hotel, agonizing over whether to go to Newark for the concert. There was a question as to whether or not there would be enough civic order to have a concert. The Newark police helped them make up their minds. They called Hendrix's management and said they feared dire consequences if Hendrix and company did *not* show. Therefore they were making a formal request that they appear.

The limo driver, upon leaving Manhattan, demanded that Jimi sit up front with him for the drive over. With the streets, highways, and tunnels devoid of normal traffic—usually heavy on a Friday night—due to martial law–like circumstances, they got to Newark from midtown in less than an hour.

On the way over, a television in the limo was turned up for part of a broadcast of a recent Martin Luther King Jr. speech entitled "Beyond Vietnam."

Martin Luther King Jr. begins his speech in an unusually somber tone. Introducing himself as a humble preacher, it does not take him long to completely topple the image he had crafted all his life and won the Nobel Prize for, his nonviolent struggle for civil rights. He is signaling a change in direction, a change that indicated a new feeling he had had about the results of his works toward integration. As he had told staunch supporter, the entertainer Harry Belafonte—whose "Banana Boat Song" from the West Indies had made him a superstar in the fifties and sixties—he was concerned that he had encouraged integration into what looked to him just days before his death as a "burning house." He announced that he was bringing Vietnam into the area of his "moral vision."

He talked about how just a few years prior, he had thought there was real "hope for the poor—both black and white—through the Poverty Program. There were experiments, hopes, new beginnings." But since that time, he saw the programs "broken and eviscerated" as if "some idle political plaything of a society gone mad on war. . . ." And he knew that "America" would never invest the necessary funds toward the elevation of poverty as long as the Vietnam War diverted such large numbers of men, skills, and money. Therefore Martin Luther King Jr. was "compelled to see the war as an enemy of the poor . . ." and he saw fit to "attack" the war on that basis.

Despite their great apprehensions the Experience and company arrived without incident in Newark. They all cleaved to Jimi: he was the only nonwhite of the party.

That fact was not lost on anyone, especially Jimi. Nor was it lost on Jimi that throughout this tour Noel, Mitch, Mark, Robert, and others were getting their first face-to-face experience with the racial realities of the United States. Mild, genteel England had nothing homegrown to compare with the tradition of slavery, forced labor, rape, lynching, segregation, discrimination, and separation that was part of the history of America. This was not lost on Jimi, either. He had had the luxury by living in London of missing most of the agonizing riots of 1967 in America. But now he had to face it. Face it with his body on the line. This was a sobering awakening.

Even though Jimi had been sitting up front with the driver in full view, those in the rear of the limo—all white—were slumped down in fear behind the tinted windows as they drove through downtown Newark to Symphony Hall.

Mark Boyle, his mind totally blown, was quite attentive to the event: "The streets of Newark were silent and deserted when we arrived except that there seemed to be an enormous black man on each corner, as though he was a sentry or policing the block or something. There was an immense crowd at the auditorium and I was terrified that Jimi was going to be killed. At the time everyone thought there was an insane conspiracy to eliminate anyone who was seen as a threat to the extreme right in America. And who was next on the list?"

Boyle watched from the wings as Jimi came on very quietly to enormous applause. Then he said softly into the microphone, "This number is for a friend of mine." He then began an improvisation that had a beauty that was simply appalling. Immediately everyone knew that the friend was Martin Luther King Jr., and this music somehow seemed to convey all the agony of the black people. The whole audience was weeping. Even the much maligned "old redneck" stagehands came to the stage and just stood there with tears streaming down their faces. It was the most harrowing lament, beyond anyone's imagining. When he finished there was no applause. Jimi just laid his guitar down and walked quietly off the stage.

Late that night, Jimi sat in the Village, at the Generation club, jamming with B. B. King and Buddy Guy. Martin Luther King Jr. was dead, shot down in Memphis. The faces of Buddy Guy and B. B. King are so much alike. The little mustaches, the straightforwardness of their gaze and talk. Southern fellows polite and direct. But now with Martin Luther King Jr. dead, Jimi read in their faces the blood thing. And he felt it. They shared the hurt that so many were feeling all across the world. A pall hung heavy in the air, in the heart, a heavy soddenness. Too easy to cry, but it was more than that. Not a momentary pain, but a dead, lasting reality. Death, the eternal reminder, especially of treachery: an assassin in the free world. B. B. King and Buddy Guy made him feel like a kid. In their grief-stricken faces he sees their age. They are ageless. In the dark underground room within the earth there is a stillness, silence. James Cleveland is up at the Apollo.

That would be the place to be if it were not for the reports of violence. You knew Harlem would blow up. But down in the Village, integrated, like King and those before him had fought so hard for, a moral force of right and good had been taken from these people, just like the people in Harlem. Yet in times like this you want to be home where your people are. But then again, he *was* home. Martin Luther King Jr. in so many ways made it possible for the Village to be his home. But danger was all around and it got into the music. There was nothing left to do but play. The music is high gospel blues directed upward. The solos are in flight. No heavy earth soddenness, although it's there. But just a taste of the danger, and then the release, soaring out of view.

They had to play. They jammed the blues. Deep into the lower Manhattan night, three guitars pulled pure emotion from the mournful faces before them. They jammed the blues for Martin. Three guitars in tear-drenched tremolos, guitars singing a down-south jazz funeral.

Later, Jimi would donate five thousand dollars to the Southern Christian Leadership Conference, Martin Luther King Jr.'s organization.

On April 8, Jimi threw a wild party at his suite in the Warwick Hotel. A caravan of cars swathed in psychedelic colors deposited an entire tribe of hippies at the hotel's entrance before a stunned doorman.

Jimi had thought he would just throw a little get-together, but *everybody* in New York showed up at his suite of rooms. A cross-section of all kinds of people—a typical hip New York party, and they were all talking about him and they were all celebrating him. It was really blowing his mind.

Tom Wilson, Bob Dylan's producer, was telling some people that Jimi was "the dominant force in pop-rock today. He combines the phantasmagoric splendor of a Hieronymus Bosch painting with the funky essence of rhythm and blues."

Harvey Cooper was comparing Jimi to the English cats: "Beck is actually better than Clapton at playing four guitar overdubs and then fusing them together. Hendrix is better than them both; he does it all at once."

Eric Burdon was in characteristic form: "Everyone likes Jimi because they think his cock is bigger than theirs."

Jimi was talking about the wah-wah. "The wah-wah pedal is great because it doesn't have any notes. Nothing but hitting it straight up using the vibrato and then the drums come through and that there feels like that, not depression but that loneliness and that frustration and the yearning for something. Like something is reaching out."

Mike Bloomfield was talking about some of the dates he played on the same bill with the Experience a couple of weeks ago on the West Coast. "We were playing a gig at the Shrine at Los Angeles—he and I were standing backstage fooling around with our guitars. And I was playing and playing. And I'm hearing these insane sounds. And Hendrix was just playing with his toggle switch. He was taking the toggle switch of the guitar, tapping the back of the neck, and he's got his vibrato in his hand and he's moving the toggle switch and tapping the neck and using the vibrato and it sounded like sirocco winds coming up from the desert. And here I am playing, hunched over and playing all these notes, and there's this guy just lightly tapping the back of his guitar and fooling with his toggle switch and these desert breezes and sounds are coming out."

Truman Capote, slightly tipsy, looking like a matron in drag, talking in his high-pitched gossipy voice about Bianca, the South American heiress who was clearly the toast of the party: "She is a totally self-invented person. One night I went to a dinner party . . . given by an *extremely* superfashionable lady who was having a dinner party for about six, no, just about eight people, and Bianca came. And she *kept* getting up from the table and going and dialing this number on the telephone continuously. And she told this woman who was giving the party, she said, 'I have a friend who is coming by here to pick me up—you mind?' She said, 'Noooo, I don't mind at all.' And finally, about eleven o'clock at night, just as we were all leaving, arrives Jimi Hendrix. And I must say I didn't know who Jimi Hendrix was at the time—I don't think anybody else there did. . . . He came in and he was very—very, ah, not like anything that I would subsequently know about him, you know. He was a very polite, subdued, rather shy guy. He stayed for about a half an hour and we all left. And she was just absolutely *maaaaadddd* about him. . . . Later in the next week or so we got all about Jimi Hendrix in the whole country. They were around that winter for about three or four months—I guess it must've broken up. She's a real adventuress—but at least she knows what it's all about."

Eric Clapton was going on and on about Jimi's "strong fingers" to jazz guitarist Larry Coryell, who laughed and agreed: "He sure knows how to shake them strings." Although Coryell knew Jimi had had no classical training, to him Hendrix "had the talent of someone like a Stravinsky or Berg."

By the time the party was over, Jimi had been notified that he was being kicked out of the hotel. The security force escorted the stragglers to the street.

Mike Bloomfield kept rapping to a journalist friend after the party ended. "The first time I saw Jimi play he was Jimmy James with the Blue Flames. I was performing with Paul Butterfield, and I was the hotshot guitarist on the block—I thought I was it. I'd never heard of Hendrix. Then someone said, 'You got to see the guitar player with John Hammond.' I was at the Cafe Au Go Go and he was at the Nite Owl or the Cafe Wha?—I went right across the street and saw him. Hendrix knew who I was, and that day, in front of my eyes, going off, flying missiles were flying—I can't tell you the sounds he was getting out of his instrument. He was getting every sound I was ever to hear him get right there in the room with a Stratocaster, a Fender Twin Reverb amp, a Maestro Fuzz Tone, and that was all. He was doing it mainly through extreme volume. How he did this, I wish I understood. He just got right up in my face with that ax, and I didn't even want to pick up a guitar for the next year.

"I was awed. I'd never heard anything like it. I didn't even know where he was coming from musically, because he wasn't playing any of his own tunes. He was doing things like 'Like a Rolling Stone,' but in the most unusual way. He wasn't a singer, he wasn't even particularly a player. That day Jimi Hendrix was laying things on me that were more sounds than they were licks. But I found, after hearing him two or three more times, that he was into pure melodic playing and lyricism as much as he was into sounds. In fact, he had melded them into a perfect blend.

"Jimi had been fooling with feedback, but when he heard the Yardbirds, he realized its huge potential. Hendrix would sustain a note and add vibrato so that it sounded just like a human voice.

"He uses an immense vocabulary of controlled sounds, not just hoping to get those sounds, but actually controlling them as soon as he produces them. I have never heard such controlled frenzy, especially in electric music. Jimi said that he went to England to wipe them out, and he did.

"I have never heard a sound on a Hendrix record that I have not seen him create in front of my eyes."

Bloomfield did not know how Jimi kept the guitar in tune. Usually if you jerked a whang bar your guitar went out of tune. "But his didn't. Apparently he could bend it in tune.

"Somehow, by tapping the back of his guitar neck (which he constantly did), and by using the bar, Jimi could control feedback. You hear a rumbling start and then Jimi hits a note he knows will feed back. He knew which note would feed back and what harmonic he was shooting for, and then he controlled it. Somehow, when he has all the notes open, he raises the pitch level by using the bar and he gets a higher note to feed back, or he makes the bass note feed back harmonically. He was listening for such things, and I believe he heard them on the English records, particularly by the Yardbirds and Jeff Beck."

But Jimi, as he was very modest, never said that he took feedback further than the Yardbirds. He said, "I fool with it, and what I'm doing now is the fruits of my fooling around."

"You can't tell what Hendrix is doing with his body. He moves with all those tricks that black guitarists have been using since T-Bone Walker and Guitar Slim—playing behind his head and with his teeth. He takes exhibi-

tionism to a new degree. He crashes his guitar against his hip. It is a bold gesture, and he would get a roaring, fuzzy, feedback sound. His body motion is
so integrated with his playing that you can't tell where one starts and where
the other leaves off.

"Many of his sounds are things that Jimi stumbled on and a lot he shopped
for. They become part of his musical language. It's not something he can just tell
you how to do. You have to understand the way he hears sound. The way he
wants to feel sound and get it out to create music."

Mike Bloomfield noticed that Jimi used two basic scales: "The blues minor
scale (E minor) and its relative major. If Jimi played A minor, he would go to C
major and make it a major seventh scale.

" 'All Along the Watchtower' is a perfect vehicle for minor- or blues-scale improvisation, while 'Bold As Love,' 'Little Wing,' and 'The Wind Cries Mary' are
perfect vehicles for major-key explorations."

Bloomfield heard Jimi defining electric music before his eyes. Jimi turned
sound into music. Sound derived from devices and gadgets that he made come
alive. "Jimi's playing went beyond music into realms of pure sound and music
combined."

Bloomfield watched Hendrix perform many times but never could understand his hand positions or the chords he used. Jimi could play left- or right-
handed with equal facility. "Sometimes he didn't even restring his guitar—he
just played it upside down."

Hendrix was, to Bloomfield, by far the greatest expert he had ever heard at
playing rhythm and blues, the styles of playing developed by Bobby Womack,
Curtis Mayfield, Eric Gale, and others. Bloomfield got the feeling there was no
guitaring of any kind that Jimi had not heard or studied, including steel guitar,
Hawaiian, and Dobro.

"In his playing I can really hear Curtis Mayfield, Wes Montgomery, Albert
King, B. B. King, and Muddy Waters. Jimi is the blackest guitarist I've ever heard.
His music is deeply rooted in pre-blues, the oldest musical forms like field
hollers and gospel melodies. From what I can garner, there was no form of black
music that he hadn't listened to or studied." But Jimi especially loved the real,
old black musical forms, and they pour out in his playing.

"Jimi's musical approach, as he explained it to me, is to lay out the entire
song and decide how it should be—horns, strings, the way it will wind up. He
plays the drumbeat on a damp wah-wah pedal, the bass part on the bass strings
of his guitar, and the pattern of the song with just the wah-wah pedal. Then he
fleshes the pattern out by playing it with chords and syncopation.

"Jimi plays a bass pattern, and then fills it in with chords, and at the exact same time he plays lead by making a high note ring out while using very

unorthodox chord positions. He has a massive thumb, which he uses like an additional finger, so his hand positions are very unconventional for every chord.

". . . He told me once that his whang [tremolo] bar was customized on all of his guitars, so he could pull it back much farther than a whole step. He wanted to be able to lower it three steps."

Bloomfield was surprised to find that Jimi was extremely interested in form. In a few seconds of playing, Jimi could give him an idea of the entire structure. "That's why he liked rhythm guitar playing so much—the rhythm guitar could lay out the structure for the whole song. Jimi would always say, 'This is a world of lead guitar players, but the most essential thing to learn is the time, the rhythm.'"

Bloomfield laughed. "He once told me he wanted to burn Clapton to death because he didn't play rhythm."

While in New York, Jimi, Noel, and Mitch were interviewed by the *East Village Other,* a New York underground newspaper run out of a storefront on Avenue A between Ninth and Tenth streets, which fed information to a growing network of underground newspapers throughout the country.

EAST VILLAGE OTHER: I'm just curious as to whether these are songs you've written over a period of time, or whether you just go into the studio.

HENDRIX: A lot of them are ideas I've had from the Village. Some of them . . . like we just got around to recording "Little Wing."

EAST VILLAGE OTHER: Noel, you do a lot of chording on the bass. Now, your bass lines are funny. I'm used to either a standard walking jazz bass or country-and-western 1/3 or a Chicago blues riffing thing. Some of the things on the album were complicated 4/4 time over.

REDDING: I like doing that . . . changing time.

MITCHELL: There you go—we don't think about time. If you want to be technically specific about it—wow! The bass player's and drummer's roles are almost completely reversed. The drummer isn't the anchor, the bass player is more of an anchor. But you've both got freedom whatever you're doing.

HENDRIX: As far as technical works of timing or trying to blow somebody's mind with a strange time.

MITCHELL: You know, we're not doing this thing: wow, we can play a number in 19/8 or whatever it is. So what . . . big deal . . . like Dave Brubeck . . . who cares? You know, you become aware of your time and forget all about it. Who wants to count time for the rest of your life?

HENDRIX: Yeah, but our music is like that jar of candy over there. Everything's all mixed up. Regardless of what the scene might be—you don't put yourself in categories or else you find yourself really unhappy because then you might want to do something else. The best way to accept some of the things that we do—if it's all that important—is to take every song for what it has to offer instead of trying to put it all in one big thing. Because our next LP is going to be completely different and, you know . . . strange. Someone from the Move sang background on "You Got Me Floating" with Noel and Mitch and our manager's footprints can be heard on the fadeout of "If Six Was Nine." [Hendrix comments that the piccolo sound on *Axis: Bold As Love* was actually a Moroccan flute he bought for two shillings.] You can get that same sound out of a guitar. We've got a gadget called the Octavia that we use on a song called "One Rainy Wish." It boosts the guitar twice as high.

As far as guitar (in terms of electronic gadgets), we use repeat echo, wah-wah, things like that. [Jimi used a hand wah-wah on *Are You Experienced?* Both Hendrix and Cream used the first wah-wah foot pedal at the same time.] On "Spanish Castle Magic" we used a guitar, bass, and drums and piano and a lot of things are in unison. Noel uses an eight-string bass plus I was playing the same thing on guitar. It didn't come out as clear as we wanted but it was a hint of what we're trying to do.

Jimi set to work on the next album. He was also customizing his new suite seventeen floors above the plush, velvet lobby of the Drake Hotel on East Fifty-sixth Street. He began to get into the New York City social scene by bringing himself up to date on the many fly ladies into various scenes all over the immense town.

Devon was on the scene. They both knew they would be getting together soon, although just when and where and how still had to be worked out. Linda Eastman showed up at the Record Plant, where he was laying some preliminary tracks for his new album. She took many photos and got them back very quickly for him to see. They were beautiful flicks. She had a relaxed, offhand manner, and with her charming blonde good looks, she helped the flow of energy move naturally and got good pictures at the same time. And she was not hung up about ten or twenty dollars. She was very cool about bread. She came from a wealthy family.

Steve Paul's the Scene was happening, so were the Hippopotamus and the Salvation discos, but while Jimi was hanging out, he had the album on his mind, too. Mike Jeffery and Chas Chandler were giving him static about costs. Studio time was more expensive in the States. They would have preferred shorter hours at the Record Plant, but Jimi was seriously thinking of booking it around the clock, twenty-four hours a day.

He could feel that he and Chas were drifting apart. Chas was married and wanted to complete their business and return home. But for Jimi, he *was* home.

He could see that Mitch and Noel were impatient to return to England, as well. They had not been scheduled to return until the autumn of 1968 anyway, but the scene was still strange to them. They did not necessarily want to groove on the scene. Their attitude was largely one of workers out to do a job. Noel had taken an inexpensive three-room suite in the nondescript but clean Penn Hotel across the street from Madison Square Garden on West Thirty-fourth Street. He was determined to save his money. He wrote down everything he spent—down to the dime, the penny. He wrote in a diary religiously. Mitch was a bit looser. He was having a better time, but he, too, was lonely for England.

Gradually Jimi took more control of the sessions. Chas felt left out, especially since he figured Jimi was wasting a lot of valuable studio time on maddening details. Jimi did take after take of seemingly irrelevant phrases and passages—even on the basic tracks. He would sit down and piece together a raggedy wah-wah pedal for hours, even though studio time cost more than a hundred dollars an hour. Mitch and Noel took to napping while they waited for Jimi. They even took to laying up with their girlfriends while they waited. Jimi would scrap seemingly perfect tracks and takes right at the point when they seemed completed. They all began to get pissed at each other.

More and more hangers-on appeared at the sessions. They effectively buffered Jimi from Mitch, Noel, Chas, and even Mike Jeffery. Jimi seemed to give a lot of control of the scene to Devon. She became an unofficial watchdog of the sessions. She would order people out when Jimi wanted the scene cleared. She would say who could stay and who could not. Her attitude was perfectly suited to the task. She seemed to enjoy her power over the scenemakers. Tall, sassy, and well put together, she also had the street shit together and was known to tote a razor—*and use it.* She was not afraid of incurring the wrath of *anyone*—even Jimi. Yet he felt that her presence and seeming omnipotence were necessary to his scene. It was obvious he needed help in the handling of many mundane tasks, and Devon was glad to do it. When he decided he wanted to get an apartment, she got right on it. It did not take much persuasion to have her put on the payroll as a kind of girl Friday to Jimi. She could check out pads and once they got one she could keep it together for Jimi while he took care of business.

Jimi let Devon handle more and more of his affairs. She became essential to the "office," as well. Relations began to break down between Jimi and his management. Chas Chandler was ready to split any day, and Jeffery was in a difficult position. Devon made no bones about serving as liaison between the two factions. Jimi did not want to hear it. All he wanted to do was make the most beautiful album imaginable.

In her platforms Devon was taller than Jimi. Beautiful, but sometimes ugly within the throes of junk, yet always charming, with a type of cunning akin to Jimi's. Never at a loss. She had the most unique set of problems imaginable. Able to be just about any way she wanted to be, she could charm and recharm with equal ease. Not one to be put off, she could usually get at any time of the night what no one else could. Be it smack, coke, or a second girl for a sexual *trois,* she could deliver. Cunning like a streetwalker, pulling chicks like a pimp, she could satisfy the mama's boy and the sadomasochistic urge. That was Devon.

Devon, a street urchin who evolved from Milwaukee, a hick in the Big Town getting over by wits and charm—the artist. Devon's art was the con with a fifty-fifty chance of delivery. Yet to her, the superwoman of the groupies, Jimi was a part of her scheme. From Duane Allman to Mick Jagger to Miles Davis to Quincy Jones, she knew the heaviest people in music and could deal the heavy shit. Survival for a beautiful woman with no special talents did not come easy. Even rich men or men with money could assume that this elegant, luscious woman had no need of bread, and it was not her game to project those needs. Yet the utter necessities of life merged with the vicious drug habit she had— inseparable from her cool and her energy—which made her subject at times to quite unwomanly conduct.

Quincy Jones had met her in Vegas, years ago in the early sixties when he worked for Sinatra. A fifteen-year-old runaway who looked like she was twenty-five, full of street hip and hustle, Devon was nevertheless a poor, confused homeless girl who had not had time to grow up. A fifteen-year-old girl may be able to hustle successfully on the streets, but she is not as hip as an older woman who *has* grown up. For Devon, tricking in the trick capital of the world often meant getting ripped off. Her lack of savvy meant that she could have a few thousand dollars in her hand one night and be without cash or a place to stay the next. Quincy took her under his wing, adopted her as his cousin, and took her on to Los Angeles, where at least she had a place and people she could relate to as a person without the exploitation of Las Vegas.

In the realm of the glamorous but hip beauties of the rock world, Devon became a counterpart of Hendrix.

As Jimi constantly practiced, whether simply jamming, writing, or sitting up in bed with the acoustic singing the old blues he loved, Devon practiced her craft, as well, constantly maintaining her mastery of the groupie technique. This took a similar degree of energy and devotion, as did the constant competition of beauty and deliverance. Trickery became one of her catchwords. Even after a rip-off, or burn, she could, unlike most other beauties of the realm, reconcile even the hardest minds to her ways and make them like it—almost. She had a way that few could reject of copping out when caught red-handed at some shit. Haughty and proud even if one were to catch her, a smile, a shrug, a twinkle of the eye, and perhaps a quick jive story or a little loving were usually enough.

•   •   •

Jimi soon found the Scene club irresistible. In London there were many hip clubs to hang out in, and they were always changing, but in New York City there was only one—the Scene. Fans did not hassle you there. It was dark and intimate, almost labyrinthine, yet you could go there and party, or play and just sit alone and drink, and no one restrained you either way. And most important of all was that he could *play* there. He could jam any time he wanted to. *He could woodshed right in the middle of New York City.*

The Scene club was like a miniforum model for every arena he would ever play. The shouting stark frenzy of the close room is what he brought with him to every stage around the world. It was always the small intimate room he was really playing to. The thousand and one nights of playing long into the Scene's night. When the chairs would finally be upside down upon the tiny tables. When Steve Paul himself would finally have to pull the plug, while Jimi, alone in his universe, would be totally unaware of the hour or of the devotees and workers who patiently waited within the exhilaration of his sound.

At the Scene, Jimi would completely let himself go—playing all he knew and didn't know, going beyond sharing—playing all. Trying to get it *all* out.

Jimi slowly but surely got to be good friends with Willie Chambers and Ray Warner of the Chambers Brothers. Sometimes it was difficult to tell the five brothers and cousins apart. They were all tall and dark with brilliant eyes. They all wore black brims in the country way, with the crown head full and the brim riding low. Willie and Ray and then Joe and Julius and silent George all made Jimi an honorary Chambers Brother. They were from Mississippi and had a beautiful rural simplicity. They still talked in southern accents, although they worked hard to round out their r's by speaking as crisply thin-lipped as possible. But when they got excited they dropped right back into their back-home raps. Their career in music began when they were teenage gospel singers, out of the black church in the early sixties. Later they found work in folk scenes, coffeehouses, and at civil rights affairs. Folksinger Barbara Dane did an album with them. Then they abandoned both gospel and folk at the same time and went straight into hard blues/rock. The Chambers Brothers then went to L.A. and became regular musicians on the *Shindig* national TV music show. After that they signed with Columbia Records—John Hammond was their producer. Their "Time Has Come Today" was a hit single.

Jimi was closest to Ray Warner. They got to talking about the meaning of "the Axis" and went on with it for hours, days, weeks. Ray Warner was well read and planned to go back to college to complete the small amount of time he had left for his degree. A psychology major with broad intellectual interests, he found through talking with Jimi that the strange title of Jimi's second album, *Axis: Bold As Love,* had far greater significance than he had imagined. Jimi had said once:

I just thought about the title. There might be a meaning behind the whole thing: the axis of the Earth turns around and changes the face of the world and completely different civilizations come about or another age comes about. In other words, it changes the face of the Earth and it only takes about one-quarter of a day. Well, the same with love. If a cat falls in love or a girl falls in love, it might change his whole complete scene. Axis: Bold As Love . . . one-two-three, rock around the clock.

Ray was curious as to what else was there. He was not satisfied that it was as off-hand and simple as all that.

Yet when he and Jimi got down and rapped seriously about it he found that Jimi's whole conversation was full of things that sounded one way yet meant something else. It was a trip just to hear the normally shy and retiring Jimi open up and really rap about where he was at. He had other speech trips. He would talk "backward," saying something was *bad* when he meant it was good, together. He would say something that sounded completely simple and normal, but by nodding his head, winking his eye, or slightly altering the sound of a word he gave it a completely different meaning. What Ray finally deduced from talking with Jimi many times was that the man had a concept that boggled Ray's mind because it encompassed so much.

Jimi's concept of the Axis was hooked up like a freeway from Earth to space to infinity. The Axis was like a bridge or crossing over a threshold from one reality to a deeper reality, or from one dimension to another. He looked upon the Earth as a single creature. Jimi wanted to help the whole world, the entire universe. The wars and the bloodshed were terrible to behold—the wounds and the swords and the poverty. But just as the Earth turned on its axis, the people turned on to the music; even the image of a record on a turntable was a representation of the Axis. It was like the Axis itself was a living form of energy music, a mass of love and creativity all rolled up into one thing that came out positive. The Axis was like a stepping-stone to a greater understanding.

He was trying to say that he could take you to a holy place without even moving your body—and he wanted to do that. It was not about LSD or any hallucinogenic—he was the drug, he was the high. He saw music in the sky. He saw his music as a living life form that had the potential to give people a direct feeling, a direct understanding—that would open their eyes to cosmic powers by simply directly experiencing his music. He had a way to work that was going to reach across the nation. And any extraterrestrial beings out there would have to pick up on it. It was a heavy communication thing. Jimi knew he could not tell a whole lot of people about where his head was at and what he wanted to do, but he could give little hints in interviews and some of it in the songs and all of it to a few. Ray Warner began getting the distinct feeling that Jimi Hendrix was not of this earth.

.   .   .

Jimi sits alone in a studio. In the dim muted lights, the white Stratocaster crosses his slender body, pointing upward.

In "Somewhere," he visualizes "hands and shades of faces" reaching upward, in search of spirituality, religious confirmation, anxiously seeking help from their God. He sees the frustration in the populations as well as in the souls of the burning cities and the killing weapons of destruction that often cause that despair. Jimi can imagine extraterrestrials in their flying saucer–like spaceships looking down from space and remarking on how "those people are so upright they sure know how to make a mess." He then muses on his personal situation and how as far as he can ascertain those who manage and market his music "may even try to wrap me in cellophane and sell me." Sell him and not even care.

Ed Kramer had gotten used to Jimi's unorthodox recording-studio style. No advance meetings, as he preferred a loose approach since he had everything in his head: from backward guitar solos to double-trackings and overdubs of various precise lengths. And this accompanied by pages and pages of lyrics that he would choose and edit after the basic tracks were layered. And he also had, for more complex compositions, notes on composition in his own language and system. Over some poetic lines there would be basic chords such as E, B, F-sharp and D, A, E with a note to "repeat twice" and then a break with guitar and bells. "Guitar 1st E string ring open as B and G strings playing slightly oriental pattern together. B string notes start on 7th fret with G string on 6th. (Like so: 7 [1, 2, 3] 10 [1, 2, 3] 12 . . . then 5 [1, 2, 3] 7 [1, 2, 3] 10.) Repeat with low clicks of bass and slide guitar coming from down notes to up—then vocal, and at the same time guitar hitting G chord and bass string and bass guitar hitting A . . . then syncopate chords of B min, C# min, D, up to G . . . then to B." Jimi wanted Kramer not to be anticipating or expecting anything. It would be revealed only when he got into the studio.

There was no question among showbiz professionals that Hendrix and company were going to be big.

A larger mania had begun, with larger crowds in Los Angeles and Montreal. And the JHE were selling a lot of records in two markets, America and Britain—the United Kingdom territories that included Ireland, Australia, and South Africa, among others. How big they would grow and for how long remained to be seen, but Hendrix, Redding, and Mitchell were all still under twenty-five years of age and had years ahead of them in the healthful flush of youth.

Jeffery and Chandler had incorporated in America on February 21, 1968, while the "British Are Coming" tour was in full sway. They definitely wanted to avoid problems with British currency regulations, especially since Jeffery had a scheme encouraged by Steve Weiss to self-promote concerts, saving agent fees, and directly receiving the income generated by often sold-out, standing-room-only concerts.

Michael Jeffery had some advanced ideas about his offices being a partner in booking concerts across America. His experience with the Animals had given him a firsthand account of the hazards of doing business with strangers. He would never forget his assistant Kathy Eberth and tour manager Bob Levine having guns placed against their heads at an Albuquerque venue and being told neither of their bands—the Animals nor Herman's Hermits—would be paid. British bands had been subject to that kind of thing in their early days of touring America. And Jeffery resented being under the thumb of the promoters while receiving the lesser share of a concert that would have been impossible without his acts.

So Jeffery and company came up with the idea to hire their own promoters and give them a flat 10 percent of the gate. All they needed was an act that was highly in demand and competent promoters, who would do well even on a small percentage. A problem with Hendrix had been that his had been dubbed an erotic act, and that hindered touring in the American hinterlands. But by self-promoting their shows the JHE organization could bypass those conservative promoters and directly engage an eager audience. A further inducement was that the standard 60/40 artist/promoter split could be avoided, with Hendrix and company coming away with as much as 85 percent of the box office.

Concerts East became the name of that operation. Originally drawn from Concerts West, it was an entity created to handle the Jimi Hendrix Experience concerts. Tom Hulett, Concerts West's mover and shaker, with assistance from booking agent Ron Terry and Jeffery's lawyer, Steve Weiss, was able to put this concept into effect.

Since Monterey and the release of the film *Monterey Pop,* Jimi Hendrix had been a top biller, so his reappearance in America made the JHE a hotly sought-after act.

"The British Are Coming" tour offered incipient publicity and a press context that let a lot of people across America know these British groups were touring America. They did splendid business returning to Bill Graham's Fillmore West and Winterland venues in San Francisco at the very beginning of the tour as a thank-you for being the first to offer the JHE a big gig after Monterey and the first to elevate the JHE to top billing.

From that point on, requests poured in and as many venues as possible were added. That left the JHE with schedules that flew them around on a blistering initial series of nineteen one-nighters in a row, and a total of forty-three gigs in two months, and they continued on well into April.

After the King assassination–truncated performance in Newark, the JHE's gig at the Westchester County Convention Center, just above New York City, was the last gig for a while. Jimi did play at the opening of Michael Jeffery's Generation Club in the Village the following night. But mostly he worked on new recordings he was calling "Electric Ladyland," in between gigs, for the next month. This time he was using more of his own ideas and techniques and using the studio in a more luxuriant way, reflecting his phenomenal success and the huge amounts of cash he generated.

Gerry Stickells had started out as a roadie, but more and more he had become a settler-of-accounts money man. He would bring bags and bags of cash, receipts from various gigs, since the JHE office as the actual promoter received the lion's share of the grosses at various venues. They would need real roadies because it became obvious that Stickells would handle the money first and foremost.

Although Hendrix's recording deals had good numbers as far as advances and promotional budgets, it was clear that the largest source of revenue would come from the JHE concerts. And this money was cash.

Accountant Michael Hecht had been hired by lawyers Steve Weiss and Henry Steingarten to help sort out the finances. He had some initial observations: "On the 1968 U.S. tour, Stickells would settle at the box office after every Experience performance, and use that money to pay bills. On his arrival in New York he would walk into our office with suitcases and paper bags full of money. We would do the accounting and then take the money down to the Franklin Bank. They would have countless slips of papers for receipts but we would always be close to ten thousand dollars short. Whatever the excuse, it just would not add up. It was an impossible way to work."

Hecht had to assess the various financial repositories that ranged from the offshore Cayman Islands accounts Jeffery had long held, to cash on hand and deposits to various bank accounts in England and America. This was in lieu of the fact that while their set-up worked well for British subjects, Jimi was an American citizen and needed an entirely different set-up. Are You Experienced? Ltd. was set up as a company to "collect and control his earnings, as well as pay his taxes and expenses."

Complicating the recording picture was a 1965 one-page contract Jimi had signed with Ed Chalpin when he was gigging and recording with Curtis Knight. While Chandler had bought up the existing contracts with a few producers and small-scale record companies for relatively small sums of money before he had departed to London with Hendrix in September 1966, the contract with Chalpin had somehow been overlooked. Now, in the wake of Monterey, and the consensus of anyone knowledgeable in the music business that Hendrix was indeed going to be huge, Chalpin had geared up for the long run. He had formally served Hendrix, Jeffery, and Chandler with papers and was suing in New York

City civil court. Jeffery and Chandler had tried to settle with him for $70,000 in mid-April. But by that time the JHE had just completed the first part of their U.S. tour as headliners, where they had broken many house records and had audiences in frenzies. There was no question, from the bottom line and the revenues he generated, that Jimi Hendrix was already, a mere year and a half from his coming to England, a major star.

Warner Bros. president, Mo Ostin, discovered during a lunch with Chas Chandler that the legal situation regarding Jimi Hendrix was different than what he had thought. The next day he had a good selection, fourteen lawyers in all, of the Warner Bros. legal department in a settlement meeting with Chandler and Jeffery in anticipation of an impending settlement with Chalpin.

Ostin had thought that regardless of who won the lawsuit, Jeffery-Chandler or Chalpin, that Hendrix would still belong to Warner Bros. Chandler pointed out that Hendrix was not signed directly to Warner Bros. but to Yameta, a holding company controlled by Jeffery and Chandler. So instead of being disinterested bystanders, Warner Bros.' fortune lay in the success of Jeffery-Chandler. It was not lost on Ostin, or any executive or lawyer in the employ of Warner Bros., that the Jimi Hendrix Experience's album sales were so in excess of the highest numbers that a Frank Sinatra or Dean Martin ever generated that the future success of their corporation was on the line in this dispute.

As soon as the lawyers got it straight that what Chandler had told them was true, there was a near immediate settlement with Chalpin. Warner Bros. was very generous. They owned the future. And they used this settlement to gain the kind of control over Jimi Hendrix they felt they needed.

It could truly be said that Hendrix's entire future was affected by this lawsuit and Warner Bros.' settlement with Ed Chalpin. It changed forever his relationship to his management. And in the face of a lot of cash floating around at that moment, Chandler chose this time to cash in and to begin his exit from the Jimi Hendrix Experience.

Warner Bros.–Reprise made it clear they wanted an exclusive artist's agreement with Hendrix and the delivery of "the master recording equivalent" of an album. For delivery of the tapes, which would be the *Electric Ladyland* album, they would pay $250,000 upon the execution of the agreement. In order for that to happen they had to also buy out certain provisions of the Jeffery-Chandler/Yameta management contract with Hendrix. A $200,000 figure was agreed upon, payable in equal amounts over four years. They would also advance Jimi Hendrix $100,000, payable to Sea Lark Music, the administrator of his publishing company, giving Hendrix a 1 percent raise on future sales of the JHE's first two albums, and a 3 percent raise in his royalties, starting with *Electric Ladyland*. They would also pay half of future recording costs, with $20,000 of those costs as advances against future royalties.

This new four-year deal still included Jeffery and Chandler as sharing responsibility with Jimi Hendrix for the delivery of those future "products." While they no longer would share producer fees as per their previous agreement, Jeffery-Chandler were still in charge of management of the JHE, which included contract negotiations, publishing arrangements, and personal services, for the original 40 percent of all earnings. Michael Hecht, accountant, business professional, and employee, not at all antagonistic to Jeffery-Chandler, considered this arrangement to be "on the high side of what was considered a normal business relationship." The agreement with Jeffery-Chandler would expire on December 1, 1970.

Ed Chalpin/PPX Productions was the big winner. Warner Bros.–Reprise settled out of court, giving Chalpin/PPX a 2 percent royalty on the suggested retail price of all Hendrix recordings sold in the USA until 1972, and retroactive, in the case of *Are You Experienced?* and *Axis: Bold As Love* ("less packaging costs of up to 54 percent per $4.79 recording"). Plus a "one percent royalty on tapes, cartridges and all Canadian sales," also retroactive. PPX was paid $50,000 immediately and was guaranteed another $200,000 by December 31, 1969. Chalpin/PPX were allowed to continue issuing an album they billed as a Curtis Knight/Jimi Hendrix collaboration. They were also given permission to issue another album of a similar nature. And the coup de grace: the right to release on Capitol Records an original album featuring the Jimi Hendrix Experience.

Aside from some small details, approval of the artwork on the Knight/Hendrix forthcoming album, and credits for the JHE album, that was essentially the settlement.

Jimi was interviewed by Meatball Fulton for ZBS Radio Syndicate. The radio syndicate distributed shows all over the country:

ZBS: What happened to you in Seattle?

HENDRIX: Seattle has a different type of cold, you know. It's a nice cold, it isn't so cutting. Anyway, there's this girl up there trying to work roots on me. Work this voodoo stuff. Keep me there, you know. I had to go to the hospital and all that stuff, you know. I couldn't make that scene.

ZBS: What do you mean, you had to go to the hospital?

HENDRIX: Well, you know, she tried workin' roots. That's a scene where . . . there's different things they can do. They can put something in your food or put some hair in your shoe. Voodoo stuff. She tried stuff like that, but she must have tried only halfheartedly because I was only sick in the hospital for a couple of days.

ZBS: Did you ever get involved in that scene . . . ?

HENDRIX: Not anymore. You know around the southern United States they have a lot of scenes like that goin' on. But if I see it happen or I feel it happen then I believe it, not necessarily if I just hear it bein' talked about.

ZBS: What about charms and things like that?

HENDRIX: Well, you know a person, they give off certain electric shocks really. So then they can actually get those things together really. If the vibrations are strong enough to get those charms working, they can actually do it.

ZBS: I was watching you when you were talking to that girl who came in. . . . I think she was going to do some clothes for you. It was nice because you were really watching her and you were really taking her in. I mean, just like sizing her up.

HENDRIX: She seemed like a nice girl, you know. I'd like to take her home and, you know, scrub her up a little bit, and get into the scene. [Jimi jokes with Colette] Get the clothes measured up maybe. You see, I don't go by . . . some girls you don't go by appearance. You go by . . . there's other things that girls have to offer besides looks that makes you maybe want to be with them. For a second or two. There's other things. I don't just go by looks. We know the story about that. Some of the worst people are . . . but you know what it is, you can just feel things. You say, "*Damn*, I might want to be with her, I don't know, let me check myself there and see what happens." That's great.

ZBS: What about this? I mean, needless to say, a lot of people are envious, me included, you know. . . .

HENDRIX: Not necessarily. Really. You shouldn't. Because if you're not used to it, well, it could kill you really. Really. 'Cause it's another way of communication. That's why other people can't understand. They say, "Well, damn! Why are you with so many people?" You know. So I say that I won't necessarily be touching those people all the time. I'll just be talking to them. Some I talk to and others . . . you know what they're *for* and what they're after. It's a scene that . . . like it's a part of you. It's nature. I don't know. I just can't help it, that's all. It's a scene like . . . it's another way of communication, though. You have your own ways, you know. Some people just communicate better by not even knowing each other's name. By sayin', "Hey, hi, how you doin' there? . . . You want to come with me for a minute?" And then you know, you do that. And you can be the best of friends then. Some even get married after that.

ZBS: How do you find you flow with it, after you started to get this image . . . ?

HENDRIX: Oh, it was worse before. Because I used to be on the block starving, you know. And girls used to help me and all that, you know. Girls are some of my best friends because they used to help me. Really help me. And ever since then that's why I say to myself, "Wow." Every girl I meet now I want to show her my appreciation for what they did for me before. Not seriously, though . . . it's just nature.

—Meatball Fulton, 1968
ZBS Radio

Backstage at the Fillmore East, Sly Stone is guffawing his hacksaw laugh, wearing a glossy white Gabriel suit, with a brief, winglike cape across the shoulders. The brothers in the band wear gorgeous Las Vegas showgirl wigs. Little Sister with a blonde Brigitte Bardot model, Larry Graham with a Jane Russell model, and Cynthia, the big round saucy trumpet player, with her California Afro au naturel. Sly's natural style rose a foot above his forehead in an elongated pompadour. They were ready to go. Sly was crazy.

Sly opened the show. He was out to kill from the git.

In a flash the Fillmore East is consumed with the baddest, ass-kickingest, hard-bopping soul music in America. Larry Graham's bass walking seven-league boots on everyone's head. Freddie, Sly's brother, next to Larry on rhythm electric guitar. Both of them gut-bucking walking kicking boogeying proscenium steps. Cynthia, in the horn section, bending her sweet red lips to the soul trumpet, calling down Jericho. Calling down Sly Stone in his Gabriel white-caped white-on-white satin suit. Sly getting down on his Beulah Baptist holiness organ, counterpointing the guitar between the peak licks of the punctuating horns.

Sly *physically* rocks the Fillmore. It is like a battleship in rocking and rolling waters. This Oakland mack man has all his pieces instrumented as rhythm. All sounds are in motion—mixed down to equal value under Sly's exhorting lyrics.

Sly didn't sing "Try a Little Tenderness" like Otis Redding, although it was Redding's arrangement. It was more like a musical shrine to Redding, like a jazz funeral, celebrating Redding's spirit in song. Redding had perished in a plane crash shortly after the Monterey Pop Festival. Sly didn't sing it exactly as *he* would have, either. He merged his voice with Redding's version, as if Otis Redding were onstage singing with him. He moved in between Redding's and his own version, yet remained true to the original. Toward the crucial climax of "Tenderness"—that beautiful building up Redding did that made you burst in anticipation of the clashing horns and Otis's plea—a screaming "got to got to try and please her"—Sly suspends "Tenderness" in a heart-sinking abyss. Sly holds the "got to got to," slowly repeating it, and then staggers the phrase. His brothers join; the pendulum swings wider and wider, and pretty soon the three brothers are into a time-suspended chant: "got to got to now now now / got to got to now now now / got to got to now now now." The chant continues and pretty soon you have ceased to hear the original words. You hear something else, something closer to the utter archetypal root of the words in the melody. And then after what seems like an eternity, a trip at the speed of light over continents and centuries, they end "Tenderness" in the resounding glory of Otis, the light-show screen's purple orbs merging and exploding into an immense twilight blue. Then Sly breaks into a fire-and-brimstone rhythm and then as quickly into the hambone (the thump of hand and chest and the slap of the palm on the thigh, dual rhythms in hump position). They do it to it. Then they jump into traditional Apollo dance steps and the freight train is off once more.

Jimi loved to play against a group as heavy as Sly and his band. Second on a two-bill show, Hendrix comes out and wastes no time. A signal twinkles in the distance, coming faster and faster, rushing atonal and crashing notes. Billows of molten metal wafting exhaust into purple plumes of funk—"Foxy Lady." And Jimi is off burning from the onset, Mitch and Noel forming a flying V.

Hendrix assaults the mind, sublimating horrible noises of the city. Subways busting through violent tunnels, exploding Mack trucks, jet exhaust fumes, buses; he turns the fascist sounds of energy exploitation into a beautiful music with a pyramid base of urban blues guitar. B. B. King's loony obbligato screams, Blind Lemon Jefferson's beautiful justice of country space, and Jimmy Reed's diddy-bop beats; Jimi exalts them all into a personal mastery of primordial sound itself, beyond ken and imagination. We hear spaceships landing in the heavy atmospheric gases of fantastic planets, we hear giant engines changing gears, we hear massive turbines that run cities, Frankenstein life-giving electric-shock blasts, jets taking off and exploding into melody. We hear the thunder of Wotan, Shango, and Shiva mixed with the ethereal melodies of our cosmic sphere, evanescent and eternal.

Jimi begins having trouble with his amps. They were great in the upper registers and shit in the lower ranges. He was trying to make like his constant going back and forth to the controls of the amps was a part of his choreo-delivery by going into a split after each visit to the amps. His exhortations to Gerry Stickells, who stands helplessly behind the amps, are to no avail. Every time he tries to get into a fusion of metals, fuzz, and feedback the system falters. He throws his white Stratocaster over his shoulder and plugs it through his legs, getting a roar from the crowd. But he cannot play what he wants. He begins to feel burned. He begins to make a few offhand comments to the crowd, presaging the moment when he'll have to tell them he can't go on due to equipment failure. Then he thinks of a song he can play that would cool out the final disappointment: "Gloria." It had little of his heavy metal pyrotechnics. Instead he can groove in upper registers on the rhythm within the ensemble.

Jimi, splendid in the lights, bumping and a-grinding to "G-L-O-R-I-A." Every move displaying total mastery over both the instrument and his body.

The sound surging, panning back and forth in huge continuous waves of vibration. Holding everything together and taking it into another realm blended into a heavy bliss within the awe. G-L-O-R-I-A . . .

Jimi plays three guitar parts simultaneously: long sustained chords, picking rhythm in electrostatic harmony, and doodling tips of fire between it all. The sound is unbelievable. You can't get enough. It's too much. You want more. You can't stand it. Sound overdriving the conscious mind and reaching right through to your subliminal centers. And then Jimi is down on his haunches weaving and bobbing like a limbo dancer to the beat and in double time. He holds the guitar up with one hand—it plays by itself.

The Underground Pop Festival (May 18, 19, 20), the brainchild of Michael Lang, a local head shop owner, had raised enough funds from investors to put on a three-day event that would become better known as the Miami Pop Festival.

The Jimi Hendrix Experience headlined a bill that featured Chuck Berry, Blue Cheer, John Lee Hooker, Frank Zappa and his Mothers of Invention, the Crazy World of Arthur Brown, and Eire Apparent, among others.

The first day was great. Twenty-five thousand attended the Gulf Stream Racetrack in the Hallandale section of Miami. The music began, but they had forgotten to pick Jimi up at the airport. The organizers were in a collective panic, when Jimi astounded them, descending via rope ladder from a hovering helicopter down to the stage—just at the moment when he was to play.

The helicopter had flown in over the racetrack as Jimi was announced. He had rented it from the airport after realizing no one was coming to get him.

Ed Kramer was there to record the JHE, and photographer Linda Eastman (who would soon marry Paul McCartney) had been hired for documentation. Jimi gave her something to shoot by burning a Sunburst Stratocaster at the end of his set.

At the Castaway Hotel in Miami proper, where all the acts stayed, Jimi's, Frank Zappa's, John Lee Hooker's, and others' jam that night at the Wreck Bar of the hotel gained instant notoriety. The next day a heavy thunderstorm forced the cancellation of the second show they were to play. Leaving the racetrack Jimi's limo got stuck in a traffic jam with Kramer and crew. He wrote "Rainy Day, Dream Away" in the limo as they crawled through the deluge.

Later, in Miami, Jimi experimented with his hair, Linda Eastman lacing several blond patches through it. She was taking pictures and Annie Fisher from *The Village Voice* was taking notes. Linda was gassed by the blond streaks she had tinted into his hair; they went well with his pink puffed-sleeve shirt. She shot in color. They were ten stories up above a swimming pool area where a square dance was about to start. Mitch ran out on the balcony with his Super 8 to get some shots. Noel was hanging out in leopard-skin skivvies. He had refused to be perturbed about having to go and get working papers, unlike Mitch, who had blown his top, shouting that nobody would expect the Beatles to go and stand in line for anything. Finally the promoter, Mike Goldstein, said that he would take care of it, and that was that.

When it came time to get paid, Arthur Brown said, "I saw Jimi go inside to get his money. A few seconds later he backed out through the door with his arms raised. There was a guy pushing him with a shotgun stuck into Hendrix's belly. He said, 'I think you'll wait, Mr. Hendrix.' Jimi took it quite calmly." Brown, a Hendrix protégé, thought the incident a "revelation about what was happening to the peace and love movement. Everything was changing."

Because two days of the three-day festival were canceled due to rain, there was a shortfall in funds. After a near shootout over the way the short funds would be paid out, with Michael Lang's Brinks guards, money collectors, and some local cops who had been hired as security, the Jimi Hendrix Experience was not paid.

The entire JHE entourage had to sneak out of the hotel without paying the hefty bill. Jimi and Trixie Sullivan, Michael Jeffery's assistant, were detained in a locked room and only managed to escape by climbing out a bathroom window.

It was quite an adventure, but the expenses incurred made it necessary for the JHE to add some gigs in Italy. They could make money at will. All they had to do was structure the offers that were constantly coming in.

A year later Michael Lang would organize and produce the historic Woodstock Festival in upstate New York.

On May 22, 1968, the Experience hustled around London looking for a road manager to replace the one they had lost at their Fillmore East concert in New York two weeks before. They had to be in Milan, Italy, the next day to play a gig at the Piper Club. Not only were they shorthanded, but the equipment was in bad shape, as well.

Noel Redding found Eric Barrett at the Speakeasy, smashed out of his mind. Barrett, who used to be road manager for the Koobas, the opening act when the JHE and the Who played the Saville, agreed to make the trip.

They went on to Rome to play the Brancaccio Theater on May 24 and 25, through Bologna on the 26th, and to Zurich, Switzerland, on May 30 for the "Beat-monster Concert." There Jimi got to jam with Stevie Winwood on organ and Chris Wood on flute from Traffic, and Carl Wayne and Trevor Burton from the infamous Move. The Move was being sued by the prime minister of Great Britain, Harold Wilson himself, for using his photo in an ad for their latest record. The photo (touched up, of course) showed Wilson in bed with a per-

sonal secretary and a caption urging the viewers to buy the latest Move single release.

The next day Jimi Hendrix split to Majorca, Spain, for a vacation.

Howard Parker, aka "H," was one of the Jimi Hendrix Experience's roadies and
equipment managers for a while during the summer of 1968. A hefty, stocky,
hard-working fellow, "H," formerly with the Pretty Things, was with Hendrix
during late spring in London. The only concert that remained for them to do
prior to their return to the States was the Woburn Festival for the Duke of
Bedford's son and *Melody Maker* outside London, and that was several weeks
away. Hendrix was keeping a low profile: The dual anxiety of leaving comfy
London to stay in the hectic USA and the wait were driving Hendrix crazy.

"H" saw Hendrix in the Bag O' Nails with Angie Burdon, Eric Burdon's estranged wife, and another girl. Used to the "cool" treatment afforded him as a
lowly roadie by the class-conscious London music world, "H" was surprised at
Hendrix's warm hello and invitation to join them. Hardly going to refuse a star,
"H" sat with them and soon sussed out that Hendrix was in "a mood." As "H"
lived in Camden Town, which was close to the club, they all retired there to get
high.

At "H's" flat Angie, Jimi, and her friend met two young groupies whom
Arthur Lee and Love had left there when they went on to Scandinavia. Angie
and Jimi seemed to be coming on to each other in a friendly way. They were jaw-
ing at each other and soon stood up in a playful fight. Somewhere along the line
the fight got serious and Angie, as drunk as Jimi, hit the floor. Hendrix got carried away. "H," reluctant to interfere, nevertheless grabbed Jimi's wrists and told
him to cool it. Jimi cooled down at once and remorsefully sat in a corner while
Angie and her friend quickly left.

Ashamed, with his face to the wall, Jimi cried. Then, to the consternation of
"H," Hendrix wanted to talk. They had a philosophical rap. "H" endured it, saying that whatever Jimi did, it was his thing, and his thing only. Hendrix was
sobered by "H" in his forthrightness and warmed to the subject. "H" said to
Hendrix: "Why do you bother with her if you hate her like you say you do?" Jimi
replied: "You see the way she walks, man, just like a cat. I dig that walk, the way
she moves—just like a cat. . . ." "H" realized that he was in over his head and retired to the couch. Hendrix took the two young girls to bed. "H" was kept awake
all night by the squeaking of the bedsprings.

Jimi got into a heavy hanging-out thing. He had been working steadily for
nearly two years straight. Recording in New York was great. For one thing,
recording freed him from touring. Although Chas was still balking because he

felt Jimi was taking too much time, Jimi was enjoying the recording of an album for a change. Not like the rush jobs on the first and second albums, but a relaxed yet intense run of sessions, which also allowed him time to reflect on what was happening in the music and to do something he had always wanted to do: compose an extended piece. And while he was recording he had the run of Manhattan, as well. Indeed, it was like a vacation.

He had his buddies who all hung out at the Scene, or the Salvation or the Hippopotamus, and he always had some fine ladies up front or on the side. He had the best recording studio on the face of the earth in the Record Plant, and several pads besides his official residence where he could disappear to, if necessary. It was a perfect set-up.

He got really tight with Hugh Masekela, who was still tripping behind his hit "Grazing in the Grass." It was the kind of hit everyone hoped for. A monster that stayed up in the charts for months. Hugh was enjoying it to the hilt. Flying back and forth between L.A. and New York, Hugh was into a heavy party scene. Sometimes he would stop what he was doing for a moment and say, "You know, I haven't slept for months!"

One day some chick who said she was from *New York* magazine talked her way into Jimi's suite at the Drake Hotel and then rushed into his bedroom and began taking pictures of him as he awoke from the commotion. Jimi was happy to find that she was a good-looking chick. They had a nice time talking and laughing and getting high. When the photo was published it appeared Jimi was in the process of receiving a blow job. The photo is from the point of view of the benefactor; Hendrix is, obviously, the delighted recipient. Next, Eric Barrett, the new road manager, came in very upset. Bad news. The equipment truck had been stolen. He looked like he expected his head to be cut off. Jimi was more philosophical. New York City was at least notorious, compared to London. Eric Barrett offered to go looking for it himself. He had already contacted the police, but their nonchalance gave him the impression that they had more important things to do. Eric rushed out, frantic. Jimi thought for a while and then called Manny's on West Forty-eighth Street.

Jimi had dealt with Manny's Musical Instruments and Accessories since he had come to New York City to live in 1964. The store was a family business. The elder Manny had given way to his son Henry after thirty years at the helm. Jimi had established an open account and would come in once a week to try out all the new instruments, distortion devices, and accessories. Usually he would take all of them home. Every other week Jimi would buy three or four guitars. He could count on Henry to deliver several guitars to him by car, or to ship the necessary stock ahead for a worldwide tour. Henry was fascinated by Jimi. Henry knew that any new little "toy" or sound effect he got hold of would be bought by Jimi on the spot.

The Fender Stratocaster, like its predecessor, the Telecaster, was designed by Leo Fender to be easy to build, play, and service. Its fretboard was standardized for accuracy down to a thousandth of an inch, the very best the tool-and-die shops could do. The cutaway body made it easy to play all twenty-one frets; its solid body made the Fender electric guitar accessible to the most modern of technology. Up until the advent of the Fender Telecaster in 1948, electric guitars (which had been inspired by the popularity of Hawaiian steel guitar music of the thirties and then through country and western music and finally popular music) were acoustic hollow-bodied instruments with pickups for amplification. Leo Fender introduced the solid-body Telecaster in 1948. Its sounds were pure-toned and accurate and were loud enough to drown out an entire orchestra. The feedback that had plagued the hollow-bodied electric guitars was virtually eliminated by the Telecaster and subsequent Stratocaster. Leo Fender had started on his quest for the perfect electric guitar by concentrating on the pickup. The pickups deliver the sound of the guitar through the amplifiers and loudspeakers by electromagnetism. The pickups are actually magnets or several magnets wound with coils of superthin wire. The guitar strings are slightly magnetized and when they are plucked they vibrate through the magnetic field, making the current pulse through the coils and on through the amps and speakers as sound.

The designed serviceability of the Stratocaster made it easy for Jimi to modify the instrument for his own use. First he would bend the tremolo bar by hand for several hours to get it to go down three steps, instead of the customary one, and also to get it near enough to the body so he could tap individual strings and raise and lower their pitch without it being an obvious manipulation, the proximity making it possible to be done quickly. Also, because of the tremolo bar's proximity to the other tone controls, he could play with all of them at once while whanging the tremolo bar. Sometimes he removed the back panel so the strings would be accessible from the back. It would achieve another kind of sound. This also enabled Gerry Stickells to change the strings onstage while Jimi continued to play. Jimi made his own adjustments at the bridge and the pickups. The adjustable solo-lead pickup had a snap-on cover that housed three elevated screws that enabled Jimi to balance the tone; this was connected to the lever switch, which had three set positions. Similarly, the rhythm pickup was adjustable by removing the pick-guard panel and working the elevated screws. The microadjustable bridge was beneath the snap-on cover. Three longitudinal screws adjusted string length for proper intonation and six elevated screws adjusted the height of each string, therefore enabling Jimi to get loose action on the bass strings for a deeper twang, and fast, close-to-the-neck action on the treble strings. Jimi varied the selection of his strings for his particular sound. He used very heavy strings on the bottom, medium gauges on his A and D, a Hawaiian G string, a light-gauge B string, and a superlight E string. The head of the Strat was styled with all the tuning pegs on one side of the neck, which made it very easy to tune the guitar even while actually playing. A neckplate was anchored by tempered steel. This extrasturdy construction made it possible for Jimi to bend the rosewood or maple-wood necks of his Stratocasters without breaking them. That way he was able to get more unique sounds. Since Jimi made sure the tremolo bar was bent down as close as possible to the control knobs, he could also manipulate the tone-control knob—which functioned as a lead pickup modifier when the lever switch was in the lead position at the same time. The lever switch had two other positions: a middle position for straight rhythm work and a forward position for deep soft rhythm. The volume-control knob was between the two; Jimi kept it at full volume, ten, at all times. Roger "the Valve" Mayer rewired all of Jimi's guitars and built him an individual and fantastic Fuzz Tone box.

In modifying his guitars, Jimi concentrated on the pickups. He also re-coiled them to get a personal sound and range. They were the tiny poles of the "axis" that propelled his sound and made his control of feedback possible.

It seemed that Jimi was trying to set an endurance record for jamming. In June of 1968 he and Jeff Beck got in two good jam sessions at the Scene. The first was with Eric Clapton, also—three incredible guitars. The patrons couldn't believe it. Soon after that Jimi and Jeff Beck's group played a benefit at the Scene for Reality House, a drug rehabilitation center. Jimi came out and played "Foxy Lady" and then got behind Beck on bass and let him blow his brains out, while he covered the bottom territory with his lightning-fast fingers.

Jimi played with the McCoys, challenging cocky young guitarist Rick Derringer. Then Derringer got on bass while the Chambers Brothers sang and Buddy Miles played drums. Jimi played with Jim Morrison and Harvey Brooks and Willie Chambers at the Scene. Jim Morrison got so excited he got down and started kissing Harvey Brooks's feet. Then Mick Taylor from John Mayall's blues band took over on drums, and Johnny Winter plugged in his guitar, and they played a strange version of "Red House" and an ultrafast version of "Sunshine of Your Love."

Jimi sat in with Muddy Waters at the Cafe Au Go Go and it was beautiful. Jimi sat in with Howlin' Wolf at the Scene but "the Wolf" put him down and really made him feel bad.

Jimi and Buddy Miles started going around jamming together at different places. They would scat Albert King solos.

Jimi and Johnny Winter got together on a Guitar Slim tune—"The Things That I Used to Do"—Winter playing slide and Jimi playing lead and singing. They went right down to the Record Plant and taped it.

Finally, Jimi got a chance to play with the entire Chambers Brothers group at the Electric Circus. Of course, they did "Time," their big hit. Jimi was glad and eager for that because the song had incredible spaces for his lead, since Willie (their only regular guitar) played only rhythm all the way through.

Jimi dug hanging out with the Chambers Brothers. They were a big family and they accepted him as another one of their brothers. Willie Chambers *looked* like a guitar.

Once they were all at the Scene club playing a benefit for the Biafra war victims, which Jimi had attended with Joan Baez on his arm. During a break, some of the people from the audience had gone out to get a "breath of air" and got busted in the parking lot. Jimi was the first guy to jump in his Stingray and go down to the police station to bail the brothers out.

Another time Jimi and Willie and Ron Hobbs, bass player for Johnny Winter, rode around New York City for hours to score some grass. They had about eight chicks back at the apartment. When they finally copped and returned to the apartment, Jimi sat up there and put on a show. He told jokes, did his Harlem queen bit—he was as loose as a goose. This was a side of him Willie had never seen before. Then Willie realized that although he had known Jimi for years they had always encountered each other before hundreds of people or backstage at a gig, but never anywhere approaching one to one. He had always thought Hendrix was shy. He was, with lots of people around. But with a few friends in the room he was truly one of the fellas.

People would always be trying to get Jimi stoned. They *assumed* he wanted to be loaded all the time. Willie and Jimi were in a bar once and someone came up and put something in Jimi's drink. Willie was astounded. They just assumed that Jimi would want to get high—and most likely he did not. A lot of people thought it was really funny to do that with acid. Willie would hear people saying that Jimi shot LSD into his temple, into the side of his head.

Jimi enjoyed recreational drugs, but not all the time. What he always wanted to do was play. He would come into the Scene at midnight or so, and at five o'clock in the morning they would try to drag him off the stage. Steve Paul would say, "Please quit, quit—I'm going to get a summons."

Sometimes Jimi and Joe Chambers would just sit at a table drinking without saying anything. Jimi had several places where he stayed. Sometimes it was not cool to go to one place, so he had others to go to. He had a place in the Village that Devon kept for him and a "business" suite at the Drake Hotel. Sometimes he kept a room in the Howard Johnson Motor Lodge on Fifty-third Street and Eighth Avenue near the Scene. He had a place in the Bronx, too. Plus a couple of others that nobody knew about. All of his pads had lovely young ladies taking care of them. They would mend his clothes and sew special things. Jimi was not at all possessive. The girls were free to see who they liked. Sometimes Willie Chambers or Hugh Masekela would be seeing the same lady at the same time. One of the ladies gave Willie a turquoise ring to wear that belonged to Jimi. When Willie became concerned that Jimi might object, she said that it was cool but if Jimi wanted it back she would just ask Willie for it.

Offstage, among his employees and ever broadening entourage, Jimi was a strange, retiring, self-effacing fellow. Not about to let fame turn his head, he seemed as if he were trained and groomed for humility from birth. Able to see through situations involving undue adulation and parasitic dependency, he would still not say anything, not rock the boat. He would not let it bother him at the moment, but he seemed to store it up and then release it all onstage, where Jimi was completely transformed. All the pent-up violence, frustrations, and personal harassments were sublimated into the music: and the audience, his fans, the lovers of his music, would come to see him with pretty much the same feelings pent up inside of them. He would provide them with their release, as well as his own.

But there were other ways in which he got release. He loved the pretty young ladies who followed him around. His pad, which had become a curse to his privacy, was at the same time a blessing for his great love appetite. He would come home to find a bevy of ladies lying all over the pad and in his bedroom, a special one naked with her legs open upon the bed.

Hugh Masekela would often come by looking for Jimi and find instead a houseful of chicks. Many times Hugh just came looking for chicks, knowing that Jimi's pad was a sure place to find them. One night he came by to find Jimi conducting his special orchestra: each chick in the place had some kind of instrument (mainly elementary percussion), and Jimi was on guitar, conducting them in a special concerto.

With all the people in his life, the only place Jimi could be alone and not hassled was onstage or in the recording studio. Many nights he roamed through Manhattan, eventually winding up at a studio. One night he recorded "Midnight," a tune that reflects his nocturnal quest. "Midnight," one of the rare instrumental recordings of Hendrix's, has a staggered shuffle beat that remains the same throughout the entire piece. Mitch's box shuffle snare is in the time dimension of midnight. Jimi begins by playing the bass line, the only sound. Climbing three steps quickly and then falling deep into a slow-motion funk abyss, Jimi's distorting fuzz delays a rag in syncopated 4/4 time. The bass, matching every shuffle/skiffle of the drums, takes off behind Jimi. It's a stately city journey. In the city, most are asleep when he is awake. His day begins in full force around midnight. Arising when the sun is down at twilight, freaky spirit thrills those who live on the other side of time: midnight, the "beginning" of the day. The midnight creatures glow resplendent through the dark nights. The midnight cruise illuminated by treble beacons and electric fire fuzz, connecting souls through the quiet caverns of midnight. To the sound-cushioned rooms where music blasts to the midnight musicians playing thousands of gigs, recording thousands of tunes, all over Earth. Up in the sky at midnight, wild stars visible by thousands and the moon reflecting sounds. A soul satellite beaming magnetic messages to the heads in midnight nirvana. Searching crosstown, the rhythm changes at the bridge. Jimi walks his bass as he transfers lightning-fast squalls to treble tremolo gliding through the night. In love upon the midnight tides, the waters and the flow of moist mucous membranes, the flush flow of fluids undammed flowing into screams of joy. A choir of soprano orgasms and unconscious atonal winds breaking bonds. A chord breaking open into three shards of feedback streaking across the sky in a flying V. The overtone of the middle note departs upward from the rest, and then all three of the notes revolve into a pure synthesizer signal. Sliding along the back of the neck in a beautiful moaning glide into a yelp, the guitar says "OH WOW," just like a girl, and then back to the life of the night as the theme returns. Jimi plays his sitarlike trademark of writhing vibrato sweeping into lissome grace figures that are then driven to the sky. And then suddenly the sound blossoms into broken feedback and a lonely aloft figure disappears beyond the sky.

Just before *Electric Ladyland*'s release, Jimi revealed a lot of thoughts and ideas he had kept to himself for a long time when he recorded various interviews at his apartment. The release would be his first United States LP, and as "produced and directed" by himself, also a mark in time where he put himself in the vulnerable position as the complete author of his work.

He spoke about the early influences of the blues, as it were, mixed with the adult life he longed to be a part of, to grow up and leave his troubled childhood behind.

But he recalled, in terms of early musical influences, that as a child he would lie in his bed awake in the dark upstairs, "while the grown-ups had parties, listening to Muddy Waters, Elmore James, Howlin' Wolf, and Ray Charles, I'd sneak down after and eat potato chips and smoke butts." Captivated by the collectively "thick sound" of those blues masters, men known for their unique contributions to what was known as the blues and rhythm 'n' blues but really the only music the blacks in the projects of Seattle would party to, Jimi would wait until everyone was gone and then he would inhabit the still warm, dark atmosphere and hear the music over in his mind, participating in his own afterparty in the only way he could. Some ultrareligious folks would say that music was the devil's music, evil. But Jimi never felt that. He thought of that music more as a dense realm of expression—something that paralleled the complicated lives of those he knew, those closest to him, his mother and his father, their relatives and friends, the community. That music was like a soundtrack to their lives.

Jimi had progressed from those early feelings he had had for the blues. He had gotten exposure in the South, living there in Kentucky and Tennessee during and after his military service and touring small venues all over the South. He had learned at the source. He had paid his blues dues. His rough experience contrasted with the current scene where the blues had become fashionable, especially after the affirmation the English rock groups had given to blues. Now there were more white American blues bands. Jimi felt that "so many groups are riding the blues bandwagon."

For many he felt it was just a stage to explore rather than what had developed out of their way of life. "The blues are easy to play but not to feel. The background of our music is a spiritual-blues thing." But Jimi also knew that blues helped to define America, to make it a nation with a distinct culture, with an art form Americans could call their own. He said, "Blues is a part of America." There was not much that could be said to be unique to the United States. Among them, blues was a major element.

From there Jimi flowed into his electric church concept. Announcing it in *Newsweek* was a scoop. Electric church was like an alternative Bible, not like one would find in a hotel, "but a Bible you carry in your heart, one that will give you a physical feeling." Jimi elaborated on his music as something that "hits your soul hard enough to make it open."

He phrased to his satisfaction what would be in his program when he headlined Royal Albert Hall just after the release of *Electric Ladyland*. He had something for England, for the world, his was the new religion. He realized it in the feeling, in the faces of the multitudes he faced.

Jimi recognized the wide frustration among the youth, and rock's ability to deliver a big, crafted sound that through volume and sometimes harshness could relieve some of the frustration. "The kids like it. . . . They become the fathers to the music."

But his music recognized blues as the basis of rock. Hendrix compared rock to a "young dragon," inferring that blues was the old, the bedrock, the papa dragon. Then Jimi laughed at what "the Establishment" would do once it could control this young dragon, making rock an extension of a Las Vegas show extravaganza.

Jimi noted that he often felt at one with many others "in our little cement beehives in this society." He felt that many of the laws were out of date, but that the establishment enforced them as if it were God administering the ten commandments.

Change the world? Jimi would love to, but a better scene would be "my own country—an oasis for the gypsy-minded people. My goal is to erase all boundaries from the world. . . . I can't withdraw to lesser goals.

"Black kids think the music is white now, which it isn't. . . . But the black kids don't have a chance too much to listen—they're too busy trying to get their own selves together. We want them to realize that our music is just as spiritual as going to church."

A long black limo drives up the West Side Highway of Manhattan, taking its time. The funk of the Hudson River breezes through the windows. A glistening ghostly-white moon shimmers over the waters. The high cliffs of the Jersey Palisades take the land higher, dispersing it into little homes and tiny lighted streets that diminish into the spread of greater America.

Living and working in New York City like any other person. Fixing up your pad with a beautiful lady who you live with who loves you. Lying back in a long, soft, smooth ride with Devon watching the river. The sky and the moon go by. And she is tall like you and slender, not lanky. Her smooth black sheath curves across her long-limbed body. Long legs bumping against each other, so warm and so cozy.

Off the highway, through the streets, to the Scene. On the edge of Times Square. Out front, a big lighted entrance; inside are narrow rectangular panels leading up to a dim box office. You sweep past into a zigzag-shaped mazelike room with tiny tables and tiny-backed chairs. But up on the tiny stage, two feet off the floor, the music happens as it happens in all major cities in the Western world.

He wears a red velvet cape that swirls about him in the dim blue lights like a red molten force field charging the air: his aura.

And there is Fayne Pridgeon, sitting with the owner of the Record Plant, Gary Kellgren, and his sister Michelle. Jimi stumbles over chairs and tables. Devon flows regally behind. Fayne is laughing already. Her long, smooth, brown, impeccably clear face with steady, mysterious, black eyes looks even more beautiful than Jimi remembered. Jimi sits in Fayne's lap. The perfect thing, as he well knows, to make her laugh uproariously, as if he were tickling her. Gary and Michelle look on pleasantly as Devon moves into a check position.

Jimi fondles Fayne and does fast-talk ecstasies aimed at Gary and Michelle. Laughter rises all around the room; some because of him directly, some because of the delight everyone now feels for being here, for being alive, for being so fortunate to be with each other, to be there when Jimi comes in cutting up 'cause he's happy.

Fayne sparkles copper gems. She is loud-talking, high-laughing, happy street people. She looks totally uptown, her up-sweeping pillared hairstyle with black locked curls illuminated against the dim air. Perfect sound system pumping rock. Devon is superelegant, her sleek black hair splaying out at the nape of her olive neck. She takes the scene in slowly, giving Gary a stroke, a slight dyke slur to Michelle, an appraisal of Fayne, who is starting to crack up all over again because Jimi is still in her lap. Then Devon checks out the adjacent tables. But she does not crane her neck; she will wait until she goes to the ladies' room to powder her nose and then she will really get a look at what's happening.

Jimi is back to Devon. He is explaining how he hasn't seen Fayne for over a year. Devon is vaguely interested. When she and Fayne have sufficient eye contact, Devon invites her to the ladies' room. This is a distinct invitation to some nice blow. Fayne is again delighted. Delights upon delights.

Devon leads the way, weaving expertly through the narrow paths. Swooping down to say a few hellos, give an occasional kiss. Fayne, much shorter even in heels, has to stop each time Devon stops, allowing enough room so she won't bump into her. Fayne is impressed. Devon moves with a measured ease and does not take too much time at any one table.

In the ladies' room Devon goes immediately for the coke. From a jeweled snuffbox case she solemnly and expertly offers Fayne a generous spoon, lifting it reverently to her nostril, as if Fayne's nose were the most beautiful part of her body. Another in the other nostril, then Devon gives herself a one-and-one. Devon takes her hits hastily, as if abhorring the delay, and then hands the entire case and spoon to Fayne for her to go for herself. A sign of healthy respect and comradeship. As the fine-ground powerful white powder connects with the mucous tissues of the sinuses they begin to talk. Devon says that Fayne looks like she knew Jimi well. Fayne laughs. "Yeah, I knew that nigger when he was uptown, just came from the South. I took him from some faggot in the Palm Cafe." Fayne laughs her constant chuckle, as if there were much more she could say. Then she goes on. "Did you see Gary's face when he sat in my lap? I nearly died. Jimi's always doing something like that. You never know what he is gonna do next."

"Yeah, we're fixing up our pad down on Twelfth Street in the Village," Devon said. "You got to come down and hang out, get loaded, and have dinner. We have a ball. You get enough? Here, for the road."

Devon leads the way back, walking right into a befuddled Eric Clapton, who looks like he had been hanging outside waiting for Devon to emerge. Devon laughs and hugs him. He continues his befuddled puppy dog kind of spaciness, very English yet very much, in a way, like Jimi. Devon introduces him to Fayne. He acts silly and shy but sweet and serious, absurd in his slick American hippie clothes.

Devon sweeps him back to the table, allowing Fayne to go first. She brandishes him like a statue of war from a London minipark. Now she will have some fun tonight. Eric really goes for her. He acted as if he didn't understand his attraction, himself, as if he were drawn to her by a mysterious force. He and Jimi were so in awe of each other, so shy and respectful, so all-giving, that she would have free rein over the situation. She could fuck with Eric and fuck with Jimi and they would smile genially at each other and be ever so polite and reserved that she would want to scream and whoop with hilarious delight. Their only respite, their only refuge would be the stage where . . . well, ain't that a bitch, where Jeff Beck stood ready to jam with the McCoys, who were set up and raring to go.

Fayne wound up coming home with Devon and Jimi and spending the night. The night's party lasted until the next day and then they crashed through the day. They awakened in twilight to eat, drink, and toot, and start the party again into the endless night. Put on your clothes and get into what happens, a fascination from moment to moment, for days. Fayne stayed for several weeks.

The Record Plant, situated very close to the Scene club, was near enough to take a good night of jamming right to the recording studio with the energy and inspiration still high. It soon became necessary to rent the Record Plant around the clock. Regulars at the Scene became the audience for several jams that appear in their entirety on the *Electric Ladyland* album.

The entire vista of his sound accelerated at the Record Plant, as it had at first in the London studios. The Record Plant had the latest equipment, young engineers with good ears, and an older, more experienced engineer who knew what could be done and what would work with Jimi on exploring new sounds. No more working night and day with two four-track machines just to layer the sound correctly. And it was great that Fayne was there; a solid crazy friend from the old days who was as excited as he amid all the debonair New Yorkers.

Long hours were spent in the studio working with the extensions of what could be done. Now there were eight tracks to work with, increasing the layers possible. And more sophisticated equalizers extended the tonality of the bass, especially in the low registers, without distorting, allowing a rounded, deeper throb. Now he was able to use three or four mikes on the drums, thus getting more subtlety on the tom-toms, high hats, and cymbals, and getting a good kick from the foot-pedaled bass drum. And he still has several tracks for himself and the voices.

But Chas was objecting to just about everything that was going on around the studio and the recording of the material. He was used to controlling the situation and saving money by being economical with studio time as he had done so well in London.

And Chas was rather appalled by the Village regulars who hung around Jimi. Many of them were from the not-so-old days when Jimi was just one of them.

Jimi could not forsake them, could not turn them away. "Like a Rolling Stone" was a philosophical edict to him. Chas was not used to so many black folks. And the regulars, including the whites, very often were not of polite society. To his way of thinking, they were not anywhere near the gentility of the average Londoner, or in possession of the self-effacing expressions the lower classes so often gave to those who had wealth, power, or status. These were black, white, Puerto Rican, and others, mostly bohemians, and a bevy of musicians from all over, most of them characters.

Besides, Chas had just married Lotta. He was a married man who needed to spend more time with his wife. And he was keeping more regular hours—not necessarily the night-to-early-morning-hour stretches in which Jimi usually preferred to record.

The time he took to launch Jimi had paid off. But in London the pubs closed at 11:00 P.M., so people led lives of rather normal hours. But New York City was a twenty-four-hour town and Jimi was used to those hours. That was more his normal cycle.

And with Concerts East, Jimi saw more of the money he was generating. More than enough for all the studio time he needed, and more.

Jimi had become aware of the large sums the posters, the T-shirts, and the book of photos, *Electric Church,* were bringing in.

He was a wealthy rock star spending his money. And, besides, Chas and Michael Jeffery were doing quite well with their large percentages of his earnings.

But he hoped Chas was only going through a temporary thing when he said he was through being the JHE's producer. He was not appreciating Jimi's approach to recording. But Jimi was involved in recognizing the studio as another instrument, another realm of sound possibilities, and he was gaining more knowledge and making more discoveries during each marathon session. He hoped Chas would see and hear and appreciate what he was trying to do. But he would hold back on his creativity for no one. Hendrix had become lord and master of his domain. And when the world heard what he was creating with *Electric Ladyland* they would know that, too. And Chas would recognize him.

On July 28, returning to the U.S. from Europe through JFK Airport, Jimi met rockabilly legend Jerry Lee Lewis, who ceremoniously refused to shake his hand.

The night they recorded "Voodoo Chile" was a gas, with streams of people going back and forth between the Scene and the Record Plant. The recording simulated a live session, and the nearness of the Scene gave the set the freshness Jimi wanted.

"Voodoo Chile" captures the atmosphere of a funky nightclub within the music. The busy sounds of the crowd are mixed into the song as if public witness to a ceremony. The ceremony, late-at-night partying, and secular blues are mixed down within a voodoo creation tale—"Voodoo chile!" There are shouts of pure joy, shouts of encouragement—"YEAH! *YEAH!*" Tinkles of glasses, small talk, and simply the alive hush of humans in a room as if their breath itself is being transferred to the grooves of the recording.

Jack Casady, the regular Jefferson Airplane bassist, starts the set off by signifying in terraplane bass growls. The mood is set. Jimi's beginning licks alternate between an octave high-unison formation with Casady and some tenor doodling, the whole effect setting up a tension of anticipation.

Jimi's guitar dubs with his voice in the ancient, sacred blues tradition. Repeating the title of the song, "Voodoo Chile," he appeals to God that he is indeed a voodoo chile. The guitar dubbing in sharp soprano every word sung. Stevie Winwood hitting a single organ note, the thrilling tonal key to the melody.

Still suspended in mystery, Jimi begins with rhythm licks at the precise staggered tempo that will carry this "song of creation" throughout. Punctuating the licks by zooming his bass strings, he hits a figure opposite his rhythm licks—it seems to talk, saying, "Okay, boys, let's go."

In a rambling, loping, yet stately stride, the rhythm section starts out. Winwood's organ blossoms into the modal underpinnings for Jimi's voice. Mitch hits like he has been waiting all his life for this moment, his double kit sounding like the clean strikes of an ax into fresh oak.

That was the sound. That was the sound he wanted. It came bopping out at him strong and round, bubbling like lava and wide and all-encompassing.

And against the ensemble sound you can feel the room. It is alive. Though all voices are hushed, you can hear the air respire, giving off a resounding southern roadhouse effect. The long banking lines of Jimi's guitar are borne through the air over great distances, over land and sea to the summit, where he begins this teaching tale, this personal catalytic of the mysteries.

He begins a story of the night of a birth, his birth, when the moon burned an incandescent red. The mother screamed and died as a fortuneteller had prophesied. He was found and aided by two highly symbolic animals, a mountain lion who discovered him as a baby and sat him upon an eagle, who then flew him "past the outskirts of infinity." When he was eventually delivered back to earth, the eagle gave him a "Venus witch's ring." The eagle told him to "fly on," because he had become a voodoo chile—no doubt, an authentic voodoo chile.

The music begins to muster, building and charging into a crescendo, the guitar stalking up ahead like a purple-flamed dragon. The organ sweeping upward. Jimi's primordial tone flashing below the organ, urging it on.

Jimi then explores his resultant powers. He can be impossible numbers of miles away and yet project himself in the same room as his love. His magic Sagittarian arrows transverse light-years from Jupiter's methane sea to earthly bedrooms and, as those arrows are made of pure desire, he can enchant from other worlds. He can make love to a woman in her sleep and she will enjoy it because, putting it mildly, he is such an amazing lover she would think she was "losing" her mind.

There is a happy energy, a buoyancy that comes through the live studio setting. Jimi has Stevie Winwood's organ pipes to play against. This gives a surprising depth-of-sound plane. The organ is a perfect opposite to Jimi's talking guitar. Mitch is kicking ass on drums—the stomp of his kick meeting the bass in its deepest tone, the shimmer of his cymbals contrasting the deep cavern echo. Winwood plays intelligent blues changes that build to Jimi's solo. Midway through, Winwood hits a series of brilliant runs and Jimi comes in at the peak to quickly drop an octave and push a liquid delay that moves beautiful deep tones into underwater depths. The shimmer of metal vibrating, atomic particles, and human tissue is in the air. The song becomes a night-train spaceship zooming off in a shimmering whine of primordial energy.

The song almost stops, but picks back up again to the cheers of the studio audience. Jimi's guitar growls in appreciation. He tags on an aside about floating in "liquid garnets" between California, where he places "honey from a flower named Blues," and a submerged New York, where he holds hands with his love as the city "drowns." All in his purview as a voodoo chile.

They had just about walked out of the studio when a camera crew rushed in. They asked Jimi to give them something they could film. Jimi and company went back to their instruments and right into "Voodoo Chile (Slight Return)."

The rhythm is brighter and nearly a hambone. The intro figure from the guitar is stark old blues. It descends as if from on high into an atomic explosion, billowing out a bottom bass of gut-bucket clouds that range, staggering and talking, across a deep terrain. Jimi has his guitar making primordial monster growls and roars. Then he gets into serpent movements, darting lizard tongues, and to cap it all off he achieves the sound of a sacrificial lamb being slaughtered.

Jimi continues the tale of the "Voodoo Chile." At this projected point he has formidable superpowers. He can destroy mountains with a blow of his hand. He also has the power to reshape that debris into an island where he just might "raise a little sand." He then apologizes for taking up the sweet time of mortals, and vows to return that time, "one of these days." And as a farewell he verbally waves good-bye, stating that if he doesn't see you anymore "in this world," he will see you again "in the next world." His final caution: "So don't be late."

August 23, 1968. The Singer Bowl, Queens, New York, former site of the World's Fair. Jimi Hendrix and Janis Joplin face each other in the narrow dressing room. Between them is a fifth of Jack Daniel's, which they share amid the hustle and bustle of the New York Rock Festival (the Chambers Brothers and Soft Machine are also on the bill). Jimi and Janis are having a little party with each other. So seldom can folks get together and relate. They cherish the moment through the twelve-year-old whiskey.

They had not planned anything. It had just happened. The Chambers Brothers had just gone on, and Jimi would follow Janis to the stage. Through the walls the crowd hummed and crackled, cheering as the lights came up on the first big chord from the Chambers Brothers.

At first Jimi just sat and listened to her talk. She had an extraordinary set of pipes. She could sound like a university-educated Texas schoolteacher one minute, and an insane, lascivious teenager the next. The more they drank, the more resonance began coming out of her voice. A subtone, like the strange intonations of a heavy drinker, yet at the same time timbres and pitches that came closer to what she sounded like when she sang. She had a squawk voice, and a husky voice that could almost sing bass. Her range increased the closer it came to the time she would go onstage. It was like her rap was a vocal exercise—the drinking, too—getting all those funky and freaky edges and vectors together.

They had started talking about the old blues. They both solemnly acknowledged how much the old music contributed to their inspiration. Then Jimi took out his stage prop for that night, a Confederate flag the size of a handkerchief, and blew his nose. That blew Janis's mind; she cracked up. She howled. Her high wheezy laugh, for a moment, reminded him of Brian Jones. She lost her breath, laughing, tears rolling down her face. That broke the ice. They talked enthusiastically about their favorite blues singers, singing little snatches from their songs. Janis's soul was into Bessie Smith, while Jimi's was somewhere among Elmore James, Robert Johnson, and Muddy Waters.

Jimi began to play some blues, like he always did before a concert. Janis fell right into the patches of melodies and runs, humming softly, repeating phrases, swaying her head to the implied beat. They were loaded. The fifth of Jack Daniel's was dead.

Then a sudden flurry of activity in the dressing room had her onstage in a flash. Her loose, funky San Francisco band, Big Brother and the Holding Company, cranking up her intro.

Her voice amazed him. He could sense the energy latent in the low tones. Her sound was Texas country crossed with Louisiana blues. The energy and the volume of her singing at full tilt in many ways matched the intensely high volume he played at. She had the voice of a wailer, a belter, who could switch to sultry blue tones with no effort. She gave all. It was not perfect and precise, but her feeling outshone everything.

She could reach up high and sing over her range, as a free jazz man would blow over his reed, producing scaling screeches. The power with which she sang produced overtones in both the upper and lower registers. Sometimes she hit three notes at once, producing weird chords of pure freak. But then she could come right down to earth and talk, singing with such naked sincerity that you *loved* her. In song she was a goddess, irresistible. Onstage now she jumps up, hollering like a field hand, pushing breath through herself seemingly at the velocity force of hurricane winds. Janis also had a foreignlike quality in her middle range that made it feel sometimes like she was not singing in English, but in languageless tongues swirling eternal. Her croony moans trailed off in unique figures you could never predict. There was something spooky about her singing that was thrilling and scary at the same time.

The huge PA system of the medium-size stadium was a perfect vehicle for her sound. You heard every piece of her eerily beautiful cries, her guttural moans, and her freaky slides as they swayed in the winds. She intertwined them all and you gave up guessing where she was coming from and totally surrendered to her power. Somewhere inside, beyond herself, she wrought it out, spread it around, and shared the power.

She was power.

Janis Joplin was total inspiration. He really felt like playing after hearing her performance.

As the Experience set up, Jimi murmurs something about "making it up in spades" for all the equipment problems he had had at Fillmore East when he played on the same bill with Sly earlier in the year. The crowd doesn't care what he is saying. They are going wild. The cops are scampering about. And wow—the stage is revolving like a lazy Susan.

Jimi goes through "Purple Haze" and "Foxy Lady." He could see how weird it must have been for Janis, facing thousands of screaming fans you can hardly see, turning all the time.

He sees Mike Jeffery and Gerry Stickells come to the edge of the stage. The house lights flash on, revealing two equipment men pulling a kid off the stage. He is resisting. They get him to the stairs and leave him there. The lights go back down. The Experience continues to play. Gerry Stickells is hassling the kid on the stairs because he is blocking the way. A cop comes up and yanks the kid off. A swarm of cops rain sticks down on the protesting kid. The crowd responds angrily. A few skirmishes start up near the stage and the momentum spreads back into the crowd. A man takes up a long two-by-ten from one of the police barricades. He is waving it at the cops. People begin to smell a riot. The audience takes in a collective breath of air. Some move toward the revolving stage area, some recoil in fear. A gang of cops quickly hustles the kid out through the musicians' entrance, and as the music continues the crowd settles back into a jagged groove.

Jimi ends his set by charging the amps like a knight, with his guitar as the lance. He skims the fretboard against the felt covers of the amps, achieving a frenzied bottleneck effect. Then he squats over his white Stratocaster and swirls it around and around under him while still playing.

Just after the completion of work on his *Electric Ladyland* album, Jimi suddenly took off for the West Coast, much to the consternation of Chas Chandler, who was used to a closer working relationship with Hendrix.

The JHE had a string of gigs on the West Coast that went from September 1 to October 31. So Jimi had decided to move his entire operation, including *Electric Ladyland* LP promotional activities, to Los Angeles. Warner Bros. rented the JHE a mansion in Beverly Hills' Benedict Canyon.

Electric Ladyland would be released nationwide September 17. Hollywood was the headquarters of Reprise and Warner Bros.; the shots would be called from there. This double LP was Hendrix's most ambitious and totally represented the spectrum of his creativity and, since Chas had retreated from the producer role, *Electric Ladyland* bore Jimi's personal signature, even in its design.

Chas Chandler, in the traditional paternal/maternal manager's role, felt that Jimi was beginning to lose control. For Chas and Noel and Mitch, England was home, England was their scene. Crazy America was like an aberration to be tolerated at best. Chas felt that England was Jimi's power base, that he had an important duty to retain England as his official and real headquarters. But Jimi, after two backbreaking years of emergence, of becoming a star, wanted to have some fun, too.

New York was hip, but L.A. was outta sight. Bevies of the freakiest and loveliest ladies, resplendent in the tropical enclosures of Hollywood/Beverly Hills. Days and days on end of parties poolside, or in someone's private jungle high above L.A. Hugh Masekela, Sly Stone, and of course Buddy Miles were on the set. The Whisky a Go-Go replaced the Scene as Jimi's chief jam stand. And Jimi's brother, Leon, arrived from Seattle for a real reunion.

Jimi and Buddy Miles quickly became legends that summer in L.A. Jimi stayed at Miles's home, which was just up the winding road past Schwab's drugstore, in the Hollywood Hills. Running with Buddy was a gas. There is nothing like two high-powered brothers on the loose who are down to party. Miles, from Minneapolis, and Jimi, from Seattle, often acted as if they had been sprung from their respective hometowns for the first time.

They hung out at a club called the Experience. It had a huge face of Hendrix painted upon the façade, with the entrance as the mouth of the likeness. Buddy was working on his first album. Hendrix was listed as producer, but he mainly sat in the booth while tracks were being laid and while Buddy sang. He produced the album by just being there and being himself, Buddy would say. Jimi did not play but just indicated his taste for the music. Jimi worked the dials some but mainly let the sessions take their own course unfettered. Jimi wrote the liner notes for the album entitled *Expressway to Your Skull* by the Buddy Miles Express. He personifies the express train as Miles, "coming on down the tracks shaking steady, shaking funk, shaking feeling, shaking life." Jimi has the train conductor announce the advent of "the electric church" where the express takes them. Where they will exist joyously and "funkily ever after." Then Jimi excuses himself with his trademark remark about hearing his own train a-coming.

The lines of young ladies waiting to see whether they would be chosen to enter Miles's handsome white Tudor house became a part of the Hollywood sightseer route. All into the night long white legs wound down the steps of the circular front entrance.

Jimi began to drink a lot, to throw some money around, and speed his silver-flecked Stingray, packed with foxes, through the winding hills of Hollywood night and day. He was having a good time. Letting it all hang out. He knew that Chas, Noel, and Mitch felt that he was being that legendary "nigger on Saturday night," but he didn't care. They treated the music as if it were a career, as if they were clerks in the British Post Office.

Jimi had a lot of fire to burn off. He had not been able to properly run the streets with a brother while he was in England. More important, he was in a highly productive and creative period.

All the hijinks in a weird way balanced with his creativity. *Electric Ladyland* was a bitch!

He smashed up his Stingray. Yeah, he had been loaded and probably shouldn't have been driving because of poor vision, but those Hollywood Hills were the weirdest roads anyone would ever want to maneuver. Trying to get back to Buddy's pad, he had to make turns up a winding one-car-wide road that swung in ninety-degree angles. He missed a turn and put the car into a wall. Well, big deal. They towed the car off and he went out and bought another one. Everybody made a big thing about it. But he *had* the money, shit, he had the cash. Why wait when you need a ride? Miles dug the limo scene, which was cool for him, but whenever possible, Jimi liked to drive his own machine. Sometimes Miles's limo bills ran into the tens of thousands, but if Jimi put up ten for a new ride everyone made a big thing about it. But what bugged Jimi most about the incident was Noel's insistence that he needed glasses. That his eyesight was poor and that was why he had the accident. Noel just wanted everyone to wear glasses, live in England, and count every penny like he did.

The brick-throwing incident was something else. Jimi didn't know whether he had thrown this brick at some chick or not. He did know that he had been getting pretty consistently loaded. Not so much acid now as booze, the hard stuff. Sometimes he wouldn't remember what he had done. And then to watch the glee of those who told him of his antics. He did know that the novelty of the chicks hanging around day and night was wearing off. They began to get on his nerves. He had given a couple of chicks a whole pocketful of money, just to get rid of them, really. He was stoned and they were nice chicks. Later, word swept the Sunset Strip that he was giving away thousands of dollars at a time. After that, traffic jams ensued outside Buddy's pad. There were hundreds of girls, and many not so nice.

But the best time he had was with the music. It was nice to do studio work in L.A. and then come out into a balmy night. It was a different perspective and he heard different things there than when he was back east or in London. The West Coast was more expansive. Sometimes he could hear his guitar bouncing off the canyons and mountain ranges and diving into the ocean.

Jimi would work late into the nights at the many amazingly modern studios in L.A. There he had the brand-new sixteen-track machines to choose from. He felt free to work within the expansiveness of L.A., especially with the extra tracks. The instrumental "Peace in Mississippi" seemed to lend itself to the L.A. lifestyle. In many ways L.A. reminded him of the last stage before the deluge. L.A., earthquake prone and absolute in its insanity, seemed to hold both great promise and imminent tragedy in a strange balance.

One night at TTG Studios on Hollywood Boulevard, Jimi completed one of the countless guitar overdubs. There were several brothers in the studios doing work, also, who were really gassed to see him there. Jimi voiced his concern over the lack of black support for his music. But the brothers told him differently. There were a lot of black people who dug his music and bought his records. They saw him perform when they could, but they were outnumbered by the simple fact of his overwhelming popularity. This was the first time Jimi had heard this point of view. It was heartening. He opened up to the brothers and told them stories about his most recent tour. He had gone through the South and found a very nice vibe there—it had surprised him. In a way it related to what the brothers were telling him about his black support. The newspapers said one thing, but once you checked it out for yourself, you discovered something closer to the truth.

Jimi had been working all day and now he wanted to play. He wanted to go to the Whisky, but rather than call a limo or cab, or call Buddy's for someone to come and get him, he put his problem on the floor and immediately got an offer of a ride. It was a gas to ride in someone's ordinary car for a change, through dark and warm Hollywood with his lovely lady companions by his side. He always sought to be as close to his people as possible, and he enjoyed this simple, innocent, brief ride a few miles down the road more than his benefactors imagined.

Jimi was interviewed by *Circus* magazine, a New York–based publication, to coincide with the mid-September release of *Electric Ladyland*. The possibility of Richard Nixon winning the presidential election was on a lot of minds.

CIRCUS: What are you working on right now?

JIMI: There's one song I'm writing that's dedicated to the Black Panthers, and that's the sort of thing we might go into. It doesn't just pertain to race but to symbolism and today's things and to what's happening today. By that time, the president will be elected.

CIRCUS: That will mean either a lot of change or absolutely no change at all.

JIMI: Well, we plan to make it a whole new thing, *regardless* of who is elected.

CIRCUS: Living in London as you do, do you get a different perspective of America?

JIMI: I was digging America so much until I went over there [to England] and came back and then went over there again and went all over Europe and came back here and saw why people put this country down. I still love America—quite naturally—but I can see why people put it down. It has so much good in it, you know, but it has so much evil, too, and that's because so much of it is based on money. That's really so sick. People here are losing their peace of mind—they're getting so lost in all of these rules and regulations and uniforms that they're losing their peace of mind. If people would just take three to five minutes a day to be by themselves to find out what they wanted to do, by the end of the week, they'd have something. If people would only stop *blaming*. You can see how frustrating it is—the black person argues with the white person that he's been treated badly for the last two hundred years. Well, he has—but now's the time to work it out, instead of talking about the past. We *know* the past is all screwed up, so instead of talking about it, let's get things together now. But that's all child's games. You know where the truth is. Quite naturally, you say, "Make love, not war" and all of these other things, but then you come back to reality—there are some evil folks around, and they want you to be passive and weak and peaceful so that they can just overtake you like jelly on bread. You have to fight fire with fire. I mean, I'm getting myself personally together in the way of music and what I'm going to do.

I'd like our next album to be a double set again and to have about twenty tracks on it. Some tracks are getting very long, that's why you can only get about twenty tracks—our type of tracks, anyway—onto two records. But, you see, our music doesn't pertain to one thing. It just happens that the white people can dig it all of a sudden because some of them are very freaky and have imagination as far as different sounds are concerned. I love different sounds as long as they're related to what we're trying to say—or if they touch me in any way. I don't like them to be gimmicky or different just for the sake of being different.

It's all going to come about soon, but the way that America is going now, it's all getting kind of lost. Those three to five minutes of contemplation I was talking about, that's how you can get yourself together and be friends with your neighbors—maybe even say hello and see if you can knock down all of those complexes. You have to go down into a really bad scene before you can come up with light again. It's like death and rebirth. After you've gone through all of the hell of dying, you've got to find out—and face—the facts to start a nationwide rebirth. But I'm not a politician, you see. All I can say is what I've been seeing: common sense.

CIRCUS: But the masses are saying just the opposite.

JIMI: You know who is *really* living in fantasy land? It's the damned masses. *The masses.* The point is, *who* is wrong and *who* is right. *That's* what the point is— not how many people.

CIRCUS: But the amazing thing is, is that the masses feel that *we* are the ones who are living in fantasy land, that we are the sick ones. . . .

JIMI: That's what I'm saying. If you want to sit around and talk about it, you can go on like this for the rest of your life. What I'm trying to say is that somebody has got to make a move. The others are just waiting around until you run to jelly. Then they tick you off.

CIRCUS: How much contact have you had with the Black Panthers?

JIMI: Not much. They come to the concerts, and I sort of feel them there—it's not a physical thing but a mental ray, you know. It's a spiritual thing. But I don't care if people are white—let me tell you something, I don't care as long as people are doing their jobs, that's what it is. Our thing is completely wide open. I'm for the masses and the underdog, but not for just trying to get the underdog to do this or to do that—because I tried that before and I got screwed so badly millions of times. So now I'm for just anybody who can do the job.

CIRCUS: Will things have to be destroyed before we can achieve a better world?

JIMI: Quite naturally, you have to destroy the ghettos. You have to destroy those. Physically.

CIRCUS: What about the mental barriers?

JIMI: Maybe we can just scare half the people with common sense. Take cancer and cigarettes on TV—we don't say yes and we don't say no, we just tell the truth. You blind your head to the TV all of the time by watching some dreary program—*really* the fantasy side of life!—and then you say, "I'll just get a joint and do this." But the problem is still there. When you come back out, it's there, the street is there.

CIRCUS: But who is going to do all of this?

JIMI: I don't know, man, I'm doing the best I can. Everybody's going to have to get off their ass. All that I can say is just common sense. We're going to use our music as much as we can. We're going to start, if people will start listening. Some things may not come yet—but they will.

CIRCUS: Was it easier for you in Europe?

JIMI: Well, everyone has problems. In Europe, people have a little more contact with one another. There's a little more communication, and everything's not all freaked out. In just saying hello and good-bye, there's more warmth. I live all over, though, so no place is really my home.

CIRCUS: When you want to relax, what kind of music do you put on?

JIMI: I dig anything that holds my interest.

CIRCUS: Thank you for a fascinating interview.

JIMI: My pleasure.

—*Circus* magazine
November 1968

At last the new album was finished. Jimi sat down and listened to the entire *Electric Ladyland* album before letting Ed Kramer send it off to be mastered.

The album opens with ". . . And the Gods Made Love," setting the tone for the sound paintings that would follow. Jimi would say the title with such serious reverence that people did not know whether to laugh or to listen more closely.

When Hendrix first played the melody of "Electric Ladyland" in the Record Plant studios, it had only a spare solo guitar feel. It sounded acoustical, crooning out a Manhattan rhapsody, the polished grace notes trilling and turning between the strangely winsome, yearning melody. Alternating chops between the bass line and the chord, and descending steps downward to break out in garlands of incredible gypsy-flavored trills. His playing indicating all four of the guitars that would be on the recording.

In the final recording, the solo intro (and also the initial mood) is sacrificed for instant vocal choirlike overdubs and layered guitars refraining with the voices. Getting to the heart of the melody at once, Jimi, in these voices, harmonizes with himself in beautiful falsetto overdubs.

"Have—you—ever been," he wonders, to the song's title, "Electric Ladyland." It is a magic carpet ride that requires precise timing. He wants to show unusual "emotions" as they flow through "sounds and motions." The "electric woman" awaits them, so it is necessary to get rid of inhibitions as they float over a sea filled with love, where before their eyes "I see the love land, soon you will understand."

Her legs open like the wings of an angel, and their lovemaking is divinely inspired.

When they recorded the song in the studio, Jimi jumped out of the barricaded enclosure where he hid himself while he sang, and shouted, "I can sing, I can sing!" He was literally jumping for joy, it sounded so pretty.

A faint whine of metal flying above the treetops fades the song out.

"House Burning Down" starts off as if it's in the middle of a splendid Hendrix solo, with the drums rolling and the bass-rumbling finale. Then it quickly breaks down into a sprightly 4/4 funk march, with Jimi shouting, "Hey . . . hey . . . hey!" over rooting treble guitar licks that harmonize with his shouts. "Look at the sky turn a hellfire red," he sings, describing somebody's house burning down, down to the ground. This is a first reference in his writing to the urban rioting that had been occurring across the United States for many a summer throughout the sixties. Almost all of the writers who insist on Jimi's so-called color blindness are British writers who rarely ever talked to any of his African-American friends who knew Jimi was extremely race conscious and proud to be so. Although careful of not appearing to be a black radical or revolutionary sympathizer as he rose in fame, once he got to superstardom he very consciously and openly endorsed and supported the Black Panthers, the SCLC, and the anti–Vietnam war movement.

Jimi tells a simple story of his going to check out on a chariot the riot situation. His supernatural elements appear to be window dressing to the main theme. He questions some of the people who had burned down the houses they lived in. In the nation's black ghettos, those who inadvertently destroyed the homes they were living in seldom owned them. Absentee landlords were an essential factor of ghetto poverty.

In "House Burning Down," he describes speaking to someone he describes as being "nineteen miles high." The man says that they were disgusted and exhausted so they set the fires. Jimi replies, sounding slightly absurd dispensing simplistic dictums, that they should try education as opposed to rioting. He notes that the "truth is straight ahead."

A latter song of Jimi's, "Straight Ahead," is an important example of his late development, where he had greatly refined his advice. For the rest of his life as an African-American superstar he would seek to send a solid message to his ghetto counterparts as perhaps trying via popular music to give some real truth to the people. In the progressively funky "Straight Ahead," which would only be issued after his death, he is telling listeners to forget about the past and go right on and "keep on straight ahead." He sings of passing knowledge on to the young and old. Tell the children the truth because they will eventually be running things. And that the love of life is the best love to have. He even sings the popular chant of the civil rights movement, "power to the people," and urges them to stand together and "organize."

Jimi takes the song out with three guitars all playing rhythm figures. One emerges across the top burning a treble pinnacle. Then Jimi growls a turn, jacking his tremolo bar to cause a slight rise in pitch that gives the effect of a great vehicle in a tortuous turn. The ending of "House Burning Down" is as thrown together as any lyric he would ever sing. He narrates about a giant ship from space coming down and taking away the dead.

"Crosstown Traffic," a bouncy back-beating boogie, reveals Jimi's ability to simply get down with amusing lyrics and basic rock 'n' roll.

Jimi cautions a young lady who seeks to waylay him: "You jump in front of my car," but that she must have some idea of the hazard she is putting herself in since she knows he is moving at a very high velocity. She tells him she can withstand the collision because she desires to ride with him. He notes with mock disdain that she is like "crosstown traffic" because he can't seem to get through to her that she would just delay his journey. He notices the "tire tracks all across" her back and surmises that she must have been recently run over by other fast-moving vehicles. She may have had fun in those encounters but he can see in her a pure traffic jam just up ahead.

Recorded in early 1968 in London, "All Along the Watchtower," by Bob Dylan, bursts forth with an enchanting sound. Later, Jimi was able to remix it in New York on advanced equipment, playing bass himself. Chanting guitars set up sharp harmonics of yearning. Settling against a flurry of back-beating drums and blossoming out with the bass, the twin rhythm guitars mew violin lines. Slightly delayed in the rotation of the beat, Jimi emphasizes breathtaking violinlike sustains and pure treble reach. His lines are so delicately drawn they seem classical in their phrasings. A high drone constantly peaks in the background. An incredibly wide expanse opens between the bass and guitar and drums. They ride upward to the tip of emotion, where Jimi shouts from the summit:

There must be some kind of way out of here
Said the joker to the thief
There's too much confusion
I can't get no relief

Businessmen they drink my wine
Ploughmen dig my earth. . . .

But let us not talk falsely now
The hour is getting late

"Watchtower" from Mount Olympus, majestic and grand the sound towers in the sky. Below, the ocean breaks against the rocks. Jimi takes off from the rhythmic theme and creates a solo that ranks with his very best.

Dew tinkling droplets, liquid electric lines, and a jazz saxophone blowing through the rhythms of the heavens begin "Rainy Day, Dream Away." The congas come out commanding a mixed-down chugging ensemble. A sleepy voice requests that the other person in the room take a look outside. A pause in space as the ensemble slowly establishes a dreamy interior. A sleepy muffled voice says, happily surprised, that it is raining. Freddie Smith's saxophone riffing bluesy against the mellow mood. Jimi's guitar trades licks and duels with the saxophone on a free terrain as the beat takes a jump in tempo and brightness.

Jimi's voice comes in, blending perfectly with the beat and the space between. He sings the title, "Rainy Day, Dream Away" in a languid tone, strangely delighted by the rain. He acknowledges the sun being on a vacation, as flowers take a bath and children frolic. He will "lay back and groove" on this rainy day. He looks out the window and sees ducks happy in their element, as dignified people are uncharacteristically on the run. The traffic is making "carnival" sounds, tire splashings echoing in the downpour. And as his gaze travels to the hotel pool he sees a woman he digs. He will definitely be able to "lay back and groove on a rainy day."

Neptunian bass throbs atmospheric fog in the cosmos, ranging along the planet of the key. Mike Finnigan's organ tightens the ensemble sound with its chords and Buddy Miles keeps the beat funky and well defined on the raining earth, fading out.

"1983 (A Merman I Should Turn to Be)" starts delicately. Hammering up fret, Jimi produces a distant vibrating peal. It sounds like fingers gliding up fretless electric violins in weird harmonics. The hammering-on goes into sonic feedback. The squealing violin sound scaling the peak of itself, the feedback tightroping distort and wobbling on the signal's edge.

A simple chord lick says, "We're about to start" within the midst, and marks the beginning of the peaked feedback coming in on a pan, getting stronger and stronger, the chord sounding like the expellation of human breath—OM. Then a perfect bluefolk run (reminiscent of "House of the Rising Sun") as the feedback and the piercing metal sounds gliss-slide up and out. The repeat of the run meets the hollow ghostlike whooze of a high wind upon a summit.

The ghostly howl pans stronger, phasing into the taxiing sound of a long-range jetliner. Then, the "deep six" submarine descending, buoy gong-bells fade into the distance, giving way to skittering plucks. The bluefolk run ends in the low registers leading to the bass line that will run for the entire piece. It dips deep in a yawning diving arc, like the culmination of a seagull's arc as it sweeps to the waters and back up to the sky.

The sound comes full up. Mitch Mitchell's chopping military snare rolls pan louder into the sound level. The bass guitar (played by Jimi) takes the bass line over from the Stratocaster and plunges the line an octave deep, creating the interior wall of an underwater mountain.

The sound comes up a bit too fast. Two wailing Crybaby sounds dub a lament, both doing the same note yet one slightly sharp, adding an echo effect.

His guitar goes out of control momentarily on a feedback whistle. The bass, the drums, and a single guitar chord dubbed in sustain a note constituting a break. The drum, picking up from its sombre taps, establishes a stately polyrhythmic march that preludes Jimi's vocal.

The ghostly swoons continue as Chris Wood comes in on flute, picking up on the ghostly *woooo*s. Playing against the effect, Wood plays single sotto lines with a variation on the key that sustains a minor mode against the finely tuned feedback effects stroked in pinks against the upper canvas. His flute is a mellow complement to what could have been a sombre song. Yet the words, although painted against the bleakest landscape, are an uplift and a relief.

Jimi croons in his most appealing pull voice as the bass plunges to its deepest range.

Hooray, I awake from yesterday
Alive but the war is here to stay

Jimi introduces his lover, Catherina, as they take their last walk to the ocean. Their intention is not to perish there but to have a rebirth away from the warring world as it is destroyed. They will live as immortals.

A flying signal wavers over the scene, hovering a moment in the break. The voice sustains in a shadowy echo reverb, tagging and extending the words the same length as the signal.

Jimi evokes missiles landing on Earth causing mayhem among humans, as the Artic region turns from a blue-tinged silver to red with blood, simultaneous with his and Catherina's feet reaching the beach. He wishes that his friends could be with them. Common thought was that their bodies could not survive underwater, and besides, they thought it was beyond God and the king's will for them to reverse evolution and live within the sea again. But they are magical beings.

He and Catherina make love on the beach, they savor their last moments on land. There are no scars or even a scratch on their well-cared-for bodies as they conclude a farewell. As they descend they take one last glimpse of "the killing noise."

Reverbing into a chamberlike passage that sounds like a Bach prelude. In three-part harmony, the bass and the guitars sound like an organ switching at the peak of its passages to overtone harmonies. Then abruptly back to the initial three-part harmony that breaks up in a slow flurry of intervals. Jimi feints a classical guitar solo while he plays over his own backward tape riffs of shimmering high frequency that space into a sustained drum solo, which presages the next movement.

The kinds of sounds the seagulls make in their orbits, circling above the waters. So similar to the sounds of metal bodies arcing in space at sonic speeds, approaching the soundlessness of space. As if the depths of the waters were synonymous with outer space.

The rhythm continues as if the drum in its spare essence is the continuance of life. More than just the beat in the pulse, but an entity against which all objects of harmony must resolve.

"1983" segues right into "Moon, Turn the Tides . . . Gently, Gently Away," which is a continuation of "1983." He and Catherina descend into the aqua world, and he cautions that they must not be late because there is a spectacle to witness: "Neptune champion games" that are very precious to this new world.

> *"Right this way" smiles a mermaid*
> *I can hear Atlantis full of cheer*

The end of "Moon, Turn the Tides . . . Gently, Gently Away" is also the end of "1983." With the return of the "1983" theme, the two guitars in harmony enliven their mournful tones. The top guitar nearly peaks into feedback with its wail, while the lower guitar is playing blue tremolo. With the thrilling qualities of a snake charmer's horn the emotion and the movement twine, wrapping themselves about you. A heightened ecstasy winding through the third-eye chakra. A cello sound joins in, perfect-toned and classical. Jimi begins to wail it all out. Returning to the "sound painting" terrain, they jam some heavy blues striking toward freedom.

Jimi Hendrix's face flaming in a red-yellow spectre fire glow is the cover of the *Electric Ladyland* album. Looking like fire elemental, the salamander that lives and glows in all that is fire—including the greatest fire of all—electricity.

The Great Britain edition of *Electric Ladyland* had another cover.

20 Nudes Disc Is Banned

Two record dealers have banned a new pop disc—because they are shocked by the record sleeve.

The LP, *Electric Ladyland,* by the Jimi Hendrix Experience, has on its cover eight lounging nude girls.

The other side of the sleeve shows twelve more in similar pose.

The owner of one of the York shops which has banned the record, Mr. Hugh Robertson, declared yesterday: "This has gone too far. There is no need for covers like this."

Artistic

A shop manager has also complained to the distributors and several shops are keeping the record cover hidden from view.

A spokesman for the company, which designed the sleeve, Track Records, of London, replied: "The cover should be looked at from an artistic point of view.

"In view of the title, we thought it appropriate to have nude women on the sleeve. I don't think it's pornographic."

— Sunday Mirror
November 1, 1968

Weeks later the British edition of the *Electric Ladyland* album was still in the news.

Disc Dealers Hit at Sexy Covers

Britain's disc dealers hit out last night at the trend towards "vulgarity" on pop record covers.

Mr. Christopher Foss, secretary of the Gramophone Retailers' Committee, said the trend could only lower the industry's image in the eyes of the public.

He claimed that twenty-one naked girls pictured on the cover of Jimi Hendrix's new LP, *Electric Ladyland,* were unnecessary. "This type of album sleeve is almost certain to reduce the sale of records," said Foss.

But a spokesman for the Jimi Hendrix Experience said last night that more than 35,000 copies were sold within four days of its release in Britain.

— Sunday Mirror
November 21, 1968

Noel and Mitch left the band at the same time that *Electric Ladyland* was becoming number one on the U.S. charts. Chas, fed up with the hassles of dealing with

Hendrix, sold his share of the JHE management to Mike Jeffery for $300,000 cash and future considerations. Chas, Noel, and Mitch returned to England. Jimi remained in New York. The Experience had officially broken up.

Jimi understood that Mitch and Noel wanted to be back home in London, especially with the Christmas holidays coming up. Jimi had to just let it hang for a while, rest for a minute. He did not have much to say to the press.

"Mitch and Noel want to get their own thing going—producing and managing other artists. In the New Year we'll be breaking the group, apart from selected dates.

"Oh, I'll be around, don't worry . . . doing this and that. But there are other scenes we want to get into."

CHAPTER 7

An Infinity of Jimis

Pretend your mind is a big muddy bowl and the silt is very slowly settling down—but remember your mind's still muddy and you can't possibly grasp all I'm saying.

Music is going to break the way. There'll be a day when houses will be made of diamonds and emeralds that won't have any value anymore and they'd last longer in a rainstorm than a wooden house. Bullets'll be fairy tales. There'll be a renaissance from bad to completely clear and pure and good—from lost to found.

The everyday mud world we're living in today compared to the spiritual world is like a parasite compared to the ocean, and the ocean is the biggest living thing you know about. One way to approach the spiritual side is facing the truth. People who make a lot of money—they get sadder and sadder 'cause deep down they feel a hurt. So they go and buy a prostitute on Saturday and go to church on Sunday and pray down on the ground in a little salt box, hearing another man who has the same problems preach—and the collection plate keeps going around and around. That man thinks he's found religion but he gets hurt more and more because he's not going toward the spiritual side, which is the way the atmosphere is.

Atmospheres are going to come through music because music is in a spiritual thing of its own. It's like the waves of the ocean. You can't just cut out the perfect wave and take it home with you. It's constantly moving all the time. It is the biggest thing electrifying the Earth. Music and motion are all part of the race of man.

I don't think what I say is abstract. It's reality. What's unreal is all those people living in cement beehives with no color and making themselves look like their gig and slaving themselves for that one last dollar and crying with millions in their pockets and constantly playing war games and making bets. They're losing themselves in big ego scenes and being above another man in some kind of form. Look at the pimps and congressmen.

But I can explain everything better through music. You hypnotize people to where they go right back to their natural state, which is pure positive—like childhood when you got natural highs. And when you get people at [their] weakest point, you can preach into the subconscious what we want to say. That's why the name "electric church" flashes in and out.

People want release any kind of way nowadays. The idea is to release in the proper form. Then they'll feel like going into another world, a clearer world. The music flows from the air; that's why I can connect with a spirit, and when they come down off this natural high, they see clearer, feel different things—don't think of pain and hurting the next person. You think of getting your own thing together. You can't be lazy. You have to look at all the faults you have.

There's no telling how many lives your spirit will go through—die and be reborn. Like my mind will be back in the days when I was a flying horse. Before I can remember anything, I can remember music and stars and planets. I could go to sleep and write fifteen symphonies. I had very strange feelings that I was here for something and I was going to get a chance to be heard. I got the guitar together 'cause that was all I had. I used to be really lonely.

A musician, if he's a messenger, is like a child who hasn't been handled too many times by man, hasn't had too many fingerprints across his brain. That's why music is so much heavier than anything you ever felt.

—Jimi Hendrix, *Life* magazine, October 3, 1969

The Experience got back together after the beginning of the New Year, 1969. Noel Redding had rehearsed a band he was calling Fat Mattress for three weeks over the holidays. It was a kind of boast, for when he split the Experience the month before, it was common knowledge that Redding had saved the most money out of everyone in the band. He achieved his mass of cash by severe penny-pinching, and he used it as part of his reason for leaving and as part of his bargaining position for returning. He knew Mike Jeffery would have him back under any terms. A tour through England, Europe, and America was already booked, from January 5 in London through June at the Newport Festival in Los Angeles.

The bargain was struck. Noel Redding's band, Fat Mattress, would be the official opening band of the tour, regardless of whether there was another band on the bill or not.

The big news of the New Year was that Cream had broken up (and remained so) over the holidays. Eric Clapton was adamant about leaving—and there could be no Cream without him.

THE GIG LIST, JANUARY 1969

1, 2	Interviews
3	Interviews
	BBC TV, Lulu Show
7	Canadian TV show
	Interviews
8	Gothenburg, Sweden, Lorensburg Cirkus—two shows
9	Press reception
	Stockholm, Sweden, Konserthus—two shows
10	Copenhagen, Denmark, Kalkoner Centeret—two shows
11	Hamburg, Musikhalle—two shows
12	Düsseldorf, Rheinhalle—two shows
13	Cologne, Sporthalle
	Jam at Storyville Club
14	Münster, Halle Münsterland—two shows
15	Interviews
	Munich, Deutsches Museum—two shows
16	Nuremberg, Meistersingerhalle—two shows
17	Frankfurt, Jahrhunderthalle—two shows
19	Stuttgart, Liederhalle—two shows
21	Strasbourg
22	Vienna, Konzerthaus—two shows
23	Berlin, Sportpalast
	Press reception

Jimi had flown into London on January 2. He had had many transatlantic telephone conversations with Kathy Etchingham, who had rented a flat for them in the Mayfair district at 25 Brook Street, a flat that was reputed to have been the former residence of the composer George Frederick Handel.

Jimi was all for it. A home. Kathy was a good, steady person who had an understanding of the many pressures he faced and was truly sensitive and sympathetic. To the surprise of Trixie Sullivan, Michael Jeffery's administrative assistant, Jimi went directly to the flat and settled in immediately, secluding himself.

He was able to catch up on some rest and avoid a lot of semipublic scenes living in a hotel would bring in increasing numbers as soon as the word got around that he was in town, living in one of those public fishbowls.

Since he would be moving around on tour a lot, Angie Burdon and Madeline Bell would be Kathy's roommates when he was on the road.

After their fabled row about food and cleanliness when they lived with

Chas and Lotta, now over a year ago, Kathy was very careful, keeping things very clean and cooking for him, as she knew he loved. A homecooked meal from a woman who loved him had been an extremely rare occasion in Jimi's young life.

They took to going to the Speakeasy every night and being back at the flat in time to go to bed by 11:30 P.M., a very unusual time for Jimi to bed down. Kathy noted that he would arise at 10:30 A.M. fully rested for a change. He was catching up on his sleep and living almost normal hours. During the day they would go around shopping—something they both enjoyed. Jimi bought lots of stuff for the flat and it began to reflect what he desired. A laid-back, colorful yet restful, almost otherworldly environment, an alternative to the common, functional, semi-industrial nature of most of London.

The JHE appeared on Lulu's TV show, which was very popular in London. She was both a hit singer and a movie star. She had costarred in *To Sir with Love* with black American Sidney Poitier, and the movie had been a smash both in London and in the States. Lulu's show was live.

Jimi, Noel, and Mitch came on, and after a bit of variety-show patter they played "Voodoo Chile (Slight Return)" from *Electric Ladyland*. Then they swung into their first hit, "Hey Joe," but midway through, Jimi startled everyone by stopping the song, announcing a tribute to Cream, and going right into a jam of "Sunshine of Your Love," which Jack Bruce had said he wrote as a tribute to Jimi. The director, the producer, the star, and the technicians all began tearing at their hair and gesturing at their throats—Jimi was going way over time, and Lulu might not be able to say a proper good-bye. Jimi, Noel, and Mitch paid them no mind as they climbed, fell, and rode through Cream's greatest hit. Jimi was tearing into the lead guitar lines that Clapton had established as a near classic. Jimi bore into the solo space with searing lines that turned up into atonals or turned over into funk moans. That was the way *The Lulu Show* ended that January day in 1969.

Hallelujah!
It's Hendrix in Handel's Old House

Another musician has moved into the London house where the great composer Handel lived and died more than two centuries ago.

Not that Jimi Hendrix pretends to know much about the old tenant.

"I didn't even know this was his pad, man, until after I got in," he said, "and to tell you the God's honest truth I haven't heard much of the fella's stuff. But I dig a bit of Bach now and again."

Luckily, Jimi's words didn't fall on the ears of some students who had come to gaze at the blue-colored plaque in memory of the old master.

Hendrix, fuzzy-haired, wild man of pop, 1969, in scarlet trousers and yellow shirt, may not meet with the approval of classical students. But millions of pop fans across the world hail him as the world's number one musician.

It is in this house in fashionable Brook Street that Handel is said to have composed "Messiah" and the "Water Music."

Hendrix promises not to let tradition down and says he, too, will compose here. Music he defines as "twenty-first century" and that "sort of scene."

Hendrix is 23, an electric man with a 240-volt electric guitar. When he plays it onstage, he may set it on fire, smash it or play it with his teeth, depending on his mood.

His music seems an uninhibited collection of jarring sounds without melody.

The grandson of a pure Cherokee Indian, he looks a rebel, and a man many could hate without meeting—someone you're sure smokes pot, has a lust for birds, and likes his hooch.

Values

Hendrix pleads guilty on all counts—or the experience of those happenings.

He laughs: "That's how I got the name of my group, the Jimi Hendrix Experience."

That's what I like about Hendrix. Not his music, but the man. His honesty. His sense of values may be wrong, but he creates his own values which, he feels, reflect the way young people want to live without suppression today.

The attic of the house, which has become Hendrix's favourite room, contains an assortment of bric-a-brac and a bed with a Victorian shawl pinned to the ceiling as a canopy.

At two in the afternoon, Hendrix is making the bed, neatly folding back the black sheets and straightening the colourful Persian bedspread. Then he grins and calls Kathy to open a bottle of wine.

Kathy Etchingham is a twenty-two-year-old redhead from the North who shares the flat. Jimi explains her presence: "My girlfriend, my past girlfriend and probably my next girlfriend. My mother and my sister and all that bit. My Yoko Ono from Chester.

"We won't marry. Marriage isn't my scene; we just live together. Those bits of paper you call marriage certificates are only for people who feel insecure."

There is no alarm in the face of Kathy, who was once a hairdresser and met Jimi by chance on his first day in England three years ago.

Groovy

"There is no shame in living with sin," she says quietly and without defiance. "My mother knows and she thinks that Jimi is groovy."

"One day I wanna become a parent," Jimi announces. "Now that is what the world is all about. Having kids. Like planting flowers . . ."

We move on to Jimi's music. "I would describe my music as electric church music," he explains. "Church meaning religion and not meaning God, that is.

"I know," he adds with a long stare at me, "that many people are blocked out but I hope they will come to understand my music soon. In fact I'm gonna write a new album which will simplify it all and bridge the gap between teenagers and parents."

Naked

"I'm moving away from what I've done so far. I don't want to play the guitar with my teeth any more or clown around, but I did it because fans, having seen me do it once, expected me to do it always and I came to do it out of self-satisfaction."

Jimi, from the cluttered mantelpiece, took a copy of his new album, *Electric Ladyland,* the sleeve of which shows twenty-one naked girls. Many record shops won't display it.

"Man, I don't blame them," said Jimi. "I wouldn't have put this picture on the sleeve myself, but it wasn't my decision. They messed about with the picture and although the girls were pretty they came out disfigured."

Jimi grew up in Seattle and was expelled from school; more recently he was given the freedom of the city.

He admits he has been in jail: "Spent seven days in the cooler for taking a ride in a stolen car. But I never knew it was."

He admits, too, that he was fined £250 for smashing a hotel room in Gothenburg when he got drunk. And once an American moral society got him banned because his act was "too erotic."

But a wild man? "No, I'm just natural all the time. What others think or say doesn't worry me, man."

Jimi says: "People still mourn when people die. That's self-sympathy. The person who is dead isn't cryin'.

"When I die I want people to play my music, go wild and freak out an' do anything they wanna do. . . ."

Obviously, Jimi Hendrix won't need a plaque for any of us to remember him by.

—Don Short
Daily Mirror
January 11, 1969

In the studio. Could be any studio in the world. The same sense of being closed in against the world. The soundproofed walls, the whir and click of advanced machinery, sensitive and delicate, smooth gloss and metallic. Soft interior light-ing, not a glance of sunlight. It was like a spaceship. The smooth dials of the electronic magnetic reproducers, perfect red, green, white. The turned-down lights make it even more cozy, more tunnel-like in the center of the Earth, mak-ing the room's true size indistinguishable. Wafts of incense. Every sound capa-ble of being captured, every vibe of the room submissive to the sound, everybody in the room supporting the sound. This was Jimi's workshop. The endless, timeless space where he was most at home.

Take after take. Seemingly for days and weeks. Getting the right sound, the right pitch and intensity. Getting a swan-diving tremolo to glide right within the ensemble sound on time. It's what he's hearing. People look at him like he's crazy. Musicians and engineers exasperated, but it's his session. But that love, when it's happening, when it's right, makes everything worthwhile. The blown minds, the beaming faces, smiles silly to behold—beatific.

Most could not hear the sounds he was after, yet were greatly touched by the final product. Its close perfection, surrendering to the final moments when it came together. Especially the electronic gadgets. He would fiddle with one for days to get it to flow with the other parts and gadgets he had hooked up. From Mellotron, to Crybaby, to wah-wah, to Fuzz Face, to Uni-Vibe, to Octavia, to Phase Shifter, Jimi had his own recipes, his own methods of combining what seemed like mumbo jumbo. Especially to the English engineers, neatly trimmed workers gazing idly through the control-room window at him on his knees in a corner, fiddling with a tiny box.

But when it was all working it was like a triumph of magic. Everything going at once and Jimi completely on top of it, dancing between foot pedals, orches-trating the frantic peaks of his sound at the speed of light.

The *Mirror* published another piece in support of the JHE's Albert Hall ap-pearances.

Jimi Wants You to Strip in the Park

He is wild, wicked—and, some say, nauseating. Yet the pop appeal of guitar man Jimi Hendrix is astounding.

His concert for February 18 at the Albert Hall is already sold out, and the hall has had to be booked again for February 24.

Not since the Beatles has there been anything like him.

Guru

But now I feel this shock-haired Twiggy-figured guru of the electric guitar, bril-liant as he is, has gone too far.

I am not talking of his current LP album with nudes galore on the sleeve.

Nor am I talking about his new LP, called (believe it or not) *Universal Bedroom.*

Nor the name of his new accompanying group: FAT MATTRESS.

As outrageous as their contributions to the pop scene might appear, his latest project tops the lot.

Mr. Hendrix tells me he is making an approach to the Royal Parks Authority for permission to hold a free concert in London in February for an audience of 100,000.

Nothing shocking in that. But, as he told me over coffee in his flat in Brook Street: "I propose to invite the whole audience to take off their clothes.

"No, I'm not mad. I think that too many people these days are hung up because they're covered up.

"The feeling in my mind is that when folks who dig my scene listen to music they have to find some way of releasing their inhibitions—and what better way than getting rid of their clothes?"

Mr. Hendrix, who makes no secret of the fact that he sells his act on sex and who openly admits that if a girl of his choice is willing, so is he, is making a fortune out of this uninhibited attitude.

In America the kids go berserk, parents fume, but it does not seem to make any difference. Pocket money is hoarded for the next sight of this man, who uses his guitar as a phallic symbol.

"What is so wrong about that?" he said. "The world revolves around sex. If I could not produce a sound that even musicians flip about, then I could understand objections.

"Audiences have been carried away in the past by swooners like Sinatra, bouncers like Glenn Miller, and the tunes of the Beatles. But now the scene must move on."

Defy

"Music should be matched with human emotions, and if you can tell me a more human one than sex, then, man, you have got me fooled . . . and there are a helluva lot of fans ready to back me up.

"Nobody puts an armlock on them to get them to see my show. I defy anybody to give me an argument on that score."

And I defy anybody to take off their clothes in a London park in February without turning blue.

—*Sunday Mirror*
February 9, 1969

• • •

February 18, 1969, Royal Albert Hall, London. The recording people and the film people had been setting up since early afternoon. The entire 4,500 capacity sold out, another show was added for February 24. Chas Chandler had been called in to help sort it out. It was a hectic scene to play against.

Jimi's proclamation "I am electric religion" appeared on the program. There was a new feeling about the Experience—their brief, recent breakup had put some distance among them, especially Noel and Jimi. Noel was into asserting himself as an individual player and the essential link between guitar and bass did not have the unified fire of a healthy Experience. And the drums, so essentially keyed into polyrhythms around the time, were off. Since Noel and Jimi both played rhythm, they had to relinquish some of their freedom to keep time, something the Experience was never known to do. Jimi took a lot more solo time than usual. The band was not really working as a unit, and Jimi's solos—as a result— were not as brilliant as when there was an ensemble sound with good ideas coming from all sides of the flying wedge. They ranged through "Lover Man," "Stone Free," "Getting My Heart Back Together," "I Don't Live Today," a thirteen-minute "Red House," "Foxy Lady," and a long version of "Sunshine of Your Love."

Then Jimi did a new song, a blues. The time was in twelve bars, very much like "Red House," but it was apparent that the song had variations that were not coming through. "Bleeding Heart"—some Elmore James.

Jimi focused on the classic blues lyric and the isolation caused by love lost. In the morning, "you can hear the willows weep and moan for me." Jimi adds his own lines, pleading for his baby to return, and hearing out the window, "the blues call my name." Misunderstandings and a woman who is no good, "that's all that caused my heart to bleed."

Then they hit "Fire," "Little Wing," "Voodoo Chile (Slight Return)," and the finale, "Room Full of Mirrors," another new song Jimi had written over the holidays, with Dave Mason, Chris Wood, and Rocki Dzidzornu joining them on-stage.

This song was a departure of sorts for Jimi, a return in a way to those early tunes he wrote in London on his first LP. Self-examining, he has a new assessment of himself. Some say it was an epiphany he had in L.A. with Devon when they visited the former home of Rudolph Valentino, the legendary Hollywood sex symbol and silent-film star. There was a large room full of mirrors. Perhaps Jimi saw how narcissistic fame could be, how damaging to the soul.

He states his realization in the opening lines that begin the details of his awareness. He used to live in a "room full of mirrors" and all he could see was himself. He smashed the mirror with his spiritual awareness. That act bared his soul in order that he could see the entire world. So now he can really search for true love. He returns to the breakthrough. The glass of the broken mirror plagued him, seeking to reestablish the narcissism by getting in his head and attacking his brain. The vengeful glass would "fall on my dreams and cut me in my bed." That made his love life "strange in my bed." But now that he is more self-aware, love will come from the four corners of the earth to find him.

Jimi ranges out in a solo against Dave Mason's scratch rhythms and Rocki's *klok-mokk*ing congas. They reach a free terrain where "Room Full of Mirrors" extends into a jam all the way out, concluding with a few bars of "The Star-Spangled Banner."

Amid the cheers and applause of the crowd emerge calls for various songs. They sound taunting, insolent, brash—as if the audience had not just sat through an entire concert. Jimi mumbles that he is not a jukebox as he slows the pace and waits out the shouted song titles, which sound like catcalls. He reannounces Chris Wood on flute, Dave Mason on guitar, and Rocki on congas. He calls for an A from Dave Mason and goes into an extended tuning-up process. It is clear that he is not happy with the crowd. Then Jimi feints two beats of "Purple Haze" (those famous two beats) and then goes into an amp-scorching, feedback-rumbling free jazz distort over free percussion accompaniment. "The Star-Spangled Banner" starts out in weird tonalities. It rages out in manic white and pink noises as full-range distortion. Audio destruct. Now he does not need to break up his guitar—he can create the effect with sound.

The concert is over.

Chas, who had come down to help out, had done so only out of friendship. The equipment found to replace the JHE's regular gear that had been left in America was below par. During soundcheck, Jimi had been having trouble with the amplifiers. The recording equipment was causing interference. It was all Chas could do to salvage the evening's performance; he found Mitch to "be totally off," often coming in so late that there seemed to be a synapse problem, and Noel was so awkward that it seemed to be on purpose. Mitch Mitchell had missed meetings and shown up late for recording sessions. Noel was preoccupied with Fat Mattress. He had never led a group before. It was widely rumored that they had squandered their substantial advance and were rather debauched as a result.

The JHE was supported by Soft Machine and Mason, Capaldi, Wood & Frog. The first appearance at Royal Albert Hall had been disappointing. Chas said that if he "had still been in charge," Noel and Mitch "would have been sacked the next day."

Chas Chandler told Jimi that the original Experience reunion had sounded as if three guys were soloing at the same time. He felt that their former unity was gone. Perhaps it would return, but they would need time and a conscious unity of purpose.

Jimi had been glad to see Dave Mason, Chris Wood, and Rocki, the African conga player, join him onstage. If they were sounding like they were jamming with three pieces, well then, they jammed properly with six. But he had to admit, it did not really hang together. The crowd was a useless monitor of how they really played. They cheered anything he did.

He was glad he had gotten a chance to hang out with Rocki and other African musicians on the London scene. They had gone to a studio before the Albert Hall concert and recorded some tunes with Jimmy Page, Denny Laine, and a lot of African percussionists, including Ginger Johnson on talking drum and Rocki on his handmade carved congas. Jimi liked experimenting with a lot of drumming sounds. It gave him different ideas from the usual power-trio rock trip. He found it a pleasure to play rhythms against their polyrhythms. They would totally get outside, into another kind of space that he had seldom been in.

He and Rocki rapped for a good while. What Rocki had to say about himself and the music fascinated him. Rocki had played with the Rolling Stones, Ginger Baker, Georgie Fame, Spooky Tooth, and with a whole lot of other people. He was considered *the* journeyman conga player of the London scene.

They went to the Speakeasy and hung out. Jimi and Rocki first played together at the Speakeasy while Jimi had been jamming with Amen Corner. He and Jimi took over the set and that was how they met and became friends.

Rocki's father was a voodoo priest and the chief drummer of a village in Ghana, West Africa. Rocki's real name was Kwasi Dzidzornu. One of the first things Rocki asked Jimi was where he got that voodoo rhythm from. When Jimi demurred, Rocki went on to explain in his halting English that many of the signature rhythms Jimi played on guitar were very often the same rhythms that his father played in voodoo ceremonies. The way Jimi danced to the rhythms of his playing reminded Rocki of the ceremonial dances to the rhythms his father played to Oxun, the god of thunder and lightning. The ceremony is called *voodoshi*. As a child in the village, Rocki would carve wooden representations of the gods. They also represented his ancestors. These were the gods they worshipped.

They would jam a lot in Jimi's house. One time they were jamming and Jimi stopped and asked Rocki point-blank, "You communicate with God, do you?" Rocki said, "Yes, I communicate with God."

Chas and Jimi had six days to make it better. For his part, Jimi got in some good jamming with Dave Mason and Jim Capaldi at the Speakeasy, which had become his solid hangout.

The hip *International Times,* London's foremost underground newspaper, dispatched their foxiest, savviest reporter, Jane de Mendelssohn, to interview Jimi. She was surprised that he answered the door himself at the flat in Mayfair, and was even more surprised to see that he was totally naked.

She followed him up to his bedroom where he got back in the bed he had apparently just gotten out of. They conducted the entire interview with him in bed, she sitting on the side of the bed, and within equal reaching distance a small table with a smorgasbord of mind-altering substances: hashish, three different types, marijuana, amyl nitrates, assorted pills, and several bottles of bourbon and whiskey. He sampled the goods throughout the interview. Jane de Mendelssohn, ever the professional, joined him to a smaller degree, so as not to lose the level of communication they had established. But "at one point he offered me some amyl nitrate and we both went out of our skulls."

JANE DE MENDELSSOHN: Tell me about your Indian heritage!

JIMI: Well, my grandmother's a full-blooded Indian, that's all. She used to make clothes for me. And everybody used to laugh at me when I went to school, you know, the regular sob story. She's full-blooded Cherokee (laughs).

JANE: And is she still around?

JIMI: Yeah. Up in Seattle, Vancouver, British Columbia now.

JANE: And does she live on a reservation?

JIMI: No, she lives in a groovy apartment building. She has a television and a radio and stuff like that. She still has her long silver hair, though.

JANE: Can't you tell me something about the whole Indian heritage scene? I don't know much about it.

JIMI: It's just another part of our family, that's all. There's not too much to know. There's a lot of people in Seattle that have a lot of Indian mixed in them.

JANE: Do they still take peyote?

JIMI: Oh yes, it's all over the place. It's mostly around the Southwest and all that, around the desert areas, you know. But you know, all Indians have different ways of stimulants, their own step toward God, spiritual forms, or whatever . . . which it should be kept as, nothing but a step, mind you.

JANE: What I'd really like to ask is . . . well, you're very big these days, you've become a real pop giant. . . .

JIMI: Oh, don't tell me those things (laughs).

JANE: Everybody's writing about you, talking about you, you won the *Rolling Stone* magazine Performer of the Year award. I want to know how it all affects you as a human being.

JIMI: Well, I'm trying not to let it affect me at all. It's nothing but a brand, it's the way the public identifies me probably with them, but I don't think that way and it's like anybody else, I just happen to have a chance to be heard.

JANE: Does it touch you?

JIMI: Yeah, it touches me and so forth.

JANE: Do you feel that it cuts you off at all?

JIMI: Yeah, a lotta times. I can't have fun like anybody else. I used to be able to go somewhere, down to the Wimpy or something like that, you know earlier on, but most of the time I go down there now, there's always people asking for autographs, somebody looking at me really strange, you know, whispering and all that. So then, quite naturally, you get complexes about that. My head's in a position now where I have to take a rest or else I'll completely crack up pretty soon, in the next few hours or days . . . (laughs).

JANE: D'you think it's true that teenyboppers don't go for you so much as the sophisticated heads?

JIMI: I've found out that just by looking for myself, you know, that you'll find almost anybody in our audience. You see a nine-year-old and you see a ninety-year-old, all ages anywhere we play. You find all kinds of people there. You find a lot of straight people there, so therefore we play twice as loud just to see where they're really at, and they dig it, the louder the better, they're just not getting into the fact that it does make you drunk if you let it.

JANE: Do you get hustled a lot by people wanting bread and hanging on your door?

JIMI: Oh constantly, yeah. I try to treat everybody fairly but if I did I wouldn't be able to buy another guitar. So therefore I just don't go around too much, except when I find a certain little scene going, and just go there if I want to go anywhere. But I stay in bed most of the time, or go to the park or somewhere. That's where I write some of my best songs, in bed, just laying there. I was laying there thinking of some when you came in. A really nice piece of music that I'm getting together for this late-summer LP that I'd like to do with this cat named Al Brown, in America. It's called *The First Ray of the New Rising Sun,* and it gives my own solution. You know, anybody can protest, for instance, like in records or whatever you use your music for, anybody can protest but hardly anybody tries to give a decent type of solution, at least a mean-time solution, you know.

JANE: You've got the reputation for being moody. I was almost afraid to come.

JIMI: Moody? Oh, that's silly (laughs). I shouldn't say that. That's what you're supposed to think. The establishment, they project a certain image and if it works, they have it made. They knock down somebody else, for instance, you know, like saying I'm moody or so-and-so is evil or saying blah blah woof woof is a maniac or something, so that everybody gets scared to actually know about me. So that's part of the establishment's games.

JANE: You were quoted in the *Sunday Mirror* as saying that it was time for a change from the pretty songs the Beatles made, time for something else.

JIMI: Aah. I don't know if I said that. Which paper is that in? *Sunday Mirror.* Well, most of those papers are all screwed up anyway, they come over here and they do their interviews, we turn the cats on, you know, give 'em wine and all that, and they go back and they're so stoned they don't know what they're writing about. No, I didn't say nothing like that. I wouldn't, there's no reason to.

JANE: What do you think about the Beatles?

JIMI: I think they're excellent and fantastic writers and musicians and so forth, you know.

JANE: Do you think their era of enormous influence has passed? Do you think another big influence is moving in?

JIMI: Well . . . yeah, people are starting to get a little more hep to music nowadays. It's not so easy to throw hogwash on anybody. The Beatles are doing their thing. I think they're going toward the past a little more. There's a lot of people that's waiting for something else to happen now anyway.

JANE: Don't you think it's you? I've got this feeling.

JIMI: Me? (laughs)

JANE: Well, it seems to me to be moving down to the animal, and that's what you are. The Beatles aren't animal.

JIMI: The Beatles are part of the establishment. They're starting to melt that way, too. We must watch out. It's just like a young cat protesting in school, for instance, saying, "That's not right, this is not right," so he goes out and says something about it and everybody says, "Yeah, man, that's what it's about, man, we're with you." Soon as he reaches about twenty-five years old and starts getting into the establishment scene, you know, he got his degree and all this, and now he's a lawyer or whatever he wants to be, and all this feeling for everybody else, well, he forgets it himself because he's comfortable now, he's nice and fat and got his little gig together, so then he just forgets about the younger people, all his friends, what they used to say when they were in school, and he melts into part of the establishment. And that's not saying nothing bad about a person at all, it's just scenes some people go through. Compare that with the Beatles' music, that's the way I look at it. It's like a person who starts out with something really on fire, you know, but now they're still good, as a matter of fact, they're better than they used to be, you know, but they seemed a little more closer to the public beforehand. Now they're doing things, like for instance, "Happiness Is a Warm Gun," bang bang shoot shoot and all these little songs.

JANE: D'you dig that?

JIMI: Not necessarily, no.

JANE: What about violence?

JIMI: I don't dig it too much, no. It's best to have violence onstage and watch it through TV than do it yourself. So what we do, we get up there and like, I found that it worked both ways; we'd do our thing, you know, and so many people would dig it, would really be turned on by it, and they don't bother their old ladies as much when they get home. They don't beat their old ladies up as much (laughs) because there's hardly anything left in them. We try to drain all the violence out of their system. That's why you watch wrestling matches and football games, you get it all out of your system, unless you want to do it for real yourself, and then you'd be a violent person. Bad. Bad.

JANE: Well, what about the violent trends in America today, the Black Power scene saying, "We've tried everything else, now we're going to slam you, baby?"

JIMI: Well, that's what the establishment's waiting for, for people to start fighting against their own selves, like for instance black against white, yellow against pink, and all that. But that's not the idea of the thing, the idea is against the new and the old, and the establishment causes this by playing games.

JANE: Well, in fact the establishment seems to get frightened by all this violence in the States because . . .

JIMI: Propaganda, propaganda, everyone has their own brand of propaganda. . . .

JANE: It still seems that if you burn down a few warehouses in the States today . . .

JIMI: Oh, they should burn down more, I think.

JANE: Well, right! That's what I was asking you!

JIMI: They should burn down the whole area.

JANE: Would you do it if you were there?

JIMI: Well, if I wasn't a guitar player I probably would, yeah. I'd probably be in jail, 'cause like, I get very stubborn, like with the police. I used to get into arguments with them millions of times, they used to tell me to be quiet and I just CAN'T be quiet, there's no reason to be, especially if I have something to say. So I'd probably wind up getting killed. But I have to feel those things. I hear about violence and all that, but really for me to say anything about that . . . I just can't jump on the bandwagon just because it might be happening today. 'Cause like for instance, how they exploit and prostitute the groupie scene, you know, that's a violent scene, it's the same thing.

JANE: But you must have an enormous amount of energy and if it weren't coming out through your music, maybe you'd be very violent.

JIMI: Well, I am very violent anyway, in defense, you know.

JANE: How liberated do you think you are?

JIMI: You mean free? I don't know. That's pretty hard to say. In music we get to do anything we want to do. But I get restricted when I get around a lot of people sometimes, or even with one person too long.

JANE: What, on a head scene?

JIMI: Yeah, like for instance on a love scene. If I stay with one person too long, I feel more obligated than I do pleased, that makes me, as it were, have to get away. So I don't know how free-feeling you can get if every time you turn around you might be with somebody. Like if you're writing a song or something like that, and you want to get the words down or you're thinking about something, and all of a sudden these people pop up . . . not saying you, because I'm digging this interview. And at least it's a different face (laughs).

JANE: It was surprisingly easy to get an interview with you. I mean, if you want one with Paul McCartney it can take weeks to set it up.

JIMI: Well, maybe 'cause I'm not Paul McCartney. You get a lot of . . . oh no, I shouldn't say that.

JANE: Why not?

JIMI: There's a lot of things I shouldn't say. But you have time, don't you? Great, we can get into a whole lot of things. There's this thing I was writing, LP sleeve notes for one of our LPs. We've got about three lined up now. Now we're trying to get them released but everybody else wants us to be released stars and so forth, so now we have to do this film, like round in August or something like that, and even before that we have to do an American tour, April and May, and we'll only have just a few weeks to edit these recordings that we did. Can I play some of those from the Albert Hall to you? Yeah? Can I? Is that all right? . . . What was the question? I forgot. What was we talking about? . . . Oh yeah, about being hard to see folks and all that. That's silly, that's the stupidest game you could ever play. It's not like, "Oh, can't see you today, far too much on, tomorrow, baby . . ."

JANE: All your songs seem to be directed at chicks. Is that from personal experience? For instance, there's one phrase, "I wanna make you mine." What d'you mean?

JIMI: Oh, just the cat would like to make love to you, that's all, whoever's singing the song, you know.

JANE: D'you see him as somebody else, outside of yourself?

JIMI: Well, sometimes. I don't look at it as me singing the song, I look at it as anybody singing the song. It's hard to say. I just don't put myself in all those positions 'cause I've already been through them already, all the things I mostly sing about. There are so many other things I like to get into myself personally, but in the meantime I can write down some other experiences, yeah, you're right, like you say. But I don't necessarily use those direct words when I'm talking to somebody (laughs). I don't say, "I wanna make you mine."

JANE: When you write songs, is it the music you hear before the words?

JIMI: Sometimes, it all depends. A lot of times I write a lot of words all over the place, anywhere, on matchboxes, or on napkins, and then sometimes music comes across to me just when I'm sitting around doing nothing. So I go back to those few words if I can find them and, you know, just get it together. Sometimes it all happens at the same time. All depends on what you might want to say. Different moods you might be in . . .

JANE: But do you sit down and think, "I want to say this to them," and then compose the song around what you want to say?

JIMI: Yeah, definitely. Sometimes, there's things I'd like to say. A lot of songs are fantasy-type songs so that people think you don't know what you're talking about at all, but it all depends on what the track before and after might have been. Like you might tell them something kinda hard but you don't want to be a completely hard character in their minds and be known for all that 'cause there's other sides of you and sometimes they leak onto the record, too, you know. That's when the fantasy songs come in. Like for instance "1983"—that's something to keep your mind off what's happening today but not necessarily completely hiding away from it like some people might do, with certain drugs and so forth.

JANE: But is this awareness actually conscious when you write this song, or do you write it, listen to it, and then realise what motivates you afterward?

JIMI: Well, honest-to-God truth, on the first LP I didn't know what I was writing about then. Most of the songs, like "Purple Haze" and "Wind Cries Mary," were about ten pages long, but then we're restricted to a certain time limit so I had to break them all down, so once I'd broken the songs down I didn't know whether they were going to be understood or not. Maybe some of the meanings got lost by breaking them down, which I never do anymore, it's such a drag.

JANE: Your songs don't tend to be analysed and intellectualised by reviewers like, for instance, the Beatles' songs.

JIMI: Mmm, which is kinda good, because our songs are like a personal diary.

JANE: Well, it's just this basicness in your music that makes me see you as the innovator of a new era.

JIMI: Yeah, but that's how it should be in any scene, though. Like I said about the carpenter, if he really digs that, he should put all his heart into really getting that together, if it means going to school or whatever it means. And in music, you gotta say something real just as quick as you can. I just say what I feel, you know, what I feel, and let them fight over it, if it's interesting enough. But that's the idea of it, make it very basic. During a certain age which was past not so long ago they started getting really superficial, and the music started getting too complicated, and in order to get into that you have to really be true to yourself, and none of those cats were doing that, they just put sounds here or sounds there.

    I don't seem like I'm busy 'cause I'm just sitting here, but after all, being busy can be just sitting here in this kind of scene, you know. I haven't had no time off to myself since I've been in this scene. People just make me so uptight sometimes, but I can't really let it show all the time because it's not really a good influence on anybody else. Oh no, don't take any pictures now 'cause my hair's all messed up. I just hate pictures, it always comes back on me later on. People are always saying, "D'you remember that picture that was in the so-and-so?" and I say, "No I don't fucking remember it." . . . Some music is such bullshit nowadays, and that's why there's so many good groups going toward establishment because it's comfortable there, it's not so hard, you don't have to keep scuffling for the rest of your life. I couldn't even save up some money and go to the hills, because there's always problems, you know, always hang-ups. Most people would like to retire and just disappear from the scene, which I'd LOVE to do, but then there's still things I'd like to say. I wish it wasn't so important to me, I wish I could just turn my mind off, you know, forget about the scene. But there's so much rubbish going by and for us trying to do our thing, there's so much rubbish said about us. I'd like to get things straight in this interview. I spend most of my time just writing songs and so forth, and not making too much contact with people 'cause they don't know how to act. They act just like the . . . the pigs that run these places, you know . . . countries. They base everything on the status thing, that's why there's people starving, because humans haven't got their priorities right. I don't feel like talking to most people because they're just bullshitting, they don't even know the difference between us and the Cream, for instance, or Blue Cheer.

JANE: Do you still take acid?

JIMI: Not necessarily, no. I don't get a chance to get into all that because I'm writing songs and so forth. Anyway I just used it for certain things, as a step toward seeing it both ways, if you like.

JANE: Do you feel good onstage?

JIMI: Oh yeah, I love to be onstage, not necessarily onstage but I love to play, that's why we play so loud 'cause it makes us feel good anyway.

JANE: Does the atmosphere in the audience affect you to the extent of changing the way you play?

JIMI: It never changes me to a negative feeling. I just ignore the negative feeling 'cause I know exactly what I'm doing when we're onstage, you know. And if the audience doesn't dig it, well, I don't know, there's nothing else we can do. Like you say, music is what it's all about, it's not us three up there facing about fifteen thousand people, it's the sounds we make that are important. Oh, I can't explain, you know what it is, you're not daft.

JANE: Well, I know what it is to me, your music is something in the middle between us, a medium between human beings, and the groovier the music the faster the communication.

JIMI: It's all spiritual. Except when the eardrums come . . .

JANE: Can you get outside of yourself enough to see the picture other people must see?

JIMI: Yeah, I can do that a lot of times. That's what makes me stay away from them, 'cause most of them have dirty minds anyway. What I see them seeing is really useless. I talked to a lot of old ladies one time, seeing exactly how they think, and wow, their impressions must really be weird.

JANE: Do you like kids?

JIMI: Yeah, I like kids. I guess I like them any age. It's a drag to grow up because you're not really growing up, you're just losing. You're only as old as you think you are, as long as your mind can still function openly you're still young.

JANE: D'you mind getting older?

JIMI: Not at all, no.

JANE: Can you think of yourself as being eighty?

JIMI: Not too much, no. I don't think I'll be around when I'm eighty. There's other things to do besides sitting around waiting for eighty to come along, so I don't think about that too much.

JANE: And death. Does it bother you?

JIMI: No, not at all. This is only here we're going through, you're not even classified as a man yet. Your body's only a physical vehicle to carry you from one place to another without getting into a lot of trouble. So you have this body tossed upon you that you have to carry around and cherish and protect and so forth, but even that body exhausts itself, so you get into a whole lot of other scenes, which are bigger. This is nothing but child's play—so-called grown-ups. Children don't play games. Well, they do, but adults play the more serious games that can get people killed for no reason at all. People who fear death—it's a complete case of insecurity. That's why the world's screwed up today, because people base things too much on what they see and not on what they feel.

JANE: They don't even know what they feel.

JIMI: Right. Well, it's time for a direction.

JANE: And did you have this awareness before you made it or has money made a difference?

JIMI: Well, listen, I could have stayed at home. I could have stayed in L.A., but I just couldn't stay in one place too long because I wanted to see other things. That's why I went in the army beforehand when I was sixteen, so I could really get all that mess over with and concentrate on the music I play, which calls for travelling all over the place in my own way. I travel most places, without any money actually. And so when the money comes along, well, it's just another part of living really. I don't dig the way the world's going these days, but it's nice to get experience out of it, that's the money, that's what I consider riches.

JANE: And do you believe that you can change anything, anybody?

JIMI: Well, the idea is trying. But I'm just gonna do it. . . .

JANE: It's really down to your music, isn't it?

JIMI: Yeah, that's it, that's what we're talking about. Music. Talking isn't really my scene. Playing is. There's certain people on this Earth that have the power to do different things, for instance in the Black Power movement they're using it wrongly. But in the musical movement you can't call that using it wrongly 'cause that's a natural talent. Protest is all over with. It's the solution everybody wants now, not just protest. The Beatles could do it, they could turn the world around, or at least attempt to. But you see, it might make them a little more uncomfortable in their position. But me, I don't care about my position. What I have to say I'd be glad to say it. You see, it comes out in my music, and then you have to go through scenes like the releasing of an LP and you can't release one every month, and you can't do this and you can't do that. And all the public-image bit . . . in my book it doesn't have to move along. People should get out of images and all that, and start getting into their own gigs, and so forth, whatever they can, in their own bags, you know, instead of laying back and digging someone else and saying, "Oh wow! Oh wow! Look at that! Such imagery!" and all that shit. That's what made me cut my hair off because of this being a slave to the public and all that, you know. . . . I used to dig all those scenes with the clothes and the hair and all that, but then people start misusing those scenes as our image and all that, which it is, but it's nothing to talk about, it's just the way I felt like going through according to my own taste. But then people start trying to prostitute that idea, and it gets to be a hang-up. You find yourself almost running away. You have to grab hold of yourself. People, they don't give me inspiration except bad inspiration, to write songs like "Crosstown Traffic" and all that 'cause that's the way they put themselves off me, the way they present themselves.

— *International Times*
London, 1969

Hendrix sat in with jazz great Roland Kirk at Ronnie Scott's club in Soho in early March. This was a very meaningful experience for Jimi. Because he was unsure of his reception among jazz artists, Roland Kirk's acceptance of Jimi's musicianship increased his confidence at an important time. While lurid details of Jimi's personality and his "threat to English culture" were circulated almost daily in the press, this meaningful exchange was ignored.

Before they played together, Kirk came to visit Jimi at his Brook Street apartment. At that time London was ablaze with Jimi Hendrix posters, rumors, and statements. Hendrix had two singles in the Top 10, and everyone knew he was the biggest new thing happening. But Hendrix, always self-deprecating, sought out Kirk, a brother, a fellow musician from the States, to simply come visit. Kirk found the flat surprisingly modest. Situated above a pub, it was the flat of a worker, not a star.

Hendrix had known of Roland Kirk's music in the States. Kirk had played at the Five Spot while Jimi was at Cafe Wha?, six blocks away. Jimi, who was able to play three different guitar parts at once, felt an affinity for Kirk, who had gained notoriety in the press for his ability to play three wind instruments at one time. Weird instruments, too, like the stritch, a medieval horn that looked like a soprano saxophone, but stretching straight down and longer, with a trumpet-like bell that curved out at the end. Kirk could play a saxophone, a mazello, and the stritch at the same time, three-part harmonizing, and also do circular breathing, which allowed unusually long sustained lines and even three-part phrases. From his neck hung a *wheee* whistle, which he would blow after an incredible solo. Kirk also played flute with his nose. The English press, of course, played up those freaky parts of Kirk's performances. Understanding the importance of novelty in attracting an audience, Kirk's and Hendrix's musical abilities were the bedrock on which these "tricks" rested.

Kirk, burly, bold, blind, outspoken, held radical views concerning jazz. Many jazz men knock the rock and blues players for doing what they consider facile music. But Kirk did not consider himself a "jazz musician," although he is considered one of the best in the business. Kirk talked only about "the music." Whether it be jazz, blues, rhythm and blues, or rock—it was the music. From the start, Kirk and Hendrix communicated on a mutual plane. Their conversations were not about what differentiated them, but about their mutuality, their involvement in the music of black people. Roland Kirk recognized Hendrix as essentially a bluesman. While it was necessary for the publicists to put the rock banner on Jimi's music, the funky syncopated foundation and wide choices of phrasings and colorings rested in the blues tradition. Kirk, who was able to deliver powerful blues blowing himself, realized, musician to musician, where Hendrix was coming from.

Jimi's flat over the pub on Brook Street bore a plaque proclaiming that Handel had once lived there. He and Kirk sat there the entire afternoon, listening to records and talking about music and about London as compared to America. They both laughed over the lack of American soul food and jammed most of the time. Jimi played what he usually played and Roland Kirk played what he usually played and it worked out fine. They were also joined by the African conga player Kwasi "Rocki" Dzidzornu.

When Kirk invited Jimi to come and sit in with him at Ronnie Scott's jazz club in Soho, they dug each other so much that they played together again the next night. No publicity, no recordings, simply the music, for the love of music—and the memories of doing it together.

Jimi returned to New York City on March 13 and checked into a suite at the Pierre Hotel on Fifth Avenue. He was joined a few days later by Kathy Etchingham on her first trip to America. She was a bit surprised by the opulence, among other things.

There was a lot for Jimi to deal with back in the States. For one, the idea had been changed from the original plan to build a club and recording studio on the site of the Generation Club, which Jimi and Mike Jeffery had formed a partnership to buy/lease. There were many problems with the club idea. Some thought the Mafia, used to running things in the West Village, would object. But then, having just a studio there would not only increase Hendrix's productivity, it would also save the tens of thousands of dollars they spent at the Record Plant or other recording studios they rented on a regular basis. And they could also sell studio time to others and have a much leaner, simpler operation than a club *and* studio.

John Storyk, the architect, was thunderstruck when he first heard the news. He had completed all the drawings and blueprints for the club. At first he thought the entire idea was scotched. But then again, recording studios could be seen as simply an extension of the original idea. The real problem was that the studio would cost about a million to build and would probably have to be built in stages since the cash was not there. A loan from Warner Bros. against the JHE's future revenues would probably fly. They could not borrow the entire amount. If they could get a quarter of the amount to start, then the JHE's four-walling appearances via Concerts East could generate substantial amounts of cash. If things went well, they could establish a cash flow and build the studio without any more stops due to lack of cash.

The Experience was scheduled to do another tour, but Jimi saw problems with the band. If they played like they played at Albert Hall, then it would be unbearable for him, and eventually for the fans, as well. Jimi had noticed that Noel was having trouble with his Fat Mattress group. He had fallen off the stage during their debut at Albert Hall because he may have been too stoned to play. Whatever the reason, Noel had a lot on his plate. Jimi would joke with Mitch, calling Noel's group "Thin Pillow." But he also sympathized with Noel. They had been through a lot together. They had written songs together. Often Noel and Mitch had been his only friends for long stretches of time, especially in those most difficult early days in London. Jimi could never be cruel to Noel. He wanted him to succeed.

Jimi had overheard Noel say, "The pressure from the public to create something even more brilliant each time, while basically expecting us to stay the same, was crushing." Jimi knew exactly what he was talking about.

But Jimi loved the challenge and the intense, frequent jamming and extended studio work helped him to envision where his music was going; and the confidence of all that had increasingly built up in him to make him feel very strong. Noel Redding still had some dues to pay before he could be what he wanted to be. But Jimi knew he himself could never forsake the ability he had worked so hard to achieve.

In late March, Jimi put together a jam at the Record Plant that included Buddy Miles on drums; Jim McCarty, the guitarist in Mitch Ryder's band; Dave Holland, who was Miles Davis's bass player; and John McLaughlin, the hot "new" guitarist on the block, who had distinguished himself with his work with Miles Davis, who had named a tune after him. McLaughlin also explored Eastern music, earning him the honorific title Mahavishnu. But actually, McLaughlin had been around for quite a while. He had played in the Georgie Fame band way before Mitch Mitchell had; that nevertheless was a bond. It was Mitch who had urged McLaughlin to come to the studio.

Jimi, jamming with these heavy jazz-oriented musicians, and Buddy Miles, with whom he had cultured a serious musical relationship, had Gary Kellgren record the jams. One of the two edited selections was an extended version of "Drivin' South," which was a derivation of Albert Collins's "Thaw Out," a composition that had had a strong effect on Hendrix when he had heard it for the first time as he was transitioning out of the army in 1962. The other jam was something he called "Everything's Gonna Be Alright."

McLaughlin, a highly schooled musician, was expertly precise in his knowledge of musical harmony. He could play, read, or write difficult changes, be it in jazz, rock, or East Indian music, with an expertness that allowed him to improvise, as well. He appreciated Jimi's humility in that it was clear he regarded himself as just another guitar player who was extremely deep into the blues tradition. He felt that Jimi's incredible imagination made up for all his shortcomings (not being able to read and write music, lack of formal academic schooling) to such an extent that he "was a beautiful guitar player" in McLaughlin's eyes.

The JHE's "gig list" for April/May 1969 was shaping up. It would begin on April 11 in Raleigh, North Carolina, at the Dalton Arena. They would stay at the Triangle Motel. The seating capacity of the arena: 9,100. Fat Mattress the supporting act. The JHE's potential gross: $45,000. The motel was at the airport, where they would fly out in the middle of the morning for Philly, to play the Spectrum. The potential gross was a high $105,000. The JHE and Fat Mattress would return to New York City, while the road crew drove the equipment down to Memphis for the April 18 gig at the Mid-South Coliseum. The next day they were due in Houston for the Sam Houston Coliseum, and the next day in Dallas at the Memorial Auditorium. The potential gross for each of the three dates was $60,000. Next they would fly to L.A. on April 21 for the Forum on April 26, for which they had a p.g. of $105,000. Next they would fly to Oakland for a show on April 27 at the Coliseum Auditorium, and back to L.A. that same night. They were due in Detroit on May 2, where they would play Cobo Hall with Cat Mother.

Mike Jeffery suddenly came up with an easy addition: a May 3 one-nighter in Toronto at the top-grossing Maple Leaf Gardens. A night of work for a possible $110,000, their largest potential gross.

On April 11, the tour officially began at the Dalton Arena in Raleigh, North Carolina, with Fat Mattress opening. Jimi met with Billy Cox on April 18 at the Sheraton Motor Inn, where the JHE was staying that one night in Memphis. He had called Billy the day before to make sure he would be there. It was a nice reunion. After sizing each other up (Billy thought Jimi looked about twenty-five pounds thinner than when they were playing together some seven years ago; Hendrix had not yet reached twenty-one), Billy looked calm, rested, living a regular life running a music publishing company in Nashville. Jimi told him he wanted Cox to work with him again. Although it was not the right time, if Cox could put his affairs in order and wait for the right time, Jimi would soon send for him. Jimi stressed that it was really about friendship, and his need for help right now, not show business but music. He would take care of Billy and it would all work out good. Jimi gave him $500 cash and said he would send for him. Billy Cox agreed; he was overjoyed to have such good fortune.

Then Jimi went on and played two shows. Noel played four, since his band, Fat Mattress, was supporting. Noel was really exhausted afterward.

On April 19, Jimi and company appeared at the Sam Houston Coliseum in Houston. Staying at the Sheraton Lincoln Hotel, they would not have much time for shut-eye since they were also playing two shows. As soon as they got to the Coliseum there was a problem. Some officials were balking at the sale of posters of Hendrix, Noel, and Mitch standing in a field fronted by two young and lovely topless blondes. It got smoothed out after a while. But that was typical of Texas hassles. And when Jimi's version of "The Star-Spangled Banner" reached the ears of not a small number of police on duty, one of them pushed Ron Terry, Concerts East's booking agent, up against the wall, demanding that he command the trio to stop playing. Terry balked, saying they could not stop in the middle of a song.

Later, Terry noted: "We got through that night but the vibes backstage after the show were terrible. We didn't know if we were going to get out of there."

And the next night in Dallas, Hendrix and company were told that, despite their reservations at the Cabana Motor Hotel, where they usually stayed when in Dallas, no rooms were available. After a lot of fussing and talking and cajoling, the reservations were restored and they were given the rooms.

Later at the Memorial Auditorium, several large white men stood before Hendrix's dressing room. Not addressing Hendrix but talking directly to Terry, a fellow white man, they were very clear in their message: "You tell that fucking nigger that if he plays 'The Star-Spangled Banner' in this hall tonight he won't live to get out of the building."

Terry replied that if something like what they were saying happened in Dallas, those responsible would not live to tell about it, and besides, a riot would be started if Jimi did not make it out of the building.

The men stalked off. Hendrix kept asking if "this" was real. Near the end of their performance, just as they usually did, Jimi, Noel, and Mitch played "The Star-Spangled Banner." They did not see those men again.

They flew back to New York for a few days before departing again for the West Coast on April 25. Jimi checked into the Beverly Rodeo Hotel. That night he and Noel attended a party for Donovan at the Factory.

On April 26, the JHE played the Forum in L.A., supported by Cat Mother and the Chicago Transit Authority (later to be known simply as Chicago). Warner Bros. threw a pre-gig party and Noel, Mitch, and Jimi got pretty well toasted before going on to play. Noel later said: "Together we relaxed and worked our way through the mountains of Mexican grass, leapers, and coke." The crowd of eighteen thousand was boisterous, the music seemed, as it would more and more with other audiences as well, to drive them into a state of mass delirium. Their reaction to Hendrix's sound surprised the Experience. The excitement generated by the music was more than the audience could take. There were a number of times when the house lights went up and the concert was in danger of being shut down. Jimi and Noel addressed the crowd directly and that had a calming effect. They were able to end with "Voodoo Chile" and with a bit of "Sunshine of Your Love" thrown in. Jimi set his guitar down, flashed the peace sign, and left the stage. That had been a close call. They had barely avoided a riot. The security had not been sufficient. And this was a Hendrix organization gig, four-walled by Concerts East, who had rented the "building" for that one night. They most certainly would have been liable had there been serious problems.

After the show, he joined Mama Cass Elliot (of the Mamas and Papas) and Mr. "B"—Billy Eckstine, the legendary jazz vocalist and band leader— and they all went to the Whisky a Go-Go on Sunset Boulevard.

The next day the JHE flew to the San Francisco Bay Area to appear at the Oakland Coliseum with Jefferson Airplane. Their bassist, Jack Casady, joined the Experience for a jam, as was becoming the custom. Jimi liked Casady's sound.

The JHE returned to Los Angeles for a photo shoot on the Warner Bros. Studios backlot. Dressed as Hells Angels and then in cowboy garb from the wardrobe department, they were photographed for the cover of the *Smash Hits* album.

Jimi had agreed to an interview with journalist Sharon Lawrence for May 1, but things were so hectic at his suite that, although she was there and ready, it did not happen. Lawrence noticed some unusual activity among those streaming in and out of Jimi's room. She took some notes. Their tour would then go back toward the East Coast, snaking through Detroit and Toronto, before heading south, then a stop in the Midwest before going back to the East Coast. They were, as usual, recording while they toured, so although they had less time on the road, the irregular patterns and frequent flights made it almost as tiring as a string of many one-nighters in a row.

Jimi turned up in New York City instead of Detroit the next day. He was mysteriously reluctant to continue to tour. Gerry Stickells showed up at the office at 27 East Thirty-seventh Street around 5:00 P.M. on May 2. He informed Bob Levine, who was responsible for Hendrix's lucrative merchandising operation and also lent his expertise in the American tour circuit, and Howard Krantz, a lawyer in the Steingarten, Wedeen & Weiss firm, which represented Hendrix, that Jimi had not made the 2:00 P.M. plane because Gerry couldn't get him to go. Jimi came in and sat down with Levine as frantic calls from the Detroit promoter began to come in. There were ten thousand people waiting for him. Detroit was a town famous for its unusually violent riots. The first act had just finished. It took Levine the better part of an hour to get Jimi to change his mind. Then there was the problem of getting Jimi to Detroit in time for his appearance. Impersonating Frank Sinatra's office, Levine contacted Butler Aviation, Sinatra's Learjet service. After some back and forth they were given a number and a gate at La-Guardia Airport. Gerry Stickells had access to the cash revenue from the show. He would be able to pay the aviation service in cash and further tip them so they would be all right with everything. Sinatra and Jimi were connected, but there had been no time to go through channels, and had there been enough time there would have been no need to. Jimi got there in time to play.

Early the next morning they all left for Toronto. For some reason there was a rumor that there would probably be a problem going through customs in Canada. Onboard the flight to Toronto, just before they were to land, Ron Terry woke Jimi up, telling him it was likely they, upon going through customs, would be detained and his luggage and possibly his person thoroughly searched. Terry took Jimi and his flight bag to the lavatory and instructed him to get rid of anything even remotely suspicious.

Upon landing, Terry was confident. "I thought he was clean." They were the last two to disembark. Tony Ruffino, carrying Jimi's bags, put one of them on the customs counter. The customs official warned Ruffino that if the bag was not his to keep his hands off of it. When Ruffino replied that he worked for Hendrix, the officer repeated that he was to keep his hands off the bag. The official turned to Jimi and asked if the bag was his. Jimi said yes, and no sooner than that, the officer had opened the bag, produced an Alka-Seltzer bottle, and opened it to reveal several glassine envelopes of what would be determined to be heroin. There was also some hashish. Jimi was immediately arrested.

Ruffino and Terry, who was also carrying one of Hendrix's bags, were also detained, although Jimi insisted that they were his bags and that the other men should be let go.

Noel had immediately tried to reach Michael Jeffery, "but he seemed to have disappeared off the face of the earth." These thoughts kept going through his mind: "Was the Toronto bust just a way for someone (from a long list of possibilities) to remind Jimi that he was very vulnerable and dependent on others to get him out of tight situations?"

Stickells finally reached the office. Jeffery was supposed to have been in Hawaii, but Michael Goldstein, the publicist, seeming to know what to do, and seeming to know what Jeffery's response would be, began immediate damage control. It is said he greased many palms, as the saying goes, paid off many people, in order to keep the story out of the national press. The absence of that story in print until it was reported in *Rolling Stone* some four weeks later is a good indication of the success of his efforts.

Interesting aspects of the power of the worldwide youth culture came into play and had an effect on the situation. For one, one of the arresting officers noted that his son had tickets for the show and that there would be hell to pay if Jimi did not show up. Not only that, but the fact that the police/customs agency had detained him might result in a riot, or to a lesser degree, the staging, perhaps that very night, of a benefit concert in support of Jimi. That would also cast an unfavorable light on the police establishment of Canada. Seeking to avoid a bad situation involving the youth culture, the decision was made to release Jimi and allow him to make the gig.

Jimi was on better time for this gig than the last one in Detroit. It began on time and the crowd was satisfied with the JHE's shaky performance. Jimi was beginning to wonder whether he was experiencing the Beatles syndrome, when they would play a concert and the fans would scream so loud and on such a sustained level that their music and songs could not be heard. Jimi's presence seemed to be enough to excite and energize the fans, regardless of the quality of his playing. For him, that was indeed a serious dilemma.

Ron Terry had heard again, as they were on their way to the Maple Leaf Gardens, a phrase he had first heard Hendrix utter after being threatened by racist Texans: "This is not real, this is not really happening." Hendrix's relationship to reality was being seriously challenged.

After the show was over and Jimi was returning to the States, the impact of his arrest really hit him. Sure, he would have the best lawyers that money could buy. Sure, it was obvious that even if he used heroin he would not be stupid enough to leave it on the top of his luggage. But the obvious had nothing to do with it. The fact remained that he could be put away for quite a long time. It came to him in a flash how he would have to change his life around with a jail sentence hanging over his head. For one, he would have to make sure that he did not get into any other hassles with the law. That meant that the house he had leased in upstate New York had become, in the space of a few hours, the most important place for him to be. Away from the New York City scene, he would be away from the influences that could possibly add to his problems with the authorities. He could keep a low profile upstate and really get into working on his music. In the event that he was put away, at least he would have some music together and in the can so he would not be forgotten.

He had the feeling that he had been set up. He searched back in his mind, trying to recall the exact circumstances of his packing. Trying to recall who was nearby, close enough to slip something into his luggage. But it was no use. He had been so rushed and enveloped by people that it was all like a whirlwind. All he saw was the expression on the customs official's face. Jimi had known something was wrong in the way the man's manner suddenly changed toward him. He had felt an icy chill in his gut that spread all over his body. Before he knew it consciously, his body had already reacted.

He knew he would have to change his music now or never. Either he would be remembered as a freaky rock 'n' roll musician or as a serious creative musician. He might have to serve time in prison. The choice was his and he had to make it—fast. He wanted to get much closer to jazz. That meant that Noel would probably have to go. Noel had strong ideas about rock 'n' roll and would not change. There was a wider range of musicians Jimi wanted to work with. He wanted to relate to musicians who were into new sounds, who were not tied down to rock 'n' roll or rhythm and blues. Jazz was what he thought of. Not pure jazz, but new elements added to his sound that would extend it and make it possible to merge with other realms of music. A house upstate would be perfect. He could have who he wanted to have up there and be free from the restrictions the city placed on him. Before he had been toying with the idea of a new direction, but now it was a serious quest. He would have to have some new music together that would appeal to more than just the fickle rock 'n' roll crowd. He did not want to be forgotten if he had to serve time in jail. The maximum sentence was seven years.

Bust or not, the tour must go on. On May 4, they played the Memorial Auditorium in Syracuse, New York. There was an ongoing black student protest at nearby Cornell University that was receiving headline attention in the news and the mood was palpable among the youthful audience. The next day Jimi had to be back in Toronto for a hearing. Luckily, Syracuse was pretty close. Jimi got a haircut, trimming his long hair into the medium Afro that would be his look throughout the entire trial. He looked like nothing approaching the image of a long-haired druggie.

Judge Fred Hayes would have Jimi back on June 19 for a preliminary hearing. It was clear this was going to be a drawn-out process.

Back on the road, the Experience, after a day in New York City, hit the South. They took the same route as when they'd gigged with the Monkees, as Noel constantly pointed out, as if he could not believe it. "We were replaying the Monkees tour, same halls, same crowds, same horror. The two-stopover Charlotte-to-Charleston flight in an old prop plane was a lesson in fear. The audiences were creepy and there were no chicks afterwards." That jaunt ended in Indiana at the State Fairgrounds Coliseum in Indianapolis.

Jimi sent for Billy Cox. Billy arrived in New York very quietly, without the limo Jimi's office usually would arrange. But no problem, Billy Cox was a down-to-earth man. He was looking forward to the kind of collaboration Jimi had mentioned. It was pretty clear that the office wanted Hendrix to remain with the original Experience.

But Jimi was really glad to see Billy for other reasons besides music. Billy was an old and trusted friend, a calming influence during these stressful times. Billy had been his friend when he was nobody. Billy was quiet, humble, and unassuming. He did not drink or use drugs, could take orders without getting pushed all out of shape, and would stay in the studio until the job was done no matter how long that was (almost like a marine of music). And he was always on time and ready.

During the four days off, Jimi hung out in New York City, often recording at the Record Plant when most people were in a deep sleep. He and Billy also worked in Jimi's suite at the Navarro Hotel for many long hours. Improvising off of patterns, with bass and guitar, they would work on ongoing compositions or discover fresh sounds within their studied jams. Later, in the studio, they would put it down. Jimi was full of ideas and it was great to have someone to share them with. He wanted to try and work with an organist, with a three- or four-piece horn section, like Buddy Miles had in his group, the Express. Jimi wanted to explore more percussion: timbales, congas, bongos, or maracas, for starters.

Jimi met Jerry Velez, percussionist, at the Scene club. He had a sister who was a singer, Martha Velez. Jimi invited Velez to a jam session at the Record Plant. Jimi liked what Jerry put down, an Afro-salsa thing, another level of rhythm. Besides, he was a cool guy, happy, and with a lot of humility.

Billy Cox, a drum-and-bass man, still in the background, increasingly a co-conspirator with Jimi on new musical directions, wondered about the feasibility of congas and timbales "competing" with what Mitch would play. But Jimi, with his big ears, had heard successful combinations of traps and other percussion, especially in New York City, where salsa was huge, and in the world of jazz, especially in Miles Davis's aggregations. Soon after Billy Cox had arrived, Juma Sultan played congas at one of their jams at the Record Plant, with an organist from Nashville, Sharon Lane. Jimi realized that Billy did not have a lot of experience with multiple percussionists and that might be a challenge for him, as well. But it would be something to work out as they went along.

Jimi was also discovering that in the success of his music many second-guessers were prematurely trying to seal it off, preserve it (that had happened with Chas Chandler, who could not see nor recognize what he was doing, where he was going, and walked away), but it *was* his music, his vision, and most challenges only strengthened his resolve to follow his head.

The JHE, supported by Cat Mother and the Buddy Miles Express, played the Civic Center in Baltimore, Maryland, on May 16; Providence, at the Rhode Island Arena on May 17; and the culminator: Madison Square Garden in New York City on May 18 with the Buddy Miles Express and Traffic, one of Jimi's favorite groups, with his good musician peers Chris Wood and Stevie Winwood added as support.

There was a discernible effort on the Hendrix organization's part to keep him as happy as possible under the circumstances.

Seattle was at the top of the list of dates on the West Coast. Jimi's family noted an exhaustion in him. It probably had more to do with stress than the rigors of the tour, which was relatively well ordered as compared to those of the recent past.

The JHE played the Seattle Coliseum supported by Fat Mattress and Ike and Tina Turner. During a particularly blistering solo under a glass dome and on a revolving stage in the center of fifteen thousand heads, lightning flashed and it joined the brilliant stage lights flashing against Jimi's white Stratocaster, creating a miraculous effect. Jimi noticed it and commented favorably to the gods in passing as he soloed on.

The next night, May 24, they were in San Diego, at the International Sports Arena. Fat Mattress opened the show. The San Jose Pop Festival was the next night, up the California coast a piece at the Santa Clara Fairgrounds. Joining Fat Mattress as supporting acts were bluesman Taj Mahal and Eric Burdon fronting his new group, War.

This particular show became legendary. Carlos Santana thought it was the best he had ever seen Jimi play, and fellow hot guitarist Santana seriously followed Jimi, the hottest guitarist on the block. Santana noted Jimi's "supreme confidence." He commanded the stage and "was all over that Strat." Many of the young women in the audience took off their tops and stood bare-breasted as Jimi's music washed over them. A truly rare event.

The highlight of this tour was the Hawaii connection, a week on the gateway islands to the South Pacific. At first Fat Mattress was not going. But Jimi insisted, saying, inscrutably, "They done the graft, they deserve the perk."

On May 26, they flew from San Francisco to Honolulu International Airport, and enjoyed three solid days off before their three-day stint at the Waikiki Shell.

The first show was abruptly terminated. There was a hum in the amplifiers that could not be subdued. After a couple of numbers, Jimi put his guitar down and went and sat in the limo and refused to reappear. Noel and Mitch were really pissed. They thought that it would have been possible to do the show. Noel, in particular, resented having to follow after Hendrix in his often subjective decisions. Many in the crowd were very angry, even though the promoters said the ticket stubs would be honored in the subsequent shows.

The next shows produced overflow crowds, many of whom said they had had tickets for the original show that was canceled but had lost them. Finally, Jimi instructed that the entire lot be allowed in. It became a free show. His playing was excellent but the overflow was a security problem and the Waikiki Shell people were not at all happy.

They flew back to L.A. with Noel and Mitch continuing on to New York and then London. They were not due back until June 20, almost three weeks away. Jimi would stay in L.A., do press, jam, record some, and further insulate himself from any more problems with the law. He sent for Billy Cox to join him so they could work on the music there.

Jimi announced his Sky Church concept to Jerry Hopkins in an interview, and further developed it in conversations with Sharon Lawrence. His playing outdoor arenas that held a lot of people, or the lightning flash while he soloed in Seattle recently, may have given him a flash of the spirituality involved in playing below the heavens, upon the earth, for multitudes. And magical concerts outside, like the San Jose Pop Festival or the most recent Waikiki Shell in Hawaii, made him feel a connection with the earth, sky, and humanity, and especially a connection with his fellow musicians onstage, as mediums for the magic. He felt he was receiving spiritual answers through music via the open air. To Sharon Lawrence, who Jimi spent a lot of time with in L.A., her home base, he further elaborated on buying land, maybe right there in Los Angeles, having a musician family with his favorite players: Rahsaan Roland Kirk was way up there, but also his regular mates: Eric Clapton, Stevie Winwood, Jeff Beck, John Mayall, Vic Briggs, Roger Mayer, the Twins Arthur and Albert Allen, Billy Cox, Jerry Velez, Juma Sultan, Mitch Mitchell, etc. They would just concentrate on music, experimentation, with the idea of bringing the music forward in a conscious, progressive way. A complex of buildings and structures. Two stages, a large one outside, a smaller one inside. A bunkhouse of sorts, a communal kitchen, with a full-time cook, an older woman (not a groupie), maybe a widow who liked music. Build a nice dining room. He just had to find the property. And there would be an office in town to conduct business in a formal, traditional way, as is often necessary.

He and Sharon Lawrence inspected Phil Spector's building on the southeast corner of Sunset Boulevard and Carol Street. It, or something like it, could be that office in town for the Sky Church concept. Some of that space might be available if he were interested. Jimi was impressed by the fact that the entire building was dedicated to Spector's vision. Its spaciousness made many activities possible. While driving back to the Beverly Rodeo Hotel he was often noticed and waved to as he sat on the passenger side of Lawrence's vehicle, and he returned little self-conscious waves back, smiling all the while.

Jimi spent some time at Stephen Stills's house in Studio City, hanging out and often jamming, one night with Stills and his drummer, Dallas Taylor, and Buddy Miles and Rick James. Taylor did not like Jimi, they were not friends. There had been a problem with a woman, Taylor's girlfriend, who was intimate with them both. Taylor assessed Jimi as, in general, "an extremely unhappy person, kind of scared," who "always had a guitar in his hands unless he was getting high or getting laid."

On June 19, Jimi appeared in court in Toronto; Judge Robert Taylor made the date for his trial: December 8, 1969.

On June 20, 1969, Jimi appeared at Devonshire Downs, a racetrack in the San Fernando Valley, for the Newport Jazz Festival–L.A. He received the highest sum ever paid a rock act for one appearance up till then: $125,000. Unsatisfied with the performance and police violence against the crowd, he returned the next day and jammed with Buddy Miles for forty-five minutes. It was the first time that Jimi and Buddy had played before a large audience together. Returning to the mobile home dressing room after the concert, Noel Redding found Jimi talking to several blacks who were said to be Black Panthers. Redding made a fuss about their discussion disrupting his dressing room. He was more uptight than usual. They left.

In L.A., Jimi finally got to meet Herbie Worthington. Buddy Miles always spoke highly of Herbie. They had been roommates once. Herbie was the kind of guy who helped you to get your thing together by his very presence on the scene. Herbie had helped Buddy Miles get his horn section together for his band. Jimi was interested in horns, too, but he was even more so interested in having a good friend. They were hard to find. Since Jimi's bust, he had begun to notice strange machinations among those who were supposed to be his friends. Herbie had a reputation in music circles as a good, solid person who could be counted on in tight spots, and who never tripped out on anything. Jimi dug

Herbie right away. Herbie was not a musician. He took photos and studied books on a wide range of subjects.

Vishwa was on the scene, also. He and Jimi and Herbie met at the hotel just as Jimi was getting ready to split for the June 29 Denver Pop concert. Vishwa, by then, was a regular member of Jimi's entourage. It was obvious that Herbie wanted to go to Denver with them, as well. Jimi finally asked him to go at the last minute. Herbie said that he would like to go but that he did not have the bread. That was a laugh. Jimi probably had about $10,000 on him at that moment. Herbie was so glad to be going that he picked Jimi up clear off the ground in a spontaneous gesture, cradling him like a baby. They all had a good laugh.

They flew in to Denver on June 29, 1969, and checked into the hotel. Herbie and Jimi dropped some fine acid just before the ride to the gig. Herbie confided to Jimi that his favorite song was "Bold As Love"—he dug the relationship of the colors to the emotions.

Mile High Stadium was in an uproar. There were forty thousand screaming kids bursting forth from the stands and not enough security. The stage was located on the infield diamond and the fans were desperate to get down close to the music.

Jimi and Herbie felt the acid coming on as they clambered onto the stage. Sedulous, fluent, and delicious waves of energy pulsated from everything.

Jimi got right into "Bold As Love." "Orange is young, full of daring/But very unsteady on the first go round." He could not resist a peek at Herbie, who stood in the wings. The acid exhilarated through the air and they had a moment of pure contact that made both of them crack up. Jimi stood on the stage laughing for a moment—then, keeping his face averted from Herbie's side of the stage, Jimi started "Bold As Love" all over again, from the top.

As Jimi rode toward the end of the song, the crowd started rushing toward the stage. The police hastily assembled on the turf. They began firing tear-gas bombs into the boisterous, onrushing crowd. The wind shifted and the tear gas began blowing onto the stage. It was not long before the crowd had completely overrun the police and security guards, and charged the stage. Barrett and Stickells and the rest of the JHE road crew raced against time and the mob. They quickly backed up the equipment truck and jammed Jimi inside, followed by Herbie, Mitch, Noel, and the others. Barrett and Stickells locked the truck and then they proceeded to slowly wade the huge truck through forty thousand rampaging kids. Jimi and Herbie giggled in the black interior of the slowly moving, rocking truck. It was wild! Some kids got up on the top of the truck and began stomping on it as if they wanted to bash it in. Others rocked the truck as if they wanted to topple it. Barrett and Stickells raced the motor so the kids would think they were going to speed off. Jimi suddenly remembered the girls he and Herbie had brought with them from the hotel. Jimi was panicked until Herbie laughed and told him that the girls were in the truck but were too scared to talk.

They went to a private party for Jimi at a club. All the best guitar pickers and the prettiest young ladies of Denver were there. Jimi jumped up on the tiny stage and played for two hours straight. Then they went to an outdoor wedding celebration and Jimi jammed until dark with the Rich Brothers and "Snip" Milton on drums. They jammed on an old Junior Walker tune: "Cornbread and Buttermilk."

Back at the hotel, Jimi, Herbie, and Vishwa shared five groupies among them.

Soon after the Denver Pop concert (the last performance of the Experience), Jimi went into virtual seclusion.

On July 2, Noel Redding and Mitch Mitchell turned up in London, announcing that they had left the Experience for good. Noel Redding told Stan Reed, of the *Evening Standard,* "I suddenly heard that Jimi was planning to expand the group, bring in other musicians, writers, and composers, and drop the name of the Experience and I hadn't been consulted." Mitch Mitchell concurred that the group had definitely split up completely.

But Jimi was more involved with the sad news from London that Brian Jones had died.

Soon after, Jimi appeared on the *Tonight* show, which was guest-hosted by Flip Wilson. Jimi—accompanied by Billy Cox on bass and Ed Shaughnessy, the drummer from Doc Severinsen's band—dedicated a new song, "Lover Man," to Brian Jones. The television studio amplifiers blew up midway through the song, something Brian Jones probably would have found amusing.

Billy Cox and Buddy Miles were eagerly waiting in the wings. Although they were still basically a jam-rhythm section for Jimi, he would make them the core of his new musical direction.

Larry Lee had been asked by Jimi to join him in New York City, and in mid-July he arrived from Nashville. Lee had served in the Vietnam War and had not been back all that long. He was very glad to get the invitation from Jimi. He flew in scared, not ready for a lot of things. It buoyed his spirits to new heights when Jimi and Buddy Miles met him in a limo. Now Jimi had a rhythm guitarist.

Jimi dug Monique as soon as he met her. Devon introduced them. Devon knew what Jimi liked and she also knew that pulling a woman like Monique for Jimi would cement their relationship even more. Monique was very much like Jimi, especially the side of him that was the fun-loving, get high and ball and laugh, and look at everything like a cosmic good time side. In so many of Monique's ways he saw himself.

Monique, long white-brown, slender, joyous, total ease in smile, and very much like Jimi. Same five-eleven height, always thin, but the kind of thin that is lithe yet soft and cuddly. A sensuous space between her even white teeth that always ranged between a kittenish smile and a full-faced Cheshire-cat grin. Of Moroccan-Jewish ancestry. Monique loved the good times. She loved Jimi, perhaps more than anyone else, in the romantic way.

Although she had been in the States for some time, her French accent was still very much there. It gave away her lack of many English words that dealt with complexities. But in the delights of the senses and the flesh she was expert.

A perfect person to have fun with. Laughter spilling from her lips as if she were a bubbling fountain of joy. She exuded a champagne high at all times. Before you knew her or even talked to her you would be impressed with her carriage; tall, graceful, and elegant, she moved in the unhurried pace of one who does not have a job to appear at. In fact, she gave the impression that she lived life totally on her own terms and did not *really* have to be anywhere at any time. Her smile was warm, at ease, and sensual. Not in the sexpot way, but just easy and warm, saying everything can happen in its own time. The affable tilt of her head when talking, her musical voice, light and soprano, making you like her immediately, making you want to be pleasant around her, to bask in her smile.

Always there, Monique's smile is her trademark. And if perhaps she knows you better, it might be a greeting or a kiss, a long luminous tongue in your mouth, directly between your lips parted in surprise. Followed perhaps by a one-and-one of coke, or whatever was being enjoyed—perhaps some excellent smoke.

A gourmet, she strikes one as always enjoying the best and seeing really no other reason for anything else. She eats like a bird and drinks lightly. She loves music, getting high, and making love the most.

Monique was a stranger to America. An outsider. She had to struggle to understand the ways. Hendrix, black, introverted, from Seattle, then the South, then Harlem, then the Village, and then London, never really felt American in the strict sense. Dislocated and estranged, he found that Monique's view of the newness and wonder of this place was close to his own outsider's awe. Jimi Hendrix was famous when he returned to America. He would choose to live in the Village, close to the pulse of the Empire City. He would live in the heart of the city, and it was Monique more than Devon who made him feel at home.

Devon had just gotten Jimi his pad and was there to help him, but they were not yet as tight as they would be later. He stayed with Monique before Devon found his apartment. But Monique was married, and her husband, who was away, would return. Jimi had to find a place of his own. So he moved up the street a couple of blocks to Twelfth Street off University Place. Monique explained to Jimi that she was intent upon maintaining her relationship with her husband but that she could come there every day and be with him a great deal of the time. She knew marriage and a home with Jimi was out of the question, but she would be with him and help him as best she could under the circumstances.

But Hendrix did not want to leave her home. He wanted her with him. The compromise they reached was more a part of their love and mutual understanding. Neither Jimi nor Monique could make a concrete and long-standing commitment. Monique was fun-loving and joyous, but she was also as shrewd and survival-oriented as her North African ancestors.

So Hendrix moved to 59 West Twelfth Street and Monique came every day and decorated his pad in neo-Moroccan. They acted like newlyweds, shopping for decorations and furnishings, going over lists, and talking with salesmen.

Hendrix was greatly insecure upon arriving back in America. Monique's love and quiet ease and sense of peace gave him confidence. She was a woman who knew how to do for a man. Though she was another man's wife—no matter—Hendrix needed her very much, and they both realized it and acted upon it. The other person who knew what he needed was Devon, and while she was not exactly "in" at that time, she would make the moves, the calls to Monique to get her to come over, as well as occasional calls to others; but for now it was Monique. Jimi soon found Devon essential to his life, even if only to make sure that Monique could be with him without blowing her life with her husband.

She knew sensuality as he knew guitar. Her long, light-brown/sun-blonde hair swirled as languorously as her long limbs. She could curl up or have him curl into her with ease, as if it were the most natural thing in the world. Her brown, steady eyes staring directly into his, her faint freckles, the lilt of her playful voice, the way she had of ducking her head and listening intently to what he was trying to say. And with music, he could feel it through her, he could listen with her and be sure she was listening and responding as he was, not only because she was with him, but also because she loved music. She had her own. She was no groupie. She was in total control of her life, at ease with life; her easy elegance gave him confidence on the street or inside the house when they were alone.

She designed clothes for him with special colors and fabrics, lots of velours and crushed velvet, soft cloths in magentas, deep blues going into purple, turquoise, starked-out reds that related to him astrologically and musically.

Monique spent a lot of time in a dress shop on the Lower East Side that was owned by two friends of hers: Colette Mimram and Stella Douglas. Jimi would sit in the shop at 321 East Ninth Street with Monique, Colette, and Stella while they did their thing with clothes. Jimi would even play salesman, blowing a customer's mind by coming out from behind the curtain that separated the back from the front and telling them how good they looked in something. It was a joke, but it was good, too. People bought things and he was glad because he wanted the dress shop to succeed. Sometimes he bought an item for a customer as a spontaneous gift. He also bought a lot of things for himself. He loved Monique and her friends.

Monique, Colette, and Stella would turn him on to expensive restaurants, good things to eat, how to order, and how to pronounce the foreign words to the waiter.

Monique decorated his apartment like she decorated him, in bluesy space colors, canopies billowing out, exotic East African fabrics and spreads, pillows spread on the floors. You had to really get down and be comfortable because there was no perching on the edge of chairs. A get-down pad. You really had to get down to enjoy Jimi's home, because if you were uptight and upright you would have to leave; there would be no place for you.

Monique, Colette, and Stella turned him on to paintings—especially the paintings of Mati, whom Colette often posed for. Mati's spacey landscapes, often with intricate designs that turned out to be people making love in all kinds of erotic positions out of the *Kama Sutra,* if you looked closely. Monique encouraged Jimi to look closer at things and appreciate finer things with the same sensibility he had for music. And he wanted that and she gave it in the laid-back, sensuous, easy way she gave everything.

Jimi got permission from the authorities to split from the USA for a vacation in Morocco. On July 31 he joined with Stella, Monique, Colette, and a woman named Luna. It was a time to reflect, away from the turmoil.

It was a strange trip. They were followed by several strange men wherever they went.

They got to Morocco and headed out into the countryside. They met up with the Living Theater people along the way; Judith Malina, Julian Beck, Rufus Collins, Jenny Hecht, and the rest of the troupe. Jimi and Colette dropped acid and tripped out in the magical countryside.

They wound up in Essaouira (formerly known as Mogador), a port city one hundred miles west of Marrakech and 180 miles south of Casablanca. Timothy Leary was there with a whole bunch of followers. So was the Art Ensemble of Chicago, a black avant-garde experimental jazz unit. It was like a prearranged pilgrimage. They partied, took acid, and generally got to know each other. They traveled all over Morocco, received and feted by aristocracy and royalty. Jimi was often mistaken for John Claude Vigon, the popular Moroccan singer. That was a switch.

Leaving Morocco he was bodysearched by their customs authorities.

Coming back to the States, Jimi and company found that they were still being followed.

The word was out that Hendrix was into something. Since the bust in Toronto he had maintained a very low profile. He was commuting between three locations, always moving fast in seemingly laid-back elegance. His new Manhattan apartment was maintained by Devon, as an employee. The Record Plant had extensive studio time reserved for him. But it was a retreat upstate, in Shokan, New York, where he was putting it all together.

Miles Davis was into something, too. He had been carefully moving his new band to a place where they could sail right into a new thing and hit it right. Miles Davis had stuck (since *ESP,* an album that signified a new "official" band of sorts) with Wayne Shorter on tenor sax, Herbie Hancock on piano, Ron Carter on bass, and Tony Williams on drums since 1965. George Benson's guitar was added to the same personnel on his *Miles in the Sky* album. *Filles de Kilimanjaro* was the summit for this band. It was also a perfect set-up to follow with something totally new.

Impeccably orchestrated, *Filles* had a song dedicated to his new wife, Betty Davis, née Mambry: "Mademoiselle Mambry." Best of friends with Devon, Colette, and just getting to be friends with Jimi, Betty Davis had just written a Chambers Brothers hit, "Uptown to Harlem," a song that celebrated the jumping black fervor of "uptown" blackness. Miles Davis was suddenly catapulted into the midst of the hip, young, funky music crowd.

Betty Davis threw a dinner party at their townhouse on West Seventy-seventh Street and invited all the finest chicks she knew. Some thought Miles Davis did not like men visiting his home, but it was understood that Jimi would escort Devon. At the last minute Miles was unable to attend the party due to a recording engagement. That left Jimi as the only male in attendance among a roomful of lovely ladies. Miles had left a sheet of music that contained part of a score for Jimi to check out. When Betty gave it to Jimi he told her that he could not read music. Miles called later and asked Betty to put Jimi on the phone. They discussed music in general but were unable to talk about the written music Miles had left.

Alan Douglas, a friend of Miles's and the husband of Stella, Colette's best friend, business partner, and confidante, was dying to get Miles and Jimi together in studio sessions. Miles Davis was said to be the more reluctant of the two, but they both were reluctant to work in public together. Aside from their mutual respect was their knowledge that the hip musical ideas they had developed independently could as readily be absorbed and applied by either one. Jimi and Miles were getting together at Jimi's Twelfth Street apartment and playing duos, exploring musical ideas without anyone else listening. But Miles was willing to help Jimi put together his new band. Horns would be the biggest problem for Jimi—and who knew horns better than Miles? Figuring out how to add horns to Jimi's virtuoso one-man-band guitar that would heighten what was already there became a cross-conversation among Jimi, Miles, Al Brown, Quincy Jones, Gil Evans, and Alan Douglas.

Jimi neither wrote nor read music. Many of his bends, runs, harmonies, cross-rhythms, and chords were not score-possible. While Jimi desired very much to be able to notate, he also knew that he wrote most of his material as he went along, culminating largely in the studio or in jams. His compositions were not based on notes as much as *sound*. His compositions compressed incredible pieces of blues funk with jazz and black classical modes, including heavy electronics. He had the ability to go down to the hardest rock 'n' roll or up to his personal improvisational signatures, where it was pure pleasure to hear his mind and imagination work out at such high speeds.

Miles Davis began to go public with his recognition of a wider spectrum of black music than just jazz. He publicly praised Jimi Hendrix, Stevie Wonder, and Sly Stone. He declared that theirs was the music he was listening to. Critics like Ralph Gleason and Leonard Feather were astounded. Miles, talking about Jimi's band, said, "It took a black cat to make two white dudes play their ass off." Miles even gave offhand praise to Mitch and Noel in the process of his growing love for Jimi's music. Jimi was astounded: Miles was the living legend of jazz. He had played with "Bird": Charlie Parker. He had helped to launch bebop.

They got into long conversations on the phone. Miles felt that Jimi was doing as well as he was. Miles was fascinated by Jimi's untrained ear—its incredible correctness in the most advanced spheres of music theory. Wilfred Mellers, the famous musicologist, often talked about how the Beatles had in their unschooled ears somehow a direct communication with ancient pagan, tribal, and magical essences of old English traditional music; some of their music he traced back to the Middle Ages. By the same token, Miles heard in Jimi solutions to the wedge that had grown over the years to separate jazz from popular music. It was difficult to explain, but then Jimi did it so well, so often, and so unconsciously that it would have done him little good to understand with words or even to try to score what he did naturally.

Miles knew it would be difficult to really help Jimi musically. Yet the problem was intriguing. You could talk about it for hours. At its center was the growth and direction of the most powerful region of black music. It was more than jazz and funk. It was the touches that Miles had already worked with while in another place. The cadences of *Sketches of Spain,* the random moods of *Filles* that often had it totally in sync with a flowing consciousness. Miles thought that Jimi would get on well with Gil Evans, his collaborator on the contemporary classic *Sketches of Spain,* among other albums and concerts. An LP that would contrast Hendrix' s virtuoso solo improvisational technique with Evans's excellent, thoughtful big-band arrangements would greatly advance black music.

Jimi Hendrix's "sound paintings" from *Electric Ladyland* had been soundly knocked by the rock 'n' roll press (including *Rolling Stone*), yet those who followed him loved "1983," "Rainy Day, Dream Away," and "And the Gods Made Love." Jimi had been painted so one-dimensionally by the rock 'n' roll press that they failed to recognize his art and his humor.

Jimi held back from doing more "sound paintings." His new works were more sculpted, celestial Sky Church guitar balanced with social realism.

But his "sound painting" concept grew stronger and stronger as *Electric Ladyland* became regarded as an album no one could sensibly be without.

Jimi was getting in a lot of jamming upstate, while in the studio he worked more with his sculpted pieces. Two prominent musicians who spent significant time jamming with Jimi on his new direction were Larry Young, the incredible keyboard jazz man, and Harvey Brooks, Fender bass whiz. Both later played on the album for Miles that was his breakthrough: *Bitches Brew.*

The land increased the farther from New York City they drove, heading north where hills merged into mountains, where trees and sky began to take over; the rough gray of Manhattan fading in the distance, fading in the mind.

They stopped off for refreshments at the Red Apple, a highway food and gas complex. Plain country folks. It seemed as if nothing hip could exist so far away from everything. Miles of highway leading into nothingness. Was this the peace he wanted?

Entering Woodstock he could see the signs: Long hair, hip restaurants, funkily painted houses, and broadly smiling, stoned people taking it easy. Right then he could feel it. The earth commanded the space of the mind.

After a couple of days of lying around, his daydreams came back. His mind quickly adapted to the country space. His visions were less frenetic and harried; long legato graceful dreams, lasting longer with more texture and involvement.

As always, he counterpointed his dream meditation with acoustical blues playing. Out of a simple bass line that flowed along endlessly, coming back to its beginning, dipping deeper, then coming back again like an eternal cycle. They were long and peaceful days, the first in a long time, and the music began to jell.

Upon reflection it seemed that in his music he had advocated a speeded-up A-head (amphetamine) feel. He strongly wanted to contrast that with another side of his existence.

It was amazing the way that simple bass line had inspired him. The peaceful yet syncopated line spun off countless variations in his mind. It was like it could go on forever. Moreover, the tune set his mind at ease. What greater gift to get from yourself than something that helps you? He decided to call the tune "Pali-gap." "Pali-gap" was like an ode to the mind, the spaces of the mind when stilled, where marvelous visions and sounds came through.

He began to call people on the phone. Musicians. He wanted to play. He wanted sound around him, not only sound to support his playing, but also musicians who were into something of their own. Jimi had met Juma Sultan, a conga-playing brother, one day while shopping in Woodstock. He had played with a lot of heavy jazz dudes, like Archie Shepp, Sonny Murray, and Larry Young. Jimi was very shy about approaching jazz musicians. Very often they had negative feelings about the kind of music he played. But talking with Juma, Jimi found his vibes were very different. Not only was Juma positive, he also was enthusiastic.

Juma had been living up there for some time. He owned a forty-acre farm. He knew all the other brothers living in the area. There were a lot of bands up there, like the Paul Butterfield Blues Band, the Band, the Blues Project, and others. Juma volunteered to help round up some cats to come and jam. In no time at all they had Ron Hicks, the brother who played bass with Paul Butterfield; Phillip Wilson, a drummer, also with the Butterfield band; Larry Young, keyboards; Larry Lee, guitar; and Jerry Velez, congas. There were also some hangers-on, like this spaced-out A-head Avocado, but everything was cool. Everyone was really into playing.

Jimi had had a conga player, Larry Faucette, on one of his cuts on the *Electric Ladyland* album, and Rocki, the African conga player, had sat in with him during a live recording session at the Albert Hall earlier that year, but Jimi had never lived with one before, playing continuously. It was a new and exciting feeling. The rhythmic complexity that Mitch had hinted at in his busy playing was resolved in the conga and bongo—African drums. Jimi could play softly and have the proper subtle effects he wanted on the percussion. And when he wailed, the African drums added to the drive without being too loud. Every trap drummer feels that he can cover all the percussive effects, and Mitch (who had returned to Jimi, leaving Noel in London) was no exception, but it was time to change and grow, and Mitch had to go along with it.

Mitch hung around, coming up regularly to "practice." It was strange hearing his hobbitlike English accent. Jimi found himself missing Noel and Chas, their accents and timbres. But he had been dominated by those English voices. Now it was different. Mitch was in the minority.

Jimi had not spent so much time with brothers for what seemed like ages. He dug it. It was like coming home. In the singular world of rock there were few blacks. Buddy Miles was one of the few. But now with a whole bunch of cats around every day he began to recapture some of the soul feelings he had been apart from.

Jimi was most impressed by Juma, college educated, well versed as a musician, and totally black, not in a militant, unyielding way, but in an intelligent, dedicated way. Juma had been operating the Society for Aboriginal Music, which was basically a promoter of serious black and African music on a research and performance level. A merging of African and American music took place during their jams, where the different elements of both had a chance to blend in an unrestricted atmosphere.

Juma organized a concert at the Tinkerville Playhouse for the jammers back at the house. Way after midnight, the Band of Gypsys assembled.

Jimi really got into it with Larry Young, who was well known on the European jazz circuit, which featured the works of the younger jazz instrumentalists and composers. He was into both avant-garde music and Herbie Hancock rhythms, electronic music and funk. He had that mystical, selfless surrender to the music they played, and his drive also made it possible for him to be himself.

The *sound* of the organ live in the wooden-walled space of the little old theater, like an old frontier church, was thrilling; merged with Jimi's Stratocaster, the combined sounds exhilarated chills in the nervous system. Tuning slightly down, using only two Marshall amps, Jimi would overdrive through the pre-amps to get the bell and gonglike effects. Then he would concentrate on the Leslie, dubbing with the organ reaching the outer ranges of the scale. Sliding up in a bottleneck trill and zooming down the neck in an all-fret distortion dive, then switching to Fuzz Tone on the way to grind in the bottom ranges as the organ droned in the deeper ranges.

The congas popped and rumbled, shaking, vibrating the wood slats of the room, the sound making one very aware of the earth beneath. The bongos sounding sometimes like the tabla, sometimes like hands slapping thighs, chasing Jimi up a run, a fraction of a beat behind him. Billy Cox on bass holding the bottom, with cautious and deep alternating phrases. At one point there were twenty-five musicians playing onstage.

Jimi exulted in the new dimensions his music was taking. He was discovering incredible new realms he could play in and invent out of. The new sounds meshed with the feelings he had been hoping for, the emotions he sought to express. He was listening to jazz a lot now, and enjoying it, too. He was into John Coltrane, Rashied Ali, McCoy Tyner, Ornette Coleman, and of course Rahsaan Roland Kirk, who was like an idol to him.

The Shokan house gave Jimi a lot of good times, especially after Big Claire came up to cook. She was a friend of Juma Sultan and could really burn. She cooked Jimi's favorite dishes. He loved to have a big pot of soup on the stove—ready to eat, with lots of goodies in it. He dug sweets, too. His favorites were tollhouse cookies made with chocolate chips and nuts. They would pick black-berries and make fresh blackberry pie.

The place had huge grounds. You could go horseback riding for miles with-out ever leaving the estate. But the grounds were not guarded and all sorts of people took to camping and hanging about near the house, hoping to get to Jimi. One chick showed up after walking miles in the rain. She parked herself in the doorway. It took days to get her to leave. There was an underage chick from Texas staying there whose father would often call at odd hours. Jimi was ex-tremely kindhearted. One cat, who had been posing as Jimi while running up an enormous hotel bill in Manhattan, wound up inside the house as a guest. Claire doubled as the one to keep people away from Jimi. Devon, who usually took care of such things, was strangely absent. There had been a big fight. No one would talk about it.

Jimi's bedroom, with beautiful Moroccan rugs and a precious French an-tique makeup table, looked out over a huge reservoir. It had a large sitting room off to the side with a wood-burning fireplace—as did all the bedrooms.

Very often at three in the morning they would go down to the Woodstock movie theater and jam. Carlos Santana came up and so did Janis Joplin. All kinds of beautiful musicians were coming up to jam.

The house was always full of chicks, besides other hangers-on. The musi-cians began staying there, too, due to the late hour at which the music began. Juma, who was staying there, began to help Claire with the house-cleaning du-ties. It was getting out of hand. It got so bad that Jimi would have to call before he came and tell Claire to clear the house. Always all of the seven or eight chicks around would claim emphatically that they were not the ones who were sup-posed to leave.

One day Jimi went to town and brought back a whole lot of Magic Markers, colored pencils, and crayons, and had everyone sitting around drawing and col-oring. Then everyone got an instrument and played; even the groupies got little percussion things. Later he grabbed an engraved Spanish guitar that Devon had given him and said, "Now I'm really gonna play y'all some music." He played a full solo concert on acoustic guitar—all pure Jimi.

Billy Cox came along slowly but very surely. He had no problems about playing Jimi's dictated bass lines. After a while Billy began to really get what Jimi was after: not just playing the notes, but also playing the sound; the contrasting double bass lines and the drum bass drone of Earth and its bodies of water that enabled Jimi to take off and soar beyond the planet's reach.

There was the feeling, especially among those in his management office, that

Jimi wanted Billy more as an old buddy, a crony, than as a bass player. While it was true that Jimi dearly needed a friend, an old friend he could trust, Jimi also felt that Billy had more potential as a bass player than Noel. Besides, Billy's progress with the music was coming along so wonderfully that it served to cement their long friendship. Unlike Noel, Billy trusted Jimi. Billy did not believe it a put-down to play dictated bass lines.

The bass lines were not difficult, but the feeling and philosophy behind them were. It was a subtle thing, string-bending nuances only brothers who had played in the South knew. More than the notes, it was the texture of the sound interwoven with the patterns the bass and guitar made in rhythm that made the sound happen.

Jimi knew that Billy Cox was a down-to-earth, southern homeboy with simple tastes and few excesses. Since their days playing in the army and in Nashville as the Casuals and the King Kasuals, they had known containment and poverty. Jimi hoped that Billy's mind would not be blown by the sudden wealth and weird scenes. Jimi hoped that he had succeeded in communicating to Billy that he was not as much into the weird scenes as it seemed, or as many thought. And Jimi hoped above all that nothing would happen through his scenes that would really trip Billy out.

Being around brothers made Jimi appreciate his relationship with Billy Cox and Buddy Miles more. They always had fun on sessions. Buddy's style was pretty predictable, but also always predictably strong. Jimi's impersonation of Elvis never failed to crack them up.

One night at the Record Plant they had some tape to use up to end the reel. Jimi played the intro to "Hoochie Coochie Man," knowing that Buddy and Billy would pick right up on it. He had one of his jokes planned for them. He sang the first lines in an imitation of the mannish "country" Delta blues phrasings of Muddy Waters, making about ten *b*'s out of the line before he was born:

> *The gypsy woman told my mother*
> *"You got a boy child coming"*

And then, in his famous Harlem drag-queen voice, Jimi pipes in falsetto:

> *"GONNA BE A SON OF A GUN!"*

Buddy and Billy burst out laughing—much against their will, as they all had a deep and abiding love for the older bluesmen; in fact, Buddy had just finished a session with Muddy Waters for the *Fathers and Sons* album. Jimi kept going, raunching the lines.

And then they all began to smoke. Jimi sliding into the first solo as he shouted the chorus about being present, here, ready.

Ed Chalpin's suit against Jimi Hendrix, Warner-Reprise Records, and Mike Jeffery for breach of contract had been going through motions, countermotions, and delays for over a year. Chalpin's evidence was a contract that consisted of merely one piece of paper.

> PPX ENTERPRISES
> Master Producers and Agents
> 1650 Broadway, New York, N.Y. 10019
> Tel.: 247-6010
> Cable: Chalprises, New York

> Agreement made as of October 15, 1965 between PPX Enterprises, Inc. and Jimmy Hendrix, Hotel America, 145 W. 47th St. New York, N.Y.
> In consideration of the sum of one (1.00) dollar and other good and valuable consideration it is agreed to as follows:
> 1. That Jimmy Hendrix will produce and play and/or sing exclusively for PPX Enterprises, Inc., for three (3) years from above date.
> 2. Jimmy Hendrix will make available his services at the request of PPX with a minimum of ten (10) days notice to produce no more than four (4) titles per session, a minimum of three (3) sessions per year.
> 3. That Jimmy Hendrix services will include singing and/or arrangements, which at the option of PPX shall be written out by other copyist or arranger.
> 4. That PPX shall pay all cost of studio, musicians, etc., and shall be reimbursed from first profits received.
> 5. Jimmy Hendrix shall receive one (1) per cent of retail selling price of all records sold for his production efforts, minimum scale for arrangements he produces.
> 6. That Jimmy Hendrix shall play instruments for PPX at no cost to PPX Enterprises, Inc.
> 7. That PPX shall have exclusive rights to assign for all masters produced in conjunction with Jimmy Hendrix.

> Agreed To:
> PPX Enterprises, Inc.
> Agreed To:
> By /s/ Jimmy Hendrix   By /s/ Ed Chalpin
>   Jimmy Hendrix   Ed Chalpin

Chalpin had had the diminutive Curtis Knight as a witness. All of Jimi's royalties due from Warner-Reprise were ordered placed in escrow by the court pending a settlement.

Instead of woodshedding, instead of working on his musical growth, instead of a measured, deep reflection and a consolidation of direction—he would have to work, work like a nigger. He would have to gig like mad to stay afloat. And there was still the Canadian bust hanging over his head.

The worry that had started in the last part of 1968 would reach a height by the end of 1969. Litigation would seemingly go on forever, weeks and months and years. But yet as he ached to soar, the weekly scorecard of suits, courts and dates, motions, and appeals began to absorb more and more of his consciousness.

Devon knew that the best way for Jimi to beat the shit against him was to move on ahead with his new musical ideas, build the studio he always talked about, and concentrate on gaining more control over his destiny. Racing against the clock. Racing before the final toll of judgments and evil human vibes.

Devon and Jimi had made up and gotten even closer, and she still kept up his New York City apartment. Devon treated Jimi's legal matters with the seasoned scorn of a junkie burn. A typical rip-off in a fucked-up world. What *concerned* her was the effect it was having on Jimi.

Her concern reached its height when Jimi's hair started coming out in clumps, in his hand, in the comb, on his sweated pillow. He began to sleep with his hat on. It was then that she gave him what she had. She gave him her most important possession: her circle of friends who kept *her* together. Included in that circle was Finney.

Finney, Miles Davis's hairdresser, was a hair specialist who was known to be able to prevent men from going bald (he had saved Miles's hair) and to enable women to have long, luxuriant locks. Miles Davis had gone through bouts of hair loss, due in large part to the conflict of trying to create amid tremendous legal and business pressures.

Jimi was in really bad shape at the prospect of losing his hair—the youthful allurement and staple part of his image. Devon called Finney in desperation. Finney had his own shop at that time and invited Jimi to come over, but Jimi did not want to go anywhere in public where the state of his hair would be exposed. After a couple of weeks, Finney finally decided to go to Hendrix. They met at Jimi's suite at the Drake Hotel.

Hendrix beat around the bush for a long time. He took Finney through his closets, showing off his wild array of stage costumes, casual togs, and fancy threads. Then he ordered dinner. While they ate he told Finney about dreaming of his mother. Jimi said that he often saw his mother while he was wide awake. Finney, strangely, had had the same experience. Finally Finney took a look at

Jimi's locks. Hendrix's hair problem was a common case. Often straightened, conked, and curled, his hair had been weakened by artificial straighteners and had begun to fall out. The fact that Jimi had begun to worry a great deal also weakened his hair. It had to be cut, the split ends pared, and allowed to grow back out fully. This was truly traumatic for Jimi—cut his hair? But it had to be done. Finney began to cut, clipping quickly and expertly with long thin scissors. Jimi was scared to death, watching much of his fabled long hair plop to the floor. He picked up a newspaper and read intensely. Once the cutting was over he sprang to the bathroom mirror. After staying a long while in the bathroom he came out smiling—it looked good.

Finney and Jimi became fast friends. Devon always said how much they resembled each other. Now, Finney, small, compactly built but spare, with a soft voice and laid-back, relaxed, totally self-controlled air, became a part of Hendrix's intimate circle.

Jim Robertson was one of Jimi's favorite engineers at the Record Plant. He put up with Jimi's eccentricities, like the dobo barricade Jimi insisted on singing behind, or his penchant for recording some vocals in the bathroom. They got stoned together, and Jimi amazed Jim by snorting meth or coke through one nostril without the aid of a straw or rolled dollar bill. Jimi often dropped several tabs of acid daily. And the thing Jimi liked most about Jim Robertson was that he could engineer while seemingly stoned.

Jim Robertson had quickly progressed beyond Tom Wilson–protégé status and had become a damn good engineer in his own right, recording Jimi at the Record Plant. Mike Jeffery began noticing him. He liked Jim's vibe. Jeffery felt he could trust him. Jim Robertson had a young naïveté and a pleasant touch of perception. He worked hard without seeming to be working at all. He had a loyalty to music, as well as to interpersonal relationships. The sessions at the Record Plant were arduous, yet Jeffery and Hendrix seemed to get on better around Robertson, who seemed to like them both equally.

Jim Robertson became very important to Jimi. He was one of the few engineers he could communicate with. Jimi and Ed Kramer had had a little falling out. The pressures of building a new studio coupled with Jimi's seemingly eccentric recording habits had taken its toll on their intense relationship. Robertson was relatively new to the business and found no problems with Jimi's philosophy regarding recording. In fact, he seemed to enjoy the long, stoned hours.

Meatball Fulton interviewed Hendrix again for his syndicated radio show. Hendrix was in the midst of a severe conflict between his music and his management. Meatball Fulton later prefaced the interview with these remarks:

I guess you could call it . . . the kind of frustrations that Hendrix went through. It was the typical artist-manager conflict, or artist-promoter, or artist-benefactor conflict. And in this segment, Hendrix really wanted to talk about things that were bugging him, but I didn't think he should talk about it into a microphone, and I didn't have the sense to stop the tape recorder. So the interview continues with Hendrix returning and returning to his frustration. And my constantly trying to avoid it and move on. And it's a very weird thing to hear. I had the impression that he had few friends if any that could see him as a person, not a pop star or a thing, and if that's true, it's really sad.

HENDRIX: I really don't care what my record does as far as chartwise. We had this one that only made number eleven, which everyone around here hated. They said it was the worst record, you know. But I think that was the best one we ever made . . . "The Burning of the Midnight Lamp." Not as far as recording, because the recording techniques are really bad, you know. You couldn't hear the words so good. Probably that's what it was.

FULTON: How are you satisfied with the recording techniques generally?

HENDRIX: Not at all.

FULTON: What about the LPs?

HENDRIX: Not at all. Even worse on the LPs. It makes me so mad. 'Cause, you see, that's a part of us. See, we record it and everything and then all of a sudden something happens and it just comes out all screwed . . . and you just get so mad, you just don't want to know about it anymore . . . our next LP, every track is gonna have to be just right or else I'm just . . . gonna forget about it. I mean, not forget about it . . . you say that but you know you're not. But that's the way I feel.

FULTON: Do you think they're better in the States as far as recording? It really depends on the engineer, though. . . .

HENDRIX: It all depends on what you want really. It all depends on where you go, too. It really depends on so many things, the cutting of it . . . that's a whole scene, the cutting of it. You can mix and mix and mix and get such a beautiful sound, and when they cut it, they can just screw it up so bad.

FULTON: I don't understand.

HENDRIX: I wouldn't understand that either 'cause we, you know . . . ooooh, it comes out so bad. 'Cause they go by levels and all that. Some people don't have any imagination. . . . See, when you cut a record, right before it's being printed, you know, when you cut the master, if you want a song where you have really deep sound, where you have depth and all this, you must . . . almost remix it again right there at the cutting place. And 99 percent don't even do this. They just say, "Oh, turn it up," so their mixture doesn't go over or their mixture doesn't go under. And there it is, you know. It's nothing but one-dimensional.

The Jimi Hendrix Experience pose with fans (*Michael Ochs Archives.com*)

Jimi and Buddy Miles in rehearsal
(© 1966–2000 David Sygall)

Band of Gypsys: Billy Cox, Jimi, and Buddy Miles (© 1966–2000 David Sygall)

Jimi as producer in the studio, 1969 (© *1966–2000 David Sygall*)

Jimi as producer in the studio
(© 1966–2000 David Sygall)

Jimi at Fillmore East—New Year's Eve, 1969 (© *Mel Wright Photo "06"*)

Jimi at Fillmore East—New Year's Eve, 1969 (© *John Brathwaite 2006*)

Jimi at Fillmore East—New Year's Eve, 1969 (© *Mel Wright Photo "06"*)

Jimi tokes at Isle of Wight Festival, August 1970 (*Laurens Van Houten/Star File*)

Jimi poses on grass on Isle of Fehmarn, Germany, September 1970 (*GT Piltz/Star File*)

Billy Cox, Jimi, and Mitch Mitchell during the last troubled tour, Isle of Fehmarn Festival (*Good Times/Star File*)

At Hollywood Boulevard star award ceremony: Al Hendrix, Jimi's father, holding plaque; to his right, Leon Hendrix, Jimi's brother; behind, in white hat and shirt, Juma Sultan, percussionist in Jimi's Woodstock aggregation. *(Vincent Zuffante/Star File)*

FULTON: Do you get the time you need? I mean . . . because it's so costly anyway.

HENDRIX: The money doesn't mean anything to me because that's what I make it for . . . to make better things happen. I don't have no value on money at all. That's my only fault. I just get things that I see and want. And try to put it into music. I want to have stereo where it goes . . . up . . . and behind and underneath. . . . 'Cause all you can get now is just across and across. Our new LP was made in sixteen days, which I'm very sad about.

FULTON: That one that's just out recently.

HENDRIX: Yeah. No use even talking about or discussing why. 'Cause it's really a bad scene. But it just makes me mad. It could have been so much better.

FULTON: It's mainly the sound quality?

HENDRIX: Well, the songs could have been better, too. You know, that's what I think though. As soon as you're finished you got a completely new idea.

FULTON: Well, it's good in a sense, because your mind's purring along, moving along nicely.

HENDRIX: It's not necessarily getting any better, but like you might move to different things, you know.

FULTON: Do you feel that the groups are free to change as they want to?

HENDRIX: No. Half of them aren't. They're all thinking about their career, about their future so much. I really don't give a damn about my future or my career. I just want to make sure I can get out what I want. That's why I say we're very lucky. Because we didn't have to, you know, make it. I said it'd be great but I really didn't care. Just as long as we could be happy with what we're doing, with what we're recording and stuff like that. With doing what we want to do . . . we're still . . . we're not really doing what we want. . . .

FULTON: What about the new LP? You've been thinking about that.

HENDRIX: Yeah. Well, I wanted to make it a double LP, you know. Which'll be almost impossible.

FULTON: Because of the cost, you mean?

HENDRIX: Yeah. Well, it's a big hassle. Nobody wants to do that. The record producers don't want to do it and companies don't want to do it. I'm willing to spend every single penny on it if I thought it was good enough. But there you go, you know. I do that and then they leave me out there.

FULTON: What about the length of the songs, too? Would you like them to be much longer?

HENDRIX: It depends on what kind of song it is. If it's a song with three or four movements . . . well, yeah. Now there's this one song I wrote named "Eyes and Imagination," that's the name of it. And it's about fourteen minutes long, but it's about, it's telling about . . . every sentence or every two sentences tells a completely different story. It's nothing but imagination . . . it starts off with a baby crying, you know, a brand-new baby has been born, and then you hear those bullets, you know (laughs), in the background. It's nothing but imagination, and every sentence tells a different story. But it goes in about four major movements, and it keeps going back to this one little thing, you must have that one little thing through it. But I don't know . . . there're so many songs I wrote that we haven't even done yet and we'll probably never do. It's because . . . oooh, I don't know, there are a lot of things around here. It's a really bad scene. . . . You know, we must be Elvis Presleys and rock 'n' rolls and Troggs. We must be that (laughs). And there'll be no smoking in the gas chamber.

FULTON: Do you think people will be doing longer numbers, or trying to?

HENDRIX: Well, I think they should if they have something to offer really . . . if the number really has to be long. If they say I have this number and it's really . . . I just can't get it together unless I have more time . . . I just need more time on it. Well, then they should. They really should. They should never hold time like that. You know the song named "Purple Haze"? That . . . had about a thousand, thousand words and oooh . . . oooh, it just gets me so mad 'cause that isn't even the "Purple Haze" you know.

FULTON: What do you mean that it isn't . . .

HENDRIX: I don't know, man. I'm just a frustrated old hen. That's all. That's what I feel like. You should have heard it, man. I had it written out. It was about going through . . . through this land. This mythical . . . because that's what I like to do is write a lot of mythical songs. You know, like the history of the wars on Neptune. And all this mess, you know. . . . They got the Greek gods and all that stuff, well, you can have your own mythology, see. Or write fiction. Complete fiction. I mean anybody can say, "I was walking down the street, and I seen an elephant floating through the sky." But it has no meaning at all, there's nothing except the elephant there, you know. And if you don't watch out you might break your neck!

FULTON: Do you think you'll be able to make more demands as you continue?

HENDRIX: Yeah. This whole thing is gonna blow wide open. . . . Can you remember when you was a little baby? I think your memory comes through, I think that's the way you come about other scenes, too. 'Cause human beings die too easily, you know.

FULTON: What about the animal? You were talking about an animal?

HENDRIX: Like you might see an animal or something like that. And also you might have a very funny feeling go through you for a second.

FULTON: You mean like looking into its eyes. Or not necessarily . . . or just the animal itself?

HENDRIX: Okay. One time I seen this deer, you know. 'Cause you know I see a lot of deers around . . . where I used to be from . . . and I said, "Wait," and something went through me for a second, like I'd seen him . . . like I had some real close connection with that deer for one split second and then it just went away like that, you know. A lot of friends of mine told me about that happening to them, you know.

Have you ever laid in bed and you was in this complete state where you couldn't move? And you feel like you're going deeper and deeper into that, and it's not sleep, but it's something else. And every time I go into that I say, "Ah hell, I'm scared as hell," and you get all scared and stuff and so you try to say, "Help, help." You can't move and so you try to say, "Help, help." You can't move and you can't speak but you say "Help, help," and you finally get out of it, you know. You just can't move. It's a very funny feeling. But one time that feeling was coming through me and I say, "Aha, here we go. This time I'm just gonna let it happen and see where I go." I just wanted to see what happens and it was really getting scary, man, it was going *whooosshhhe,* like that, you know. And I said, "I'm not even asleep, this is really strange." And then somebody knocked on the door. I said, "Oh," . . . because I wanted to find out.

FULTON: Can you remember some things really far back? Like when you were a baby?

HENDRIX: Yeah, I can remember the nurse putting the diaper . . .

FULTON: Can you really?

HENDRIX: Yeah. When the nurse . . . I don't know what I was there for, but I remember when I used to wear diapers. And then she was talking to me. She took me out of this crib . . . or something like that. And then she held me up to this window . . . this was in like Seattle, and she was showing me something up against the sky. It was fireworks or something like that. It must have been the Fourth of July, you know. . . . I remember her putting the diaper on me and almost sticking me. . . . I remember I didn't feel so good, you know. I musta been in the hospital sick about something, and I had a bottle and all that kinda stuff and then she held me up to the window and she was saying something about . . . I was looking, and the sky was all WHEW . . .

FULTON: Almost an acid thing.

HENDRIX: Wow. That's right. That's what it was. Only beforehand . . . (laughing). That nurse still turns me on.

FULTON: Can you remember any other things?

HENDRIX: Well, I can remember when I was small enough to fit in a clothes basket. You know those straw clothes baskets they have in America, that they put all the dirty clothes in? It's only about like that (gestures).

FULTON: They call them hampers or something.

HENDRIX: Yeah. Hampers. I remember when my cousin and I was playing around. I must have been about three or something. Like sometimes when you're sitting around and you start remembering things. . . . Those are the first two that come to my mind. And some dreams that I had when I was real little, you know. Like my mother was being carried away on this camel. And there was a big caravan and she was saying, "Well, I'm gonna see you," and she was going under these trees, and you could see the shade . . . you know the leaf patterns . . . crossing her face. You know how the sun shines through a tree, and if you go under the shadow of the tree the shadows go across your face! Well, these were in green and yellow. Shadows. And she was saying, "Well, I won't be seeing you too much anymore, you know." And then about two years after that she died. And I said, "Where you going?" I remember that, I always will remember that.

There are dreams you never forget. Like one dream. There's this one dream where you go down like that, you go down this real big hill, but it has this real long grass and there are a whole lot of bananas on the floor, on the floor of this hill, but they're all growing from the ground . . . each one separate. I remember that, and we was skating across that . . . I don't know how we were, but what we did was we poured out this stuff that we made. You know, these big bags. We poured it out across the bananas. And it fills up all the gaps between the bananas and we skate across it. I remember those things.

FULTON: You must have been dreaming in color when you were very young.

HENDRIX: Oh yeah. I was. I don't remember too many. . . . The closest thing to a black-and-white dream I ever had was in pastel shades like . . . maroon and ah . . . dark, you know, then very light maroon. And then this big gold chick—I don't know her. It was great. And that was the closest I ever got to black and white.

—Meatball Fulton
ZBS Radio, 1969

The new jamming with the Band of Gypsy Suns and Rainbows was also helping Jimi with his laborious studio work. It seemed to take seasons just to move from one point to the next—the final mix was always elusive. Continuously laying down new tracks, working on older tracks, mixing, adding touches, remixing. The thought that he had new music before him and a studio under construction made him more efficient with his open-schedule account at the Record Plant. He could not wait until Electric Lady Studios was completed.

His office (Mike Jeffery and crew) really froze on his upstate jams. They resented him taking on other directions when they were burdened from day to day with the details of building Electric Lady Studios. They had just found out that the site (formerly the Generation Club on West Eighth Street in the Village) was over a subway tunnel. Extra soundproofing would now be essential, at outrageous cost.

He felt that Mitch might be spying on him for the office. Mitch's loyalties were to the rock 'n' roll star sound, as were the loyalties of the office. Jimi *knew* that Devon was shaky sometimes. But you never know who can be bought. Even Juma, as much as Jimi respected him, could be a spy. Jimi even asked Juma. Juma laughed, "Man, you're really paranoid."

Jimi told Juma why he was paranoid. A very bizarre and frightening act of violence has happened to him recently. He has told no one about it except Big Claire. One early morning, alone in his apartment in the Village, he answers the doorbell. Strange men are at the door. He is taken forcibly from his apartment and stuffed in the back of a car by four dudes. They act tough yet they still handle him more gently than would be expected. He is blindfolded. One of the guys kneels on him, his knee in his back. He is shunted and reeled through black vectors to a dry, brick-smelling bare cement floor. In very tough voices the guys tell him how they are going to hurt him. His mind has resigned itself to that. He waits. But they don't hurt him. He just sits and sits. Then after a while there is a commotion. Sounds of struggle. Shouts and curses. Doors slamming and feet running. He hears people running toward him. His blindfold is ripped off. It is Mike Jeffery and the guys from the office. His bonds are untied. He is relieved. He is grateful. They hustle him out of the building, talking some shit. He is dazed, wondering . . . "What kind of shit is this? How did they know where I was? What happened?" They jabber a story at him, but he is too busy wondering in his mind . . . Was it a set-up or was it for real?

It was hard to tell. The atmosphere around the music was always too spacey and trippy. It was hard to tell what kind of influence the office had over the people close to him. Any type of official business that went down involving anybody put them in direct touch with the office. Jeffery would not even pay the weekly salaries that had been agreed upon for his jam band, nor even help them with transportation.

But Jimi could not let that bother him. His obligation to the music was where he was at. But he could see his office's point about rock: They had made a lot of money with it and they wanted to continue.

He had met over the past year new people who were into his music and were very sure of his abilities: Tom Wilson, Jim Robertson, Al Brown, Quincy Jones, Miles Davis, Gil Evans, Alan Douglas, and, on another level, Timothy Leary. Alan Douglas had produced Eric Dolphy and other jazz artists, usually in their formative stages. Douglas was the producer of the infamous Last Poets, who had entered the national charts with poetic chants set to African drum accompaniment. *Performance*, the movie that starred Mick Jagger, used a cut from their album in the movie and in the soundtrack album.

Douglas was also recording at the Record Plant at the same time as Jimi.

They knew each other fairly well through Stella, Douglas's wife, whose partner was Jimi's private designer, Colette, from the dress shop on the Lower East Side that Monique frequented. Alan Douglas had Timothy Leary in the studio doing a spoken-word album entitled *You Can Be Anyone This Time Around*. Jimi visited their sessions a few times and even contributed a few guitar licks and effects to a varied montage score that played behind the voice.

Jimi remembered some of the lines Leary spoke. The title of the LSD/expanded consciousness sermon "You can be anyone this time around," was repeated as a refrain-like passage, alternating "be anyone" with "do anything" and "be anything" in this incarnation. "You're the first generation in human history to know how to control your own nervous system, change your own reality. Blow your own mind. Make up your own mind."

Douglas took to acting as a go-between for Jimi in various transactions. Douglas knew many jazz musicians. He brought Tony Williams, the brilliant jazz drummer, by while Hendrix was doing some solo overdubbing. Hendrix and Williams jammed for a while, feeling each other out. Tony Williams was the young prodigy who had joined Miles Davis's band at seventeen years of age. That had been almost six years ago. Tony Williams was in the process of recording his own band. He had sent for John McLaughlin, the English electric guitarist, to record with him, but Miles had used him on the *In a Silent Way* sessions. Williams preferred McLaughlin's colorless high technique to Hendrix's free-flowing funk and blue noise. Williams and Hendrix did not click together. They stopped jamming after several minutes.

Even though they had not hit it off, Hendrix had been impressed that Douglas had come up with Tony Williams and brought them together. Douglas felt that Miles Davis would eventually come in the studio and record with Jimi. Although *In a Silent Way* had just gotten in the can, word was out that Miles had gone very strongly toward rock. This was earth-shaking news in the music world. Tony Williams rebelled against it. Herbie Hancock stood on the fence. But Miles was completely into *his* new sound. Hendrix was impressed with just the fact that Miles had moved musically in a way few jazzmen had the guts to move: to challenge rock's dominance over popular music. In Jimi's mind, it endorsed what he was trying to do in moving closer to jazz and African percussive realms. At one point Douglas had Hendrix, Tony Williams, and Miles Davis ready to record together. The deal fell through after Miles and Williams demanded $50,000 for the sessions.

Back at the house in Shokan, word had begun to come through the grapevine about a proposed rock festival to end all rock festivals. They were calling it "Woodstock" and it would be given somewhere in upstate New York. People were beginning to freak out over it already. Woodstock—oh well, he had some new shit for them.

The cars began coming weeks before. Everybody in the thirty-mile radius had strangers' cars parked out in front of their houses, visitors from all over. Traffic in Woodstock got noticeably thicker day by day. The single-lane roads that branched off to other small towns nearby, like Boiceville and Liberty, began to look like Twelfth Street and University Place in Manhattan.

The week before Woodstock, even more cars began to show up parked and locked on the side of the roads. Backpackers trudged through the fields. The Woodstock area was miles from Max Yasgur's farm, the actual site of the festival. Three days before Woodstock the roads were closed to automobiles. Cars were backed up for ten miles.

The day before Woodstock was insane. Everybody was in town. Stevie Stills came by plucking out a song on acoustic that Joni Mitchell had just written for the occasion. Stills was part of a new band, Crosby, Stills, and Nash; Woodstock would be their first appearance together. Jimi felt that Woodstock was also his first appearance with a new band, as well. It seemed amazing that Woodstock was happening at this time, when so many new things were coming together in the music.

But then again, it was the last summer of the sixties.

The day Woodstock opened was manic. The producers still had not finalized their agreement with Jimi's office. The phone rang all day. Cars were now lined up for thirty miles in all directions. Folks were beginning to abandon them en masse. Jimi's friends were coming by and leaving so quickly their names began to melt into a faceless procession.

The deal was finalized that night: $18,000, promise of $42,000 more (which they would probably get burned for); a helicopter would have to bring the band. There was no other way. Jimi would play last, as usual. Ever since Monterey, and then the Fillmore (when the Jefferson Airplane refused to follow him), no group would follow him on any stage in the world.

The vibes were high. The air was charged with mass magnetism. Instead of taking the helicopter, they wound up in a funky caravan. Big Claire's Dodge Dart and someone's Rambler station wagon, led by and followed through the countryscape by the loony-sirened cruisers' flashing lights and the motorcycles of the state troopers.

The day Woodstock officially opened, Miles Davis assembled the most creatively ambitious group of musicians in his musical history to record at Columbia Studios in New York City: August 19, 1969.

Missing from his basic unit of the past six years were Herbie Hancock and Tony Williams. Replacing Hancock on keyboards were Chick Corea, who had made the last session (*In a Silent Way*), Joe Zawinul, of the Cannonball Adderley band, and most notably Larry Young, straight from the Shokan jams with Jimi Hendrix. Miles employed several drummers of different textures to cover for Tony Williams (Jack DeJohnette, Lenny White, and Charles Alias); most notable was the addition of a percussion man, Jim Riley, who played everything from bells to bongos to congas to triangles.

There was also Wayne Shorter on soprano sax instead of tenor and Dave Holland on bass, both carry-overs from Miles's last band. Bennie Maupin appeared on bass clarinet. John McLaughlin again on electric guitar. And the biggest surprise was Harvey Brooks, the journeyman rock bassist, on Fender.

The title of the sessions was *Bitches Brew*. It was to make musical history as the first serious synthesis of jazz and rock. It was to be Miles's biggest-selling album to date. And strangely enough, it was recorded under the full influence of the Woodstock vibes.

Jimi came out on the Woodstock stage following Sha Na Na, with Jerry Velez on bongos, Larry Lee on rhythm guitar, Juma Sultan on congas, Billy Cox on bass, and Mitch Mitchell on drums. Since they had arrived at Jimi's, it had been a hard three days of getting the music together and partying. Jimi had not slept the whole time. Big Claire held his full purple cape in the wings, looking on very anxiously. Everyone was stoned but keyed entirely into the incredible vibes of history staring at them.

Jimi and company go into "Spanish Castle Magic" and then "Red House." Then an upbeat instrumental improvisation, with everyone getting in some good licks. They segue into a formal jam called "Villanova Junction Blues" and another jam by Mitch called "Jam Back at the House," which is governed by Mitch's rhythmic patterns rather than melody. They hit "Izabella," one of Jimi's new songs, as a bit of rock in the midst of their jam fever. And then they go back to the train station for "Getting My Heart Back Together," Jimi tearing out huge chunks of pure blues soloing off the two-chord changes. With the bass string tuned down a fifth, Jimi really gets into his own bass accompaniment, bending the bass string to gut-trembling vibratos while he hits weird modal pitches in fast eighth-note runs, then quickly repeats them twice as fast in sixteenth notes and triplets, as well. Like sixteenth notes to the second power, as if he is splitting the atoms of the notes, which then come out in thirty-second-note cascading waterfalling runs. They slide into distort at the edge of overamplification where Jimi's speed-of-light attack overloads the amps. Jimi takes that distort, just at the peak of feedback, and glissandos back down into the modal space-station pitch and then back down to the two-chord blue earth.

Jimi allows Larry Lee to sing lead on "Gypsy Woman" and a new tune "Mastermind." They go into a jam pattern with Jimi's lead mixed far out in front on the monitors. They bomp into "Purple Haze" on a nice groove. There is a full battery of percussion and rhythmic sounds going behind Jimi. He is exulting in the heights of the sound. Jimi leads a segue into "The Star-Spangled Banner," the congas and bongos and the military-drum kit all rolling strong, polyrhythmic statements, Billy Cox holding the bottom drone and Larry Lee hitting key notes of the changes as he and Jimi sustain long lines in the all-time greatest hit of the USA. Jimi moves from a raging finale into a genuflectingly lyrical improvisation melody told in sparse Spanish-Moorish tones that is both sad and beautiful, almost mournful yet exquisitely sculptured, the melody making the total more than any of its emotional parts. This is the last set of the festival, the last festival of the summer, of the year, of the sixties—and Hendrix's solo is a lament, through human cries of divine ecstasy.

The African holy drums confer a blessing upon all.

Woodstock is over.

Jimi walks offstage and collapses. He had played a far longer set than he ever had—well over two hours. Panic ensues. A doctor runs up and checks him out. Severe exhaustion. Jimi is helicoptered to a hotel suite near Woodstock, with a lovely young lady named Lesley, who stays there with him. Jimi sleeps for three days.

The recordings of the Woodstock performance were disappointing. As usual, Jimi's guitar dominated the sound; Larry Lee's rhythm guitar, Billy Cox's bass, Juma's congas, and Jerry Velez's bongos were hardly heard above Mitch's drum kit. The sound the African drums made in the air was lost, an entire acoustical realm dispersed in the air.

He wished he had done more with Wally Heider and his crew in hipping them to the new kind of sound he wanted recorded. It had sounded fine onstage. But it was disappointing that it did not *all* get on tape.

The rock 'n' roll press was very cautious about Jimi's new band. He had not come out with a new album in 1969, although *Electric Ladyland* had spanned the bridge between 1968 and 1969. Rumors were beginning to crop up about this being the end of Jimi Hendrix. He knew better than that. He continued to work on the new album and push through the completion of Electric Lady Studios. His office was nervous about his new band. They clearly wanted Noel and Mitch back with him, and there were few dates lined up for the autumn of 1969. Jeffery felt that the fielding of an all-black band would ruin his image.

Jimi was interviewed by English journalist Ritchie Yorke, who had come over for Woodstock.

I plan to use different people at my sessions from now on; their names aren't important. You wouldn't know them anyway. It really bugs me that there are so many people starving, musicians who are twice as good as the big names. I want to try and do something about that.

I feel guilty when people say I'm the greatest guitarist on the scene. What's good or bad doesn't matter to me; what does matter is feeling and not feeling. If only people would take more of a true view and think in terms of feeling. Your name doesn't mean a damn, it's your talent and feeling that matters. You've got to know much more than just the technicalities of notes, you've got to know sounds and what goes between the notes.

When you first make it, the demands on you are very great. For some people, they are just too heavy. You can just sit back, fat and satisfied, or you can run away from it, which is what I did. I don't try to live up to anything anymore.

Really, I'm just an actor—the only difference between me and those cats in Hollywood is that I write my own script. I consider myself first and foremost a musician. My initial success was a step in the right direction, but it was only a step, just a change. Now I plan to get into many other things.

What it all comes down to is that albums are nothing but personal diaries. When you hear somebody making music, they are baring a naked part of their soul to you. *Are You Experienced?* was one of the most direct albums we've done. What it was saying was, "Let us through the wall, man, we want you to dig it." But later, when we got into other things, people couldn't understand the changes. The trouble is, I'm a schizophrenic in at least twelve different ways, and people can't get used to it.

Sure, albums come out different. You can't go on doing the same thing. Every day you find out this and that and it adds to the total you have. *Are You Experienced?* was where my head was at a couple of years ago. Now I'm into different things.

There's a great need for harmony between man and Earth. I think we're really screwing up that harmony by dumping garbage in the sea, air pollution, and all that stuff.

And the sun is very important; it's what keeps everything alive. My next album, coming out in late summer, will be called, *Shine on Earth, Shine On,* or *Gypsy Sun.*

There might also be a couple of other albums in between. A live album, which we cut at the Royal Albert Hall in London, and a greatest hits thing. But I have no control over those. All I know is that I'm working on my next album for summer release.

We have about forty songs in the works, about half of them completed. A lot of it comprises jams—all spiritual stuff, all very earthy.

I couldn't possibly take a year off. Even though I am very tired. In reality, I might get a month off somewhere but there's no way for a year. I spend a lot of time trying to get away but I can't stop thinking about music. It's in my mind every second of the day. I can't fight it so I groove with it.

To each his own. In another life the people who were trying to do it may have been Beethoven or one of those cats. But this is a rock 'n' roll era, so the people get into rock. Every era has its own music.

What I don't like is this business of trying to classify people. Leave us alone. Critics really give me a pain in the neck. It's like shooting at a flying saucer as it tries to land without giving the occupants a chance to identify themselves. You don't need labels, man. Just dig what's happening.

A couple of years ago all I wanted was to be heard. "Let me in" was the thing. Now I'm trying to figure out the wisest way to be heard.

—Jimi, interviewed by Ritchie Yorke,
September 1969

Hendrix made his management cancel the big, *big* outdoor concert planned for the Boston Common in September 1969. They prepared a press release that said that he was suffering from nervous exhaustion and would have to have at least a month's convalescence. They even got two doctors' names on it.

Jimi was tired of being run all over the country without any concern for how he felt. That he had had to cancel a benefit for the Young Lords, a radical political organization that emerged spontaneously out of Spanish Harlem opposing police brutality and championing Puerto Rican identity, to appear on *The Dick Cavett Show* really got Jimi's goat. His management was all in an uproar over his alleged "Black Power" turn of mind, as if it were unnatural for him to have concern about his people in a political way.

There were other things. All the money he was supposed to be making failed to jibe with his bank account. He never quite understood why all the publishing money had to go to the Bahamas. He had been pressured into signing a release that freed Jeffery from any liability in the settlement with Chalpin. The lawyers would go into their raps and he would feel like a kid. It seemed like what they were saying was that while he could make the money, it was beyond his ability to handle it. He knew he would have to get his own lawyers. Lawyers who worked for him, who could not be bought and who he could trust. He shared Henry Steingarten's law firm with Jeffery. This did not seem right from a commonsense viewpoint, although his present lawyers were indignant when he voiced even the slightest reservations about the set-up.

While the word was going out about his "nervous exhaustion," he sat up with Jeanette Jacobs, an old friend from his Village days, laughing and watching television. Finally the boredom got to him and they went to the Scene. Eric Barrett was amazed to see him. Barrett thought Jimi was sick. Jimi laughed it off, saying that there was no particular time limit on getting well—was there?

But in the back of his mind he realized that he would have to make a complete stand against all the bullshit. He was getting hustled and bled dry. Jeffery complained about all the hangers-on and how they were hustling Jimi. But a couple of drinks, or dinner, or some exotic treats were chicken feed compared to the money that his trusted coworkers were losing, or seeming to lose.

Mike Jeffery took some friends along with him when he traveled to the house in Shokan to talk with Jimi about the problems that had forced cancellation of the Boston Common concert. Juma and others who were part of the Gypsy Suns, Moons, and Rainbows had been alerted that there might be trouble.

Jeffery drove up to the house with several tough-looking men. He and Jimi went upstairs to confer privately while the others in his party stayed in the yard. Jeffery had booked Jimi into the Salvation club and was insisting that he make the gig. Many of Jimi's musical cohorts speculated that the Salvation was Mafia-controlled and balked at playing there. Jeffery knew that he had to have local support if Electric Lady Studios was to be a reality. The Salvation, on Sheridan Square, was less than two blocks away from the site of the studios.

As Jimi and Jeffery conferred, a member of Jeffery's party began to take some target practice. He emptied his Beretta into the side of a tree in the yard. He reloaded and did it again. Meanwhile, the Gypsys assumed battle stations throughout the compound. One of them, hatchet in hand, stole around the house in case Jimi needed help.

Jeffery and Jimi finally came downstairs, appearing well disposed toward each other. Jimi would make the gig.

Jimi got to play in Harlem in September 1969 at an outdoor street fair hosted by Eddie O'Jay, the popular DJ of WWRL, the black R&B station that reached all over New York City. The musicians from back at the house up in Shokan were on hand.

Jimi found the intimacy of this unheralded street affair fascinating. Thousands of faces, it was almost another Woodstock, only the faces were all black and instead of being in a meadow, they were in the streets.

Jimi waited behind a police barricade to go on. Some little black kids beckoned him over; he went to the end of the barricade and talked with several ten-year-olds. They were vibrant and fresh. They were awed by him but did not stand off. They touched his clothes, his pink pants and yellow blouse, his Moroccan vest, and stared at his Indian moccasins. They touched his hair and his wide-brimmed black hat and stared wide-eyed and innocent into his face. Jimi felt strangely serious. Although he could have just as easily laughed and jived, he felt a strange obligation to impart something meaningful. They had never heard of him before.

As Eddie O'Jay introduced Jimi, O'Jay seemed to be, amid his upbeat DJ patter of praise for Jimi's music, apologizing for the fact that he did not play Jimi Hendrix's records on his popular daily show.

In many ways, Jimi Hendrix's appearance in Harlem brought up the true paradox of his fame. Jimi was known worldwide, but not in Harlem, his symbolic hometown. Both he and Eddie O'Jay knew that this reality was the result of corporate conferences. Eddie O'Jay nearly had to admit to the crowd that he did not control his own play list (a horrible admission for any DJ). In fact, his play list was controlled by the Sonderling Corporation of Dallas—a white-owned corporation with a string of the biggest black radio stations in America, which they ran as a component of specialized radio for black markets. Their seven-day, twenty-four-hour air time was the heaviest advertisement-saturated format in radio. Their interests in the cultural development of their listeners did not go beyond airing the R&B Top 10 and the highest density of ads legally allowable. Hendrix's music was out of the question.

Jimi followed Big Maybelle, a perennial Harlem favorite, to the portable stage. With Larry Lee laying down a nice rhythm guitar texture, and Juma's congas bouncing off the tenement walls, Jimi roared out of his Marshall amps, playing his ass off. He did his complete showtime routine while all the while wrenching the echo of human sounds from atonals, distortions, and feedback. He could imagine being able to play loud enough so that all of Harlem could hear. They played "Fire," "Foxy Lady," "The Star-Spangled Banner," "Purple Haze," "Red House," and then the finale (which he announced as "the Harlem National Anthem"), "Voodoo Chile."

As he was walking back to the equipment truck after the set, a black nationalist type came up to Jimi and said, "Hey, brother, you better come home." Jimi quickly replied, "You gotta do what you gotta do and I gotta do what I got to do *now.*"

Back in L.A., Jimi was interviewed by Jim Brodey, a poet who also wrote for the *Los Angeles Free Press*. A court decision on the Toronto bust was imminent.

LOS ANGELES FREE PRESS: Tell me a little about your bust in Toronto.
JIMI: I can't tell you too much about that because my lawyer told me not to. Anyway, I'm innocent, completely innocent.
F.P.: Do you think it was a frame?
JIMI: It must have been or either it was just a very bad scene, because it ain't anything it was. But anyway, I can't talk too much about it now.

F.P.: How about your retirement? I understand you're going to . . .

JIMI: Oh well, see this is what the negative folks are trying to tell you. That's what the establishment is telling you. They're trying to blow us all up and give us awards and all that so that they can just dust us away, but we're not here to collect awards, you know, we're here to turn people on to the right way because there is some really strange scenes coming up, though. . . . Hey, I can't do this with other people in the room.

F.P.: You mean the rumor then, about your going into a year's retirement?

JIMI: No, I don't think it'll take that long actually, because now is the time when a year's retirement would be just completely wasted, you know, at the rate our pace is going now.

F.P.: What objective do you have? Just sort of to get back together again?

JIMI: No, no, not again. There's other moves I have to make now, you know. A little more toward a spiritual level through music. It's not the idea of basing yourself on different religions and so forth. There's no such thing really. All those are nothing but games they play upon themselves, but you know the drag of it is there are a lot of good people that are aware of the games being played. They play just as many but are not doing anything about it, you know, for their own selves. Not necessarily taking violent means; that's just another game. That's what they want you to do. They want you to be extra weak; fight amongst yourselves—so they can have complete control, you know.

Some of the vibrations people claim they are getting now, it is true considering the fact that the Earth is going through a very, what do you call it, physical change soon. A physical change basically. I mean, like since the people are part of Earth, they are going to feel it, too. In many ways they are a lot of the reason for causing it.

There really are other people in the solar system, you know, and they have the same feelings, too, not necessarily bad feelings, but see, it upsets their way of living, for instance, and they are a whole lot heavier than we are. And it's no war game because they all keep the same place. But like the solar system is going through a change soon and it's going to affect the Earth in about thirty years, you know. And I'm not just talking about this room; I'm talking about the Earth itself. This room is just a crumb from the crust of the pie. And like there's no moving from any one land to another to save yourself in that respect.

So I think a person should try to get his own thing because he should get a certain faith with one link. There's no whole lot of religions. Just one link, because there's only a few chosen people that supposedly are to get this across; these chosen people, in the process, are now being distracted and they are drowning themselves. So, therefore, they've got to take a rest. Not a rest, but a break from people. In order to properly save them, they've got to take a break from people. There's no good people or bad people; it's actually all lost and found. That's what it all boils down to. There's a lot of lost people around and like there are only leaders in times of crises, but that's just what's happening now. It's not just a fad that's going on; it's very serious.

If you revert back in time, there's Egypt. It's very dusty now, but it used to be green. It's that they had a great flood and the world used to be flat, so they say, I mean, you know. And like they found memorandums on the moon, but no telling when they are going to get there, but when they do, they are going to find memorandums from other civilizations that have been there before and think nothing of it because the moon is there in the first place.

I mean, it's hard to say really quickly, but all they can do . . . the only answer they can find is through music now. That's not a good scene or a bad scene, this is the truth. They have to face up to the complete, constant truth. Music is in a state now where it's getting rid of all the rubbish, and in order to do these things, mostly the musicians that are here for a purpose are not out to satisfy themselves because in that case, that is when they get distracted with the fame, imagery, and all that stuff. Actually this is when the kids get more distracted by trying to follow the changes that a musician might go through because they look like that person. Like when they come here to see us, which is wrong. That is what we are trying to get across. It's very easy right now because, like I say, I haven't had this time to get away yet.

F.P.: Will it actually be an absence from the rock scene then?

JIMI: I don't look at things like the "rock scene" and "folk scene." I don't look at those terms at all. But, therefore, nothing can explain what I'm going to do later on. I will have to use some sort of brand name. So like, I guess I will call it the spiritual scene. But it's not a hazy thing out of frustration or bitterness that I'm trying to build up. It's out of what's directing me. What I was here in the first place to do.

It does mean I am going to strip myself from my identity because this isn't my only identity. I was foolish to cut my hair, but that was part of the step of me learning what I was really here for. I see miracles every day now. I used to be aware of them maybe once or twice a week, but some are so drastic that I couldn't explain them to a person or I'd probably be locked up by this time.

F.P.: Through what means do you see these miracles?

JIMI: From all different types, because you may not necessarily be one of the chosen few to help. Everybody can't or else there would be nothing but every single person having his own different religion, and pretty soon they would wind up fighting and we would go right back to the same thing again. I'm not better than you in this sense. It's just that maybe I'm not going to say it until a wider range of people see it. It's a universal thought; it's not a black or white thing, or a green and gold thing.

F.P.: It might be used as a vehicle. . . .

JIMI: Yeah. I would like to say to close, there are a few chosen people that are here to help to get these people out of this certain sleepiness that they are in. There are some people running around with long hair preaching the word "love," and they don't know what the fuck they are talking about because there's no such thing as love until truth and understanding come about. All they're doing is making themselves weaker and weaker until their negatives come and just take them away. And that's what's gonna happen. Then you are going to have no world to live on. The establishment's going to crumble away.

This only happens when a person has his own thing. If he is a carpenter, for instance, or whatever, he has to work toward what he really digs. Like someone is going to have to go back to his childhood and think about what they really felt, really wanted before the fingerprints of their fathers and mothers got ahold of them or before the smudges of school or progress. . . . Most of them are sheep. Which isn't a bad idea. This is the truth, isn't it? That's why we have the form of Black Panthers and some sheep under the Ku Klux Klan. They are all sheep and in the beginning they were all following a certain path.

F.P.: But you feel the Black Panthers are necessary, though?

JIMI: Yeah, only to the word "necessary." You know, in the back of their minds they should be working toward their own thing. They should be a symbol only to the establishment's eyes. It should only be a legendary thing.

F.P.: Is it necessary as a step on the road to liberation and freedom?

JIMI: It all depends on what freedom means. Some people don't even know the meaning.

F.P.: How about for each individual that's involved in the Black Panthers?

JIMI: No, see, most of that comes from any kind of aggressive group like that. It's good when you start adding up universal thoughts, and it's good for that second. The rest of it should probably be in a legendary figure. In a, what do you call it, a symbol, or whatever. So what they are doing now is fighting among their individual selves. There's nothing we can explain to them. Most of it is from bitterness. There's no color part now. There's no black and white. It's very small. It's just like animals fighting among each other—then the big animals will come and take it all away.

F.P.: But someone who has been crippled for years?

JIMI: Other people have no legs, have fought in wars, and have no eyesight.

F.P.: Psychologically crippled?

JIMI: Right, that's what it's all about. They have to relax and wait to go by feeling.

If you are going to be psychological, you have to go by the psychological feeling. If you start thinking negative, it switches to bitterness, aggression, hatred, whatever.

Al Brown, a highly educated and experienced composer, arranger, violist, and violinist, was a stable influence, a mentor to the young crowd that formed loosely around Devon. Al Brown, a roundish chocolate-brown man, had a wonderful beaming smile. Older—speckled-gray, short black hair, the beginnings of a gray beard when he didn't shave—he was animated and joyous, very much the father figure. Upon greeting always a warm hug to heart and chest. Being a one-to-one person, Al Brown was closest to Devon. She brought him together with Jimi and he extended his personal one-to-one warmth to Jimi, including the run of his rambling apartment at Fifty-seventh Street and Tenth Avenue, which became Jimi's home away from home.

Jimi, subject to the vicious food of the road and many missed meals, glossed over with amphetamines, cocaine, cigarettes, and whiskey, had developed ulcers. Al Brown cooked well, especially West Indian dishes from his native Nevis. A particular dish made with beef, chicken, dumplings, and carrots was Jimi's favorite. Al Brown would have that dish every time Jimi showed up. Jimi would invariably meander into the kitchen and peek into the big kettle. "Is it okay if I have a little?" he would always ask, to the exasperation of Al Brown, who had to continuously repeat to Jimi that he was to treat the place as his own home. Al insisted they were sharing the place rather than being guest and host, but Jimi always acted as if he had come for the first time. Apologetic and sorry for every minuscule transgression even after he had many of his possessions there—jackets, notes, a red-velvet caftan with a hood, a guitar—enough stuff to actually be able to claim residence, he still continued his self-effacing, apologetic attitude.

One day when Jimi was leaving after an extended stay he said, "Thank you," to Al at the door. Al chose that moment to lecture him. "Jimi," he said, "this is your home. We share this home. Ever since you first came I have always told you to treat this place as if it were your own. You are always free to come whenever you want to and stay as long as you like. You don't have to give me any thank-yous; it is understood that this is your house as well as mine—we share it. No more thank-yous, Jimi, this is your home." Chagrined, all Jimi could say was, "I'm sorry." They had a good laugh.

Jimi's running buddies began to note a drastic change in him. There was something deep going on around his career that made him more and more depressed as 1969 went on. There was some finagling going on with his head. He began to come into the Scene or Ungano's, a new club on West Seventy-first Street, and be so deep in thought that it looked like he was going to freak out. Jimi would be sitting and drinking and then all of a sudden split out the door and get in his car and take off. At times it seemed like he could not handle a public place where there were other people. It would get so heavy that Jimi would jump up in a second and run out the door, leaving his chick and everything.

His friends saw the apparent torment and began to wonder what was really bothering him. It was more than an occasional depression, more than just being under the weather. It became obvious that it was something very, very deep. To his friends, his career was apparently going well, he was playing as excellently as ever, he had the love of many wonderful people—yet something deep down inside was eating away at his mind and his thoughts. And anyone who saw him could not fail to register Jimi's deep unhappiness. But his friends respected him so much that they never brought it up—and Jimi never volunteered. Very often they wanted to ask what was bothering him—but they did not dare.

Devon knew what was happening. For all the hassles Jimi and Devon had, she was still his confidante. She kept many of his most valued possessions and his New York apartment, as well. She knew a lot about his business and what was bothering him, but she did not talk about it, either.

One night at Ungano's, Jimi sat with Devon, digging on Buddy Guy. Hendrix was supposed to sit in with the renowned Chicago blues guitarist. But when Guy introduced Jimi, he had already left. Buddy Guy was very hurt. He had been put on the spot in front of the crowd. Buddy Guy was near tears as he began his next tune.

There were many things that burdened Jimi during this period and probably intensified his erratic behavior. Jimi was worried about the impending court case in Canada, which might send him to jail for seven years (he was recording at a breakneck pace, so at least he would be heard on LPs if he was jailed). In addition, there was the lawsuit Chalpin had against him, a great deal of money that he had earned was not accounted for by his management, he was not gigging, his record royalties were in escrow, the studio he was building was months behind schedule and running way over projected costs, and Devon was fucking with smack again.

The out-of-court settlement with Chalpin would cost him a complete album, to be delivered to Capitol Records for distribution for PPX. Chalpin received a cash settlement of one million dollars and a percentage of all past and future royalties earned by Hendrix. Warner Bros. had softened the blow by assuming payment of Chalpin's percentage of future royalties. They also bought out Jeffery's interest in Hendrix's royalties so that Jimi was actually better off from that point of view. Instead of having to give Jeffery the bulk of his royalties, Hendrix now would receive almost 10 percent for himself, instead of the 3 percent he previously shared with Mitch and Noel. But it was Warner Bros. and his management and legal advisers who had urged the settlement upon him. They did not want to fight it out in court. Jimi was still convinced that the contract was not legal and that he could have won the case, but he had no one on his side. The problem with Jimi was not the money, but control over his music. This situation ate at his consciousness.

Many people thought he was on top of the world, but his problems were monumental. For the first time in years he dreaded his upcoming birthday, his twenty-seventh.

On November 27, 1969, Devon threw a birthday party for Jimi in producer Monte Kay's duplex on the Upper East Side of Manhattan. Devon invited all the guests, including the Rolling Stones, who, it just so happened, had opened at Madison Square Garden that night. Jimi had attended the concert, sitting in partial view onstage in a place of honor. Devon and Mick Jagger had been linked romantically before. This was a subject not often brought up to Jimi, but whenever he was down on Devon he would always bring it up, not angrily, but with a grunting acknowledgment—calling her Dolly Dagger, punning on Jagger.

The hassles over whether Devon was his woman, his employee, his roommate, his running buddy—or just what—often came up. She played each role with great verve, as she went from one to the other according to Jimi's disposition toward her. Like Fayne, Devon was first associated with Jimi on a simple level, which then became complex. Like Fayne, Devon was an independent woman who could run dudes like Hendrix ran chicks.

Mick Jagger swaggered in dressed up like a gangster in a black-and-white checkered zoot suit and a Mafia-size ruby ring on his pinky. Although it was Jimi's birthday, Devon paid uncommon attention to Jagger. The professional competition between Jagger and Hendrix had always been high, and so was their lover-man competition. Hendrix had tried to pull Marianne Faithfull from Jagger a few years ago in London. That Marianne dug Jimi was apparent from the public support she had given him. But Jagger had pulled Devon in the public eye. According to the gossip, Jagger had an uncanny possession of Devon. She was unable to go to anyone but him whenever he was on the scene.

Except for Devon's attention to Jagger, the party was rather uneventful.

When Mick and Jimi went downstairs together, some speculated that they might be about to fight over Devon. But Mick wanted to speak to Jimi privately about his court case, assuring him that he and the Stones were behind him and that he, too, had been busted but it turned out all right. He wanted to make sure Jimi knew how he felt with the trial coming up so soon.

Jimi was extremely embarrassed by Mick's uncharacteristic behavior. There was no doubting his sincerity.

Mick and Keith Richards had been busted by British police invading Richards's home. Mick had four amphetamine pills in his pocket that had actually belonged to his girlfriend Marianne Faithfull. Richards was found guilty of having suspicious substances in his home. Mick admitted that he had cried when the English judge sentenced him to a year at Lewes Prison, and Richards to three months at Wormwood Scrubs—but people had been supportive of them. An editorial in the *Times* had pointed out the unfair severity of the sentences, and they were soon released.

Jimi felt that the British dealing with other Brits was one thing, but a black man up against a foreign court, even a Canadian one, was something else. However, he vowed not to cry in court if found guilty.

Mick had come to the heart of Jimi's dilemma. But he insisted that the publicist they shared, Les Perrin, was an invaluable ally who had helped Keith and him immeasurably, had surely influenced the *Times,* and would help Jimi, as they all would, if it came to that.

Jimi knew that fans and groupies often thought that artists such as the Rolling Stones or Jimi Hendrix were invincible, but the truth was that they were extremely vulnerable, and easy prey, especially to police and criminals.

Finney and Al Brown were also at the party. Devon had scored some soma and everyone seemed spaced. Someone kept repeating a quote of Madame Blavatsky's, "And those who are aware of the nature of the soma know the properties of other plants, as well. . . ." Someone else was explaining that Marianne Faithfull had recently run off with an Italian count.

They just sat around listening to sides, getting stoned, watching Devon go through her thing with Jagger. Flip Wilson, who lived upstairs, was telling jokes. Hendrix disappeared downstairs later in the evening. Finney, after waiting around for a while, exchanged small talk with the various Stones, especially Jagger, who he sat next to on the couch. He then excused himself to Jagger and picked up Sally, his date. He wanted to go somewhere else before the night was over where he could possibly have a better time.

They went downstairs to look for Jimi. The room was dark and his eyes had to get adjusted. He spied Hendrix and was surprised that he sat alone in the middle of the room. Sensing a delicate situation, Finney and Sally asked Jimi what was wrong. He said he was depressed, that's all. Finney and Sally quickly said good-bye.

They went back upstairs and through the party on their way out. It was clear to them that Devon and Jagger were leaving together. Not wishing to be around for the results, they hustled out.

Walking down the streets of New York, rather early in the night, they discussed the scene at the party. They both were grieved that Jimi obviously did not have a good time, and would be left alone on his birthday for the remainder of the night. Before they had gotten too far away, Sally decided to go back.

She returned to the party to find it just about over and Hendrix still downstairs alone. He didn't have much to say, but he was glad that she had returned. She left with him and they went to his pad. There he told her how so many chicks come on to him just wanting to do a physical thing. They laughed. Sometimes, he said, he just wanted to talk. They talked for a while, he venting his hurt. Sally told him she was from Antigua. She gave him a bottle with her picture on it as an impromptu birthday present. Then he said, "You know what? You know what I'd really like now more than anything? Some ice cream and cake."

They ate birthday cake and ice cream together with great relish. Then they spent the night together.

Jimi arrived in Toronto on December 12 for, perhaps, the last trial of his career. With him was Lynne Bailey, who testified on his behalf, and his old friend Jeanette Jacobs. Jimi, with his hair cut short and in a conservative sports jacket and slacks, looked like a lamb. He and Jeanette looked like newlyweds on honeymoon in Canada.

Jimi was questioned by his own attorney in a very unusual way. He did not try to hide the fact that Hendrix was involved with, and had used, drugs. He certainly took that thunder away from the Canadian (British) Crown's prosecutor. But Hendrix's legal strategy may have also been in part a reaction to a recent headline in a Toronto daily proclaiming Hendrix had admitted he had taken drugs, but not heroin. Jimi's questioning by his Canadian attorney, Mr. J. O'Driscoll, a former prosecutor, was tough but straightforward and honest.

Hendrix said it was not unusual to receive gifts from fans and that he often took them to be polite and agreeable, and to not alienate them (the implication being that fans were essential to his success). He said that he had received all sorts of things as gifts, from bits of yarn to paintings to stuffed animals, and he admitted that sometimes fans would also give drugs or marijuana.

When confronted with the contraband evidence, Jimi thought the hash pipe with illegal residue could have also easily been a peashooter. The Bromo-Seltzer canister containing heroin could have been, during a hectic scene at his hotel suite, thrown in his bag by himself after being given it by a fan after he had complained of a stomachache. The fact that it had heroin in it was unknown to him.

O'Driscoll went down a list:

O'DRISCOLL: How many times have you used hashish yourself?
JIMI: I really couldn't tell you how many times.

O'DRISCOLL: So many times that you could not remember?

JIMI: No.

O'DRISCOLL: You cannot even approximate it?

JIMI: I would say about three times.

O'DRISCOLL: Have you ever used LSD?

JIMI: Yes. Five times.

O'DRISCOLL: Have you ever used heroin?

JIMI: No.

O'DRISCOLL: Have you recently smoked marijuana?

JIMI: Not recently.

O'DRISCOLL: What do you burn incense for?

JIMI: For the nice smell.

O'DRISCOLL: Would you agree with me that, knowing about marijuana users, that it is sometimes used to cover the marijuana smell?

JIMI: Yes. It is sometimes used for that and for bad kitchen odors.

O'DRISCOLL: Am I safe in saying it was not for your bad kitchen odors?

JIMI: No, I don't have a kitchen.

O'DRISCOLL: Can you give us any idea of how often you receive drugs from your fans?

JIMI: Most every time that we play a show, you know.

Sharon Lawrence, a journalist with the Associated Press, testified that she was at Jimi's hotel suite trying to interview him just before he left for Toronto. She spoke of the confusion in his suite and the steady stream of unidentified strangers coming in and out. She distinctly remembered a seventeen- to twenty-year-old woman with "long, blondish-brown hair" dressed stereotypically like a hippie giving him a Bromo-Seltzer bottle after he complained of a stomachache, saying, "This will make you feel better." She noted the incident because she was taking mental notes that would provide an introduction to her interview with Jimi by describing the scene happening at the time.

When O'Driscoll asked her for any example of strange gifts being given to other music personalities, she told of receiving some envelopes from fans for the Beatles. She opened some and found some marijuana cigarettes and something that looked like LSD.

After eight and a half hours of deliberation, the jury returned a verdict of not guilty. Jimi was more than relieved—it was like he had been born again, brought back from death to life.

Because of the possibility of his serving time in a Canadian prison, he had not really known whether he would be able to play at the Fillmore East on New Year's Eve.

Hendrix and His Band of Gypsys

"No, you didn't get me out of bed, man. I'm in bed," said Jimi Hendrix, relaxing in his Toronto hotel after being acquitted of the drugs charge that had been hanging over his head for months.

Even over three thousand miles of transatlantic telephone cable it was obvious he wasn't too keen to talk about the case. When I said how delighted we were at the *MM* that things had worked out OK for him, he contented himself with: "I've been having kind of a hard time over it all."

I let the matter drop and told him the *MM* had reported that he was trying to get Noel Redding and Mitch Mitchell—the other two thirds of his Experience—back with him for a major tour.

"I've been thinking about that for a long time," he agreed. "All I'm waiting for is for Noel and Mitch to make up their minds and we can get everything fixed.

"I saw Noel at the Fillmore and I think everything is working out fine with him. Now I am looking to see Mitch. He has been over there in England getting himself together."

Will the tour include England if Noel and Mitch agree to return for the six weeks necessary—at a reported figure of half a million pounds?

"It would certainly include Britain and I'd hope to be there around February, or maybe March, at the latest," said Jimi. "The way I see it is we would start in England, then do the rest of Europe, America, Hawaii, Canada, and maybe end up back in England."

The conversation halted while Jimi went into paroxysms of sneezing that must have had the cable writhing on the ocean bed.

" 'Scuse me," he snorted when silence finally reigned. "Seems like I've got a chill."

I asked what he had been doing recently, apart from worrying about the court case. "We've been recording with my new group, the Band of Gypsys," he said. "It's a three-piece and we have Buddy Miles on drums and Billy Cox on bass. How to describe the group? Very funky! Sort of a blues and rock type of thing.

"Hey, what's happening over there in England? Who's making it happen? Somebody sent me a record by that Blue Mink. Nice. I need to get back there. I need to hear some of those new groups. And I need some new vibrations."

I wondered if Jimi had found any time to write new material recently.

"I've been writing a whole lot of things," he told me, after another, but lesser, bout of sneezing. "In fact, we've got enough material now for another two LPs. We are trying to decide what to release and at what time.

"We've started recording and you should be receiving a single around the end of January. The title? It should be another 'Trying to Be a Man' or 'Room Full of Mirrors.'"

Jimi repeated that he was looking forward to playing with Noel and Mitch again. I said Buddy Miles wasn't exactly a bad dep.

"Buddy is more of a rock drummer," he replied. "Mitch is more of a classic drummer—more of a funky R&B-type drummer."

Jimi has always been a man for catching up on what other groups and musicians are doing. I asked him if he had heard anyone new in the States that we ought to know about.

"I don't know about anybody new, I'm still digging Jethro Tull," he told me. "I heard them here and I was impressed.

"Have you heard of the Blues Image?"

I admitted that I hadn't.

"Or Eric Mercury?"

This time I was able to say that Peter Frampton had mentioned in last week's *MM* that Humble Pie had been working with him in the States.

"He's like all the R&B figures you ever heard all wrapped up together," said Jimi.

"To be honest, I'm not too up to date on what's been happening here. I've been working too hard rehearsing and recording with the Band of Gypsys. We are really getting it together now."

I thanked him and said good-bye.

"Hey," came Jimi's voice. "Just tell everybody over there a Happy New Year and a Merry Christmas from me and I'm really looking forward to coming back home."

> —Bob Dawbarn
> *Melody Maker*
> December 20, 1969

Jimi and Al Brown would talk for long hours about plans for the guitar concerto they were writing together. This subject, as a plan for part of Jimi's musical future, made him glad, and he talked eagerly about the direction he wanted to go in. He loved the idea of his guitar backed by an entire orchestra, and especially the violins, violas, and cellos that Al had mastery over. Horns and voices, a higher plateau of sound. Right away several of the tunes he was working on took on the measured and thought-out pace of the concerto. Just thinking about it inspired him in his writing.

He had affirmed his African-American mystical/magical heritage in "Voodoo Chile" and was readying "Machine Gun," a protest against police establishment oppression, with Buddy Miles. His space thoughts had attracted many American mystics, spiritualists, and alternative-minded groups. Foremost among them was the Sufi group from Tucson and its Hollywood counterpart led by Chuck Wein, who were getting together *Rainbow Bridge,* a movie intended to offer America a spiritual alternative through yoga, vegetarianism, psychicism, consciousness-expanding drugs, and an affirmation of intelligent and advanced life in outer space.

But for Jimi his magic was in the music, and the collaboration with Al Brown promised to move Jimi's music to a higher spiritual plane, which would at the same time take the growing stigma of being a rock 'n' roll star off Jimi's back.

Hendrix and Buddy Miles are in the studio with Alan Douglas listening to Alafia of the Last Poets run down this poem that was orally composed by black inmates. *Doriella du Fontaine* is a story about a chick, the choicest of the pimp's chicks, who sets out to make her man, her pimp, the baddest pimp of them all, the man of men. Like *Shine* or *Stagolee,* the poem is an epic toast from "the people," a true folk expression, dealing metaphorically with the black man's relationship with his women, as expressed through the pimp and the whore. Two lovers living under oppression, underground, illegally—the ill-fated romance.

It was so ironic that this tale, this saga with its force and power, would remind Hendrix of Devon. She probably really loved him, and like a prostitute to her pimp, their understanding was inclusive of the myriad chicks he had. For a pimp the chicks are strictly monetary, but for Hendrix the chicks were release, part of his creative fashion, a way for him to maintain his drive and keep his energy peaked.

Doriella du Fontaine thus became a kind of parallel to Hendrix's life with Devon. Devon, who tricked at fifteen in Vegas, the big time for prostitutes, was fully aware of that role. She would trick and procure for Hendrix and then in the next minute do some shit to enrage him. But that was part of it: the prostitute demands the hard-edged discipline of the pimp, and the gentle Hendrix was sometimes prompted into "heavy" acts by the devilish, mischievous Devon.

Their mutual attraction seemed to have occurred in spite of themselves. Neither particularly wanted a romantic attachment. Devon, as efficient as she was devious, commanded enough presence to keep the creeps away, get him to the show on time, score some blow with minimal effort at any time, keep track of his shit, and help to maintain some line of intelligible contact and communication between Hendrix and his estranged management. Perhaps she would not have done that except for love, but she was paid to do that and paid well from the start. Perhaps her pulling him and getting his nose open was to her also a part of her job security. But she had her own shit going, too. Bisexual, it was said that she loved only women until Hendrix came along and "straightened her out"—or else she straightened out for him. At one point she even tried to have a baby by him. But she did not give up her female lovers for Hendrix; in fact, she often served both Hendrix and another woman in their famous threesomes. Her initial meeting with Hendrix had involved a train, with her and Angie calling up Quincy Jones in the process to announce the train they were running on Jimi. They also said that Hendrix's joint "was damn near big as his guitar."

Devon also had a vicious heroin habit, a habit that cost plenty and cost every day, as well. Maintaining it with rare cool, she did get uptight on occasion and put people through some very weird changes. In addition to keeping up the glamorous image of the supergroupie, she also had to score and stock big. She required more bread than the occasional cab fare. She required bread that paralleled the turning of tricks, and she got it. Whether her love for Hendrix was part of the intrigue or not, it did cause them some very bad moments. But her tremendous appeal, mixed with her boldness and charm, always got her over.

Jimi had hoped that Fayne would be able to help Devon get her shit together and drop heroin, but Fayne came back with some weird stories. It was hopeless. Fayne talked about Devon needing a fix, going out in the street; fly, tall, and lean, getting some trick to go for a ten-minute blow job in an alley. To Devon it was a joke, yet a fact of life not too distant from where she was at the moment. Junk tends to erase memory, but in the throes of needing a fix, it all comes back. She had the bravado of a streetwalker. No happening could be *that* far out as to blow her mind. Her head erect like the Sphinx's, regal and tall, her chin slightly jutted in arrogance, her black hair swept back severely framing her serene eyes. She was the Cleopatra of the groupies.

Jimi talked about Cleopatra as the absolute temptress. Cleo had been a fantasy, a fantasy that myriad women who surrounded him all sought to emulate. But most imaginations were lacking. Devon was a Cleo incarnate, but not the fanciful fantasy that seemed to come out of Jimi's dreams. She was a weird temptress-demon of the times whose being had edges he could only vaguely comprehend. A super femme fatale. He could understand the occasional perfidies, and even understand the frequent bouts of lovemaking, but the middle and outer grounds, the gray areas, often seemed to suffuse the entire polarity. At times it seemed that her lies were a simple mistake, while at other times they seemed like vast conspiracies. Her lovemaking often made her seem as true as the sloppiest love story, but then she would turn another side and become the biggest dyke, the biggest sadomasochist, the biggest whore, the most relentless nymphomaniac, and the heaviest doper—all rolled into one.

What began to scare Jimi most about Devon was the smack.

He had no trouble staying away from heroin. First he found out that Devon snorted a little bit now and then. Well, fine, lots of people do. Then he gradually found out she was doing a little chipping, using the needle, "a little bit." But his time was always so fucked-up he could not really check on her properly. After a while it became obvious that she was heavy into smack. Usually he kept enough space between himself and the ladies to be clear of whatever trip they were into. But Devon was close, very close. She had gotten next to him. Many times he remembered himself unconsciously accepting the smack's presence. This he realized was dangerous.

Devon wanted the public thing to confirm their relationship. As much as Jimi loved her, he knew she could destroy him.

Bill Graham, grand impresario of rock, had booked Hendrix in the Fillmore West right after his historic performance at Monterey in 1967. He had steadily booked him every time he appeared in the States, but always inconveniently by long distance. When Hendrix moved to downtown Manhattan, he lived very conveniently less than ten blocks from the Fillmore East.

With the new year approaching, Graham planned a big one for the beginning of the seventies—the end of the decade of the sixties, where rock and soul really took their rightful berths in worldwide music. Who better than Jimi Hendrix, Buddy Miles, and Billy Cox: the Band of Gypsys?

But Graham was nervous about it. Hendrix was always very standoffish, keeping to himself with his own personal friends; and now with the estrangement of his management at an all-time high, it would be necessary to approach Hendrix directly with an offer of such an important date. Graham had to be sure. The only way would be to deal directly with Hendrix and then back through the management.

The good fortune of Hendrix staying right there in the Village paid off. A couple of days later Graham went over to the west side of the Village to a rented garage where Jimi, Buddy Miles, and Billy Cox rehearsed and jammed. They had made a deal—Fillmore East New Year's Eve and Day—two shows each. And then, for the first time, they actually broke open a bottle, sat down, lay back, and rapped for a while. In the dark of a practice-studio garage, they laughed and talked for the first time without being in a gig situation.

The night of the first concert, New Year's Eve, Luther Rabb, who had been in the Velvetones with Jimi when they were teenagers, opened with his group Ballin' Jack. Then Hendrix and Miles and Cox *rocked* the Fillmore. The audience was jubilant, cheering Hendrix's every move. And Jimi put on a classic two-hour soul show—a minihistory of showtimes all over the USA in black towns, villages, and ghettos. The crowd was screaming when Hendrix came in after the third encore.

Bill Graham recalled standing solemnly offstage feeling unhappy about the performance. Exuberant, Hendrix, passing through the wings, asked bosslike Graham, "How was it?" Graham, swarthy and terse, said, "All right, Jimi, all right." Taken aback a bit by the formal, almost prosaic rebuttal to his enthusiasm, Jimi took a strange look at Graham as he kept on to his dressing room. After drying off, changing, Hendrix sought Graham out in his office. Again, he asked Graham, "How was it?" Graham again gave a noncommittal, "It was all right, Jimi, fine." Jimi couldn't believe his ears. He had had three encores, the crowd had screamed, they were still whooping in the streets of Sixth Street and Second Avenue below. He wanted to know why Graham was so contradictorily reserved.

Graham, on record as preferring Latin and soul music to rock, was outspoken: no bullshit. A shrewd, streetwise New York businessman of Jewish origins, he was aware (as he was aware of every phase of the multimillion-dollar history of rock) that this historic occasion would go down in eternity through the live recording being done by Wally Heider's remote crew outside.

"You really want it?" Graham said. Hendrix quickly agreed. The staff, sensing another typical Graham-artist confrontation and wanting none of it, left just as quickly.

It seemed to Graham that just as they had gotten a bit close as people, in a wink they were on the verge of a confrontation that could ruin their business relationship. But he also wanted a good performance for the recording and he felt Hendrix's wild showtime movements often slowed and stumbled the music. The crowd did not mind, they were enthralled by the spectacle and seemed to forget about the music completely as Hendrix moved so incredibly across the proscenium, under the light show's great washes of rose and white violet lights, the huge tentlike screen exploding billows of sub-scan molecules, atoms, DNA, RNA, LSD pyrotechnics. Graham, behind the stage only hearing the concert, wanted more. He told Hendrix that the crowd would have loved him no matter what he did, and that his wild cavorts, swoops, and sex play allowed him to play, in actuality, only much below par.

Again, Hendrix couldn't believe his ears. And Graham elaborated on the theme. If he got cheers for only his antics, then the thing to do at the end of the show was to ask the crowd if they liked it. And when they cheer and scream, to slowly intone in the mike, "Oh yeah? Well, you are full of shit!" Hendrix tried to interrupt, but Graham, on his high horse, said, "You asked me, right? So let me talk." Graham intoned on about the responsibility of the great and truly gifted to avoid the trap of mass adulation, which is surface and illusory, to avoid that deception and *play* their very best at all times.

Jimi Hendrix had always loved his movements onstage—since he was a kid. He loved to go out like that before a crowd. But everyone had hated it, except the fans. His fellow musicians in the service and even in high school would complain that he was making a fool out of himself and all of them, as well. In England and the USA, it had helped establish his uniqueness as a performer—

the press always scandalized, the promoters always bugged. Graham had questioned and challenged his integrity as a performer and also as a star who had earned the right to choose what he presents.

The next set Hendrix played stock-still, hardly moving at all. The crowd was breathless all the way through. Bill Graham danced in the wings. Sweeping back to the wings, after the tremendous ovation that seemed to pervade the walls, every nook and cranny of the great theater, Hendrix walks over to Graham and says, "All right, motherfucker?" Then he walks out and plays a fifteen-minute encore doing nothing but bumps and grinds and humps and tongue flickings.

That classic second set, which Hendrix played standing stock-still, formed the basis for the album *Band of Gypsys*.

"Who Knows?" and "Machine Gun" from the second set became the first side of the *Band of Gypsys* album. The other side was drawn from material recorded during the three other sets of the two-night performances. "Who Knows?," a new song, begins the set as Bill Graham's dramatic introduction nears its end. It is a bouncy, bopping tune with a lilting flow that is aided by a close call-and-response lyric sung by Jimi and Buddy. After an incredible ovation, Jimi intones, "This next song is dedicated to all the troops fighting in Harlem, Chicago, and, oh yes, Vietnam. A little thing called 'Machine Gun.'"

Never before had Jimi sounded more funky. But it was also a scary funk. Syncopating the heartbeat in the hypnotic drone of an eternal caravan, the Band of Gypsys hit an awe-inspiring power. No psychedelic soars, no bump-and-grind humor. Jimi's tonalities grow from bending E-minor modes into the Eastern drone-sounding tonic and leap octaves into screams and howls. Slurring from deep within his range, Jimi uses his body between the amps and his Stratocaster to undulate a slowly building feedback howl. His sound over the drone shifts from a woman's scream to a siren to a fighter plane diving, all amid Buddy Miles's Gatling-gun snare shots, building in intensity by Buddy's sheer power. His broad-girthed arms slowly rising on each beat to smash the dual cymbals, which dangle in position above his head. His arms fall slowly, like a conductor's, to his snares, beating out percussive licks that sound like marching music amid the report of a point-blank gun. Jimi sings, his voice almost breaking with sadness, as he tells of the bullets of the "machine gun" tearing apart bodies of his buddies and himself. He says, "Evil man make me kill you" just as the same evil man will "make you kill me" although "we're only families apart." Jimi tells of picking up his ax to fight like a farmer—Ax is slang for guitar. Although he is defenseless against the machine gun, he is nonetheless shot down. But karma will return to the perpetrator many times over the pain he experiences.

Throughout the song, Jimi's voice veers at tenor peak to the pentatonic intonations of a Vietnamese or Bangkok nightclub singer.

Buddy Miles pauses, eyes closed, like a Buddha within a silver metal bubba flowing outward, his snare shots wide and strong. He beats into the depths of a groove, the snare shots *ratatat*ting stronger and stronger. Miles captures and entrances you with his repetition. The intensity of his shots rings out on a par with Jimi's guitar.

At the bridge, the pace of the song turns upside down into the juicy middle, where it gets more buoyant and funky. Jimi momentarily stops playing to go over and turn both Marshall stacks to their utter limits, and then in total feedback the maestro takes over. As Buddy Miles screams in the background a Delta moan, Hendrix lightly fingers the amp-busting guitar, his very touch emitting the cries of a woman beyond pleasure to the threshold of pain, the screams of electric fire, the looney cacophony of siren scream alarm pain planes in space bombing, people screaming.

Jimi's Stratocaster emits very light high harmonic pings. And then the guitar gets to haranguing and shit. Double picking. Going back and forth between runs, cross-running them faster and faster. Filling with a rhythm-lick turn, Jimi evokes a speed rush, a coke rush, a grass rush, a DMT rush. It's total recall, total awareness, total light streaming, and you understand it all in the feeling.

They had a beautiful time. Jimi, Buddy, and Billy got off and made a political statement, as well. It was a classic concert; they *rocked* the joint and said something, too. Bill Graham, a great showman, had urged them to make a historical musical statement, as well, playing their best straight to the music. The end-of-the-sixties concert, Jimi, their prince, and Graham, their field marshal, taking them into the seventies.

But something was haunting Jimi that night. He was hurt and angry, and the vibes had made him take it out in the music. A big hurt hung over the 1970s for Jimi.

The recording of the performance was "owed" to Ed Chalpin of PPX Productions as part of the out-of-court settlement. An album (*Band of Gypsys*) would be released on Capitol Records. A large cash settlement and a percentage of all past and future record royalties was also part of the agreement with Chalpin.

Even Hendrix's original management contract with Chas Chandler and Michael Jeffery had been exploitative. They—Chandler and Jeffery—had received 40 percent of all of Hendrix's earnings. In addition, they had received 7 percent of his record royalties. Hendrix controlled 3 percent, he kept 1 percent and split the remaining 2 percent between Mitch Mitchell and Noel Redding. Hendrix's management had received 40 percent of his 1 percent record royalty earnings, as well.

For live concerts, after management had deducted their 40 percent off the top, Hendrix had received 50 percent of the remainder and Mitch Mitchell and

Noel Redding each received 20 percent of that. All expenses were, of course, deducted from earnings. Now with the Band of Gypsys, Billy Cox was on salary. So was Buddy Miles, who had officially joined Jimi in October of 1969. Buddy received a large salary plus other benefits.

The influence that the constant jamming and rehearsing with Billy Cox and Buddy Miles had on Jimi's writing was borne out in "Message to Love," "Power of Soul," "Who Knows?," and the incredible "Machine Gun."

"Machine Gun" was a big departure from Jimi's usual celestial and/or love themes. The Vietnam War; the national repression of the Black Panthers, who for many were a symbol of the black struggle for self-determination within the United States; and Jimi's exploitation contributed to his sombre, highly political mood. The FBI, aided by other intelligence agencies and local police forces, was waging war on the Panthers in an attempt to separate them from the youth culture and the peace movement. J. Edgar Hoover, the FBI's head, was determined to stop their momentum, which was garnering more and more public support every day.

Many influential and popular entertainers were becoming more and more outspoken in their support of the Panthers and the peace movement. Many of Hollywood's top entertainers such as Warren Beatty, Jack Nicholson, Jean Seberg, Jane Fonda, and Donald Sutherland supported both movements. Rock musicians and groups from the San Francisco Bay area had been the first to openly avow some sort of revolutionary stance. Folksingers like Joan Baez, Bob Dylan, Pete Seeger, and Peter, Paul, and Mary had supported the civil rights movement in the early sixties. By the time Dylan went electric in 1965, San Francisco musicians were discovering acid and protest as one and the same. The coinciding of the Monterey Pop Festival of 1967 with the great Human Be-ins in New York and San Francisco had made rebels almost overnight of the majority of the youthful attendees.

By 1969, the sides were clearly drawn. Many within the establishment vowed that the seventies would be a different story. And with Richard Nixon in power, the secret and uniformed police began a program of harsh repression. By the end of 1969, many Hollywood stars of consequence to the youth culture were attending peace rallies and Panther fund-raisers, and donating significant sums of money to both movements, as well.

This was the popular mood of the time, and Jimi Hendrix as the *top* musical performer was called upon in various ways to contribute. To put his body on the line.

From all the evil and disturbing things that were happening to him as 1969 closed, Jimi began to feel the emotions of the struggle the Black Panthers were going through. He began to really feel what the brothers up at the house in Woodstock said about repression and racism.

Jimi felt he was being robbed by people close to him, people whom he trusted; and he could not be sure who was doing it, how it was being done, or why. It was hard for Jimi to relate to basic criminal greed. Everyone around him mouthed the same feelings about love and peace and getting high and hating the police—yet some of those very same people were robbing him blind. And some of those very same people who said that they were his friends—who swore it—were full of shit. Jimi really began to feel the presence of evil close by.

He had been set up for a bust at an international crossing. He would never be so stupid as to take heroin *anywhere*—much less across a border. Heroin was an evil drug that he avoided; he even found it hard to be with people who used it. That was one of the factors that made him so ambivalent about Devon. He had been sued by someone who had said he was his friend, whose chief witness was another person who said he was his friend (a fellow musician, yet). The settlement of the lawsuit had taken more money from him than he had thought he would ever make in a lifetime. But the biggest drag was that he had to give an entire album over to them—that hurt. That meant that he had to give of himself something he dearly loved—his music. That contract on one piece of paper had given him all of one dollar for his signature. It had been "between friends."

It was ironic, to say the least, that the debut of the Band of Gypsys, doing his new "protest" and teaching songs of social concern, would be recorded for release in order to pay off this settlement. It seemed that everyone was against him in the judgment: not only the party that sued, but also the record company and even his own lawyers. How could such a settlement come down? He truly felt evil around him like he had never felt evil before. "Evil man make you kill me/Evil man make me kill you. . . ."

It was January 1, 1970.

CHAPTER 8

The Cop of the Year

How do you get Mick Jagger when you're already living with Jimi Hendrix? Or as one green-eyed groupie put it when Devon walked off with the cop of the year after the Stones' Madison Square Garden concert, "But Mick usually goes for those skinny, scrawny blondes, those English birdie types." Nobody had thought Devon could possibly cut it. Sitting in Jimi's West Village apartment, she was more than happy to share her experiences. Hendrix's place is decorated in contemporary casbah with Oriental rugs, canopied couches, tapestries, brass hookahs. It's moon over Marrakech as jasmine incense floats through soft blue light. Devon, Jimi, and Colette (a beautiful Moroccan friend of Devon and Jimi's personal couturiere) are spending a normal afternoon at home. The ultimate rock ménage à trois: Star Musician/Star Groupie/Star Designer. Jimi is hanging around, unsure of whether he's wanted, maybe a little jealous that Devon is being interviewed. The doorbell rings. The groceries. Devon tells Colette to unload them and she disappears. Jimi splits to the bedroom. Posed on harem pillows in a tasty Ossie Clark hostess gown, Devon's movie starts to roll.

I met the Stones a couple of years ago at their press party at the Playboy Club, where I was working. I went out with Brian Jones first. I was closer to him than any of the others. He was the true Rolling Stone.

Last year when I heard that the Stones were coming for a tour I knew I would hear from Mick. He called and asked me to go to Philadelphia for their concert. Then we spent the week together in New York. Six beautiful days and nights. Everyone was really happy for me. Colette used to help me get dressed before I'd go out with Mick. A lot of chicks were envious. But I'd get calls from my friends who'd congratulate me and say, "Hey, you did it!" Like *heavy* score, right?

What did Jimi think? Oh, he loved it, but he was jealous, too. Mick and Jimi like each other a lot. The night of the Stones' concert, I gave a surprise birthday party for Jimi at the apartment. Mick came in an out-of-sight black-and-white checkered zoot suit and a Mafia-size ruby ring on his little finger. It was their big night out and everyone had a fantastic time.

Most of the time, Mick and I didn't do much of anything. I'd go up to the hotel or we'd visit friends of mine. He didn't want to go to any clubs. He loved to order from room service. Coffee, toast, and crepes. One night we watched an old, old Errol Flynn movie. It was a gas.

Mick is a very sexually electric person. Especially his mouth and eyes. I think he's had his fair share of sex, don't you? He told me he likes either fourteen-year-old girls who look like little boys, or thirty-year-old women, excepting me, of course. I think he's into a heavy spade trip, which had a *little* something to do with us. He was getting telegrams from famous models and calls from hundreds of chicks who wanted to sleep with him. He knows his appeal to women. He's the biggest sex symbol ever. I've heard a lot of stories from the girls about him, but mine are probably closer to the truth. I tease him about it and he said he wasn't into sex scenes anymore. But he did say he was still open for all suggestions.

I think he meant it when he said he didn't come to the States to sleep with teenyboppers. A lot of girls I know—who are considered groupies—he's known for a long time. He commented on how some hadn't changed, they were just taking different drugs.

You know the song "Stray Cat Blues"? He told me he wrote it about a certain chick. He said he usually doesn't write like that but he had this one particular lady in mind. When he was in California the girl called him and said, "Thanks for writing that song about me." He was shocked because he didn't think she could have recognized herself. But she did and it completely freaked him.

He understands blues so well because he's into spades. He digs Tina Turner, Taj Mahal, Jimi. He wrote a song about me. "Your mother she was a country girl / Where's your father, he done left this world? / Every brown girl has to pay a due / Every white boy he just sings the blues."

He loved being on the road. The Stones like the New York audiences better than the California ones. It seemed to Mick that the California kids had saved up all their heavier drugs for the Stones' concert and said, "Let's freak out," and didn't get into the music. The Madison Square Garden crowd was much more responsive.

The Beatles are like the British Supremes. The Stones are hard and funky. They're like that as people and their music is them. The words "Rolling Stones" have come to symbolize their freedom, weirdness, and honesty.

I think Mick would make a great husband. He loves children. He's very attached to Marianne's four-year-old son. I don't know why he hasn't married her.

What I like about Mick is that he doesn't get up very early. The thing we have most in common is that neither of us like to get up before two in the afternoon.

So what can I do for an encore? I don't know, probably marry Jimi . . . Will you publish my wedding pictures?

Rags, 1970

.   .   .

Although Jimi had mixed feelings about the New Year's Eve concert, favorable comments swept the grapevine. Never before had Jimi been so funky and so political, as well. "Machine Gun" was the talk of the town. The song fused the international horror of the Vietnam War with the local horrors perpetrated against the Black Panthers.

The Panther 21 had been in jail in New York City since April 2, 1969, when they were charged with conspiracy to bomb various sites in New York and the tristate area. While the New York dailies sensationalized the upcoming trial, others close to the Panther Party were beginning to wonder if the Panther 21 and others were not the victims of infiltrators, provocateurs, and organized police and intelligence-agency repression.

Jimi was acquainted with Black Panthers on both the East and West coasts. Several high-ranking Panther Party members had had discussions with Jimi about a benefit performance. The bail for the New York Panther 21 had been set at $100,000 each, far too much money for the party to raise in the usual ways. The trial began in February of 1970. Hendrix, engrossed in building Electric Lady Studios and having legal battles of his own, was still willing to do a benefit, but Mike Jeffery was dead set against it. He was having enough trouble without Hendrix becoming more identified with the Black Panthers.

Others close to Hendrix were worried that he might be attracting the very same infiltrators and provocateurs who were operating within the black liberation movement. Those who knew about such things knew that if any one of the intelligence agencies decided to go after Jimi they would do so with only the most subtly crafted plan. Not only would it be difficult to detect such an operation, but also such an operation would wreak havoc upon Jimi's creative life—after all, he was an artist. The kind of pressure well-seasoned political activists were used to could destroy Jimi. With Jimi's estrangement from his office at an all-time high it would be incredibly easy to manufacture incidents. And with Jimi's easygoing, unable-to-say-no personality, he could well be duped by almost any person who got within his good graces. All it took was persistence. The streetwise wit of Devon became very important. She more than anyone else would hopefully be able to deal with such a situation if it ever came to that.

Jimi had been approached to play a benefit by people connected with the Vietnam Moratorium Committee. They were supporting negotiations between the warring factions in Vietnam. Negotiations would have more of a chance of success if there was a moratorium in the fighting. Jimi was all for it. It was not the violent faction of the antiwar community that was sponsoring the event, but a group that lobbied for diplomatic, peaceful negotiations. They would have the benefit kick off a nationwide campaign.

• • •

The poster for the Winter Festival for Peace that was organized by the Vietnam Moratorium Committee, read as follows:

Wednesday Jan. 28
(5 Hour Festival)
One Performance Only

WINTER FESTIVAL FOR PEACE

Harry Belafonte
Blood, Sweat & Tears
Dave Brubeck
Judy Collins
Richie Havens
The Cast of HAIR
Jimi Hendrix and his Band of Gypsys
Mother Earth
Peter, Paul and Mary
The Rascals

All net Proceeds to Moratorium Fund

On January 28, 1970, at Madison Square Garden, the vibes were very high. Jimi's public endorsement and financial support for the anti–Vietnam War movement was a very big deal.

It was his first concert of the new year after the debut of the Band of Gypsys at the Fillmore East. Many personalities on the New York scene were backstage. It was not the usual professionally organized concert. Bill Graham would have never allowed so many unaccounted-for people backstage with the performers, but the amateur producers for this show had allowed many politicos and marginal persons to mingle backstage.

Jimi stood with his entourage and looked as if he were dead. He had been given some powerful and horrible acid by someone he did not know. In the hectic rush of backstage just before showtime, Jimi's head hung down.

Bad acid is the worst of all possible things to take anytime, and much more so before an important concert. It would have been better if he had been stone drunk.

While the opening speeches were going on, Jimi sat on his dressing-room couch with his head in his hands. It was unusually bad acid. Not only did it make him physically sick, but also the trip itself was a vicious psychic downer.

But Jimi struggled with it. It was important for him to be there, it was an important statement for him to make. He had not been able to do any major benefits to aid the progressive forces that were fighting for reform. Although he felt like shit, he went on anyway, with Billy Cox on bass and Buddy Miles on drums.

Jimi tried to play, but his body and his mind were in agony. After a few minutes he had to say to the twenty thousand in the audience, "I'm sorry, we just can't get it together. . . ." Jimi walked off, followed by Buddy and Billy. The entire place was in an uproar. They did not know what had happened.

Buddy Miles would say, "I personally witnessed Michael Jeffery give him [Jimi] two tabs of Purple Haze, acid, before we went on the stage at Madison Square Garden. Jimi, from the very start, was not himself. After that eighteen minutes, Jimi humped over, like he was gonna throw up. And then when he got up something scared him. He went off the stage. Michael Jeffery had a smile on his face. And I said, 'Michael, you did what you set out to do, didn't you?' No comment."

Jimi was quoted in the press as having said at some point between the stage and the dressing room, "That's what happens when earth fucks with space."

But author Sharon Lawrence said Jimi told her it was Devon who gave him the bad acid. Whatever it was, it effectively severed his public connection to the anti–Vietnam War movement.

The next day in the press Hendrix made a statement to the effect that he was not happy with the Band of Gypsys. He singled out Buddy Miles as having too much "earth" for his taste. Still recovering from the effects of the amazingly bad acid, Jimi, in one comment, totally alienated Buddy Miles, who was also a close friend. And to the delight of Mike Jeffery, Jimi seemed receptive to rejoining Mitch and Noel for the spring tour. Jeffery immediately arranged for *Rolling Stone* to interview Jimi.

Buddy Miles was dismissed as a member of the Jimi Hendrix organization by Mike Jeffery, who seemed to enjoy the heavy role. "This trip is over," he told the large and muscular drummer.

For Buddy, the biggest disappointment was that Jimi had not come to him and told him himself.

Billy Cox quit, leaving immediately for his home in Nashville.

Jann Wenner, young editor of *Rolling Stone*, dispatched crack reporter John Burks to interview Hendrix and company at Mike Jeffery's apartment on February 4, 1970.

Hendrix had been quoted late in 1969, by a *Rolling Stone* correspondent, Sheila Weller, as being sympathetic to the Black Panthers' plight. Mike Jeffery had been after Hendrix to clarify his position regarding the Black Panthers in the press. The almost protestlike songs of his Fillmore East concerts and his in-volvement in the benefit for the Vietnam Moratorium Committee had, in Jeffery's view, given Hendrix the image of a radical rock singer. And, in fact, Hendrix had just been acquitted of a serious drug charge in Toronto. In Jeffery's mind, Hen-drix had changed his music so radically since moving back to America that he was in danger of losing the audience that had propelled him to fame. Not only did Jeffery feel that the original Experience sound was the right sound for Jimi, but he also felt that Noel and Mitch were the perfect completion of the image.

Even before Woodstock in August of 1969, Jeffery had been dead set against Hendrix appearing with black sidemen, especially when all of them were black. He had made sure they were far to the back of the stage at Woodstock. He did not like the wild-haired African-named Juma, nor the addition of his congas to Hendrix's sound. Jeffery marshaled a powerful argument against Hendrix going any further in the direction he had been going: Jimi had the lawsuit settlement to pay off and he had the Electric Lady Studios to pay for. They had little money coming in. Jimi could not take the chance of alienating people; and in Jeffery's mind, Jimi had already alienated his fans quite a bit in the past year.

Less than seven days after he had walked off the stage with Billy and Buddy, Jimi was being interviewed with the original Experience by John Burks for *Rolling Stone* magazine. Jimi, Noel, and Mitch were sprawled on the floor before a gas-burner fake fireplace. Burks felt it was a set-up, like those done for fan magazine reporters to give an image of solidarity and fellowship. Yet less than a week ago, Jimi had gone onstage at Madison Square Garden with the Band of Gypsys as his permanent band. The Band of Gypsys' marathon jamming sessions had been the talk of the town. Their performance at Fillmore East had been highly praised throughout the grapevine and everyone was looking forward to a return perfor-mance. So it was kind of embarrassing for all involved to greet each other and sit down as if it were not unusual for Jimi, Noel, and Mitch to be sitting around a fireplace together. They were close enough to hold hands. The power trio.

Jimi wore a dark green satin V-neck shirt, with a finely jeweled pendant bal-anced within the deep-cut V. Violet pinstripe bell-bottoms and pink loafers with high insteps that made them look like elf boots.

The presence of their press agents made it very clear that the Hendrix orga-nization felt a dire need for some favorable publicity. The haste with which the interview had been arranged also pointed to that. And when a smiling Mike Jef-fery entered with a tray of choice wine and wondrous cognac to counteract the bitter cold outside, Burks got the message. But Burks knew that it would be im-possible for them to totally manipulate *Rolling Stone* for their own purposes. They knew it, too. So there was a curious edge to the balance of desires in the room. Jimi seemed embarrassed while Mitch and Noel plunged right into Burks's questions.

Jimi seemed content just to listen. Then it was Burks's turn to be embarrassed a bit; although it was significant that Mitch and Noel were there, Burks's questions actually were only for Hendrix.

"Well, this is the band that you're going to record with? And not Billy Cox or Buddy Miles? Or will they [Noel and Mitch] be recording too?"

Jimi expected the question. "Yeah, we have some tracks that we did, some jams we did with them. That's another thing. You know, you overdub the piano."

"I guess you'd call this the Experience and you'd call that the Band of Gypsys?" Burks pinned.

Jimi laughed.

John Burks addressed the room. "What I'd like to do is just launch into a whole thing here if you . . . How much time we got?"

"As long as you want," Mike Jeffery replied.

Burks plowed right in, noting that there had been a lot of talk that Jimi "may be forming closer ties with black militant groups, possibly the Panthers, and all that."

Mike Jeffery led Mitch and Noel in laughter. The press agent stuttered incoherently. Jimi was focused. He murmured, "Start with a shovel, end up with a spoon." And then to Burks, "I heard that too—tell me all about it." Then he laughed.

"I don't know, I didn't write that," Burks said quickly.

Mitch piped, "We got the White Tigers."

Everyone laughed except Jimi who cooed, "White-on-white."

Burks persisted, "But that's not—that's not so?"

Jimi was ready for him and he was not going into specifics. "No man, listen. Everyone has wars within themselves. So like, you know, we form different things and it comes out to be war against other people and so forth and so on."

There was laughter and joking Jimi looked Burks in the face.

"Well, what do you do, man?" Burks insisted.

Jimi, still laughing: "I can't solve that. I don't know. Anything: the Fat Gypsys and all those other cats."

Jimi had subtly conflated the Black Panther question with the personnel of his band. It could as well be the same thing.

Everyone laughed and talked.

Burks wanted to know about the jammers back at the house in Woodstock where Jimi had "a bunch" of blues guitarist and jazz players.

"Well, it was like a jam. They had different types of music coming in and out, mixing it with different types of sounds." Jimi named the main jammers back at the house: his old buddy from the south, Larry Lee, the percussionist, Juma Sultan and Jerry Velez, and of course Billy Cox. But he was not ready to go public with that sound, it had taken somewhat of a hit at Woodstock. Although his playing had been superb, the sound mix through the giant stadium speakers did not give justice to the sound they were able to make together.

When pressed about public performances of that jam group, recording, or simply what they sounded like, Jimi replied, "I'd like to say it's not effeminate." But he could see that Burks needed more on this; after all, he was a working journalist.

Jimi gave him some more: "I don't know. It's just like a jam I'd like to get together for a gig or something." He went on to mention the new material he was working on. "We're gonna take some time off and go out somewhere in the hills and woodshed, or whatever you call it, until I get some new songs and new arrangements and stuff like that, so we'd have something to offer. You know, something new. Regardless of if it's different or not."

Burks wanted to know how long Jimi would be doing that: "Next month or two months?" Noel jumped in. "Carry up until the end of the year at least . . . play at places we never worked at before maybe."

Jimi was amused. This interview for *Rolling Stone* was at Jeffery's insistence, but the music was Jimi's and he made all the decisions in that regard. Just as Buddy was out of the group, so was Noel. The jammers back at the house were a part of his new direction. They were beginning to record together and would be ready when his own Electric Ladyland studios opened later in the year.

He listened to Noel and Mitch chirp away. Mitch was talking about playing in Czechoslovakia, and other places the Experience had never played before. Jimi smiled, he was amused. He watched Burks politely extricate himself from Mitch and Noel's banter and got back to the Panthers. That was obviously the journalistic hook of the day.

Did Jimi feel the black Panthers were a good thing, or did he not relate to them at all—did he feel a part of what they were doing?

"Yeah, I naturally feel a part of what they're doing, in certain respects. But everybody has their own way of doing things. I just don't know. They get justified as they justify others in their attempts to get personal freedom. That's all it is."

"And to the extent they do that—you're with them?" Burks was relentless.

Jimi cut to the chase: "Yeah, but not for aggression or violence . . . I'm not for guerilla warfare."

Mitch Mitchell decided to lighten it up. Hunching up his shoulders, he said, "I'm a gorilla."

Jimi laughs. "I got a pet monkey named Charlie Chan."

His improvisation takes the subject out. Burks melds the death of R&B star

Otis Redding, who was starting a black recording company before he died in a plane crash, with Jimi's bust in Toronto. Mitch said they had played a club Otis Redding had just left a few weeks before he died. Jimi said it was less than a week after.

Would Jimi have any hang-up about returning to Toronto?

"Of course not. My *hang-up* is getting hung up with things that happened in the past."

Burks insisted that Hendrix, "of all the black musicians I can think of in the country," would be in the best situation to do his own recording and promotion company as Redding intended. Mitch and Noel responded with levity. Burks repeated the question but Jimi brushed it off. That was exactly what he was doing and he knew better than to announce it.

Burks got into Hendrix's testimony after his bust. "You told the court in Toronto that you'd, in your own term, had outgrown dope.

Jimi murmured, "At least stopped it from growing." He laughed softly.

Hilarity ensued. Comments were traded, and then silence.

"Is it true?"

Jimi asked, "What is that?

"About outgrowing dope."

"I don't know, I'm too . . . *wrecked* right now." Laughter all around. "I'll have to check into it." Then, seriously, "Oh yes, it's true, it's true, I don't take as much. That's what I was trying to tell them."

The interview began to mellow out as Jimi talked about his music. He was writing: "Mostly just cartoon material. Make up this one cat who's funny, who goes through all these strange scenes. I can't talk about it now. You could put it to music, I guess. Just like you can put blues into music."

But was Jimi getting into "long extended pieces or just songs?"

"Yeah, I want to get into what you'd probably call 'pieces,' yeah—pieces, behind each other to make movements, or whatever you call it. I've been writing some of those."

Then Jimi continued talking about these pieces going into movements—compositions he heard in his head. "The music I might hear I can't get on the guitar. It's just a thing of just laying around daydreaming or something. You're hearing all this music and you just can't get it on the guitar. As a matter of fact, if you pick up your guitar and just try to play, it spoils the whole thing. I can't play the guitar that well to get all this music together, so I just lay around. I wish I could have learned how to write for instruments, I'm going to get into that next, I guess."

Burks wanted to know how his fabled long Band of Gypsys rehearsals, "twelve to eighteen hours a day," factored into his new musical direction.

"Yeah we used to go and jam. Actually, we'd say 'rehearsing' just to make it sound, you know, official. We were just getting off, that's all. Not really eighteen hours—say about twelve or fourteen maybe [laughs]. The longest we [the Experience] every played together is going onstage. We played about two and a half hours, almost three hours one time."

Jimi tried summing it all up: "I like electric sounds, feedback and so forth, static."

Burks wanted to know how would he handle his concerts with the Experience so that he "won't feel hemmed in."

"As long as we three agree to it. I'd like for it to be permanent." Jimi summed up what he saw as a future direction. It was not the time to be "putting other groups on the tour, like our friends . . . because we're in the process of getting our own thing together as far as a three-piece group. But eventually, we have time on the side to play with friends. That's why I'll probably be jamming with Buddy and Billy; probably be recording too, on the side, and they'll be doing the same."

Burks got Jimi to talk about jazz. Jimi mentioned a jam of avant-garde jazz musicians he had seen in Sweden. Followers of that style of music were almost like cultists who had come from different spots in Europe—Copenhagen, Amsterdam, Stockholm—to play together. "Some of these cats we had never heard before . . . were actually in little country clubs and little caves blowing some sounds that, you know, you barely imagine. . . . Every once in a while they start going like a wave. They get into each other every once in a while within their personalities, and the party last night, or the hangover [laughs], and the evil starts pulling them away again. You can hear it start to go away. Then it starts getting together again. It's like a wave, I guess, coming in and out."

But Jimi was still in awe about jazz master multi-reed man Rahsaan Roland Kirk, although it had been years since they played together. "I had a jam with him at Ronnie Scott's in London, and I really got off. It was great. It was really great. I was so scared! It's really funny. I mean *Roland* [laughs]. That cat can get all those sounds. I might just hit one note and it might be interfering, but like we got along great, I thought. He told me I should have turned it up or something."

It was necessary for Burks to go to another touchy subject, the recent walk-out at the Madison Square Garden concert for the antiwar Vietnam Moratorium. "It's like it's the end of a beginning. I figure [it] was like the end of a big long fairy tale, which is great. It's the best thing I could possibly have come up with. The band was out of sight as far as I'm concerned."

"But what happened to you?" Burks persisted. Was Jimi going to divulge his obvious poisoning?

"It was just something where the head changes, just going through changes. I really couldn't tell, to tell you the truth. I was very tired. You know, sometimes there's a lot of things that add up in your head about this and that. And they hit you at a very peculiar time, which happened to me at that peace rally, and here I am fighting the biggest war I've ever fought in my life—inside, you know? And like that wasn't the place to do it, so I just unmasked appearances."

The interview closed on a musical note, as Burks commented that Jimi's musical tastes seemed "broader than the typical rock 'n' roll fan or listener."

Jimi responded, "This is all I can play when I'm playing. I'd like to get something together, like with Handel and Bach, and Muddy Waters, flamenco type of thing [laughs]. If I could get that *sound*. If I could get *that* sound, I'd be happy."

On February 21, the Hendrix office's press agent called John Burks back to see if it was too late to change his story. According to the press agent, Noel Redding had decided to tour with Jeff Beck, and Billy Cox would be the bass player on the spring tour. The press agent said that Redding would probably return to the group, so nothing really had changed.

It would be called Electric Lady Studios. It brought to mind the beautiful period during the recording of the *Electric Ladyland* album at the Record Plant and the grand experimentation that went on. From the environmental setting for "Voodoo Chile" to the sound-painting composition "1983—A Merman I Should Turn to Be," the sounds of the depths of the ocean, sonar, buoys, gull cries, and submarine hydraulics included some monstrous engineering feats that both Hendrix and Ed Kramer, individually and together, fought for, including the burning-guitar sound of "House Burning Down," and the sound of space in ". . . And the Gods Made Love."

He wanted Electric Lady Studios to be physically as beautiful as the sounds of music to be made within it. The outside would have a distinct shape—like a giant guitar wedged into the row of four-story brownstones that lined West Eighth Street. The studios would be below in the cavernous basement. They would be designed along circular cyclical lines that curved onward and out of sight in the dim light. Only the most modern equipment would be in the engineering booths and beyond on the studio floor. The three stories above would house the offices of Jimi's organization, as well as the offices for the running of the studio, which would book groups for sessions just like the Record Plant. John Storyk designed the physical layout for the studio in collaboration with Jimi.

Had Jimi known how much of a hassle building a studio would turn out to be, he might have changed his mind, or at least given it more thought. Although the site had housed the Generation (the same club where Jimi and B. B. King and Buddy Guy had played their blues guitar laments the night Martin Luther King Jr. was killed), all the walls of the basement had to be ripped out. The contractors took delight in charging superextra fees for circular walls that were ultrasoundproof, as well. Even before they began to build, incredibly extensive alterations had to be made on the building at 55 West Eighth Street, both inside and outside. Permits to build a uniquely designed exterior were an incredible hassle to get. Jimi insisted on special colors for the walls downstairs in the studio section, whose building he was personally supervising. The walls had to be white carpet so they could reflect varicolored lights totally, green, red, purple, pink. A Hawaiian artist painted the mural of a space voyage on the hallway walls. Jimi ordered the best of everything for recording purposes, including the largest Moog synthesizer on the East Coast and thirty-six Dolbys. There were two studios, A and B. All the mirrors on the walls faced each other, reflecting infinity. And then they discovered that the studio was over a subway tunnel. It would be even more expensive to soundproof.

There was another problem with the studios: the neighbors. Not the bookstore next door or the Nedick's hot dog shop on the corner, but the Mafia. It was rumored that they controlled the businesses along the commercial strip of West Eighth Street. There are subtle ways neighbors can make trouble. Jimi was glad that he had friends in the area, even glad the brother who sold the Panther newspaper was there.

It was said that the Mafia did not want Electric Lady Studios on West Eighth Street. Jimi's management was only able to obtain a five-year lease on the space, and they could not buy it. Although Jimi had no real contact with his management, who were actually controlling the day-to-day operations concerning the building of the studio, he was held personally responsible by the Mafia. The Mafia did not want too much police concentration on the street. They knew that there was a drug scene connected with musicians and rock music. The Mafia also knew that the FBI had been sniffing around the studios already. They felt that Jimi would make it too hot for them to run business as usual. It was kind of unusual for the FBI to be involved in drugs; that was usually the domain of the local police. The Mafia sensed that something heavier was happening than just smoking pot or snorting coke. The Mafia had unusual trouble finding out the real reasons for the FBI's snooping around.

All was not lost. Jimi had a go-between, Tom Nitelife, a small-time pimp and dealer, who talked to the Mafia regularly. Nitelife often assisted in the purchase of prime grass and coke and was a personal taster for Jimi. Not only did he help get it but he also guaranteed it through his internal system. He was a mainstay in Washington Square Park and was known as a person who could "fix things." The presence of the FBI on the scene put the Mafia in a double bind. Although they had control over most of the strip between Fifth and Sixth Avenues, they had no control over Electric Lady, and if they tried to use some muscle they would have to out-sleuth the FBI. Jimi's studio existed in limbo between two very powerful adversaries.

One night Jimi showed up at a gig some friends were playing at an out-of-the-way club in downtown Manhattan. They were surprised to see him just come in, out of the blue. He did not have his ax or his two TEAC recorders, so they knew he did not come to sit in.

As soon as they left the bandstand he popped a question to them: "Do you know of a hit man I can contact?" They hushed him up right away and whisked him out of there to a nearby place where they could talk privately. They knew that if word got out that Jimi was looking for a hit man then *his* life would be in danger—whether he meant it or not. Also, they did not want to know about the situation and they did not ask. If they gave him the name of someone and something had gone down, then they would have not only been involved but also be guilty of whatever outcome occurred.

They sat down and talked about it. The friends said, "Hey, there are hit men all over the place, but we're not going to turn you on to one because you'll get yourself in trouble." Then they talked over the situation in general. The main concern from their point of view was Jimi's depression, the way he would just up and leave places where his friends were. The way he seemed to be so overcome with unhappiness. They felt that a hit man was not the answer. That Jimi's state of mind would not be assuaged by hiring a killer. It would not end there.

Finally Jimi said, "Fuck it." It was kind of incredible to them that someone was messing with his head so bad that he wanted to have them done away with. He decided to put it in a song, in his music instead. Like sublimation, he would work it out where he was powerful and confident—in the music. Not in the underworld.

April 25, 1970, the Forum, Los Angeles. Jimi and company launched "The Cry of Love tour," a selective tour that would last until August 1. Then the completion, hopefully, of the album *First Rays of the New Rising Sun* for worldwide release sometime that fall.

All the wild party times in L.A. now ceased without Buddy Miles around. It was kind of lonely secluded in the penthouse above Beverly Hills, facing out over Los Angeles, the amorphous smog making an infinite gray haze right in front of your face.

This is the first big gig with Mitch Mitchell back on his oversize double-kit drum. Jimi hopes Mitch's chops are up. They have not been on a stage together since the Denver Pop Festival nearly a year ago.

The crowd is enthusiastic at the sold-out Forum. It almost seems strange to Jimi. His thoughts about his music are far from where the audience is at. The last album release, *Electric Ladyland,* clashes with Jimi's new material that will be on the new albums, *Band of Gypsys* and *First Rays of the New Rising Sun.* The material for *First Rays* is considerable, enough for a double album, actually. He will include some new numbers in this concert and see.

Jimi starts out with "Spanish Castle Magic." There are cheers of recognition as he drones the intro. The staggered beat of the first few lines fades into the long boogie lines of the chorus. The crowd is happy at once. He could play this tune for the entire show and no one would complain.

The boogie is continued with "Foxy Lady." Mitch is not drumming with the confidence he had had in the past. Billy Cox on bass is consistent and steady as a rock, without the adventurism of a Noel Redding. Billy continues to improve the more he plays. As an extension of Jimi's guitar in the lower registers, he can be counted on to always be there for Jimi's frequent unison and harmony lines.

Jimi announces a song that he has been lately calling "Getting Your Brothers' Shoes Together." Actually it is "Lover Man." The significance of this title selection is in regard to the increasing struggle he is having in bringing the music to the public. Segueing into "Getting My Heart Back Together," which is better known as "Hear My Train A-comin'," Jimi has outlined his metaphysical dilemma: love is the emotion that commands his devotion to the struggle to take the music around. Like in the blues, shoes, a difficult acquisition for the rural black, signified the ability to move and to do. Like Hermes, the early Greek messenger of the gods, who flew with wings attached to his feet to render absolute love in his deliverance of the sacred words, which like sacraments nourished the multitudes.

In "Getting My Heart Back Together," Jimi is even more direct. Death is his adviser. Death, like the mythological train, chugs in the piston beats of boogie, measured and deliberate. Death is a celebration in that it propels him toward his destiny.

"Room Full of Mirrors," Jimi's theme song of sorts for the new year, is a twenty-two-minute-long set that includes, in medley, "Hey Baby (New Rising Sun)," a jam that ends in a drum solo, and then "Freedom." The wide range of the medley removes the sharp-edged drive from each tune, but overall it is a tour de force.

"Voodoo Chile (Slight Return)" includes a section of a new song, "Midnight Lightning." The two songs flow into each other effortlessly, creating an added message to his natal song of creation.

"Machine Gun" is played like a hypnotic stately caravan with meditative delays in the beat. Military taps, the drape, the rolls of a state funeral. Fading down, the beat lowers like a flag in the wind, as Jimi's solo comes up like human cries, screams, and emotional feelings of tragedy produced by his Stratocaster. Then he goes into the intro to "The Star-Spangled Banner," spinning off into the blues with a satirical Yankee twang to it.

It becomes clear that the cumulative message of the new Jimi Hendrix is much heavier than ever before. No longer straight-up boogie myths and rock 'n' roll blues, but now the political and occult overtones engender more meditative ponderance and less release and abandon. The cheers of the audience, though not the howls of Monterey, are nevertheless totally supportive. But it is difficult to assess from onstage the penetration that has been made into the ongoing consciousness of the crowd.

Jimi went into virtual seclusion after the first L.A. Forum concert. The feedback from the concert was muted but favorable. But of more concern to Jimi was a quiet contemplation in the penthouse above Beverly Hills. His mood was expressed in the sheaves of hotel stationery he filled with his thoughts. This hotel stationery would join other papers in his Morocco leather case where he kept all of his writing, his journals, lines, some for songs, some just thoughts. Some drawings flowing from his elegant handwriting that was full of flourishes and revealed many of his innermost thoughts, the themes that he continuously worked with, coming from his own personal experience, and his spiritual goals, some melding into songs, some of which would be performed and others that would remain more rumination and reverie, sometimes poetry.

He flipped through the papers in the Morocco leather case. He stopped and studied the line "You'd think I found the lost chord" before going on. A few lines from a long passage made him stop: "Love is being tested here." He did not mean familial love, but love "for our *whole* world." People "must never be afraid of paths chosen by God" because, he wrote, they could see the path better with their hearts than through their eyes. Jimi had his own creation theory that had humanity originally living on an asteroid belt that was like a planet the "approximate size of Earth." It was a virtual paradise. But although Venus was "the ultimate physical power of that world . . . it was then believed that love itself did not exist." But that changed when the different races met; they were like different worlds coming together. But their hubris was attempting to go to other planets by building "rockets the size of Maine."

"O transistor feeder can you hear me thank you."

He saw an entire poem tucked into the back, about Love and God, his big themes: "Love is trying / Thank the Lord." His concern for the people expanded outward into space. He felt the moon as a sensate being: it was "wounded, crying" but at the same time "bleeding an infant sword." He would weave in and out of a theme he called "Moondust." It was a part of "a giant production of heaven" he felt he was a participant of. "Heaven in reality is a rocket-ship, always swirling through space looking for a stepping-stone." He liked the concept of a stepping-stone and was writing a composition with lyrics around it. He regarded the races of Earth's humanity as also interchangeable with worlds, planets—"but needing to clear every world of hate and repression." Earth he considered "the last to be called" a most troublesome world—"the vision of earth's tears are rivers of futures being born." He would have to constantly ask himself, and also as an often unstated question to those close to him, "Is this the only world you care about?"

He would always reread the source of what he wrote for the Royal Albert Hall program. It expressed exactly what he felt. "No, I believe in myself more than anything. And I suppose, in a way that's also believing in God. If there is a God and He made you, then if you believe in yourself, you're also believing in Him. So I think that everybody should believe in himself. That doesn't mean you have to believe in heaven and hell and all that stuff. But it does mean that what you are and what you do is your religion. . . . When I get up on stage—well, that's my whole life. *That's* my religion. My music is electric church music, if by 'church' you mean 'religion.' I am electric religion."

But this night he wrote intensely, urging himself on to "ride instead the waves" of his interpretation of his belief in God. The hypnotic music, a sound of God, that he represents as truth, life, "regardless of your questionable timid compromises." It was as if Jimi were both fan and star. The boy he used to be who was unsure, but seeking, and the fans who flock to him, his music—seeking. Jimi wants to "erase" that which holds back. He regards himself as "a messenger" to those in various aspects of their evolution who could be called "sheep in process." There are lines that repeat all though this leather binder. His concentration on his mission as a spiritual messenger of God and the need to constantly monitor the deep sadness always with him due to his rough, poverty-stricken, emotionally unstable childhood, the death of his mother when he was still a boy—"almost at death with yourself and on the staircase of birth." He was the timid fan with the guitar and a dream. And now he was at a pinnacle of a difficult and exhilarating wave of popularity, of recognition of his unique musical intelligence. But sadness and depression also dogged him: "Soon you may also forget the smell of your family."

Meryl, a lovely Eurasian doe, shared his quiet suite with him in hushed reverence. Her Zen attitude was reflective of his mood. Vishwa was around, too. Sincere and intuitive, he sought to bring to Jimi what would help him to be happier.

Vishwa ran into Taj Mahal in Hollywood at the old Ashgrove, where for years Taj had been a fixture in a range of tasks, from doorman to performer. Taj sensed an urgency when Vishwa asked him to come to see Jimi. Taj went right away, driving up with Vishwa through the cityscape foothills into the semirural, suburblike expanse of Beverly Hills. He sensed a heavy mood before he got there.

On several occasions before, Taj had expressed, in his understated way, his concern for Jimi and his disdain for the scene Jimi was surrounded by. The hangers-on were legion and, in a way, were understood to be part of his rock-star imagery. But Taj also saw a carelessness behind it that bothered him. He loved Jimi brother to brother, and as a brother also saw that "Jimi's back was not covered." This left Jimi open to a number of dangers that could eventually culminate in his being snuffed—and only because of carelessness. Being surrounded by people who were into very unnatural ways, Jimi was walking a tightrope, which was painful for Taj to see.

Devon was considered, by Taj, to be walking in a similar way. Her confusion, masked by bravado, concealed an intelligent and sensitive soul. That she was beautiful, as well, made her all the more poignant. She and Colette would come by to see Taj whenever they were in the same town. They always brought a little present. Some wine and cheese, some good smoke, and in a way Devon brought herself—as if she were available for whatever might help him along. Taj, unused and unwilling to being approached in that way, would always rebel. He wanted her to show *herself* some respect. So *he* could in turn respect her. Otherwise, it was impossible for them to get together on any meaningful level. Her heroin, her sex thing ("with all her body hanging out of her clothes"), her strange desperation, made him unwillingly ambivalent. He respected Jimi for taking a lot of time with Devon, but feared that Jimi would be sucked into a deathful void.

As he and Vishwa neared the hotel, Taj recalled the last time he and Jimi had been together: the previous year at Devonshire Downs, in the San Fernando Valley, for the Newport Jazz Festival. They were on the same bill with the Chambers Brothers and had ridden to the site together in two limos. As they rolled up to the gate the Los Angeles Police Department was seriously busting heads with specially prepared billy clubs. As Jimi and Taj coasted by in their limos their windows became life-size TV screens through which they saw the upfront violence of heads being directly smashed, blood splattering on the windshield, young people recoiling in panic, bodies falling, screams, and agonized groans. This is what they were entering. This is what the music was making happen. They all had been sick. Jimi had not really been able to play. He had had to come back the next day to make up for his truncated performance. Taj's revulsion had been steeled. He had no illusions about the violence, but he felt that Jimi's whole spiritual stance had not prepared him for the true human nature that was apparent in what surrounded the music. Festival producer George Wein wanted the crowd and the money. The surplus crowd got the shit kicked out of them. Jimi was still not prepared for these facts. And the time was late. He was too open. Too trusting. Too naïve. Taj hoped he would simply be able to survive.

Taj was surprised by the austerity of the penthouse suite at the Beverly Rodeo Hotel. Jimi's mood was as austere as the standard plush hotel furnishings. Taj had brought his Dobro acoustic, and Jimi was glad he had. Subdued by a light nervousness but still self-effacingly polite, Jimi got out his acoustic and turned on his reel-to-reel TEAC recorder. Taj put on his cassette recording of crickets singing in Topanga Canyon as background. Taj set the pace with a ruminating standard country blues. Taj liked to lie back and savor the meaning of the blues with an economy of notes that you could feel in the air. To him this was the strength and reason within the acoustic guitar. To feel the vibrations in the air, and within. But Jimi soon took over the pace. He could not seem to relax within the dictates of the blues of the old masters they both loved so much. Jimi took to playing fast runs and atonalities against the measure. Taj still stayed in his economy, not letting Jimi take him over. Seeming to give Jimi the lead, but this was not the case. Taj was sticking to his guns, and Jimi was moving all over the place—each to his own head. Objectively, it was probably an interesting contrast, but subjectively, Taj was further troubled by Jimi and where his head was at. The rural blues was like a test to a musician, like Muddy Waters would say. Taj dedicated himself to the axioms of the blues masters. And that was why his concern for Jimi went sky high. Jimi's *feel* was off. Whether because of depression, troubles, or worries—whatever—his feelings were off. Jimi's few other guests were being unnaturally thoughtful. Then, as if to punctuate and nail down his apprehensions, several Mafia-looking dudes swept into the room without knocking and proceeded to spread out on the coffee table a smorgasbord of killer dope. Taj was taken aback by the insult to the sanctity of the music and the space. Jimi was, as usual, apologetic and polite to all.

The next day Vishwa came by the penthouse with Ananda Shankar, the nephew of Ravi Shankar (who had dropped them off there). Ananda was very pleased to meet Jimi, and the feeling was mutual. Ananda had brought his sitar, of which he was a master, just as his uncle was. Ananda sat on the floor of the sumptuous room and tuned the sitar. He began to play, sitting Indian fashion, commanding the meditation it takes to play the difficult timings of the age-old ragas. Jimi soon plugged in his Princeton practice amp and began to play along. He played over, under, and around Ananda's timing. This truly astounded Ananda. It usually took years to master the timing of the raga. At the end of their session Ananda expressed his amazed pleasure at playing with someone as versatile as Jimi. They parted with a great musical respect for each other.

The night after the last Forum concert of the tour, Jimi was in a strange mood when he returned to the penthouse. Vishwa was inclined to leave him be—he had noticed that Jimi's nerves were raw these days—but when Vishwa heard screams coming from the bedroom he ran in. Jimi had the beautiful Eurasian girl, Meryl, down on the floor and was beating her head against it. Vishwa tackled Jimi and held him as Meryl ran naked out of the door. Jimi turned on Vishwa and began beating him. Although Vishwa was larger than Jimi and could have probably made a fight out of it, he elected to take Jimi's blows, defending himself as best he could without fighting back. Soon Jimi's rage was over.

The next day Jimi was all apologetic. Vishwa understood. He had a large sympathy for Jimi and the frustrations he faced as an artist. He also understood the great restraint that Jimi had to have in public and how the opposite would sometimes come out when Jimi was with his friends. It was not everyone to whom Jimi could vent his feelings of frustration. Vishwa forgave Jimi and forgot the incident. But he had seen the violent side of Jimi before and was more worried about his state of mind than about a few blows.

That night Herbie Worthington came by and gave Jimi a lovely ring that he had made out of petrified moss.

"What are you giving me this for?" Jimi asked.

"For your birthday," Herbie replied.

"It's not my birthday today."

"Well, keep it until your birthday."

Jimi was so touched that he looked like he wanted to cry. He tried the ring on. It was too big.

"That's all right," he said. "I'll eat more so my fingers will get fatter."

He rides with Devon and Colette in the deep black limo, Vishwa on the jump seat, the bright sun of Berkeley, California, washing their dark clothes in white light. They are dressed for night. Devon's black lace blouse is open down the front, Saks Fifth Avenue supershades, hair back but loose. Jimi's glossy black shirt merges into his hair, which covers his ears in a medium-long stylishly cut Afro. Clean-shaven, his high cheekbones are stark against his lean face. Indian countenance. The trace of a goatee gives his pale, dark-sand-colored face even more angularity. Devon could be his sister, they look so much alike. She wears crazy chic jeans with embroidered erratic patches in blues and greens. Jimi walks through the Berkeley Community Theater stage door in low moccasins that look cartoonish, turquoise beads across the top like rows of corn kernels.

The soundcheck is also a rehearsal. He goes over the bass lines with Billy Cox, playing higher octaves on his guitar as he gives eye and head signals, the same signals he occasionally uses onstage. They play the intro phrases to "Dolly Dagger," the bridge to "Freedom," a snatch from "The Star-Spangled Banner." Billy and Mitch run them over while Jimi checks the amps and the bottoms. He always depends on Eric Barrett to instantly fix problems with the sound system. Ten electricians and engineers scramble behind stage and scamper on knees across the facing bank of the giant stacks of Marshall cabinets. The dual stadium PA system's mammoth speakers are directed straight out across three thousand empty seats. They hit a song, the intro goes to a peak, where it stops. Jimi shouts, "Eric, the amps, man!"

Berkeley was close to being under martial law on May 30, 1970. The People's Park protest coupled with the Cambodian invasion had led to rioting and trashing. There was an obvious beefing up of police everywhere.

Bill Graham sensed an even stranger mood among the crowd as he entered the Berkeley Community Theater later that afternoon.

Gate crashings common to many eastern arenas did not usually occur in northern California. The restraint of the Bay Area's rock music lovers was one of the major reasons Graham had stayed on the West Coast and terminated the fabled Fillmore East. By 1970, Bill Graham was phasing out the operation of his own halls, opting for the larger and easier to operate Winterland in San Francisco, the Berkeley Community Theater, the huge Cow Palace just outside San Francisco, and the modern Oakland Arena and Coliseum.

Graham's staff had noticed an unusual and continued demand for tickets. That night several thousand fans surrounded the Berkeley Community Theater.

It was an agitated, unruly, bellicose crowd, which began breaking windows, leaping walls, and charging the front doors when the announcement came that the two concerts were sold out.

Graham was shocked. They were the same mellow people who always came to his concerts. This was not like them. The crowd breathed an urgency that turned into manic disappointment that verged on mass hysteria. Many felt that it would be the last time they would have a chance to see Jimi play.

When the doors opened, Graham's security force was confronted with the most serious crowd-control problem they had ever encountered. The crowd was not only trying to rush the doors, breaking glass in the process and making it difficult for ticket holders to gain entry, but they were also on the roof of the theater. Some had scaled the thirty-foot windows and broken them trying to get in. Chaos reigned for the entire double concert, further compounded by Wally Heider's remote recording crew outside, and a film company shooting what was to be the film *Jimi Plays Berkeley*.

Jimi dedicates the concert to the Black Panthers and those fighting in People's Park. The first song was "The Star-Spangled Banner." It was greeted with a great ovation. It so befitted the mood of the entire city, the entire nation—at war. Using the guitar as a synthesizer, Hendrix gliss-slides rapidly up and down the neck of the guitar while he whangs the tremolo bar and shakes the instrument rudely, sometimes banging it against his hip. He does not *play* in the classic sense, but goes straight to the basic synthesizer sounds produced by the interplay between the guitar and amps. He begins with a crackling feedback effect, manipulating the position of his body in relation to the mike and amplifiers so that he gets a sound that is the sum total of all the systems in overload situations. The sound is rerouted through the mike monitors, setting up an independent sound that Hendrix plays against. The cry of the system is heard from the onset, going out of concert key on ". . . dawn's early light." Slightly bending the neck, Jimi brings it back into control, but it is clear that he intends to play against the distort of the system. Even though the words are not sung, everyone follows in their minds the lyrics so ingrained in their consciousness since childhood. Jimi wheezes his guitar on ". . . proudly . . ." staggering the sound into baroque figures. The feedback single tone is an atonal in strange harmony with the melody. Beginning with ". . . hailed . . ." the single feedback tone establishes itself in solitary station above Jimi's sound, to merge with it at certain peaks. At ". . . the twilight's last gleaming? . . ." the feedback tone entirely takes over the sound for two beats. At ". . . whose broad stripes and bright stars," he sustains "stars" as if it is a shooting star attempting to maintain its height, but plummeting and wavering in flight. Then at "And the rockets' red glare . . ." he lets the system implode. The sound screams like a fighter plane strafing, coming out of a deep dive, the impact of bombs striking the earth, the cries of the Cambodian peasants merging with the impact of the bombs, metal striking metal, the high whine of machine guns chattering, the bombers fighting out of their dives to be able to strike again. At ". . . The bombs bursting in air," Jimi plays bonking, monotonous sounds of civilization back home going on as usual, traffic and machines, crowds going home after work, all safe and complacent amid the master machines. On "Gave proof through the night," Jimi strings through in straight melody with no feedback tone at all. At ". . . that our flag," he sustains the note "still there" and then slowly ascends ever so subtly into a piercing peal, where Jimi says, ever so casually into a perfect break, "Big deal!" The crowd cracks up at his humor. "O say does that star-spangled banner yet wave," he produces a sirocco wind coming up from the desert by flicking the toggle switch. "O'er the land of the free" breaks into a lovely figure produced by both the feedback of the system and his single-note sustain; "and the home of the brave," Jimi grinds his Stratocaster's strings against the mike stand in rude bottleneck.

As the crowd begins to applaud, Jimi jumps right into "Purple Haze." The crowd voices forming a single sound of pure delight.

Jimi hits the intro run to "Johnny B. Goode" and the crowd roars with approval. And at that moment Berkeley becomes the rock 'n' roll capital of the world. Upbeat on the tempo, Jimi faces his Stratocaster to the crowd, picking incredibly fast and hitting chords that require superhuman stretches of his large hands up the frets. He moves between picking and rhythm chordings that run the entire fret board. Between the rapid-fire lyrics, the chorus *"GO JOHNNY GO!"* becomes a chant, like an ancient high school cheer. Yet it is so keyed to the warfare outside the theater, in the world, on the campus, in the streets. This archetypal scene of rock 'n' roll history, thousands of young heads in high school auditoriums moving to the beat that changed the world. *"Go Johnny Go!"* The war will end: the spirit of the people is too high. *"Go Johnny Go!"* The song could have also been Jimi's life story.

Chuck Berry, the author, placed the song way down in Louisiana—close to New Orleans, the birthplace of jazz—where, in an old cabin deep in the evergreen woods, lives a "country boy named Johnny B. Goode." He had not learned to read or write very well, "but he could play a guitar" with amazing ease, "just like ringing a bell." Berry tells of how Johnny B. Goode would carry his guitar in a common brown fabric bag used for bulk grain or beans, often called a gunnysack. The term goes back to the time of slavery. Jimi had carried his guitar in a gunnysack when he joined Little Richard's band for the first time, and got ridiculed for it. But as with people's comments about Johnny B. Goode, everyone had to say Jimi really could play. Johnny's mother encouraged him by saying that when he became a man he would be the head of a "big ol' band." The song ends with his mother's words continuing to prophesy: many would come from all over to hear her son's music and that perhaps someday her son's name would be in lights on a big marquee that would say JOHNNY B. GOODE TONITE.

The album entitled *Band of Gypsys,* recorded live at Fillmore East, was released in June 1970. Jimi was not entirely satisfied with it. He had no control over the mixing and mastering, and no control over the album cover or the liner notes. Capitol Records could do virtually whatever they wanted. The ugly album cover made it look as if he were bowing in supplication.

Jimi's record royalties were still in escrow until the cash settlement owed Ed Chalpin had been entirely paid. Yet Jimi desperately needed cash to pay for the studio's completion. That meant that he would have to gig like mad wherever the bread was right. His management wanted the album out because they feared he would not draw as well without a new album, since the last album, *Electric Ladyland,* had been released well over a year ago. Jimi did not want *Band of Gypsys* to be thrown out like that, yet there was nothing he could do. A feeling of powerlessness welled up in him. And he had no way of expressing it.

The first total session at Electric Lady Studios took place on July 1, 1970. Not everything was finished yet. There was still a lot to do with the three floors of office space above. But behind the guitar-shaped front brickwork that rolled out at you like the hips of a vivacious lady, and down the long flight of stairs seemingly into the earth, the main studio was ready to go. The rest would have to be completed as they went along. Everyone agreed that the first step would be to have a functioning studio where Jimi could work in earnest.

Big Claire commemorated the event with a big feed, just like in the brief good old days upstate—days not really that long ago.

Jimi recorded important songs that he had nurtured through the long winter up in Shokan. "Pali-gap" was a stone meditative piece flowing in rural magic. "Hey Baby" was the song that signified his new musical head direction. Subtitled somewhere between "First Rays of the New Rising Sun" and "Land of the New Rising Sun," "Hey Baby" was conceived as a piece that would form the basis of a concerto.

"Dolly Dagger" was a slick-flowing, capricious funk achieved through incredibly tight ensemble playing that got a unified and clear sound without the heavy metal bridges. It was about Devon, to Devon (in a way), and kind of cleared his head about her.

A lively diddy-bop bass line dubbing with lead guitar tools out the three-tiered theme. The Fuzz-Toned talking bass starts out in harmony with the bass drum's kicks—a mock sinister intro, the bass grinding down the octave. Jimi beckons Devon. She is crazy but always at his beck and call. "Here comes"—Jimi sings quickly, and then the loving legato vibrato—"Doll-ie Dagger." And then a quip as if an aside, "Her love's so heavy, gonna make you stagger." He repeats "Dolly" and the Ghetto Fighters come in with flowing, pretty male voices, singing harmony with Jimi on "Dagger." They hold the name as a theme. Jimi intones knowledgeably that she drinks her blood from a jagged edge, an image of the vampirism of shooting dope: blood flowing through a tube, flowing in and out back and forth between body and tube, blood full of heroin and the final plunge. Billy's bass winds the theme down to the ground.

Juma's congas filled the interludes with Jimi's rap on top. The bass takes over and fuzzes down to the utter bottom as Jimi says, *"Drink up, baby."*

Then Jimi sings of her background as a girl on her own at fifteen, earning her witch's symbolic vehicle of mobility. He was also emotionally isolated as a teen and found love as a way to cope and overcome. However it came about, Devon became a dominant player in the game, compelling both men and women. In the next verse Jimi asks if words of love ever touch "Dolly Brown." He gives her a common name to indicate her basic nature as an everyday person, but then the question turns out to be rhetorical because the narrator recommends taking an expressway out of town without waiting for an answer. The capriciousness of Jimi's lead against the sinister bass bottom is in high contrast. But at the end, as Jimi intones about her conquering drive contrasting with her ultimate master, he eggs her on to drink up that jagged-edged blood, and his last aside is sotto and to the point: "Watch out Devon, and give me a little bit of that heaven." Jimi pulls out into a solo that is light and whimsical, with a touch of sinister on the bends.

Devon would pull shit. She would cop sympathy and love and hate, all the while knowing very well her wit and courage would get her over. Loving her, not wanting to hurt her, her friends and detractors called her "queen of the groupies." Her lovers called her the teacher of sex.

Jimi eventually went out on her and beat her ass, but even that extreme behavior could not tip the scales irrevocably against Devon in his mind. The song he wrote for her was bittersweet, but he knew she'd like it. She would be scandalized in ecstasy.

"She drinks her blood from a jagged edge. . . ." Dolly Dagger, Mick Jagger's black wife, sucking his blood from a cut on his finger. But all in all, the song showed a real love for her life, her verve, her motion, her funk, but in bitter sarcasm. Jimi hated the choices she made, for they revealed her values.

Billy Cox on bass, Mitch Mitchell on drums, and Juma on percussion, with the Ghetto Fighters (the Allen twins) doing vocal harmonic effects on "Dolly Dagger." The sound of the congas fit the sound of the brand-new studio perfectly. Juma said it was because they were underground, with the earth's spirit.

July 1970, Maui, Hawaii. This was the last leg of the brief tour that had seemed to take an eternity. The tour had exhausted him. And suddenly you are in a plane, staring at an incorporeal self in the conical window, the landscape of sky merging with your reflection. Going yet another place, no matter where your head was at. Another terminal. Another set of changes. Another row of limos waiting, motors running.

Chuck Wein, son of producer George Wein, was not exactly the mogul type. He was round and soft, though not fat, slightly tipsy, yet happily in control. "Jimi," he gasped, as if he were in the presence of a Greek god.

The island was physically impressive. Maui. He recalled reading and talking about the lost civilizations: Lemuria, Atlantis. He would have dearly loved to hang out, but he was working. Whatever sentiments to the contrary, he was indeed working—every minute.

One of the ceremonies upon Jimi Hendrix's arrival was to have his fortune told by the resident soothsayer. Clara Schuff, a German émigré octogenarian would intuit through the midsection navel area. She draws an etheric representation of Jimi, his past and present and future lives, on an ordinary piece of paper. She draws in red and blue colored pencils as she talks. Circles, bodies and heads, all circular and cyclical. Down through the ages, heads of Jimi's past lives, or those who have deeply affected his earthly sojourns.

She tells him to be careful of women. They mean him no good. She repeats this several times. She tells him also that he is descended from Egyptian and Tibetan royalty, and that his next life will be most concerned with the magical systems of Tibet. She repeats the warning about women. For a moment "Bold As Love" comes into his mind. He had written of the queen behind him in jealousy and envy. It sounds so simple. No big mystical thing. What Clara Schuff told him was what he had once told himself.

He had the feeling that she was in touch with something deep. Not by her appearance, which was grandmotherly and old Germanic, but by her utter simplicity. She obviously enjoyed the fuss being made over her by all the young hippies. Yet what they talked about sounded much more complex and much more unreal. She was down-to-earth, uncomplicated, and very real.

But the place was a mess. Mostly everyone was stoned, even the camera crew shooting the film. He did not know what the sound would be like. Warner Bros. was paying for part of the flick and the recording, but Jimi was paying the bulk of the cost, through some weird machination of Mike Jeffery's to get him film exposure. Something did not seem right. There seemed to be no thought-out thing about what was to be done or who was in charge. Oh no!

Chuck Wein had introduced Touraine to Jimi a month before the concert. She was physically beautiful and heavy of mind, as well. She had a three-hundred-page book that contained Jimi's music decoded into color vibrations that corresponded to internal bodily functions, neurological and philosophical elements, and radiant-energy levels. She was into color-sound healing and found that Jimi's music fit perfectly with her activities in that field. She and Jimi got into an instant and extended spellbinding rap. They talked about magic and the occult. They fantasized about being able to beam sounds of music over five thousand square miles. Touraine believed that the work she had done on color and sound healing would have a profound effect on all of the people who were within the sound of Jimi's music. Jimi told her that he was from another planet, an asteroid belt off Mars, and that he had come here to show people some new energy. They talked about the Axis a lot. They finally decided to buy an Arabian horse (Touraine was also an Arabian horse costume designer), name it Axis: Bold As Love, give it a purple haze as a third eye, and never have it ridden. She would train the horse according to her sound and color charts to respond to those vibrations rather than the usual horse-trainer ones.

"The Rainbow Bridge Vibratory Color-Sound Experiment" was largely the inspiration of Touraine. The assembled sat in circles grouped into their astrological signs so Jimi could feel their celestial vibes. They were right on the side of the Olowalu Volcano, the Crater of the Sun. Jimi wore a special Hopi Indian medicine-man shirt, which was turquoise and black, that Touraine had gotten for him. Chuck Wein made the introductory remarks.

"Welcome, cosmic brothers and sisters of Maui, to the Rainbow Bridge Vibratory Color-Sound Experiment. We're here for a very, very particular purpose. I think it applies to all our brothers and sisters all across the planet. The Rainbow Bridge is not just a bridge. Just as there are cells that make up our body, we are cells in the body of the planetary beings. And the purpose of the humanity for being on this planet is to build that bridge between the heart and the higher mental and spiritual centers of the planetary being. And every higher thought and higher action that each of us participates in builds that bridge. And the reason that we've all kind of dropped out to here; it's the first time that anybody has dropped out in any large numbers since the Christians dropped out of Rome, then we want to convey that vow to everyone else. So instead of just being like a reflective, groovy audience that we have at every love-in and concert forever and ever up to now, if we just turn on harmony so Jimi can stick it to that and lead us across that bridge and everybody all over the world is going to pick up on that. So we're all counting on you and here's your chance, and Jimi should be here in a few minutes. Thank you."

After Chuck Wein's intro everyone does "om" until Jimi comes onto the portable stage. The volcano looms in the background. Everyone, including the film and sound crew, is pretty well wrecked on LSD, hash, and booze, but most manage to function. The audience is rather stoned and laid-back. They hardly remember to applaud.

"We have Billy Cox on bass. Billy Cox. Mitch Mitchell on drums and me, Jimi, on public saxophone." He mumbles something about playing an instrumental because the words are not quite together. The seasoned Hollywood film crew cannot hide their amusement with the scene.

Jimi starts out with a majestic-sounding theme that does not seem possible to be coming from an electric guitar. More like cellos, several cellos and violas churning. The orchestra sound swells, rises, and falls, seemingly with no connection to any song or melody. Then seemingly out of nowhere, Billy kicks down on the bass in a slow, moderate, yet funky rocking bottom that refers back to the theme in the last figures of the run as Jimi plays, fills, and augments the sound on top of a melody that sounds simple compared to the intro. Jimi steps to the mike and raps/sings, slurring words over the appropriate beats: "Hey Gypsy Baby." He wants to know where she is coming from. She answers that she is from "the land of the new rising sun." He then asks about her mission, and she replies that she simply wants to distribute love and peace of mind to everyone. Jimi's request is a refrain that spirals between the lovely melody: he simply wants to come along with her. Can he "come along"? The reply is in the affirmative and continues with the refrain. This is the essence of the lyrics of this deceptively straightforward song, which points the way to a new kind of Hendrix tune: extended instrumental ensemble playing along with the words. "We're gonna go across the Jupiter sun."

Jimi hits "In from the Storm" with great zest; it rides up and crests beautifully, just like the fury and emotion of a storm, with Jimi getting off on top waves. He is in fantastic form.

"Foxy Lady" is dedicated "to that lady over there, Pat Hartley." Although it is the same song, Jimi plays it completely differently. He has a new treble sound that wings high-scaling freaky peaks.

Jimi, totally stoned, raps an intro to "Getting My Heart Back Together." Jimi is bending strings over a wide tonal range. Not in the blues sense but in elongated notes that stretch beyond the B. B. King clichés and explore the meaning of the tonal range in between. Then he turns the exploration into cascading, waterfalling runs that are blocked against chords that move easily into pure electronic sounds. They all move so quickly against each other, producing a three-dimensional sound. The densities produced are a result of the linear clustering of notes that have a vertical effect because of Jimi's amazing technique. The lines move into pure sound distortion that obliterates all the notes into one sound.

Then through that distortion Jimi segues into "Voodoo Chile (Slight Return)," with Billy Cox hitting the change right on the head. Then they segue into "Purple Haze," with Billy Cox right on top of the action. And behind that they go into "The Star-Spangled Banner" to clear the smoke. And then they return to "Getting My Heart Back Together," where Jimi sings the line: "Even tried my hand at being a voodoo chile, baby."

"Red House" becomes more than just a twelve-bar blues. Jimi extends the blues vibrato, playing the most complex of the blues guitar clichés, molding them into multinote runs and then blasting them away with feedback distort.

Jimi played three forty-five-minute sets. After each set he retired to a special sacred Hopi Indian tent.

Later, witnesses on Maui testified that they heard musical tones emanating from rocks and stones. UFOs were also sighted over the volcano by people who called in to a local radio show. A cameraman on the set said that he fell from his perch after seeing a UFO through his lens.

Chuck Wein was a film director of the Andy Warhol school. Not much script, hand-held cameras, and a lot of improvisation. The film was to be called *Rainbow Bridge*. Jimi shot his only scene the same day as his performance.

Wein and actress Pat Hartley, a key figure in Hendrix's inner circle during his emergence in London, were having a rapid, meandering exchange when Jimi walked onto the set.

Jimi characteristically enters with a shy, weary, " 'Scuse me." Chuck Wein, in the absence of a script, greets Jimi with the title of one of Jimi's favorite science-fiction novels: "Aha! Stranger from a strange land." Pat, who was very sped up for some reason, slurred her words unintelligibly. Even though it was a film, and therefore make-believe, Jimi's powerful presence overwhelms.

Chuck said, "I got rid of my wizard's hat because . . . you don't need a leader anymore, there's no more leader." "Leader for what," Jimi wanted to know. And he was half serious.

They go through a rapid back-and-forth where there is talk of the presence or the absence of a temple. Then Chuck mentions pyramids. When Jimi says, "Maybe it was one of my past lives or something," Wein does not seem to understand. Jimi explains, "I'm stoned now, so I have a little trouble."

But Pat Hartley picked up on the past-lives thing and says something about Jimi not having "to come back this way again. You wouldn't have any past lives."

Jimi's reply: "Only this one? Is that all you're looking forward to?"

Pat Hartley begins stuttering profusely. "The thing is . . ." She continues to stutter something about "coming back in the same trip?"

Wein, speechless, manages a "Well."

Jimi goes on the attack. "What is this all about you being a wizard? And all this, throwing in your hat." He asks, "You used to be a wizard, I take it?" To Chuck's yeah, Jimi continues: "Well, show me a trick. Show me you have enough guts to get out of your overalls."

Wein asks for a beer, and then brings up Jesus. Jimi begins to improvise. "I thought there was a death going on around here."

Faced with the near hysterical chatter of Chuck and Pat, Jimi begins riffing on his days in public school, and how his fascination with the planets, especially Mars, got him in trouble.

When Chuck asks him about out of body experiences, Jimi takes a long, improvisatory solo. "I don't know, man, it seems like there's this little center in space that's just rotating, you know, constantly rotating, and there's these souls on it, and you're sitting there like cattle at a waterhole and there's no rap actually going on, there's no emotions that are strung out, so you're just sitting there and all of a sudden the next thing you know you'll be drawn to a certain thing and the light gets bright and you see stuff, a page being turned, and you see yourself next to a Viet Cong, you know, a soldier being shot down, and all of a sudden you feel like helping that soldier up, but you're feeling yourself held in another vibe, another sense of that soldier. It seems like the soul of him, you know, and then you whisk back to the waterhole or the oasis and you're sitting there and you're rapping again or something, eating a banana cream pie and sitting on the gray hardwood benches and so forth, and all of a sudden somebody calls out again, but this is without words, that whole scene, and all of a sudden the next thing, you know, you see yourself looking down at the left paw of the Sphinx and the tomb of King Blourr and his friendly falcons and these all-night social workers with mattresses tied around their backs screaming "Curb service! Curb service! Curb service!" You know, with a third eye in the middle of the pyramid. Ah, then we find ourselves drifting across the desert sands dry as a bone but still going toward home and then finally things look up as Cleopatra is here giving you demands, and at the same time begging for fetishes. "Invent something or else I'll kick your ass." Those kind of scenes. A girl who claims to be Pio Cleopatra, Pio What? And all of a sudden the Hawaiian mountains open up and rise another thirteen thousand feet, and we go higher and higher, and Cleopatra has this beautiful raven hair and what are you supposed to do, man, except lay there and play the part? And so I'm laying there playing the part and a grape chokes me almost, but I can't let the choke come out, because, you know, I have to be together. Right? So I say, "*Pttt,* groovy grape wine you have there, Cleo. Ah hell, I mean let's get it on. Forget about all that stuff back there and forget about you and your scene. Let's just go up in the hills and relax and live. No, I have the conscience, I must do this. I must do that, I must . . . Oh, forget about it, Cleo, man, you're a woman, I'm a man, come on, let's get it on. Let's go out and get ourselves a grapevine out in the valley somewhere on the side of Mount Vesuvius or something. I don't know, hell. No, no, no. My parents, my traditions, my snake. Ooh, you bit me in the ass again, you naughty asp." Then we found ourselves wrapped up in carpets, which was fine. And here I am."

Jimi had his management cancel his trip to London set for August 13, saying that he had sustained injuries in a surfing accident while filming in Hawaii.

He hung out in Hawaii in seclusion in a small house by the sea with Melinda Merryweather. Grateful for her help in achieving this and for her company during this very necessary break, he made a recording just for her, entitled, "Scorpio Woman," and gave it to her as a one-of-a-kind gift.

Those in London had no way of knowing that he had been on the set of *Rainbow Bridge* for only one day. Jeffery was very pissed about it. He felt that Jimi would not be able to get the proper exposure and promotion for the upcoming European tour. He had not been to London for almost a year and a half. The expenses of the studio, in the final stages of completion, were enormous; Jimi would need this tour and even more work to cover the bills.

Back in New York, Jimi put the final touches on "Belly Button Window," overdubbing wah-wah effects as touches over a straight blues accompaniment that had the feel of an acoustic guitar.

Inspired by being around a very pregnant woman, Jimi takes the point of view of the baby inside in order to comment on his everyday world. Both Jimi and the baby have the question present in their minds of whether they are wanted.

> If you don't want me now
> Give or take, you only got two hundred days.

As somber and melancholy as this song is, the mysteriousness of the two-hundred-day deadline remains a mystery. Jimi, as the person up in that womb, makes it clear that if he is not wanted he is quite willing to return to spirit land and that he may never come through these earthly parts again.

Jimi wanted to be sure the studio was finished. He had been there night and day. He even did a little painting himself. People thought he was really freaking out over the studio. It was said that he went about at night and talked to the machines and petted them and whispered to them. An observer said that Hendrix was able to make the oscilloscope's signal configure the words "Fuck this shit." Jimi had been able to record there since the spring, and he used the full facilities from July 1. He was there all the time. Recording and remixing for hours on end. When the recording stopped, he would spend hours upon hours mixing and remixing. The engineers knew he was crazy. Only Ed Kramer was accustomed to his fastidiousness, and it was Kramer whom Hendrix preferred to be with in the studio. But Edwin H. Kramer had a life of his own to lead and Jimi was known to work around the clock until he collapsed.

Bob Dylan was riding his bike through the Village one afternoon when he came across Jimi slouched in the back of a limo. They had not seen each other since they were hanging with John Hammond Jr. in the Kettle of Fish on MacDougal Street some five years ago, although Jimi had subsequently recorded Dylan's "All Along the Watchtower." Dylan referred to that time, praising Jimi's "The Wind Cries Mary" as a beautiful tune that was far from where he was at back in the day when Jimi was emerging and really wasn't even writing songs. But to Dylan this encounter was "strange," and almost "eerie." He saw both himself and Jimi as having been propelled forward as if they were "fireballs" having been "shot out of cannons." Dylan had come so far he was practically retired from that crazy intensity. Here he was riding a bike and there was Jimi, in a limo, as Dylan had been when they first met. It was like a reversal on another level. He could see Jimi was preoccupied with the heavy matters fame brought. Far from the worship Jimi had for Dylan back in the day. It was as if they were passing each other, going in opposite directions. They would not see each other again.

Jimi called Les Paul, the electric-guitar virtuoso and electronic whiz. Les Paul had done things with the electric guitar and studio electronics in the 1950s that people were still trying to catch up with in 1970. Jimi wanted to know some things about the recording board that only a guitarist who also knew electronic engineering would know. He wanted to know how Les Paul went into the board himself. And in general, any tips Les Paul might have about building a studio. Jimi found Les Paul to be very, very friendly, almost familiar. Paul's approach to electronics was as personal as Jimi's, so it was difficult to explain in one conversation how he went about doing things. But Les Paul wanted to let Jimi know that he had heard him play in Lodi, New Jersey, way back in 1964. Even then Les Paul thought that Jimi was one of the most radical guitar players he had ever heard. He had dug the way Jimi was bending strings and getting a powerful funk sound out of his Fender. Paul had had to deliver some tapes to Columbia Records in New York, but he rushed back to the club only to find that Jimi had only been auditioning and that the club had not hired him because they said he played too crazy and too loud and too wild. That's what had really impressed Les Paul about him. So Paul started a search of his own, going all over New Jersey and Manhattan, even going up to Harlem asking around for him. Paul was interested in helping Jimi get recorded. Les Paul and his sons looked everywhere for Jimi. Finally they gave up. Jimi laughed out loud. "You mean I was that close and didn't know it?" he said.

Jimi had an idea he wanted to try out on Paul to see how it sounded to him. Would it be possible to mike a guitar amp from far away, like across a room, while having the guitar connected to the board at the same time? Les Paul knew what he meant in terms of sound. He wanted to get the same signal directly from the amp and directly into the board at the same time. There might be some delay in it akin to a kind of phasing, the same signal at different mike sources giving something like an echo of two different qualities of sound. Of course, the only way to find out about it was to do it, but it was interesting to talk about. After all, they both were after unique sounds. Les Paul told him how important the mastering of a record was, and how he used to sit in the parking lot while they mastered his recordings, listening to it through his car radio speakers. While most studios had the equivalent of a car-radio speaker inside the studio, it was usually only used to listen back to the mixes. But Les Paul knew how much of the sound could be lost during the mastering stage. He told Jimi to be at the mastering of his albums and to try to have them remaster it two or three times so that the depths of sound and the heights of sound are true. Then you'd be able to hear them on a regular five-inch car-radio speaker, and that is how you'd know that it's being mastered properly.

Hendrix had changed a lot in the nearly two years he had been back in the USA. More and more assertive, he was openly challenging his management, which had made just about every decision for him before.

Not only was he booking his own concerts, beginning in Pago Pago in late September, but also it was common knowledge that his management contract, up for renewal in October 1970, would be terminated. He also had a reputable lawyer checking his royalties and other financial statements. Now with the studio complete he could really do his Gypsy Suns and Rainbows, Electric Church Caravan thing.

The best bands, musicians, and singers in the world would be attracted to Electric Lady, paying top dollar for the facilities and the vibes. Juma knew nearly all the young jazz musicians. He could offer Electric Lady to people who could use a top-flight studio but, like many jazz musicians, could not afford the top prices. Now the tables could be turned on all those people who had made millions because of Jimi. People he didn't even know. People he didn't want to know. People who cared very little about the music or the progress of his music, people who only cared about the cash money at the record shop or ticket taker's booth. He did not need all the bullshit connected with his concerts anymore. His "caravan" idea was that all he had to do was show up and already they had an ample audience to fill any arena. All those middlemen made money just on the fact that he would be there. Now he could distribute the money more equitably, to the people who really needed it, and record and tour and have it all in front of his eyes instead of cut up and mystified through lawyer talk in somebody's office.

The official opening of Electric Lady Studios was celebrated with a hastily put-together bash. Jimi went all out to complete all the arrangements before he went on his tour of England and Europe. Electric Lady was one of his greatest achievements—a modern yet laid-back studio with the latest equipment. It spelled the Record Plant as the hippest place to record in New York. In the short month they had to record there, Jimi had burst out with a great wealth of material, as if he had been holding back for that moment. The tracks done at Electric Lady were the best work he had done to date.

The work on Electric Lady had gone on under great pressure: personnel changes within the group, lawsuits, and lack of communication between Hendrix and his management, still headed by Michael Jeffery. But it was a great victory, they were able to complete the studio in spite of all the hassles. To celebrate would be a morale booster, as well.

Jimi personally called up certain people for the party. He especially wanted the lovely ladies he was very close to, especially Monique, Colette, Betty Davis, and even Devon. After all, the studio was called Electric Lady. He wanted to make sure everybody he loved came to his studio: a massive guitar growing out of the earth.

The carpeted stairway led to an underground reception area that was shaped like a flying saucer. A low, round, cubicled mini-office was encircled by a soft, low couch. Passageways led to the first studio and, curving around a bend, to the second. Curving passageways disappeared in muted lights, spacey spectrum colors gave the effect of endlessness. A sound-buffered, upholstered, cozy underground lab.

Jimi, Juma, Billy, Arthur and Albert Allen (aka the Twins, aka the Ghetto Fighters) sat in Studio A listening to the tapes of the music that would be on the next album while the opening bash for Electric Lady Studios bashed on. Tom Nitelife is not with them as he usually is. He has turned up dead. A mysterious OD. They refuse to let that dampen their spirits, but the strange death hangs in the air anyway.

As the tapes play, Juma comments on the conga sound he plays that is integrated within the sound, the Twins go through some of their background harmonies, laughing at the prettiness, and Billy bops his head along with the bass lines. Jimi is silent, totally into the sound, listening as if he were alone. When the tapes stop, another is put on, Jimi speaks in his fluttering rush about how it will be necessary to remaster the album and maybe master it again to get the desired depth-of-sound terrain that balances the high sounds with greater contrast. *First Rays of the New Rising Sun* would be completely what he wanted it to be. No one would do work on it other than Jimi, with Ed Kramer at his side.

First Rays of the New Rising Sun was to be an official end to the rock 'n' roll image Jimi had cultivated and the beginning of a new direction. Jimi had been working on the tracks for well over a year. The songs were more sculpted than free-flowing; there were a couple of pure instrumentals that had classical flamenco and concerto-type movement, as in "Pali-gap" and "Hey Baby (New Rising Sun)." He also had a funky instrumental called "Midnight," which had been in the can for a while, as had been "Tax Free." "Belly Button Window," "Somewhere," and the old session of "My Friend" were almost straight poetic lyric with only touches of accompaniment, almost as if he were playing solo acoustic guitar. "Hey Baby (The New Rising Sun)" contrasted with "Dolly Dagger." One was about the ideal woman and the other about the demon woman. "Freedom," "Ezy Ryder," and "Stepping Stone" are rocking message songs, while "Drifting," "Nightbird," and "Angel" (with fifties R&B changes) are straightforward love songs. "Earth Blues" and "Room Full of Mirrors" had been recorded seemingly ages ago, although they had been done at the Record Plant only that last winter. They had a different sound, very busy, lush, and very freaky. Jimi had a wide range of material, more than enough for one album, enough for a double album at least, although his management was against it, but he would see how they flowed together when he returned from England. And since his management contract would be over by then, he would legally be the one to totally make the decisions.

The party was like a christening, not only of the studios, but of the music he had forged into a new personal statement. He listened to his new music, fixing it in his mind so as to hold him through the duration of the tour. That mad road. Warrior within, he listened.

Billy Armstrong's tabla-sounding congas blending with the strong rhythms of Buddy Miles's drum kit begin "Ezy Ryder," recorded a year earlier at the Record Plant. This is the just completed final mix. Buddy is respectful of the African drums and uses more cymbal than snare bash to complement the added percussion. They establish a hand-jive rhythm as Jimi comes in sustaining a wailing blue-note howl. Jimi on another guitar track plays through two Fuzz Tones patched together, producing a mellow fuzz that jacks the rhythm at the same time as Billy Cox comes in playing double time against the bass drum in a way only he can. Jimi is still sustaining the blue howl against his own staggered rhythm jags. Buddy begins to kick as the rhythm guitars announce the turn into the song proper. The hand-jive rhythms really become dominant as Jimi plays the lead lines in his new violin-like treble sound. The sustain ends as Jimi begins the lyrics but comes back to punctuate the end of his phrases in abrupt metal howls.

Stevie Winwood and Chris Wood on backing vocals fill out the sound of what could have been the Band of Gypsys. Jimi summons "Ezy Ryder" who is "riding down the highway of desire," just as in the popular film of the sixties starring as a hippie motorcyclist, Peter Fonda, who commissioned this song. Exulting in the free winds of the open road, searching for love. "Today is forever" our hero claims, and Jimi affirms, "We got freedom coming our way."

Buddy Miles's power is great on the toms, pure on the funky syncopation of the kick bass drum.

The instrumental "Pali-gap" is three guitars blending beautifully, delicately, yet with a funky bottom. The lead guitar touches off a fuzzy feedback that is tastefully developed at the tips of phrases. A background guitar with a wonderful rhythm and strange yet appealing echo and yet another guitar track adds straight-chord touches at random yet consistently delayed intervals. The yearning of the lead lines develops the emotion, building and shaping.

There are Moorish flamenco flavors in the irregular repetitions of the two major phrases alternating against the meshings of Billy's kick-down bass lines and Mitch's shuffling, stately drums. The Andalusian Gypsy rhythm is tipped by a dervish fervor at points in Jimi's playing where he breaks with the beautiful harmonies of his guitars and peaks away in rapid triple meter. Jimi double-picks through a Leslie organ speaker, getting sounds of water flowing. In the last passages Jimi completely changes the lead tonality. He goes into horn lines, then into ragtime, then a blues flurry, and then into celestial chordings that take off from Wes Montgomery, tagging out with a melody that could go on forever.

When Jimi had first written "Hey Baby" he was calling it "Gypsy Boy," and it sounded real pretty on the refrains, "Can I come along?" going into lazy evanescent boy sopranos mixed back and flowing against the beat.

But it was pretty, too pretty, *too* laid-back, winsome, and evanescent. Better to take it out and leave the weight with the song and the singer up front talking about it, like a testimonial rather than pretty slow-drag R&B.

A two-vamp song, the African change in melody is indicated by the blue-note stride slurring into nomadic pan-Saharan vibratos. It gives the English words and instrumentation an African feeling, with the rhythmic and tonal meanings implicit in the flamenco style.

Fine harmonies of high-nut treble bending strings against a separate arcing feedback ring. Then the haunting Moorish sound that is basic to flamenco, hesitating in its deliverance, a saga of a search spread across Saharan sands and winds. Ecclesiastical tones of High Church emotions. Jimi's virtuoso picking cascades run into microtonal notes. Then back to the swaying, sauntering rhythm, and then as if from out of nowhere, in surprise: *"Hey . . . baby . . ."*

Not limiting himself to major or minor scales, Jimi changes keys at will, sometimes on each note, in weird modes. Since the Fuzz Tone changes the harmonics, and there are more harmonics in distortion, Jimi gets Eastern scales and pure freak sounds out of nowhere.

In "Earth Blues" the Ronettes are a joy of pure harmony, and combined with the maleness of the Ghetto Fighters (the Twins) they get into a really nice sound. The engineer has the licks panning from one speaker to the other. Billy Cox's bass lines have the feel of Charlie Mingus playing bottom runs in his "Fables of Faubus."

Billy Cox has really arrived within Jimi's music; no more the treble frenzy of Noel Redding as a frustrated guitarist. Billy Cox is terse and tough. He covers the bottom without any yearnings for the top. He has an understated funk groove that is so subtle that even when he gets into off tonalities it all flows in a fluid groove. He can rev and snarl, strut and talk, and never blow the groove. His steady jazzlike presence fuses together the wide range of tonals on the bottom shelf . And that was just what Jimi wanted, so he could have complete freedom on top: a steady and consistent, yet creative, bottom presence.

Jimi evokes multitudes seeking salvation via hands and faces seeking upward. "Saying, 'Please, Lord, give us a helping hand.' " The rhythm of the music and the voice of the chorus are full of cheer, the spirit of salvation can be within the music. Jimi cautions to be wary of a long hot summer, as freedom is speeding on a parallel plane, coming their way. Jimi notes that he too often has his "head in the clouds" and he warns himself and others, "Don't get too stoned, please remember you're a man." The choral take-out encourages joy and faith and remaining in the light to deal with those "earth blues."

"Drifting" is a slow ballad with beautiful, layered violin-sounding guitar tracks. Jimi's lush-life vocal is one of his best.

Drifting—
On a sea of forgotten teardrops

On a lifeboat
Sailing for
Your love
Sailing home

Jimi loved the studio, his electric lady. He used to sleep with his guitar; now he could sleep *in* his studio amid the subdued fires of electricity, magnetism, and radiance.

They talked in the streets of dawn the morning after the party, Jimi, Juma, Billy, and the Twins.

Juma and the Twins would not be making the tour. Jimi sat in the passenger seat of his Stingray, his feet dangling out on the curb where the others sat. The silence of New York City at blue dawn. A quiet time when words and thoughts come together. The party had been a success, one of the "events of the season," like the newspapers say. They were not tired but they had no energy. They knew they would be tired sometime in the future, but in the euphoria of the christening of Electric Lady they huddled, drawing strength from one another like little boys in the street. They had just gotten through recording a few things over. In a way it was sad that Jimi was leaving so soon after triumph. Bread was needed. They talked of touring Pago Pago, and the American Samoan Islands. They wore that Hawaiian-type hula stuff there. Headdresses and thin soft material wrapped around themselves when they really got into celebrating their ancestral thing. But many related as Afro-American brothers. Some of them had Afros that were out of sight. They grew to tremendous sizes, especially the men, and the women, too. A three-hundred-pound Samoan was no big thing. Giving a concert in Pago Pago was an unusual move, but that's what the Caravan was about. The trial run would begin in the South Pacific. When they got it together they would be able to take the top names in jazz, rock, and blues anywhere and knock them out on short notice. Gypsy Suns and Rainbows, Electric Church Caravan. The bread for their concerts in Pago Pago was Jimi's responsibility, and he was going out to get it.

Digging one another, reluctant to let go of that moment, they finally had to say good-bye. Jimi had become, strangely enough, a true leader, a leader of men. Their last words to each other were: "See you in Pago Pago."

Later four New York City Police Department motorcycles met Jimi's limo in front of the hotel. Two in the front and two in the back, full lights flashing, sirens wailing, they speed out for Kennedy Airport. Jimi smiles as he watches the early morning New York City landscape whiz by. He really did not think Jim Marron, Michael Jeffery's right-hand man, could pull this off.

CHAPTER 9

T hree or four different worlds went by within the wink of an eye. Things were happening. There was this cat came around called Black Gold. And there was this other cat came around called Captain Coconut. Other people came around. I was all these people. And finally when I went back home, all of a sudden I found myself bein' a little West Coast Seattle boy—for a second. Then all of a sudden when you're back on the road again, there he goes, he starts goin' back. That's my life until somethin' else comes about.

There are a lot of things you have to sacrifice. It all depends on how deep you want to get into whatever your gig is. Whatever you're there for. So like the deeper you get into it the more sacrifices you have to do, maybe even on your personality or your outward this and that. I just dedicate my whole life to this whole art. You have to forget about what other people say. If it's art or anything else, whatever you really, really dig doing, you have to forget about what people say about you sometimes. Forget about this or forget about that. When you're supposed to die or when you're supposed to be living. You have to forget about all these things. You have to go on and be crazy. That's what they call craziness. Craziness is like heaven. Once you reach that point of where you don't give a damn about what everybody else is sayin', you're goin' toward heaven. The more you get into it, they're goin' to say, "Damn, that cat's really flipped out. Oh, he's gone now." But if you're producin' and creatin' you know, you're gettin' closer to your own heaven. That's what man's trying to get to, anyway.

What's happening is, you, we, we have all these different senses. We've got eyes, nose, you know, hearing, taste and feeling and so forth. Well, there's a sixth sense that's comin' in. Everybody has their own name for it, but I call it Free Soul. And that's more into that mental kind of thing. That's why everything is beyond the eyes now. The eyes only carry you so far out. You have to know how to develop other things that will carry you further and more clear. That's why the fastest speed . . . what's the fastest speed you can think of? They say the speed of light is the fastest thing—that's the eyes—but then there's the speed of thought, which is beyond that. You can get on the other side of this theme in a matter of thinkin' about it, for instance.

Sometimes you might be by yourself writing something. And you come across *some words and you just lay back and dig the words and see how that makes you feel. And you might take it at practice or rehearsal or something like that, and get together with it there, in music—see how the music feels. Or either sometimes you might be jammin'—when I mean you, I mean the group—the group is jammin' or something, and then you might run across somethin' really nice. And then you keep runnin' across that, then you start shoutin' out anything that comes to your mind, you know, whatever the music turns you on to. If it's heavy music, you start singin' things.*

Once you have the bottom there you can go anywhere. That's the way I believe. Once you have some type of rhythm, like it can get hypnotic if you keep repeating it over and over again. Most of the people will fall off by about a minute of repeating. You do that say for three or four or even five minutes if you can stand it, and then it releases a certain thing inside of a person's head. It releases a certain thing in there so you can put anything you want right inside that, you know. So you do that for a minute and all of a sudden you can bring the rhythm down a little bit and then you say what you want to say right into that little gap. It's somethin' to ride with, you know. You have to ride with somethin'. I always like to take people on trips.

That's why music is magic. Already this idea of living today is magic. There's a lot of sacrifices to make. I'm workin' on music to be completely, utterly a magic science, where it's all pure positive. It can't work if it's not positive. The more doubts and negatives you knock out of anything, the heavier it gets and the clearer it gets. And the deeper it gets into whoever's round it. It gets contagious.

Bach and all those cats, they went back in there, and they had caught a whole lot of hell. All they could do was get twenty-seven kids and then dust away. Because the way the society was they didn't respect this. They didn't know how to say, "Well, yeah, he's heavy. We'll go to his concerts. We'll dig him on the personal thing." But like, see, you're not supposed to judge a musician or composer or singer on his personal life. Forget about that. I like Handel and Bach. Handel and Bach is like a homework type of thing. You can't hear it with friends all the time. You have to hear some things by yourself. You can listen to anything that turns you on, that takes you for a ride. People want to be taken somewhere.

I wish they'd had electric guitars in cotton fields back in the good old days. A whole lot of things would have been straightened out. Not just only for the black and white, but I mean for the cause!

They keep sayin' things are changin'. Ain't nothin' changed. Things are going through changes, that's what it is. It's not changes, it's going through changes.

That's the way evolution happens. You have little bumps here. That's why you have the number seven after six. You have six smooth and all of a sudden a little bump. There's gonna be sacrifices. You get a lot of Black Panthers in jail, a lot of—what do you call that war thing?—the moratorium. A lot of those people who are goin' to get screwed up, for instance, here and there. But the whole idea, the whole movement is for everybody to appreciate. It's not only for young people to get it together by the time they're thirty. It's for anybody who's livin' to really appreciate.

It's just like a spaceship. If a spaceship came down if you know nothin' about it, the first thing you're goin' to think about is shootin' it. In other words, you get negative in the first place already, which is not really the natural way of thinking. But there's so many tight-lipped ideas and laws around, and people put themselves in uniform so tightly, that it's almost impossible to break out of that.

Subconsciously what all these people are doin', they're killin' off all these little flashes they have. Like if I told you about a certain dream that was all freaked out, and you'll say, "Oh wow, you know, where is this at?" That's because you're cuttin' off the idea of wantin' to understand what's in there. You don't have the patience to do this. They don't have the patience to really check out what's happenin' through music and what's happenin' through the theater and science.

It's time for a new national anthem. America is divided into two definite divisions. And this is good for one reason because like somethin' has to happen or else you can just keep on bein' dragged along with the program, which is based upon the past and is always dusty. And the grooviest part about it is not all this old-time thing that you can cop out with. The easy thing to cop out with is sayin' black and white. That's the easiest thing. You can see a black person. But now to get down to the nitty-gritty, it's gettin' to be old and young—not the age, but the way of thinkin'. Old and new, actually. Not old and young. Old and new because there's so many even older people that took half their lives to reach a certain point that little kids understand now. They don't really get a chance to express themselves. So therefore they grab on to what is happening. That's why you had a lot of people at Woodstock. You can say all the bad things, but why keep elaboratin'? You have to go to the whole balls of it. That's all you can hold on to, in the arts, which is the actual earth, the actual soul of earth. Like writin' and sayin' what you think. Gettin' into your own little thing. Doin' this and doin' that. As long as you're off your ass and on your feet some kind of way. Out of the bed and into the street, you know, blah-blah, woof-woof-crackle-crackle—we can tap dance to that, can't we? That's old hat.

We was in America. We was in America. The stuff was over and startin' again. You know, like after death is the end and the beginnin'. And it's time for another anthem and that's what I'm writin' on now.

— Jimi Hendrix
from *Superstars*

Flying above the Atlantic to London, Jimi felt as he had felt when he had been a paratrooper. The same anticipation of descent, the same tingling in his belly. And he knew that this was the most important jump of his life. Yet it was not like a physical risking of his life, it was more that his heart, his spirit, his soul were being put up to risk for his music, his song. All he wanted to do was play. He would do anything as long as he could play. He thought of the plane crashing. Then from his window he saw the clouds break, they were low across the ocean as the plane pointed toward a land mass amid the waters.

Jimi checked into a suite at the Londonderry Hotel. Because he had delayed his arrival in London to virtually the last minute before the Isle of Wight festival was to occur, Jimi felt especially obligated to spend as much time as possible with the press, the promoters of his tour, and various people on the London music scene. Somehow he wound up with his old nemesis Angie Burdon, and their love-hate relationship resumed. She was with another girl. They both bedded down with Jimi, making a happy threesome, and stayed on and spent the night.

Jimi, upon awakening from a not-so-restful night, was anxious to take care of the press interviews and the many other things that had to be done in preparation for his performance only two days away. But the girls wanted to sleep in and perhaps fool around some more. There Jimi and Angie's old chemistry kicked in and he went ballistic, smashing the girls' heads together, chasing them from his bedroom as well as breaking a few things, including the glass coffee table. He locked himself in the bedroom. Nude and frightened in the wrecked sitting room, Angie called Kathy Etchingham. Jimi had beaten them up and locked them out of the bedroom, where their clothes were; would Kathy come over and help sort things out?

Kathy arrived in twenty minutes and immediately went inside the bedroom. She found Jimi sitting up on the bed. He was not feeling well. He had a fever and had a lot of anxiety about returning to England after such a long time. Kathy felt his forehead and, noticing he was feverish, got him a cool compress and placed it on gently. She gathered up the girls' clothes and delivered them, returned to Jimi, and told him not to worry, everything was going to be all right.

She departed, having calmed him down, cleared the girls out, and left him in better shape than she had found him. She was married now and could not afford any more than that, but he was grateful.

He went on without really sleeping, seeing folks, partying, and giving interviews to the papers and magazines in London and to reporters who reported for other points on the tour, which included London, Sweden, Denmark, Germany, and France.

The next day Karen Davies, a friend from New York, brought Kristen Nefer by to meet him. Nefer, an angelic, spritely Danish model who was breaking into films, was in her early twenties and a rare beauty. Jimi fell in love with her immediately. The feeling was mutual. Nefer, who appreciated his music but had detested his image, thinking him short and portly, totally changed her mind when confronted with the real man. "I couldn't believe it—he was tall, he was skinny, and he was beautiful."

He kept the women there with him all day and through the night, talking and interacting with the press as he dealt with the many details of his upcoming appearance—all in a kingly style.

He would not let Kristen leave his sight and insisted she accompany him to the Isle of Wight Festival.

The Isle of Wight was a massive thirty-three acre festival site. The crowd was estimated to be over half a million, making it the largest crowd Jimi would ever play before.

Vishwa waited for Jimi as the helicopter landed at the Isle of Wight. He had not seen Jimi since the spring, when they were filming *Jimi Plays Berkeley*. Vishwa was an old hand at traveling with Hendrix. Since Jimi first came to Los Angeles after Monterey as a star, Vishwa often accompanied Jimi and company as a part of the entourage and helped out where he could. He had helped put together the deal for the film *Jimi Plays Berkeley* and had introduced Jimi and Jeffery to the special-effects man for the Kubrick film *2001*.

Jimi spied him as soon as he disembarked and waved Vishwa into his dressing room. The dressing room was a portable type that had a long history. Opulent and spacious, it folded out from its railroad-car size like an accordion. During World War II it had been used to smuggle arms.

Vishwa noticed Jimi's weariness right away. But it seemed like more than weariness. Jimi seemed resigned, down, almost fated. His vibe was the lowest Vishwa had ever seen, and as a highly trained TM master, Vishwa would not let something like that pass. At first Jimi and Vishwa talked excitedly about what they had been doing and seeing since they had last been together. Then Jimi changed. Suddenly he seemed to go back into himself.

Vishwa helped some friends get through the security force into the dressing room. Jim Morrison was one. Jimi was happy to see them, but there was something on his mind.

Besieged as usual by the press, Jimi continued to answer questions.

He told the *Times* reporter: "If I'm free, it's because I'm always running. I tend to feel like a victim from public opinion. They want to know about these girls, kicking people in the ass, doing the 'Power to the People' sign. I cut my hair—they say, 'Why'd you cut your hair, Jimi?' It was breaking up. 'Where'd you get those socks?' 'What made you wear blue socks today?' Then I started to ask myself questions. Did I take too much solo? Should I have said thank you to that girl? I'm tired. Not physically. Mentally. I'm going to grow my hair back, it's something to hide behind. No, not to hide. I think maybe I grow it long because my daddy used to cut it like a skinned chicken.

"When they [the audiences] feel, and smile with that sleepy, exhausted look, it's like being carried on a wave. We mostly build on bar patterns and emotion. Not melody. We can play violent music, and in a way, it's like watching wrestling or football for them—it releases their violence. It's not like beating it out of each other, but like violent sick. I mean, sadness can be violent."

He told freelance writer Stephen Clarkson: "I am all alone and I say, 'What are you doing here dressed up in satin shirts and pants?' I've got this feeling to have a proper home. I like the idea of getting married. Just someone who I could love."

It was evident Jimi was very tired, near exhaustion.

Soon the reporters left and Jimi prepared for the show. It was dead in the middle of night, seemingly nowhere in time and place, only the darkness of the expansive field, the roar of the crowd, and the surges of the giant sound system. Richie Havens was on. He sounded good. He always sounded good, his unique baritone swelling out over the assembled.

Jimi did not have much to say to Vishwa, which was strange. They were as tight as a star performer and a non-show-business friend could be.

The Isle of Wight crowd was huge and loud. By the time Jimi was to go on, many who had been unable to get in had succeeded in breaking in through barricades after a grenade had blown a hole in the fence. The large security force with its trained dogs were unable to prevent the widespread gate crashings. Jimi instructed Kristen to stay in the wings, always in his view.

Just before going on, Jimi said to no one in particular that he would play until someone in the audience booed. It was a strange statement for him to make, since he was obviously exhausted. The statement both indicated a weary bravado and his insecurities at facing a large British audience after a nineteen-month absence.

Jimi comes onstage with flushed and youthful cheerfulness, his voice wafting high greetings. Methedrine rushing through exhausted limbs.

Isle of Wight. Lying below the British Isles, longitude 50° 30'N by latitude 001° 16'W. One degree from the end of time—Greenwich, England.

Late night, early morning. Staring into depths of darkness, black shrouded crowd, lit only by the tortured surge of night fires, a few bodies visible in the haze. Blackness. The presence of thousands as far back as the eye can see merging with the horizon facing east toward the zero point of time.

Weird not seeing anyone—only voices from a black void. No faces staring back in the dead of night.

"Yes," Jimi says. "It has been a long time, hasn't it?

"Stand up for your country and the police. Maybe you should sing along. Well, if you don't want to stand, then fuck you. . . ."

Crowd laughs. Voices up front speaking for the muted roar from the back, sounding like approval yet not really sounding like anything. The huge outdoor area of the Isle of Wight meant the volume had to be extremely loud in order to cover the vast distances.

"God Save the Queen" comes on in a crash of volume, then drones downward. Almost like "The Star-Spangled Banner," but not as freaky. The same melody he used to sing as a schoolchild, "My country 'tis of thee/Sweet land of liberty . . . Let freedom ring." Only this is the original "God Save the Queen." The melody is so much like Handel, the anthem of long tradition and world domination.

Mitch beats out a brief drum solo as they segue into "Sgt. Pepper," then the true national anthem of young England. The jaunty fanfare of the song is replaced by Jimi's weird vibrato treble peaks that trail off close to feedback rather than bend roundly. He's rushing, but he can't stop. He is fighting the exhaustion, his body tone bone-weary. Harmonics begin to pop up. Playing against the amps, his weariness seems to be reflected in the strangest electric tones he's ever played. Sharp to piercing, the sound seems to want to take off from harmonics straight up into feedback, like a knife's edge sharpened to razor intensity.

Harmonizing with himself, fretting rhythm on the bottom strings and wild-trilled atonal licks on top—the sound was freaky, amphetamine-intense. Yet it swung, swung almost insanely. Teetering on the edge of manic annihilation.

He goes into "Machine Gun" and gets his mind blown. Cutting right through the introductory guitar phrases a clear, middle-class Englishman's voice intoning, "Security force, security force . . . come in. . . ." He was floored. He almost stopped playing. He kept the show going, nodding at Billy and Mitch to keep on going. Sgt. Pepper had invaded his amps! Somehow the frequencies of the PA systems and the security-police band were feeding into each other. That was why he was having so much trouble controlling the sound. He was actually in circuit with the operating frequencies of the security police. Too much. At another time he might have laughed it off, but right then it was all he could do to remain standing. Every time his eyes would blink he was afraid he would fall. Head bobbing, directing Mitch and Billy, he was also directing himself, keeping himself going.

Mitch begins missing on his drums. The steady drone of "Machine Gun" seems to be eluding him. There are very weird vibes in the air. Jimi nods anxiously at him to pick up. But before he does he misses two entire beats. Mitch had stopped for two whole beats! Jimi could not believe it. Gritting his teeth, he turns to the crowd and grimaces in pyrotechnic agony and dances, taking his, the band's, and the audience's minds away from the pause. He moves into "Midnight Lightning," as he and Billy position themselves behind Mitchell in order to hear better and to drive him on.

> *I get stoned and I can't go home*
> *but I'm callin' long distance on a public saxophone*

Jimi goes on about being shook up, upset as if his past has taken him over and public opinion is ruling his life. His strategy is to keep moving and remain positive, in love as well as in perception. But love is the sweetest, and he will make love even on his "dyin' bed."

Suspended between Sunday and Monday, Greenwich Mean Time. Receding in time as if the sound that sprang from the giant amps and speakers rushed over the curve of the Earth into a vortex that separated other worlds.

"There must be some kind of way out here. . . ." "Watchtower" stole up on him. Before he knew it, he was singing it. He had completely forgotten about the band, although he nodded unconsciously at them. The words of "Watchtower" seemed to come straight from his unconscious. In the past he had forgotten those words several times onstage. But this time they sailed out into the darkness of the Isle of Wight, their meaning becoming clear as if he were hearing them for the first time. His voice almost breaking: "But you and I we've been through that and this is not our fate/So let us not speak falsely now/The hour's getting late. . . ." His guitar screams out in solo, rushing ahead of Mitch and Billy.

His heart thumps against his chest. The rhythm driving manic. When he hears himself he sounds as if he were crying. As if something within had ripped from its moorings. He sings against the strange deep sleep that seems to tempt him to collapse. He sings his ass off. Lest he cease to exist.

> *Watchtower in the cold distance*
> *A wildcat did growl*
> *Two riders were approaching*
> *And the wind began to howl. . . .*

Jimi's freaky vibratos spiraling out seaward toward the sonic sonority so close to the feedback range that they began to clash in peak vibratos that straighten out every so often into flat peals of pure signal. An earnestness clenched tight in fatigue. Nearly unconsciously he plays, pulling out his reserves to deliver what his top fee demanded. The bottom range of fatigue, one step from falling out, yet pushing forward in the black, bleak night, keeling seaward, signal distorting into fog.

Jimi played another version of "Hey Baby (New Rising Sun)," an instrumental seeming to explore the melody's every conceivable note and sound possibility. Jimi ad-libbed new lyrics:

> *Coming back to England*
> *Thank you, baby, for making it so easy*
> *Going through changes in New York, Chicago*
> *Thank you, baby, for staying with me. . . .*

They cheer. They always cheer. The blank faces he hates to face. No one to point at in the absolute blackness. No little girl to cun his tongue at. Only banks of nearly blinding super stage lights. Only screams of the same fatigue he feels in his bones coming back. One moment he feels he is playing lousily, the next moment it sounds okay. But he is dissociated from time, unaware of the lapses, wondering if he forgot a verse or movement. Trying to stay totally on top, lest his systems stop and recede into nothingness.

He tries to listen to his voice. Then he stops trying to listen. It sounds strained, forced, a little higher than usual, emotions creeping in that he can't control. Songs sounding differently. All sounding new, yet far away, as if it might not be him onstage at all. Tears of frustration and rage are close to his surface, as close as the waters of the Atlantic. Tears of exhaustion and a burgeoning fear for what lies ahead.

"Red House," a blues, establishes a calm within the eye of the storm. Wishing, conjuring, feeling it, he tries to gather himself back together.

Jimi begins the lyrics of "Hey Joe," his first hit in England. Even though weary, he injects some musical humor into his solo when he starts off with a few riffs from the guitar intro to "I Feel Fine" by the early Beatles and then goes into the tune of an old English dance song called "Country Manor." And then on the tag-out ending, instead of singing, "I'm going way down south," he shouts, "Good-bye, baby, good-bye."

"In from the Storm." The last number and he is so glad. He feels like a boxer in the last round pushing through, wondering what the outcome will be. Shrouds of depression sweeping across his consciousness like the predawn fog that moved through the arena, casting the lights garish.

He found himself singing in the same modality as "Watchtower." He could not help the emotion in his tone. Overtones close to tears. The song struck something within. It was true. It was what he wanted to say. It was the way he felt right there at that moment. He wished Emmaretta Marks, a friend from Greenwich Village who had sung background vocals on "In from the Storm," were there to sing it with him. He feels so lonely, so isolated—and it was only the beginning of the tour. Yet, strangely, he does not want to leave the stage.

Billy Cox was finally getting that really good tone in live performances that Jimi wanted. Billy was resolving his playing in relation to the ongoing happening-now music. Getting that good tone consistently. Bulbous blue funk in a bottom abyss. Mitch's drumming notwithstanding, Jimi and Cox had gotten into some nice things. They were riding very high on that teetering tip that Jimi was used to but that Billy was not.

Jimi's tired face shows the bones of his high cheeks in stark relief. Hair bouffant in soft curls slightly combed out. Eyes slightly closed, he directs Billy and Mitch: eye contact bone-weary. Each blink of the eye could bring sleep. Head keeping time, nodding to the beat. Keep the beat for Billy and Mitch, widen the eyes for the change, sway abruptly for the solo entrance.

Standing on an elevation looking out. Thousands of heartbeats through thousands of amps. Pure sound oscillating. Oscillating slow for bass, fast for guitar. Electric throb through him spiraling outward.

Peering into the darkness. Standing up there screaming, screaming like a madman. Screaming like a toad, kneecaps all up in the chest, to the emptiness to the darkness. Flying into the darkness beyond the continental shelf.

I just came back from the storm
It was so cold and lonely
The cryin' blue rain was tearing me up . . .

In the dressing room, exhausted, Jimi stands in the onslaught. The security guards are admitting anyone into the tiny room. Jimi, trying to catch his breath, smiles mechanically at the well-wishers. He can hardly see. He feels he has played poorly, but then he does not really know. He wishes there were someone there like Chas to tell him, to talk it over. But now he is in the crush of the temporal world. A star whom they touch and stand in the face of.

A helicopter awaits.

There is no rest. Monday, August 31, they would be at Gröna Lunds Tivoli, Stockholm, Sweden. Tuesday, September 1, Liseberg, Gothenburg, Sweden. Wednesday, September 2, Vejlby Risskov Hall, Arhus, Denmark. Thursday, September 3, K.B. Hallen, Copenhagen, Denmark. Friday, September 4, Deutschlandhalle, West Berlin, West Germany. Sunday, September 6, Isle of Fehmarn Festival, West Germany . . .

Jimi and company begin to move toward the helicopter, through the throngs of well-wishers. Vishwa looks expectantly at Jimi as they wade through. The dawn is breaking. Vishwa has never had to ask to accompany Jimi anywhere, but this time he senses a reservation in Jimi's demeanor. He searches Jimi's face for a nod of the head, a twinkle of the eye, a smile, some kind of resumption of their usual camaraderie—but it is not there. Vishwa has his traveling bag on his shoulder. Either he goes with Jimi or else he heads to France to join the crew that will shoot *Le Mans,* a racing-car film. But Vishwa would really like to groove along with Jimi through Europe on tour. Finally they are standing at the door of the helicopter. Jimi turns and faces Vishwa. Expectancy plays on Vishwa's face as they study each other. Finally Jimi says, "What are you—my old lady?" and disappears into the chopper.

Standing there as the helicopter created its infernal racket in the takeoff, Vishwa thought through all the times Jimi and he had spent together, through good times and bad. They had shared women and had fought physically. Jimi had hit him in a frustrated night of rage once, but Vishwa felt the blow of Jimi's final words more than anything.

At Tivoli Gardens in Stockholm, August 31, Jimi was so out of it he shocked the manager of the amusement park, who sought to restrict the length of his set. Chas Chandler surprised Jimi by being there, but to the former manager's seasoned eye Jimi was "a wreck." Jimi would start a song and then forget which one it was they were playing when they got to the solo section. He would go into a different tune. Chas thought the gig "disastrous" and he found it "awful to watch." Before the concert Jimi had chug-a-lugged a small bottle of whiskey. Something was markedly wrong.

The following day, September 1, in Gothenburg, Sweden, the show was satisfactory. But Billy Cox somehow consumed some bad LSD and began a rapid downward spiral, and thought that he would be killed by a stranger at any moment.

Wednesday, September 2, Vejlby Risskov Hall, Arhus, Denmark. They start the set with "Freedom." Moving abruptly into another tune, something is obviously very wrong. Jimi stops playing. Mitch and Billy wonder at him. To Kristen Nefer, looking on from the wings, he looked exhausted and scared as he shook and trembled.

Never before had he come so close to falling out onstage. He felt that it was more than fatigue. There was a vicious vibe affecting him. Billy Cox was beginning to pick up on it. Jimi had been physically followed by strange people before, but this time, although he detected no one out of the ordinary, he felt marked.

He stands on the far end of the stage almost teetering over the edge. He is in a leaning crouch, his right hand sweeps the frets of his Stratocaster, his white-jacketed arm a blur of white. Never before, in any concert, has he manifested this level of physical exhaustion. He had had to be helped onstage, so weak were his legs, his energy. Billy Cox, bravely struggling along, believes he himself had been dosed by some neurotoxic substance the night before in Sweden. Had Hendrix been dosed, as well?

The song is "Come On (Part 1)," a song he used to play a long time ago in

Seattle in his high school days. Only this time it hardly sounds like the song Earl King wrote. Instead of progressive R&B it is manic slurring chords and elongated drones that peak in a freak treble peal that is constant and foreboding. He seems to be exhorting the traditionally mild Danish audience. He stops playing and barks out at the crowd between some teeth-gnashing grace notes. Then he smooths on off into a rap. He continues to fret wildly, zooming the length of the white Strat. He goes into "Room Full of Mirrors," singing the lyrics as if he were telling something about himself. There is a weird strain in the song. He goes into "Hey Baby (New Rising Sun)." It is nothing like that mellow tune he penned up in Woodstock. It sounds a lot like the previous song. It is almost as if something otherworldly is playing his guitar. As if some force were bending the notes toward a melody they wanted to hear. Only the melody being approached is like nothing he has ever played before. He has seldom had trouble controlling the feedback. It has always worked for him. Yet at the Isle of Wight three days ago and now in Arhus there is an added element to his feedback sound. An element that has never before entered his sound. It is peaked to freak out. The other side of "Laughing Sam's Dice." He segues quickly into "In from the Storm," and it is right there. It is unbelievable. It sounds like some crazy manic metallic sonics, bleeding, eating through the amps. That tone is totally opposite to the emotion of the song. It comes out of nowhere, screaming at him something crazy.

Jimi moves into "Message of Love," "We're traveling a speed of a reborn man . . ." He stops abruptly and walks off the stage and collapses. The concert is over.

In his dressing room he told reporter Anne Bjorndal, "I am not sure I will live to be twenty-eight years old." That birthday was less than three months away.

Kirsten Nefer witnessed something very strange when they returned to their hotel. "Jimi was in so much pain and not talking. When we get into the room, there was a girl sitting in a chair, apparently she was Danish. They start talking together and she tells some horrific story about a guy from the Vanilla Fudge who was killed somewhere in the countryside in England. And I can see Jimi got really scared. I got so mad, you know. Three or four times I tell her in Danish, 'You'd better fuck off, you're just scaring him.' I don't know who this girl is or how she got in. After this Danish girl left, Jimi said to me that we had to talk all night."

Jimi finally told Kirsten that he had toured with the guy who was killed. They were managed by the same man—Michael Jeffery. He and Kirsten talked until 7 A.M.

The next day was all right. They sweated through a well-received date at K.B. Hallen in Copenhagen and even did an encore.

The next day they were in West Berlin, at Deutschland Halle. Jimi was besieged by U.S. Armed Forces Radio personnel. Military brass were all over the place. The U.S. troops who occupied the American section of West Berlin were, as usual, starved for any contact with the homeland.

Jimi, exhaustion telling in his voice, stumbled through an interview with Chris Romberg, a very nice cat from Armed Forces Radio whom he had known before.

They filmed an interview in Jimi's dressing room. The interviewers, assorted personnel from Armed Forces Radio, and a few other journalists, were all nervous. The room was crowded and overlit. Jimi was bone-tired. His replies were in weary drawls between long, weary pauses.

JIMI: . . . because nobody can beat . . . right now . . . until the next wave of musicians and artists and . . . come along . . .

Q.: What is your point of view on the Isle of Wight Festival you just played a few nights ago?

JIMI: The people are really groovy. People are really groovy. But I really hate to play at night. You know what I mean? 'Cause you can't see 'em, especially outside.

Q.: You couldn't see the audience?

JIMI: Not too good. I couldn't see anybody. And that's what I play off of. Especially musicians and . . . (incoherent mumbles). Then second of all the audience.

Q.: We're not seeing you for very long—what have you been doing?

JIMI: I been doing like Yogi Bear. I been hibernating. It surprises me . . . (incoherent mumbles). Because we received a lot of static in New York. A lot of aggravation in New York.

Q.: You mean . . . your music today, has it changed?

JIMI: We play a whole vacuum, a whole wall of sound. A wall of feeling. That's what we're trying to get across. Whew! I haven't slept in two days.

Q.: In all this time when you've not appeared in Europe—what have you been doing in the States?

JIMI: Well, we've been working real hard on other projects. Well (incoherent mumbles) . . . Billy Cox, our bass player, has been doing a lot of song writing.

Q.: You've written songs along with him, as well?

JIMI: Well, you know, we're starting to do that now. We're getting, we're starting to make really good contact with each other. Because we realize how important a friend is in this world.

Q.: Are a lot of your songs recorded waiting for release?

JIMI: We have a whole LP. We have a single called "Dolly Dagger" and another one called "Nightbirds Flying." It's going to be released as soon as possible.

Q.: About your appearance in the film *Woodstock,* especially the scene at the end with the National Anthem.

JIMI: I guess they could have showed some other songs probably (incoherent mumbles) . . . they shot the end of it. I wish they could've caught more of the musical side, really.

Q.: You think they tried to make a political issue out of it?

JIMI: I don't know, I don't know—not really—I don't think so (tired laughter). That's just the way it is, you know.

Q.: What about festivals like Woodstock—you think there'll ever be another gathering of people that large that have the same kind of vibes?

JIMI: I don't know because like, uh, it's pretty hard for a sound to get to all those people—it's such a big crowd. Like if they had smaller crowds we would really get next to them more.

Q.: How do you feel about playing to, say, 400,000 people?

JIMI: That's what I mean—it's just too big, you know. You know you're not getting through to all of them and, uh, the idea to play to them is to try to turn them on or something.

Q.: Do you think that large music festivals are actually just an extension of the commercialism angle? Is it too commercial?

JIMI: Oh, I don't know. I don't think that we'll play too many more of those anyway, you know, so there's really not too much to talk about. It's just too much, it's just too many things going and not enough you know, love or concentration on one certain thing.

Q.: Jimi, you've just come from the Isle of Wight, which is another of these large festivals—do you enjoy that?

JIMI: Well, you know, I enjoy playing anywhere. But like, it was dark. You know, it was very night time—I couldn't see anybody. If I could see the people, instead of just lines of bonfires up there, you know . . . as everyone could tell (incoherent mumbles) . . . back up there (laughs, as if telling a joke no one got) . . . Oh well, that's all right. . . .

Q.: Do you prefer playing at a concert like this one where the accent is more coming and listening to the music than gathering in a folk festival?

JIMI: Yeah . . . I guess so.

Q.: You think you're more appreciated here?

JIMI: Oh, I don't know—it's really hard to say. Sometimes it's easier in playing different places, you know. At different times. Germany in the summertime is beautiful.

Q.: Do you enjoy playing in Germany?

JIMI: Yeah . . . yeah . . .

Q.: Do you think German audiences differ from English ones?

JIMI: I don't know. It's pretty hard to say. We haven't played in England in a long time. We have two albums . . . but you know, it's pretty hard to say.

Q.: Is there really anyone in pop music or rock music when you hear their stuff who you say, "Wow, they really knock me out"?

JIMI: Yeah. Sly (laughs).

Q.: Sly Stone?

JIMI: Yeah, 'cause I like his beat, I like his pulse. You know, "Music Lover" and "Dance to the Music" and all those types of things. And Richie Havens, which is out of sight.

Q.: I was wondering about the Experience that's appearing here in Berlin tonight . . . this is really . . . there's only one main difference from the original Jimi Hendrix Experience—that being your bass player, Bill Cox. . . . I was wondering how, um . . .

JIMI: And we have a new road manager, too, don't forget. Jim McFadden. Besides Gerry Stickells and Eric Barrett. And you can't forget because they're . . . those are the ones who keep it together. Everybody forgets about that side of it really.

Q.: That's true. That's something I'd like to try and find out more about. Behind-the-scenes people normally do a lot more than . . .

JIMI: It's like that beautiful airplane. Everybody forgets about the pilot sometimes, you know. But I think that's one way to look at it (sighs inaudible words).

Q.: I was wondering about the group itself, however, and the reason that the original Experience broke up with Noel Redding and Mitch Mitchell and now that you are back together with your old drummer, Mitch, how Bill Cox came to you?

JIMI: You know he and I, we used to play together before. We're doing a lot of bass unison, bass and guitar unison things, you know. Which makes—is nothing but a lot of rhythms, we call it. It's like patterns, you know. And like, I don't know, see, Noel he had his own thing. He gets his own group. He has his own group. And he's into his own thing. He's more of an individual himself, I guess, and so forth like that (mumbles incoherently) . . . the bottom be just a little solid. Noel is more of a melodic player, you know. And Billy plays more of a solid bass.

Q.: Do you think that the Monterey Festival back in '67 was the original starting point for what we could say is the amount of fame of Jimi Hendrix?

JIMI: Yeah . . . (incoherent mumbling)

Q.: And as far as the Monterey Festival goes, I was there. I know that there were a lot of fantastic performances there. Will there ever be anything in pop music like Monterey again?

JIMI: I'm not sure. I really don't know . . . about . . . pop music . . . you know . . . no telling . . . you know . . . It'd be nice if it was. That's the next wave around though, you know. The next time around . . . You see . . . (starts to say something but changes his mind). Oh well . . . that's too much (laughs sadly).

Q.: How do you feel when you're on tour? How do you feel at the moment?

JIMI: Right now, you mean? I'm just worried a bit now. I sound . . . like a frog. Because last night we were playing so loud. I was just shouting on my tip-toes. I felt like my kneecaps were up in my chest (laughs). And just right now I feel a little nervous—but I think it will be all right. 'Cause now we're gonna go on and do our little gig. Like Mitch'll be playing drums and Billy will be playing bass and I will be playing guitar (laughter) . . . and I'll still be up there screaming.

Q.: Do you get very worn-out?

JIMI: Yeah, certain things we try to do in an instant and we get worn-out in an instant, too.

Q.: Like interviews . . .

JIMI: Sometimes they're fun (laughs apologetically). I wish you would have caught me at a more unnervous time, because right now we have to go on soon. . . . (Sergeant Keith Robin of Armed Forces Radio enters after the interview is officially over; his question brings laughter from everyone within hearing distance.)

SGT. ROBIN: Why does that name always spark laughter? Whenever I say "Mungo Jerry," everybody busts out laughing.

JIMI: I think that's a happy song. It's a great way to (clears voice, sings), "You got women/you got women/on your mind. . . ." I think it's a beautiful summer-time type of song. And you know . . . I don't know about the group but the song is clear, it's nice and light and, uh, you know, they just laid it down. I didn't know it was a group, I thought they just got together to make that one record. But you know, best of luck to anybody who, you know, wants to get together. Mungo Jerry . . .

The Isle of Fehmarn Festival, located on a dark and misty island on Kiel Bay, just west of the Baltic Sea, had succumbed to mob rule by the time Hendrix and company got there. Mad German bikers were shooting up the place, including the medical tent and even the stage itself, where the emcee had fled just prior to Hendrix's scheduled appearance. The bikers had robbed the box-office receipts and were charging exorbitant parking fees. They had taken over the Isle of Fehmarn.

Late and tired and unwilling to go on in the madness, Hendrix, Mitchell, and Cox stayed in their camper while violence flared all around them. Rescheduled for the next morning at ten, Hendrix again failed to appear. Again the crowd was set to riot until Alexis Korner got up onstage and began to talk. By that time Korner was the sole emcee. He had been sharing the duties with another fellow, but when the shooting started, he had disappeared. Korner, who spoke fluent German, told the crowd that Hendrix was not there and that they'd have to listen to him play acoustic guitar or nothing. By noon the crowd was quieted down enough and Hendrix, Cox, and Mitchell came on.

"No more nights," Jimi had been saying, but now coming on in the daylight of the Straits of Fehmarn, he is wishing for darkness to shield the ugliness of the scene. Many of the crowd stayed only because Jimi Hendrix was scheduled to play.

People who had been beaten, people who had been robbed, staring, waiting for Hendrix to appear onstage. Along with the people who had done the robbing, the beating, the pillaging. No sympathy. Not even outrage or horror, just a weird acceptance on everyone's part, it seemed.

Alexis makes the intro. He tries to fanfare the occasion. But it is obvious that the crowd is in such agitation that only the music itself has a chance of getting through the grim mists. Jimi comes on out as usual: an octave-higher voice vocally waving to the crowd, "Peace, peace, anyway." The crowd is divided between polite, cheerful applause and lusty boos. Jimi boos back. The booers in the crowd switch to that favorite Yankee-inspired phrase: "GO HOME . . . GO HOME." Jimi continues, "We were to come on last night but . . . it was just too unbearable. We couldn't make it together." As those who came to listen wait for the music, the booers take advantage of the lull in applause to fill the hush with raucous "GO HOME GO HOME GO HOME." Almost funny, almost ready to laugh—that's just where he would like to be, home. Hurriedly he whips through the platitudes: "Mitch Mitchell on drums, Billy Cox on bass, and Jimi on public saxophone. Like to play some music for you." As the boos and "GO HOME"s continue, he announces in German the title of the first tune: "Killing Floor," and then in English, "I Should Have Quit You a Long Time Ago," and here he appends a personal message to the booers, "You mothers . . ." Jimi sets the tempo, as usual playing both lead and rhythm, and takes an upward climb progressing to the crest where the song proper begins. The tune is light-sounding but the message is quite clear.

While "Killing Floor" was originally Howlin' Wolf's comparison of a slaughterhouse for cattle with a domestically violent scene where death was close at hand. Now Jimi presented it in an actual scene—what was before him—where there had been violence and murder, and where there was still danger of more. He stood there as probably the only thing that held the rioting in check. The song had manifested, Jimi rushed through. It was entirely too relevant, a true lament that reflected his feelings at that precise moment: *And now you got me cry-ing on the killing floor.*

The applause outsounds the boos. Again the music is in power, but those who love the music and have stayed here in violence's midst will have to find their way out at the end.

Jimi ends the quick snappy set with "Voodoo Chile (Slight Return)." No en-cores, no delay. They run for the camper, they speed to the helicopter that will take them across the Straits of Fehmarn to Hamburg and the airport.

The bikers continued to loot the money, shake down the audience, and gen-erally shoot up the place.

Billy Cox continued to have visions of people coming to kill them, to kill Jimi. And he was certain that people would be killed at Fehmarn. On returning to London he was proved correct. There had been ensuing deaths at Fehmarn. The island had been been sealed off. One of Jimi's roadies had received a gunshot wound to the leg as he cleared the stage, and Stickells had been struck in the head with a plank that had left a bloody wound.

Jimi was exhausted and visibly depressed. His mood plunged further when he was denied a suite at the Londonderry Hotel because of the recent distur-bance with Angie Burdon and the other young woman. He checked instead into the Cumberland Hotel near Marble Arch. Suite 507/508.

They had checked Billy into the Airways Hotel, but he was acting so strange that they immediately took him to a doctor. It was clear he could not be left alone.

Jimi was glad to get back to his suite and rest. It had been nonstop since the Isle of Wight. He was cheered to see Kristen and Karen arrive, but he got a call about Billy and they had to go right away to the Airways Hotel and calm him down. They took Billy out to dinner at a nearby Indian restaurant. He was act-ing so strangely that Jimi brought him back to his suite and they just adminis-tered to Billy. It was a round-the-clock affair. Billy kept saying, "I'm gonna die." Jimi would constantly assure him that there would be no such thing happening.

After two days and nights with Jimi, Stickells decided Billy could stay with him for a while and they would take it from there. Jimi, Kristen, and Karen took a break and went to the movies. It was a relief to escape the reality they had been through. They took in Antonioni's *Red Desert* and it was great. They were all happy to have been successfully transported outside of their immediate con-cerns.

The next day it was decided Billy should return home. The drugs he had been given at the hospital dispensary had silenced him. That was almost as bad as his ravings.

But Jimi had to get back to work. It was necessary to deal with the press, since they probably would not be able to continue the tour. Calls had been made for a replacement bass player. Ric Grech of Blind Faith was contacted, Jack Casady of the Jefferson Airplane. But one thing was firm with Jimi: he would not reassemble the old Experience by having Noel Redding come back. Calls continued to be made, but it did not look promising and Jimi did not want to increase the uncertainty around his music.

On September 10, Les Perrin arranged a few interviews with the press, enough to get some print out there on the status of Hendrix and his music. The decision to let Billy go home made Jimi very thoughtful about his entire journey to this point. He summed it up in *Melody Maker*'s offices when he told a small group, "I've turned full circle. I've given this era of music everything." But he insisted that nothing had changed in his sound, his music that had propelled him to stardom. "My music's the same." He assured them that he could not think of "anything new to add to it in its present state." But then he went on to talk about the future, "thinking that this era of music sparked off by the Beatles had come to an end." Whatever the new expression would be, "Jimi Hendrix will be there." He contemplated a possible future for himself. "I want a big band . . . full of competent musicians I can conduct and write for." He wanted to be able to "marry earth rhythms with celestial pictures."

But he also knew he was there to reassure his British public. He revealed that he thought he had been forgotten in England, maybe they did not want him anymore. He termed his long stay in the States "a vanishing act." After the last American tour, he had just concentrated on writing and recording in New York, all the while feeling he was "through here." But he had continued to think that perhaps he had relied on too much of "a visual thing." When he did not do his patented stage routine, people must have "thought I was being moody, but I can only freak when I really feel like doing so." He wanted an audience to be able to "sit back and close their eyes" and experience the music in their minds "without caring a damn what we were doing onstage."

But in general he thought he was a better guitarist because he had learned a lot and was still learning, not resting on recently gained laurels.. With a bigger band he would not be playing as much guitar: "I want other musicians to play my stuff. I want to be a good writer." And then he floated the idea about not doing as many live gigs and instead having an "audiovisual thing that you sit down and plug into and really take it through your ears and eyes. I'm so happy. It's gonna be good."

But upon leaving *Melody Maker* with upbeat, positive message, his depressed mood had returned by the time he got to ex-Monkee Mike Nesmith's party in Hyde Park at the posh Inn on the Park Hotel for his new band's LP release promotion. Keith Altham had urged him to come and he was glad he did. Nesmith said to Jimi that he had "invented" something in music. That Jimi was "one of the most important musical powers to come along in decades. And you're the fulcrum for a major shift in the landscape—not of popular music, but just of music in general." Jimi customarily demurred, saying that he was working on his singing. Nesmith was astounded. He was certain that Jimi "had no idea who he was or where he fit." It was clear to Nesmith that Jimi was at the center of a "hurricane."

Kristen and Karen joined Jimi and they went back to his suite, where he was to be interviewed formally by Altham, who had become more of an ally and a friend rather than a workaday journalist. Kristen was relaxed and easy with him. It was if they had been together for a long time. He liked that feeling. They all relaxed, drinking some excellent light wine, Mateus Rosé, and watched Karen and Kristen's favorite TV show, *The Kenny Everett Explosion*. It was one of his best and they laughed heartily throughout. Jimi openly praised the show as the best he had ever seen. This pleased Altham. Jimi knew how important it was to Altham, to most Londoners, that their entertainment be appreciated by Americans.

They finally got started. Altham expected to go through the obvious questions. After all, he was working press. He asked Jimi if he was satisfied about the Isle of Wight performance. Jimi sputtered an answer that went all over the place. He mentioned being confused and mixed up and that he wouldn't base his whole future on that one gig. He mentioned playing "God Save the Queen" but then faced with an actual Brit instead of a black sky he was a bit embarrassed, and laughed nervously. After all, he was not British—"The Star Spangled Banner" was his own. It seemed that his version of "God Save the Queen" also suffered from the group not having played together since midsummer in Hawaii. It was a hasty decision, not well played, and if he had thought about it he probably would have left it alone; it had not been the best way to reenter England.

Altham mentioned that Billy Cox had returned to the States. That was the story and Jimi did not have much to say besides a monosyllabic yeah to that question, and to the obvious follow-up as to whether he'd be looking for a new bass player. Of course.

Jimi could not really talk about his new direction because it was so much up in the air. Altham knew this but could not avoid the obvious questions. He probed Jimi about "the new, subdued, mature Jimi Hendrix." His haircut, his extensive studio work, his absence from London where he had left as a psychedelic wild thing, and had returned as a thoughtful, sophisticated New Yorker. "I felt like I was changing and getting into a heavier music and it was getting unbearable with the three pieces." Jimi again floated the notion of a larger group. "I always wanted to expand . . . but I think I'll go back to three pieces again" with a new bass player, "and I'll probably be loud again." He laughed. It was so obvious he was reassuring his old fan base.

Altham was bringing up the obvious aspects of Jimi's new image that Jimi, so comfortably accepted in New York City, had failed to properly prepare the British public for. They were still into Jimi as the Experience, with two locals, Mitch and Noel, and the frizzy, frilly Afros and frilly clothes. As Altham termed it: "The days of the baubles and bangles and the freaky hairstyle have all disappeared." Was Jimi worried that his "quieter approach now may lose a little of the mystique" that first attracted his huge fan base?

Jimi could only say "everybody goes through those stages." New groups breaking in like Mountain or Cactus were growing their hair longer and longer and "strangling themselves with beads and jewelry and stuff." But for himself, Jimi thought it had gotten out of hand and that he was "being too loud." He laughed because the connection with loudness of color and audio volume converged. But "my nature just changes, you know . . . I just started cutting my hair." He laughed. "Rings disappearing one by one." He did not want to just be "hyped up on all the visual things, you know." He wanted his audience to hear him too, "like, listen too."

Altham wanted to know if the early Jimi Hendrix " 'freak' thing was really a kind of publicity hype." Jimi had to demur. He was doing what he wanted to do, it was his scene: burning guitars, destruction. He had not known it was anger-related until the press termed it such. But he believed that everyone should have a room "where they can do a release at. So my room was a stage." He laughed.

Altham brought him back to the subject of the Isle of Wight and the need for a new bass player. Jimi, aware of the show business aspects of the whole thing, did not want to rule out being the same wild man the British had known and loved. He let it be known there would be an upcoming tour of England and that he could get "very wild, though, and wrapped up into that other scene again, you know. Like with the hair and so forth, or the visuals."

Altham knew that Jimi was close to Pink Floyd. They had toured the States together and perhaps their thing was something Jimi wanted to get closer to. Jimi saw Pink Floyd as playing a different kind of music, "like a space type of thing, like an inner-space type of thing." But if he were to get into something like that it would be "a little more easier," but with a "solid beat." Not only would he have more beat, but "more music."

Jimi agreed with Altham's suggestion, in the form of a question, of having "an organist, and a vocalist . . ." Jimi interrupted this foray, agreeing with that augmentation and adding another guitarist. If he could do it, "that would be out of sight." They segued into the subject of songwriting, and Jimi's humbleness was in evidence. He was still trying to get that together. "All I'm writing is just what I feel, that's all." But "I don't really round it off too good, you know, I just keep it almost naked." He laughed, a little embarrassed. He thought that a lot of songs currently in circulation and coming out were "too heavy—almost to the state of unbearable." But he had "this one little saying: When things get too heavy, just call me helium, the lightest gas known to man." He laughed delightedly.

Keith Altham seemed to be casting about for Jimi to make a statement about the future of "music, popular music" changing the world or "as a reflection of the world." Jimi replied, "But like if they, see, then, well their reflection of the world is like blues." He added, "That's where that part of the music is at." But there was another kind of music coming around, "not sunshine music" but more of "an easier type of thing, with less words and more meaning to it." He thought of Flower Power, the love generation of the immediate past, the sixties, "And you don't have to be singing about love all the time, to give love to the people."

Did Jimi "ever want to change the world?" Jimi gave the question a thoughtful pause. He would want to be a part of a changing world in such a way that it would improve, and "where young and old don't clash so much together." But a big problem was conformity on all fronts. The "human race" was carrying the same old burdens around. Jimi was certain that "you have to be a freak in order to be different, and even freaks, they're very prejudiced. You have to have your hair long and talk in a certain way in order to be with them, you know." But in order to be with the more establishment, traditional people, "you have to have your hair short and wear ties. So we're trying to make a third world happen." He laughed seriously. "You know what I mean?"

Altham went into Jimi's music as expressing anger and rage against the establishment's principles. Jimi interrupted that flow. He denied raging against it. "If it were up to me, there would be no such thing as establishment." He laughed at his verbal audacity. "But see that's nothing but blues, that's all I'm singing about, today's blues."

Altham asked about Jimi's personal politics. Jimi replied that he had started to get seriously into politics, but now he considers that as a stage he was going through like everybody else. For him, "It all comes out in the music most of the time." He was on a roll of sorts. 'We have this one song called 'Straight Ahead' and it says, like, 'Power to the people, freedom of the soul, pass it on to the young and old. And we don't give a damn if your hair is short or long, Communication's coming on strong.' "

Altham jumped from there to the standard question of Hendrix's relationship with the "Black Panther movement in the States." Had he had any problems? "Problems, no." Jimi maneuvered away saying that there are many political situations out there he has to get away from because they boxed him in. "If I had anything to say I'd have a say to everybody."

Altham charged, "Have they ever demanded of you that you play a concert for the Panthers?" Jimi was up front: "Well actually they asked us, which I was really, you know, I was happy for them to ask us. I was honored." But it had not happened yet. And here Jimi pointed to that situation as one of many problems with his management. "Ah, Mike Jeffery, he's taking care of that side of it, so I don't know if we'll ever." Jimi could have easily added his wish to get away from that brand of controlling management. He knew what he wanted to do, he didn't need Jeffery to decide anything about his music, or who he associated with, or played a benefit for.

Altham switched the subject back to music, noting that it has been said that Jimi "invented psychedelic music." Jimi got a kick out of that, he laughed—"A mad scientist approach." Altham persisted, asking whether Jimi intentionally wrote "for psychedelic purposes?" Jimi went back to his most popular song identified with psychedelics "Purple Haze," that after three years had also become a famous name for a brand of LSD. But he did not think it an "invention of psychedelic." Rather, the song "was just asking a lot of questions. It says damn, wait a minute. I feel, you know, 'scuse me while I do this, you know, for a second. Then you feel yourself like going in different, strange areas, and all this— like most curious people do, and I just happen to put it on 'Purple Haze.' " He liked to contrast reality and fantasy: "You have to use fantasy in order to show different sides of reality. That's how it can bend. . . ." Reality is nothing but each individual's own way of thinking. And then the Establishment grabs a big piece of that, you know, and the Church of England and so forth, on down the line."

He thought that he would release "this thing called 'Horizon. Between Here and Horizon.' " "Room Full of Mirrors" was "more of a mental disarrangement that a person might be thinking. This says something about broken glass used to be all in my brain and so forth." Jimi pondered over other new tracks he was working on at Electric Lady. Of "Astro Man," a new kind of superhero who was "saying something about living in peace of mind," but who could also "leave you in pieces." He also mentioned "Valleys of Neptune Arising," pointing out that none of those new songs could be considered psychedelic. Altham seemed intent on making the connection between LSD and Jim's music, perhaps he was also giving him a chance to talk about the growth of his work. Jimi responded, mentioning "one little 'Bolero' type of thing." He tried to describe its movement: "It breaks down into a very simple pattern, asking this one question. Like where you coming from or where you going to, and then this little girl answers, you know. But like it's not really into the really big mass movement in music that I want to do." But then again he had in mind other kinds of sounds that were going in a different direction. What Europeans called classical music he conceived of in another way. "I don't plan to just go out there with a ninety-piece orchestra and play, you know, two and a half hours of classical music." His own music would meld rock and classical "without even knowing that it's rock and classic. With it being a whole 'nother theme then."

They had to return to the Isle of Wight festival, the immensity of it was just sinking in. Now it was recent history. "The Isle of Wight was great, you know, people milling about, digging each other . . . so many mixtures of different countries." The only trouble came not from those people, but "from the other people that can't understand the idea of mixing so many different people together under the name of music." Jimi had been to many countries in Europe and could not fail to note that in "World War Two, all these countries were completely against each other." But now "we're getting them all together through the idea of music." Jimi was awed by the attendees. "Five hundred thousand people. That's way larger than the average city, for instance, in England." Those numbers would contain everything any city would have, outcasts, gate-crashers. "You're gonna have the other side of everything. All of it." But it was up to the people "if they want to keep it going." Because the festivals are really for them "to dig themselves, and so forth, you know. Just mingle around meeting different, other people. That's groovy. That's why they should give more to a festival, they should have not only music, but theater and, you know, selling things, and circuses and so forth."

They went into how it could be possible to have free festivals. Jimi had given a lot of thought to touring for expenses only, even down to controlling ticket prices in order to keep them affordable.

They concluded by talking about money: Did Jimi have enough to live comfortably from here on out, even if he would no longer have the income of a "professional entertainer"? That was a joke, Jimi's income was so tied up between paying for the recording studio, with Jeffery's huge percentage of all of his income, and with the settlements that Chalpin was getting, he could hardly stop working. But he humored Altham. If he did have enough money to live a fantasy life he would, upon awaking, "just roll over in my bed into an indoor swimming pool, and then swim to the breakfast table," even swim into the bathroom to "shave and whatever." But on the other hand it could just as well be "a tent, maybe overhanging a mountain stream." He had to laugh at that image of himself as some kind of nature guy.

Finney had returned to London to do Hendrix's hair. Finney was now Miles Davis's official hairdresser but often doubled on Hendrix's head when the two's schedules did not conflict. He had gotten Miles's permission to stay on in Europe after the great jazzman's tour, which had included the Isle of Wight, also, and do Jimi's hair for a while, before joining Miles again in time for his West Coast tour in the States. Finney found that Hendrix's tour had been canceled and that Hendrix was hiding out. Billy Cox was virtually a vegetable.

Billy Cox had not spoken a word that made sense since being out of the hospital several days.

Cox had to have someone he knew with him around the clock in Gerry Stickells's flat. They needed the privacy and also needed to avoid the press. Finney prepared Hendrix's hair daily and generally helped out. There was little else to do.

Since Billy had never before had acid or whatever that was he'd taken, there was no way to reorient him, so he had to be taken to a hospital where the customary Thorazine was administered. From the shock of acid-rush revelation to the sudden all-the-way-down of Thorazine—the drug given to settle him—Cox had become a vegetable of sorts. Several concerts, including the one at De Doelen of September 13, 1970, were canceled, and Hendrix took Cox to London to rest and work out the vicious combination of drugs that had made Cox like a walking, paranoid zombie.

Although it would have been better for Jimi and Billy to return to the United States, Jimi knew that Billy could not make the trip in the state that he was in. Fearing that Billy might freak out in public, where he would run the risk of being institutionalized, Jimi hid Billy out in London. Jimi was the only person there Billy knew well and trusted totally. He felt responsible for Billy's condition and was determined to make sure that Billy got back home safely. He would wait until Billy came back to himself. Until he was fit to travel, no matter how long that took.

Jimi was caught in a bind. It was a very bad time for him to stay in London. Ed Chalpin of PPX Productions, the same concern that had been awarded the settlement, had pressed his fight to London, where Hendrix still had not been taken to court. Other lawyers were after him to give blood in two paternity lawsuits. Dodging messengers, process servers, and subpoenas, Hendrix was forced to live an underground existence while tending to the needs of Billy Cox.

Waiting for Billy to come around was rough on the nerves. He had much more time on his hands than he had had during his first days in London back in 1966. He checked out several friends on a regular basis. He spent a good deal of his time with Kristen, until Alvenia Bridges caught up with him.

Alvenia had been staying at Pat Hartley's mansion up on Elvinstone Terrace since the spring. When Jimi first got to London, before the Isle of Wight, he called Pat Hartley's and got Alvenia instead (Pat was still in Hawaii). He was glad to hear Alvenia's voice. They had not seen each other in two years, since Alvenia had split New York for Switzerland. They had a lot to catch up on. They met at Pat Hartley's place and talked, bringing each other up to date.

Alvenia, an attractive sister with a soft voice and cozy air, who had gone to Switzerland with such love and hope, now nursed a broken heart. But she was happy to be back on the London scene with her old running buddies.

Jimi was extremely tired, in a way she had never seen before, but he was all right. That Michael Jeffery had arrived in London that day brought into focus the problems with his management not doing the right things for him, but Electric Lady Studios was a proud reality. But right then Jimi's mood shifted and he went into an anxiety attack Alvenia had never even guessed he was capable of. Alarmed, she hugged him and kissed him and calmed him the best she could. He rambled on about being kidnapped in New York City and taken to a house in up-state New York. There was a strange involvement of his management, Michael Jeffery, although that scenario ended with his supposed rescue by Jeffery.

He was very emphatic about something that was stuck in his mind to the ef-fect that his management would stop at nothing, would do absolutely anything to keep him under control.

Alvenia, a sensitive soul, realized how unhappy Jimi was in London. She thought he needed a whole lot of love just to maintain equilibrium. She wished she could do more for him, realizing that her hugs and kisses, whatever she could do, "wasn't enough."

There was no way for Jimi to avoid the fact that Michael Jeffery had arrived in London. Jimi's road manager and assistant, Stickells and Barrett, were em-ployees of his and Jeffery's, and were paid by Jeffery out of the money Jimi earned. The London office had long ceased to exist. The office had shifted to America, where the bulk of their revenues came from. The fact that Billy was in-communicado and staying at Stickells's place was certainly an extension of Stickells's employee status with Jeffery and Hendrix. It was his job to take care of things. They were on the road in London, luckily where Stickells had his home. But Jimi, as the star, could move any way he wanted, see who he wanted, when he wanted—so he would be able to avoid Jeffery in London. But the mere fact that Jeffery was in town and that Ed Chalpin had also arrived filled him with a dread that went beyond the mere facts of the legalities of the situation.

Sunday evening, September 13, Kristen joined Jimi at his hotel suite at the Cumberland. Angie Burdon and several others Kristen did not know were there, too. Soon after her arrival, Kristen called the director of the film she was starring in. He had expected her to be back Sunday night, but she was extend-ing the return date that she had already extended several times since she had met Jimi. The director accused her of being "a fucking groupie" so loudly that everyone in the room could overhear his voice from the telephone. Jimi became furious. He wanted her not to return at all. But she smoothed things over. She had worked on the film for six months. She owed it to all the people working on it and to her own professionalism to return. Jimi calmed down and agreed. Somehow they had become close enough for her to risk her career and for them to be making mutual decisions about her movements.

Monday, September 14: that morning as Kristen was preparing to leave, Jimi did not want her to go. He said he wanted her to leave the film, get away from the influence of the director. But it was probably the fact that they had been together solidly from the day after he had arrived in London on August 28 until now—with him through all the crazy goings on, she had been there steady as a rock. She had even taken him to her mother's home, where he had indeed been sheltered from the storm. But now after almost three weeks (an eternity for his relationships) she was leaving him. His separation anxiety was quite intense, and when he gripped her with his unconscious, overpowering strength, he unknowingly bruised her. He became desperate and bitter and, grasping at straws, accused her of sleeping with the director. Tearful, Kristen had no choice but to return to the production to which she was essential and into which many millions of dollars had been invested. But his accusations were also an insult. The only way for her to leave was to abruptly stalk out in anger. But as she walked down the corridor, Jimi had implored her to call him that night.

Alvenia had taken to hanging out at the Speakeasy. It was an exciting atmosphere. Most of the people there were into music and into the Isle of Wight, which was being touted as England's Woodstock. It was like hanging out at the Scene club. In fact, Alvenia met the girl who used to take the tickets at the Scene. She had married one of the members of Chicago.

Alvenia had been having lunch on Monday, September 14, when Monika Dannemann came over to her. They had known each other a couple of years ago when they both had spent time at a posh Italian resort; Monika had had to make Alvenia remember her. Somehow Dannemann knew Alvenia knew Jimi.

Dannemann said that she had known Jimi very well. They had been lovers. He had been the first man ever to make love to her; she had been a virgin when they met. She began to cry. If Alvenia saw Jimi would she tell him that Monika was trying desperately to get in touch with him?

At that point Alvenia left the table and called Jimi, although she did not let Monika know what she was going to do. Alvenia said that there was this German chick named Monika Dannemann sitting at her table at the Speakeasy who said she was a good friend of his. Jimi laughed and made arrangements to meet them.

They all got together. Monika and Jimi seemed to get along very well. The three of them had dinner together that night. Then they dropped Alvenia off in Monika's blue sports car, which was a great convenience.

Eric Burdon, another old London friend, was due in from L.A. to appear with a new band called War. The band consisted of brothers from L.A. and they were known to really cook. Jimi was looking forward to meeting up with some stateside brothers who could blow. He dearly missed being able to play and record regularly.

Stella and Alan Douglas, Colette, Luna, and Devon were due in town any day now. Jeanette Jacobs, who was so kind in helping out with Billy, was cool. Kathy Etchingham was as vibrant as ever.

Wire service journalist and author Sharon Lawrence was surprised to see Jimi at Ronnie Scott's for Eric Burdon and War's opening the evening of September 5. She thought he would still be touring. She had been dividing her time between the Rolling Stones tour and accompanying Jimi's tour, but had left before they had gone into Germany to rejoin the Stones in Copenhagen. Although aware of Billy Cox's dosing, she did not know that things had continued to deteriorate to the point where the tour had to be canceled. She saw Jimi was with "a heavily but perfectly made-up, expensively dressed" Monika Dannemann, "her face glowing with pride." But Jimi moved slowly, as if he were having trouble keeping his balance. When she came up to him he did not seem to recognize her. He was in a daze, she thought. She had to say her name to him several times. Billy Cox's condition had often required the same protocol. Jimi appeared extremely tired, his skin had no tonality, his eyes strange and afraid. Looking at her directly, something he seldom did, he had only one thing to say to her: "I'm almost gone."

Lawrence sensed something very awful happening to Jimi. She could not say what, but it at once made her very upset. She left immediately, missing Burdon's second set, which Jimi had just arrived for.

Jimi made his way backstage. Burdon was glad to see his friend. He was worried about him. Eric Barrett, Jimi's road manager, had expressed serious concern about Jimi to Burdon earlier that day, saying Jimi was in really bad shape. But Burdon would not intervene. He reasoned that Jimi would not listen to him, as he was in no shape to be advising anyone else, nor would Jimi listen to anybody else anyway. But as the members of War watched Jimi barely able to walk through the dressing room, they found it hard to believe that he wanted to sit in with them. Burdon dodged the question, noting aloud that Jimi was wobbling. Terry McVay, former Animal road manager who now performed the same function for War, picked up on it right away. He was the one who had carried Jimi's guitar when he first arrived in London nearly four years ago. McVay told Jimi he couldn't allow him to play. Eric joined in, suggesting he come back the next night and sit in. That was very strange—usually a superstar was never denied.

But Jimi was so uncharacteristically out of control, nearly unable to walk, that there was no way he could have played. The brothers in War did not get into it, but to them Jimi had looked definitely "smacked out," having had too much heroin, or perhaps tweaking right after a hit, or simply stone drunk.

Jimi left, still practically being held up by Monika Dannemann, who seemed unaware of how bad off he was. They passed Rolling Stones guitarist Ron Wood, who noted how unnaturally slowly Jimi was moving. He had to shout to make Hendrix look at him and return his good-night wishes.

Later, alone, Jimi finally went by the old place that Chas, Lotta, Kathy, and he had shared not too long ago. Now Chas was there with his family. Jimi wanted very much to meet their baby boy Stephen, who he had not yet seen. Chas and Lotta were glad to see him. Their surprise dissipated as they made their dear old friend comfortable. The shelter of a real home did wonders for Jimi: It did not take long for him to come down from the remaining throes of a crazy high and be himself. He was feeling totally exposed in a London he had lost touch with in the nearly two years he had been gone. He was back in the home he had known the best, and it felt very good.

They played Risk, like in the old days, and they talked about the business of the music. Jimi hoped Chas would eventually (sooner than later) come back as his manager. Jimi definitely needed someone to take some of the weight from his shoulders. He was doing it all himself. Jeffery was getting the gigs and taking his percentage and that was pretty much it. But Jimi was handling everything else, including the day-to-day stuff, pretty much by himself, and the burden was breaking him down, especially when things went wrong. And there was no one watching his back.

He even called Electric Lady Studios and talked with Ed Kramer. He wanted to impress upon Chas the seriousness of his desire to bring him back, not only as manager but also as coproducer. He was aware that Chas felt he should have received at least coproducer credit on the *Electric Ladyland* album. And there he was, demonstrating that he would have the tapes for his forthcoming album shipped to London for them to resume their old relationship just by verbal agreement, a handshake, their words.

Of course, the brief conversation with Kramer revealed the absurdity of the request. They had just built a state-of-the-art studio for Jimi and he had recorded the bulk of the album there.

Kramer gave the phone to one of the Twins, who was within earshot. Jimi quickly told him about Billy, but he did not reveal that Billy was still in London. Word was that Billy had flown home, but that was to prevent the intervention of any authorities who might insist Billy be institutionalized in England.

Jimi had made the call as a gesture for Chas, and Chas had gotten excited. He would book time at Olympic Studios Monday or Tuesday at the latest, and they could get in there after he brought his family back from a weekend in-law trek north.

Jimi knew that Chas could handle Jeffery and would do anything to protect his artists.

Jimi returned to Stickells's flat Wednesday, September 16, where Billy Cox was being kept. He was saddened to see that Billy had not improved, although he had kept constantly abreast of his condition. Billy had still not uttered a sensible word.

Jimi took Billy to his suite at the Cumberland and instructed the desk to admit no one except his hairdresser, Finney. That noon Finney came by to do Jimi's hair. Billy and Jimi sat in the kitchen while Finney set up shop. Jimi had some hashish, which he was reluctant to offer to Finney because he did not want to smoke around Billy. Finney began to curl Jimi's hair, which he would eventually comb out into flowing waves. Although Jimi had been pretty much into the Afro, he seemed to favor a slight modification of the older style in London. Jimi, the perfect, polite host, finally offered Finney some hashish. He was relieved when Finney refused it. Finney had dug Jimi's hesitation and understood the circumstances. It all went by Billy, who watched Finney press curl after curl with almost moronic intensity. After one particularly pretty curl, Finney and Jimi were startled to hear Billy Cox say, "That was a good one." Jimi could not believe his ears. Finney was blown away. It was a great moment. Billy had finally broken through his dreadful silence. That meant they all could return to the States. Jimi and Finney were overjoyed. They tried to act as if it was no big thing, but a big load had been taken off their minds.

Jimi and Finney made plans to meet that night at Ronnie Scott's to celebrate. Finney went back to his hotel room to prepare for his return to the States. He had a tour to do and he wanted to get some rest in his New York apartment. Jimi went over to see Stella, Alan, and Devon, who were staying at Danny Secunda's apartment. They had been in London since Monday and he was long overdue for a visit with his running buddies. He felt liberated now that Billy was all right. He wanted to talk over some business with Alan. He wanted to be clear of a lot of the bullshit when he returned to the States, and Alan, as a friend and adviser, would help.

Devon was pissed off at Jimi. She had been looking for him for two days. Stella was her usual calm and intelligent self. It was like being home. They had been concerned for him and now they were all together, happy and at ease. Devon, who always had an attitude, cooled down and began to take Jimi through some familiar changes. She teased him about the Danish woman he had been with. It seemed to her that he had to have a blonde a week or he was not satisfied. Jimi asked her about Mick Jagger. Devon said that he was in Düsseldorf, Germany. They traded Mae West impersonations and suddenly everything was all right between them again. Jimi got a limo and took the girls shopping.

Jimi met Monika and Alvenia at Judy Wong's birthday party, an impromptu afternoon affair at Pat Hartley's mansion. Alvenia and Judy resided in a couple of the many rooms, as did several other guests (model Amanda Lear, designer Johnny Make, and writer Andrew Cockburn), while Hartley and her husband were in residence in Hawaii working in postproduction on the film *Rainbow Bridge*. Wong had recently broken up with her boyfriend Glen Cornick, who played with the band Jethro Tull, and there was a concerted effort among the "girls," led by Alvenia, to cheer her up. Monika gladly contributed to the cost of finger sandwiches, cakes, and drinks. She made the most of the occasion by announcing that she and Jimi were engaged and showing off a snake ring he had given her as something tantamount to an engagement ring.

Jimi sang "Happy Birthday" just for Judy's ears and then bussed her on the cheek. He also told her that he and Monika were getting married.

That night they all met at Ronnie Scott's to check out Eric Burdon and War. Alvenia, Finney, Devon, Stella, Alan, Judy, and Angie Burdon were all sitting together. Finney had not known Devon was in town and expected Jimi to be furious when he found out. Jimi walked in with Monika Dannemann, came by the table, and said hello, bussing Finney's hair and grasping Devon's neck in a mock stranglehold. He took a nearby table for two and then went backstage. He was very anxious to play.

During the last set, with Eric Burdon sitting in the audience, Jimi and War played an extended version of the Memphis Slim song "Mother Earth." It's a straight-up blues, and they played it with no affectations, shouting the choruses in unison.

Mississippi born, Memphis Slim had died just seven years before, in 1963, at the age of 45, at a time when he was just beginning to receive the recognition for his blues lyrics and innovative slide guitar technique. He died relatively young, especially for a blues musician,

Elmore James uses the image of mother earth as the source to which everyone must return. The concept of the mother refers to birth; mother earth, as the source of life of humanity, is also the repository of the body, of human remains. Elmore James lists achievements that a person can attain: owning most of a city, personal aircraft, racehorses, precious metals, gems and stones. But no matter how high a status one has achieved, how much they may own, or how great their personal worth:

When it all ends up
You got to go back to mother earth.

It would be the last song Jimi ever played.

Howard Scott and Jimi traded guitar leads and rhythm. Jimi got off a decent solo and enhanced the changes with skillful manipulations of the melody. Lee Oskar's harmonica and Charles Miller's saxophone blended remarkably well, with both taking excursions out over the melody. Miller tagged the tune out with a mellow solo and that was it.

Jimi returned to Monika and found that she and Devon had had a tiff. Monika had shown off the snake ring Jimi had given her recently and declared that she and Jimi were planning to get married. Devon called her on that. Monika glossed over the threat, but those who knew Devon made sure the ladies said no more to each other.

Devon simply did not like Monika. She had bad vibes about her. It was beyond simply dealing with Jimi's various women. She did it all the time, often getting rid of the ones he had tired of, or helping him to get new, strange, or exotic ones. Sometimes they did threesomes. They also had a thing with each other, but she and Jimi did as they pleased. It was not about jealousy. But this was different. Monika Dannemann set things off in Devon and she refused to suppress those bad feelings.

Jimi left with Monika and Alvenia. Alvenia seemed to be more upset than anybody about the argument. She wished she had known that Devon and Jimi had had a thing going in the States ever since she had been gone; she most certainly would not have helped Monika and Jimi get together.

Later Jimi joined Danny Secunda, Devon, Stella, and Alan at dinner at a Moroccan restaurant on Fulham Road. Jimi, it was obvious, was quite worried about Michael Jeffery. Secunda felt that Alan Douglas was "hustling" Jimi to take over as his manager. Jimi did not say much, Alan Douglas did most of the talking. Secunda noted that "Jimi and the girls were so smacked out," in the intense portion of a heroin high, that "they barely ate anything or even said a word." They all went back to Secunda's place and "Jimi went off to bed with Stella and Devon. He loved a ménage à trois." It was clear to Secunda that Jimi was stressed, but as a veteran of the music business, Secunda did not find that unusual.

In the morning, Jimi rode with Alan Douglas in a cab to the airport. They talked about what Douglas could do for Jimi in terms of the new direction he wished to head in.

Stella, Alan, Colette, and Devon—they were all like some kind of strange extended family. He and Alan could talk about his future plans, although sometimes it felt that Alan was taking advantage of that extended family connection.

But Alan was better than a sounding board. He was a facilitator in Jimi's new musical direction involving more musicians and more involved compositions, in which he would not have to be the superstar and primary instrumentalist. Alan was having some success outside of his usual jazz thing with the Last Poets LP he had produced, which was in the *Billboard* Top 30 best-selling albums.

Alan Douglas had performed various favors for Jimi. Their informal arrangement involved Douglas as a semiproducer and a semimanager. There was no doubt that Douglas wanted a more formal relationship from a business point of view. After all, he was no novice in the music world. He had pulled off some very interesting feats. Jimi was wondering whether they could operate on a more formal level in spite of Jeffery. Jimi talked about what he wanted to do when he returned to America and Douglas sought to see where he could fit in. It seemed that all plans stopped at Jeffery. He had such control over Jimi to the extent that it had been impossible for Jimi to even see the legal papers spelling it all out. Every time Jimi had requested to see the legal documents that governed his and Jeffery's relationship as client and manager, he was put off one way or the other. Jimi and Alan had bumped heads with Jeffery more than once. The last time was that spring when they had a big showdown meeting with Mo Ostin, president of the Warner Bros. music division. The meeting had resolved with Jimi staying with Jeffery. It had been embarrassing, as if the meeting had been called to just let Jimi let off some steam. Whenever Jimi and Alan discussed his management they got bogged down, but when they talked about future projects ideas flew. There was a question of whether the Caravan thing could happen now that Billy had had a bad experience, but he would find a suitable bass player sooner or later. But instead of having Jimi do a heavy touring thing they talked of doing a tour for every season, autumn, winter, spring, and summer. They would film everything and then send the films of the concerts around in between the seasonal tours. Jeffery still remained the big hang-up. Finally they had a solution: agree to pay Jeffery his management percentage for the remainder of the contract. It was a great idea, they felt. If it was only money preventing them from moving on, then they would pay Jeffery his money so they could do what they wanted. Their agreement expired in December 1970. They got really excited. Douglas would fly back to the United States the next day and meet with Steingarten and Mo Ostin. Steingarten would, as Jeffery's lawyer, be informed as to what they intended to do. Mo Ostin would be informed that Jimi wanted to release a double album that winter, not the single LP Warners expected. Jimi had trouble communicating that to Warner Bros. through his present management, so Douglas would do it.

Jimi rode the cab back into town and went to his suite at the Cumberland Hotel, where he ordered a meal from room service and also had them take his shoes and clean them.

That early afternoon he went over to Monika Dannemann's place at the Samarkand Hotel. They hung out in the garden having tea and she took some photos of him. She was telling him she was trained as an artist and could use the photos to make paintings that could perhaps be covers for his albums. Jimi laughed. He got that a lot. He was a little surprised. They drank tea and hung out for a while, then decided to go to Kensington Market. He had been buying a bunch of clothes in anticipation of his return to New York, which, now that Billy was taken care of, would probably be in two or three days, Sunday or Monday.

Finney was in the gift shop of the Kensington Market doing some last-minute shopping when he bumped into Devon and Angie. He had just purchased an antique guitar pin for Jimi. They told him that they had just seen Jimi and Monika in another part of the market. Finney would have liked to give Jimi the gift himself but he realized that he only had enough time to catch a cab to the hotel, where his bags waited in the lobby, and continue on to the airport. He asked Devon if she would give the gift to Jimi and when she agreed, he inscribed a note on the tiny card. It said, "I wish I were a guitar." He gave the package to Devon and split for the States, taking Billy Cox with him.

Devon and Angie found Jimi and gave him the package. He had not seen them before and was surprised they were there. He excused himself from Monika and went with them to find Stella. They all greeted each other and went outside to chat. One of the older but hip wealthy Londoners they knew, Peter Cameron, was giving a dinner party that evening; the girls wondered if Jimi would like to go. Sure he did. He knew people who would be there. They decided to meet and go together. While they talked Stella was struck by Jimi's eyes. They were fantastic, deep and wise. Stella, who knew Jimi well, had not seen his eyes like that often. He seldom looked in anyone's eyes, but today he seemed to be staring into Stella's soul. Devon picked up on it, too. They saw something very special happening inside of him.

Stella was surprised when Jimi just tripped on with them back to their flat while she and Devon changed clothes. They were just hanging out, enjoying one another's company. Then Jimi had Monika pick him up. He had to get things together for his return to the States now that Billy was on his way back.

While driving to the hotel, Jimi and Monika pulled up next to a well-dressed young man driving a stylish white 1968 Mustang with two pretty young teenage girls inside, who waved very excitedly at Jimi. Philip Harvey was an obviously upper-class young man. His father was in the House of Lords. He invited Jimi and Monika for tea at his home, which was nearby. Jimi was agreeable but first they had to stop at his hotel for him to change clothes and pick up messages. At the hotel, Jimi called Mitch Mitchell regarding the arrival of Sly Stone in London that evening and getting together with Sly, Ginger Baker, and Mitch to jam. Jimi was very excited, as Sly was one of his personal favorite performers. They went to Harvey's home and the two young women made food and rolled joints and treated Jimi with great yet delicate respect. This seemed to anger Dannemann, who had by then drunk a good amount of wine. After Jimi and one of the women went off to a small room together, Dannemann stormed out and Jimi followed her. A loud argument ensued; Dannemann was screaming that Jimi was a fucking pig. Since Harvey lived on a street with other wealthy homeowners he was afraid someone would call the police. He went out to try and get them back in the house, but Dannemann would not move. He went back inside. Soon Jimi came in and apologized and departed. It was obvious Jimi was quite disturbed by Dannemann's behavior.

Monika dropped Jimi at the dinner party. He went in alone.

There were several groups of people in various rooms of the large floor-through when he got there. Stella, Devon, and Jimi found friends in the bedroom: Bert Kleiner, the financier; David Saloman, heir to the Wimpy fast-food chain; and Pete Cameron, music publisher, who was an old friend of Alan and Stella's. Jimi and Bert got into a long rap, both supine on the bed. There was nothing to get high with there, only liquor and conversation. Stella and Devon knew that Jimi, like them, wanted to get high. Devon came up with two black-bombers (amphetamines). She took one and Jimi took one. Later someone else came up with some pure Owsley powdered sunshine LSD in a small gold box. There was not much, but the benefactor warned that it was very powerful. Jimi, Stella, and Devon took some hits of it through their nostrils. It got them all high. Stella stared at the crystals of her necklace for a long time, Devon seemed to almost pass out, and Jimi continued to rap.

The food came and Stella took charge. She pulled the food out of the bags and containers and served up several bowls, but no one seemed to be interested in food. Stella called Jimi to the phone; she thought it might be Monika calling. After the call Jimi appeared to be about to leave. Stella saw him trying to get Devon to come with him, but Devon was dozing off from the effects of two powerful chemicals. Stella heard a horn honk outside and, going to the window, she saw long blonde hair in a blue car. She went and told Jimi that she thought someone was there to pick him up. Stella tried to let Devon know that Jimi was leaving and Jimi was telling her to come along with him, but Devon did not break out of her lethargy. Jimi went back into the kitchen with Stella and talked and joked with her for a good while. He heard people on the balcony heckling Monika, it was getting nasty. Finally he walked out of the door after sampling from the bowl of food Stella held in her hands. Stella went to Devon and asked her if she wanted to follow him and catch up. Devon said no. Stella said, "You know, you're terrible." Devon replied, "It's okay, it's all right—I'll find him later," and went back to sleep.

Jimi rode off with Monika driving her blue sports car.

•   •   •

Lansdowne Crescent has come alive. Porters sweep the outsides of their buildings, the black cabs grind up Notting Hill Gate Road, pedestrians on their way
to work pop from every doorway, and the birds have muted their songs as the
humans take over the day. Twenty-two Lansdowne Crescent. The dim trees of
the gray day. The birds of dawn rest on the block of the consulates. In the Scandinavian hotel no politics, only ancient Buddha *zazen* on the door. The dawn
comes creeping up with birdsong and pastel blues.

As Alvenia Bridges recalls: She awoke to the phone ringing. Eric Burdon picked
it up. She had wound up spending the night in his hotel suite. It was Monika
Dannemann on the phone. She was saying that Jimi would not wake up. Eric
shouted into the telephone, "CALL THE FUCKING AMBULANCE!" Alvenia
grabbed the phone. Monika was frantic, she did not know if she should, she was
worried that Jimi might get mad. Alvenia spoke to her very nicely, "Call the ambulance, call the ambulance right now." Monika said she couldn't wake Jimi, he
seemed to be sick in his sleep. Alvenia said, "I'll be right over. Hang up and call
the ambulance." Alvenia hung up and began dressing hurriedly. Clothes on, she
dialed Monika back. Monika was hysterical. "What hospital are you going to?"
Alvenia asked. Monika had not called the ambulance yet. Alvenia was astounded. "CALL THE AMBULANCE."

Eric grabbed the phone and again screamed, "CALL THE FUCKING AMBU-
LANCE!" Monika did not know if she should, Jimi might be mad about the
scandal. Alvenia got hysterical, too, and said, her voice on an emotional par
with Monika's, *"There's no time to lose. You have to call an ambulance."*

His body lies fully clothed on the bed. He is soaked in cheap red wine and a
huge amount of vomit. The door is wide open. There are policemen and men in
white coats. They roll him onto a stretcher, the ambulance takes off, the knell-
like wail of its siren clearing the busy streets. He is rushed from the ambulance
into St. Mary's Abbot Hospital. The doctors work on him.

Alvenia tried, she recalled, to call Jimi's road manager, Eric Barrett, then she
tried to reach Noel or Mitch. She could not seem to get the numbers right. She
reached Steve Gold, Eric Burdon and War's manager. He gave her a car to use and
she drove to the hospital. Monika was crying hysterically in the parking lot. She
said that Jimi's heart had stopped and his lung had collapsed but that there was a
good chance the doctors could revive him. Alvenia rushed off to call Eric and
Gerry Stickells. When she returned from the phone Monika was crying, "No,
no," and being physically restrained by a nurse. The nurse looked in Alvenia's

eyes and said, "Jimi Hendrix is dead." Monika cried, "You're lying, you're lying." Alvenia pulled her well-put-together body up and with all the sister in her, grabbed the nurse and said, "I don't believe you. You have to show me."

Someone finally let them see him. Alvenia and Monika went into a very clean and quiet white room, which was dimly lit and strangely peaceful. They saw Jimi lying there.

"He looked so beautiful."

CODA

Much more than the initial seven years of research and writing went into this biography. I traveled to London, Amsterdam, Seattle, Vancouver, New York, and Los Angeles and conducted over one hundred interviews. Reams of press material were collected, studied, and charted, as well as related articles, tape recordings, and books. The music of Jimi Hendrix was my active inspiration and abides as such.

In most cases I have fused the information derived from all sources into a narrative. I also used Hendrix's own words in informing the narrative at crucial junctures. I have refrained from editorializing both the subtle and the obvious in my desire to be objective. I have used some quotations of what others have said about Hendrix in the construction of several scenes that serve to coalesce bodies of fact. There are also some scenes that are biographically interpretive, yet they, too, are informed by facts and sources that lend themselves to such construction. In the few instances when I have been asked not to reveal the sources of information, names have been left out or changed. Where I have found source information to conflict, I have included both versions, or several versions.

Jimi Hendrix was a classic black ghetto "smoothie" whose mania and genius was electric guitar. He achieved an unmatched virtuoso style and became a musician's musician, a player's player, and a priest of the new age in Afro-American ceremonial music.

His music and words, studio or live, written or sung, are the best way of figuring him out—if that is the goal desired. Witnessing Jimi Hendrix playing live was a joy for many.

The particulars of his secular existence parallel everyman's. He ate, he slept, he made love, he worked (often harder than most men work), he made his mistakes and had his triumphs. The key to his life was creation. The most important thing in life for Jimi Hendrix was to create. And with pen and guitar, voice and ensemble, he kept his beliefs' bargain with his soul and left a wonderful legacy to us all.

In an intimate social setting, Jimi Hendrix appeared slender, elfin, and seemed even smaller with his traditional guitar-player slouch than his five-foot-ten-inch, broad-shouldered frame. He appeared "girlish" and even "jivey" to some, yet once Hendrix got onstage and played, he underwent a complete transformation. His body seemed to grow into the gargantuan sound the powerhouse amplifiers gave his guitar. Ablaze in the brilliant stage lights, his long arms and large hands were magnified. His Indian-boned jaw, high cheekbones, Tlaloc-like nose and mouth (that often chewed on a piece of gum), his slanted Afro-Asian eyes (and bouffant Afro, curls, or conk) gave him an incredible presence. Long-legged and tautly muscled in the trunk, he had a dancer's body that choreoed effortlessly with his music.

In these pages I quote liberally from his interviews, public and intimate. The reason is clear: Hendrix documented his life through his verse and through his oral improvisation on the interview.

Perhaps it was the contemplation of his mother's death and her love of music when she had been alive that inspired Hendrix to fall so deeply in love with music—to the extent that he often lost himself completely within its magic. Both he and his mother died at age twenty-seven.

Hendrix demonstrated a high order of voodoo. Not the pulp magazine tales of horror or the elementary sympathetic formulas—Hendrix showed the voodoo that related to the stars and to magical transformations. Milo Rigaud, an authority on Haitian voodoo, has written of the crossovers between voodoo and Freemasonry and other high orders of Western mystical systems. *Voudou* is an ancient African religion of tremendous power that unites the land by the codification of every tribe's drum battery rhythm to the solar offices: to the solar chromosphere, photosphere, and nucleus. Voodoo, as a religion, has been forced to dwell underground in America, as have other cultural and artistic manifestations of black people.

The song "Voodoo Chile" is a tale of creation that unites the religion with its transition to the West and its relationship to the solar systems. It speaks of legacy and transformation upon a "place of power" (a mountain summit), and then upon the wings of an eagle we are transported to the near planets. There we partake of the funk of life (methane seas) and the talismanic gems of love and power. At the beginning of the song Hendrix's mother's death is related in symbolic terms. At the end of the song supernatural powers are celebrated.

Jimi Hendrix often used death as his adviser. From "Hear My Train A-comin'" to "Voodoo Chile (Slight Return)," where Hendrix sets up a meeting in the next world if it cannot be accomplished in this one, the message is clear, as he intones, "If I don't meet you in this world, I'll meet you in the next world, so don't be late."

As a warrior, his sword and his salvation were his guitar. Throughout his life Hendrix produced an amazing amount of songs, chronicling them with a running philosophical commentary that ranged from the joys of sex to the mysteries of the universe. His musical compositions and performances coalesced all his words and beliefs into pure energy at a stellar level of creativity. His is a wonderful example of a gifted and productive artist.

Jimi Hendrix was one of the few top rock stars to come out against the war in Vietnam and in support of the black liberation movement in the United States. His "Machine Gun," recorded live at the Fillmore East during the height of the Vietnam War, was a devastating antiwar statement. Jimi made his declarations as an individual artist, he had no group to support his public stance.

He told Buddy Miles and Sue Cassidy Clark:

> In American riots you see these masochist kids. Some of 'em will say, "Well, we don't have nothin' else to live for anyway. This is our scene now." They go in there with no shelter, no anything. They get beat. I mean, you can see, you see how desperate the whole case must be if a kid's goin' to go out there and get his head busted open. Without no protection. Just gettin' things together. But then you look over in Japan. Now these students got it together and you must put this in the book, 'cause I'm tired of seein' Americans get their heads split open for no reason at all. The kids in Japan, they buy helmets, they got their little squadrons. The pink helmets for the left side, and they go in wedges like this. They got all their stuff together. They've got their shields. They're wearin' steel supports—protection. You have to have all these things if you're goin' to go up there; you might as well make it together. Just go on and do it together. I'd like to see these American kids with helmets on and big Roman shields and then do their thing! Really together. America. That music is goin' to tell 'em anything they want to know, really.

He did not seclude himself from the populace like most other superstars. He was not into Dylanesque reclusions, Rolling Stones traveling fortresses, or English countryside retirements like the Beatles. In Greenwich Village, Jimi was out there among the people who loved the music as much as he loved performing his own. At the Salvation disco on Sheridan Square, on Eighth Street where he was building his dream studio, or at Ungano's or the Scene, both in midtown, Jimi walked among the people. And although he was extremely shy he was always ready to talk to those who came up to him in the street or in a club. Most of the time he was virtually alone in public with a couple of girlfriends and a male friend or two. But he had no full-time bodyguards or entourage to protect him. He did not design his public movements to shield him from the people. He had no fear of rapping with a stranger. He took every chance imaginable, from his music to his love life to the safety of his person.

Jimi Hendrix left no will. His father was the sole heir of his estate. Al Hendrix named Henry W. Steingarten as administrator of Jimi Hendrix's estate at a court hearing in New York City. It was soon reported that the estate was worth some $400,000. This figure shocked many close to Hendrix, who knew that he had amassed much more than that in royalties alone. The $400,000 seemed to be only the monies Hendrix had earned on the last tour of England and Europe.

Al Hendrix was straightforward in declaring his lack of ability to handle the various legal and economic decisions required of him. He quickly fell victim to a couple of charity scams, and the estate, as headed by Henry Steingarten, was unable to add substantially to the $400,000 figure originally left. Al Hendrix began to ponder other courses of action.

Leo Branton took over the Hendrix estate after Herbert Price, Jimi's former valet, urged Al Hendrix to retain him. Immediately Branton took action. Henry Steingarten cooperated by stepping aside as administrator of the estate after Branton threatened to take him before the bar because of the obvious conflict of interest implicit in the fact that his partner, Steve Weiss, was the lawyer for Michael Jeffery, Hendrix's personal manager. Ed Chalpin's suit against Hendrix in the English courts had been hanging the estate up, but Branton broke the contract by pointing out the obvious exploitation of the one-dollar contract.

Leo Branton felt that if Steingarten and Warner Bros. had fought the litigation of Chalpin in America they would have won easily. That would have saved Jimi a lot of heartache.

Electric Lady Studios was sold to the Michael Jeffery estate. The Jimi Hendrix estate began receiving updated royalties from Warner Bros. A Bahamian tax shelter scheme that Jeffery and Steingarten had advised Hendrix to join had taken in considerable revenue from Hendrix's music publishing companies. The money had disappeared. Noel Redding and Mitch Mitchell received $100,000 and $300,000, respectively, as settlements for alleged oral agreements between them and Hendrix regarding record royalties. A paternity suit in Sweden was adjudicated in favor of Eva Sundquist and son. It had no bearing on heirs to Hendrix's estate since paternity suits in Sweden are traditionally settled on the sole testimony of the mother.

The posthumous manipulation of Jimi Hendrix's music is somewhat depressing to his true fans and followers. One of his biggest battles in life was the production, merchandising, and packaging of his music. It is a shame that *Electric Ladyland* is his only LP totally controlled and produced by himself. Of the albums after that, only *Band of Gypsys* was not issued after his death. The *Cry of Love* and *Rainbow Bridge* albums were more or less the tracks that would have been on the double album *First Rays of the New Rising Sun,* had Hendrix remained alive. Two of the studio-recorded songs on *Rainbow Bridge* ("Pali-gap" and "Hey Baby") form the nucleus of the live concert performed in Maui that was supposed to have been the live soundtrack album for the motion picture *Rainbow Bridge*. But Chuck Wein, director and producer of the movie, lost the soundtrack to thieves after Hendrix died. *Loose Ends* was the last album put together by Ed Kramer, Mitch Mitchell, and others who were on top of his music at the time of his death. *Hendrix in the West, War Heroes,* and *Loose Ends* give pure Hendrix tracks. Although not up to the level Hendrix would have preferred, they offer some splendid surprises like "Midnight," an instrumental "Hoochie Coochie Man," "Bleeding Heart," "Drifter's Escape," a Dylan song, "Look Over Yonder," and "Room Full of Mirrors," among others.

First Rays of the New Rising Sun would have been a fabulous album, rivaling *Electric Ladyland* in popularity. The tracks reveal a lovely range and a new direction for Hendrix. Yet without his final mixes, follow-through mastering techniques, and other touches, there are subtle and obvious lapses and flaws that Hendrix would not have permitted.

Jimi and Devon Wilson were a love story unto themselves. Their love, hate, and ambivalence created a parallel legend. Many related to Jimi through Devon, more than they related to him through his music. Jimi vacillated about his deep feelings for Devon, as he did in many other essential areas of his life. But it was clear that he had a concern for her he could not shake. Devon impressed the women on the rock superstar scene almost as much as Jimi. Betty Davis, a close friend of Devon's who was married to Miles Davis during a good deal of their friendship, remembered Devon through a song: "I. Miller Shoes."

She could have been anything she wanted
Truly fine from her head down to her toes
Instead she chose to be nothing
So nothing flew from the East to the West Coast

Became a thief
She was a dancer
Became a harlot
She was a black diamond queen
Music men wrote songs about her
Some said her sweet
And some said her very mean
Rock music played loud and clear for her
Rock music took her youth and left her very dry
She was abused and used by many men
Ask the guitar grinder
He'll tell you why

She could have been anything she wanted
She had bells from her head down to her toes
But instead she chose to do nothing
So nothing flew from the West back to the East Coast

She rendered her services easily
'Cause her services were all she had to give
But after the passing of her savior
She did and tried everything she could to stay here
Dark glasses used to hide her mourning face
Dark marks found a place upon her arm
And when they told me that she had died
They didn't have to tell me why or how she'd gone

She came to the jungle from Milwaukee
Stepping high in her I. Miller shoes
She came to the jungle from Milwaukee
And she stepped out in her I. Miller shoes

Following Hendrix's death it seemed as if every guitarist in the public eye was making a personal testament to the beauty of the man's style. Many of his licks became immediate additions to every electric guitarist's vocabulary. All of what was possible was absorbed.

Robin Trower, former lead guitarist of Procol Harum, became a devotee of Hendrix's. While staying clear of Hendrix's compositions he often captured similar moods and effects. Frank Marino, lead guitarist of the Canadian group Mahogany Rush, played several of Hendrix's compositions almost verbatim. Marino claims to have been visited by the spirit of Jimi Hendrix soon after his death. Ronnie Isley, of the Isley Brothers, acknowledges his debt to Hendrix in many of their early seventies releases.

This task seemed impossible when I first started. Jimi Hendrix's inner circle of friends was even tighter than I had realized. Many had been put off by the poor and notorious accounts of his life that were published soon after his death. Hendrix kept no diaries. His notebooks, letters, collections of poems, and the myriad scraps of paper and matchbooks he wrote lines for lyrics on were all missing. His apartment had been raided and all of his personal effects distributed without any supervision or thought toward keeping his stuff together for posterity. Much of his wardrobe was traced to various itinerant clothes freaks. His priceless, private tape-recorded collection of jams in clubs, in concerts, and solo (alone in his room at home or on the road) was gone. The two people closest to him on a personal and business level, Devon Wilson and Michael Jeffery, both died strange and violent deaths soon after he left this world. Other close associates died, got strung out, or went mad soon after his death.

He was as much into himself offstage as he was flamboyant onstage. He knew many people and many people knew him, yet many of his closest friends had been his friends long before his fame. Buddy Miles, Billy Cox, Fayne Pridgeon, the Twins, Jennie Dean, Jeanette Jacobs, Bobby Taylor, Tommy Chong, Linda Keith, Devon, and others all were his oldest friends and knew him well before he made it big. With the exception of Chas Chandler, his relationship with his English management and band that formed the Experience was as close to a purely business arrangement as could be in the small world of high international rock. His relationship with his American recording company was distant. One of his European labels, Track, distributed by Polydor, never paid him a royalty at all, according to Leo Branton. But it came to pass that close friends, record companies, and personal management all played a crucial role in his death.

Most of the people who were closest to Jimi Hendrix denied a close knowledge of him. Very often those who were somewhat removed from his ongoing intimacy felt they knew him better than their information indicated. One person who was interviewed early in the research said that those who knew Jimi Hendrix the best were those who loved his music. It took years, literally, to win the trust and confidence of many of those who formed Hendrix's inner circle of friends.

At first I was incensed by his death (like many who dearly loved his life, his music, and his style) to the point that I clearly bore a visible anger. It took me two full years and a trip to England to get over that hard-boiled, almost private eye–like intensity. Once it entered my mind that the most important thing about the man was his life, I was home free. I must have encountered every causeway and roadblock imaginable. But I found it was more trial than error, because every effort toward uncovering his essence was almost magically rewarded. Many beautiful people came forth to help me out, especially Herbie Worthington of Los Angeles and all of the Chambers Brothers. Also helpful were Caesar Glebbeek and Don Foster of the Jimi Hendrix Information Centre in Holland and, especially, James "Vishwamitra" Scott. Because of their help and the help of many others, instead of hating his death, I began enjoying Jimi Hendrix's life again.

LIFE AFTER DEATH

On April 7, 1993, a touring art show featuring representations of Hendrix's image entitled "The Jimi Hendrix Exhibition" opened at a gallery in New York City's SoHo district. Also that day, Al Hendrix, Jimi's father, as reported in the *Los Angeles Times,* sued to regain control of the Jimi Hendrix estate. His lawyer for over twenty years, Leo Branton, who was named as one of the defendants in the suit, was involved with the organizers of the show, most notably Alan Douglas, who represented the anonymous legal owners of Jimi Hendrix's music, works, and image. At the exhibition, the representatives of the anonymous owners of Hendrix's oeuvre were promoting him solely in the retrosphere of the white rock world that Hendrix had rejected long before his death. In preponderance, those in charge, and those who worked for those in charge, and other art-world types, avoided talk of his death; they were not interested in anything about the strange circumstances of Hendrix's death. They were celebrating his life. Or, more precisely, they were celebrating Jimi Hendrix's life after death.

Jimi Hendrix is now recognized as a major force in twentieth-century music. It was not until the eighties that Hendrix began to be widely acknowledged, beyond the rock category, as a musical genius. His compositions and unique guitar technique have withstood the test of time: levels of achievement regarding speed and precision of playing, inventiveness, improvisational skills, the control of feedback as a melodic element, his compositions (which are of the best of his era), his ability to dance, sing, and play all at the same time, which is amazingly difficult to do at all, much less beautifully. His poetry, lyrics, and serious writings are now becoming available as a body of work. His studio technique, where he was able to layer several guitar tracks with techniques of weaving rhythm figures, blues tips going into pink noise, guitar choirs, and backward mixed-down solo techniques and hot ten-second solos made him a stellar electric guitarist/producer on a par with no one.

The public's appreciation of Hendrix's music has soared yearly since his death and especially after the piecemeal posthumous release of what would have been his masterpiece: *First Rays of the New Rising Sun,* which became a compilation due to complications with the material that, among other things, lacked his finishing touches. His other music—which consists of the albums/

CDs, jazz jams, instrumentals, many blues pieces, the recent release of all of his Woodstock set and outtakes of recording sessions—is now largely available. Somewhere are more recordings of solo acoustic jams he performed endlessly in dressing rooms and alone and with company in his rooms; the film of the twelve-string acoustic version of "Hear My Train A-comin'" is the only taste available. But his "opera," *Black Gold*, is available, although unfortunately only to collectors.

But the direction in which he was headed was beyond the narrow rock world to which he had been confined. Miles Davis understood where Hendrix was trying to go with the Band of Gypsys and recognized that "Jimi Hendrix came from the blues, just like me. We understood each other right away because of that. He was a great blues guitarist." Davis talked about the extension of that blues foundation in his autobiography.

I first met Jimi when his manager called up and wanted me to introduce him to the way I was playing and putting my music together. Jimi liked what I had done on Kind of Blue *and some other stuff and wanted to add more jazz elements to what he was doing. He liked the way Coltrane played with all those sheets of sound, and he played the guitar in a similar way. Plus, he said he had heard the guitar voicing that I used in the way I played the trumpet. So we started getting together. Betty [Mabry] really liked his music—and later I found out she liked him physically, too—and so he started to come around.*

He was a real nice guy, quiet but intense, and was nothing like people thought he was; he was just the opposite of the wild and crazy image he presented on the stage. When we started getting together and talking about music, I found out that he couldn't read music. Betty had a party for him sometime in 1969 at my house on West Seventy-seventh. I couldn't be there because I had to be in the studio that night recording, so I left some music for him to read and then we'd talk about it later. (Some people wrote some shit that I didn't come to the party for him because I didn't like having a party for a man in my house. That's a lot of bullshit.)

When I called back home from the studio to speak to Jimi about the music I had left him, I found out he didn't read music. There are a lot of great musicians who don't read music—black and white—that I have known and respected and played with. So I didn't think less of Jimi because of that. Jimi was just a great natural musician—self-taught. He would pick up things from whoever he was around, and he picked up things quick. Once he heard it he really had it down. We would be talking and I would be telling him technical shit like, "Jimi, you know, when you play the diminished chord . . ." I would see this lost look come into his face and I would say, "Okay, okay, I forgot," I would just play it for him on the piano or on the horn, and he would get it faster than a motherfucker. He had a natural ear for hearing music. So I'd play different shit for him, show him that way. Or I'd play him a record of mine or 'Trane's and explain to him what we were doing. Then he started incorporating things I told him into his albums. It was great. He influenced me, and I influenced him, and that's the way great music is always made. Everybody showed everybody else something and then moving on from there.

In well-publicized pretrial press interviews, Al Hendrix contended that he was unaware of the nature of the documents when he signed away, not long after his son's death, all future considerations regarding his son's music and likeness. Leo Branton contends that Al Hendrix was well aware of the sales. But Al Hendrix says he was unaware that he was selling his son's musical legacy. He thought he was leasing it, but retaining ownership as sole heir (he has retained ownership over everything else his son left him).

In the summer of 1995, nearly twenty-five years after the death of Jimi Hendrix, Al Hendrix and his daughter, Janie Hendrix-Wright, in an out-of-court settlement of their lawsuit, took control of the Jimi Hendrix estate, which was valued at somewhere between forty and one hundred million dollars.

Today the Jimi Hendrix estate is valued in the range of one billion dollars.

Hendrix's life, as it was with his music, has blossomed under the attention his work demands. There are college-level courses being taught on his works. He has a star on Hollywood Boulevard. Various researchers have reconstructed a virtual diary of his life as a music star. Some authors and researchers regard themselves as Hendrix scholars, as experts on his life, but most have come to him after death. Jimi Hendrix has many followers, some of whom regard him as a philosopher, a visionary, a man of high magic. Miles Davis has placed Hendrix within his pantheon, which includes Charlie "Bird" Parker and Dizzy Gillespie, giants of the jazz idiom. Today Jimi Hendrix approaches avatar status as a recognized spiritual being and master of the music world.

Jimi Hendrix indeed lives on.

—David Henderson

A SELECTED DISCOGRAPHY OF THE RECORDINGS OF JIMI HENDRIX

Jimi Hendrix released only six albums during his lifetime; they were issued by Warner Bros. Reprise, which was his official label in the United States, and by Polydor and Track, his official labels in Europe and the United Kingdom. They are: *Are You Experienced?* (Reprise RS6261) September 1967, *Axis: Bold As Love* (RS 6281) January 1968, *Electric Ladyland* (Double 2RS 6307) September 1968, *Smash Hits* (MSK 2276) June 1969, and *Otis Redding/Jimi Hendrix Experience at Monterey* (MS 2029) July 1970. *Band of Gypsys* was released by Capitol (STAO 472) after the tapes from the historic Fillmore East New Year's Eve concert of 1969 were used to settle a lawsuit.

After his death, several albums appeared under varying circumstances, all of which were compromised to some extent by the lack of Hendrix's participation in the postproduction process, which he often considered the most crucial phase in the making of an album. These albums are also available through his official companies: *The Cry of Love* (MS 2034) January 1971, *Rainbow Bridge* (MS 2040), *Hendrix in the West* (MS 2049), *War Heroes* (MS 2103), *Sound Track Recording from the Film Jimi Hendrix* (2RS 6481) June 1973, and *Loose Ends,* which was only available in England (Polydor Super 2310 301) and Europe.

Loose Ends was not released in America because his official company felt that the tracks given them by the Jimi Hendrix estate were of inferior quality. This led the Hendrix estate to contract independent producer Alan Douglas to spin off some albums from a mass of some six hundred hours of raw, unedited tapes that Hendrix had left in his Electric Lady Studios and elsewhere. *Crash Landing* (MS 2204) and *Midnight Lightning* (MS 2209) were released as a result of the agreement in February and November 1975. Both albums sparked controversy because of Douglas's decision to erase tracks featuring original sidemen (Buddy Miles, Noel Redding, Juma Sultan, Larry Lee, and others) in favor of Los Angeles studio musicians and background singers. Many who were close to the tracks recorded by Hendrix that appear on the latest LPs state that the originals were far superior to their subsequent "versions." Douglas cited problems in the tracks themselves, which often changed key or tempo suddenly.

SCUSE ME WHILE I KISS THE SKY

The Essential Jimi Hendrix Vol. I (2RS 2245) July 1978, and *Vol. II* (HS 2293)—including the seven-inch EP "Gloria" (EP 2293)—July 1979, are anthology compilations of songs and compositions released in prior official albums. *Nine to the Universe* (HS 2299), produced by Douglas, was released in 1980. It is a splendid album featuring largely instrumental tracks. Jazz keyboard man Larry Young is featured along with guitarists Jim McCarty and Larry Lee and bass player Roland Robinson. It was recorded at the Record Plant in late 1969. The triple LP *Woodstock* (Cotillion SD 3-500) has only a brief selection of Hendrix and the fabled Band of Gypsys, Suns and Rainbows performance. But the difficult-to-obtain *Woodstock Two* (Cotillion SD 3-500 Double) contains an entire side of their work. The *Isle of Wight* performance of Hendrix is available only in the United Kingdom (Polydor Super 2302 016) and in Europe. It was the first gig of his last tour. In Germany, Polydor has released a twelve-volume set of all official European albums, including a "maxi" single of "Gloria": *Jimi Hendrix* (2625038).

Early in his career Hendrix participated in recording sessions with Arthur Lee (of the sixties group Love), Little Richard, Curtis Knight, the Isley Brothers, and Lonnie Youngblood. "My Diary," 45 rpm (Revis 1013 mono), as sung by Rosa Lee Brooks and produced by Arthur Lee, was recorded in 1965 in Los Angeles and is the earliest known recording of Jimi Hendrix. The LP with Lonnie Youngblood entitled *Rare Hendrix* (TLP 9500), from Trip Records, was recorded in the United States in 1963–64.

The following selection of tapes exists in private collections and archives:

WITH NOEL REDDING, BASS, AND MITCH MITCHELL, DRUMS

January 19, 1967, London, England. *Top of the Pops* show: "Hey Joe," with the Breakaways, background vocals.

February 5, 1967, London, England. The Flamingo Club. Entire concert. JHE plays R&B standard "Have Mercy."

March 2, 1967, London, England. Marquee Club. "Hey Joe," "Purple Haze."

June 18, 1967, Monterey, California. Monterey International Pop Festival. "Killing Floor," song left off official release.

September 5, 1967, Stockholm, Sweden. Radiohus Studio. Entire concert.

October 6, 1967, London, England. *Top Gear* show. "Radio One Theme (BBC)" and a jam with Stevie Wonder on drums, "Midnight Hour/I Was Made to Love Her."

October 9, 1967, Paris, France. L'Olympia. "Hey Joe," "Wind Cries Mary," "Purple Haze."

October 17, 1967, London, England. *Rhythm and Blues* show. "Please Crawl Out Your Window," "Hoochie Coochie Man," "Drivin' South."

December 15, 1967, London, England. *Top Gear* show. "Spanish Castle Magic," "Daytripper."

February 25, 1968, Chicago, Illinois. Civic Opera House. Thirty minutes.

August 23, 1968, Queens, New York, Singer Bowl. Entire concert.

November 28, 1968, New York City. Philharmonic Hall, *An Electric Thanksgiving*. Entire concert.

January 17, 1969, Frankfurt, West Germany. Jahrhunderthalle. Entire concert.

May 25, 1969, Santa Clara, California. San Jose Pop Festival. Entire concert.

June 20, 1969, Northridge, California. Newport Pop Festival/Devonshire Downs. Thirty minutes.

July 10, 1969, New York City. *Tonight* show, hosted by Flip Wilson. Billy Cox, bass, and Ed Shaughnessy, house band drummer. "Lover Man," dedicated to Brian Jones.

BAND OF GYPSYS: BILLY COX, BASS, AND BUDDY MILES, DRUMS

December 1969, New York City. Record Plant. "Auld Lang Syne," "Silent Night/Little Drummer Boy."

December 31, 1969, Fillmore East. First show. Entire concert.

WITH MITCH MITCHELL, DRUMS, AND BILLY COX, BASS

April 25, 1970, Los Angeles, California. Forum. Entire concert.

May 30, 1970, Berkeley, California. Berkeley Community Theater. Second show. Entire concert.

July 4, 1970, Atlanta, Georgia, Atlanta Pop Festival. Entire concert.

July 30, Maui, Hawaii, Rainbow Bridge concert. Forty-five minutes.

August 30, 1970, Isle of Wight, England. Isle of Wight Festival. Entire concert.

September 1, 1970, Gothenburg, Sweden. Liseberg. Entire concert.

September 2, 1970, Arhus, Denmark. Vejlby Risskov Hall. Twenty-five minutes.

September 3, 1970, Copenhagen, Denmark. K.B. Hallen. Entire concert.

September 6, 1970, Isle of Fehmarn, West Germany. Love and Peace Festival. Entire concert.

MISCELLANEOUS

October 1969, Woodstock, New York. Various house jams with Juma Sultan, percussion, and Michael Ephron, electric piano.

March 1968, New York City. Scene club. Live jam with Harvey Brooks, bass, Buddy Miles, drums, an unidentified guitarist, and Jim Morrison, vocals.

April 1970, Los Angeles, California. Beverly Hilton Hotel. Taj Mahal and Hendrix accompanied by a tape of Topanga Canyon crickets.

1969–1970, New York City. Apartment house jams. Solo acoustic blues, electric guitar duos with unidentified guitarist, and songs such as "Neptune Rising," "Astro Man," "Room Full of Mirrors," and an acoustic version of "Manic Depression."

1969–1970, New York City. Record Plant. Jam with John McLaughlin, guitar, Dave Holland, bass, and Buddy Miles, drums.

1972, New York City. Electric Lady Studios. Ed Kramer, engineer, breaks down the tracks of "Dolly Dagger" and explains the mix and the various effects.

1974, London, England. *Crawdaddy* Radio Review. Johnny Winter accompanies Hendrix on "Things I Used to Do." Also some jams with Larry Young.

1979 and 1980, Berkeley, California. The Third World Department of KPFA-FM Radio produced a twelve-hour documentary, *Jimi Hendrix: A Slight Return.*

Nowadays Music Corporation of America is Jimi Hendrix's parent company, taking over from Warner Bros. Hendrix's official releases: *Are You Experienced?, Axis: Bold As Love,* and *Electric Ladyland* are, of course, available from them. The recent CD *Jimi Hendrix: Woodstock* MCA (MCAD 11603) is significant because he had fielded his most ambitious band ever. Although the recording is not Hendrix's complete show, and does not give a proper mix to the ensemble, which featured two additional percussionists, Juma Sultan and Jerry Velez (who gave Hendrix's sound that African drum-battery effect), and a second guitarist, Larry Lee, along with regulars Billy Cox and Mitch Mitchell, it is nevertheless an important record of the last set at the original Woodstock.

Jimi Hendrix: Blues MCA (MCAD 11060)—I had always thought Hendrix should have an all-blues album out. We used to feature a solid blues section when we did marathon celebrations of Hendrix's birthday at KPFA-FM in Berkeley. I would have selected perhaps a few different cuts. Perhaps some Dylan tunes Hendrix did so bluesily, reflecting his philosophical ideas about new blues, personal blues, albeit postmodern blues.

Someday I'd like to hear an all-instrumental Hendrix CD. I have compiled my own tape and it is very satisfying.

Jimi Hendrix: The Ultimate Experience MCA (MCAD 10829) is a standard greatest hits type release. But *Jimi Hendrix: Voodoo Soup* (MCAD 11236) is a compilation from what I believe would have been Hendrix's stellar album had he lived: *First Rays of the New Rising Sun.* But it was dispersed over several posthumous releases. This is a very credible assemblage, beginning with a very avant-garde instrumental, "The New Rising Sun," then "Belly Button Window," "Stepping Stone," "Freedom," "Angel," "Room Full of Mirrors," "Midnight" (a great instrumental), "Night Bird Flying," "Drifting," "Ezy Ryder," "Pali-gap" (another great instrumental), "Message to Love," "Peace in Mississippi" (a rousing instrumental), and "In from the Storm."

There is now in the new millennium a trademark of sorts called "Experience Hendrix" and it goes with a range of recent CDs under the heading "Authorized Hendrix Family Editions." This no doubt reflects the Hendrix family's control over most of Jimi's oeuvre, which is now pretty much (at last) completely available to the public.

The following is an array of recent releases under "Authorized Hendrix Family Editions":

First Rays of the New Rising Sun MCA (MCAD 11599)

Finally, at last, Hendrix's last album as CD. Not with the master's final touches and revisions, but what he had down before the last tour. And it feels pretty complete. "Final studio recordings . . . digitally remastered from the original 2-track mixdown master tapes." "17 tracks, 70 minutes compiled as an album for first time ever." Wonder what Jimi would have thought of digital remixes?

Jimi Hendrix Live at Woodstock MCA (MCAD 11987)

Supersedes *Jimi Hendrix: Woodstock* (MCAD 11603). It has "more than 30 minutes of previously unreleased music." There is also a VHS video and DVD (MCAD 11988).

Hendrix: Band of Gypsys Live at the Fillmore East MCA (MCAD 11931).

Looks like the entire historic concert at the Fillmore East, New Year's Eve, 1969, with Buddy Miles and Billy Cox. "Almost 2 hours of previously unreleased music. 2 CDs mixed from the original masters. 16 extended tracks, 13 previously unreleased." It looks like there will be a VHS video/DVD available soon.

The Jimi Hendrix Experience BBC Sessions MCA (MCAD 11742). Live sessions on BBC radio and TV. "2 CDs, 30 tracks, 13 previously unreleased."

OTHER THAN THE "AUTHORIZED" . . .

The Jimi Hendrix Experience: Original Soundtrack to the Motion Picture Experience.

Recorded at the Royal Albert Hall on February 24, 1969, it is available from the Brilliant label (BT 33045).

Jimi Hendrix: A "Rockumentary"

An excellent biopic by Joe Boyd, John Head, and Gary Weiss is available in the DVD format on Warner Bros.: 11267.

Discography Addenda

The Jimi Hendrix Estate, better known as Experience Hendrix, L.L.C., releases Hendrix's music through MCA Records. They include *Live at the Fillmore East*, *BBC Sessions*, and The Jimi Hendrix Experience box set. They also release through Dagger Records.

Dagger Records releases include:

Jimi Hendrix Experience: Paris 1967/San Francisco 1968
Jimi Hendrix: The Baggy's Rehearsal Sessions
The Jimi Hendrix Experience: Live in Ottawa
The Jimi Hendrix Experience: Live at the Oakland Coliseum
The Jimi Hendrix Experience: Live at Clark University
Morning Symphony
Hear My Music
The Jimi Hendrix Experience: Live at the Isle of Fehmarn

Hear My Music and *Jimi Hendrix Experience: Paris 1967/San Francisco 1968* are also available on long-playing records: 180-gram, audiophile-grade vinyl releases, each title pressed in colored vinyl as opposed to the traditional black.

Just about all of the music released on two recent CDs—*Jimi Hendrix: Woodstock* (MCAD 11063) and *Jimi Hendrix: Blues* (MCAD 11060)—have been available for some time to collectors or aficionados via bootlegs, often from those friends of various music industry personnel who have had access to board tapes of concerts or dubs or outtakes from recording sessions, or copies of jams and audience-taped performances recorded on a wide array of sound machinery.

To those music fans unaware of Hendrix's broad range, *Jimi Hendrix: Blues* must be amazing. It places him well within the pantheon of blues greats. The CD cover has, collaged against Hendrix's profile, small portraits of B. B. King, Chuck Berry, Howlin' Wolf, John Lee Hooker, Little Walter, Robert Johnson, Willie Dixon, Jimmy Reed, T-Bone Walker, Ike Turner, Lightnin' Hopkins, Robert Jr. Lockwood, Guitar Slim, Son House, Elmore James, Otis Rush, and others. For those who knew Hendrix's music well, this "status" was never an issue. Hendrix was not all that sold on singing but knew what he had to do. You can hear him when he did not want to sing on the Isle of Wight performance and on many legs of what turned out to be his last tour, in the early autumn of 1970.

Hendrix could impersonate Albert King's vocal style and play him lick for lick, as he could Muddy Waters and just about any other living bluesman of that time. But Hendrix and Albert King, both left-handed guitarists, gave something very subtle to the sound. In *Jimi Hendrix: Blues* we hear "Hear My Train

A-comin'" on an acoustic version of twelve string, an instrument we never heard enough of from the man; "Born Under a Bad Sign," Albert King's tune; "Red House," Hendrix's signature blues composition, where the love is the woman and the guitar, and if he can't have her, then he'll try her sister, and when all else fails, he still has his guitar—the ever faithful lover; "Catfish Blues," from *Rollin' and Tumblin'*, and "Rolling Stone," which Hendrix introed as "Muddy Waters's Blues," since they are blues of the maestro, by and large, of whom Hendrix remarked: "The first guitarist I was aware of was Muddy Waters. I heard one of his old records when I was a little boy and it scared me to death." "Voodoo Chile Blues" is Hendrix's signature fusion of the blues with the African and African-American religious-magical tradition—blues and jazz here form a sort of postmodern voodoo; the title could be more precisely "Hoodoo Chile." "Mannish Boy" is another Muddy Waters tune that includes some of its precursor, Bo Diddley's "I'm a Man," and some more contemporary rock repertoire flourishes. "Once I Had a Woman" is Hendrix in a "Red House" extension. "Bleeding Heart" is more Elmore James than anyone else, although the CD literature deems it "traditional," with a new arrangement by Hendrix. That "traditional" label has long been a device employed to get around crediting and paying blues lyricists and composers. "Jelly 292" is another take of "Jam, 292" on the 1974 *Loose Ends* LP. "Electric Church Red House" is Hendrix's, a studio jam, and "Hear My Train A-comin'," electric version, was recorded live at the Berkeley Community Theater in Berkeley, California, blocks from the housing project where Hendrix spent significant years of his early childhood. A full-blown riot was occurring in Berkeley over People's Park while this recording was being made.

Hendrix came on last at Woodstock, at nine o'clock in the morning, after everyone had been up all night and was in the process of leaving. Pissed off, yet professional, Hendrix brought to the stage the most extended and personalized band he had ever assembled: Mitch Mitchell on drum kit; Billy Cox, bass; Larry Lee, guitar; Juma Sultan and Jerry Velez, percussion. He finally had the bottom he wanted with the addition of congas and bongos, a second rhythm guitarist who could help approximate the complex layers he laid down by himself in the studio, and a bedrock of a bass player who could match his improvisational flamboyance with a wit and subtlety in repetition only known to truly bad bassists. They do "Fire," "Izabella," "Hear My Train A-comin' (Getting My Heart Back Together)," "Red House," "Jam Back at the House (Beginnings)," "Voodoo Chile (Slight Return)/Stepping Stone," "The Star-Spangled Banner" (which Ornette Coleman called a work of true genius), and "Purple Haze." And then, after an extended solo improvisation, "Villanova Junction." The last leg of Hendrix's

Woodstock performance is a great example of Hendrix's jamming ability. Hendrix playing alone, going through the ideas in his head as they happen and delving deeply into the improvisational mode where blues and jazz truly intersect, is the place Hendrix listeners rarely have access to. That this intimacy is from one of the largest concerts in music history is an indication of how very close Hendrix felt to his audience. He wrote, at Woodstock:

> *500,000 halos . . .*
> *outshined the mud and history*
> *We washed and drank in God's tears of joy*
> *And for once . . . and for everyone . . .*
> *the truth was not a mystery—*
>
> *Love called to all . . . music is magic*
> *As we passed over and beyond the walls of nay*
> *Hand in hand as we lived and*
> *made real the dreams of peaceful men—*
>
> *We came together. . . . Danced with*
> *the pearls of rainy weather*
> *Riding the waves of music and*
> *Space—music is magic. . . .*
> *Magic is life. . . .*
> *Love as never loved before . . .*
> *Harmony to son and daughter . . . man and wife*

PERMISSIONS

Page 111: "Hey Joe" written by Billy Roberts. Published by Third Palm Music (BMI).

Pages 136–139: © IPC+Syndication.

Pages 142–53: Hendrix conversation with Eric Clapton—David Henderson transcript (transcribed by David Henderson from a recording). Permission: © 1978 David Henderson.

Page 153–54: © Mirrorpix.

Pages 169–70: Lyrics from "Like a Rolling Stone" by Bob Dylan. Copyright © 1965 by Warner Bros. Inc. All Rights Reserved. Used by permission.

Page 171: "Wild Thing"—Words and Music by Chip Taylor © 1965 (Renewed 1993) EMI BLACK-WOOD MUSIC INC. All Rights Reserved. International Copyright Secured. Used by Permission.

Pages 185–86: © Mirrorpix.

Page 189: "A Genuine Nightmare," *New York Times,* November 12, 1967 © 1967 *The New York Times.* All Rights Reserved. Used by permission and protected by the Copyright Laws of the United States. The printing, copying, redistribution, or retransmission of the Material without express written permission is prohibited.

Pages 196–99: Interview with Jimi Hendrix by Professor Jay Ruby reprinted by permission of Jay Ruby.

Pages 208–9: © Mirrorpix.

Pages 218–19: Interview *East Village Other* reprinted by permission.

Pages 228–30: Interview with Hendrix by "Meatball Fulton" on ZBS Radio (1969) reprinted by permission of Meatball Fulton, ZBS Media.

Pages 257–58: Lyrics from "All Along the Watchtower" by Bob Dylan. Copyright © 1968 by Dwarf Music. Used by permission. All Rights Reserved.

Page 261: © Mirrorpix.

Pages 263–64: "Infinity of Jimis" by Robert Richman, October 3, 1969, LIFE magazine. Copyright 1969 Life Inc. Reprinted with permission. All Rights Reserved.

Pages 266–68: © Mirrorpix.

Pages 269–70: © Mirrorpix.

Pages 274–82: Interview with Jimi Hendrix by Jane de Mendelssohn, which appeared in the *International Times* March/April 1969. Copyright © 1969 by Lovebooks Limited. Reprinted by permission.

Pages 310–14: Interview with Hendrix by "Meatball Fulton" on ZBS Radio (1969) reprinted by permission of Meatball Fulton, ZBS Media.

Pages 320–321: Interview with Jimi Hendrix by Ritchie Yorke, which appeared in the *L.A. Times,* September 7, 1969. Reprinted by permission of Ritchie Yorke.

Pages 323–27: Interview with Jimi Hendrix from the *Los Angeles Free Press,* November 1969. Reprinted by permission.

Pages 333–34: © IPC+Syndication.

Pages 379–81: Interview of Jimi Hendrix by Sue Cassidy Clark in *Superstars,* reprinted by permission of Sue Cassidy Clark.

Pages 391–94: David Henderson transcription. Public domain.

Pages 420–21: Lyrics from "I. Miller Shoes" by Betty Davis. Reprinted by permission of Betty Davis.

Pages 424–25: Reprinted with the permission of Simon & Schuster Adult Publishing Group, from *Miles: The Autobiography* by Miles Davis and Quincy Troupe. Copyright © 1989 by Miles Davis. All rights reserved.

Pages 431–33: Excerpt of review of CDs: *Jimi Hendrix: Woodstock* (MCAD11063) and *Jimi Hendrix: Blues* (MCAD11060) entitled: "Jimi Hendrix Deep Within the Blues and Alive Onstage at Woodstock . . ." from *African American Review,* volume 29, number 2, Summer 1995 © *African American Review,* Indiana State University, 1995. The official publication of the Division on Black American Literature and Culture of the Modern Language Association. Reprinted by permission.

INDEX

ABOUT THE AUTHOR

DAVID HENDERSON was born in Harlem, later moving to the Lower East Side of Manhattan where he was one of the original members of Umbra, an African American literary group. He was active in the civil rights and peace movements. An award-winning poet who has recorded his work for the permanent poetry archives at the Library of Congress, he has been poet-in-residence at the City College of New York, and a visiting professor of English and African American studies at the University of California at Berkeley. He has performed and recorded with jazz musicians Ornette Coleman, Sun Ra, David Murray, and "Butch" Morris, and wrote the book and lyrics for the funk opera *Ghetto Follies*, which premiered in San Francisco. He is the author of *Felix of the Silent Forest*, *De Mayor of Harlem*, *The Low East*, and *Neo-California*, and his work has been widely published in anthologies and in magazines, which include *The Paris Review*, *Essence*, *African Voices*, *Black Scholar*, *Tribes*, and *The London Poetry Review*.